Microsoft Office
365

Microsoft Office 365

365

A SKILLS APPROACH

2019 Edition

Cheri Manning

Catherine Manning Swinson

Triad Interactive, Inc.

MICROSOFT OFFICE 365: A SKILLS APPROACH

Published by McGraw-Hill Education, 2 Penn Plaza, New York, NY 10121. Copyright © 2020 by McGraw-Hill Education. All rights reserved. Printed in the United States of America. Previous editions © 2017, 2014, 2012. No part of this publication may be reproduced or distributed in any form or by any means, or stored in a database or retrieval system, without the prior written consent of McGraw-Hill Education, including, but not limited to, in any network or other electronic storage or transmission, or broadcast for distance learning.

Some ancillaries, including electronic and print components, may not be available to customers outside the United States.

This book is printed on acid-free paper.

1 2 3 4 5 6 7 8 9 QVS 24 23 22 21 20 19

ISBN 978-1-260-07944-9 (spiral-bound edition)
MHID 1-260-07944-9 (spiral-bound edition)
ISBN 978-1-260-70888-2 (loose-leaf edition)
MHID 1-260-70888-8 (loose-leaf edition)

Portfolio Manager: *Wyatt Morris*
Product Developers: *Alan Palmer*
Marketing Manager: *Corban Quigg*
Content Project Manager: *Harvey Yep*
Buyer: *Susan K. Culbertson*
Design: *Egzon Shaqiri*
Content Licensing Specialist: *Traci Vaske*
Cover Image: *Volodymyr Krasyuk/Shutterstock*
Compositor: *SPi Global*

All credits appearing on page or at the end of the book are considered to be an extension of the copyright page.

Library of Congress Control Number: 2019950598

mheducation.com/highered

brief contents

contents

chapter **3**
Formatting Documents   WD-78

chapter **4**
Working with Pictures, Tables, and Charts   WD-122

access 365

chapter 1
Getting Started with Access   AC-2

Content

How well do you know Microsoft Office? Many students can follow specific step-by-step directions to re-create a document, spreadsheet, presentation, or database, but do they truly understand the skills it takes to create these on their own? Just as simply following a recipe does not make you a professional chef, re-creating a project step by step does not make you an Office expert.

The purpose of this book is to teach you the skills to master Microsoft Office 365 in a straightforward and easy-to-follow manner. But *Microsoft® Office 365: A Skills Approach* goes beyond the how and equips you with a deeper understanding of the what and the why. Too many times books have little value beyond the classroom. The *Skills Approach* series has been designed to be not only a complete textbook but also a reference tool for you to use as you move beyond academics and into the workplace.

WHAT'S NEW IN THIS EDITION

With Office 365, Microsoft changed the delivery method for new features for users who have an Office 365 subscription. Rather than waiting for the next version of Office to be released, users with a 365 subscription will now receive new features through automatic updates to their account. Why does this matter to you? Because while we feel this book is still a solid reference for you to use, it could mean that certain content in this book may be out of date. But there is hope! If you signed up for a SIMnet account along with purchasing this book, the electronic version of this textbook (the SIMbook) will be updated along with Microsoft's updates. This means the text in the SIMbook, along with the simulated environment used for the exercises, will reflect any changes made to Office 365. In addition, your SIMbook may include additional content that could not be accommodated in the printed version of the textbook.

ABOUT TRIAD INTERACTIVE

Triad Interactive specializes in online education and training products. Our flagship program is SIMnet—a simulated Microsoft Office learning and assessment application developed for McGraw-Hill Education. Triad has been writing, programming, and managing the SIMnet system since 1999.

about the authors

CHERI MANNING

Cheri Manning is the president and co-owner of Triad Interactive. She is the author of the Microsoft Excel and Access content for the *Skills Approach* series and SIMnet. She has been authoring instructional content for these applications for more than 20 years.

Cheri began her career as an Aerospace Education Specialist with the Education Division of the National Aeronautics and Space Administration (NASA), where she produced materials for K–12 instructors and students. Prior to founding Triad, Cheri was a project manager with Compact Publishing, where she managed the development of McGraw-Hill's Multimedia MBA CD-ROM series.

CATHERINE MANNING SWINSON

Catherine Manning Swinson is the vice president and co-owner of Triad Interactive. She is the author of the Microsoft Word and PowerPoint content for the *Skills Approach* series and SIMnet. She also authors SIMnet content for Computer Concepts, Microsoft Outlook, Windows, and Web browsers. She has been authoring instructional content for these applications for more than 20 years.

Catherine began her career at Compact Publishing, one of the pioneers in educational CD-ROM–based software. She was the lead designer at Compact and designed every edition of the *TIME Magazine Compact Almanac* from 1992 through 1996. In addition, she designed a number of other products with Compact, including the *TIME* Man of the Year program and the *TIME 20th Century Almanac*.

CONTRIBUTORS

- Kelly Morber, *Saints Philip and James School, English Teacher and Malone University, M.A.Ed.*
- Timothy T. Morber, *MEd, LPCC-S, Malone University*

Instructor Walkthrough

Microsoft Office 365: A Skills Approach

> **1-1 Content in SIMnet for Office 365**

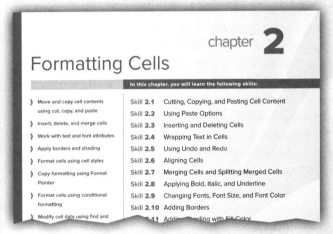

> **At-a-glance Office 365 skills**
> *Quick, easy-to-scan pages, for efficient learning*

> **Introduction—Learning Outcomes are clearly listed.**

Fix It

On Your Own

Skill Review

> **Diverse end-of-chapter projects**

Projects that relate to a broad range of careers and perspectives, from nursing, education, business, and everyday personal uses.

Features

From the perspective of. . .

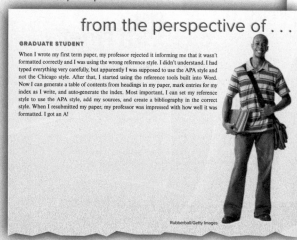

from the perspective of . . .

GRADUATE STUDENT

When I wrote my first term paper, my professor rejected it informing me that it wasn't formatted correctly and I was using the wrong reference style. I didn't understand. I had typed everything very carefully, but apparently I was supposed to use the APA style and not the Chicago style. After that, I started using the reference tools built into Word. Now I can generate a table of contents from headings in my paper, mark entries for my index as I write, and auto-generate the index. Most important, I can set my reference style to use the APA style, add my sources, and create a bibliography in the correct style. When I resubmitted my paper, my professor was impressed with how well it was formatted. I got an A!

Rubberball/Getty Images

Tips & Tricks

tips & tricks

You can choose to always show specific formatting marks on-screen even when the Show/Hide button is inactive. To show specific formatting marks:

1. Click the **File** tab and select **Options**.
2. In the *Word Options* dialog, click the **Display** category.
3. Select the formatting marks you want to display in the *Always show these formatting marks on the screen* section.
4. Click **OK**.

tell me more

Tell Me More

tell me more

❭ Some of the other character effects available from the Ribbon include:
- **Strikethrough**—draws a horizontal line through the text.
- **Subscript**—draws a small character below the bottom of the text.
- **Superscript**—draws a small character above the top of the text

❭ The *Font* dialog contains other character formatting options not available from the Ribbon. These effects include **Double strikethrough**, **Small caps**, and **All caps** among others. To open the *Font* dialog, on the *Home* tab, in the *Font* group, click the dialog launcher. Select an option in the *Effects* section and click **OK** to apply the character effect to the text.

another method

Another Method

another method

❭ The following keyboard shortcuts can be used to apply the bold, italic, and underline effects:
- Bold = Ctrl + B
- Italic = Ctrl + I
- Underline = Ctrl + U

❭ To access the bold, italic, or underline commands, you can also right-click the selected text and click the **Bold**, **Italic**, or **Underline** button on the Mini toolbar.

❭ To apply an underline style, click the **Underline** button arrow and select a style.

let me try

Open the student data file **wd2-01-SpaNewsletter** and try this skill on your own:
1. Select the text **free smoothies** in the first paragraph of the newsletter.

Let Me Try

let me try

Open the student data file **wd2-01-SpaNewsletter** and try this skill on your own:
1. Select the text **free smoothies** in the first paragraph of the newsletter.
2. Apply the **bold** character formatting to the text.
3. Select the text **online appointment booking system** in the second paragraph of the newsletter.
4. Apply the **italic** and **underline** character formatting to the text.
5. If you will be moving on to the next skill in this chapter, leave the document open to continue working. If not, save the file as directed by your instructor and close it.

❭ **Instructor materials available in the SIMnet course manager.**

- Instructor Manual
- Instructor PowerPoints
- Test Banks

SIMnet for Office 365 Online Training & Assessment

❭ Includes:

- Microsoft® Office Suite
- Computer Concepts
- Windows 10
- File Management
- Web Browsers

EASY TO USE

SIMnet is McGraw-Hill's leading solution for training and assessment of Microsoft Office skills and beyond. Completely online with no downloads for installation, SIMnet is accessible for today's students through multiple browsers and is easy to use for all. Now, SIMnet offers SIMbook and allows students to go mobile for their student learning. Available with videos and interactive "Guide Me" pages to allow students to study MS Office skills on any device. It's consistent, clean user interface and functionality will help save you time and help students be more successful in their course.

LIFELONG LEARNING

SIMnet offers lifelong learning. SIMnet is designed with features to help students immediately learn isolated Microsoft Office skills on demand. Students can use SIM-Search and the Library to learn skills both in and beyond the course. It's more than a resource; it's a tool they can use throughout their entire time at your institution.

MEASURABLE RESULTS

SIMnet provides powerful, measureable results for you and your students. See results immediately in our various reports and customizable gradebook. Students can also see measurable results by generating a custom training lesson after an exam to help determine exactly which content areas they still need to study. Instructors can use the dashboard to see detailed results of student activity, assignment completion, and more. SIMnet Online is your solution for helping students master today's Microsoft Office Skills.

SIMNET FOR OFFICE 2016

. . . **Keep IT SIMple!** To learn more, visit www.simnetkeepitsimple.com and also contact your McGraw-Hill representative.

office 365

Essential Skills for Office

In this chapter, you will learn the following skills:

❯ Learn about Microsoft Office and its apps Word, Excel, Access, and PowerPoint

❯ Learn the difference between Office 365 and Office 2019 on-premises

❯ Demonstrate how to open, save, and close files

❯ Recognize Office common features and navigation elements

❯ Use Microsoft Help and Tell Me features

❯ Create new files

❯ Share files through OneDrive

❯ AutoSave documents and manage versions

❯ Modify account information and the look of Office

❯ Customize the Quick Access Toolbar

Skill **1.1**   Introduction to Microsoft Office

Skill **1.2**   Opening Files

Skill **1.3**   Closing Files

Skill **1.4**   Closing the App

Skill **1.5**   Using the Start Page

Skill **1.6**   Getting to Know the Office User Interface

Skill **1.7**   Getting Help

Skill **1.8**   Using Smart Lookup

Skill **1.9**   Working in Protected View

Skill **1.10** Picking Up Where You Left Off

Skill **1.11** Working with File Properties

Skill **1.12** Creating a New Blank File

Skill **1.13** Saving Files to Your PC

Skill **1.14** Saving Files to OneDrive

Skill **1.15** Using AutoSave

Skill **1.16** Sharing Files Using OneDrive

Skill **1.17** Using the Account Page

Skill **1.18** Changing the Look of Office

Skill **1.19** Customizing the Quick Access Toolbar

skills

introduction

This chapter introduces you to Microsoft Office. You will learn about the versions of Microsoft Office and how they differ. You will learn about the shared features across the Office apps and how to navigate common interface elements. You will learn how to open and close files as well as different ways to save and share files, including through your OneDrive account.

Skill 1.1 Introduction to Microsoft Office

Microsoft Office is a collection of business "productivity" apps (computer programs designed to make you more productive at work, school, and home). The most popular Office apps are:

Microsoft Word—A word processing program. Word processing software includes powerful formatting and design tools that allow you to go beyond simple text files and create complex documents such as reports, résumés, brochures, and newsletters.

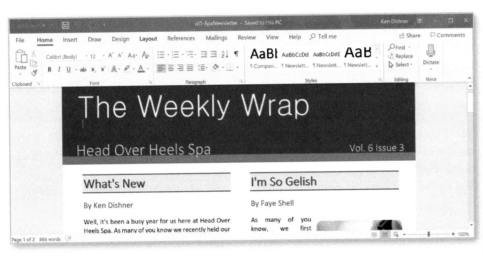

FIGURE OF 1.1
Microsoft Word

Microsoft Excel—A spreadsheet program. Originally, spreadsheet apps were viewed as electronic versions of an accountant's ledger. Today's spreadsheet apps can do much more than just calculate numbers—they include powerful charting and data analysis features. Spreadsheet programs can be used for everything from managing personal budgets to calculating loan payments.

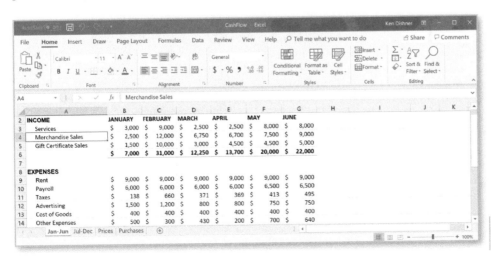

FIGURE OF 1.2
Microsoft Excel

Microsoft Access—A database program. Database apps allow you to organize and manipulate large amounts of data. Databases that allow you to relate tables and databases to one another are referred to as *relational* databases. As a database user, you usually see only one aspect of the database—a *form*. Database forms use a graphical interface to allow a user to enter record data. For example, when you fill out an order form online, you are probably interacting with a database. The information you enter becomes a record in a database *table*. Your order is matched with information in an inventory table (keeping track of which items are in stock) through a *query*. When your order is filled, a database *report* can be generated for use as an invoice or a bill of lading.

FIGURE OF 1.3
Microsoft Access

Microsoft PowerPoint—A presentation program. Presentation apps are used to create robust multimedia presentations. A presentation consists of a series of electronic slides. Each slide contains content, including text, images, charts, and other objects. You can add multimedia elements to slides, including animations, audio, and video.

FIGURE OF 1.4
Microsoft PowerPoint

To open one of the Office apps in Windows 10:

1. Click the Windows **Start** button (located in the lower left corner of your computer screen).

2. Scroll the list of apps on the Start menu.

3. Find the app in this list and click the app you want to open.

office 365   Essential Skills for Office

There are two main ways to license and pay for the installed version of Microsoft Office:

Office 365—This version allows you to download and install Office and pay for it on a yearly or monthly subscription basis. Office 365 includes full versions of the Office apps along with online storage services for your files. Microsoft is continually updating Office 365 with security and bug fixes. In addition, the apps are updated with new features twice a year. If you have an Office 365 subscription, Office will prompt you when an update is available.

Office 2019 (on-premises)—The on-premises version of Office allows you to install Office and pay for it once. The on-premises version of Office receives security and bug fixes, but does not receive new feature updates. In addition, certain features available in Office 365 are not available in Office 2019 on-premises, including the Editor in Word and PowerPoint's Designer feature.

Because this book is written for Office 365 which is continually being updated, your version of the software may look different than the screenshots shown here. For example, after the Office 2019 on-premises version of the software was released, Microsoft updated the look of the Ribbon and Backstage in the apps.

If you have the 2019 on-premises version of Office, the Ribbon will look like this:

FIGURE OF 1.5

If you have the updated Office 365 version, the Ribbon looks more like this:

FIGURE OF 1.6

Be aware that although the interface has changed, the steps to complete the skills are the same. SIMnet (the software that accompanies this textbook) is updated with the new feature and interface changes twice a year.

tell me **more**

Office apps are available to you on a variety of platforms. The features available depend on which version of the apps you are using:

〉 Desktop apps—Full-featured version of the Office apps that you download and install on your computer. If you are creating complex documents or presentations or performing complicated calculations on large amounts of data, you will most likely need the desktop version of the app. If you purchase an Office 365 subscription or the Office 2019 on-premises version, you will be downloading and installing the Desktop app version of the software.

〉 Online apps—Available at https://office.com. These apps are accessed through a Web browser (no installation required) and allow you to create and save files online using your OneDrive account (Microsoft's cloud storage service). The online apps have a limited set of features, but depending on your needs that may be enough.

〉 Mobile apps—Free apps available for your tablet device. Similar in features and functionality to the online apps, these apps are designed to run on the iOS and Android operating systems. They offer limited functionality compared to the installed desktop apps.

let me **try**

Try this skill on your own:

1. Display the Start menu.
2. Open the **Word** app.
3. Keep the app open to work on the next skill.

Skill 1.2 Opening Files

Opening a file retrieves it from storage and displays it on your computer screen. Files can be stored online, such as in your OneDrive, or on the hard drive of your computer. The steps for opening a file are the same for Word documents, Excel spreadsheets, PowerPoint presentations, and Access databases.

To open a recently opened file:

1. Click the **File** tab to open Backstage view.
2. Click **Open**.
3. The *Open* page displays the recently opened files.
4. Click a file in the list to open it.

If you do not see the file you want to open in the *Recent Files* list, you can navigate to find the file you want to open:

1. Click the **Browse** button to open the *Open* dialog.
2. Navigate to the folder containing the file you want to open.
3. Select the file name you want to open and click the **Open** button.

FIGURE OF 1.8

tips & tricks

❭ If the file you want to open is located in your *Documents* folder, click the **This PC** option in the list of locations. The contents of the *Documents* folder will display on the right. Click a file to open it.

❭ To open files from recently used folders, click the **Folders** option at the top of the *Recent* page. Click a folder to display its contents in the *Open* page.

❭ If you use a file frequently, you can pin the file to the list of files to open. Pinned files appear at the top of the list and do not go away until you unpin them.

tell me **more**

OneDrive is Microsoft's free cloud storage where you can save files and access those files from any computer or device or share the files with others. When you save files to your OneDrive, they are stored locally on your computer and "synched" with your OneDrive account and stored online where you can then access the files from another computer or device that has OneDrive capability.

another **method**

❭ To display the *Open* page in Backstage view, you can also press (Ctrl) + (O) on the keyboard.

❭ To open the *Open* dialog from the *Open* page in Backstage view, you can also double-click **This PC** at the left side of the *Open* page under *Other locations*.

❭ You can also click **Home** in Backstage view to display a list of recently opened files.

let me **try**

Try this skill on your own:

1. Open the student data file **of1-SpaNewsletter**.

   NOTE: You may see a yellow security message at the top of the window. See the skill *Working in Protected View* to learn more about security warning messages.

2. Keep the file open to work on the next skill.

Skill 1.3 Closing Files

Closing a file removes it from your computer screen and stores the last saved version for future use. If you have not saved your latest changes, most apps will prevent you from losing work by asking if you want to save the changes you made before closing.

To close a file and save your latest changes:

1. Click the **File** tab to open Backstage view.
2. Click **Close**.
3. If you have made no changes since the last time you saved the file, it will close immediately. If changes have been made, the app displays a message box asking if you want to save the changes you made before closing.

   - Click **Save** to save the changes.
   - Click **Don't Save** to close the file without saving your latest changes.
   - Click **Cancel** to keep the file open.

FIGURE OF 1.9

another **method**

To close a file, you can also press (Ctrl) + (W) on the keyboard.

let me **try**

If you do not have the data file from the previous skill open, open the student data file **of1-SpaNewsletter** and try this skill on your own:

1. Close the file
2. Keep the app open to work on the next skill.

Skill 1.4 Closing the App

When you close a file, the app stays open so you can open another file to edit or begin a new file. Often, when you are finished working on a file, you want to close the file and exit the app at the same time. In this case, you will want to close the app.

To close an app:

1. Click the **Close** button in the upper right corner of the app.
2. If you have made no changes since the last time you saved the file, it will close immediately. If changes have been made, the app displays a message box asking if you want to save the changes you made before closing.
   - Click **Save** to save the changes.
   - Click **Don't Save** to close the file without saving your latest changes.
   - Click **Cancel** to keep the file open.

Click the **Close** button to exit the application.

Click **Save** to save any changes made.

Click **Don't Save** to exit without saving.

FIGURE OF 1.10

tell me **more**

Next to the **Close** button in the upper right corner of the app you will see two other buttons:

Minimize ▭ —hides the window from view, but does not close the app. The app button is still active on the Windows taskbar. Click the button on the taskbar to display the window again.

Maximize ☐ —resizes the app window so it fills the screen. When the window is maximized, the window cannot be moved around the screen and the *Maximize* button is replaced with the *Restore* button ❐. Click the **Restore** button to reduce the size of the window and move it around on the screen.

another **method**

To close the app, you can also right-click the title bar and select **Close**.

let me **try**

Open the student data file **of1-SpaNewsletter** and try this skill on your own:

1. Make a change to the document.
2. Close the app.
3. Do not save the change you made.

Skill 1.5 Using the Start Page

Before you can begin working in an app, you must have a file to work on. This can be a file you have worked on in the past, a new blank file, or a new file based on a template. When you launch an Office app you are first taken to the **Start page**. By default, the *Start* page opens to the to the **Home page** which displays a list of recently opened files along with templates for creating new files.

To open a recent file from the *Home* page:

1. Launch the app.
2. The *Start* page opens with the *Home* page displayed.
3. On the right side of the screen, click a template to create a new file or select a file in the list of recent files to open it.

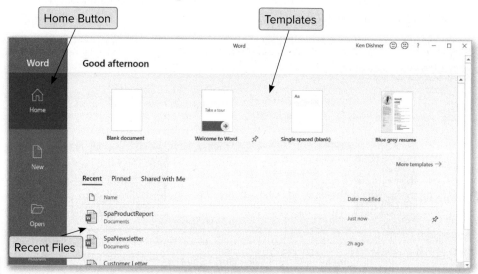

FIGURE OF 1.11

tips & tricks

If you do not see the file you want to open on the *Home* page, click the **Open** option in the left pane. This will display the *Open* page that includes buttons for finding and opening files from other locations such as your computer or your OneDrive.

If you do not see a template you want to use on the *Home* page, click the **More templates** link or the **New** option in the left pane. Either of these will display the *New* page that includes more templates to choose from and the ability to search for templates online.

tell me more

In previous versions of Office when you launched an app, a blank file opened ready for you to begin working. If you want to start a new blank file, click the blank file template in the list of templates. It is always listed as the first option on the *Home* page and the *New* page.

let me try

To try this skill on your own:

1. Launch **Microsoft Word**.
2. Click the **of1-SpaNewsletter** file in the list of recently opened files. If you do not see this file, open a file of your choice.
3. If you will be moving on to the next skill in this chapter, leave the document open to continue working. If not, close the file.

Skill 1.6 Getting to Know the Office User Interface

THE RIBBON

Beginning with Office 2007, Microsoft redesigned the user experience for the Office apps–replacing the old menu bar/toolbar interface with a Ribbon interface that makes it easier to find app functions and commands.

The **Ribbon** is located across the top of the app window and organizes common features and commands into tabs. Each **tab** organizes commands further into related **groups**. The **dialog launcher** appears in the lower right corner of some groups. Clicking this button opens the primary dialog for working with commands in the group. For example, clicking the dialog launcher in the *Font* group will open the *Font* dialog.

FIGURE OF 1.12

Figure OF 1.12 represents the 2019 version of the Office 365 Ribbon.

If you have the Office 2019 on-premises version, your Ribbon may look more like Figure OF 1.13. Although the look of the Ribbon is different, the steps to complete the skills covered in this textbook are the same.

FIGURE OF 1.13

When a specific type of object is selected (such as a picture, table, or chart), a contextual tab will appear. **Contextual tabs** contain commands specific to the type of object selected and are visible only when the commands might be useful.

Each app includes a **Home tab** that contains the most commonly used commands for that app. For example, in Word, the *Home* tab includes the following groups: *Clipboard*, *Font*, *Paragraph*, *Styles*, and *Editing*, while the Excel *Home* tab includes groups more appropriate for a spreadsheet program: *Clipboard*, *Font*, *Alignment*, *Number*, *Styles*, *Cells*, and *Editing*.

tips & tricks

If you need more space for your file, you can minimize the Ribbon by clicking the **Collapse the Ribbon** button in the lower right corner of the Ribbon (or press `Ctrl` + `F1`). When the Ribbon is minimized, the tab names appear along the top of the window (similar to a menu bar). When you click a tab name, the Ribbon appears. After you select a command or click away from the Ribbon, the Ribbon hides again. To redisplay the Ribbon permanently, click the **Pin the Ribbon** button in the lower right corner of the Ribbon. You can also double-click the active tab to hide or display the Ribbon.

BACKSTAGE

Notice that each app also includes a **File tab** at the far-left side of the Ribbon. Clicking the **File** tab opens **Backstage view**, where you can access the commands for managing and protecting your files, including *Save*, *Open*, *Close*, *New*, *Print*, and *Share*.

To return to your file from Backstage view, click the **Back** button located in the upper left corner of the window.

KEYBOARD SHORTCUTS

Many commands available through the Ribbon and Backstage view are also accessible through keyboard shortcuts and shortcut menus.

Press and hold **Ctrl** and then press **V** to paste text or item in a file.

FIGURE OF 1.14

Keyboard shortcuts are keys or combinations of keys that you press to execute a command. Some keyboard shortcuts refer to **F** keys or function keys. These are the keys that run across the top of the keyboard. Pressing these keys will execute specific commands. For example, pressing the F1 key will open Help in any of the Microsoft Office apps. Keyboard shortcuts typically use a combination of two keys, although some commands use a combination of three keys and others only one key. When a keyboard shortcut calls for a combination of key presses, such as Ctrl + V to paste an item from the *Clipboard*, you must first press the modifier key Ctrl holding it down while you press the V key on the keyboard.

tell me **more**

Many of the keyboard shortcuts are universal across all apps—not just Microsoft Office apps. Some examples of universal shortcut keys include:

Ctrl + C = Copy
Ctrl + X = Cut
Ctrl + V = Paste
Ctrl + Z = Undo
Ctrl + O = Open
Ctrl + S = Save

SHORTCUT MENUS

Shortcut menus are menus of commands that display when you right-click an area of the app window. The area or object you right-click determines which menu appears. For example, if you right-click in a paragraph, you will see a shortcut menu of commands for working with text; however, if you right-click an image, you will see a shortcut menu of commands for working with images.

FIGURE OF 1.15

THE MINI TOOLBAR

The **Mini toolbar** gives you access to common tools for working with text. When you select text and then rest your mouse over the text, the Mini toolbar fades in. You can then click a button to change the selected text just as you would on the Ribbon.

FIGURE OF 1.16

another **method**

To display the Mini toolbar, you can also right-click the text. The Mini toolbar appears above the shortcut menu. The Mini toolbar that appears at the top of the right-click shortcut menu includes buttons for the features most commonly used in the app, not just text options.

QUICK ACCESS TOOLBAR

The **Quick Access Toolbar** is located at the top of the app window above the *File* tab. The Quick Access Toolbar, as its name implies, gives you quick one-click access to common commands. Some of the commands include *Save*, *Undo*, and *Redo*.

FIGURE OF 1.17

ENHANCED SCREENTIP

A **ScreenTip** is a small information box that displays the name of the command when you rest your mouse over a button on the Ribbon. An **Enhanced ScreenTip** displays not only the name of the command, but also the keyboard shortcut (if there is one) and a short description of what the button does and when it is used. Certain Enhanced ScreenTips also include an image along with a description of the command.

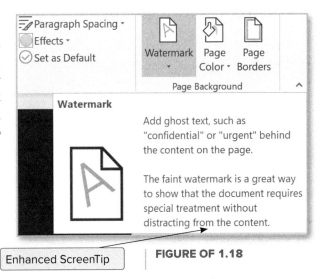

FIGURE OF 1.18

THE OPTIONS DIALOG

The **Options dialog** is where you can control settings for the Office app. When you make a change in the *Options* dialog, the setting applies to the app, not the current active file. This means when you exit the app and open it again, any changes you made in the *Options* dialog will remain.

Although each app has a slightly different set of controls, the *Options* dialog includes areas for controlling proofing options, save options, language, the Ribbon, and Quick Access Toolbar, as well as a general section where you can control some of the user interface features.

You can enable and disable some of the user interface features through the *Options* dialog:

1. Click the **File** tab to open Backstage view.
2. Click **Options**.
3. Make the changes you want, and then click **OK** to save your changes
   - Check or uncheck **Show Mini toolbar on selection** to control whether or not the Mini toolbar appears when you hover over selected text. (This does not affect the appearance of the Mini toolbar when you right-click.)
   - Check or uncheck **Enable Live Preview** to turn the live preview feature on or off.
   - Make a selection from the *ScreenTip style* list:
     - **Show feature descriptions in ScreenTips** displays Enhanced ScreenTips when they are available.
     - **Don't show feature descriptions in ScreenTips** hides Enhanced ScreenTips. The ScreenTip will still include the keyboard shortcut if there is one available.
     - **Don't show ScreenTips** hides ScreenTips altogether, so if you hold your mouse over a button on the Ribbon, nothing will appear.

FIGURE OF 1.19

LIVE PREVIEW

The **Live Preview** feature in Microsoft Office allows you to see formatting changes in your file before committing to the change. When Live Preview is active, rolling over a command on the Ribbon will temporarily apply the formatting to the currently active text or object. To apply the formatting, click the formatting option.

Use Live Preview to preview the following:

Font Formatting—Including the font, font size, text effects, and font color

Paragraph Formatting—Including numbering, bullets, line spacing, and shading

Styles and Themes Table Formatting—Including table styles and shading

Picture Formatting—Including correction and color options, picture styles, borders, effects, positioning, brightness, and contrast

SmartArt—Including layouts, styles, and colors

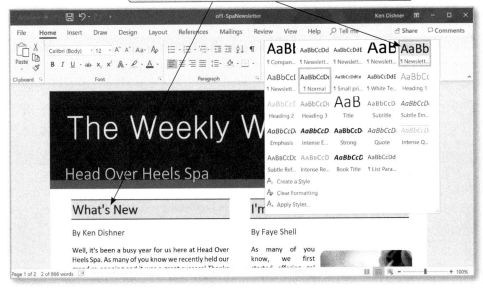

The Live Preview feature allows you to see formatting changes in your file before committing to them.

FIGURE OF 1.20

let me try

If you do not have the data file from the previous skill open, open the student data file **of1-SpaNewsletter** and try this skill on your own:

1. Explore the Ribbon. Click on different tabs and observe how commands are arranged together in groups.
2. Click the picture to display the *Picture Tools* contextual tab.
3. Right-click an area of the file to display the shortcut menu.
4. Explore the Mini Toolbar at the top of the shortcut menu. Click away from the menu to hide it.
5. Click the **Insert** tab. In the *Pages* group, roll your mouse over the **Cover Page** button to display the Enhanced ScreenTip.
6. Display **Backstage** view.
7. Click **Options** to open the *Options* dialog.
8. Disable **Live Preview** and change the **ScreenTips** so they don't show feature descriptions. Close the *Options* dialog and save your changes.
9. Click the **Back** button to return to the document.
10. If you will be moving on to the next skill in this chapter, leave the document open to continue working. If not, close the file.

Skill 1.7 Getting Help

The **Tell Me** feature offers a quick way to access commands that you do not know how to find in the Office interface or that take several clicks to get to. By using the *Tell Me* box to access commands, you can save time and frustration by quickly getting to the features you need.

To use *Tell Me* to access a command:

1. Type the word or phrase you want to look up in the **Tell me what you want to do...** box at the top of the window.

2. Office displays a list of commands that match your search.

3. Options with a triangle have a gallery or menu of options associated with it. Point to the option to display more commands from which to choose.

4. Click an option on the list to access that command.

Type the command you are looking for in the *Tell Me* box.

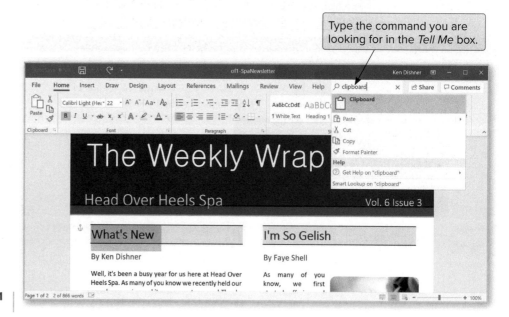

FIGURE OF 1.21

If you want to learn more about a command, you can look it up using the **Help task pane**. Each app comes with its own Help topics specifically tailored for working with that app.

To look up a topic using the *Help* task pane:

1. Type the word or phrase you want help on in the *Tell Me* box.

2. At the bottom of the menu, point to the *Get Help on [topic]* option.

3. A list of Help topics appears.

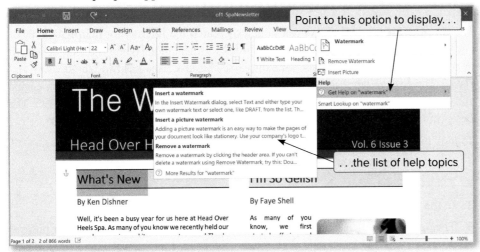

FIGURE OF 1.22

4. Click a topic to display it in the *Help* task pane.

FIGURE OF 1.23

tips & tricks

At the bottom of the list of options, you will see options for **Smart Lookup**. Click the **Smart Lookup** link to search for information on the Internet on the word or phrase you typed.

another **method**

To open the *Help* task pane, you can also:

❭ Press `F1` on the keyboard.

❭ Click the **Help** tab and then click the **Help** button.

let me **try**

If you do not have the data file from the previous skill open, open the student data file **of1-SpaNewsletter** and try this skill on your own:

1. Type **Clipboard** in the *Tell Me* box and display the *Clipboard* task pane.

2. Click the **X** in the upper right corner of the task pane to close it.

3. Type **Watermark** in the *Tell Me* box and display the topic for inserting a watermark in Word in the *Help* task pane.

4. Close the file.

Skill 1.8 Using Smart Lookup

The **Smart Lookup** tool allows you to quickly search the Internet for information about any word or phrase in a document, spreadsheet, or presentation. When you look up a word or phrase, the *Smart Lookup* task pane displays. This task pane has two tabs—*Explore* and *Define*. The *Explore* tab displays search results powered by Microsoft's Bing search engine and returns results from Wikipedia, Bing image search, and other sources on the Web. The *Define* tab displays a definition of the word or phrase from the Oxford Dictionaries.

To look up information about a word or phrase using the *Smart Lookup* tool:

1. Select the word or phrase.
2. Click the **References** tab.
3. In the *Research* group, click the **Smart Lookup** button.
4. The *Smart Lookup* task pane opens displaying information about the word or phrase.

FIGURE OF 1.24

tips & tricks

You can also display the *Smart Lookup* task pane from the *Tell Me* box. First, type the word or phrase in the *Tell Me* box at the top of the screen. Click the **Smart Lookup on** link on the menu. The *Smart Lookup* task pane opens with the information displayed.

tell me **more**

Smart Lookup relies on Microsoft Office's **intelligent services** to retrieve the most up to date search results. You may need to turn on intelligent services in order to use the *Smart Lookup* feature. You can turn on intelligent services by clicking **Options** in Backstage view and then checking the **Enable services** check box in *Office intelligent services* section the *Options* dialog.

another **method**

To look up a word or phrase using Smart Lookup, you can also right-click the word or phrase and select **Smart Lookup** from the shortcut menu.

let me **try**

If you do not have the data file from the previous skill open, open the student data file **of1-SpaNewsletter** and try this skill on your own:

1. Select the words **Dead Sea** in the middle of the first paragraph of the newsletter.
2. Display the **Smart Lookup** task pane.
3. Review the information on the *Explore* tab.
4. Click the **X** in the upper right corner of the task pane to close it.
5. Close the file.

Skill 1.9 Working in Protected View

When you download a file from a location that Office considers potentially unsafe, it opens automatically in **Protected View**. Protected View provides a read-only format that protects your computer from becoming infected by a virus or other malware. Potentially unsafe locations include the Internet, email messages, or a network location. Files that are opened in Protected View display a warning in the Message Bar at the top of the window, below the Ribbon.

To disable Protected View, click the **Enable Editing** button in the Message Bar.

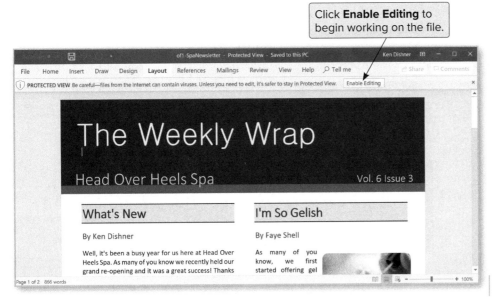

Click **Enable Editing** to begin working on the file.

FIGURE OF 1.25

You can also enable editing from the *Info* page in Backstage view.

1. Click the **File** tab to open Backstage view.
2. Click **Info**.
3. The *Info* page provides more information about the file. If you are sure you want to remove it from Protected View, click the **Enable Editing** button.

tips & tricks

To learn more about the security settings in Office, open the Trust Center and review the options. To open the Trust Center, click the **File** tab and select **Options**. In the *Options* dialog, click **Trust Center** on the left side of the dialog. We do not recommend changing any of the default Trust Center settings.

let me try

Open the student data file **of1-SpaNewsletter** and try this skill on your own:

1. If you downloaded the file from the Internet, the file will open in Protected View.
2. Click the **Enable Editing** button to begin working with the file.
3. Navigate to the second page of the document.
4. Close the file.

Skill 1.10 Picking Up Where You Left Off

When you are working in a long document or a presentation and reopen it to work on it, you may not remember where you were last working. The **Pick up where you left off** feature automatically bookmarks the last location that was worked on when the file was closed.

To pick up where you left off in a document or presentation:

1. Open the document or presentation.

2. A message displays on the right side of the screen welcoming you back and asking if you want to pick up where you left off. The message then minimizes to a bookmark tag.

3. Click the **bookmark tag** to navigate to the location.

FIGURE OF 1.26

tips & tricks

The bookmark tag displays only until you navigate to another part of the document. If you scroll the document, the bookmark tag disappears.

tell me more

The bookmark tag is available only in Word and PowerPoint. This feature is not necessary in Excel, since Excel automatically opens to the last active cell position when the workbook was last closed.

let me try

Open the student data file **of1-SpaNewsletter** and try this skill on your own:

1. Navigate to the last location of the file when it was last closed.

2. If you will be moving on to the next skill in this chapter, leave the document open to continue working. If not, close the file.

Skill 1.11 Working with File Properties

File Properties provide information about a file such as the location of the file, the size of file, when the file was created and when it was last modified, the title, and the author. Properties also include keywords, referred to as **tags**, that are useful for grouping common files together or for searching. All this information about a file is referred to as **metadata**.

To view a file's properties:

1. Click the **File** tab to open Backstage view.

2. Properties are listed at the far right of the *Info* page.

3. To add keywords to a file, click the text box next to *Tags* and type keywords that describe the file, separating each word with a comma.

   The Author property is added automatically using the account name entered when you installed and registered Office. You can change the author name or add more names by editing the Author property.

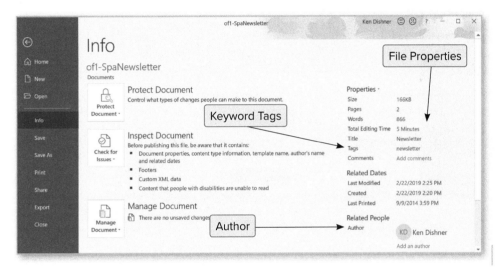

FIGURE OF 1.27

tips & tricks

Some file properties are generated automatically by Windows and cannot be edited by the user, such as the date the file was created and the size of the file.

let me try

If you do not have the data file from the previous skill open, open the student data file **of1-SpaNewsletter** and try this skill on your own:

1. Add a tag to the document that reads **newsletter**.

2. If you will be moving on to the next skill in this chapter, leave the document open to continue working. If not, close the file.

Skill 1.12 Creating a New Blank File

When you first open an Office app, the *Start* page displays giving you the opportunity to open an existing file, create a new blank file, or create a new file based on a template. But what if you have a file open and want to create another new file? Will you need to close the app and then launch it again? The **New command** allows you to create new files without exiting and reopening the program.

To create a new blank file:

1. Click the **File** tab to open Backstage view.
2. Click **New**.
3. The first option on the *New* page is a blank file. Click the **Blank document** thumbnail to create the new blank file.

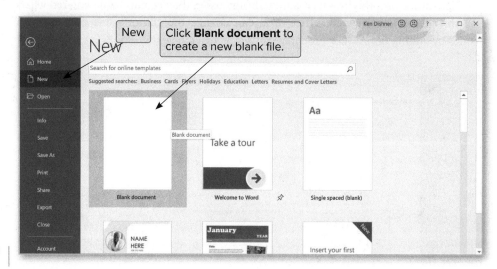

FIGURE OF 1.28

tell me **more**

In addition to a blank file, you can create new files from templates from the *New* page.

another **method**

❯ To bypass the Backstage view and create a new blank file, press `Ctrl` + `N` on the keyboard.

❯ You can also create a new blank file by clicking the **File** tab to display Backstage view, clicking **Home**, and then clicking the **Blank document** template at the top of the page.

let me **try**

If you do not have the data file from the previous skill open, open the student data file **of1-SpaNewsletter** and try this skill on your own:

1. Create a new blank file.
2. If you will be moving on to the next skill in this chapter, leave the document open to continue working. If not, close the file.

Skill 1.13 Saving Files to Your PC

As you work on a new file, it is displayed onscreen and stored in your computer's memory. However, it is not permanently stored until you save it as a file to a specific location. The first time you save a file, the *Save As* page in Backstage view will display. Here you can choose to save the file to your OneDrive, your local computer, or another location.

You can also choose to save the file in different formats, including templates and macro-enabled files. This table lists the default and template file formats for Word, Excel, and PowerPoint:

APP	DEFAULT FORMAT	TEMPLATE
Word	Word Document (*.docx)	Word Template (*.dotx)
Excel	Excel Workbook (*.xlsx)	Excel Template (*.xltx)
Powerpoint	PowerPoint Presentation (*.pptx)	PowerPoint Template (*.potx)

To save a file to your PC:

1. Click the **Save** button on the Quick Access Toolbar.
2. The *Save As* page in Backstage view appears.
3. On the left side of the page, click **This PC** to save the file to a local drive.
4. At the top of the right side of the page, you will see the name of the folder the file will be saved in. If you want to save the file in this location, type the name of the file in the *Enter file name here* box.
5. If you want to change the file type, click the box below the file name and select an option.
6. Click the **Save** button to save the file.

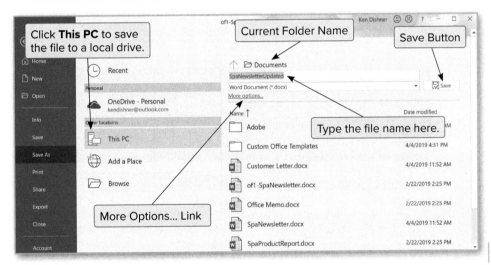

FIGURE OF 1.29

To save the file to a new folder:

1. On the *Save As* page, click the **More options...** link under the *Enter file name here* box.
2. The *Save As* dialog opens.
3. If you want to create a new folder, click the **New Folder** button near the top of the file list. The new folder is created with the temporary name *New Folder*. Type the new name for the folder and press ⬅ Enter.
4. Double-click the folder to open it.
5. Click in the **File name** box and type a file name.
6. Click the **Save** button.

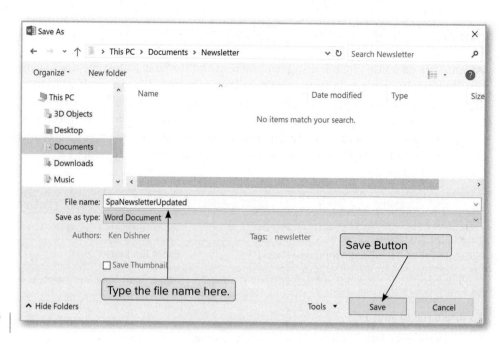

FIGURE OF 1.30

If you are working on a file that has already been saved, click the **Save** button on the Quick Access Toolbar or press Ctrl + S on the keyboard to quickly save the file as you make changes. The file will be saved to the same location with the same name.

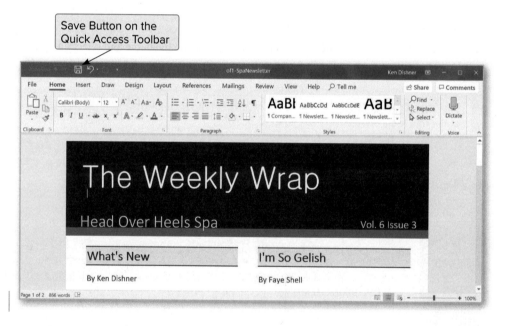

FIGURE OF 1.31

tips & tricks

❯ If the location where you want to save the file is not listed on the right side of the *Save As* page, click the **Browse** button to open the *Save As* dialog. Navigate to the location where you want to save the file.

❯ If you are working on a file that you want to save but not overwrite the original file, you should save the file with a new name. When you save a file with a new name, the original file still exists in its last saved state and the new file you save will include all the changes you made.

another **method**

let me **try**

from the perspective of . . .

A BUSY PARENT

Learning Microsoft Office was one of the best things I did to help manage my family's busy lifestyle. I use Word to write up and print a calendar of everyone's activities for the week. I keep a handle on the family finances with a budget of all expenses in an Excel spreadsheet. I used PowerPoint to create a presentation for my family of our summer vacation pictures. Once I became more familiar with Access, I used it to help organize my family's busy schedule. I created a database with one table for activities, another for parent contact information, another one for carpooling, and another one for the schedule. Being able to organize all the information in a database has been invaluable. And the best part is now I can share and view these files with everyone, even on my tablet. I always thought Office was only for businesses, but now I can't imagine running my household without it!

George Doyle & Ciaran Griffin/
Stockbyte/Getty Images

Skill 1.14 Saving Files to OneDrive

OneDrive is Microsoft's free **cloud storage** where you can save documents, workbooks, presentations, videos, pictures, and other files and access those files from any computer or share the files with others. When you save files to your OneDrive, they are stored locally on your computer and then "synched" with your OneDrive account and stored in the "cloud" where you can then access the files from another computer or device that has OneDrive capability.

To save a file to your OneDrive:

1. Click the **File** tab.
2. Click **Save As**.
3. Verify the OneDrive account is selected on the left side of the page.
4. A list of OneDrive folders appears on the right. Click the **folder** you want to save to.
5. Type the name of the file in the *Enter file name here* box and click the **Save** button.

FIGURE OF 1.32

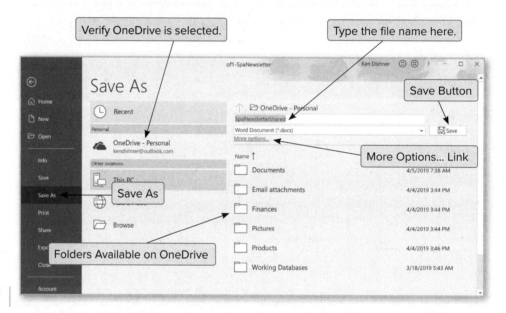

You can also save the file through the *Save As* dialog:

1. On the *Save As* page, click the **More options...** link under the *Enter file name here* box.
2. The *Save As* dialog opens to your OneDrive folder location on your computer.
3. Click in the **File name** box and type a file name.
4. Click the **Save** button.

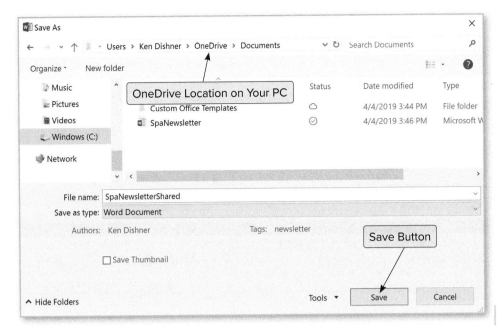

FIGURE OF 1.33

tips & tricks

By default, your OneDrive includes folders for documents, pictures, and files you want to make public. You can save your files in any of these folders or create your own. To create a new folder in your OneDrive, click the **New Folder** button near the top of the file list in the *Save As* dialog. The new folder is created with the temporary name *New Folder*. Type the new name for the folder and press (← Enter).

tell me **more**

When you are working on a file that has been saved to your OneDrive, others can work on the file at the same time as you. The app will mark the area being worked on as read only so others cannot modify the same information you are working on.

let me **try**

Open the student data file **of1-SpaNewsletter** and try this skill on your own:

NOTE: You will need a OneDrive account to complete this exercise. In addition, if you are using this in class or in your school's computer lab, check with your instructor before completing this exercise.

1. Save the file to the **Documents** folder on your OneDrive.
2. Name the file: **SpaNewsletterShared**
3. If you will be moving on to the next skill in this chapter, leave the document open to continue working. If not, close the file.

Skill 1.15 Using AutoSave

When a file is saved to your OneDrive, the **AutoSave** toggle is on by default. This means you no longer need to continually save your files in order to not lose your work. Each time your file is saved on your OneDrive, a version of the file is saved in that state. The title bar displays the last saved date and time next to the file name.

To turn the *AutoSave* feature off, click the toggle so it appears in the "Off" state. Click the toggle again to return it to the "On" state and have the files automatically save to your OneDrive.

FIGURE OF 1.34

You can access previous saved **versions** of files from the *Version History* task pane. You can then open those versions and copy and paste content you need or save the version with a new name to create a new file from that version.

To open a previously saved version of a file:

1. Click the arrow next to the title in the title bar and select **Version History**.

2. The *Version History* task pane opens displaying the saved versions of the file.

3. In the list of files, click the saved version of the file you want to open.

4. The file will open as read-only. Save the file with a new name to remove the read-only status.

FIGURE OF 1.35

> **Office 2019 Note:** If you have the Office 2019 on-premises version of Office, you will not have the *AutoSave* toggle in the title bar. In addition, you will not be able to restore versions of files using the method described here.

tell me **more**

Files that are saved locally to a computer and not to a OneDrive or SharePoint account will not display the last saved date and time next to the file name. Instead, you will see *Saved to my PC*.

another **method**

To display the *Version History* task pane, you can also:

1. Click the **File** tab.
2. Verify you are on the *Info* page.
3. Click **View and restore previous versions** under *Version History*.

let me **try**

If you do not have the data file from the previous skill open, open a file you have saved to your OneDrive account and try this skill on your own:

NOTE: You will need a OneDrive account to complete this exercise. In addition, if you are using this in class or in your school's computer lab, check with your instructor before completing this exercise.

1. Turn the **AutoSave** feature off.
2. Turn the **AutoSave** feature back on.
3. Make a change to the file and save the file.
4. Open the **Version History** task pane.
5. Open a previously saved version of the file.
6. Close the version you opened.
7. If you will be moving on to the next skill in this chapter, leave the document open to continue working. If not, close the file.

Skill 1.16 Sharing Files Using OneDrive

One of the benefits of saving files to your OneDrive is the ability to share files with others. The first step in sharing a file using OneDrive is to save the file to your OneDrive folder. To learn how to save a file to a OneDrive account, see *Saving Files to OneDrive*. Once the file is saved to your OneDrive, you can share it with others from the Ribbon.

To share a file using OneDrive:

1. Click the **Share** button at the far-right side of the Ribbon.
2. The *Share* task pane displays.
3. Type the email address of the person you want to share the file with in the *Invite people* box.
4. Click the drop-down arrow under the box and select whether the recipient(s) can edit or only view the file.
5. If you want to include a note to the recipient(s), click in the message box and a type a message.
6. Click the **Share** button.

FIGURE OF 1.36

REAL-TIME COLLABORATION

When you share files through OneDrive, you can take advantage of Office's **online collaboration** tools. This means multiple people can work on a file at the same time and all the changes are made to one file. When a person works on a shared file, their user account icon appears to the left of the *Share* button for anyone else who also has the file open. Office locks any section of the file currently being worked on. This prevents overlapping changes when multiple people are working on the same file. Office also marks the area being worked on by others and displays a flag at the site of the change with the user's name.

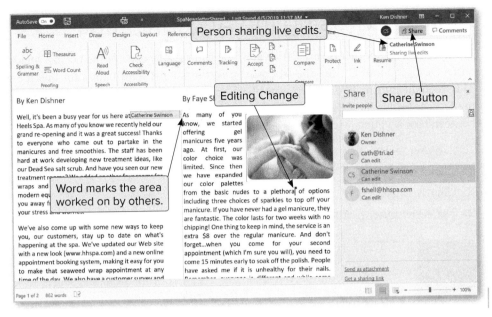

FIGURE OF 1.37

tips & tricks

❯ To share the file with more than one person, enter the email addresses for each recipient separated by a comma.

❯ If the file has not been shared, you will be prompted to share the file to your OneDrive or to send the file as an attachment.

tell me **more**

You can also share a file through a **sharing link**. A sharing link creates a link to your OneDrive that others can access to either view or edit the file. Click the **Get a sharing link** option at the bottom of the *Share* task pane to create a sharing link you can send to others.

another **method**

To open the *Share* task pane, you can also:

1. Click the **File** tab.
2. Click **Share**.
3. Verify *Share with People* is selected on the left side of the page. Click the **Share with People** button on the right side of the page.

let me **try**

If you do not have the data file from the previous skill open, open a file you have saved to your OneDrive account and try this skill on your own:

NOTE: You will need a OneDrive account to complete this exercise. In addition, if you are using this in class or in your school's computer lab, check with your instructor before completing this exercise.

1. Display the **Share** task pane.
2. Share the document with **fshell@hhspa.com** and include the message **Please review and edit**. The recipient should be able to edit the document.
3. If you will be moving on to the next skill in this chapter, leave the document open to continue working. If not, close the file.

skill 1.16   Sharing Files Using OneDrive

Skill 1.17 Using the Account Page

In the upper right corner of any Office app, you will see the name of the person who is currently logged into Office. The **Account page** lists more information for that user. This account information comes from the Microsoft account you used when installing Office. From the *Account* page, you can view your Microsoft user profile, switch between user accounts, view your product information, and connect to online services.

To view user information:

1. Click the **File** tab.
2. Click **Account**.
3. The current user profile is listed under *User Information*.

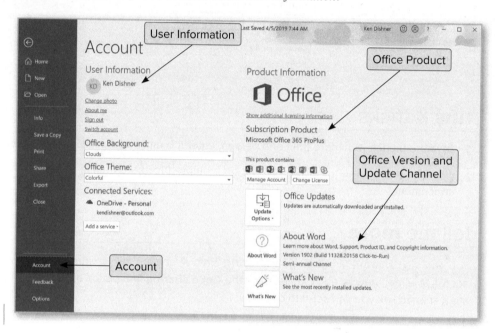

FIGURE OF 1.38

On the right side of the *Account* page, you will see product information, including the product you have installed (Office 365 or Office 2109). If you have an Office 365 subscription, you or the account administrator (if you are using a school or work account) can choose how often Office is updated (the update channel):

❭ **Semi-annual channel**—updates in January and July with new features from the Semi-annual (targeted) release. At this point, all users have the new features.

❭ **Semi-annual (targeted) channel**—updates in September and March with what is expected to be the feature set that will be rolled out to everyone in the semi-annual release.

❭ **Monthly channel**—updates once a month with new features. These features have not been thoroughly tested and are released to Monthly channel users for feedback.

office 365   Essential Skills for Office

Office will alert you when a new update is available. You can also check to see if your version is up to date from the *Account* page.

To check for Office updates:

1. Go to the *Account* page.
2. Click the **Update Options** button and select **Update Now**.
3. If there are new updates, follow the prompts to install the updates. If there are no new updates, close the message box that appears.

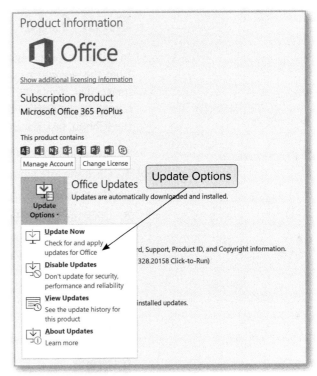

FIGURE OF 1.39

tips & tricks

Click **Change photo** or **About me** under user information to navigate to *live.com* where you can change the image that appears with the user profile and change information for that user as well.

tell me **more**

Depending on the version of Office you have, multiple accounts can use the same installation of Office. When you switch accounts, any personalization that person has done to Office will be applied. The account will also have access to that person's OneDrive account and all files that have been saved there.

another **method**

To display the *Account* page, you can also click the user name in the upper right corner of the window and select the **Account Settings** link.

let me **try**

If you do not have the data file from the previous skill open, open the student data file **of1-SpaNewsletter** and try this skill on your own:

1. Open the **Account** page in Backstage view.

   NOTE: If you are using this in class or in your school's computer lab, check with your instructor about permissions before completing the following steps.

2. Check for new updates to Office.

3. If you will be moving on to the next skill in this chapter, leave the document open to continue working. If not, close the file.

Skill 1.18 Changing the Look of Office

In addition to managing the Office account, you can also control the look of Office from the *Account* page. Changing the **Office background** changes the background image that displays in the upper right corner of the window near the user profile. Changing the **Office theme** changes the color scheme for Office, affecting the look of the Ribbon, task panes, and main working areas.

To change the look of Office:

1. Click the **File** tab to open Backstage view.
2. Click **Account**.
3. Click the **Office Background** drop-down list and select an option to display as the background.
4. Click the **Office Theme** drop-down list and select a color option for your apps.

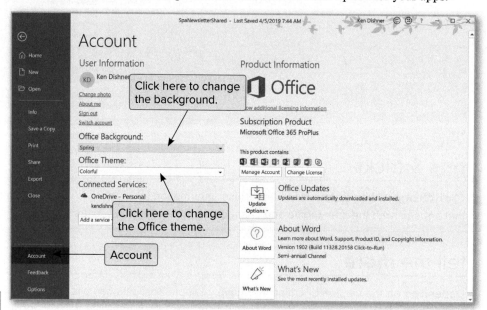

FIGURE OF 1.40

tell me **more**

In Office 2016, Microsoft added new backgrounds and themes. The new default theme is the *Colorful* theme. This theme recolors parts of the user interface to match the color of the app. For example, in Word the area above the Ribbon appears blue when the *Colorful* theme is applied.

another **method**

To display the *Account* page, you can also click the user name in the upper right corner of the window and select the **Account Settings** link.

let me **try**

If you do not have the data file from the previous skill open, open the student data file **of1-SpaNewsletter** and try this skill on your own:

1. Open the **Account** page in Backstage view.

   NOTE: If you are using this in class or in your school's computer lab, check with your instructor about permissions before completing the following steps.

2. Change the Office background to the **Spring** background.
3. Change the Office theme to **Colorful**.
4. If you will be moving on to the next skill in this chapter, leave the document open to continue working. If not, close the file.

office 365   Essential Skills for Office

Skill 1.19 Customizing the Quick Access Toolbar

The Quick Access Toolbar gives you a fast way to access commands that you use often. By default, the Quick Access Toolbar displays the *Save*, *Undo*, and *Redo* commands. If you use different commands often, you can add commands to and remove commands from the Quick Access Toolbar.

To modify the Quick Access Toolbar:

1. Click the **Customize Quick Access Toolbar** button located on the right side of the Quick Access Toolbar.

2. Options with checkmarks next to them are already displayed on the toolbar. Options with no checkmarks are not currently displayed.

3. Click an option to add it to or remove it from the Quick Access Toolbar.

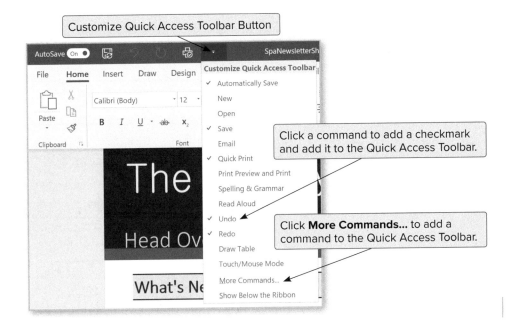

FIGURE OF 1.41

If a command does not appear on the *Customize Quick Access Toolbar* list, you can still add it to the Quick Access Toolbar:

1. Click the **Customize Quick Access Toolbar** button and select **More Commands…**

2. The *Options* dialog opens to the *Customize the Quick Access Toolbar* page.

3. Scroll the list of popular commands or expand the **Choose commands from** list and select an option.

4. Select the command you want to appear on the Quick Access Toolbar and click the **Add** button.

5. You can reorder commands by selecting a command in the list and using the **Move Up** and **Move Down** buttons.

6. When you are finished customizing the Quick Access Toolbar, click **OK**.

FIGURE OF 1.42

tips & tricks

The *Quick Print* option on the Quick Access Toolbar allows you to print with a single mouse click. If you do not need to change any print settings, this is by far the easiest method to print a file because it doesn't require opening Backstage view first.

tell me **more**

To reset the Quick Access Toolbar to its original state:

1. In the *Options* dialog, *Customize the Quick Access Toolbar* page, click the **Reset** button and select **Reset only Quick Access Toolbar**.

2. A message displays to verify that you want to reset the Quick Access Toolbar customizations. Click **Yes**.

another **method**

To open the *Customize Quick Access Toolbar* page:

❭ Click the **File** tab and click **Options** to open the *Options* dialog. Click **Quick Access Toolbar**.

❭ Right-click the **Quick Access Toolbar** and select **Customize Quick Access Toolbar...**

let me **try**

If you do not have the data file from the previous skill open, open the student data file **of1-SpaNewsletter** and try this skill on your own:

NOTE: If you are using this in class or in your school's computer lab, check with your instructor about permissions before completing the following steps.

1. Add the **Quick Print** command to the Quick Access Toolbar.
2. Open the **Word Options** dialog from the *Quick Access Toolbar* page.
3. Add the **Insert Comment** command to the Quick Access Toolbar.
4. Close the file.

office 365   Essential Skills for Office

key terms

Microsoft Word
Microsoft Excel
Microsoft Access
Microsoft PowerPoint
Office 365
Office 2019 (on-premises)
Desktop apps
Online apps
Mobile apps
Start page
Home page
Ribbon
Tab
Groups
Dialog launcher
Contextual tabs
Home tab
File tab
Backstage view
Keyboard shortcuts
Shortcut menus
Mini toolbar
Quick Access Toolbar

ScreenTip
Enhanced ScreenTip
Options dialog
Live Preview
Tell Me
Help task pane
Smart Lookup
Intelligent services
Protected View
File Properties
Tags
Metadata
New command
OneDrive
Cloud storage
AutoSave
Versions
Online collaboration
Sharing link
Account page
Office background
Office theme

concept review

1. Which Microsoft Office application is a spreadsheet program?

    a. Word

    b. Excel

    c. Access

    d. PowerPoint

2. Which tab do you click to display Backstage view?

    a. File

    b. Home

    c. View

    d. Contextual

3. To display a shortcut menu _____ an area of the file.

    a. left-click

    b. right-click

    c. double-click

    d. drag over

4. If you have downloaded a file from the Internet and it opens in Protected View, you should never open the file.

    a. true

    b. false

5. Which part of the Office interface is located across the top of the application window and organizes common features and commands into tabs?

a. Menu bar

b. Toolbar

c. Title bar

d. Ribbon

6. The _____ provide(s) information about a file such as the location of the file, the size of file, when the file was created and when it was last modified, the title, and the author.

a. file properties

b. user profile

c. account information

d. Options dialog

7. When you save files to your OneDrive, they are available to access from other computers that have OneDrive capability. If you are working on an Excel or Word file, others can be working on the same file at the same time you are working on the file.

a. true

b. false

8. You can change user information from which page in Backstage view?

a. Account

b. Options

c. Share

d. Info

9. Which keyboard shortcut allows you to paste an item from the Clipboard?

a. Ctrl + C

b. Ctrl + X

c. Ctrl + V

d. Ctrl + P

10. Which part of the Office interface gives you quick one-click access to common commands and is located at the top of the application window above the File tab?

a. Ribbon

b. Quick Access Toolbar

c. Options dialog

d. Backstage view

Source of screenshots: Microsoft Office 365: Word, Excel, Access, and PowerPoint.

word 365

chapter 1

Getting Started with Word

In this chapter, you will learn the following skills:

❯ Enter, select, and delete text

❯ Use the spelling and grammar features

❯ Use Undo and Redo

❯ Find and replace text in a document

❯ Cut, copy, and paste text

❯ Apply different paste options

❯ Use the Clipboard

❯ View document statistics

❯ Change how the document displays in the window

❯ Print documents

skills

introduction

This introductory chapter will teach you some of the basic editing features of Microsoft Word, such as entering, selecting, and deleting text. You will also learn how to correct spelling and grammar errors; find and replace text; and use the cut, copy, and paste commands. In addition, you will look up document statistics, change the magnification of a document by using the Zoom feature, and change the document view. Finally, you will print a document using the typical print settings.

Skill 1.1 Introduction to Word

Microsoft Office Word is a word processing program that enables you to create many types of documents including letters, résumés, reports, proposals, flyers, personal cards, and more. Word's advanced editing capabilities allow you to quickly and easily perform tasks such as checking your spelling and finding text in a long document. Robust formatting allows you to produce professional documents with stylized fonts, layouts, and graphics. Printing and sharing can be managed directly from the Word window. In short, everything you need to create polished professional and personal documents is available in Microsoft Word.

Here are some basic elements of a Word document:

〉 **Font**—also called the typeface, refers to a set of characters of a certain design. You can choose from several preinstalled fonts available.

〉 **Paragraph**—groups of sentences separated by a hard return. A hard return refers to pressing the ← Enter key to create a new paragraph. You can assign a paragraph its own style to help it stand out from the rest of the document.

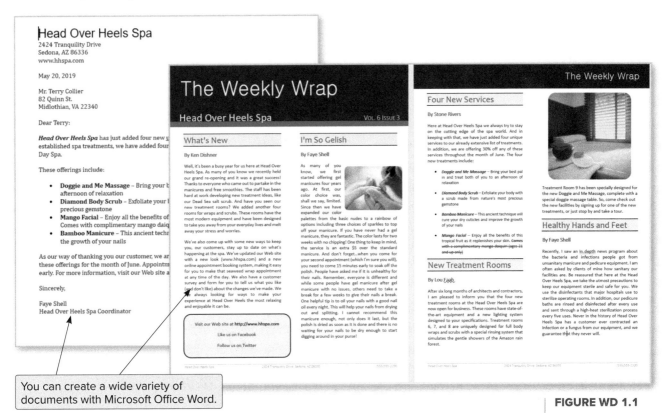

You can create a wide variety of documents with Microsoft Office Word.

FIGURE WD 1.1

> **Styles**—complex formatting, including font, color, size, and spacing, that can be applied to text. Use consistent styles for headings, body text, notes, and captions throughout your document. Styles also can be applied to tables and graphics.

> **Theme**—a group of formatting options that is applied to an entire Word document. Themes include font, color, and effect styles that are applied to text, tables, graphics, and other elements in the document.

> **Table**—used to organize data into columns and rows.

> **Chart**—transforms numerical data into a visual representation.

> **Graphics**—photographs, SmartArt, icons, 3-D models, or line drawings that can be added to documents.

> **Header**—text that appears at the top of every page in a document.

> **Footer**—text that appears at the bottom of every page in a document.

> **Page Break**—marker in a document that identifies where one page ends and another page begins.

> **Margin**—the blank areas at the top, bottom, left, and right of a page.

> **Citations**—automatically insert references to external sources in the proper format for use in a bibliography.

> **Comment**—a note you add to a document that is not meant to be a part of the document.

> **Track Changes**—feature that marks any changes made to a document by reviewers. Such changes include deletions, insertions, and formatting.

tips & tricks

Microsoft Office includes many other features that can further enhance your documents. If you would like to learn more about these features, begin typing in the **Tell Me** box to the right of the Ribbon tabs. Click the **Get Help on** link at the bottom of the menu to open the *Word Help* task pane.

tell me **more**

Some basic features of Microsoft Word include:

> **Word Wrap**—places text on the next line when the right margin of the page has been reached.

> **Find and Replace**—searches for any word or phrase in the document. Also, allows all instances of a word to be replaced by another word.

> **Editor**—checks for spelling and grammar errors, as well as writing style issues, and offers solutions to the problem.

> **Document Formatting**—allows the enhancement of the appearance of the document.

> **Draw Tools**—on touch devices, allows for drawing on documents using a pen or your finger.

> **Intelligent Services**—cloud-enhanced features in Office that can offer recommendations to help you work more efficiently. In Word, the *Editor* and *Smart Lookup* features rely on intelligent services.

> **Mail Merge**—creates several documents based on a main document, specified fields, and a list of recipients.

let me **try**

1. From the Start menu, open the **Word** app.
2. Open the student data file **wd1-01-FourNewServices** to review the formatting of a simple letter.
3. Open the student data file **wd1-01-SpaNewsletter** to review the formatting of a more complex document. Close this file when you are finished.
4. If you will be moving on to the next skill in this chapter, leave the **wd1-01-FourNewServices** document open to continue working. If not, close the file.

Skill 1.2 Entering and Deleting Text

The basic function of a word processing application like Microsoft Word is to create written documents. Whether the documents are simple, such as a letter, or complex, such as a newsletter, one of the basic tasks you will perform in Word is entering text. **Word wrap** is a feature in Microsoft Word that automatically places text on the next line when the right margin of the document has been reached. There is no need to press ⬅ Enter to begin a new line in the same paragraph. Press ⬅ Enter only when you want to create a break and start a new paragraph.

To enter text in a document:

1. Place the cursor where you want the new text to appear.

2. Begin typing.

3. When the cursor reaches the end of the line, do not press ⬅ Enter. Keep typing and allow word wrap to move the text to the next line.

If you make a mistake when entering text, you can press the ⬅ Backspace key to remove text to the left of the cursor, or press the Delete key to remove text to the right of the cursor.

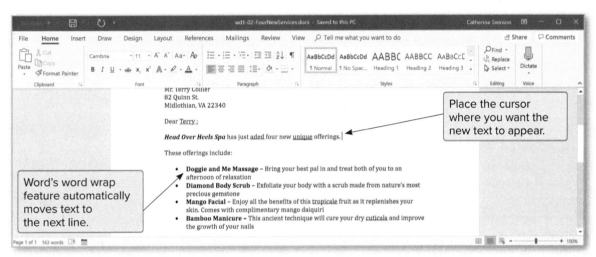

FIGURE WD 1.2

tips & tricks

If you want to force text onto a new line, but do not want to start a new paragraph, press ⬆ Shift + ⬅ Enter. This will insert a soft return where the text is moved to a new line without creating a new paragraph.

tell me **more**

The cursor indicates the place on the page where text will appear when you begin typing, indicated by a blinking vertical line. If you want to edit text you have typed, click in the text to place the cursor anywhere in the document. When you begin typing, the new text will be entered at the cursor point, pushing out any existing text to the right. You can also use the arrow keys to move the cursor around in the document and then begin typing.

let me **try**

If you do not have the data file from the previous skill open, open the student data file **wd1-02-FourNewServices** and try this skill on your own:

1. Place your cursor at the end of the first paragraph and type the following text: **In addition to our longstanding spa services, we have added four new offerings truly unique to Head Over Heels Spa.**

2. Delete the word **truly** from the sentence you typed.

3. If you will be moving on to the next skill in this chapter, leave the document open to continue working. If not, save the file as directed by your instructor and close it.

Skill 1.3 Selecting Text

When you select text in a document, a shaded background appears behind the selected text. You can then apply commands to the text you've selected, such as changing the font or applying the bold effect.

There are several methods for selecting text in a document:

》 Click and drag the cursor across the text.

》 **To select a single word:** double-click the word.

》 **To select a paragraph:** triple-click a word in the paragraph you want to select.

》 **To select a line of text:** point to the left margin next to the line you want to select. When the cursor changes to an arrow, click once to select the line of text.

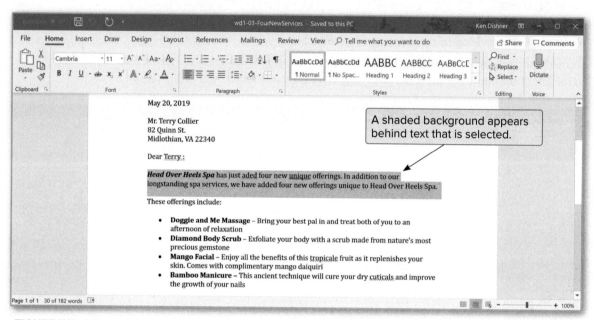

FIGURE WD 1.3

tips & tricks

To select all the text in the document, you can press (Ctrl) + (A) on the keyboard or triple-click the left margin of the document.

another **method**

To select a paragraph of text, you can also double-click in the left margin next to the paragraph you want to select.

let me **try**

If you do not have the data file from the previous skill open, open the student data file **wd1-03-FourNewServices** and try this skill on your own:

1. Select the word **Tranquility**.
2. Select the line **Mr. Terry Collier**.
3. Select the paragraph beginning with **Head Over Heels Spa has just**.
4. If you will be moving on to the next skill in this chapter, leave the document open to continue working. If not, close the file.

Skill 1.4 Checking for Writing Errors as You Type

Microsoft Word can automatically check your document for writing errors as you type. Writing errors include misspellings and grammatical errors. Word can also check for clarity and conciseness and make suggestions to improve your writing. Misspelled words, words that are not part of Word's dictionary, are indicated by a wavy red underline. Grammatical errors appear double-underlined in blue and are based on the grammatical rules that are part of Word's grammar checking feature. Writing suggestions are underlined with a dotted purple line and rely on Office's intelligent services to obtain ever-changing options to improve the writing in your document. When you right-click any type of error, a shortcut menu appears with suggestions for correcting the error and other options.

To correct a writing error:

1. Right-click the red, blue, or purple underlined word.
2. Choose a suggested correction from the shortcut menu.

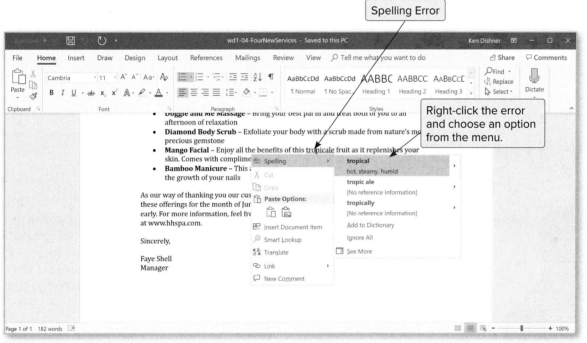

FIGURE WD 1.4

tips & tricks

Although having Word check for writing errors as you type is useful when creating documents, there are times when you may find it distracting. You can choose to turn off the tools for checking for spelling errors or grammar errors. To turn the *Check spelling as you type* and *Mark grammar errors as you type* features on and off:

1. Click the **File** tab.
2. Click the **Options** button.
3. In the *Word Options* dialog, click the **Proofing** button.
4. In the *When correcting spelling and grammar in Word* section, deselect the **Check spelling as you type** option for spelling errors or the **Mark grammar errors as you type** option for grammatical errors.

tell me **more**

> ❯ Word will not suggest spelling corrections if its dictionary does not contain a word with a similar spelling, and Word will not always be able to display grammatical suggestions. In these cases, you must edit the error manually. If the word is spelled correctly, you can choose the **Add to Dictionary** command on the shortcut menu. When you add a word to the dictionary, it will no longer be marked as a spelling error.

> ❯ Word's intelligent services rely on communicating with the cloud to provide ever-changing options for improving your documents. A number of Office features rely on intelligent services, including Word's *Editor* feature. When intelligent services are enabled, Word provides spelling and writing suggestions based on the surrounding content of the document and provides additional information beyond the spelling suggestion. You can enable and disable the intelligent services through the Word options dialog.

let me **try**

If you do not have the data file from the previous skill open, open the student data file **wd1-04-FourNewServices** and try this skill on your own:

1. Using the right-click method, replace the misspelled word **tropicale** with the correction **tropical**.

2. If you will be moving on to the next skill in this chapter, leave the document open to continue working. If not, save the file as directed by your instructor and close it.

from the perspective of . . .

ADMINISTRATIVE ASSISTANT

It seems like every time I write a memo or a letter, I use all the basic Word skills I learned when I first started using Word. Shortcuts like triple-clicking to select a paragraph of text and cutting and pasting to move text around in a document are tricks I use over and over every day. My boss has terrible eyesight, so every time I review a document with him I am sure to take the zoom up to 150% so he is able to read it better. And trust me, I don't know where I would be without Word's spelling and grammar checker, but no matter what, I always give my documents another read before sending them out to clients.

Ryan Mcvay/Getty Images

Skill 1.5 Using the Editor

Regardless of the amount of work you put into a document, a **spelling error** or typo or **grammar error** can make the entire document appear sloppy and unprofessional. All the Office applications include a built-in spelling checker, but Word also includes a grammar checker and writing style checker. In Word, the **Editor** analyzes your entire document for spelling, grammar, clarity, and conciseness errors and displays any potential errors for you to decide how to handle.

To check a document using the *Editor*:

1. Click the **Review** tab.

2. In the *Proofing* group, click the **Spelling & Grammar** button.

3. The first error appears in the *Editor* pane:

   - Potential spelling errors appear with the *Spelling* label near the top of the pane. Review the spelling suggestions and then select an action:

     - Click the correct spelling in the list of suggestions to replace the misspelled word.

     - Point to the correct spelling in the list of suggestions, click the arrow that appears, and select **Change All** to correct all instances of the misspelling in your document.

     - Click **Ignore Once** to make no changes to this instance of the word.

     - Click **Ignore All** to make no changes to all instances of the word.

     - Click **Add to Dictionary** to make no changes to this instance of the word and add it to the main dictionary, so future uses of this word will not show up as misspellings. When you add a word to the main dictionary, it is available for all of the Office applications.

   - Potential grammar errors appear with the *Grammar* label near the top of the pane. Review the grammar suggestions and then select an action:

     - Click a suggestion to make the correction.

     - Click **Ignore Once** to skip the grammar error.

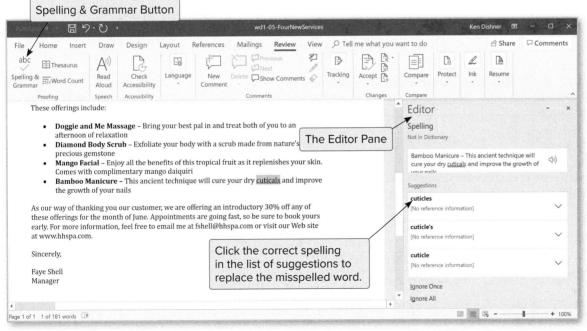

FIGURE WD 1.5

- Potential writing errors appear with the *Clarity and Conciseness* label near the top of the pane. Review the suggestions and then select an action:
  - Click a suggestion to make the correction.
  - Click **Ignore Once** to skip the grammar error.

4. After you select an action, the next suspected error is displayed.

5. When the checker finds no more errors, Word displays a message telling you the check is complete. Click **OK** to close the message box and return to your file.

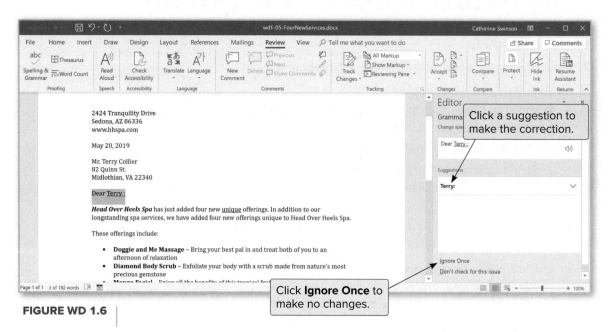

FIGURE WD 1.6

tips & tricks

❭ Whether or not you use the *Editor*, you should always proof-read your files. Spelling and grammar checkers are not fool-proof, especially if you misuse a word, yet spell it correctly—for instance, writing "bored" instead of "board."

❭ If you have repeated the same word in a sentence, Word will flag the second instance of the word as a possible error. In the *Editor* pane, the *Change* button will switch to a *Delete* button. Click the **Delete** button to remove the duplicate word.

another method

To check for spelling and grammar errors in a document, you can also:

❭ Press the F7 key

❭ Click the **Proofing Errors** icon on the status bar.

let me try

If you do not have the data file from the previous skill open, open the student data file **wd1-05-FourNewServices** and try this skill on your own:

1. Click at the beginning of the first paragraph in the document.

2. Open the **Editor** to review misspelling and grammar errors in the document.

3. Change the misspelled word **aded** to **added**.

4. Change the misspelled word **cuticals** to **cuticles**.

5. Fix the grammar error, so there is no space before the colon in the greeting line of the letter.

6. If you will be moving on to the next skill in this chapter, leave the document open to continue working. If not, save the file as directed by your instructor and close it.

Skill 1.6 Using Undo and Redo

If you make a mistake when working, the **Undo** command allows you to reverse the last action you performed. The **Redo** command allows you to reverse the *Undo* command and restore the file to its previous state. The Quick Access Toolbar gives you immediate access to both commands.

❭ To undo the last action taken, click the **Undo** button on the Quick Access Toolbar.

❭ To redo the last action taken, click the **Redo** button on the Quick Access Toolbar.

To undo multiple actions at the same time:

1. Click the arrow next to the *Undo* button to expand the list of your most recent actions.

2. Click an action in the list.

3. The action you click will be undone, along with all the actions completed after that. In other words, your document will revert to the state it was in before that action.

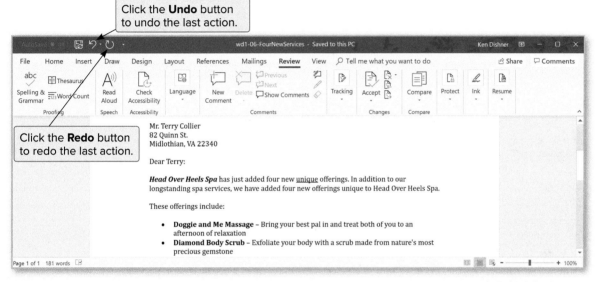

FIGURE WD 1.7

another **method**

❭ To undo an action, you can also press (Ctrl) + (Z) on the keyboard.

❭ To redo an action, you can also press (Ctrl) + (Y) on the keyboard.

let me **try**

If you do not have the data file from the previous skill open, open the student data file **wd1-06-FourNewServices** and try this skill on your own:

1. In the first sentence of the first paragraph, select the word **unique**. Press the **Delete** key to delete the word.

2. Click the **Undo** button to restore the word to the document.

3. Click the **Redo** button to remove the word again.

4. If you will be moving on to the next skill in this chapter, leave the document open to continue working. If not, save the file as directed by your instructor and close it.

Skill 1.7 Finding Text

The **Find** command opens the *Navigation* pane and allows you to search a document for a word or phrase. When you search for a word or phrase in a document using the *Navigation* pane, Word highlights all instances of the word or phrase in the document and displays each instance as a separate result in the pane.

To find a word or phrase in a document:

1. On the *Home* tab, in the *Editing* group, click the **Find** button.

2. The *Navigation* pane appears.

3. Type the word or phrase you want to find in the *Search document* box at the top of the *Navigation* pane.

4. As you type, Word automatically highlights all instances of the word or phrase in the document and displays any results.

5. Click a result to navigate to that instance of the word or phrase in the document.

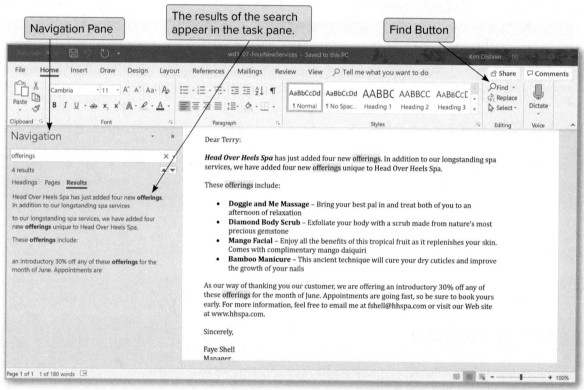

FIGURE WD 1.8

word 365   chapter 1 Getting Started with Word

tips & tricks

❭ The magnifying glass in the *Search document* box gives you access to more search options. You can choose to search only specific elements in your document, such as tables, graphics, footnotes, or comments. From this menu, you can also open the *Find Options* dialog. From the *Find Options* dialog you can set the preferences for searching the document, including matching capitalization, ignoring punctuation, and using wildcard characters in the search.

❭ Clicking the **X** next to a search word or phrase will clear the search, allowing you to perform a new search.

❭ To perform more complex searches in your documents, you can use the *Find and Replace* dialog. To open the *Find and Replace* dialog, start on the *Home* tab. In the *Editing* group, click the **Find** button arrow and select **Advanced Find...** The *Find and Replace* dialog opens with the *Find* tab displayed. Click the **More >>** button to expand the *Find and Replace* dialog and view more search options. Here you can choose to find exact matches of words or phrases (including capitalization), search for whole words only, search for special characters, or find formatting in your document. Click the **<< Less** button to collapse the dialog and hide these options.

tell me **more**

In older versions of Microsoft Word, searching for text was performed through the *Find and Replace* dialog. In Word 2010, Microsoft introduced the *Navigation* pane as the default method for searching for text in a document.

another **method**

To display the *Navigation* pane with the *Results* section displayed, you can also:

❭ Click the **Find** button and select **Find** on the menu.

❭ Press Ctrl + F on the keyboard.

let me **try**

If you do not have the data file from the previous skill open, open the student data file **wd1-07-FourNewServices** and try this skill on your own:

1. Use the **Find** command to search the document for instances of the word **offerings**. You should see four results.

2. If you will be moving on to the next skill in this chapter, leave the document open to continue working. If not, close the file.

Skill 1.8 Replacing Text

The **Replace** command in Word allows you to locate specific instances of text in your document and replace them with different text. With the **Replace All** command, you can replace words or phrases all at once throughout the document.

To replace instances of a word in a document:

1. On the *Home* tab, in the *Editing* group, click the **Replace** button.

2. Type the word or phrase you want to change in the *Find what* box.

3. Type the new text you want in the *Replace with* box.

4. Click **Replace** to replace just that one instance of the text.

5. Click **Replace All** to replace all instances of the word or phrase.

6. Word displays a message telling you how many replacements it made. Click **OK** in the message that appears.

7. To close the *Find and Replace* dialog, click the **Cancel** button.

FIGURE WD 1.9

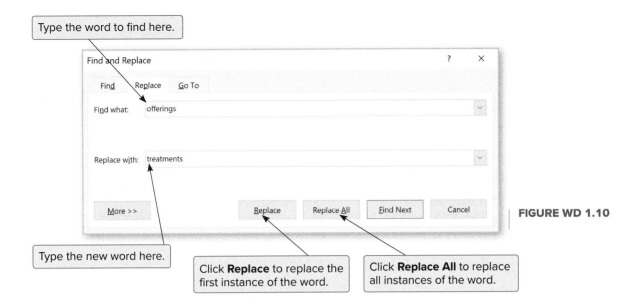

Type the word to find here.

Type the new word here.

Click **Replace** to replace the first instance of the word.

Click **Replace All** to replace all instances of the word.

FIGURE WD 1.10

tips & tricks

In addition to text, the *Replace* command can also operate on formatting characters such as italicized text and paragraph marks. The *More >>* button in the *Find and Replace* dialog displays additional options, including buttons that allow you to select formatting and other special characters in the document.

tell me **more**

The *Go To* tab in the *Find and Replace* dialog allows you to quickly jump to any page, line, section, comment, or other object in your document.

another **method**

To open the *Find and Replace* dialog with the *Replace* tab displayed, you can also press (Ctrl) + (H) on the keyboard.

let me **try**

If you do not have the data file from the previous skill open, open the student data file **wd1-08-FourNewServices** and try this skill on your own:

1. If necessary, place the cursor at the beginning of the document.
2. Open the **Find and Replace** dialog with the *Replace* tab displayed.
3. Replace all instances of **offerings** with **treatments**. There will be four replacements.
4. Click **OK** to close the message box.
5. Click the **Close** button to close the *Find and Replace* dialog.
6. If you will be moving on to the next skill in this chapter, leave the document open to continue working. If not, save the file as directed by your instructor and close it.

Skill 1.9 Using Copy and Paste

The **Copy** command places a duplicate of the selected text or object on the **Clipboard** but does not remove it from your document. You can then use the **Paste** command to insert the text or object into the same document, another document, or another Microsoft Office file, such as an Excel workbook or a PowerPoint presentation.

To copy text and paste it into the same document:

1. Select the text to be copied.
2. On the *Home* tab, in the *Clipboard* group, click the **Copy** button.
3. Place the cursor where you want to insert the text from the *Clipboard*.
4. On the *Home* tab, in the *Clipboard* group, click the **Paste** button.

These same steps apply whether you are copying and pasting text, pictures, shapes, video files, or any type of object in a Word file.

FIGURE WD 1.11

another **method**

To apply the *Copy* or *Paste* command, you can also use the following shortcuts:

❯ *Copy* = Press Ctrl + C on the keyboard, or right-click and select **Copy**.

❯ *Paste* = Press Ctrl + V on the keyboard, or right-click and select **Paste**.

let me **try**

If you do not have the data file from the previous skill open, open the student data file **wd1-09-FourNewServices** and try this skill on your own:

1. In the last sentence of the last paragraph, select the text **fshell@hhspa.com**.
2. Copy the text to the *Clipboard*.
3. Place the cursor in the blank line at the end of the document (under the word *Manager*). Paste the copied text.
4. If you will be moving on to the next skill in this chapter, leave the document open to continue working. If not, save the file as directed by your instructor and close it.

Skill 1.10 Using Cut and Paste

The *Copy* command is great if you want to duplicate content in your document, but what if you want to move content from one place to another? The **Cut** command is used to move text and other objects within a file and from one file to another. Text, or an object that is cut, is *removed* from the file and placed on the *Clipboard* for later use. You can then use the *Paste* command to insert the text or object into the same document, another document, or another Microsoft Office file.

To cut text and paste it into the same document:

1. Select the text to be cut.
2. On the *Home* tab, in the *Clipboard* group, click the **Cut** button.
3. Place the cursor where you want to insert the text from the *Clipboard.*
4. On the *Home* tab, in the *Clipboard* group, click the **Paste** button.

FIGURE WD 1.12

another **method**

To apply the *Cut* or *Paste* command, you can also use the following shortcuts:

❭ *Cut* = Press (Ctrl) + (X) on the keyboard, or right-click and select **Cut**.

❭ *Paste* = Press (Ctrl) + (V) on the keyboard, or right-click and select **Paste**.

let me **try**

If you do not have the data file from the previous skill open, open the student data file **wd1-10-FourNewServices** and try this skill on your own:

1. Select the last bullet point in the bulleted list in the document. It is the *Bamboo Manicure* bullet point.
2. Cut the selected text. If necessary, delete the extra empty bullet point at the end of the list.
3. Place the cursor at the beginning of the **Mango Facial** bullet point.
4. Paste the cut bullet point. If necessary, press (← Enter) to create two bullet points in the list.
5. If you will be moving on to the next skill in this chapter, leave the document open to continue working. If not, save the file as directed by your instructor and close it.

Skill 1.11 Using Paste Options

When you cut or copy an item, whether it be a piece of text, a chart, or an image, Word gives you a variety of ways to paste the item into your document. If you click the bottom part of the *Paste* button (the *Paste* button arrow), you can control how the item is pasted. Each type of object has different paste options. The four **paste options** for pasting text include:

》 **Keep Source Formatting**—pastes the text and any formatting that was applied to the copied text.

》 **Merge Formatting**—pastes the text to match the formatting of the surrounding text.

》 **Picture**—pastes the text as a single picture object rather than individual characters.

》 **Keep Text Only**—pastes the text without any formatting that was applied to the copied text.

To paste text using paste options:

1. Place your cursor where you want to paste the text.

2. On the *Home* tab, in the *Clipboard* group, click the **Paste** button arrow.

3. Roll your mouse over each of the paste options to see how the text will appear when pasted. Click an option to paste the text.

Click the **Paste** button arrow to display the *Options* menu.

FIGURE WD 1.13

tips & tricks

When you paste text using the *Paste* button, Word pastes the text using the *Keep Source Formatting* option.

another method

To paste text using paste options, you can also right-click and select an option under *Paste Options* on the menu.

tell me more

Different object types have different paste options to choose from. Pictures, shapes, SmartArt diagrams, and charts can all be pasted using the same formatting as the original source object or can be pasted as a picture. If the object is pasted as a picture, any formatting or customization applied becomes part of the pasted object and cannot be removed. So, if you want to be able to modify the pasted object, you should use the *Keep Source Formatting* paste option.

let me try

If you do not have the data file from the previous skill open, open the student data file **wd1-11-FourNewServices** and try this skill on your own:

1. Select the text **Head Over Heels Spa** at the beginning of the first paragraph and copy the text to the *Clipboard*.

2. Place the cursor before **Manager** in the second to last line of the document.

3. Paste the text using the **Keep Text Only** paste command.

4. If you will be moving on to the next skill in this chapter, leave the document open to continue working. If not, save the file as directed by your instructor and close it.

Skill 1.12 Using the Clipboard

When you cut or copy items, they are placed on the *Clipboard*. The *Clipboard* can store up to 24 items for use in the current document or any other Office application. The most recently copied items appear at the top of the pane while the oldest items appear at the bottom of the pane. The *Clipboard* is common across all Office applications—so you can cut text from a Word document and then paste that text into a PowerPoint presentation or copy a chart from Excel into a Word document.

To copy and paste an item from the *Clipboard* into a document:

1. On the *Home* tab, in the *Clipboard* group, click the **Clipboard** dialog launcher to display the *Clipboard* pane.

2. Select the item you want to copy. This can be in the current Word document or in a file open in another application.

3. Click the **Copy** button to copy the item.

4. Place your cursor where you want to paste the item in the Word document.

5. Click the item in the *Clipboard* you want to paste in the document.

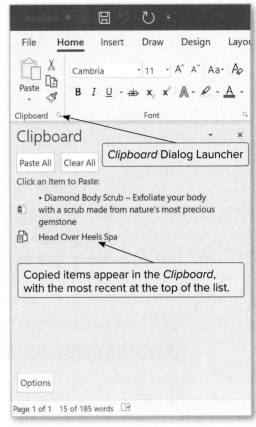

FIGURE WD 1.14

tips & tricks

> To remove an item from the *Clipboard*, point to the item, click the arrow that appears, and select **Delete**.

> To add all the items in the *Clipboard* at once, click the **Paste All** button at the top of the pane.

> To remove all items from the *Clipboard* at once, click the **Clear All** button at the top of the pane.

another method

To paste an item, you can also point to the item in the *Clipboard* pane, click the arrow that appears, and select **Paste**.

let me try

If you do not have the data file from the previous skill open, open the student data file **wd1-12-FourNewServices** and try this skill on your own:

1. Display the **Clipboard**.

2. Select the text **Head Over Heels Spa** in the signature line (before the word *Manager*) and copy it to the *Clipboard*.

3. Select the **Diamond Body Scrub** bullet point and copy it to the *Clipboard*.

4. Place the cursor in the blank line at the top of the document.

5. Paste the **Head Over Heels Spa** text from the *Clipboard*.

6. If you will be moving on to the next skill in this chapter, leave the document open to continue working. If not, save the file as directed by your instructor and close it.

Skill 1.13 Zooming a Document

When you first open a document, you may find that the text is too small to read, or that you cannot see the full layout of a page. Use the **zoom slider** in the lower-right corner of the window to zoom in and out of a document, changing the size of text and images onscreen. **Zooming** a document affects only how the document appears on-screen. It does not affect how the document will print.

To zoom in on a document, making the text and graphics appear larger:

❭ Click and drag the **zoom slider** to the right.

❭ Click the **Zoom In** button (the button with the plus sign on it) on the slider.

To zoom out of a document, making the text and graphics appear smaller:

❭ Click and drag the **zoom slider** to the left.

❭ Click the **Zoom Out** button (the button with the minus sign on it) on the slider.

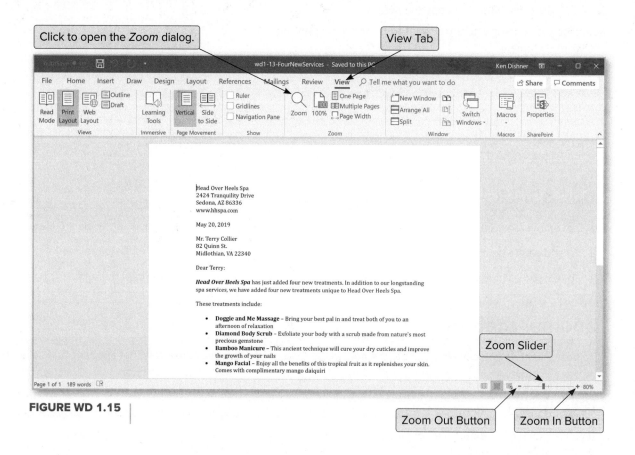

FIGURE WD 1.15

You can use the *Zoom* dialog to apply a number of display presets:

❭ **Page width**–changes the zoom so the width of the page including margins fills the screen.

❭ **Text width**–changes the zoom so the width of the page not including margins fills the screen.

❭ **Whole page**–changes the zoom so the entire page, both vertically and horizontally, displays on the screen. This is a helpful view when working with a page's layout.

❭ **Many pages**–changes the zoom to display anywhere from one to six pages on the screen at once.

FIGURE WD 1.16

tips & tricks

As you move the slider, the zoom level displays the percentage the document has been zoomed in or out. When zooming a document, 100% is the default zoom level. If you work on a large monitor at a high resolution and need to display your document at a higher zoom percentage, Word will retain the zoom level you set as the new default when opening documents. You won't need to increase the zoom level every time you open a document.

another **method**

You also can change the zoom level through the *Zoom* dialog. To open the *Zoom* dialog:

1. Click the **zoom level number** next to the zoom slider OR click the **View** tab. In the *Zoom* group, click the **Zoom** button.
2. Click a **zoom preset** or type the **zoom percentage** in the *Percent* box.
3. Click **OK**.

let me **try**

If you do not have the data file from the previous skill open, open the student data file **wd1-13-FourNewServices** and try this skill on your own:

1. Change the zoom level of the document to **80%**.
2. Change the zoom level of the document back to **100%**.
3. If you will be moving on to the next skill in this chapter, leave the document open to continue working. If not, close the file.

Skill 1.14 Using Word Count

Have you ever had to write a 250-word essay or submit a 3,000-word article? You don't need to guess whether your Word document is long enough (or too long). Word's **Word Count** feature provides the current statistics of the document you are working on, including the number of pages, number of words, number of characters (with and without spaces), number of paragraphs, and number of lines.

To view document statistics:

1. From the *Review* tab, in the *Proofing* group, click the **Word Count** button.
2. The *Word Count* dialog opens and displays the statistics for the document.
3. By default, the document statistics include the text in text boxes, footnotes, and endnotes. To exclude text in these areas, click the **Include textboxes, footnotes, and endnotes** check box to remove the checkmark.
4. Click **Close** to close the dialog.

Click to open the *Word Count* dialog.

Review Tab

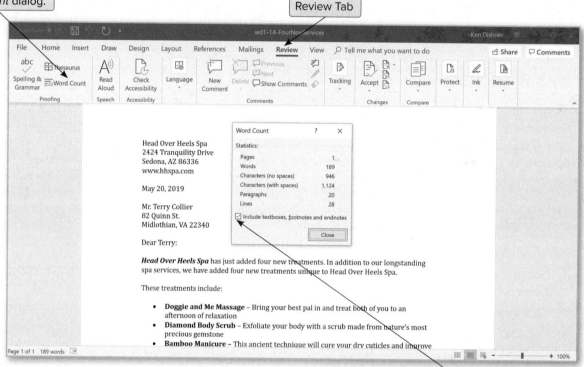

FIGURE WD 1.17

Click this check box to exclude text boxes, footnotes, and endnotes in document statistics.

tips & tricks

The number of words and the number of pages in the document are also displayed on the status bar at the bottom of the Word window and as part of the document properties available from the *Info* tab in Backstage view.

another method

To open the *Word Count* dialog, you can also click **Words** on the status bar at the bottom of the Word window.

let me try

If you do not have the data file from the previous skill open, open the student data file **wd1-14-FourNewServices** and try this skill on your own:

1. Open the **Word Count** dialog.
2. Note the number of words in the letter along with other document statistics.
3. Close the **Word Count** dialog.
4. If you will be moving on to the next skill in this chapter, leave the document open to continue working. If not, close the file.

Skill 1.15 Using Views

By default, Microsoft Word displays documents in Print Layout view, but you can display your documents in a number of other ways. Each view has its own purpose, and considering what you want to do with your document will help determine which view is most appropriate to use.

To switch between different views, click the appropriate icon located in the lower-right corner of the status bar next to the zoom slider.

⟩ **Read Mode**—Use this view when you want to review a document. Read Mode presents the document in an easy-to-read format. In this view, the Ribbon is no longer visible. To navigate between screens, use the navigation buttons on the left and right side of the window.

⟩ **Print Layout view**—Use this view to see how document elements will appear on a printed page. This view will help you edit headers and footers, and adjust margins and layouts.

⟩ **Web Layout view**—Use this view when designing documents that will be viewed on-screen, such as a web page. Web Layout view displays all backgrounds, drawing objects, and graphics as they will appear on-screen. Unlike Print Layout view, Web Layout view does not show page edges, margins, or headers and footers.

FIGURE WD 1.18

tell me **more**

In previous versions of Word, *Outline* view and *Draft* view were accessible from the status bar. In Word, you access these views only from the *View* tab:

⟩ **Outline view**—Use this view to check the structure of your document. In Outline view, you can collapse the document's structure to view just the top-level headings or expand the structure to see the document's framework. Outline view is most helpful when you use a different style for each type of heading in your document.

⟩ **Draft view**—Use this simplified layout view when typing and formatting text. Draft view does not display headers and footers, page edges, backgrounds, or drawing objects.

another **method**

To switch views, you also can click the **View** tab and select a view from the *Views* group.

let me **try**

If you do not have the data file from the previous skill open, open the student data file **wd1-15-FourNewServices** and try this skill on your own:

1. Switch to **Read Mode**.
2. Switch to **Web Layout** view.
3. Switch back to **Print Layout** view.
4. If you will be moving on to the next skill in this chapter, leave the document open to continue working. If not, close the file.

Skill 1.16 Previewing and Printing a Document

In Word, all the print settings are combined in a single page along with a preview of how the printed document will look. From the **Print page** in Backstage view, you can preview and print all the pages in your document.

To preview and print a document:

1. Click the **File** tab to open Backstage view.
2. Click **Print**.
3. At the right side of the page is a preview of how the printed document will look. Beneath the preview there is a page count. If there are multiple pages, click the next and previous arrows to preview all the pages in the document.
4. Verify that the correct printer name is displayed in the *Printer* section.
5. Click the **Print** button to print.

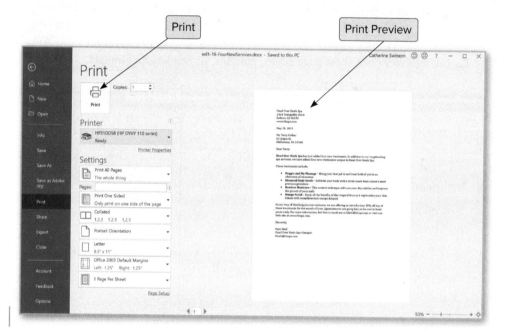

FIGURE WD 1.19

another **method**

To display the *Print* page, you can also press (Ctrl) + (P).

let me **try**

If you do not have the data file from the previous skill open, open the student data file **wd1-16-FourNewServices** and try this skill on your own:

1. Display the **Print** page in Backstage view.
2. Print the document. **NOTE**: If you are using this in class or in your school's computer lab, check with your instructor about printing permissions before completing this step.
3. Save the file as directed by your instructor and close it.

Font
Paragraph
Styles
Theme
Table
Chart
Graphics
Header
Footer
Page Break
Margin
Citations
Comment
Track Changes
Intelligent Services
Word wrap
Spelling error
Grammar error
Editor

Undo
Redo
Find
Replace
Replace All
Copy
Clipboard
Paste
Cut
Paste options
Zoom slider
Zooming
Word Count
Read Mode
Print Layout view
Web Layout view
Outline view
Draft view
Print page

concept review

1. Which of the following actions is used to select a paragraph of text?

a. single-click the paragraph

b. double-click the paragraph

c. triple-click the paragraph

d. click in the left margin next to the paragraph

2. Grammatical errors in a document are represented by a _____.

a. red double underline

b. blue double underline

c. red wavy underline

d. blue wavy underline

3. Which feature in Word automatically places text on the next line when the right margin of the document has been reached?

a. styles

b. zoom slider

c. word wrap

d. status bar

4. Which command would you use to copy text to the *Clipboard* and remove it from the document?

a. Copy

b. Cut

c. Undo

d. Redo

5. Which paste option pastes the text with the original formatting of the copied text?
   a. Keep Source Formatting
   b. Merge Formatting
   c. Keep Text Only
   d. Picture

6. Which command would you use to replace all instances of a word with another word?
   a. Find
   b. Replace
   c. Replace All
   d. Paste All

7. The primary method for finding text in a document is to use the _____.
   a. Find and Replace dialog
   b. Navigation pane
   c. Clipboard pane
   d. Go To dialog

8. In the *Editor* pane, which command will prevent the word from being marked as a misspelling in all the Office applications, not just Word?
   a. Ignore
   b. Ignore All
   c. Change All
   d. Add to Dictionary

9. Which would you use to magnify the text on-screen, making the text appear larger?
   a. Zoom Out button
   b. Zoom In button
   c. Page Width command
   d. 100% command

10. In addition to the number of words in a document, the *Word Count* dialog also displays _____.
    a. the number of tables
    b. the number of charts
    c. the number of pages
    d. the number of images

projects

skill review **1.1**

In this project you will be editing the text of a brochure for the Suarez Agency. First, you will reset the magnification of the document. You will then enter, select, and delete text. You will fix spelling and grammar errors in the document. You will edit the document using the *Find* and *Replace* commands as well as the *Cut* and *Paste* commands. Finally, you will review the document statistics using the *Word Count* dialog.

Skills needed to complete this project:

- Zooming a Document (Skill 1.13)
- Entering and Deleting Text (Skill 1.2)
- Selecting Text (Skill 1.3)
- Checking Writing Errors as You Type (Skill 1.4)
- Using the Editor (Skill 1.5)
- Finding Text (Skill 1.7)
- Replacing Text (Skill 1.8)
- Using Cut and Paste (Skill 1.10)
- Using Word Count (Skill 1.14)

1. Open the start file **WD2019-SkillReview-1-1** and resave the file as: **[your initials] WD-SkillReview-1-1**

2. If the document opens in Protected view, click the **Enable Editing** button in the Message Bar at the top of the document so you can modify the document.

3. Change how the document is displayed on your computer by clicking the **Zoom Out** button next to the *Zoom slider* one time so the magnification is **decreased by 10%**.

4. Add text to the document.

a. Place the cursor on the empty line following the phone number.

b. Type the following heading: **Our Goal**

c. Press **Enter**.

d. Type the following text: **We are dedicated to listening to your needs and working with you to develop a strategic plan to grow your business.**

5. Select and delete text from the document.

a. In the paragraph under the *Experience* heading, select the text **small** by double-clicking the word.

b. Press the **Delete** key to remove the text.

6. Check spelling and grammar as you type. Notice how words that Word does not recognize are underlined in red and potential grammar errors are underlined in blue.

a. Right-click the word **mesage** in the *Experience* section. A list of suggested changes is shown.

b. Click **message**. Word corrects the spelling of this word.

c. Right-click the word **is** in the *Client Quotes* section.

d. Click **are**.

7. Correct spelling and grammar errors using the *Editor* pane.

a. Press ⌨Ctrl + ⌨Home to move to the top of the document.

b. Click the **Review** tab.

c. In the *Proofing* group, click the **Spelling & Grammar** button. The *Editor* pane will open.

d. For the first error, the text should be **Communication** not **Comunication**. Click **Communication** in the *Suggestions* list to fix the misspelling.

e. Next, Word finds a grammar error. Click the suggestion in the *Editor* pane to fix the error.

f. **Morriss** is spelled correctly. Click the *Ignore Once* option in the *Editor* pane.

g. For the next error, the text is supposed to be **goal** not **gol**. Click **goal** in the *Suggestions* list to fix the misspelling.

h. A message box appears letting you know the spelling and grammar check is complete. Click **OK** in the message box to close it.

8. Find and replace text in a document.

a. On the *Home* tab, in the *Editing* group, click the **Find** button.

b. Type **savvy** in the *Search document* box. You will see two results.

c. On the *Home* tab, in the *Editing* group, click the **Replace** button.

d. Notice **savvy** appears in the *Find what* box. If you do not see this, delete any text in the *Find what* box and type the word **savvy** in the box.

e. Type **know-how** in the *Replace with* box.

f. Click **Replace All** to replace both instances of the word.

g. Word displays a message box, indicating that two replacements have been made. Click **OK** in the message box to close it.

h. Click the **Close** button in the *Find and Replace* dialog.

9. Cut and paste text from one part of the document to another.

a. Select all the text in the **Suarez Marketing Belief System** at the end of the document (from *The Suarez Marketing Belief System* through *results with integrity*).

b. On the *Home* tab, in the *Clipboard* group, click the **Cut** button to remove the text and copy it to the *Clipboard*.

c. Navigate back to the first page and place the cursor at the beginning of *Client Quotes*.

d. On the *Home* tab, in the *Clipboard* group, click the **Paste** button to paste the text. If necessary, press **Enter** to place *Client Quotes* on its own line.

10. View the statistics for the document.

a. Click the **Review** tab.

b. In the *Proofing* group, click the **Word Count** button.

c. Review the number of pages, words, and paragraphs in the document. Click the **Close** button to close the *Word Count* dialog.

11. Save and close the document.

In this project, you will be editing the agenda for the Tri-State Book Festival. First, you will change views and adjust the zoom level for the document. You will add and remove text from the document, move text around using the cut and paste commands, and find and replace snippets of text. Finally, you will ensure there are no spelling and grammar errors in the document and then print the document.

Skills needed to complete this project:

- Using Views (Skill 1.15)
- Zooming a Document (Skill 1.13)
- Entering and Deleting Text (Skill 1.2)
- Selecting Text (Skill 1.3)
- Finding Text (Skill 1.7)
- Replacing Text (Skill 1.8)
- Using Copy and Paste (Skill 1.9)
- Using Cut and Paste (Skill 1.10)
- Checking for Writing Errors as You Type (Skill 1.4)
- Using the Editor (Skill 1.5)
- Previewing and Printing a Document (Skill 1.16)

1. Open the start file **WD2019-SkillReview-1-2** and resave the file as:
   `[your initials] WD-SkillReview-1-2`

2. If the document opens in Protected view, click the **Enable Editing** button in the Message Bar at the top of the document so you can modify the document.

3. Click the **Read Mode** button on the status bar to view the document in *Read Mode*. Click the **Print Layout** button on the status bar to switch back to Print Layout view.

4. Change how the document is displayed on your computer by clicking the **Zoom In** button next to the *Zoom slider* one time so the magnification is **increased by 10%**.

5. Add text to the document.

   a. Place the cursor on the empty line between *Authors* and *Fiction*.

   b. Type the following text: `The following is a list of authors who will be attending the festival and will be participating in moderated panels. Check the festival agenda for times and locations.`

6. Select and delete text from the document.

   a. In the list of authors, there are two entries for **David Chase**. Select one of the instances of the name.

   b. Press the **Delete** key to remove the text. If there is an extra blank line, press the **Delete** key again to remove it.

7. Find and replace text in a document.

   a. Press `Ctrl` + `Home` on the keyboard to navigate to the beginning of the document.

   b. On the *Home* tab, in the *Editing* group, click the **Find** button.

   c. Type **event** in the *Search document* box. You will see three results.

   d. On the *Home* tab, in the *Editing* group, click the **Replace** button.

   e. Notice **event** appears in the *Find what* box. If you do not see this, delete any text in the *Find what* box and type the word **event** in the box.

   f. Type **festival** in the *Replace with* box.

g. Click **Replace All** to replace all instances of the word.

h. Word displays a message box, indicating that three replacements have been made. Click **OK** in the message box to close it.

i. Click the **Close** button in the *Find and Replace* dialog.

8. Copy and paste text in a document.

   a. Select the text **Showcased work:** in the *Authors* section of the document. Be sure to select the space after the colon as well.

   b. On the *Home* tab, in the *Clipboard* group, click the **Copy** button to copy the text to the *Clipboard*.

   c. Place the cursor before the text *Living with Big Foot*.

   d. On the *Home* tab, in the *Clipboard* group, click the **Paste** button to paste the text.

9. Cut and paste text from one part of the document to another.

   a. On the second page of the document, select the text **Catherine Cartwright**.

   b. On the *Home* tab, in the *Clipboard* group, click the **Cut** button to remove the text and copy it to the *Clipboard*.

   c. Place the cursor before *Showcased work: A Guide to Eating Out and Eating Well*.

   d. On the *Home* tab, in the *Clipboard* group, click the **Paste** button to paste the text. If *Showcased work: A Guide to Eating Out and Eating Well* appears on the same line as the pasted text, press **Enter** to move the text to a new line.

10. Check spelling and grammar as you type. Notice how words that Word does not recognize are underlined in red and potential grammar errors are underlined in blue.

    a. Press (Ctrl) + (Home) on the keyboard to navigate to the beginning of the document.

    b. Right-click the word **attende** in the second paragraph on the first page of the document. A list of suggested changes is shown.

    c. Click **attendee**. Word corrects the spelling of this word.

    d. Right-click the word **non fiction** in the first paragraph.

    e. Click **nonfiction**.

11. Correct spelling and grammar errors using the *Editor* pane.

    a. Click the **Review** tab. In the *Proofing* group, click the **Spelling & Grammar** button. The *Editor* pane will open.

    b. The first error in the document is a grammar error; the text should be **an**, not **a**. Click the correct option in the list of suggestions.

    c. Next, Word finds a spelling error. Correct the misspelling to **available**.

    d. Next, Word thinks there is a repeated word in the title *Drawing in Real Real Life*. There is no error. Click the **Ignore Once** button to move on and not make any changes.

    e. If Word flags the name *Swinson* as a misspelling, click the **Ignore Once** button.

    f. Word finds another spelling error. Correct the misspelling to **Better**.

    g. A message box appears letting you know the spelling and grammar check is complete. Click **OK** in the message box to close it.

12. Print the document.

    a. Click the **File** tab and click **Print**.

    b. Click the **Print** button. **NOTE:** If you are using this in class or in your school's computer lab, check with your instructor about printing permissions before completing this step.

13. Save and close the document.

In this project you will be editing a cover letter for a marketing manager position. You will edit the content of the letter by adding and deleting text and replacing text within the document. You will move text around using the *Cut* and *Paste* commands. You will use the spelling and grammar checker to find and fix spelling and grammar errors.

Skills needed to complete this project:

- Zooming a Document (Skill 1.13)
- Selecting Text (Skill 1.3)
- Using Copy and Paste (Skill 1.9)
- Using Paste Options (Skill 1.11)
- Entering and Deleting Text (Skill 1.2)
- Finding Text (Skill 1.7)
- Replacing Text (Skill 1.8)
- Using Cut and Paste (Skill 1.10)
- Using the Editor (Skill 1.5)
- Using Word Count (Skill 1.14)

1. Open the start file **WD2019-ChallengeYourself-1-3** and resave the file as: `[your initials] WD-ChallengeYourself-1-3`

2. If the document opens in Protected view, click the **Enable Editing** button in the Message Bar at the top of the document so you can modify the document.

3. If necessary, change the zoom level to view the document at 100% magnification.

4. Select the name **Suarez** from the address block and copy it to the *Clipboard*.

5. Place the cursor after *Dear Ms.* in the salutation. Paste the copied text using the *Keep Text Only* paste option. Add a colon after the name.

6. Place the cursor at the end of the first paragraph (after the text *marketing manager position.*) Press the **Spacebar** one time and type the following text: `After reviewing the job description, I am certain that my marketing expertise is a perfect match for this position with your organization.`

7. Add `, including:` at the end of the second paragraph, beginning with *I am certain.*

8. Remove the typing using the *Undo* command.

9. Re-apply the typing using the *Redo* command.

10. Select the word **urgently** in the last paragraph of the document and delete it.

11. Use the **Find** command to locate all instances of the word **skills** in the document.

12. Use the **Replace** command to replace the third instance of the word **skills** with the word **experience**.

13. Use the **Cut** and **Paste** commands to move the first bullet point in the list, the one beginning with *Extensive proficiency*, so it appears below the bullet point beginning with *Ability to think.*

14. Copy the last name **Smith** from the address block.

15. Place the cursor after the name Jessica at the bottom of the document. Paste the copied text using the *Keep Text Only* paste option.

16. Check spelling and grammar in the letter.
    a. Ignore the misspelling of the word **Streecker** in the address block.
    b. Correct the misspelling of the word **dicuss** in the first sentence of the last paragraph.
    c. Correct the grammar mistake **you're** in the third sentence of the last paragraph.
17. Use the **Word Count** dialog to review the number of words, paragraphs, and pages in the document.
18. Save and close the document.

challenge yourself **1.4**

In this project, you will be editing a safety strategies report for the Spring Hills Community. You will change the view and adjust the zoom level to make working in the document easier. You will fill in information and correct errors in the document. You will practice copying and pasting text. You will check the document for spelling and grammar errors and use the *Find* and *Replace* commands to substitute one word for another. Finally, you will check the document's statistics and print the document.

Skills needed to complete this project:
- Using Views (Skill 1.15)
- Zooming a Document (Skill 1.13)
- Selecting Text (Skill 1.3)
- Using Copy and Paste (Skill 1.9)
- Entering and Deleting Text (Skill 1.2)
- Checking for Writing Errors as You Type (Skill 1.4)
- Using the Editor (Skill 1.5)
- Finding Text (Skill 1.7)
- Replacing Text (Skill 1.8)
- Using Word Count (Skill 1.14)
- Previewing and Printing a Document (Skill 1.16)

1. Open the start file **WD2019-ChallengeYourself-1-4** and resave the file as: `[your initials] WD-ChallengeYourself-1-4`
2. If the document opens in Protected view, click the **Enable Editing** button in the Message Bar at the top of the document so you can modify the document.
3. Switch to **Read Mode**, and then switch back to **Print Layout** view.
4. Adjust the zoom level so it is set to **110%**.
5. Navigate to the list of full-time officers on the second page of the document.
6. Select **(5 years)** next to *Tyler Fuller* and copy the text to the *Clipboard*.
7. Place the cursor after *Emile Berry* and paste the text you copied. Be sure there is a space between the name and the opening parenthesis.
8. Navigate to the beginning of the document and select the text **simple and easy** in the first sentence of the first paragraph. Delete the text.
9. Place the cursor at the end of the first paragraph. Type the following text:
   `The following are basic safety tips provided by our security team to help you stay safe when going out into the community.`

10. Check for and fix all spelling and grammar errors in the document.

11. Find all instances of the word **Manager**.

12. Replace all instances of the word **Manager** with **Supervisor**.

13. Use the **Word Count** dialog to review the number of words, paragraphs, and pages in the document.

14. Print the document. **NOTE**: If you are using this in class or in your school's computer lab, check with your instructor about printing permissions before completing this step.

15. Save and close the document.

on your own 1.5

In this project, you will be working on a marketing sheet for a landscape company. You will change the view and adjust the zoom level to make working in the document easier. You will fill in information and correct errors in the document. You will practice copying text and using the *Clipboard.* You will use the *Find* and *Replace* commands to substitute one word for another.

Skills needed to complete this project:

- Using Views (Skill 1.15)
- Zooming a Document (Skill 1.13)
- Entering and Deleting Text (Skill 1.2)
- Selecting Text (Skill 1.3)
- Using Copy and Paste (Skill 1.9)
- Using the Clipboard (Skill 1.12)
- Using Undo and Redo (Skill 1.6)
- Using Cut and Paste (Skill 1.10)
- Finding Text (Skill 1.7)
- Replacing Text (Skill 1.8)
- Checking for Writing Errors as You Type (Skill 1.4)
- Using the Editor (Skill 1.5)
- Using Word Count (Skill 1.14)
- Previewing and Printing a Document (Skill 1.16)

1. Open the start file **WD2019-OnYourOwn-1-5** and resave the file as: [your initials] WD-OnYourOwn-1-5

2. If the document opens in Protected view, click the **Enable Editing** button in the Message Bar at the top of the document so you can modify the document.

3. If the document opens in *Read Mode,* switch to **Print Layout** view.

4. Adjust the zoom level to one of your choice.

5. On the second page of the document, type the following on the blank line between *Pricing* and *Greenscapes' Service and Pricing*: Our prices are competitive with other companies in the area. Each of our technicians is trained to provide the highest quality of service in his or her area of specialty.

6. Practice selecting text by dragging and clicking. Select a word, paragraph, and line in the document.

7. On the second page, change the text **$89.00 per treatment** to read **$119.00 per visit**.

8. Copy several pieces of text to the *Clipboard*. Paste a text piece into the document and then undo the action.

9. Use the **Cut** and **Paste** commands to rearrange the items in the bulleted list in the *Lawn Maintenance* section.

10. Find all instances of the word **unprocessed** and replace each instance with a word of your choice.

11. Fix all the grammar and spelling errors in the document. *Hint*: *Greenscapes* is not misspelled in the document.

12. Check the number of words and pages in the document.

13. Print the document. **NOTE**: If you are using this in class or in your school's computer lab, check with your instructor about printing permissions before completing this step.

14. Save and close the document.

fix it 1.6

In this project, you will be fixing the résumé of an applicant for a marketing assistant position. There are a number of issues with the document that need correcting. First, you will need to adjust the view and zoom level to be able to work comfortably in the document. Next, you will add missing content and correct incorrect content in the résumé. You will move text using the *Cut* and *Paste* commands and find and replace words to help with readability. Finally, you will correct all grammar and spelling errors in the document.

Skills needed to complete this project:
- Using Views (Skill 1.15)
- Zooming a Document (Skill 1.13)
- Entering and Deleting Text (Skill 1.2)
- Selecting Text (Skill 1.3)
- Using Copy and Paste (Skill 1.9)
- Using Cut and Paste (Skill 1.10)
- Finding Text (Skill 1.7)
- Replacing Text (Skill 1.8)
- Checking for Writing Errors as You Type (Skill 1.4)
- Using the Editor (Skill 1.5)

1. Open the start file **WD2019-FixIt-1-6** and resave the file as: [your initials] WD-FixIt-1-6

2. If the document opens in Protected view, click the **Enable Editing** button in the Message Bar at the top of the document so you can modify the document.

3. Switch to **Read Mode,** and then switch back to **Print Layout** view.

4. Adjust the zoom level to **110%**.

5. The summary section is missing. Type the following paragraph under *Summary*.

   I am an accomplished professional offering a solid history of top performance in the field of marketing with a focus on the health care and publishing industries. I am skilled in managing multiple projects, meeting deadlines, and resolving issues prior to escalation. I am also detail-oriented, well organized and an effective communicator; I enjoy working on a team, but I also work well independently.

6. Copy the text: **Expert-level knowledge** and paste it after **Microsoft Excel:** and **Microsoft PowerPoint:**.

7. Copy the text **Experienced-level knowledge** and paste it after **Microsoft Project:**.

8. Cut the text **WordPress: Content management**. If there is a blank bullet after cutting the text, delete the extra line.

9. Place the cursor at the beginning of the bulleted item *Microsoft Word: Expert-level knowledge* and paste the text you cut. If necessary, press **Enter** to move *Microsoft Word: Expert-level knowledge* to a new line.

10. At the end of the document, the GPA for Templeton University should be **3.6**. Fix the error.

11. Use the **Find** command to find all instances of **Microsoft**.

12. All five instances of **Microsoft** should read **Microsoft Office 365**. Use the **Replace** command to fix this error.

13. Cut the line **Trained fellow employees in how to use accounting system** and paste it above **Created and maintained a database of customer information**. If necessary, delete any extra blank lines.

14. Right-click the spelling error **Digetal** and fix it using a suggestion on the shortcut menu.

15. Use the **Editor** pane to correct the remaining misspellings and grammar errors in the document. *Hint*: Both *ETech* and *UniHealth* are the names of corporations and are not misspelled.

16. Save and close the document.

chapter 2

Formatting Text and Paragraphs

In this chapter, you will learn the following skills:

❭ Apply fonts and style text

❭ Copy and paste formatting using the Format Painter

❭ Use bulleted and numbered list to organize information

❭ Use styles to format text

❭ Change paragraph alignment and spacing to effectively use white space

❭ Format the look of paragraphs by adding shading and borders

❭ Set and use tabs and indents to improve document layout

skills

introduction

This chapter will cover character and paragraph formatting and alignment to enhance the presentation, professionalism, and readability of documents. You will change the look of text by changing the font, font size, and font color. You will use styles and the *Format Painter* tool to copy formatting and apply it to text. You will convert text into numbered and bulleted lists. You will format paragraphs including changing alignment and spacing. Finally, you will indent text both from default commands on the Ribbon as well as from custom tabs that you set.

Skill 2.1 Using Bold, Italic, and Underline

You can call attention to text in your document by using the **bold**, *italic*, or underline effects. These effects are called **character effects** because they are applied to individual characters or words rather than paragraphs. Remember that these effects are used to emphasize important text and should be used sparingly—they lose their effect if overused. You can apply these effects using similar steps:

1. Select the text you want to emphasize.

2. On the *Home* tab, in the *Font* group, click the button of the effect you want to apply:

   - **Bold**—gives the text a heavier, thicker appearance.
   - **Italic**—makes text slant to the right.
   - **Underline**—draws a single line under the text.

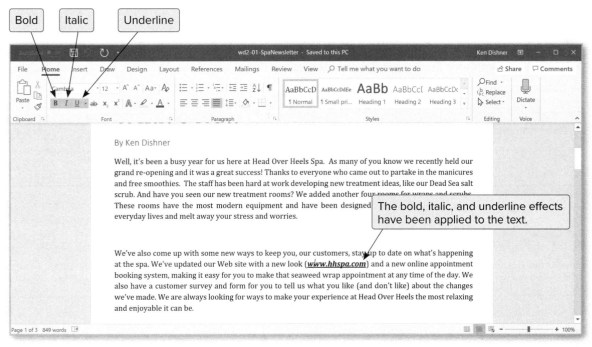

The bold, italic, and underline effects have been applied to the text.

FIGURE WD 2.1

tips & tricks

When text is bolded, italicized, or underlined, the button appears highlighted on the Ribbon. To remove the effect, click the highlighted button, or press the appropriate keyboard shortcut.

tell me **more**

》 Some of the other character effects available from the Ribbon include:
  - **Strikethrough**—draws a horizontal line through the text.
  - **Subscript**—draws a small character below the bottom of the text.
  - **Superscript**—draws a small character above the top of the text

》 The *Font* dialog contains other character formatting options not available from the Ribbon. These effects include **Double strikethrough**, **Small caps**, and **All caps** among others. To open the *Font* dialog, on the *Home* tab, in the *Font* group, click the dialog launcher. Select an option in the *Effects* section and click **OK** to apply the character effect to the text.

another **method**

》 The following keyboard shortcuts can be used to apply the bold, italic, and underline effects:
  - Bold = Ctrl + B
  - Italic = Ctrl + I
  - Underline = Ctrl + U

》 To access the bold, italic, or underline commands, you can also right-click the selected text and click the **Bold**, **Italic**, or **Underline** button on the Mini toolbar.

》 To apply an underline style, click the **Underline** button arrow and select a style.

let me **try**

Open the student data file **wd2-01-SpaNewsletter** and try this skill on your own:

1. Select the text **free smoothies** in the first paragraph of the newsletter.
2. Apply the **bold** character formatting to the text.
3. Select the text **online appointment booking system** in the second paragraph of the newsletter.
4. Apply the **italic** and **underline** character formatting to the text.
5. If you will be moving on to the next skill in this chapter, leave the document open to continue working. If not, save the file as directed by your instructor and close it.

Skill 2.2 Changing Fonts

A **font**, or typeface, refers to a set of characters of a certain design. The font is the shape of a character or number as it appears on-screen or in a printed document.

To change the font:

1. Select the text to be changed.

2. On the *Home* tab, click the arrow next to the *Font* box.

3. As you roll over the list of fonts, the Live Preview feature in Word changes the look of the text in your document, giving you a preview of how the text will look with the new font applied.

4. Click a font name from the menu to apply it to the text.

Word offers many fonts. **Serif fonts**, such as Cambria and Times New Roman, have an embellishment at the end of each stroke. **Sans serif fonts**, such as Calibri and Arial, do not have an embellishment at the end of each stroke. Sans serif fonts are easier to read on-screen and should be used for the main body text for documents that will be delivered and read electronically, such as a blog. Serif fonts are easier to read on the printed page and should be used for documents that will be printed, such as a report.

> Cambria is a serif font.
> Calibri is a sans serif font.

FIGURE WD 2.2

FIGURE WD 2.3

tips & tricks

If you want to change the font of an individual word, you can place your cursor in the word you want to modify, then select the new font.

another **method**

To change the font, you can also right-click the text, click the arrow next to the *Font* box on the Mini toolbar, and select a font from the list.

let me try

If you do not have the data file from the previous skill open, open the student data file **wd2-02-SpaNewsletter** and try this skill on your own:

1. Select the article title **What's New** on the first page of the newsletter.

2. Change the font to **Calibri Light (Headings)**.

3. If you will be moving on to the next skill in this chapter, leave the document open to continue working. If not, save the file as directed by your instructor and close it.

Skill 2.3 Changing Font Sizes

When creating a document, it is important not only to choose the correct or best font, but also to use the appropriate font size. Fonts are measured in **points**, abbreviated "pt." On the printed page, 72 points equal one inch. Different font sizes are used for the words in the paragraphs and for the headers in a document. The paragraphs of text typically use 10 pt., 11 pt., or 12 pt. fonts. Headers often use 14 pt., 16 pt., or 18 pt. fonts.

To change the size of the font:

1. Select the text to be changed.
2. On the *Home* tab, in the *Font* group, click the arrow next to the *Font Size* box.
3. Scroll the list to find the new font size.
4. Click the size you want.

FIGURE WD 2.4

tips & tricks

Sometimes when you are formatting text, you may not be sure of the exact size you want your text to be. You can experiment with the look of text in your document by incrementally increasing and decreasing the size of the font. Use the *Grow Font* or *Shrink Font* button, available in the *Font* group, to change the font size by one increment.

another **method**

To change the font you can also right-click the text, click the arrow next to the *Font Size* box on the Mini toolbar, and select a font size from the list.

let me **try**

If you do not have the data file from the previous skill open, open the student data file **wd2-03-SpaNewsletter** and try this skill on your own:

1. If necessary, select the article title **What's New** on the first page of the newsletter.
2. Change the font size to **22 pt**.
3. If you will be moving on to the next skill in this chapter, leave the document open to continue working. If not, save the file as directed by your instructor and close it.

Skill 2.4 Changing Text Case

When you type on a keyboard you use the [↑ Shift] key to capitalize individual letters and the [Caps lock] key to type in all capital letters. Another way to change letters from lowercase to uppercase, and vice versa, is to use the **Change Case** command. When you use the *Change Case* command in Word, you are manipulating the characters that were typed, changing how the letters are displayed. There are five types of text case formats you can apply to text:

〉 **Sentence case**–formats text as a sentence with the first word being capitalized and all remaining words beginning with a lowercase letter.

〉 **lowercase**–changes all letters to lowercase.

〉 **UPPERCASE**–changes all letters to uppercase, or capital letters.

〉 **Capitalize Each Word**–formats text so each word begins with a capital letter.

〉 **tOGGLE cASE**–formats text in the reverse of the typed format, converting uppercase letters to lowercase and lowercase letters to uppercase.

To apply text case formatting to text:

1. Select the text you want to change.

2. On the *Home* tab, in the *Font* group, click the **Change Case** button.

3. Select a text case option from the menu to apply it to the text.

FIGURE WD 2.5

tips & tricks

Headers and titles often use the *Capitalize Each Word* format. One way to ensure that your headers and titles are consistent in text case is to use the *Change Case* command.

tell me **more**

From the *Font* dialog, you can apply the *All caps* or *Small caps* character formatting to text. Although the *All caps* command produces the same visual results as the *UPPERCASE* command, the core text is different. *All caps* applies character formatting keeping the underlying text the same, while *UPPERCASE* changes the underlying text that was typed to capital letters.

let me **try**

If you do not have the data file from the previous skill open, open the student data file **wd2-04-SpaNewsletter** and try this skill on your own:

1. Select the text **Vol. 8 Issue 4** in the first line of the document.

2. Use the **Change Case** command to change the letters to all uppercase letters.

3. If you will be moving on to the next skill in this chapter, leave the document open to continue working. If not, save the file as directed by your instructor and close it.

Skill 2.5 Changing Font Colors

Unless you are creating a basic business letter, most documents include graphics, illustrations, and color text. Adding color to text in your document adds emphasis to certain words and helps design elements, such as headers, stand out for your reader.

To change the color of the text:

1. Select the text to be changed.
2. On the *Home* tab, in the *Font* group, click the arrow next to the *Font Color* button.
3. Click the color you want from the color palette.

FIGURE WD 2.6

tips & tricks

When you change the color of text, the *Font Color* button changes to the color you selected. Click the **Font Color** button to quickly apply the same color to other text in the document.

another **method**

You can change the font color from the Mini toolbar. To display the Mini toolbar, right-click in the text you want to change. Click the arrow next to the *Font Color* button and select the color you want.

tell me **more**

A color theme is a group of predefined colors that works well together in a document. You can apply a color theme to change the color of a number of elements at once. When you change the color theme, the color palette changes and displays only colors that are part of the color theme.

let me **try**

If you do not have the data file from the previous skill open, open the student data file **wd2-05-SpaNewsletter** and try this skill on your own:

1. Select the text **I'm So Gelish** on the first page of the document.
2. Change the text to the **Blue, Accent 1, Darker 25%** color. It is the fifth option in the fifth row under *Theme Colors*.
3. If you will be moving on to the next skill in this chapter, leave the document open to continue working. If not, save the file as directed by your instructor and close it.

Skill 2.6 Applying Highlights

Text in a Word document can be highlighted to emphasize or call attention to it. The effect is similar to that of a highlighting marker. When text is highlighted, the background color of the selected area is changed to make it stand out on the page.

Highlighting is very useful when you are sharing a document with coworkers or reviewers. It calls the other person's attention to elements that most need his or her attention. However, highlighting can sometimes be distracting as well. Be careful when using the highlighter in Word; use it only for small amounts of text.

To highlight text in a document:

1. Select the text to be highlighted.
2. On the *Home* tab, in the *Font* group, click the arrow next to the *Text Highlight Color* button.
3. Click the color you want to use.

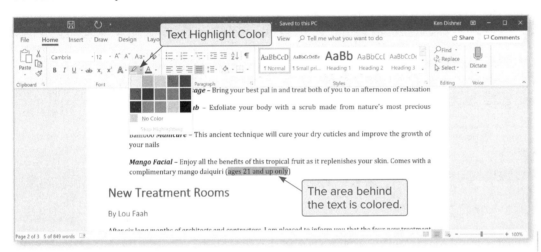

FIGURE WD 2.7

tips & tricks

❯ Be careful when selecting colors to use for highlighting. If both the color of the text and the highlight color are dark, the text will be hard to read. If the highlight color is too light, it may not give the text enough emphasis.

❯ To remove highlighting from text, select the highlighted text and then select the **No Color** option at the bottom of the *Text Highlight Color* palette.

another **method**

You can highlight text from the Mini toolbar. First, select the text you want to highlight; right-click the selected text to display the Mini toolbar. Click the arrow next to the *Text Highlight Color* button and select the color you want.

tell me **more**

Rather than applying highlighting to text you have already selected, you can use the highlighter to apply highlighting to text throughout your document. Click the **Text Highlight Color** button without selecting any text first. Your cursor changes to a highlighter shape. Click and drag across text with the highlighter cursor to highlight text. To change your cursor back, click the **Text Highlight Color** button again.

let me **try**

If you do not have the data file from the previous skill open, open the student data file **wd2-06-SpaNewsletter** and try this skill on your own:

1. Select the text **ages 21 and up** in the *Mango Facial* description on the second page of the newsletter. Do not select the opening and closing parentheses.
2. Apply the **Bright Green** highlighting to the text.
3. If you will be moving on to the next skill in this chapter, leave the document open to continue working. If not, save the file as directed by your instructor and close it.

Skill 2.7 Using Format Painter

When you want to copy text from one part of your document to another, you use the *Copy* and *Paste* commands. What if you don't want to copy the text but instead copy all the formatting from text in one part of your document to text in another part of your document? The **Format Painter** tool allows you to copy formatting styles that have been applied to text. You can then "paste" the formatting, applying it to text anywhere in the document.

To use *Format Painter*:

1. Select the text that has the formatting you want to copy.
2. On the *Home* tab, in the *Clipboard* group, click the **Format Painter** button.
3. Select the text that you want to apply the formatting to.
4. The formats are automatically applied to the selected text.

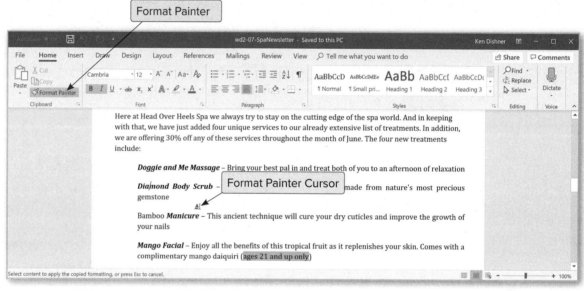

FIGURE WD 2.8

tips & tricks

> If you want to apply the formats more than once, double-click the **Format Painter** button when you select it. It will stay on until you click the **Format Painter** button again or press **Esc** to deselect it.

> If the text you are copying the formatting from is formatted using a paragraph style, then you don't need to select the entire paragraph. Just place the cursor anywhere in the paragraph and click the **Format Painter** button. To apply the same paragraph style formatting to another paragraph, click anywhere in the paragraph to which you want to apply the formatting.

another **method**

To activate *Format Painter*, you can right-click the text with formatting you want to copy and click the **Format Painter** button on the Mini toolbar.

let me **try**

If you do not have the data file from the previous skill open, open the student data file **wd2-07-SpaNewsletter** and try this skill on your own:

1. Use the **Format Painter** to copy the formatting of the text **Diamond Body Scrub** in the *Four New Services* article.
2. Apply the copied formatting to the word **Bamboo**.
3. If you will be moving on to the next skill in this chapter, leave the document open to continue working. If not, save the file as directed by your instructor and close it.

Skill 2.8 Clearing Formatting

After you have applied a number of character formats and effects to text, you may find that you want to return your text to its original formatting. You could perform multiple undo commands on the text, or you could use the **Clear All Formatting** command. The *Clear All Formatting* command removes any formatting that has been applied to text, including character formatting, text effects, and styles, and leaves only plain text.

To remove formatting from text:

1. Select the text you want to remove the formatting from.
2. On the *Home* tab, in the *Font* group, click the **Clear All Formatting** button.

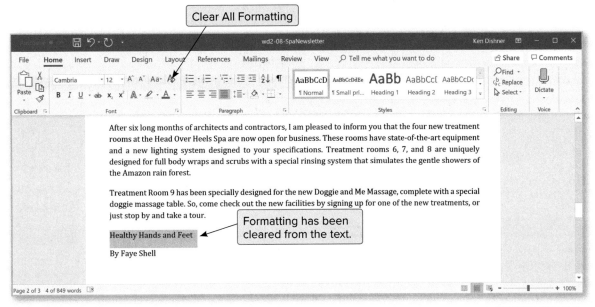

FIGURE WD 2.9

tips & tricks

If you clear the formatting from text and then decide that you want to keep the formatting that was removed, you can use the **Undo** command to apply the previous formatting to the text.

another **method**

To clear the formatting from text, you can also:

1. On the *Home* tab, in the *Styles* group, click the **More** button.
2. Click **Clear Formatting**.

tell me **more**

The *Clear All Formatting* command does not remove highlighting that has been applied to text. In order to remove highlighting from text, you must click the **Text Highlighting Color** button and select **No Color**.

let me **try**

If you do not have the data file from the previous skill open, open the student data file **wd2-08-SpaNewsletter** and try this skill on your own:

1. Select the **Healthy Hands and Feet** article title.
2. Clear the formatting from the text.
3. If you will be moving on to the next skill in this chapter, leave the document open to continue working. If not, save the file as directed by your instructor and close it.

Skill 2.9 Creating Numbered Lists

Some lists, such as directions to complete a task, need to have the items displayed in a specific order. **Numbered lists** display a number next to each list item and display the numbers in order. Numbered lists help you organize your content and display it in a clear, easy-to-understand manner.

To create a numbered list:

1. Select the text you want to change to a numbered list. In order to appear as separate items within a numbered list, each item must be followed by a hard return (press (←Enter)).

2. On the *Home* tab, in the *Paragraph* group, click the **Numbering** button arrow and select an option.

3. Click outside the list to deselect it.

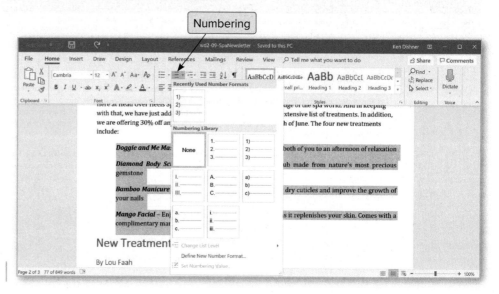

FIGURE WD 2.10

tips & tricks

❯ Sometimes you will want to add more items to an existing list. To add another item to the list, place your cursor at the end of an item and press (←Enter) to start a new line. The list will renumber itself to accommodate the new item.

❯ You can turn off the numbering feature by pressing (←Enter) twice.

❯ You can create new numbered list styles by selecting **Define New Number Format...** at the bottom of the Numbering menu.

another **method**

You can start a numbered list by:

❯ Typing **1.**, a space, and your list item, then pressing the **Enter** key.

❯ Clicking the **Numbering** button, typing your list item, then pressing the **Enter** key.

You can convert text to a numbered list by right-clicking the selected text, pointing to *Numbering* on the Mini toolbar, and selecting an option.

let me **try**

If you do not have the data file from the previous skill open, open the student data file **wd2-09-SpaNewsletter** and try this skill on your own:

1. Select descriptions of the four new services on the second page of the newsletter. Select starting from **Doggie and Me Massage** and ending at **(ages 21 and up only)**.

2. Apply the **a), b), c)** number style to the text.

3. If you will be moving on to the next skill in this chapter, leave the document open to continue working. If not, save the file as directed by your instructor and close it.

Skill 2.10 Creating Bulleted Lists

When typing a document you may want to include information that is best displayed in list format rather than paragraph format. If your list does not include items that need to be displayed in a specific order, use a **bulleted list** to help information stand out from surrounding text. A **bullet** is a symbol that is displayed before each item in a list. When a bullet appears before a list item, it indicates that the items in the list do not have a particular order to them.

To create a bulleted list:

1. Select the text you want to change to a bulleted list. As with numbered lists, in order to appear as separate items within a bulleted list, each item must be followed by a hard return (press ⬅Enter).

2. On the *Home* tab, in the *Paragraph* group, click the **Bullets** button.

3. Click outside the list to deselect it.

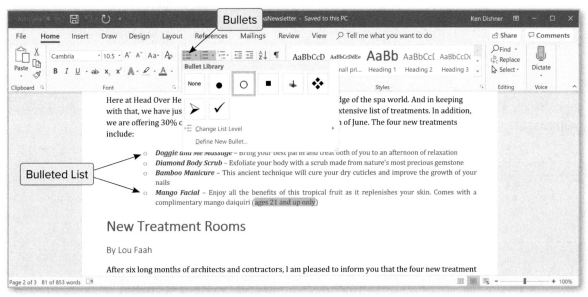

FIGURE WD 2.11

tips & tricks

❭ Sometimes you will want to add more items to an existing list. Place your cursor at the end of a list item and press ⬅Enter to start a new line. A bullet will automatically appear before the list item.

❭ You can turn off the **Bullets** formatting feature by pressing ⬅Enter twice.

another **method**

❭ You can start a bulleted list by typing an asterisk, a space, and your list item, then pressing the ⬅Enter key.

❭ You can convert text to a bulleted list by right-clicking the selected text, pointing to *Bullets*, and selecting an option.

tell me **more**

To change the bullet type, click the **Bullets** button arrow and select an option from the *Bullet Library*. You can create new bullets by selecting **Define New Bullet...**

let me **try**

If you do not have the data file from the previous skill open, open the student data file **wd2-10-SpaNewsletter** and try this skill on your own:

1. Select the numbered list on the second page of the newsletter.

2. Apply the **open circle** bullet style to the text.

3. If you will be moving on to the next skill in this chapter, leave the document open to continue working. If not, save the file as directed by your instructor and close it.

Skill 2.11 Using Styles

A **style** is a group of formatting, including character and paragraph formatting, that you can easily apply to text in your document. Styles can be applied to body text, headings, quotes, or just about any type of text you may have in your document.

It is a good idea to use styles to format text in your documents. When you use styles to format text, you can quickly change the look of that style across your document by changing the document's theme. Certain styles, such as headings, are also used by other features in Word, such as creating a table of contents and the *Navigation* task pane.

The *Styles* group on the *Home* tab displays the latest styles you have used. If you want to apply a recently used style, you can click the option directly from the Ribbon without opening the *Styles* gallery.

FIGURE WD 2.12

To apply a style to text:

1. Select the text you want to change.
2. On the *Home* tab, in the *Styles* group, click the **More** button.
3. Select an option from the *Styles* gallery.

FIGURE WD 2.13

tips & tricks

❭ If you modify a style, you can save the style with a new name and then use it throughout your document. To save a new text style, open the *Styles* gallery and select **Create a Style**.

❭ Click the **dialog launcher** in the *Styles* group to open the **Styles** pane where you can work with and modify styles.

tell me **more**

When you select a new style, it replaces the formatting of the text. If you want to clear all the formatting from text, open the *Styles* gallery and select **Clear Formatting**.

let me **try**

If you do not have the data file from the previous skill open, open the student data file **wd2-11-SpaNewsletter** and try this skill on your own:

1. Select the text **Healthy Hands and Feet** article title on the second page of the newsletter.

2. Apply the **Heading 1** style to the text.

3. Select the text **By Faye Shell** on the next line.

4. Apply the **Heading 2** style to the text.

5. If you will be moving on to the next skill in this chapter, leave the document open to continue working. If not, save the file as directed by your instructor and close it.

from the perspective of . . .

COLLEGE GRADUATE

When creating my résumé to send out to potential employers, I always make sure I use the right combination of fonts and styles to create the most eye-catching and professional document. I use tab stops and indents to align text just the way I want it and add space before and after paragraphs to control the layout on the page. I learned my lesson with the first résumé I sent out. Apparently, using a different color font for each section and using pink highlighting on my achievements was not the way to land an interview at the firm I applied to.

Mark Andersen/Rubberball/Getty Images

Skill 2.12 Changing Paragraph Alignment

Paragraph alignment refers to how text is aligned with regard to the left and right margins.

> **Left alignment** aligns the text on the left side, leaving the right side ragged.
>
> **Center alignment** centers each line of text relative to the margins.
>
> **Right alignment** aligns the text on the right side, leaving the left side ragged.
>
> **Justified alignment** evenly spaces the words, aligning the text on the right and left sides of the printed page.

It is important to understand common uses of different alignments. Paragraph text and headers are typically left aligned, but titles are often centered. Newspaper columns are often justified, and columns of numbers are typically right aligned.

To change the alignment of text:

1. Click in the paragraph you want to change.
2. On the *Home* tab, in the *Paragraph* group, click an alignment button—**Align Left**, **Center**, **Align Right**, or **Justify**.

FIGURE WD 2.14

another **method**

The following keyboard shortcuts can be used to apply horizontal alignment:

- ❯ Align Left = `Ctrl` + `L`
- ❯ Center = `Ctrl` + `E`
- ❯ Align Right = `Ctrl` + `R`
- ❯ Justify = `Ctrl` + `J`

let me **try**

If you do not have the data file from the previous skill open, open the student data file **wd2-12-SpaNewsletter** and try this skill on your own:

1. Select the **Four New Services** article title.
2. Change the text so it is **left aligned**.
3. Select the **first paragraph** of text in the *Four New Services* article.
4. Change the paragraph text so it is **justified**.
5. If you will be moving on to the next skill in this chapter, leave the document open to continue working. If not, save the file as directed by your instructor and close it.

Skill 2.13 Changing Line Spacing

Line spacing is the white space between lines of text. The default line spacing in Word is 1.08 spacing. This gives each line the height of single spacing with a little extra space at the top and bottom. This line spacing is a good choice to use for the body of a document. Other commonly used spacing options include single spacing, double spacing, and 1.5 spacing. To change line spacing:

1. Select the text you want to change.
2. On the *Home* tab, in the *Paragraph* group, click the **Line Spacing** button.
3. Select the number of the spacing you want.

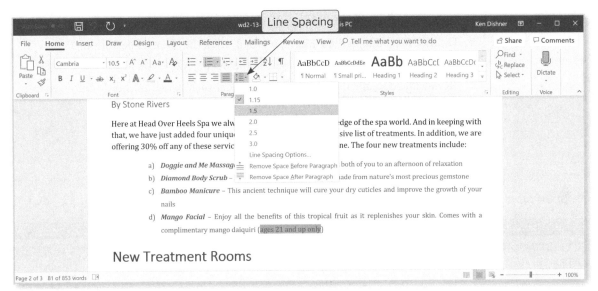

FIGURE WD 2.15

tips & tricks

To change the line and paragraph spacing for the entire document, you can select an option from the *Paragraph Spacing* gallery in the *Document Formatting* group on the *Design* tab.

tell me **more**

In Word 2007, Microsoft changed the default line spacing from single space to 1.15 lines. This option is still available from the *Line Spacing* menu. However, in Word 2013, the default was changed to 1.08 lines. The new default line spacing is designed to help with readability of online documents on a number of devices, including traditional desktop and laptop computers, tablets, and smartphones.

another **method**

❯ To apply single spacing, you can also press Ctrl + 1 on the keyboard.
❯ To apply double spacing, you can also press Ctrl + 2 on the keyboard.

let me **try**

If you do not have the data file from the previous skill open, open the student data file **wd2-13-SpaNewsletter** and try this skill on your own:

1. Select bulleted list on the second page of the newsletter. Select starting from **Doggie and Me Massage** and ending at **(ages 21 and up only)**.
2. Change the line spacing from double spaced to **1.5 spacing**.
3. If you will be moving on to the next skill in this chapter, leave the document open to continue working. If not, save the file as directed by your instructor and close it.

Skill 2.14 Revealing Formatting Marks

When creating a document it is important to use consistent formatting, such as a single space after the period at the end of a sentence. As you create a document, Word adds **formatting marks** that are hidden from view. For example, a paragraph mark, ¶, is created every time the (← Enter) key is pressed.

When creating professional documents, it is considered bad practice to use extra line breaks to add space between paragraphs in a document. By displaying formatting marks, you can quickly see where these extra line breaks occur in your documents and then easily delete them. Formatting marks appear on-screen only. They do not appear in the printed document.

To display formatting marks in a document:

1. On the *Home* tab, in the *Paragraph* group, click the **Show/Hide** button.

2. The formatting marks are displayed in the document.

3. Review the document for extra ¶ symbols between paragraphs or for more than one dot between words or after punctuation.

4. Use the **Delete** key to remove extra paragraph marks or spaces.

5. Click the **Show/Hide** button again to hide the formatting marks.

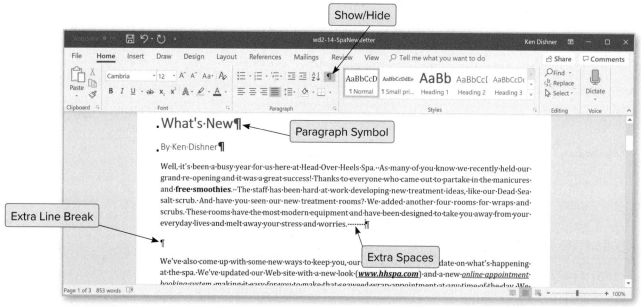

FIGURE WD 2.16

Formatting marks include symbols that represent spaces, nonbreaking spaces, tabs, paragraphs, and page breaks. The following table shows examples of formatting marks and the keyboard commands used to create them:

CHARACTER	FORMATTING MARK	KEYSTROKE/COMMAND
Space	·	Spacebar
Paragraph	¶	Enter
Tab	→	Tab
Line Break	↵	Shift + Enter
Nonbreaking Space	°	Ctrl + Shift + Enter
Page Break	...........Page Break..........¶	Ctrl + Enter

tips & tricks

You can choose to always show specific formatting marks on-screen even when the Show/Hide button is inactive. To show specific formatting marks:

1. Click the **File** tab and select **Options**.
2. In the *Word Options* dialog, click the **Display** category.
3. Select the formatting marks you want to display in the *Always show these formatting marks on the screen* section.
4. Click **OK**.

tell me **more**

❭ A nonbreaking space is a space between two words that keeps the words together and prevents the words from being split across two lines.

❭ A line break forces the text onto a new line, but does not treat the text as a separate paragraph.

another **method**

To show formatting marks, you can press (Ctrl) + (↑ Shift) + (8).

let me **try**

If you do not have the data file from the previous skill open, open the student data file **wd2-14-SpaNewsletter** and try this skill on your own:

1. Show the formatting marks in the document.
2. On the first page, there is an extra blank line. Remove the extra blank line from the document.
3. In the *I'm So Gelish* article, there should be no spaces after punctuation at the end of a paragraph. Remove the extra spaces from the article.
4. Hide the formatting marks.
5. If you will be moving on to the next skill in this chapter, leave the document open to continue working. If not, close the file.

Skill 2.15 Adding Borders and Shading to Paragraphs

If you have an important paragraph of information in a document and want it to stand out from the rest of the text, you can format it using **borders** and **shading**. Shading refers to color that appears behind the text of the paragraph. Borders are lines that appear along the top, bottom, left side, and right side of the paragraph. You can quickly apply borders and shading to paragraphs directly from the Ribbon.

To apply shading:

1. Place the cursor in the paragraph you want to format.

2. On the *Home* tab, in the *Paragraph* group, click the **Shading** button.

3. Click a color in the color palette to apply the shading.

To apply borders:

1. Place the cursor in the paragraph you want to format.

2. On the *Home* tab, in the *Paragraph* group, click the **Borders** button.

3. Select a border option on the menu to apply it to the paragraph.

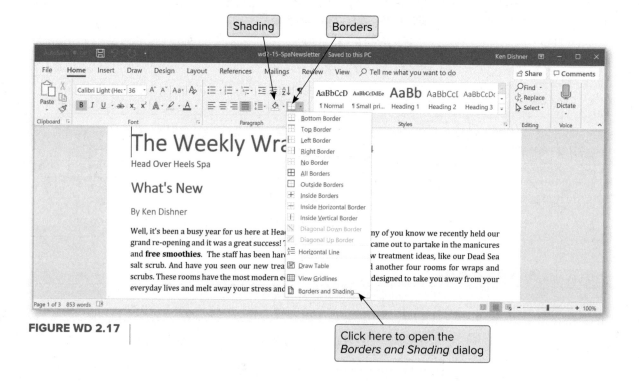

FIGURE WD 2.17

Click here to open the *Borders and Shading* dialog

You can also apply borders and shading to paragraphs through the *Borders and Shading* dialog. To apply a simple border from the *Borders and Shading* dialog:

1. Place the cursor in the paragraph you want to add the border to.

2. On the *Home* tab, in the *Paragraph* group, click the **Borders** button, and select **Borders and Shading…**

3. Select **Box** under *Setting*.

4. A preview of the border appears in the *Preview* area. Click the **Top Border**, **Bottom Border**, **Left Border**, or **Right Border** buttons to turn that part of the border on and off. The *Preview* area will display the changes as you make them.

5. Click **OK** to apply your changes.

FIGURE WD 2.18

To apply shading from the *Borders and Shading* dialog:

1. Open the *Borders and Shading* dialog and click the **Shading** tab.

2. Click the **Fill** arrow and select a color from the palette.

3. Click **OK** to apply your changes.

FIGURE WD 2.19

tips & tricks

Notice that when you apply shading and borders from the buttons on the Ribbon, each button updates to reflect the most recently used option. To apply the same option again, just click the button on the Ribbon rather than opening the menu and making a selection.

let me try

If you do not have the data file from the previous skill open, open the student data file **wd2-15-SpaNewsletter** and try this skill on your own:

1. Place the cursor in the title of the newsletter.

2. Change the paragraph shading to **Gold, Accent 4, Lighter 80%**. It is the third to last option in the second row under *Theme Colors*.

3. Add an **outside border** to the paragraph using the default settings.

4. If you will be moving on to the next skill in this chapter, leave the document open to continue working. If not, save the file as directed by your instructor and close it.

Skill 2.16 Adjusting Spacing Before and After Paragraphs

The default spacing after paragraphs in Word is 8 pt. This creates an evenly spaced document with some spacing between paragraphs to make it easier to tell when one paragraph ends and another begins. Sometimes you will want to increase the amount of space after paragraphs or add space above the paragraph in addition to below the paragraph.

To adjust the amount of white space that appears above and below paragraphs:

1. Place the cursor in the paragraph you want to change.
2. Click the **Layout** tab.
3. In the *Paragraph* group, click the up and down arrows next to the *Before* box to adjust the spacing above the paragraph.
4. Click the up and down arrows next to the *After* box to adjust the spacing below the paragraph.

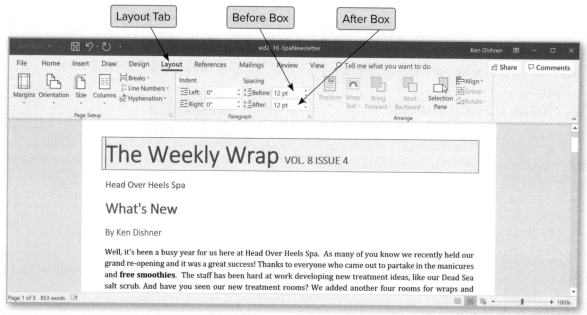

FIGURE WD 2.20

You can also adjust the spacing around paragraphs from the *Line Spacing* menu:

1. On the *Home* tab, in the *Paragraph* group, click the **Line Spacing** button.
2. Select **Add Space Before Paragraph** to add space above the paragraph.
3. Select **Remove Space After Paragraph** to remove space below the paragraph.

While this is a quick way to adjust spacing before and after paragraphs, be aware that with this method you cannot customize the amount of space added before or after the paragraph.

FIGURE WD 2.21

tips & tricks

〉 When you click the up and down arrows, the value for the spacing adjusts by 6 pts. You can also type a value in the box to apply more precise spacing.

〉 If you want to adjust how paragraphs appear on the page, add space before or after the text rather than pressing ⏎ Enter to add space. Pressing ⏎ Enter adds unnecessary line breaks and can cause issues with the page layout if future edits are made to the document.

another **method**

To adjust spacing before and after paragraphs, you can also open the *Paragraph* dialog and change the spacing in the *Before* and *After* boxes in the *Spacing* section.

let me **try**

If you do not have the data file from the previous skill open, open the student data file **wd2-16-SpaNewsletter** and try this skill on your own:

1. Place the cursor in the first line of the document (beginning with **The Weekly Wrap**).

2. Change the spacing before the paragraph to **12 pt**. and the spacing after the paragraph to **12 pt**.

3. If you will be moving on to the next skill in this chapter, leave the document open to continue working. If not, save the file as directed by your instructor and close it.

Skill 2.17 Applying Indents

When you create a document, the margins control how close the text comes to the edge of a page. But what if you don't want all your paragraphs to line up? Indenting paragraphs increases the left margin for a paragraph, helping it stand out from the rest of your document.

To change the indentation of a paragraph:

1. Place the cursor anywhere in the paragraph you want to change.

2. To increase the indent of the paragraph by one level, on the *Home* tab, in the *Paragraph* group, click the **Increase Indent** button.

3. To reduce the indent of the paragraph and bring it closer to the edge of the page by one level, click the **Decrease Indent** button.

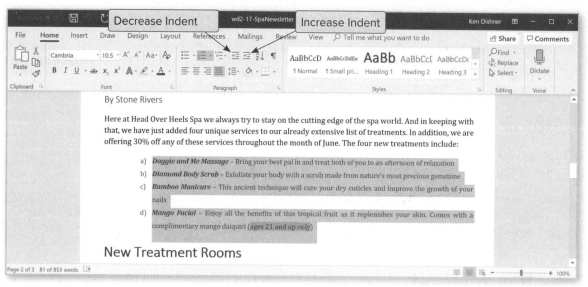

FIGURE WD 2.22

Using the *Decrease Indent* and *Increase Indent* commands allows you to indent only from the left side of the paragraph and only in set amounts. You can adjust both the right and left indents, each by one-tenth of an inch, from the *Layout* tab, giving you more control over the layout of your document.

To increase and decrease the left and right indentation for a paragraph:

1. Click the **Layout** tab.

2. In the *Paragraph* group, click the up arrow next to *Left* and *Right* to increase the indentation by one-tenth of an inch at a time.

3. Click the down arrow next to *Left* and *Right* to decrease the indentation by one-tenth of an inch at a time.

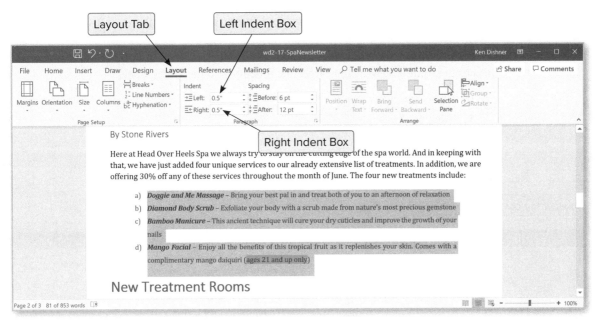

tell me **more**

The *Indent* commands indent all lines in a paragraph the same amount. If you want only the first line of a paragraph to be indented and the remainder of the paragraph to be left-aligned, use a **First Line Indent**. If you want the first line of a paragraph to be left-aligned and the remainder of the paragraph to be indented, use a **Hanging Indent**.

In the *Format Paragraph* dialog, you can precisely set options for first line indents and hanging indents. To open the *Format Paragraph* dialog, click the **Dialog Launcher** in the *Paragraph* group on the *Home* tab or in the *Paragraph* group on the *Layout* tab.

let me **try**

If you do not have the data file from the previous skill open, open the student data file **wd2-17-SpaNewsletter** and try this skill on your own:

1. Select the four bullet points on the second page of the newsletter.
2. Increase the indent for the text by one level.
3. Decrease the indent for the text by one level.
4. Change the right indent to be the same as the left indent.
5. If you will be moving on to the next skill in this chapter, leave the document open to continue working. If not, close the file.

Skill 2.18 Displaying the Ruler

When working with documents, it is helpful to display the **ruler**. The ruler displays horizontally across the top of the window just below the Ribbon and vertically along the left side of the window. The ruler gives you a quick view of the margins and position of elements in your document. From the ruler you can also control other document layout controls such as tabs, first line indents, and hanging indents.

To display the ruler:

1. Click the **View** tab.
2. In the *Show* group, click the check box next to **Ruler** so a checkmark appears.
3. To hide the ruler, click the check box again so the checkmark disappears.

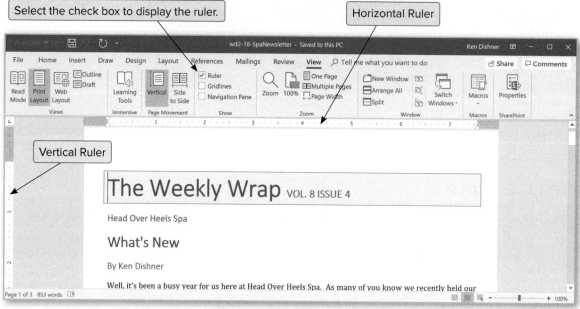

FIGURE WD 2.24

tips & tricks

Double-click the ruler to open the *Page Setup* dialog where you can control page layout elements such as margins and page orientation.

tell me **more**

Gridlines are a series of vertical and horizontal lines that divide the page into small boxes, giving you visual markers for aligning graphics, tables, and other elements on the page. Click the *Gridlines* check box on the *View* tab to show and hide the gridlines on the screen.

let me **try**

If you do not have the data file from the previous skill open, open the student data file **wd2-18-SpaNewsletter** and try this skill on your own:

1. Practice showing and hiding the ruler from the *View* tab.
2. If you will be moving on to the next skill in this chapter, leave the document open to continue working. If not, close the file.

Skill 2.19 Using Tab Stops

A **tab stop** is a location along the horizontal ruler that indicates how far to indent text when the (Tab ⇆) key is pressed. There are five types of tab stops:

> ⌞ **Left Tab**—displays text to the right of the tab stop

> ⊥ **Center Tab**—displays text centered over the tab stop

> ⌟ **Right Tab**—displays the text to the left of the tab stop

> ⊥. **Decimal Tab**—aligns the text along the decimal point

> ⎸ **Bar Tab**—displays a vertical line through the text at the tab stop

To set a tab stop:

1. Select the text in which you want to set a tab stop.

2. Click the **tab selector** at the far left of the horizontal ruler until it changes to the type of tab you want.

3. Click the horizontal ruler where you want to set a tab stop.

FIGURE WD 2.25

tips & tricks

> To clear a tab stop, drag the tab marker down from the horizontal ruler to remove it.

> To move a tab stop, drag the tab marker to the right or left along the horizontal ruler to its new position.

tell me more

The tab selector also includes two options for adding indents to your document:

> ▽ **First Line Indent**—Controls where the first line of a paragraph begins.

> △ **Hanging Indent**—Controls where the remainder of the paragraph is indented.

let me try

If you do not have the data file from the previous skill open, open the student data file **wd2-19-SpaNewsletter** and try this skill on your own:

1. Place the cursor before the text **Vol. 8 Issue 4** in the first line of the document.

2. Click the **tab selector** two times so the right tab icon appears.

3. Click the ruler at the **6.5"** mark.

4. Use the (Tab ⇆) key to indent the **Vol. 8 Issue 4** text and align it along the right side of the tab stop.

5. If you will be moving on to the next skill in this chapter, leave the document open to continue working. If not, save the file as directed by your instructor and close it.

Skill 2.20 Using the Tabs Dialog

FIGURE WD 2.26

You can quickly add tabs to a document by selecting a tab stop type and clicking the ruler where you want the tab to appear. Another way to set tabs in your document is through the *Tabs* dialog. From the *Tabs* dialog, you can add new tabs or modify or clear existing tabs.

To set tabs in the *Tabs* dialog:

1. Select the text in which you want to set a tab.
2. On the *Home* tab, in the *Paragraph* group, click the **dialog launcher**.
3. In the *Paragraph* dialog, click the **Tabs...** button.
4. The *Tabs* dialog opens.
5. In the *Tab stop position* box, type the number of where you want the tab stop to appear.
6. Click a radio button in the *Alignment* section.
7. Click **OK**.

tips & tricks

> Click the **Clear All** button to clear all the tabs displayed in the *Tabs* dialog.

> To add the tab stop and continue working in the *Tabs* dialog, click the **Set** button instead of **OK**.

tell me more

A tab leader fills the tabbed space with dotted, dashed, or solid lines. Tab leaders are helpful if there is a long distance in the tabbed space in a list of items, like in a table of contents or an index.

another method

To open the *Tabs* dialog, you can double-click a tab stop on the ruler.

let me try

If you do not have the data file from the previous skill open, open the student data file **wd2-20-SpaNewsletter** and try this skill on your own:

1. Press Ctrl + A on the keyboard to select the entire document.
2. Open the **Paragraph** dialog.
3. Open the **Tabs** dialog.
4. Add a **left tab stop** at .3".
5. Place the cursor before the text *By Ken Dishner* under the *What'sNew* article title. Press the Tab key. Notice the text is indented **.3"** inches.
6. Use the Tab key to increase the remaining bylines in the newsletter. There are an additional four lines of text that will be indented.
7. Save the file as directed by your instructor and close it.

Character effects
Bold
Italic
Underline
Font
Serif fonts
Sans serif fonts
Points
Change Case
Highlighting
Format Painter
Clear All Formatting
Numbered lists
Bulleted list
Bullet
Style
Paragraph alignment
Left alignment
Center alignment

Right alignment
Justified alignment
Line spacing
Formatting marks
Borders
Shading
Increase Indent
Decrease Indent
First Line Indent
Hanging Indent
Ruler
Gridlines
Tab stop
Left Tab
Center Tab
Right Tab
Decimal Tab
Bar Tab

concept review

1. Which type of font has an embellishment at the end of each stroke to lead the eye from one character to the next?

a. heading

b. theme

c. serif

d. sans serif

2. Which command would you use to change the text from uppercase to having each word capitalized?

a. Shrink Font

b. Change Case

c. Change Font

d. Grow Font

3. Which command would you use to call attention to text by coloring the background behind the text?

a. Text Highlight Color

b. Text Effects

c. Font Color

d. Format Painter

4. Which command is used to copy the styles from one word to another?

a. Format Painter

b. Text Effects

c. Styles

d. Text Highlight Color

5. Styles ensure parts of your document, such as headings, all use the same formatting.

   a. true

   b. false

6. Which kind of list would you use for instructions that do not need to be performed in a certain order?

   a. bulleted list

   b. numbered list

   c. multilevel list

   d. justified list

7. To evenly space words, aligning the text on the right and left sides of the printed page, use the command _____.

   a. Align Left

   b. Center

   c. Align Right

   d. Justify

8. Which command displays hidden formatting marks in a document, including paragraph and spacing marks?

   a. Formatting dialog

   b. Show/Hide

   c. Clear All Formatting

   d. Styles

9. You can adjust the amount of space that appears before and after paragraphs from the *Design* tab on the Ribbon.

   a. true

   b. false

10. Which tab stop displays the text to the left of the tab stop?

   a. Center Tab

   b. Decimal Tab

   c. Left Tab

   d. Right Tab

skill review **2.1**

In this project you will be adding basic formatting to a brochure for the Suarez Agency. First, you will remove unwanted formatting in a line of text. Next, you will change the font and line spacing for the entire document. You will remove extra lines and spaces in the document. You will apply styles to text as well as use the _Format Painter_ tool to copy and paste formatting from one selection to another. You will also convert text into a numbered list and a bulleted list.

Skills needed to complete this project:

- Clearing Formatting (Skill 2.8)
- Changing Fonts (Skill 2.2)
- Changing Font Sizes (Skill 2.3)
- Changing Line Spacing (Skill 2.13)
- Revealing Formatting Marks (Skill 2.14)
- Using Styles (Skill 2.11)
- Adjusting Spacing Before and After Paragraphs (Skill 2.16)
- Using Bold, Italic, and Underline (Skill 2.1)
- Changing Font Colors (Skill 2.5)
- Using Format Painter (Skill 2.7)
- Creating Numbered Lists (Skill 2.9)
- Applying Indents (Skill 2.17)
- Creating Bulleted Lists (Skill 2.10)
- Changing Paragraph Alignment (Skill 2.12)
- Adding Borders and Shading to Paragraphs (Skill 2.15)

1. Open the start file **WD2019-SkillReview-2-1** and resave the file as:
   `[your initials] WD-SkillReview-2-1`

2. If the document opens in Protected view, click the **Enable Editing** button in the Message Bar at the top of the document so you can modify the document.

3. Clear the formatting on text.
   a. Select the third line in the document. The one beginning with _Phone:_.
   b. On the _Home_ tab, in the _Font_ group, click the **Clear All Formatting** button.

4. Change the font and size on all the text in the document.
   a. Press Ctrl + A to select all text in the document.
   b. On the _Home_ tab, in the _Font_ group, click the arrow next to the _Font_ box and choose **Calibri Light**.
   c. In the _Font_ group, click the arrow next to the _Font Size_ box and choose **12**.

5. Change the line spacing on all the text in the document.

    a. Verify the entire document is still selected.

    b. On the *Home* tab, in the *Paragraph* group, click the **Line and Paragraph Spacing** button and select **1.5** to change the line spacing.

6. Show formatting marks and remove extra spaces and blank lines.

    a. On the *Home* tab, in the *Paragraph* group, click the **Show/ Hide** button to reveal formatting marks in the document.

    b. Delete the extra spaces at the end of the first line of the document.

    c. Delete all the extra blank lines between paragraphs in the document. *Hint*: There are four blank lines that need to be deleted.

    d. Click the **Show/Hide** button again to hide the formatting marks.

7. Use styles to apply a heading format to a section heading in the document.

    a. Select the **Our Goal** heading on the first page.

    b. On the *Home* tab, in the *Styles* group, click the **Heading 1** style to apply it to the text.

    c. Apply the **Heading 1** style to the following lines of text:

        1. **Experience**

        2. **Why Suarez?**

        3. **The Suarez Marketing Belief System**

        4. **Client Quotes**

        5. **Professional Credentials**

8. Change the spacing before the paragraph on the selected heading.

    a. Select the **Our Goal** heading on the first page.

    b. Click the **Layout** tab.

    c. In the *Paragraph* group, click the **Before** down arrow three times to change the spacing before the text to **6 pt**.

    d. Use this method to change the spacing before all the headings in the brochure.

9. Change the character formatting, font, and color of text.

    a. Select the text **The Suarez Agency** at the top of the document.

    b. Click the **Home** tab.

    c. In the *Font* group, click the **Bold** button.

    d. In the *Font* group, click the arrow next to the **Font** box and select **Verdana**.

    e. In the *Font* group, click the arrow next to the **Font Size** box and select **22**.

    f. In the *Font* group, click the **Font Color** button and select **Orange, Accent 2** (it is the sixth color in the first row under *Theme Colors*).

10. Use the Format Painter to change the format of text.

    a. With the text *The Suarez Agency* still selected, on the *Home* tab, in the *Clipboard* group, click the **Format Painter** button.

    b. Select the text **"Putting Your Needs First"** to apply the copied formatting.

    c. On the *Home* tab, in the *Font* group, click the arrow next to the **Font Size** box and select **12** to change the size of the text.

11. Add a numbered list to and decrease the indent on a section of the brochure.

    a. In the *Why Suarez?* section, select all of the text below the heading.

    b. On the *Home* tab, in the *Paragraph* group, click the **Numbering** button arrow and select the **1), 2), 3)** option to apply the numbering style to the selected text.

    c. Click the **Decrease Indent** button once to change the left indent to **0"**.

12. Add a bulleted list to sections of the brochure.

   a. In the *The Suarez Marketing Belief System* section, select all of the text below the heading.

   b. On the *Home* tab, in the *Paragraph* group, click the **Bullets** button arrow and select the **open circle bullet** option to apply the bullet style.

   c. In the *Professional Credentials* section, select all of the text below the heading.

   d. Apply **open circle bullet** style to the text.

13. Apply a style to text.

   a. In the *Client Quotes* section, select the first quote and include the quotation marks.

   b. On the *Home* tab, in the *Styles* group, apply the **Quote** style. You might have to click the **More** button to locate this style.

   c. Select the second quote in the section and apply the same style.

14. Change the paragraph alignment and apply a style on selected text.

   a. Select -**Jason Brown, Chesterfield, MO**.

   b. On the *Home* tab, in the *Paragraph* group, click the **Align Right** button.

   c. On the *Home* tab, in the *Paragraph* group, apply the **Subtle Emphasis** style. You might have to click the **More** button to locate this style.

   d. Select the text -**Scott Morris and Associates, St. Louis, MO** and apply the same formatting.

15. Add shading and borders to paragraphs of text.

   a. In the *Client Quotes* section, place the cursor in the first quote.

   b. On the *Home* tab, in the *Paragraph* group, click the **Shading** button, and select **Blue, Accent 1, Lighter 80%**. It is the fifth option in the second row under *Theme Colors*.

   c. In the *Paragraph* group, click the **Borders** button, and select **Top Border**.

   d. Apply the same formatting to the second quote in the section.

16. Save and close the document.

skill review 2.2

In this project you will be adding text and paragraph formatting to the Tri-State Book Festival agenda. First, you will clear the formatting from the entire document. You will then change the font, font size, and line spacing for the document. You will use the *Show/Hide* command to display formatting marks and remove extra line breaks and spaces in the document. You will apply styles, adjust font formatting, and then copy and paste text formatting using the *Format Painter* tool. Finally, you will set tabs both from the ruler and the *Tabs* dialog, and then apply those tabs to text.

Skills needed to complete this project:

- Clearing Formatting (Skill 2.8)
- Changing Fonts (Skill 2.2)
- Changing Font Sizes (Skill 2.3)
- Changing Line Spacing (Skill 2.13)
- Revealing Formatting Marks (Skill 2.14)

- Changing Text Case (Skill 2.4)
- Using Styles (Skill 2.11)
- Adjusting Spacing Before and After Paragraphs (Skill 2.16)
- Changing Paragraph Alignment (Skill 2.12)
- Changing Font Colors (Skill 2.5)
- Adding Borders and Shading to Paragraphs (Skill 2.15)
- Using Format Painter (Skill 2.7)
- Applying Highlights (Skill 2.6)
- Using Bold, Italic, and Underline (Skill 2.1)
- Displaying the Ruler (Skill 2.18)
- Using Tab Stops (Skill 2.19)
- Using the Tabs Dialog (Skill 2.20)

1. Open the start file **WD2019-SkillReview-2-2** and resave the file as:
   [your initials] WD-SkillReview-2-2

2. If the document opens in Protected view, click the **Enable Editing** button in the Message Bar at the top of the document so you can modify the document.

3. Clear formatting from the entire document.
   a. Press (Ctrl) + (A) to select the entire document.
   b. On the *Home* tab, in the *Font* group, click the **Clear All Formatting** button.

4. Change font and font size for the entire document.
   a. Verify the entire document is still selected.
   b. On the *Home* tab, in the *Font* group, click the arrow next to the **Font** box and choose **Century Gothic**.
   c. In the *Font* group, click the arrow next to the **Font Size** box and choose **11**.

5. Change the line spacing for the entire document.
   a. Verify the entire document is still selected.
   b. On the *Home* tab, in the *Paragraph* group, change the line spacing to **1.15**.

6. Reveal formatting marks and remove extra line breaks in the document.
   a. On the *Home* tab, in the *Paragraph* group, click the **Show/Hide** button to reveal formatting marks in the document.
   b. Delete the extra spaces at the end of the first paragraph.
   c. Delete the extra spaces before *Agenda* and before *Authors*.
   d. Delete all the extra blank lines between paragraphs in the document. *Hint*: There are five blank lines to delete.
   e. Click the **Show/Hide** button again to hide the formatting marks.

7. Change the text case for the title of the document.
   a. Select the first line of text in the document.
   b. On the *Home* tab, in the *Font* group, click the **Change Case** button, and select **Capitalize Each Word**.

8. Apply styles.
   a. Verify the first line of text is still selected.
   b. On the *Home* tab, in the *Styles* group, click the **Title** style to apply it to the text.
   c. Place the cursor in the *Agenda* heading. It appears after the first two introductory paragraphs of the document.

    d. On the *Home* tab, in the *Styles* group, click the **Heading 1** style to apply it to the text.

9. Adjust the space that appears before and after the paragraph.

    a. Verify the cursor still appears in the *Agenda* heading.

    b. Click the **Layout** tab.

    c. In the *Paragraph* group, click the **Before up arrow** once so **18 pt**. appears in the box.

    d. Click the **After up arrow** four times so **24 pt**. appears in the box.

10. Change the alignment of text.

    a. Click the **Home** tab.

    b. In the *Paragraph* group, click the **Align Right** button.

11. Change the color of text.

    a. On the *Home* tab, in the *Font* group, click the **Font Color** arrow.

    b. Select **Orange, Accent 4**. It is the third option from the right in the first row under *Theme Colors.*

12. Add a border to a paragraph.

    a. On the *Home* tab, in the *Paragraph* group, click the **Borders** button.

    b. Click **Bottom Border**.

13. Copy and paste formatting using the *Format Painter* tool.

    a. With the cursor in the *Agenda* heading, on the *Home* tab, in the *Clipboard* group, click the **Format Painter** button.

    b. Apply the copied formatting to the **Authors** heading by clicking on the heading.

14. Apply another style to text.

    a. Place the cursor in the *Fiction* heading.

    b. On the *Home* tab, in the *Styles* group, click the **Heading 3** style to apply it to the text.

    c. Place the cursor in the *Nonfiction* heading.

    d. Apply the **Heading 3** style to the text.

15. Add space before paragraphs of text.

    a. Select the first two paragraphs of text (from *The Tri-State Book festival will take place* to *additional $25.00 per attendee.*).

    b. Click the **Layout** tab.

    c. In the *Paragraph* group, click **After up arrow** two times so **18 pt**. appears in the box.

16. Bring attention to text using the highlighter tool.

    a. In the first sentence of the first paragraph, select the text **September 6-9**.

    b. Click the **Home** tab.

    c. In the *Font* group, click the **Text Highlight Color** button. Select the **Bright Green** option.

17. Apply character formatting.

    a. Scroll down to the *Fiction* section.

    b. Under the name *Max Wallace,* select the text **Showcased work:**.

    c. On the *Home* tab, in the *Font* group, click the **Italic** button.

    d. Apply the italics character formatting to the text **Showcased work:** under each author's name in the *Fiction* and *Nonfiction* sections.

18. Display the ruler and set a tab stop.

    a. Select the text in the *Fiction* and *Nonfiction* sections (be sure to select the headings as well).

    b. Click the **View** tab. In the *Show* group, click the **Ruler** check box to select it.

    c. Verify the tab at the left side of the ruler is the *Left Tab*.

    d. Add a tab stop at the **1"** mark.

19. Set tab stops using the *Tabs* dialog.

    a. Click the **Home** tab.

    b. In the *Paragraph* group, click the **dialog launcher**.

    c. In the *Paragraph* dialog, click the **Tabs...** button.

    d. In the *Tabs* dialog, type **.75** in the *Tab stop position* box.

    e. Verify the tab will be a left tab and click **OK**.

20. Apply the tabs you set.

    a. Place the cursor before the author name *Max Wallace*. Press the (Tab ⇆) key one time.

    b. Repeat this for all the author names in the *Fiction* and *Nonfiction* sections.

    c. Place the cursor at the beginning of the line below *Max Wallace* (before the *Showcased work:*). Press the (Tab ⇆) key two times.

    d. Repeat this for all the lines beginning with *Showcased work:*.

21. Save and close the document.

challenge yourself 2.3

In this project, you will be formatting a safety report from the Winter Springs Community. You will be updating the font, font size, and line spacing for the entire document. You will remove unnecessary line breaks and apply styles. You will modify paragraphs by changing alignment, applying shading, and adjusting the space that appears before and after the paragraphs. You will then copy that formatting and paste it to other text using the Format Painter tool. You will apply character formatting and change the case of text. Finally, you will convert text to both a bulleted list and a numbered list.

Skills needed to complete this project:

- Changing Fonts (Skill 2.2)
- Changing Font Sizes (Skill 2.3)
- Changing Line Spacing (Skill 2.13)
- Revealing Formatting Marks (Skill 2.14)
- Using Styles (Skill 2.11)
- Changing Paragraph Alignment (Skill 2.12)
- Adding Borders and Shading to Paragraphs (Skill 2.15)
- Adjusting Spacing Before and After Paragraphs (Skill 2.16)
- Using Format Painter (Skill 2.7)
- Changing Text Case (Skill 2.4)

- Using Bold, Italic, and Underline (Skill 2.1)
- Creating Bulleted Lists (Skill 2.10)
- Applying Indents (Skill 2.17)
- Creating Numbered Lists (Skill 2.9)

1. Open the start file **WD2019-ChallengeYourself-2-3** and resave the file as:
   `[your initials] WD-ChallengeYourself-2-3`

2. If the document opens in Protected view, click the **Enable Editing** button in the Message Bar at the top of the document so you can modify the document.

3. Change font on the entire document to **Times New Roman** and the size to **14 pt**.

4. Change the line spacing on the entire document to **1.15** line spacing.

5. Display the formatting marks for the document and delete all the extra blank lines between paragraphs in the document including the extra blank line at the end of the document. When you are finished, hide the formatting marks.

6. Apply the **Title** style to the first line of text in the document.

7. Change the font size to **26 pt**.

8. **Center** the title.

9. Apply the **Heading 1** style to the text **INTRODUCTION**.

10. Apply the **Blue, Accent 3** shading to the section heading. It is the fourth option from the right in the first row under *Theme Colors*.

11. Change the spacing before the paragraph to **18 pt**. and the spacing after to **6 pt**.

12. Use the *Format Painter* to apply the formatting of the first section heading to the other two section headings in the document (*Most Targeted Electronic Devices* and *Guidelines For Staying Safe*).

13. Use the **Change Case** tool to change the title text to **Uppercase**.

14. Select the text **basic safety procedures** in the first paragraph and **underline** the text.

15. Select the text **Winter Springs** in the first paragraph and **italicize** the text.

16. Select the text **most targeted** in the second paragraph and **bold** the text.

17. Select all the five targeted electronic items in the *Most Targeted Electronic Devices* section (from *Smartphones* to *Laptop computers*). Apply the **1), 2), 3)** number format to the text.

18. Select all the lines in the *Guidelines For Staying Safe* section (from *Avoid walking* to *reflective clothing*). Apply the **black square** bullet style.

19. Select the items in the numbered list and increase the indent of the list by one level.

20. Select the items in the bulleted list and increase the indent of the list by two levels.

21. Place the cursor at the beginning of the numbered list (before the word *Smartphone*). Change the spacing before the text to **18 pt**.

22. Place the cursor at the beginning of the numbered list (before the word *Avoid*). Change the spacing before the text to **18 pt**.

23. Save and close the document.

challenge yourself 2.4

In this project, you will be adding text and paragraph formatting to a section of a research paper on alternative assessments for students. You will change the font, font size, and line spacing for the entire document. You will then show formatting marks and remove unnecessary line breaks and spaces. You will apply a style, and then add additional formatting to the text and apply that formatting to other text using the *Format Painter* tool. You will convert text to a bulleted list and add emphasis to text by adding bold and italics character formatting.

Skills needed to complete this project:

- Changing Fonts (Skill 2.2)
- Changing Font Sizes (Skill 2.3)
- Changing Line Spacing (Skill 2.13)
- Revealing Formatting Marks (Skill 2.14)
- Using Styles (Skill 2.11)
- Using Bold, Italic, and Underline (Skill 2.1)
- Adding Borders and Shading to Paragraphs (Skill 2.15)
- Adjusting Spacing Before and After Paragraphs (Skill 2.16)
- Using Format Painter (Skill 2.7)
- Creating Bulleted Lists (Skill 2.10)
- Applying Indents (Skill 2.17)
- Changing Text Case (Skill 2.4)

1. Open the start file **WD2019-ChallengeYourself-2-4** and resave the file as: **[your initials] WD-ChallengeYourself-2-4**

2. If the document opens in Protected view, click the **Enable Editing** button in the Message Bar at the top of the document so you can modify the document.

3. Change the font on the entire document to **Calibri** and **11 pt**.

4. Change the line spacing for the entire document to **single** line spacing.

5. Display the formatting marks for the document.

6. Delete all the extra blank lines between paragraphs in the document.

7. Text has been indented by adding spaces. Delete the extra spaces before each line of text.

8. When you are finished, hide the formatting marks.

9. Apply the **Heading 1** style to the **Introduction** heading at the beginning of the document.

10. Bold the **Introduction** heading.

11. Apply a top border and a bottom border to the **Introduction** heading.

12. Change the spacing before the **Introduction** heading to **24 pt**. and the spacing after the heading to **12 pt**.

13. Use the *Format Painter* to copy the formatting from the **Introduction** heading and copy it to the following lines of text:
    - Alternate Assessment
    - No Child Left Behind (NCLB)
    - Modified Achievement Standards

- Which Students Will Benefit
- Who is Eligible
- Conclusion

14. Select the four learning tasks in the *Introduction* section (beginning with *Taking a test*) and convert the text to a bulleted list using the closed circle bullet style.

15. Increase the indent on the bulleted list by two levels.

16. Bold the text **basic educational tasks** in the last paragraph of the introduction section.

17. In the first paragraph in the *Alternate Assessment* section, italicize the word **learning** and italicize the phrase **ability to show what they know and can do**.

18. Find the text **(iep)** in the document. Use the *Change Case* command to change the text to uppercase letters.

19. Find both instances of **C-Baas** in the document and use the *Change Case* command to change the text to uppercase letters.

20. Save and close the document.

on your own 2.5

In this project, you will be formatting a service document from Greenscapes, a landscaping company. First, you will remove all formatting from the document and then show formatting marks and remove all extra line breaks and spaces. You will change the font, font size, and line spacing on the entire document. You will then apply a style, modify the formatting, and copy and paste the formatting using the *Format Painter* tool. Finally, you will create a list and add and apply tabs where appropriate.

Skills needed to complete this project:

- Clearing Formatting (Skill 2.8)
- Revealing Formatting Marks (Skill 2.14)
- Changing Fonts (Skill 2.2)
- Changing Font Sizes (Skill 2.3)
- Changing Line Spacing (Skill 2.13)
- Using Styles (Skill 2.11)
- Changing Font Colors (Skill 2.5)
- Adding Borders and Shading to Paragraphs (Skill 2.15)
- Using Format Painter (Skill 2.7)
- Creating Bulleted Lists (Skill 2.10)
- Applying Indents (Skill 2.17)
- Displaying the Ruler (Skill 2.18)
- Using Tab Stops (Skill 2.19)
- Using Bold, Italic, and Underline (Skill 2.1)
- Changing Text Case (Skill 2.4)

1. Open the start file **WD2019-OnYourOwn-2-5** and resave the file as: [your initials] WD-OnYourOwn-2-5

2. If the document opens in Protected view, click the **Enable Editing** button in the Message Bar at the top of the document so you can modify the document.

3. Select the entire document and clear all formatting from the text.

4. Show formatting marks and delete extra spaces from the beginning and end of paragraphs.

5. Delete the extra line breaks between paragraphs.

6. Change the font, font size, and line spacing for the entire document to selections of your choice.

7. Apply the **Title** style to the first line of the document.

8. Change the font color for the title to a color of your choice.

9. Apply the **Subtitle** style to the second line of the document.

10. Change the font color for the subtitle to a color of your choice.

11. Adjust the font size of the subtitle to a size of your choice.

12. Apply the **Heading 1** style to the three main headings (*Our Way of Life*, *What We Provide*, and *Costs and Pricing*).

13. Apply the **Heading 2** style to the first subheading under the *What We Provide* heading (*Lawn Care Plans*).

14. Change the font color for the **Lawn Care Plans** heading to a color of your choice.

15. Add shading and a border of your choice to the **Lawn Care Plans** heading.

16. Copy the formatting from the **Lawn Care Plans** heading and paste it to the remaining three subheadings in the *Services* section (*Lawn Maintenance*, *Leaf and Debris Removal*, and *Unique Services*).

17. Convert the four items under **Lawn Maintenance** into a bulleted list using a style of your choice.

18. Adjust the indentation on the bulleted list to an appropriate level.

19. In the *Unique Services* section, indent the five services by setting a tab stop on the ruler and pressing (Tab ⇥) to indent the text.

20. In the *Unique Services* section, bold each of the service names.

21. In the *Unique Services* section, use the *Change Case* command so all five service names have the same capitalization as *Nature paths*.

22. Save and close the document.

fix it 2.6

In this project, you will be fixing the formatting for the résumé of an applicant for a marketing manager position. There are several issues with the document that need correcting. First, you will clear all formatting from the document. You will then show formatting marks and remove unnecessary line breaks and extra spaces. You will adjust the font and font size for text as well as apply appropriate styles. You will format paragraphs and copy and paste formatting using the *Format Painter* tool. You will display the ruler and apply tabs. You will create a bulleted list and adjust the indentation of text. Finally, you will adjust the line spacing to ensure the document fits on a single page.

Skills needed to complete this project:

- Clearing Formatting (Skill 2.8)
- Revealing Formatting Marks (Skill 2.14)
- Changing Fonts (Skill 2.2)

word 365   chapter 2 Formatting Text and Paragraphs

- Changing Font Sizes (Skill 2.3)
- Using Styles (Skill 2.11)
- Adjusting Space Before and After Paragraphs (Skill 2.16)
- Changing Paragraph Alignment (Skill 2.12)
- Changing Font Colors (Skill 2.5)
- Using Format Painter (Skill 2.7)
- Displaying the Ruler (Skill 2.18)
- Using Tab Stops (Skill 2.19)
- Using Bold, Italic, and Underline (Skill 2.1)
- Creating Bulleted Lists (Skill 2.10)
- Applying Indents (Skill 2.17)
- Changing Text Case (Skill 2.4)
- Changing Line Spacing (Skill 2.13)

1. Open the start file **WD2019-FixIt-2-6** and resave the file as:
   `[your initials] WD-FixIt-2-6`

2. If the document opens in Protected view, click the **Enable Editing** button in the Message Bar at the top of the document so you can modify the document.

3. Clear the formatting from all the text in the document.

4. Reveal the formatting marks in the document and remove any extra blank lines and spaces.

5. Change the font and font size for the text in the document. Select all the text in the document and change the font to **Verdana**. Change the font size to **10 pt**.

6. Select the **name at the top of the document** and apply **Heading 1** style.

7. Change the font color of the name to **Blue-Gray, Text 2** (it is the fourth option in the first row under *Theme Colors*).

8. Place your cursor in the first line of the address. Change the spacing after the paragraph to **0 pt**.

9. Select the name and address at the top of the document (from *James Houseman* to *44333*). **Center** align the text.

10. Select the first section heading (**Summary**) and apply the **Heading 1** style.

11. Change the font color of the section heading to **Blue-Gray, Text 2, Darker 25%** (it is the fourth option in the fifth row under *Theme Colors*).

12. Change the spacing after the heading to be **6 pt**.

13. Use the **Format Painter** to copy and paste the formatting from the first section heading to the other section headings (*Skills and Capabilities*, *Experience*, and *Education*).

14. Select the text **Computer** and apply the **Heading 2** style.

15. Change the font color of the heading text to **Blue-Gray, Text 2** (it is the fourth option in the first row under *Theme Colors*).

16. Place the cursor in the first paragraph in the *Summary* section. Display the ruler and set the left tab stop at the .5" mark. Use the `Tab ⇥` key to indent the paragraph to the tab stop you just set.

17. In the *Experience* section, bold the **dates** and italicize the **position titles** and the **company name**.

18. Select the four lines under *Skills and Capabilities* (from *Marketing* to *Social Media Marketing*) and change the text into a bulleted list using the round open circle bullet style.

19. Decrease the indent on the bulleted items by one level.

20. Apply the same bulleted list style to the items under *Computer*.

21. Apply the same bulleted list style to items listed under each job experience.

22. Increase the indent on the lines under each degree by one level (the *school name* and the *GPA*).

23. Use the *Change Case* command to change the text case on the text **BUSINESS ADMINISTRATION** so only the first letter of each word is capitalized.

24. Change the line spacing for the entire document to **1.5**.

25. Save and close the document.

Source of screenshots: Microsoft Office 365: Word, Excel, Access, and PowerPoint.

chapter **3**

Formatting Documents

In this chapter, you will learn the following skills:

❭ Add consistency to document fonts and colors by using themes

❭ Use headers and footers to display page numbering and the date/time

❭ Control document layout by adjusting margins, using page breaks, and adding columns

❭ Enhance document formatting by using page borders, watermarks, and hyperlinks

❭ Use building blocks and property controls to save time and provide consistency

❭ Print multiple copies of a document and specific pages within a document

skills

Introduction

This chapter provides you with the skills needed to format and print documents. The first step is to apply and work with document themes. Once you have applied themes, you will add document elements, including headers, footers, page numbers, and automatic dates. Next, you will add building blocks and property controls as well as hyperlinks. You'll learn how to modify the layout of a document by adding breaks, adjusting the margins, and displaying text in columns. You will add a cover page and page borders to add graphic elements to the document. Finally, you will preview and print the document, including printing multiple copies and specific page ranges.

Skill 3.1 Applying Document Themes

A **theme** is a group of formatting options that you apply to an entire document. Themes include font, color, and effect styles that are applied to specific elements of a document. Theme colors control the colors available from the color palette for fonts, borders, and backgrounds. Theme fonts change the fonts used for built-in styles—such as *Normal* style and headings. Theme effects control the way graphic elements in your document appear. Applying a theme to your document is a quick way to take a simple piece of text and change it into a polished, professional-looking document.

To apply a theme to a document:

1. Click the **Design** tab.
2. In the *Document Formatting* group, click the **Themes** button.
3. Click a theme option in the gallery to apply it to your document.

tips & tricks

To reset the theme to the original theme that came with the document's template, click the **Themes** button and select **Reset to Theme from Template**.

FIGURE WD 3.1

tell me **more**

You can modify any of the existing themes and save this as your own custom theme. The file will be saved with the *thmx* file extension. The theme will be saved in the *Document Themes* folder and will be available from Excel, PowerPoint, and Outlook as well as Word.

let me **try**

Open the student data file **wd3-01-SpaProductReport** and try this skill on your own:

1. Change the theme of the document to the **Office** theme.
2. If you will be moving on to the next skill in this chapter, leave the document open to continue working. If not, save the file as directed by your instructor and close it.

Skill 3.2 Applying Style Sets

Each theme comes with a number of style sets you can choose from. A **style set** changes the font and paragraph formatting for an entire document. Style sets apply formatting based on styles. So, in order to see your changes, the text in your document must be formatted using styles. To learn more about applying styles to text, see the skill *Using Styles*. The *Style Set* gallery displays thumbnails of how the text will appear when the style set is applied.

To change the style set:

1. Click the **Design** tab.

2. In the *Document Formatting* group, click the **More** button to open the *Style Set* gallery.

3. Click a style set from the gallery to apply it to the document.

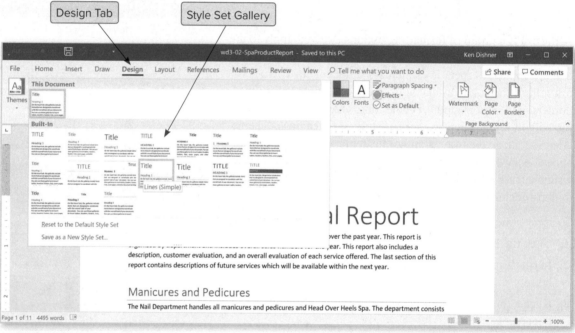

FIGURE WD 3.2

tell me **more**

The first thumbnail in the *Style Set* gallery displays the style set that is currently in use for the document.

let me **try**

If you do not have the data file from the previous skill open, open the student data file **wd3-02-SpaProductReport** and try this skill on your own:

1. Apply the **Lines (Simple)** style set to the document.

2. If you will be moving on to the next skill in this chapter, leave the document open to continue working. If not, save the file as directed by your instructor and close it.

Skill 3.3 Using Color Themes

When creating a document, it can sometimes be difficult to choose colors that work well together. Documents can end up monochromatic or with too many colors that clash with each other. A **color theme** is a set of colors that are designed to work well together in a document. A color theme will change the color of text, tables, and drawing objects in a document. When you apply a theme to a document it includes a color theme, which has default theme colors for document elements. You can change the color theme without affecting the other components of the theme.

To apply a color theme to a document:

1. Click the **Design** tab.
2. In the *Document Formatting* group, click the **Colors** button.
3. Click a color theme option to apply it to your document.

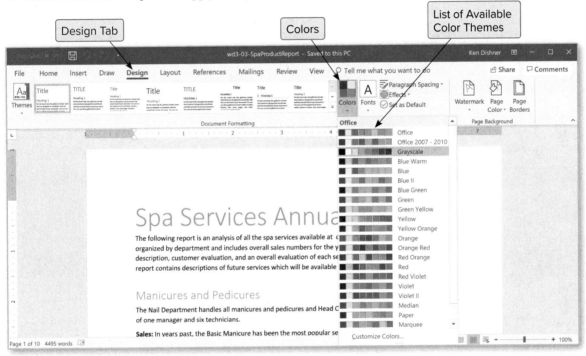

FIGURE WD 3.3

tell me **more**

When you change the color theme for a document, the color options for document elements will change. The theme colors will appear in the *Font Color* menu, as well as in the *Table Styles* and *Shape Styles* galleries. Choose your colors from these preset theme colors to ensure your document has a consistent color design.

let me **try**

If you do not have the data file from the previous skill open, open the student data file **wd3-03-SpaProductReport** and try this skill on your own:

1. Change the color theme to **Grayscale**.
2. Notice that the color change is too monochromatic. Click the **Undo** button on the Quick Access Toolbar to reverse the change.
3. If you will be moving on to the next skill in this chapter, leave the document open to continue working. If not, save the file as directed by your instructor and close it.

Skill 3.4 Using Font Themes

There are thousands of fonts for you to choose from to use in your documents. Some fonts are designed to work well as header text, such as Calibri Light and Cambria, and others are designed to work well as body text, such as Calibri. When you apply a theme to a document, this includes a **font theme**, which includes default fonts for body text and header text. As with color themes, you can change the font theme without affecting the other components of the theme.

To apply a font theme to a document:

1. Click the **Design** tab.

2. In the *Document Formatting* group, click the **Fonts** button.

3. Click a font theme option to apply it to your document.

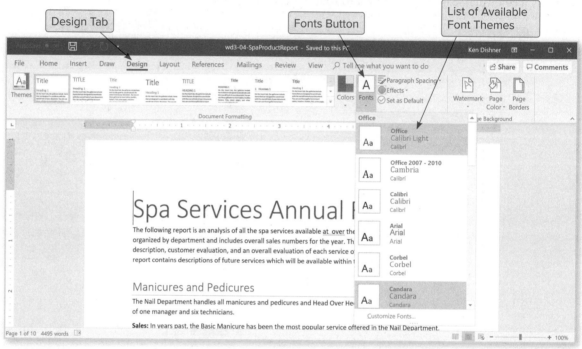

FIGURE WD 3.4

tell me **more**

The font theme menu displays a preview of the header font (on top) and the body font (on bottom). Notice that some themes include two different fonts, but others include the same font, only in different sizes. The default font theme for Word is the *Office Calibri Light/Calibri* font theme.

let me **try**

If you do not have the data file from the previous skill open, open the student data file **wd3-04-SpaProductReport** and try this skill on your own:

1. Change the font theme to **Candara**.

2. Change the font theme back to the **Office font theme** by clicking the **Undo** button on the Quick Access Toolbar.

3. If you will be moving on to the next skill in this chapter, leave the document open to continue working. If not, save the file as directed by your instructor and close it.

Skill 3.5 Creating Watermarks

A **watermark** is a graphic or text that appears as part of the page background. Watermarks appear faded so the text that appears on top of the watermark is legible when the document is viewed or printed.

There are three categories of watermarks:

Confidential–Includes the text "Confidential" or "Do Not Copy" in different layouts.

Disclaimers–Includes the text "Draft" or "Sample" in different layouts.

Urgent–Includes the text "ASAP" or "Urgent" in different layouts.

To add a watermark to a document:

1. Click the **Design** tab.

2. In the *Page Background* group, click the **Watermark** button and select an option from the gallery.

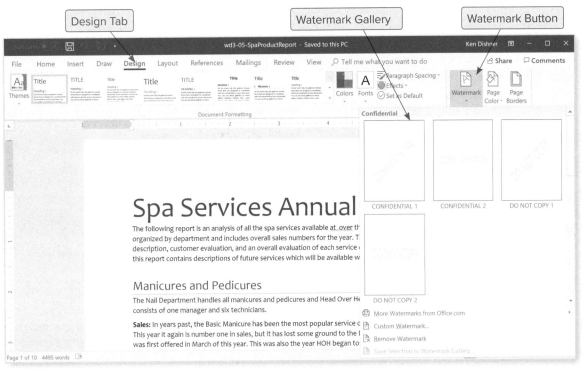

FIGURE WD 3.5

tips & tricks

You do not have to use one of the built-in watermarks from the *Watermark* gallery. You can create your own custom watermark, displaying whatever text or image you like. Click the **Custom Watermark...** command to open the *Printed Watermark* dialog and choose different options for the text watermark. You can add pictures as watermarks from this dialog. When you add a picture as a watermark, it appears faded so any text on top of it is still legible.

let me **try**

If you do not have the data file from the previous skill open, open the student data file **wd3-05-SpaProductReport** and try this skill on your own:

1. Apply the **CONFIDENTIAL 1** watermark to the document.

2. If you will be moving on to the next skill in this chapter, leave the document open to continue working. If not, save the file as directed by your instructor and close it.

Skill 3.6 Inserting Page Breaks

When text or graphics have filled a page, Word inserts a soft page break and goes on to a new page. However, at times you may want to manually insert a **hard page break**—forcing the text to a new page no matter how much content is on the present page. Typically, hard page breaks are used to keep certain information together.

To insert a hard page break:

1. Click the **Layout** tab.

2. In the *Page Setup* group, click the **Breaks** button, and select **Page**.

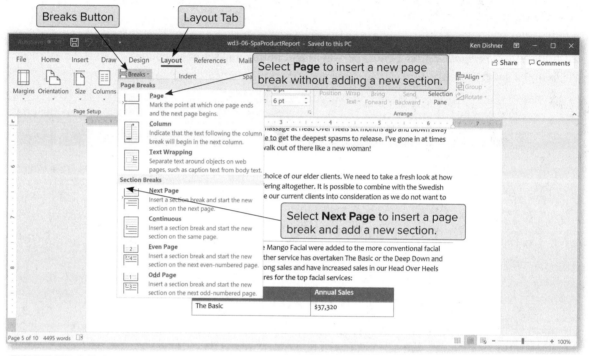

FIGURE WD 3.6

Another type of page break is a **section page break**. A section page break inserts a hard page break and starts a new section in the document. A **section** is a designated part of a document that can be formatted separately from the rest of the document. For example, if you have a large table that needs more horizontal space than the rest of your document, you can add the table in its own section and set the margins for the section to the narrow margin settings while keeping the remaining document with the normal margin settings.

To add a section to a document:

1. Click the **Layout** tab.

2. In the *Page Setup* group, click the **Breaks** button.

3. In the *Section Breaks* section, click **Next Page** to insert a new section and a hard page break.

tips & tricks

> To delete a page break, switch to Draft view. Here all the page breaks are displayed. Select a page break and press the [Delete] key on the keyboard to delete the break. When you delete a section break, the content from the section takes on the formatting from the preceding section.

> If you want to add a new section, but do not want to add a page break, select **Continuous** in the *Section Breaks* area of the *Breaks* menu.

tell me **more**

There are two basic types of breaks you can add to a document:

Page Breaks—These breaks create visual breaks in your document but keep the content in the same section. Page breaks include *Page*, *Column*, and *Text Wrapping*.

Section Breaks—These breaks create new sections in your document. Section breaks include *Next Page*, *Continuous*, *Even Page*, and *Odd Page*.

another **method**

To insert a hard page break:

> On the *Insert* tab, in the *Pages* group, click the **Page Break** button.

> Press [Ctrl] + [← Enter] on the keyboard.

let me **try**

If you do not have the data file from the previous skill open, open the student data file **wd3-06-SpaProductReport** and try this skill on your own:

1. Place the cursor at the end of the paragraph before the *Facials* heading. It is located near the bottom of page 5.
2. Insert a **page break**.
3. A blank line appears at the top of the new page. Delete the blank line.
4. Place the cursor at the end of the paragraph before the *Future Products* heading. It is located near the bottom of page 10.
5. Insert a **next page section break**.
6. A blank line appears at the top of the new page. Delete the blank line.
7. If you will be moving on to the next skill in this chapter, leave the document open to continue working. If not, save the file as directed by your instructor and close it.

Skill 3.7 Adding Headers

A **header** is text that appears at the top of every page, just below the top margin. Typically, headers display dates, page numbers, document titles, or authors' names. Word comes with several predesigned headers that you can add to your document and then modify to suit your needs. When you add one of Word's predesigned headers, the header will include fields for you to add content to. Some of these fields, such as author name and title, will auto-populate from the document's properties. For others, simply click the field you want to add content to and begin typing.

To add a header to a document:

1. Click the **Insert** tab.

2. In the *Header & Footer* group, click the **Header** button and select a header format from the gallery.

3. Word displays the *Header & Footer Tools Design* tab and inserts a header with content controls for you to enter your own information. Click a content control and enter the information for your header.

4. To close the header and return to your document, click the **Close Header and Footer** button on the contextual tab.

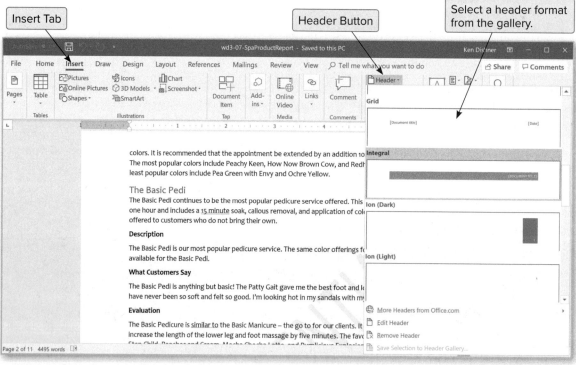

FIGURE WD 3.7

If the first page of your document is a title page, you won't want the header text to display on the page. To display a header on the first page of the document that is different from the header in the rest of the document, display the *Header & Footer Tools* tab. In the *Options* group, select the **Different First Page** check box.

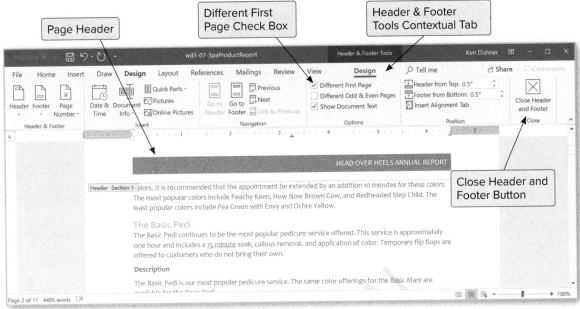

FIGURE WD 3.8

tips & tricks

Headers appear faded out in *Print Layout* view. If you want to edit a header, double-click it and make your changes. Click the **Close Header and Footer** button to return to the document.

another method

To close the header and return to the document, you can also double-click on the main document area below the header.

let me try

If you do not have the data file from the previous skill open, open the student data file **wd3-07-SpaProductReport** and try this skill on your own:

1. Navigate to **page 2** of the document.
2. Add a header to the document using the **Integral** style.
3. Click the **[Document title]** control and type HEAD OVER HEELS ANNUAL REPORT
4. Have the header display differently on the first page of the document.
5. Close the header and footer.
6. If you will be moving on to the next skill in this chapter, leave the document open to continue working. If not, save the file as directed by your instructor and close it.

Skill 3.8 Adding Footers

A **footer** is text that appears at the bottom of every page, just below the bottom margin. Typically, footers display dates, page numbers, author names, or disclaimers. Word comes with a number of predesigned footers that you can add to your document and then modify to suit your needs. When you add one of Word's predesigned footers, the footer will include fields for you to add content to. Just as with headers, some of these fields will auto-populate from the document's properties. For others, click the field you want to add content to and begin typing.

To add a footer to a document:

1. Click the **Insert** tab.
2. In the *Header & Footer* group, click the **Footer** button and select a footer format from the gallery.
3. Word displays the *Header & Footer Tools Design* tab and inserts a footer with fields for you to enter you own information.
4. Click a field and enter the information for your footer.
5. To close the header and return to your document, click the **Close Header and Footer** button on the contextual tab.

FIGURE WD 3.9

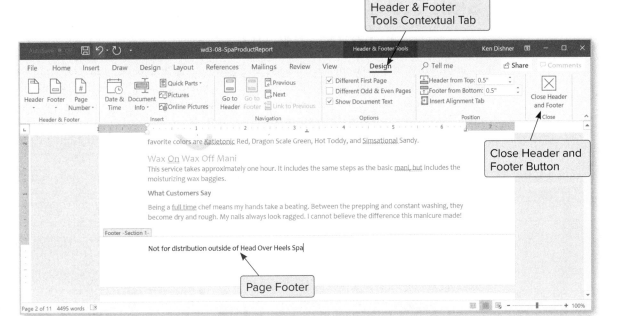

Header & Footer Tools Contextual Tab

Close Header and Footer Button

Page Footer

FIGURE WD 3.10

tips & tricks

When you add a header or footer to your document, the *Design* tab under *Header & Footer Tools* displays. This is called a contextual tab because it displays when a header or footer is the active element.

another **method**

To close the footer and return to the document, you can also double-click on the main document area above the footer.

let me **try**

If you do not have the data file from the previous skill open, open the student data file **wd3-08-SpaProductReport** and try this skill on your own:

1. Place the cursor anywhere on the second page of the document.
2. Add a footer to the document using the **Blank** style.
3. Click the **[Type Here]** control and type `Not for distribution outside of Head Over Heels Spa`.
4. Close the header and footer.
5. If you will be moving on to the next skill in this chapter, leave the document open to continue working. If not, save the file as directed by your instructor and close it.

Skill 3.9 Adding an Automatic Date Stamp

In addition to information such as the company name and page numbers, headers and footers typically include the current date. You could manually type the date in the header or footer and then update the date every time you work on the document, or you could add an **automatic date stamp**. This pulls the current date from the computer's system clock and displays the date in the document. The date is then automatically updated when the computer's date changes.

To add an automatic date stamp to the header of a document:

1. Double-click the header to switch to header view. Place the cursor where you want the date to appear.
2. Under the *Header & Footer Tools Design* tab in the *Insert* group, click the **Date & Time** button.
3. In the *Date and Time* dialog, select a date format in the *Available formats* list.
4. Select the **Update automatically** check box.
5. Click **OK**.
6. To close the header and return to your document, click the **Close Header and Footer** button on the contextual tab.

FIGURE WD 3.11

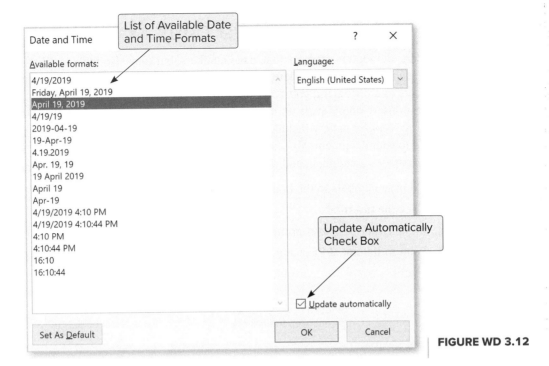

FIGURE WD 3.12

tips & tricks

If all your documents use a date format other than Word's default MM/DD/YYYY format, you can change the date and time format that is preselected in the *Date and Time* dialog. First, select the format you want to set as the default and then click the **Set As Default** button. When you open the dialog, the format you selected and set will be automatically selected for you.

another **method**

You can also use *Quick Parts* to add the date and time to the header or footer of your document:

1. Double-click the header to make it active.
2. Under the *Header & Footer Tools Design* tab, in the *Insert* group, click the **Quick Parts** button and select **Field...**
3. In the *Field* dialog, click the **CreateDate** or the **Date** field.
4. Select a format for the date.
5. Click **OK**.

let me **try**

If you do not have the data file from the previous skill open, open the student data file **wd3-09-SpaProductReport** and try this skill on your own:

1. Double-click the header area on page 2 of the document to switch to header view.
2. Open the **Date and Time** dialog.
3. Add a date that will update automatically and use the format **Month Day, Year**. For example, January 1, 2020.
4. Close the header and footer.
5. If you will be moving on to the next skill in this chapter, leave the document open to continue working. If not, save the file as directed by your instructor and close it.

skill 3.9   Adding an Automatic Date Stamp

Skill 3.10 Inserting Page Numbers

Headers and footers often include page numbers, but they also include other information, such as author name, date, and document title. If all you want to do is add page numbers to a document, you don't need to use the header and footer feature. Instead, you can insert simple page numbers to a document through the *Page Number* gallery. The *Page Number* gallery includes everything from simple numbers to complex designs to add to your document. You can choose to display page numbers in the page's margin or the cursor's location, in addition to the traditional header or footer of the document.

To add page numbers to the bottom of pages of a document:

1. Click the **Insert** tab.
2. In the *Header & Footer* group, click the **Page Number** button.
3. Point to **Bottom of Page** and click a page number format from the gallery.

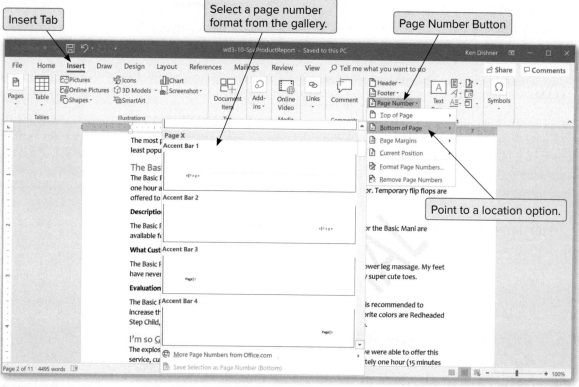

FIGURE WD 3.13

To remove a page number:

1. On the *Header & Footer Tools Design* tab, in the *Header & Footer* group, click the **Page Number** button.
2. Select **Remove Page Numbers**.

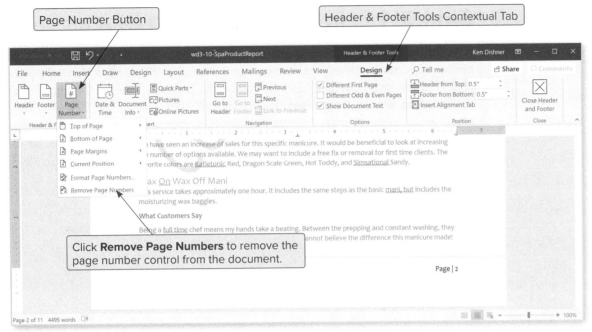

Page Number Button

Header & Footer Tools Contextual Tab

Click **Remove Page Numbers** to remove the page number control from the document.

FIGURE WD 3.14

tips & tricks

❯ When adding page numbers to a document, you should always use Word's built-in page numbers. If you type page numbers into your document manually, they will not update when you add or remove pages.

❯ When choosing a page numbering option, be sure to choose a design that fits with your document. For example, if you are writing a research paper, you will want to use simple page numbering in the header or footer of the document. On the other hand, if you are designing a brochure, you can try using one of Word's more ornate page numbering options and place the page number in the margin rather than the traditional header or footer.

let me try

If you do not have the data file from the previous skill open, open the student data file **wd3-10-SpaProductReport** and try this skill on your own:

1. Place the cursor anywhere on the second page of the document.
2. Add a page number to the bottom of the page using the **Accent Bar 2** format.
3. Remove the **page number**.
4. Close the header and footer.
5. If you will be moving on to the next skill in this chapter, leave the document open to continue working. If not, save the file as directed by your instructor and close it.

Skill 3.11 Inserting Building Blocks

A **building block** is a piece of content that is reusable in any document. Building blocks can be text, such as page numbers, or they can include graphics, such as a cover page. You can insert building blocks from specific commands on the Ribbon or from the **Building Blocks Organizer**. The *Building Blocks Organizer* lists all the building blocks in alphabetical order by which gallery they appear in and includes bibliographies, cover pages, equations, footers, headers, page numbers, table of contents, tables, text boxes, and watermarks.

To insert a building block from the *Building Blocks Organizer*:

1. Click the **Insert** tab.

2. In the *Text* group, click the **Quick Parts** button and click **Building Blocks Organizer...**

3. Select a building block in the list.

4. A preview of the selected building block displays on the right.

5. Click the **Insert** button to add the building block to the document.

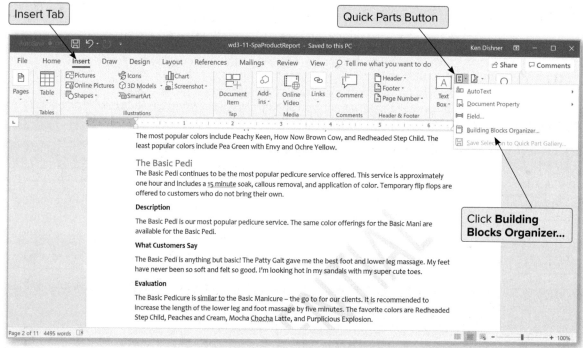

FIGURE WD 3.15

word 365   chapter 3 Formatting Documents

Building Blocks List

A preview of the selected building block displays here.

Insert Button

FIGURE WD 3.16

tips & tricks

If you find that the list of building blocks is too long, you can remove building blocks you don't use. To remove a building block from the *Building Blocks Organizer*, select a building block and click the **Delete** button. Be aware that the *Building Blocks Organizer* is used across all of Word. If you delete a building block from the *Building Blocks Organizer*, it will no longer be available when you are working on other documents.

tell me **more**

You can sort the list of building blocks by clicking the **Name**, **Gallery**, **Category**, or **Template** button at the top of the *Building Blocks Organizer*. You can also modify the properties of a building block, changing properties such as the name or which gallery the building block appears in.

let me **try**

If you do not have the data file from the previous skill open, open the student data file **wd3-11-SpaProductReport** and try this skill on your own:

1. Place the cursor anywhere on the second page of the document.

2. Open the *Building Blocks Organizer* dialog.

3. Insert page numbers using the **Three Lines** building block.

4. Close the header and footer.

5. If you will be moving on to the next skill in this chapter, leave the document open to continue working. If not, save the file as directed by your instructor and close it.

Skill 3.12 Inserting Property Controls

A **property control** is an element you can add to your document to save time entering the same information over and over again. Property controls can be used as shortcuts for entering long strings of text that are difficult to type. For example, instead of typing the company name *Head Over Heels Spa,* you can insert the *Company* property control. Many of the built-in property controls, such as company name and author, pull their information from the document's properties.

Before adding a property control, first add the information in the document's *Properties* panel:

1. Click the **File** tab.
2. A brief list of the document's properties is displayed on the left side of the *Info* page.
3. Click the **Show All Properties** link at the bottom of the properties to expand the list and show all the properties for the document.
4. Click the text box next to a property and either type the new text or edit the existing text for a property.

FIGURE WD 3.17

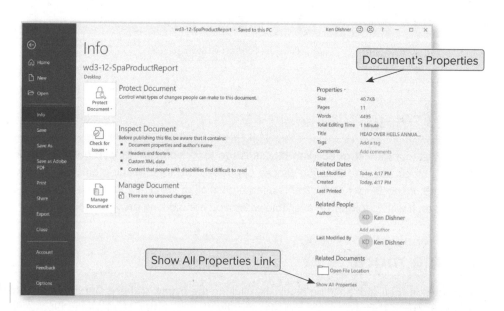

When you add a property control, Word will add the text to the document and update the text automatically if any changes are made to the property control. By using property controls, you can be assured that all the information throughout the document is consistent.

To add a property control to a document:

1. Click the **Insert** tab.
2. In the *Text* group, click the **Quick Parts** button, point to **Document Property**, and select a control.

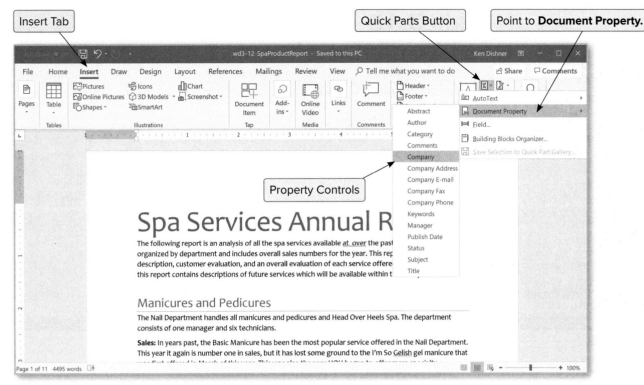

Insert Tab

Quick Parts Button

Point to **Document Property.**

Property Controls

FIGURE WD 3.18

tips & tricks

If you need to update a property control, you need to either update the control on the *Info* page or type the change once in any property control in the document. As you update any property control, all the other controls created from the same property control as well as the document's properties will update.

let me try

If you do not have the data file from the previous skill open, open the student data file **wd3-12-SpaProductReport** and try this skill on your own:

1. Display the **Info** tab in Backstage view.

2. Type **Head Over Heels Spa** in the *Company* property control.

3. Click between the words **at** and **over** in the first sentence of the first paragraph of the document.

4. Insert a **Company** property control.

5. Add a space between property control and the surrounding text to fix any spacing issue.

6. If you will be moving on to the next skill in this chapter, leave the document open to continue working. If not, save the file as directed by your instructor and close it.

Skill 3.13 Inserting Hyperlinks

A **hyperlink** is text or a graphic that, when clicked, opens another page or file. You can use hyperlinks to link to a section in the same document, to a new document, or to an existing document, such as a web page.

To insert a hyperlink:

1. Select the text or graphic you want to use as the link.
2. Click the **Insert** tab.
3. In the *Links* group, click the **Link** button to open the *Insert Hyperlink* dialog.
4. Select an option under *Link to* and select the file to which you want to link.
5. Type the text of the link in the *Text to display* box.
6. Click **OK** to insert the hyperlink into your document.

FIGURE WD 3.19

FIGURE WD 3.20

After you have added a hyperlink to your document, you can modify the hyperlink:

) To edit a hyperlink, right-click the link and select **Edit Hyperlink...** from the menu. Make any changes in the *Edit Hyperlink* dialog.

) To remove a hyperlink, right-click the link and select **Remove Hyperlink** from the menu.

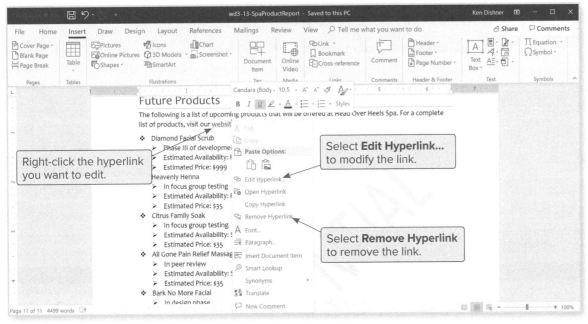

Right-click the hyperlink you want to edit.

Select **Edit Hyperlink...** to modify the link.

Select **Remove Hyperlink** to remove the link.

FIGURE WD 3.21

tips & tricks

If you do not have your window size at full screen, the *Links* group may be collapsed on the Ribbon. Click the **Links** button on the *Insert* tab to display the commands in the group, including the *Hyperlink* button. If you are using the SIMnet program along with this textbook, the *Links* button may appear in its collapsed state.

tell me **more**

Some hyperlinks include ScreenTips. A **ScreenTip** is a bubble that appears when the mouse is placed over the link. Add a ScreenTip to include a more meaningful description of the hyperlink.

another **method**

To open the *Insert Hyperlink* dialog, you can:

❭ Right-click the text or object you want as the link and select **Hyperlink...** from the shortcut menu.

❭ Press Ctrl + K on the keyboard.

let me **try**

If you do not have the data file from the previous skill open, open the student data file **wd3-13-SpaProductReport** and try this skill on your own:

1. Place the cursor at the end of the first paragraph and press the spacebar one time.
2. Add a link to the *Future Products* section of the document.
3. Change the link text to read **See Our Future Products** and add the link.
4. Navigate to the *Future Products* section.
5. Remove the hyperlink from the word **website** in the first paragraph.
6. If you will be moving on to the next skill in this chapter, leave the document open to continue working. If not, save the file as directed by your instructor and close it.

Skill 3.14 Adjusting Margins

Margins are the blank spaces at the top, bottom, left, and right of a page. Word's default margins are typically 1 inch for the top and bottom and 1 inch for the left and right. Word comes with several predefined margin layout options for you to choose from, including normal, narrow, wide, and mirrored.

To adjust the margins for a document:

1. Click the **Layout** tab.
2. In the *Page Setup* group, click the **Margins** button, and select an option for the page layout.

FIGURE WD 3.22

If you don't want to use one of Word's preset margins, you can set your own margin specifications in the *Page Setup* dialog.

To set custom margins:

1. On the *Layout* tab, in the *Page Setup* group, click the **dialog launcher**.
2. The *Page Setup* dialog opens.
3. Click the up and down arrows next to each margin (*Top*, *Bottom*, *Left*, and *Right*) to adjust the width and height of the margins.
4. Click **OK** to close the dialog.

FIGURE WD 3.23

tips & tricks

While most documents you create will use the *Normal* or *Moderate* settings for margins, some documents will require either less or more space around the text. If you have a large exhibit or table, you may want to make the margins narrow so the content will still fit in portrait orientation. On the other hand, if you are writing a letter, you may want to increase your margins to accommodate preprinted stationery.

tell me **more**

A gutter is additional space you can add to one side of the document when you plan to have the document bound. You can enter the amount of extra space you need for binding in the *Gutter* box in the *Page Setup* dialog. You can then choose how your document will be bound—along the left side or along the top.

another **method**

❭ To open the *Page Setup* dialog, you can also click the **Margins** button and select **Custom Margins...**
❭ To adjust margins in the *Page Setup* dialog, you can also type the number in the box.

let me **try**

If you do not have the data file from the previous skill open, open the student data file **wd3-14-SpaProductReport** and try this skill on your own:

1. Verify you are on **page 1** of the document.
2. Change the margins for the document to use the **Moderate** margin settings.
3. Open the **Page Setup** dialog.
4. Change the left margin to **0.8"**. Change the right margin to **0.8"**.
5. If you will be moving on to the next skill in this chapter, leave the document open to continue working. If not, save the file as directed by your instructor and close it.

Skill 3.15 Applying Columns

Newsletter pages are often laid out in **columns**. The text of these pages continues from the bottom of one column to the top of the next column. Word comes with a number of preset column options, making it easy to create columns of text in a document.

To apply columns to text:

1. Click the **Layout** tab.
2. In the *Page Setup* group, click the **Columns** button and select an option.
3. Selecting *One*, *Two*, or *Three* will create evenly spaced columns. Choosing *Left* or *Right* will create a two-column layout with one column narrower than the other.

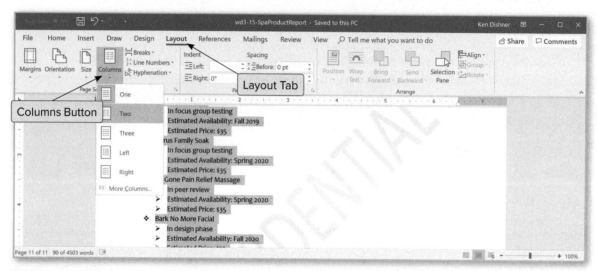

FIGURE WD 3.24

tips & tricks

If you know you want your document to appear in column format, set the columns before you enter the document text. When you type the text for your document, it will automatically be formatted in columns.

tell me **more**

The *Columns* dialog gives you more control over the display of the columns in your document, including changing the width of columns and adjusting the space that appears between columns. To open the *Columns* dialog, click **More Columns...** at the bottom of the *Columns* gallery.

let me **try**

If you do not have the data file from the previous skill open, open the student data file **wd3-15-SpaProductReport** and try this skill on your own:

1. Navigate to the *Future Products* section of the document and verify the ruler is displayed.
2. Select the list of future products (from *Diamond Facial Scrub* through *Estimated Price: $25*).
3. Apply the two-column layout to the text.
4. You may not see a visual change in the selected text, but notice on the ruler that two columns have been applied.
5. If you have an empty bullet item in the list, place the cursor next to the item and press the (Delete) key to remove it.
6. If you will be moving on to the next skill in this chapter, leave the document open to continue working. If not, save the file as directed by your instructor and close it.

Skill 3.16 Inserting a Column Break

After you have added columns to your document, you may find that the text does not break across the columns exactly as you would like. In this case, you can add a column break where you want the bottom of the column to be. A **column break** marks where one column ends and moves the following text to the top of the next column.

To insert a column break:

1. Place the cursor before the text you want to appear at the top of the next column.

2. Click the **Layout** tab.

3. In the *Page Setup* group, click the **Breaks** button and select **Column**.

A column break is added. The text following the break now appears at the top of the next column.

FIGURE WD 3.25

tips & tricks

❯ To view column breaks in a document, click the **Show/Hide** button in the *Paragraph* group on the *Home* tab.

❯ If you are displaying a list of items across multiple columns, use column breaks to create columns that contain the same number of items.

another **method**

To insert a column break, you can also press Ctrl + ⇧ Shift + ← Enter.

let me **try**

If you do not have the data file from the previous skill open, open the student data file **wd3-16-SpaProductReport** and try this skill on your own:

1. In the *Future Products* section, place the cursor before the text **Citrus Family Soak**.

2. Insert a column break.

3. If you will be moving on to the next skill in this chapter, leave the document open to continue working. If not, save the file as directed by your instructor and close it.

Skill 3.17 Adding Page Borders

Page borders are graphic elements that can give your document a more polished look. **Page borders** draw a decorative graphic element along the top, right, bottom, and left edges of the page. Borders can be simple lines or 3-D effects and shadows. You can modify borders by changing the style and color. You can apply a border to the entire document or parts of a section.

To add a border to a document:

1. Click the **Design** tab.
2. In the *Page Background* group, click the **Page Borders** button.
3. The *Borders and Shading* dialog opens with the *Page Border* tab displayed.
4. Click a setting for the border.
5. Select a style, color, and width for the page border.
6. The *Preview* area shows how the border will look.
7. Click **OK** to accept your changes and add the page border to the document.

FIGURE WD 3.26

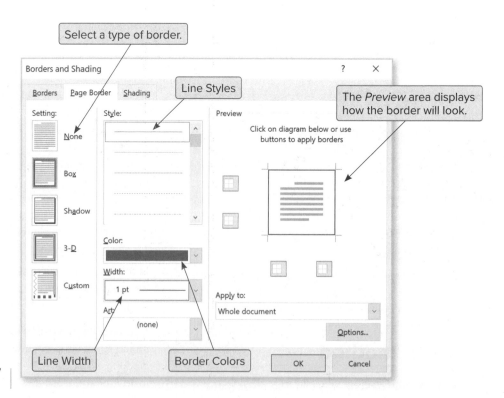

FIGURE WD 3.27

tips & tricks

You can further adjust the look of page borders from the *Borders and Shading* dialog:

❭ Click on the **Preview** area diagram to add or remove parts of the border.

❭ Click the **Art** drop-down menu to select graphic elements for the border.

another **method**

You can also open the *Borders and Shading* dialog from the *Home* tab. In the *Paragraph* group, click the arrow next to the *Borders* button and select **Borders and Shading...** Click the **Page Border** tab in the dialog to add a page border.

let me **try**

If you do not have the data file from the previous skill open, open the student data file **wd3-17-SpaProductReport** and try this skill on your own:

1. Navigate to **page 1** of the document.
2. Open the **Borders and Shading** dialog with the **Page Border** tab displayed.
3. Change the border to use the **Box** style.
4. Apply the **Blue-Gray, Text 2** color. It is the fourth option in the first row under *Theme Colors*.
5. Change the width of the border to **1 pt**.
6. If you will be moving on to the next skill in this chapter, leave the document open to continue working. If not, save the file as directed by your instructor and close it.

from the perspective of . . .

MARKETING MANAGER

When writing a report, I use Word's built-in themes and style sets to create a cohesive document. A cover page and page borders add visual zing to my report that really grabs the attention of my readers. Before I send it out for review, I always add a footer and watermark to the report to let others know not to share the information outside our organization. Using the *Company* property control has been invaluable, especially when I realized I misspelled our company name in the report! And when it comes to printing, I am often printing at least 10 copies to hand out, but then can easily reprint an individual page when minor edits come in from my boss—which they always do.

Ryan McVay/Getty Images

Skill 3.18 Adding a Cover Page

When creating documents such as reports, proposals, or business plans, it is a good idea to include a **cover page** that contains the title of the document and the date. You can also add other information such as a subtitle, a short description of the document, and company information. Word comes with a number of prebuilt cover pages that you can quickly and easily add to your documents.

To add a cover page:

1. Click the **Insert** tab.
2. In the *Pages* group, click the **Cover Page** button and select an option.
3. Word inserts a cover page with content controls for you to enter your own information.
4. Click a content control and type the information for your document.

FIGURE WD 3.28

tips & tricks

Most content controls include instructions for adding text to the cover page. However, some content controls, such as the author, do not include text and are hidden from view. One way to see all the fields available in a cover page is to use the *Select All* command by pressing (Ctrl) + (A) on the keyboard.

tell me **more**

When you click a date content control, you will notice a calendar icon next to the text area. Click the icon to display the calendar to select a date to add to the cover page.

let me **try**

If you do not have the data file from the previous skill open, open the student data file **wd3-18-SpaProductReport** and try this skill on your own:

1. Insert a cover page using the **Ion (Light)** style.
2. In the *Year* content control, type **2020** as the year.
3. In the *Subtitle* control, type **SERVICE BY SERVICE REVIEW**
4. If you will be moving on to the next skill in this chapter, leave the document open to continue working. If not, save the file as directed by your instructor and close it.

Skill 3.19 Printing Multiple Copies of a Document

When creating documents, sometimes you will need only one printed copy, but other times you will need to print more than a single copy. From the *Print* page in Backstage view, you can print multiple copies of a document.

To print multiple copies of a document:

1. Click the **File** tab to open Backstage view.
2. Click **Print**.
3. Type the number of copies you want to print in the **Copies** box.
4. Click the **Print** button to print.

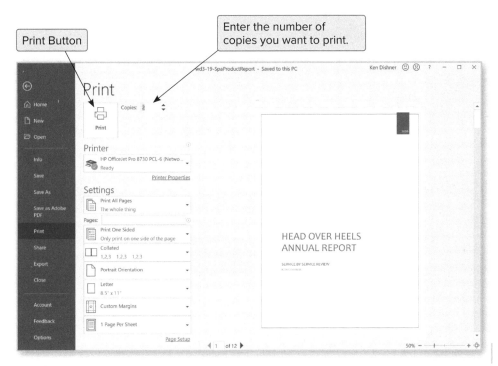

FIGURE WD 3.29

another **method**

You can also change the number of copies to print by clicking the up and down arrows next to the *Copies* box.

let me **try**

If you do not have the data file from the previous skill open, open the student data file **wd3-19-SpaProductReport** and try this skill on your own:

1. Display the **Print** page in Backstage view.
2. Print **two copies** of the document. **NOTE**: If you are using this in class or in your school's computer lab, check with your instructor about printing permissions before completing this step.
3. If you will be moving on to the next skill in this chapter, leave this document open to continue working. If not, save the file as directed by your instructor and close it.

Skill 3.20 Printing Page Ranges

When designating which pages to print, you can print a range of pages or individual pages. To print sequential pages, type the number of the first page you want to print, followed by a hyphen, followed by the last page you want to print. For example, if you want to print pages 3 through 8 in your document, type **3-8** in the *Pages* box. To print individual pages, type each page number you want to print separated by a comma or semicolon. For example, if you want to print page 3, page 5, page 8, and page 10, type **3,5,8,10** in the *Pages* box.

To print specific pages in a document:

1. Click the **File** tab to open Backstage view.
2. Click **Print**.
3. In the *Settings* section, click in the **Pages** box and type the range of pages you want to print.
4. Click the **Print** button to print.

FIGURE WD 3.30

tips & tricks

If you want to print only part of a page, you can choose to print selected content. First, select the content you want to print. On the *Print* page, click the first button under *Settings* and select **Print Selection**. Click the **Print** button to print the selected content only.

tell me more

When you enter a range of pages in the *Pages* box, the first button under *Settings* automatically changes to *Custom Print*.

let me try

If you do not have the data file from the previous skill open, open the student data file **wd3-20-SpaProductReport** and try this skill on your own:

1. Display the **Print** page in Backstage view.
2. Print the **first four pages** of the document. **NOTE**: If you are using this in class or in your school's computer lab, check with your instructor about printing permissions before completing this step and step 3.
3. Now print **pages 2 and 5**.
4. Close the file.

Theme   Building block
Style set   Building Blocks Organizer
Color theme   Property control
Font theme   Hyperlink
Watermark   ScreenTip
Hard page break   Margins
Section page break   Columns
Section   Column break
Header   Page borders
Footer   Cover page
Automatic date stamp

concept review

1. Which of the following is a group of formatting elements you apply to a document?

a. theme

b. style

c. building block

d. property control

2. A(n) _____ changes the font and paragraph formatting for an entire document based on styles.

a. font theme

b. color theme

c. effects theme

d. style set

3. A _____ is a graphic or text that appears as part of the page background and is usually faded in appearance.

a. cover page

b. watermark

c. margin

d. property control

4. The text that appears at the top of every page, just below the top margin is known as what?

a. header

b. footer

c. title

d. cover page

5. A piece of content that is reusable in any document, such as a cover page or a watermark, is known as a _____.

a. building block

b. property control

c. field

d. style set

6. Which of the following would you use to add your company's name over and over again in a document without typing it every time?

   a. style set

   b. theme

   c. building block

   d. property control

7. What are the blank spaces at the top, bottom, left, and right of a page known as?

   a. borders

   b. margins

   c. page breaks

   d. columns

8. Which of the following will add text that when clicked will take you to another place in the document?

   a. hyperlink

   b. building block

   c. field

   d. property control

9. What would you use to force text onto a new page that will have its own settings separate from the rest of the document?

   a. page break

   b. section break

   c. column break

   d. none of these

10. What would you type in the *Pages* box on the *Print* page to print only the fourth and seventh page in a document?

   a. 4-7

   b. 4,7

   c. 4:7

   d. 47

Data files for projects can be found by logging into your SIMnet account and going to the *Library* section.

projects

skill review **3.1**

In this project you will be formatting and printing a brochure for Suarez Marketing. First, you will apply a document theme and then adjust the look of the document by changing the style set, color theme, and font theme. You will change the layout of the document by adjusting the margins and adding a page break. You will add a page border as a visual element, as well as add a header and footer. You will mark the document as a draft copy by adding a watermark.

Skills needed to complete this project:

- Applying Document Themes (Skill 3.1)
- Applying Style Sets (Skill 3.2)
- Using Color Themes (Skill 3.3)
- Using Font Themes (Skill 3.4)
- Inserting Property Controls (Skill 3.12)
- Adjusting Margins (Skill 3.14)
- Inserting Page Breaks (Skill 3.6)
- Adding Page Borders (Skill 3.17)
- Adding Headers (Skill 3.7)
- Adding Footers (Skill 3.8)
- Adding an Automatic Date Stamp (Skill 3.9)
- Creating Watermarks (Skill 3.5)
- Printing Multiple Copies of a Document (Skill 3.19)

1. Open the start file **WD2019-SkillReview-3-1** document and resave the file as: `[your initials] WD-SkillReview-3-1`

2. If the document opens in Protected View, click the **Enable Editing** button in the Message Bar at the top of the document so you can modify it.

3. Apply a theme to a document.

   a. Click the **Design** tab.

   b. In the *Document Formatting* group, click the **Themes** button and select **Metropolitan**.

4. Change the style set for the document.

   a. Verify you are still on the **Design** tab.

   b. In the *Style Set* gallery, click the **Lines (Distinctive)** option.

5. Change the color theme.

   a. On the *Design* tab, in the *Document Formatting* group, click the **Colors** button.

   b. Select the **Median** color theme.

6. Change the font theme.

   a. On the *Design* tab, in the *Document Formatting* group, click the **Fonts** button.

   b. Select the **Candara** font theme.

7. Add a company property control.

   a. Place the cursor after *Phone:* and press the Spacebar one time.

   b. Click the **Insert** tab.

   c. In the *Text* group, click the **Quick Parts** button. Point to *Document Property* and select **Company Phone**.

   d. Type **314.555.0144** in the control. Click outside the control to deselect it.

8. Change the margins for the document.

   a. Click the **Layout** tab. In the *Page Setup* group, click the **dialog launcher** to open the *Page Setup* dialog.

   b. Type **1.3"** in the *Left* box. Type **1.3"** in the *Right* box. Click **OK**.

9. Add a page break.

   a. Click before the heading *Client Quotes.*

   b. On the *Layout* tab, in the *Page Setup* group, click the **Breaks** button and select **Page**.

10. Add a page border to the document.

    a. Navigate to the top of the document.

    b. Click the **Design** tab. In the *Page Background* group, click the **Page Borders** button.

    c. Under *Setting*, change the option to **Box**. Click the **Color** arrow and select **Blue-Gray, Accent 6** (it is the last option in the first row under *Theme Colors*). Click the **Width** arrow and select **1 pt**. Click **OK**.

11. Add a header to the document.

    a. Click the **Insert** tab.

    b. In the *Header & Footer* group, click the **Header** button and select the **Banded** header option.

    c. Edit the text in the *Title* property control to read **PUTTING YOUR NEEDS FIRST**

    d. On the *Header & Footer Tools Design* tab, click the **Close Header and Footer** button.

12. Add a footer to the document.

    a. Click the **Insert** tab.

    b. In the *Header & Footer* group, click the **Footer** button and select the **Blank** footer option.

13. Add an automatic date stamp.

    a. In the footer area, click the **Type here** control to select it and press the (Delete) key.

    b. On the *Header & Footer Tools Design* tab, click the **Date & Time** button.

    c. In the *Date and Time* dialog, click the **Month DD, YYYY** option (the third option in the list).

    d. Verify the **Update automatically** checkbox is selected.

    e. Click **OK**.

14. Set a different first page header and footer.

    a. On the *Header & Footer Tools Design* tab, in the *Options* group, click the **Different first page** check box so it appears with a checkmark in it.

    b. Click the **Close Header and Footer** button.

15. Add a watermark to the document.

    a. Navigate to the beginning of the document.

    b. Click the **Design** tab.

    c. In the *Page Background* group, click the **Watermark** button and select the **DRAFT 2** option.

16. Print multiple copies of the document.

   a. Click the **File** tab and click **Print**.

   b. Click the **Copies** up arrow two times, so **3** appears in the box.

   c. Click the **Print** button. **NOTE**: If you are using this in class or in your school's computer lab, check with your instructor about printing permissions before completing this step.

17. Save and close the document.

skill review **3.2**

In this project you will be formatting and editing a paper on alternate assessments for students. You will apply a theme and then alter the theme by changing the style set and color theme. You will adjust the margins for the document. You will add information to the footer of the document and a page number and date to the header of the document. You will link to a section in the document. You will add a cover page and then edit the information displayed. Finally, you will print a range of the pages in the document.

Skills needed to complete this project:

- Applying Document Themes (Skill 3.1)
- Applying Style Sets (Skill 3.2)
- Using Color Themes (Skill 3.3)
- Adjusting Margins (Skill 3.14)
- Adding Footers (Skill 3.8)
- Inserting Page Numbers (Skill 3.10)
- Adding an Automatic Date Stamp (Skill 3.9)
- Inserting Hyperlinks (Skill 3.13)
- Creating Watermarks (Skill 3.5)
- Inserting Page Breaks (Skill 3.6)
- Adding a Cover Page (Skill 3.18)
- Printing Page Ranges (Skill 3.20)

1. Open the start file **WD2019-SkillReview-3-2** document and resave this document as: **[your initials] WD-SkillReview-3-2**

2. If the document opens in Protected View, click the **Enable Editing** button in the Message Bar at the top of the document so you can modify it.

3. Apply a theme to a document.

   a. Click the **Design** tab.

   b. In the *Document Formatting* group, click the **Themes** button and select **Facet**.

4. Change the style set for the document.

   a. Verify you are still on the **Design** tab.

   b. In the *Style Set* gallery, click the **Elegant** option.

5. Change the color theme.

   a. On the *Design* tab, in *Document Formatting* group, click the **Colors** button.

   b. Select the **Blue Green** color theme.

6. Adjust the margins for the document.

   a. Click the **Layout** tab.

   b. In the *Page Setup* group, click the **Margins** button and select **Moderate**.

7. Add footer text.

   a. Click the **Insert** tab.

   b. In the *Header & Footer* group, click the **Footer** button and select **Ion (Light)**.

   c. Click the **[Title]** control at the far left side of the footer.

   d. Type **ALTERNATE ASSESSMENT**

   e. Click the **[Author]** control in at the far right side of the footer.

   f. Type **ALEXANDER MIRANDA**

   g. Click the **Header & Footer** tab.

   h. Click the **Close Header and Footer** button.

8. Insert page numbers and display a different first page for the header.

   a. Click the **Insert** tab.

   b. In the *Header & Footer* group, click the **Page Number** button arrow, then click **Page Number**. Select **Top of Page (Header)** for the *Position* and **Left** for the *Alignment.*

   c. Deselect the check box for **Show number on first page**.

   d. Click **OK**.

9. Add an automatic date stamp.

   a. Navigate to **page 2** and double-click the header area to activate it.

   b. Place the cursor after the word *Page* and press the (Tab ⇥) key two times.

   c. On the *Header & Footer* tab, click the **Date & Time** button.

   d. Add a date to the header using the **MM/DD/YY** format (for example, 01/01/20). Have the date update automatically.

   e. Click the **Close Header and Footer** button.

10. Add a hyperlink to another place in the document.

    a. Navigate to the *Modified Achievement Requirements* section.

    b. Place the cursor after the third sentence (ending in to *receive an alternate assessment.*) and press the spacebar one time.

    c. Click the **Insert** tab.

    d. In the *Links* group, click the **Link** button.

    e. Click the **This Document** button.

    f. In the *Text to display* box, type **(See the Who is Eligible section)**

    g. Click the arrow next to *Headings* to expand the list of headings, and select **Who is Eligible**.

    h. Click **OK**.

11. Add a watermark to the document.

    a. Click the **Design** tab.

    b. In the *Page Background* section, click the **Watermark** button. Click the **Text** radio button, and select **DRAFT** in the *Text* drop-down list. Click the **Diagonal** radio button under *Orientation*. Click **OK**.

12. Insert a page break.

 a. Navigate to the *Summary* heading and place the cursor at the beginning of the line.

 b. Click the **Layout tab**.

 c. In the *Page Setup* group, click the **Breaks** button and select **Page**.

13. Add a cover page.

 a. Click the **Insert** tab.

 b. In the *Pages* group, click the **Cover Page** button and select **Facet**.

 c. Select the **[Abstract]** control and press **Delete**.

 d. Select the **[Document Subtitle]** control and type MAKING SURE NO CHILD IS LEFT BEHIND

14. Preview and print a specific page range.

 a. Click the **File** tab and click **Print** to display the Print page.

 b. Under *Pages*, click the **From**: radio button, and type **2** in the *From:* text box. Type **5** in the *to:* textbox.

 c. Verify the name of your printer appears under **Printer**.

 d. Click the **Print** button. **NOTE**: If you are using this in class or in your school's computer lab, check with your instructor about printing permissions before completing this step.

15. Save and close the document.

challenge yourself 3.3

In this project you will be formatting and editing a document for the Tri-State Book Festival. First, you will adjust the look of the document by changing the theme, style set, color theme, and font theme. You will add header and footer information and insert a property control. You will adjust the margins on the document and add a page break. You will display text in columns and adjust how the text is displayed by inserting a column break. Finally, you will add a page border and then print multiple copies of the document.

Skills needed to complete this project:

- Applying Document Themes (Skill 3.1)
- Applying Style Sets (Skill 3.2)
- Using Color Themes (Skill 3.3)
- Using Font Themes (Skill 3.4)
- Adding Headers (Skill 3.7)
- Adding an Automatic Date Stamp (Skill 3.9)
- Adding Footers (Skill 3.8)
- Inserting Property Controls (Skill 3.12)
- Adjusting Margins (Skill 3.14)
- Inserting Page Breaks (Skill 3.6)
- Applying Columns (Skill 3.15)
- Inserting a Column Break (Skill 3.16)
- Adding Page Borders (Skill 3.17)
- Printing Multiple Copies of a Document (Skill 3.19)

1. Open the start file **WD2019-ChallengeYourself-3-3** document and resave this document as: **[your initials] WD-ChallengeYourself-3-3**

2. If the document opens in Protected View, click the **Enable Editing** button in the Message Bar at the top of the document so you can modify it.

3. Apply the **Integral** theme to the document.

4. Change the style set to **Lines (Simple)**.

5. Change the color theme to **Green**.

6. Change the font theme to **Century Gothic**.

7. Add a header using the **Sideline** format.

8. Add a footer using the **Retrospect** format.

9. Delete the **Author** property control in the footer and insert a date stamp that will update automatically. Use the **MM/DD/YYYY** format (for example 1/1/2019).

10. Change the header and footer so the first page is different from the rest of the document.

11. Change the margins for the document to the following:
    - *Top*: **1.2"**
    - *Bottom*: **1.2"**
    - *Left*: **1.1"**
    - *Right*: **1.1"**

12. Place the cursor at the beginning of the *Friday September 7* heading in the *Agenda* section. Add a page break.

13. Place the cursor at the beginning of the *Authors* heading at the bottom of page 2. Add a page break.

14. In the *Authors* section, select the text from the heading **Fiction** through **Showcased work: The PM Handbook**. Display text in **two columns**.

15. Add a page border to the document with the following settings:
    - *Setting*: **Box**
    - *Style*: **Solid line** (default option)
    - *Color*: **Green, Accent 1** (it is the fifth option in the first row under *Theme Colors*)
    - *Width*: **1½pt**

16. Print three copies of the document. **NOTE**: If you are using this in class or in your school's computer lab, check with your instructor about printing permissions before completing this step.

17. Save and close the document.

challenge yourself 3.4

In this project you will be editing the text of a safety memo from the Winter Springs. You will change the theme for the document and then adjust the theme by changing the style set and color theme. You will add content to the footer and the header of the document. You will link to another place in the document. You will adjust the layout of the document by adding a page break and displaying text in columns. Finally, you will add a watermark and then print multiple copies of a specific page range.

Skills needed to complete this project:

- Applying Document Themes (Skill 3.1)
- Applying Style Sets (Skill 3.2)

- Using Color Themes (Skill 3.3)
- Using Font Themes (Skill 3.4)
- Adding Footers (Skill 3.8)
- Adding Headers (Skill 3.7)
- Adding an Automatic Date Stamp (Skill 3.9)
- Inserting Hyperlinks (Skill 3.13)
- Adjusting Margins (Skill 3.14)
- Applying Columns (Skill 3.15)
- Inserting a Column Break (Skill 3.16)
- Inserting Page Breaks (Skill 3.6)
- Adding a Cover Page (Skill 3.18)
- Creating Watermarks (Skill 3.5)
- Printing Multiple Copies of a Document (Skill 3.19)
- Printing Page Ranges (Skill 3.20)

1. Open the start file **WD2019-ChallengeYourself-3-4** document and resave this document as: **[your initials] WD-ChallengeYourself-3-4**

2. If the document opens in Protected View, click the **Enable Editing** button in the Message Bar at the top of the document so you can modify it.

3. Apply the **Retrospect** theme to the document.

4. Change the style set to **Simple**.

5. Change the color theme to **Blue Warm**.

6. Change the font theme to **Candara**.

7. Add a footer using the **Banded** format.

8. Add a header using the **Blank** format. Select the placeholder on the left and insert the document title.

9. On page 2, press tab twice and add an automatic date stamp on the right side of the header using the **MM/DD/YYYY** format. Be sure the date will update automatically.

10. Add a hyperlink to another place in the document.

    a. Navigate to the *Our Safety Vision* section.

    b. Place the cursor after the second sentence (ending in *overlapping shifts.*) and press the spacebar one time.

    c. Add a hyperlink to the **Round the Clock Officers** section of the document. Have text for the link read **(See the list of officers)**

11. Change the margins for the document to the following:
    - *Top*: **1.1"**
    - *Bottom*: **1.1"**
    - *Left*: **1.2"**
    - *Right*: **1.2"**

12. Navigate to the beginning of the document and change the font size of the text *Winter Springs Safety News* to **36 pt**.

13. In the *Round the Clock Officers* section, select the text from the heading **Amy Stephens (12 years)** through **Jeannie Smith (4 years)**. Display the text in **two columns**.

14. In the *Day Shift Officers* section, select the text from the heading **Harriet Hollow (7 years)** through **Gordan Beagle (2 years)**. Display the text in **two columns**.

15. Insert a page break before the *Upcoming Safety Improvements* section.

16. Add a cover page.

    a. Insert a cover page using the **Whisp** design.

    b. Change the **Document subtitle** to read `The latest safety news for you`

    c. Delete the **Date** control on the cover page.

17. Navigate to the *Introduction* section and add a watermark using the **SAMPLE** text with diagonal orientation.

18. Print two copies of all the pages except the cover page. **NOTE**: If you are using this in class or in your school's computer lab, check with your instructor about printing permissions before completing this step.

19. Save and close the document.

on your own 3.5

In this project you will be formatting and printing a marketing sheet for a landscape company. You will apply a theme of your choice and adjust the theme by changing the style set, color theme, and font theme. You will add a property control to ensure consistent spelling of the company name. You will add content to the header and footer of the document. You will change the layout by adjusting margins and adding a page break. You will add a page border and a cover page. Finally, you will practice printing multiple copies and page ranges.

Skills needed to complete this project:

- Applying Document Themes (Skill 3.1)
- Applying Style Sets (Skill 3.2)
- Using Color Themes (Skill 3.3)
- Using Font Themes (Skill 3.4)
- Inserting Property Controls (Skill 3.12)
- Inserting Page Numbers (Skill 3.10)
- Adding an Automatic Date Stamp (Skill 3.9)
- Adding Headers (Skill 3.7)
- Adjusting Margins (Skill 3.14)
- Inserting Page Breaks (Skill 3.6)
- Adding Page Borders (Skill 3.17)
- Adding a Cover Page (Skill 3.18)
- Printing Multiple Copies of a Document (Skill 3.19)
- Printing Page Ranges (Skill 3.20)

1. Open the start file **WD2019-OnYourOwn-3-5** document and resave this document as: `[your initials] WD-OnYourOwn-3-5`

2. If the document opens in Protected View, click the **Enable Editing** button in the Message Bar at the top of the document so you can modify it.

3. Apply a theme of your choice to the document.

4. Change the style set to one of your choice.

5. Choose a new color theme

6. Choose a new font theme.

7. Insert a **Company** property control at the beginning of the first paragraph. Be sure a space appears between the property control and the next word.

8. There are four instances where the company name is spelled **GreenScapes**. Find each instance, delete the text, and replace the text with a **Company** property control. Be sure a space appears between the property control and the next word.

9. Add a page number to the bottom of the document. Use a format of your choice.

10. Add an automatic date stamp to the footer of the document. Use a format of your choice.

11. Add a header that will display the **document title**. If there are other property controls in the header, delete them.

12. Change the header and footer so they do not appear on the first page of the document.

13. Adjust the margins for optimal layout.

14. If necessary, insert a page break before any *Heading 1* so the section starts on a new page and does not break across two pages. Be sure to delete any extra lines. **NOTE**: Depending on the margin settings you used, you may not need to insert a page break.

15. Add a page border of your choice. Modify the color and width of the border.

16. Print three copies of the document. **NOTE**: If you are using this in class or in your school's computer lab, check with your instructor about printing permissions before completing this step.

17. Save and close the document.

fix it 3.6

In this project you will fix a report on classroom behavior. First, you will fix the margins and apply a new theme and style set. You will then apply styles to text and adjust the color and font themes. You will replace manually entered page numbers and add an author property control to the header of the document. You will add information to the footer including an automatic date stamp. You will add a section break and cover page. Finally, you will add a watermark and print multiple copies of the document.

Skills needed to complete this project:

- Adjusting Margins (Skill 3.14)
- Applying Document Themes (Skill 3.1)
- Applying Style Sets (Skill 3.2)
- Using Color Themes (Skill 3.3)
- Using Font Themes (Skill 3.4)
- Adding Headers (Skill 3.7)
- Inserting Property Controls (Skill 3.12)
- Adding Footers (Skill 3.8)
- Adding an Automatic Date Stamp (Skill 3.9)
- Inserting Page Breaks (Skill 3.6)
- Adding a Cover Page (Skill 3.18)
- Creating Watermarks (Skill 3.5)
- Printing Multiple Copies of a Document (Skill 3.19)

1. Open the start file **WD2019-FixIt-3-6** document and resave this document as: **[your initials] WD-FixIt-3-6**

2. If the document opens in Protected View, click the **Enable Editing** button in the Message Bar at the top of the document so you can modify it.

3. Change the margins to use the **Normal** preset.

4. Change the document theme to **Ion**.

5. Change the style set to **Simple**.

6. On page 1, apply the **Title** style to the text **Behavior Modification Project**.

7. Apply the **Heading 1** style to section titles beginning with a roman numeral:
   - I. Identify the target behavior
   - II. Define the target behavior in measurable terms
   - III. Collect and chart baseline data
   - IV. Implement the behavior change program
   - V. Evaluate the result
   - VI. Evaluation and conclusion

8. Change the color theme to **Blue**.

9. Change the font theme to **Office**.

10. The author Joseph Marquez typed his name and a page number at the top of each page. Delete this line from the top of each page. There are four instances of this mistake. **NOTE**: After you have deleted the first instance of this mistake, the remaining instances will no longer appear at the top of the following pages.

11. Review the document and remove any extra line breaks.

12. Add the **Ion (Light)** header to the document.

13. Adjust the header so it does not appear on the first page of the document.

14. In the *Document Properties*, add the name **Joseph Marquez** as the author.

15. In the header area on page 2, add an **Author** property control to the left side of the page.

16. Add a footer to the document using the **Blank (Three Columns)** design. Replace the first instance of [**Type here**] with the text **Not for Distribution**

17. Delete the second instance of [**Type here**].

18. In the footer, replace the third instance of [**Type here**] with an automatic date and time field using the **MM/DD/YY** format.

19. Insert a next page section break before the *V. Evaluate the result* section.

20. Add a cover page.
    a. Insert a cover page using the **Banded** design.
    b. Change the **Document Title** to read **Behavior Modification Project**
    c. Delete the **COMPANY NAME and Company address** controls on the cover page.

21. Navigate to the next page and add a watermark using the **CONFIDENTIAL** text and horizontal orientation.

22. Print two copies of the document. **NOTE**: If you are using this in class or in your school's computer lab, check with your instructor about printing permissions before completing this step.

23. Save and close the document.

chapter 4

Working with Pictures, Tables, and Charts

In this chapter, you will learn the following skills:

❯ Insert pictures and add alt text to pictures

❯ Resize, move, and change the layout of pictures

❯ Apply Quick Styles to objects

❯ Insert SmartArt, shapes, icons, and WordArt

❯ Create a table

❯ Enter data in a table

❯ Modify the structure of a table

❯ Sort data in a table

❯ Add borders to a table

❯ Create and modify a chart

skills

introduction

This chapter provides you with the skills to add and modify pictures, graphic elements, tables, and charts. You will learn to insert pictures from an online source as well as from your own computer and add alt text to images. Once you have added pictures to a document, you will manipulate them by resizing, positioning, and changing the text wrapping. You will then stylize pictures using Quick Styles. You will learn about other graphic objects you can add to documents including icons, shapes, WordArt, and SmartArt diagrams. You will create and enter data in a table and then modify the table by adding and deleting rows and columns. You will change the display of data in a table by merging and splitting cells and sorting the data within a table. You will modify the look of a table by applying a table Quick Style and then changing the display of table borders. Finally, you will add a chart to a document and then modify the look of that chart.

Skill 4.1 Inserting a Picture

You can insert pictures that you created in another program into your document. There are a number of graphic formats you can insert into a Word document. Some of the more common file types include JPEG, PNG, BMP, and GIF. By default, Word inserts pictures as embedded objects, meaning they become part of the new document. Changing the source file will not change or affect the newly inserted picture.

To insert a picture from a file:

1. Click the **Insert** tab.
2. In the *Illustrations* group, click the **Pictures** button.

FIGURE WD 4.1

3. The *Insert Picture* dialog opens.
4. Navigate to the file location, select the file, and click **Insert**.

To delete a picture, select it and press the **Delete** key on the keyboard.

FIGURE WD 4.2

tell me **more**

When you insert a picture to a document, the *Format* tab under *Picture Tools* displays. This tab is called a contextual tab because it displays only when a picture is the active element. The *Format* tab contains tools to change the look of the picture, such as picture style, brightness and contrast, cropping, and placement on the page.

another **method**

To insert the file from the *Insert Picture* dialog, you can also click the **Insert** button arrow and select **Insert**.

let me **try**

Open the student data file **wd4-01-SpaProductReport** and try this skill on your own:

1. Place the cursor on the blank line after the first paragraph in the document.
2. Open the dialog where you can insert a picture from your computer.
3. Navigate to the location where you saved the data files for this book.
4. Insert the **foot soak** picture.
5. If you will be moving on to the next skill in this chapter, leave the document open to continue working. If not, save the file as directed by your instructor and close it.

Skill 4.2 Positioning Pictures

When you first add a picture to your document, Word inserts the picture at the insertion point and displays the picture in line with the text. More often than not, you will want to place the picture somewhere else on the page. Word comes with a number of preset picture positions that place the picture at a specific location on the page with text wrapping applied.

To position a picture on a page with text wrapping:

1. Click the **Picture Tools Format** tab.
2. In the *Arrange* group, click the **Position Object** button.
3. In the *With Text Wrapping* section, select an option. The picture is placed on the page according to the option you chose.

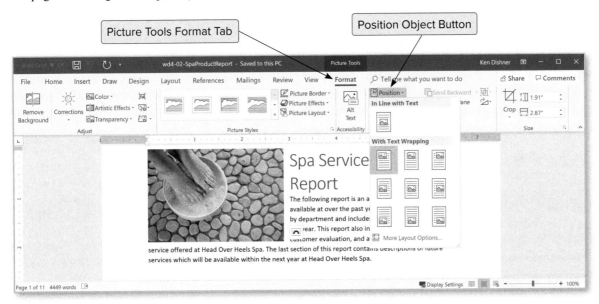

FIGURE WD 4.3

tips & tricks

When you position a picture, the location you choose is for the page the picture is on. If you want the picture to appear on another page, move the picture to that page and then use the **Position Object** command to place it.

another **method**

You can also position pictures on the page from the *Layout* tab. In the *Arrange* group, click the **Position Object** button and select an option.

let me **try**

If you do not have the data file from the previous skill open, open the student data file **wd4-02-SpaProductReport** and try this skill on your own:

1. Select the picture on the first page of the document.
2. Use the **Position Object** command that will place the picture in the upper left corner of the page with square wrapping applied.
3. If you will be moving on to the next skill in this chapter, leave the document open to continue working. If not, save the file as directed by your instructor and close it.

Skill 4.3 Adding Alt Text to Pictures

Adding alt text to pictures in your documents makes your documents accessible to a wider audience, including those that are blind. **Alt text** is a description of a picture, chart, or other object that can be read by screen readers. When creating alt text, write a description that is thorough and to the point. Do not include any unnecessary words. A good rule of thumb is to think of how you would describe the picture to someone who cannot see it.

To add alt text to a picture:

1. Right-click the picture and select **Edit Alt Text...**

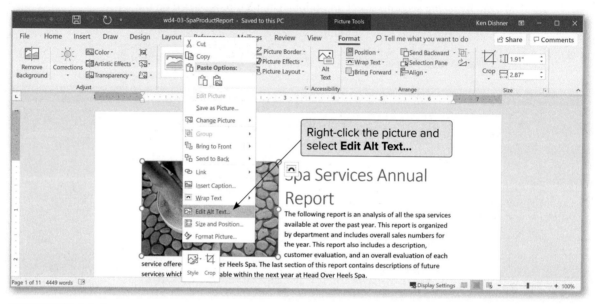

FIGURE WD 4.4

2. In the *Alt Text* task pane, type a detailed description of the picture in the text box.

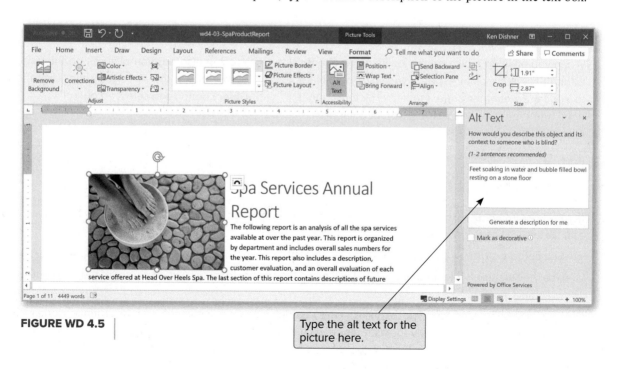

FIGURE WD 4.5

tips & tricks

Word's *Accessibility Checker* feature reviews your document looking for anything that does not meet accessibility standards. To run the *Accessibility Checker*, click the **Review** tab. In the *Accessibility* group, click the **Check Accessibility** button. Issues that might interfere with a screen reader's ability to read the document appear in the *Warnings* section, including any figures that do not include an alt text description.

tell me **more**

If you have an Office 365 subscription, Word's intelligent services automatically analyzes any picture that is added to the document and creates an alt text description for the picture. However, the description that Word's intelligent services creates is not always accurate. It is important to check the alt text for the pictures in your documents and edit the pictures as necessary.

another **method**

To add alt text to images, you can also:

1. Select the picture to which you want to add the description.
2. Click the **Picture Tools Format** tab.
3. In the *Accessibility* group, click the **Alt Text** button.

let me **try**

If you do not have the data file from the previous skill open, open the student data file **wd4-03-SpaProductReport** and try this skill on your own:

1. Select the picture of the feet on the first page of the document.
2. Open the **Alt Text** task pane.
3. Add the following description as alt text and then close the task pane when you are done: **Feet soaking in water and bubble filled bowl resting on a stone floor**
4. If you will be moving on to the next skill in this chapter, leave the document open to continue working. If not, save the file as directed by your instructor and close it.

Skill 4.4 Inserting Online Pictures

In addition to adding pictures from your computer, you can also search for **online pictures** to add to documents. You can search for pictures from different online sources, including the Internet or from your OneDrive. When searching for online pictures, you are responsible for understanding copyright issues and obtaining permission from the copyright owner if necessary.

To insert a picture from an online source:

1. Click the **Insert** tab.

2. In the *Illustrations* group, click the **Online Pictures** button.

FIGURE WD 4.6

3. The *Online Pictures* dialog opens.

4. Type a word describing the picture you want to search for in the *Search* box and press ⏎ Enter.

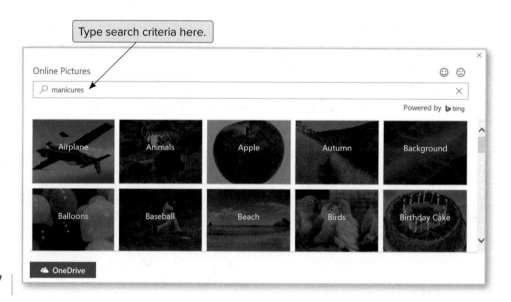

FIGURE WD 4.7

5. Word displays thumbnail results that match the search criteria.

6. Click a thumbnail to select it and click the **Insert** button to add the picture to your document.

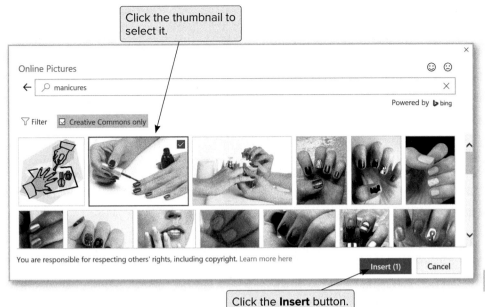

Click the thumbnail to select it.

Online Pictures

← 🔍 manicures   ×

Powered by ▶ bing

▽ Filter   ☑ Creative Commons only

You are responsible for respecting others' rights, including copyright. Learn more here

Insert (1)   Cancel

Click the **Insert** button.

FIGURE WD 4.8

If you do not have an updated version of Office 365, your *Online Pictures* dialog may look different than the one here, but the general steps for searching for online images still apply.

tips & tricks

⟩ When you insert a picture from Creative Commons, Word will automatically insert the source information along with the picture. Be sure to select both the source and the picture when you move or resize the picture.

⟩ You can add more than one image at a time in the *Online Pictures* dialog. As you select images, a checkmark appears next to the selected image and the number on the *Insert* button updates to reflect the number of images that will be added to the document.

⟩ To insert pictures from your OneDrive, click the **OneDrive** button at the bottom of the *Online Pictures* dialog. Navigate to the folder where you have saved the picture you want to insert, select the picture, and click the **Insert** button.

tell me more

If you use Bing search, you will be searching for pictures from across the Internet and Word will return pictures that have the **Creative Commons** licensing tag. However, the results you see may include pictures that are not royalty free. Always check the source of the picture to be sure you use only pictures in your documents that you know you have the proper rights to use.

let me try

If you do not have the data file from the previous skill open, open the student data file **wd4-04-SpaProductReport** and try this skill on your own:

1. Place your cursor in the empty line under the first paragraph of the document.

2. Open the dialog where you can insert a picture from an online source.

3. Use *Bing* to search for pictures of **manicures**.

4. Insert the picture that is selected in Figure WD 4.8. If you do not see this picture in your results, insert a picture of your choice.

5. If you will be moving on to the next skill in this chapter, leave the document open to continue working. If not, save the file as directed by your instructor and close it.

Skill 4.5 Resizing Pictures

When you first add a picture to a document, you may find it is not the right size. The picture may be too large for the page, or it may be too small for the page layout. You can resize pictures in a document by either manually entering the values for the size of the picture or by dragging a **resize handle** on the picture to resize it.

To resize a picture by manually entering values:

1. Select the picture you want to resize.
2. Click the **Picture Tools Format** tab.
3. In the *Size* group, type a value in the *Width* or *Height* box to resize the picture.
4. Press ⬅ Enter to resize the picture.

To resize a picture by dragging:

1. Select the picture you want to change.
2. To resize a picture, click a **resize handle** and drag toward the center of the picture to make it smaller or away from the center of the picture to make it larger.

FIGURE WD 4.9

tips & tricks

When resizing by dragging, be sure to use one of the resize handles on the four corners of the picture to maintain the aspect ratio of the picture. This means that as the width is increased or decreased, the height of the picture is increased or decreased proportionally. To maintain the aspect ratio when entering values, click the dialog launcher in the *Size* group and verify the *Lock aspect ratio* checkbox is selected in the *Layout* dialog.

let me try

If you do not have the data file from the previous skill open, open the student data file **wd4-05-SpaProduct-Report** and try this skill on your own:

1. Select the picture of the manicure on the first page of the document.
2. Resize the picture so it is **2″** in height and **2.68″** in the width.
3. If you will be moving on to the next skill in this chapter, leave the document open to continue working. If not, save the file as directed by your instructor and close it.

Skill 4.6 Changing Picture Layouts

When you first add a picture to your document, Word inserts the picture at the insertion point and displays the picture in line with the text. This causes the picture to be treated as its own paragraph. But what if you want the text in your document to wrap around the picture? Word comes with a number of layout options for you to choose from. When a picture is selected, you will see the **Layout Options** button. This button gives you one-click access to text layout options for the picture.

To adjust the layout of a picture:

1. Click the picture to select it.
2. Click the **Layout Options** button.
3. Select a wrapping option.

FIGURE WD 4.10

tips & tricks

As you roll the mouse over each layout option, Live Preview will display how the document will look with the text wrapping applied.

another **method**

To change the layout of pictures, you can also click the **Layout** tab or the **Picture Tools Format** tab. In the *Arrange* group, click the **Wrap Text** button and select an option.

let me **try**

If you do not have the data file from the previous skill open, open the student data file **wd4-06-SpaProductReport** and try this skill on your own:

1. Select the picture of the manicure on the first page of the document.
2. Change the text wrap option of the picture to the **Tight** layout option.
3. If you will be moving on to the next skill in this chapter, leave the document open to continue working. If not, save the file as directed by your instructor and close it.

Skill 4.7 Moving Pictures

When you first add a picture to a document, you may find it is not positioned where you want it. You can change the position of pictures by dragging and dropping the picture where you want it on the page. When you drag a picture, you will see horizontal and vertical green lines called the **alignment guides**. They appear when the picture's edge is aligned with another element on the page.

To move pictures in a document:

1. Select the picture you want to move.

2. Rest your mouse over the picture.

3. When the cursor changes to the **move cursor**, click and drag the picture to the new location.

4. When an alignment guide appears aligning it with the desired element on the page, release the mouse button to snap the picture in place and align it on the page.

FIGURE WD 4.11

tips & tricks

If you don't see alignment guides when you move a picture, they may be turned off. To turn on alignment guides, click the **Picture Tools Format** tab. In the *Arrange* group, click the **Align** button and select **Use Alignment Guides** so a checkmark appears next to the menu item. Click **Use Alignment Guides** again to turn off the feature.

let me try

If you do not have the data file from the previous skill open, open the student data file **wd4-07-SpaProductReport** and try this skill on your own:

1. Select the picture of the manicure on the first page of the document.

2. Move the picture to the right of the first paragraph so the top of the picture aligns with the top of the first paragraph in the *Manicures and Pedicures* section and the right side of the picture aligns with the right margin of the page. You will see horizontal and vertical alignment guides as shown in Figure WD 4.11.

3. If you will be moving on to the next skill in this chapter, leave the document open to continue working. If not, save the file as directed by your instructor and close it.

word 365   chapter 4 Working with Pictures, Tables, and Charts

Skill 4.8 Applying Quick Styles to Pictures

Quick Styles are combinations of formatting that give elements of your document a more polished, professional look without a lot of work. Quick Styles for pictures include a combination of borders, shadows, reflections, and picture shapes, such as rounded corners or skewed perspective. Instead of applying each of these formatting elements one at a time, you can apply a combination of elements at one time using a preset Quick Style.

To apply a Quick Style to a picture:

1. Select the picture you want to apply the Quick Style to.
2. Click the **Picture Tools Format** tab.
3. In the *Picture Styles* group, click the **More** button.
4. In the *Picture Quick Styles* gallery, click an option to apply it to the picture.

FIGURE WD 4.12

tell me **more**

The same steps for applying Quick Styles to pictures can be used to apply Quick Styles to other drawing objects, such as shapes.

another **method**

To apply a Quick Style to a picture, you can also right-click the picture, click the **Picture** button, and select a Quick Style from the gallery.

let me **try**

If you do not have the data file from the previous skill open, open the student data file **wd4-08-SpaProductReport** and try this skill on your own:

1. Select the picture of the **foot soak** on the first page of the document.
2. Apply the **Center Shadow Rectangle** Quick Style to the picture.
3. If you will be moving on to the next skill in this chapter, leave the document open to continue working. If not, save the file as directed by your instructor and close it.

Skill 4.9 Adding Icons

Icons are SVG (Scalable Vector Graphics) images you can add to your documents. They are simple drawings and because they use the SVG format, they can be enlarged, colored, and rotated without losing image quality.

To insert an icon:

1. Navigate to the location where you want to add the icon.
2. Click the **Insert** tab.
3. In the *Illustrations* group, click the **Icons** button.

FIGURE WD 4.13

4. The *Insert Icons* dialog appears. Click a category on the left to navigate to that section.
5. Click an icon to select it.
6. Click the **Insert** button.

FIGURE WD 4.14

All icons are inserted with a black fill color, but you can modify icons from the *Graphics Tools Format* tab. This tab contains commands for changing the look of the icon, including applying a preset graphics style. Preset graphic styles are a combination of fill and outline settings that can be applied to a graphic at the same time.

To apply a preset graphics style to an icon:

1. With the icon selected, on the *Graphics Tools Format* tab, click the **Graphics Styles More** button.

2. The *Graphics Styles* gallery displays. Click a style in the gallery to apply it to the icon.

tell me **more**

You can select more than one icon to insert. Selected icons appear with a box around the icon and a checkmark in the upper right corner.

another **method**

〉 You can also scroll the icons in the *Insert Icons* dialog rather than using the category list to jump to a section.

〉 To apply a preset graphics style, you can also click an option in the gallery on the Ribbon.

let me **try**

If you do not have the data file from the previous skill open, open the student data file **wd4-09-SpaProductReport** and try this skill on your own:

1. Navigate to the end of the document and place the cursor on the blank line above the last line of text.

2. Add the icon of the **three test tubes**. It is in the *Education* category.

3. Apply the **Colored Fill – Accent 1, Dark 1 Outline** graphics style to the icon. It is the second icon in the third row of the gallery.

4. If you will be moving on to the next skill in this chapter, leave the document open to continue working. If not, save the file as directed by your instructor and close it.

Skill 4.10 Inserting SmartArt

SmartArt is a way to make your ideas visual. Where documents used to have plain bulleted and ordered lists, now they can have SmartArt, which are visual diagrams containing graphic elements with text boxes in which you can enter your information. Using SmartArt not only makes your document look better, but also helps convey the information in a more meaningful way.

To add SmartArt to a document:

1. Click the **Insert** tab.
2. In the *Illustrations* group, click the **SmartArt** button.

FIGURE WD 4.16

3. In the *Choose a SmartArt Graphic* dialog, click a **SmartArt** option and click **OK**.
4. The SmartArt is added to your document.
5. If necessary, click the arrow tab on the left side of the diagram to display the *SmartArt Text* pane.
6. Click in the first item of the *SmartArt Text* pane and type your first item.
7. Enter the text for each item.
8. Click outside the SmartArt graphic to hide the *Text* pane.

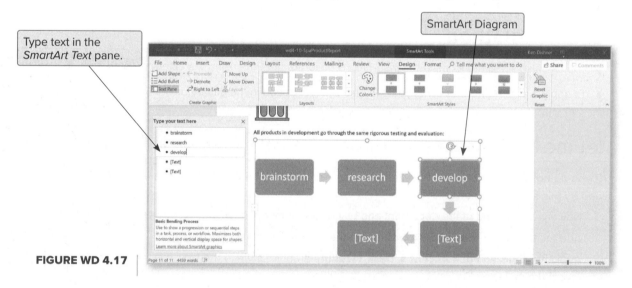

FIGURE WD 4.17

There are eight categories of SmartArt for you to choose from:

List—Use to list items that do not need to be in a particular order.

Process—Use to list items that do need to be in a particular order.

Cycle—Use for a process that repeats over and over again.

Hierarchy—Use to show branching, in either a decision tree or an organization chart.

Relationship—Use to show relationships between items.

Matrix—Use to show how an item fits into the whole.

Pyramid—Use to illustrate how things relate to each other with the largest item on the bottom and the smallest item on the top.

Picture—Use to show a series of pictures along with text in the diagram.

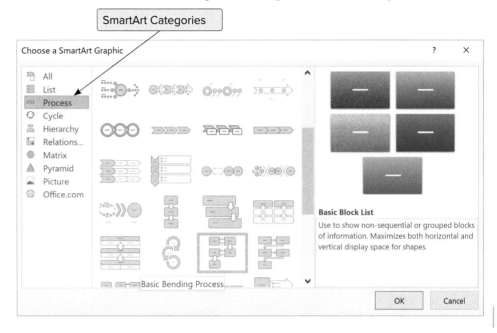

FIGURE WD 4.18

tips & tricks

When choosing a SmartArt diagram, it is important that the diagram type suits your content. In the *Choose a SmartArt Graphic* dialog, click a SmartArt type to display a preview of the SmartArt to the right. The preview not only displays what the diagram will look like, but also includes a description of the best uses for the diagram type.

another **method**

To enter text in SmartArt, you can click in a text box on the SmartArt diagram and type your text.

let me **try**

If you do not have the data file from the previous skill open, open the student data file **wd4-10-SpaProductReport** and try this skill on your own:

1. Navigate to the end of the document and place the cursor at the end of the last line of text and press ⏎ Enter .
2. Insert a **Basic Bending Process** SmartArt diagram. See Figure WD 4.18.
3. Enter the following information in the diagram:
   - `brainstorm`
   - `research`
   - `develop`
   - `focus test`
   - `produce`
4. If you will be moving on to the next skill in this chapter, leave the document open to continue working. If not, save the file as directed by your instructor and close it.

Skill 4.11 Inserting a Shape

A **shape** is a line drawing that you can quickly add to your document. Word comes with a number of shapes for you to choose from, including lines, block arrows, callouts, and basic shapes such as smiley faces, rectangles, and circles.

Insert Tab

Shapes Button

Select an option from the *Shapes* gallery.

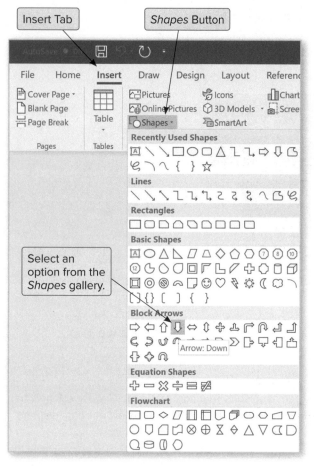

FIGURE WD 4.19

To add a shape to a document:

1. Click the **Insert** tab.

2. In the *Illustrations* group, click the **Shapes** button and select an option from the *Shapes* gallery.

3. The cursor changes to a crosshair.

4. Click on the document to add the shape with default sizing. If you want to control the size of the shape, click and drag on the document. As you are dragging, you will see an outline of the shape. When the shape is the size you want, release the mouse button.

A shape added to a document.

FIGURE WD 4.20

tell me **more**

When you insert a shape into a document, the *Drawing Tools Format* tab displays. This is called a contextual tab because it displays only when a drawing object is the active element. The *Format* tab contains tools to change the look of the shape, such as shape styles, effects, and placement on the page. You can apply Quick Styles to shapes by selecting an option in the *Shape Quick Styles* gallery in the *Shape Styles* group. Click the **More** button for the gallery to expand it and view all the Quick Style options you can apply to shapes.

let me **try**

If you do not have the data file from the previous skill open, open the student data file **wd4-11-SpaProductReport** and try this skill on your own:

1. On the last page of the document, add an **Arrow: Down** shape above the *Brainstorm* box in the SmartArt diagram.

2. If necessary, move the shape so it is centered above the *Brainstorm* box. See Figure WD 4.20.

3. If you will be moving on to the next skill in this chapter, leave the document open to continue working. If not, save the file as directed by your instructor and close it.

Skill 4.12 Adding WordArt to Documents

Sometimes you'll want to call attention to text you have added to your document. You could format the text by using character effects, or if you want the text to really stand out, use **WordArt**. WordArt styles are predefined graphic styles you can apply to text. These styles include a combination of color, fills, outlines, and effects.

To add WordArt to a document:

1. Click the **Insert** tab.
2. In the *Text* group, click the **Insert WordArt** button and select a style from the gallery.
3. Replace the text *Your text here* with the text for your document.

After you have added WordArt to your document, you can modify it just as you would any other text. Use the **Font** box and **Font Size** box on the *Home* tab to change the font or font size of WordArt.

FIGURE WD 4.21

tips & tricks

When you insert WordArt into a document, the *Drawing Tools Format* tab displays. You can modify the look of the WordArt from commands in the *WordArt Styles* and *Text* groups on this tab, including adjusting fill and outline colors and changing the alignment and direction of the text.

let me try

If you do not have the data file from the previous skill open, open the student data file **wd4-12-SpaProductReport** and try this skill on your own:

1. Place the cursor at the top of the last page in the document.
2. Add WordArt to the document using the second option of the first row of the WordArt gallery.
3. Replace the text *Your text here* with: **Future Products**
4. Move the WordArt object so it appears above the list aligned with the left side of the left column of text. See Figure WD 4.21.
5. If you will be moving on to the next skill in this chapter, leave the document open to continue working. If not, save the file as directed by your instructor and close it.

Skill 4.13 Creating a Table

A **table** helps you organize information for effective display. Tables are organized by **rows**, which display horizontally, and **columns**, which display vertically. The intersection of a row and column is referred to as a **cell**. Tables can be used to display everything from dates in a calendar to sales numbers to product inventory.

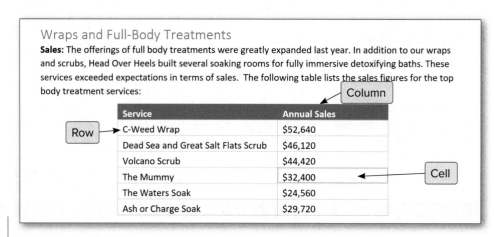

To create a simple table:

1. Click the **Insert** tab.

2. In the *Tables* group, click the **Table** button.

3. Select the number of cells you want by moving the cursor across and down the squares.

4. When the description at the top of the menu displays the number of rows and columns you want, click the mouse.

5. The table is inserted into your document.

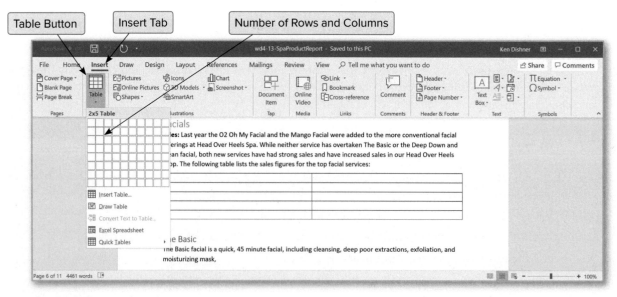

FIGURE WD 4.23

tips & tricks

Rather than inserting a table and then adding data, you can convert existing text into a table. After selecting the text to be converted, click the **Table** button and click **Insert Table…**. The number of rows and columns will automatically be determined by the tabs and paragraphs in the selection.

tell me **more**

Word comes with a number of **Quick Tables** building blocks. These templates are preformatted for you and include sample data. To insert a Quick Table, click the **Tables** button, point to **Quick Tables**, and select a building block option from the gallery. After you insert a Quick Table, just replace the sample data with your own.

another **method**

To insert a table, you can also:

1. Click the **Table** button and select **Insert Table…**
2. In the *Insert Table* dialog, enter the number of rows and columns for your table.
3. Click **OK**.

let me **try**

If you do not have the data file from the previous skill open, open the student data file **wd4-13-SpaProductReport** and try this skill on your own:

1. Navigate to the *Facials* section of the document (it is located on page 6 of the document) and place the cursor on the blank line under the first paragraph of the section.
2. Insert a table that has **two columns** and **five rows**.
3. If you will be moving on to the next skill in this chapter, leave the document open to continue working. If not, save the file as directed by your instructor and close it.

from the perspective of . . .

A COMMUNITY NEWSPAPER INTERN

When I first started working for the newspaper, articles were text with all the photographs arranged either above or below the text of the article. The text was well formatted, but didn't convey the information in an exciting, visual manner. We do the layout in Word for delivery either in print or online. So, one of the things I did was jazz up the photographs by adding text wrapping and Quick Styles. I also changed our boring lists into vibrant SmartArt diagrams. I finally convinced my editor to format tables in the newspaper using Quick Styles. No more boring black and white! Now our newspaper has the visual punch that really grabs our readers' attention.

Comstock Images/Getty Images

Skill 4.14 Working with Tables

Once you have inserted a blank table, you will need to enter data. When entering data in a table, it is a good idea to use the first row as a heading row by typing a short description of the content for the column in each cell. After you have labeled each column, continue entering the data into your table.

To enter data in a table:

1. Place the cursor in the cell where you want to enter the data.

2. Type the data just as you would in normal text.

3. Press (Tab ⇆) to move to the next cell and enter more data.

4. When you reach the last cell in the last row of a table, pressing (Tab ⇆) on the keyboard will create a new row in the table.

5. Continue pressing (Tab ⇆) until all data is entered.

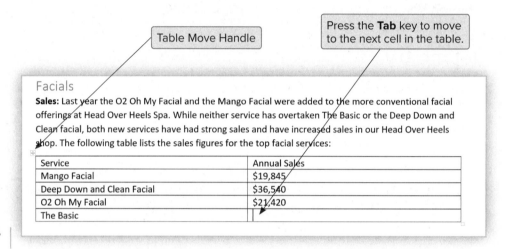

> Table Move Handle

> Press the **Tab** key to move to the next cell in the table.

Facials

Sales: Last year the O2 Oh My Facial and the Mango Facial were added to the more conventional facial offerings at Head Over Heels Spa. While neither service has overtaken The Basic or the Deep Down and Clean facial, both new services have had strong sales and have increased sales in our Head Over Heels shop. The following table lists the sales figures for the top facial services:

Service	Annual Sales
Mango Facial	$19,845
Deep Down and Clean Facial	$36,540
O2 Oh My Facial	$21,420
The Basic	

FIGURE WD 4.24

After you have entered data in a table, you will most likely want to manipulate all or part of the table. You can select individual rows, columns, or the entire table:

❭ To select a row, point to the left side of the row you want to select. When the cursor changes to a white arrow icon (↑), press the mouse button. The selected row will appear highlighted.

❭ To select a column, point to the top of the column you want to select. When the cursor changes to a black, down-pointing arrow icon (↓), press the mouse button. The selected column will appear highlighted.

❭ To select the entire table, click the **table move handle** that appears at the upper left corner of the table when it is active.

tips & tricks

When working with tables be sure you have the correct part of the table selected. If you want to change the formatting on a row or column, you must select the row or column first. If you place the cursor in a cell or select a cell, the formatting will apply only to that cell.

tell me **more**

When working with tables, the conventional way to identify a cell is by column and row. Columns are typically referred to by letters and rows by numbers. Thus, the first cell in the third row would be identified as "cell A3" and the third cell in the first row would be identified as "C1."

another **method**

⟩ To enter data in another cell in a table, you can also click in the cell and begin typing.

⟩ To select parts of a table, you can also click the **Table Tools Layout** tab. In the *Table* group, click the **Select** button and select an option.

let me **try**

If you do not have the data file from the previous skill open, open the student data file **wd4-14-SpaProductReport** and try this skill on your own:

1. Navigate to the table in the *Facials* section.

2. Practice selecting a row, a column, and the entire table.

3. Enter the following information in the table. Press (Tab ⇤) to move between cells in the table.

Service	Annual Sales
Mango Facial	$19,845
Deep Down and Clean Facial	$36,540
02 Oh My Facial	$21,420
The Basic	$37,320

4. If you will be moving on to the next skill in this chapter, leave the document open to continue working. If not, save the file as directed by your instructor and close it.

Skill 4.15 Inserting Rows and Columns

Once you have created a table, you often find you need more rows or columns. In Word, you can quickly add rows and columns to tables with **insert controls**. Insert controls appear when you roll your mouse over the left edge of a row or the top edge of a column.

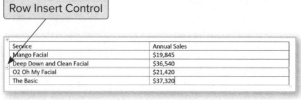

FIGURE WD 4.25

To add a new row using an insert control:

1. Roll your mouse along the left side of the table.

2. When the *insert control* appears where you want to add the new row, click the **control**.

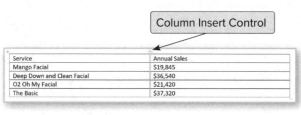

FIGURE WD 4.26

To add a new column using an insert control:

1. Roll your mouse along the top of the table.

2. When the *insert control* appears where you want to add the new column, click the **control**.

tips & tricks

A quick way to insert a new row at the end of a table is to place the cursor in the last cell in the last row and then press Tab. A new row is automatically added to the table, with your cursor in its first cell.

another method

> To insert an additional row and column, you can also click the **Table Tools Layout** tab. In the *Rows & Columns* group, click the **Insert Above** or **Insert Below** buttons to insert a new row. Click the **Insert Left** or **Insert Right** buttons to insert a new column.

> You can also insert rows and columns by right-clicking in a cell, pointing to *Insert*, and selecting **Insert Rows Above**, **Insert Rows Below**, **Insert Columns to the Left**, or **Insert Columns to the Right**.

> You can also insert rows and columns by right-clicking in a cell, clicking the **Insert** button on the Mini toolbar, and selecting an option.

let me try

If you do not have the data file from the previous skill open, open the student data file **wd4-15-SpaProductReport** and try this skill on your own:

1. Navigate to the table in the *Facials* section.

2. Insert a new row between the third and fourth row in the table.

3. Insert a new column between the two columns in the table.

4. If you will be moving on to the next skill in this chapter, leave the document open to continue working. If not, save the file as directed by your instructor and close it.

word 365   chapter 4 Working with Pictures, Tables, and Charts

Skill 4.16 Deleting Columns, Rows, and Cells

After you have added information to your table, you may find that you no longer want to include everything you added. Even if you delete the text in a table row or column, the empty row or column still remains. To remove the row or column from the table, you must delete the row or column, not just the text. When you delete a row or column from a table, the content along with the table element is removed.

To delete a row or column:

1. Select the row or column you want to delete.
2. The Mini toolbar displays.
3. Click the **Delete** button and select an option.

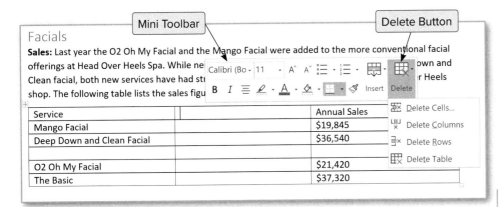

FIGURE WD 4.27

tips & tricks

You can also delete individual cells from a table. When you delete a cell, the *Delete Cells* dialog appears. Here you can choose to shift the cells to the left or up. You can also choose to delete the entire row or column the cell belongs to.

another **method**

To delete rows and columns you can also:

❯ Select the row or column you want to delete. Right-click in the row or column and select **Delete Row** or **Delete Column**.

❯ Click in the row or column you want to delete. Click the **Table Tools Layout** tab. In the *Rows & Columns* group, click the **Delete** button and select an option.

let me **try**

If you do not have the data file from the previous skill open, open the student data file **wd4-16-SpaProductReport** and try this skill on your own:

1. Navigate to the table in the *Facials* section.
2. Delete the **fourth row** in the table.
3. Delete the **second column** in the table.
4. If you will be moving on to the next skill in this chapter, leave the document open to continue working. If not, save the file as directed by your instructor and close it.

Skill 4.17 Sizing Tables, Columns, and Rows

When you insert a table, it covers the full width of the page and the columns and rows are evenly spaced. Once you have entered your data, you will probably find the table is larger than it needs to be and the columns and rows need adjusting. You can resize your table using Word's **AutoFit** commands.

To adjust the width and height of cells using the AutoFit command:

1. Click in the table you want to resize.
2. Click the **Table Tools Layout** tab.
3. In the *Cell Size* group, click the **AutoFit** button.
4. Select **AutoFit Contents** to resize the cell to fit the text of the table. Select **AutoFit Window** to resize the table to the size of the page.

FIGURE WD 4.28

Rather than using the *AutoFit* command, you can specify a width and height for table cells from the Ribbon.

To adjust the width and height of cells:

1. Click in the row or column you want to resize.
2. On the *Table Tools Layout* tab, in the *Cell Size* group, adjust the numbers for the **Table Row Height** and **Table Column Width** by clicking the up and down arrows in the control box.

To resize all the rows in a table so they have the same height, in the *Cell Size* group click the **Distribute Rows** button. Click the **Distribute Columns** to resize all the columns in a table so they have the same width.

FIGURE WD 4.29

tips & tricks

Once you have resized a table, you will probably want to position it better on the page. You can do this by using the **table move handle** tool that appears at the top-left corner of the table when the mouse pointer is placed over the table. Click the move handle and drag the table to where you want it.

tell me **more**

Each cell is set up as one line, but if you type more data than will fit in one line, Word will automatically wrap and create another line within the cell, making the row taller. If this happens, all the cells in that row will be affected.

another **method**

To resize a table, you can also:

1. Select the table you want to resize.

2. When the **resize handle** appears at the bottom right corner of the table, click and drag it until you achieve the desired size. This method can also be used to resize columns and rows.

let me **try**

If you do not have the data file from the previous skill open, open the student data file **wd4-17-SpaProductReport** and try this skill on your own:

1. Navigate to the table in the *Facials* section.

2. Place the cursor in the *Annual Sales* column. Use the **AutoFit** command to resize the table so it fits the content in the column.

3. Change the **column width** of the *Annual Sales* column to: **2.5"**

4. Change the height of the first row to: **.6"**

5. Use the distribute command to change all the rows to the same height.

6. Use the distribute command to change all the columns to the same width.

7. If you will be moving on to the next skill in this chapter, leave the document open to continue working. If not, save the file as directed by your instructor and close it.

Skill 4.18 Merging and Splitting Cells

When you first create a table, it is a grid of rows and columns. But what if you want to display your content across columns or across rows? For instance, if the first row of your table includes the title for the table, then you will probably want to display the title in a single cell that spans all the columns of the table. In this case, you will want to *merge* the cells in the first row into one cell. On the other hand, if you have a cell that contains multiple values, you may want to *split* the cell so it can display each value in a separate row or column. Use the **merge cells** and **split cells** commands to customize the layout of tables. Merging cells entails combining multiple cells into one; splitting a cell divides the cell into multiple cells.

To merge cells in a table:

1. Select the cells you want to merge into one.
2. Click the **Table Tools Layout** tab.
3. In the *Merge* group, click the **Merge Cells** button.

To split a cell in a table:

1. Select the cell you want to split.
2. In the *Merge* group, click the **Split Cells** button.
3. In the *Split Cells* dialog, enter the number of columns and rows.
4. Click **OK** to split the cell.

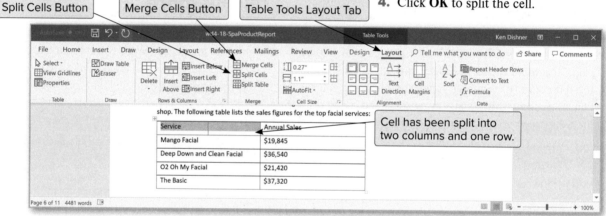

FIGURE WD 4.30

tips & tricks

In addition to splitting cells, you can also split a table, creating two tables from one. To split a table into two tables:

1. Place the cursor in the row where you want to split the table.
2. In the *Merge* group, click the **Split Table** button.

another **method**

❯ To merge cells, you can right-click the selected cells and select **Merge Cells** from the menu.

❯ To split cells, you can right-click a cell and select **Split Cells...** from the menu.

let me **try**

If you do not have the data file from the previous skill open, open the student data file **wd4-18-SpaProductReport** and try this skill on your own:

1. Navigate to the table in the *Facials* section.
2. Split the first cell of the table into two columns and one row.
3. Merge the two cells back into a single cell.
4. If you will be moving on to the next skill in this chapter, leave the document open to continue working. If not, save the file as directed by your instructor and close it.

Skill 4.19 Sorting Data in Tables

After you have entered data in a table, you may decide they need to be displayed in a different order. **Sorting** rearranges the rows in your table by the text in a column or columns. Word allows you to sort data based on the first character of each entry. You can sort in alphabetical or numeric order, in either ascending (A-Z) or descending (Z-A) order.

To sort a column:

1. Click the **Table Tools Layout** tab.
2. In the *Data* group, click the **Sort** button.

FIGURE WD 4.31

3. The *Sort* dialog opens.
4. Click the **Sort by** arrow and select a field to sort by.
5. The *Ascending* radio button is selected by default. If you want to sort the text in reverse order, from Z to A, click the **Descending** radio button.
6. Click the **Type** arrow and select what to sort by: *Text, Number,* or *Date.*
7. If your table has a header row that you do not want to include in the sort, select the **Header row** radio button.
8. Click **OK** to sort the text in the table.

FIGURE WD 4.32

tips & tricks

Word can sort uppercase and lowercase letters differently. Click the **Options...** button in the *Sort* dialog and then click the **Case sensitive** check box in the *Sort Options* dialog.

another **method**

To open the *Sort* dialog, from the *Home* tab, in the *Paragraph* group, click the **Sort** button.

let me **try**

If you do not have the data file from the previous skill open, open the student data file **wd4-19-SpaProductReport** and try this skill on your own:

1. Navigate to the table in the *Facials* section and place the cursor in the first row of the table.
2. Open the **Sort** dialog and sort the table in **descending** order based on the number values in the **annual sales** column.
3. If you will be moving on to the next skill in this chapter, leave the document open to continue working. If not, save the file as directed by your instructor and close it.

Skill 4.20 Applying Table Quick Styles

Just as you can apply complex formatting to paragraphs using styles for text, you can apply complex formatting to tables using Quick Styles for tables. Using Quick Styles for tables, you can change the text color along with the borders and shading for a table, giving it a professional, sophisticated look without a lot of work.

To apply a Quick Style to a table:

1. Click the **Table Tools Design** tab.
2. In the *Table Styles* group, click the **More** button ⤓.
3. Select a style from the *Quick Styles* gallery.

FIGURE WD 4.33

By default, the Word *Table Styles* gallery displays styles that include header rows, banded rows, and first column layouts. Depending on the information in your table, you may not want to format your table using all these options.

To change the options that display in the *Table Styles* gallery:

1. Click the **Table Tools Design** tab.
2. In the *Table Style Options* group, select an option so it appears with a checkmark in the box to include that option in the *Table Styles* gallery.
3. Click an option again to remove the checkmark and remove the option from the *Table Styles* gallery.
4. As you check and uncheck options, open the *Table Styles* gallery to see how the changes affect the available table styles.

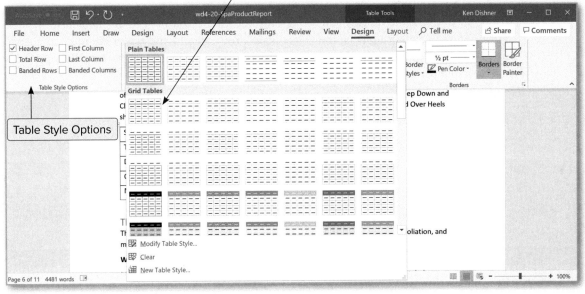

Notice the options in the *Quick Style* gallery have changed.

FIGURE WD 4.34

tips & tricks

To create your own table style, click the **More** button and select **New Table Style....** In the *Create New Style from Formatting* dialog, you can create a new table style based on an existing table style, changing options such as gridlines and shading to suit your needs. When you save the style, it will appear in the *Table Styles* gallery.

tell me more

In addition to applying a Quick Style to a table, you can change the shading, or background color, applied to the table. Adding shading to a table helps it stand out on a page. To apply shading to a table, click the **Shading** button in the *Table Styles* group. A palette of colors displays. Select a color to change the background color for the table.

another method

The *Table Styles* group on the Ribbon displays the latest Quick Styles you have used. If you want to apply a recently used Quick Style, you can click the option directly from the Ribbon without opening the *Quick Styles* gallery.

let me try

If you do not have the data file from the previous skill open, open the student data file **wd4-20-SpaProductReport** and try this skill on your own:

1. Navigate to the table in the *Facials* section.
2. Change the *Quick Style* gallery display so formats with **first column** and **banded row** formatting do not display. Only *Header row* should be selected.
3. Apply the **List Table 3-Accent 1** Quick Style to the table. It is in the *List Tables* section of the gallery (see Figure WD 4.34).
4. If you will be moving on to the next skill in this chapter, leave the document open to continue working. If not, save the file as directed by your instructor and close it.

Skill 4.21 Adding Borders to a Table

When you first create a table, it uses the simple grid style. You can apply a Quick Style to your table to quickly add formatting, but what if you want to further adjust the look of a table after applying the Quick Style? You can add and remove borders to change the look of the entire table or just parts of the table. The *Border Styles* gallery provides a number of predesigned **border styles** from which to choose.

To change the border style for a table:

1. Click the **Table Tools Design** tab.
2. In the *Borders* group, click the **Border Styles** button.
3. Select an option from the gallery.

FIGURE WD 4.35

To change the borders for a table:

1. Select the table you want to change.
2. Click the **Table Tools Design** tab.
3. In the *Borders* group, click the **Borders** button arrow.
4. Click a border option to apply it to the table.

If your table does not show borders, you can display **gridlines** to give you a visual guide. The gridlines appear as a dotted line onscreen but do not print as part of the final document. To display gridlines, click the **Borders** button and select **View Gridlines**.

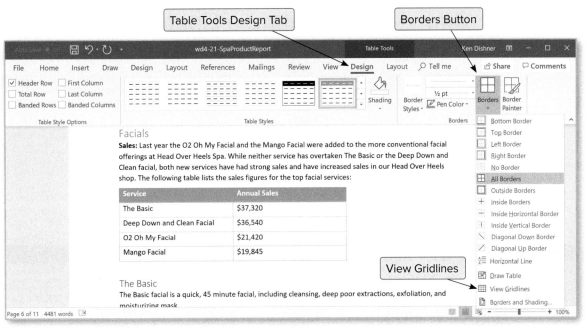

FIGURE WD 4.36

tell me more

When you select a border style, the **Border Painter** becomes active. This feature allows you to quickly apply borders to tables. When the *Border Painter* is active, the cursor changes to a paintbrush. Click a border along the edge of a cell to apply the selected border style to that cell's border.

another method

〉 You can also change the borders of a table by clicking the **Home** tab. In the *Paragraph* group, click the arrow next to the **Borders** button and select an option.

〉 You can change borders and shading through the *Borders and Shading* dialog. To open the *Borders and Shading* dialog:

- From the *Home* tab or from the *Design* tab, click the arrow next to the *Borders* button and select **Borders and Shading....**
- Right-click on the table and select **Borders and Shading...** from the menu.

let me try

If you do not have the data file from the previous skill open, open the student data file **wd4-21-SpaProductReport** and try this skill on your own:

1. Navigate to the table in the *Facials* section and select the table.
2. Display **gridlines** in the table.
3. Change the *Border Style* to **Single solid line, ½ point, Accent 1**.
4. Apply the **all borders** option to the table.

skill 4.21   Adding Borders to a Table

Skill 4.22 Creating a Chart

Charts allow you to take raw data and display them in a visual way. A **chart** takes the values you have entered in a spreadsheet and converts them to graphic representation. In Word, you can create a wide variety of charts, including bar charts, pie charts, column charts, and line charts.

To add a chart to a document:

1. Click the **Insert** tab.
2. In the *Illustrations* group, click the **Chart** button.

FIGURE WD 4.37

3. In the *Insert Chart* dialog, click a chart type category to display that category in the right pane.
4. Click a chart type in the right pane to select it.
5. Click **OK** to add the chart to the document.

FIGURE WD 4.38

Word automatically opens the *Chart in Microsoft Word* dialog. Think of this dialog as a simplified spreadsheet where you can enter the data for your chart. The dialog opens with sample data entered for you.

1. Replace the sample data with your own data.
2. Click the **Close** button to return to Word to see your finished chart.

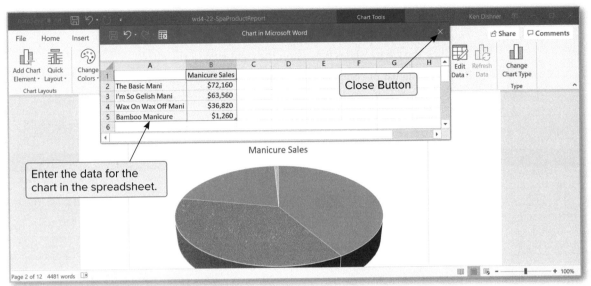

FIGURE WD 4.39

tell me **more**

As you enter data in the *Chart in Microsoft Word* dialog, Word will update the chart as you enter data and move from cell to cell in the spreadsheet.

let me **try**

If you do not have the data file from the previous skill open, open the student data file **wd4-22-SpaProductReport** and try this skill on your own:

1. Navigate to the *Manicures and Pedicures* section and place the cursor in the blank line below the table.
2. Insert a **3-D pie chart** into the document.
3. Enter the following information for the chart:

	Manicure Sales
The Basic Mani	$72,160
I'm so Gelish Mani	$63,560
Wax On Wax Off Mani	$36,820
Bamboo Manicure	$ 1,260

4. If you will be moving on to the next skill in this chapter, leave the document open to continue working. If not, save the file as directed by your instructor and close it.

Skill 4.23 Modifying a Chart

When you insert a chart, Word displays the chart based on the chart type and the document's theme. But what if you want to change the look of your chart? Word includes a number of **chart styles** for you to choose from. These styles are a combination of chart layout styles and formatting options.

To change the style of a chart:

1. Select the chart you want to change.
2. Click the **Chart Styles** button on the right side of the chart.
3. Scroll the list of styles. Click a style to apply it to the chart.

FIGURE WD 4.40

Chart Styles Button

Select a chart style to apply to the chart.

Showing and hiding chart elements, such as the chart title, legend, and data labels, can make a chart easier to read. The **chart title** is a text box that overlays the chart and is typically located above the chart. The **chart legend** tells you which color represents the categories in the chart. **Chart data labels** display the values that go with the categories in the chart.

To show and hide chart elements:

1. Select the chart you want to change.
2. Click the **Chart Elements** button on the right side of the chart.
3. Click the check boxes to show or hide chart elements.

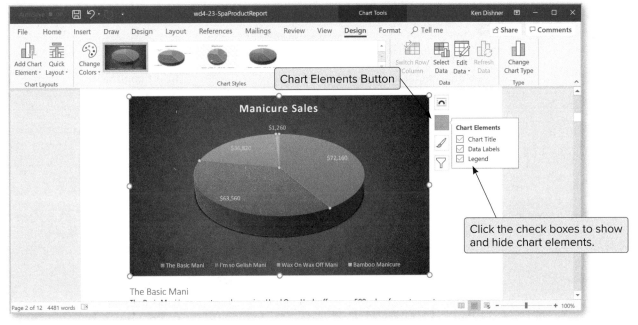

FIGURE WD 4.41

tips & tricks

To change the color of the chart, click the **Color** button in the *Chart Styles* pane. Word displays a number of color sets for you to choose from. These color sets are based on the color theme applied to the document. Select a color set to apply to the chart.

tell me **more**

The available chart elements will change depending on the type of chart in your document. For example, bar charts include *axes*, *axis title*, and *gridlines* as chart elements you can turn on and off.

another **method**

❯ To change the chart style, you can also click the **Chart Tools Design** tab. In the *Chart Styles* group, click the style you want to use, or click the **More** button to see all of the chart styles available.

❯ To show and hide chart elements, you can also click the **Chart Tools Design** tab. In the *Chart Layouts* group, click the **Add Chart Elements** button, point to the chart element you want, and click an option.

let me **try**

If you do not have the data file from the previous skill open, open the student data file **wd4-23-SpaProductReport** and try this skill on your own:

1. Select the chart in the *Manicures and Pedicures* section.

2. Apply the **Style 7** chart style to the chart.

3. Show the **data labels** on the chart.

4. Save the file as directed by your instructor and close it.

key terms

Alt text
Online pictures
Creative Commons
Resize handle
Layout Options
Alignment guides
Move cursor
Quick Styles
Icons
SmartArt
Shape
WordArt
Table
Rows
Columns
Cell
Quick Tables

Table move handle
Insert controls
AutoFit
Distribute Rows
Distribute Columns
Merge cells
Split cells
Sorting
Border styles
Gridlines
Border Painter
Chart
Chart styles
Chart title
Chart legend
Chart data labels

concept review

1. Which of the following is a description of a picture, chart, or other object that can be read by screen readers?

   a. ToolTip

   b. text box

   c. alt text

   d. AutoText

2. Which button would you click to add a picture you have saved to your OneDrive account?

   a. *Pictures*

   b. *Online Picture*

   c. *Icons*

   d. *Shapes*

3. Which button would you click to wrap text around a picture?

   a. *Layout Options*

   b. *Group*

   c. *Align*

   d. *Rotate*

4. Alignment guides are lines that are always visible onscreen and help you align pictures with other elements in the document.

   a. true

   b. false

5. Which of the following is a combination of formatting, including color, shadows, and reflections, that you apply to pictures?

   a. Quick Style

   b. Style Set

c. Picture Effect

d. Artistic Effect

6. Which of the following are added to a document as an SVG image?

a. pictures

b. SmartArt

c. icons

d. shapes

7. Visual diagrams containing graphic elements with text boxes for you to enter your information in are called SmartArt.

a. true

b. false

8. Which of the following are preset drawing objects, such as block arrows and callouts, that you can quickly add to your document?

a. charts

b. SmartArt

c. pictures

d. shapes

9. Which key would you press to move to the next cells in a table?

a. Enter

b. Tab

c. Shift

d. Alt

10. The Distribute Columns command resizes all the columns in a table so they are the same width.

a. true

b. false

projects

skill review **4.1**

In this project you will be editing a marketing brochure for Suarez Marketing. You will add graphic elements to the brochure such as an icon, pictures, and SmartArt. You will then modify the pictures by applying a style and changing the layout, size, and placement. You will organize information in a table and then modify the table.

Skills needed to complete this project:

- Adding Icons (Skill 4.9)
- Inserting Online Pictures (Skill 4.4)
- Resizing Pictures (Skill 4.5)
- Changing Picture Layouts (Skill 4.6)
- Moving Pictures (Skill 4.7)
- Inserting SmartArt (Skill 4.10)
- Creating a Table (Skill 4.13)
- Working with Tables (Skill 4.14)
- Inserting Rows and Columns (Skill 4.15)
- Merging and Splitting Cells (Skill 4.18)
- Sizing Tables, Columns, and Rows (Skill 4.17)
- Applying Table Quick Styles (Skill 4.20)
- Adding Borders to a Table (Skill 4.21)
- Inserting a Picture (Skill 4.1)
- Positioning Pictures (Skill 4.2)
- Adding Alt Text to Pictures (Skill 4.3)

1. Open the start file **WD2019-SkillReview-4-1** and resave the file as: [your initials]WD-SkillReview-4-1

2. If the document opens in Protected View, click the **Enable Editing** button in the Message Bar at the top of the document so you can modify the document.

3. Insert an icon.

    a. Place the cursor at the beginning of the heading *Our Goal*.

    b. Click the **Insert** tab.

    c. In the *Illustrations* group, click the **Icons** button.

    d. Navigate to the *Analytics* category and click the icon of the **target with an arrow**.

    e. Click the **Insert** button.

4. Modify an icon.

    a. With the icon selected, on the *Graphics Tools Format* tab, in the *Size* group, type **.5"** in the *Height* box and **.5"** in the *Width* box.

    b. On the *Graphics Tools Format* tab, in the *Graphics Styles* group, click the **More** button and select the **Colored Fill – Accent 6, No Outline** option. It is the last option in the second row of the gallery.

5. Insert an online picture.

    a. Place the cursor in the blank line above the *Client Quotes* heading.

    b. Click the **Insert** tab.

    c. In the *Illustrations* group, click the **Online Pictures** button.

    d. In the *Bing Search* box, type **company communication** and press ⏎ Enter .

    e. Select a photograph of your choice and click the **Insert** button.

6. Resize a picture.

    a. Verify the picture and credit that were inserted are selected.

    b. Click and drag a corner resize handle until the height of the object is approximately **1.5"** tall.

7. Change the layout on a picture.

    a. With the picture and credit still selected, click the **Layout Options** button.

    b. Select the **Tight** wrapping option.

    c. Click outside the *Layout Options* box to hide it.

8. Move a picture.

    a. Click and drag the picture and credit to the right.

    b. Using the alignment guides, place the object so the top of it is aligned with the top of the first quote in the *Client Quotes* section and the left side of it is aligned with the left side of the quote text. See Figure WD 4.42.

FIGURE WD 4.42

9. Insert a *SmartArt* diagram.

    a. Place the cursor in the empty line in the *Our Process* section.

    b. Click the **Insert** tab.

    c. In the *Illustrations* group, click the **SmartArt** button.

    d. Click the **Cycle** category and click the **Circle Arrow Process** option. Click **OK**.

    e. In the upper left segment, type: **Analyze Needs**

    f. In the upper right segment, type: **Design Project**

    g. In the lower segment, type: **Implement Campaign**

    h. Click outside the diagram to deselect it.

10. Add a table to the document and enter text into the table.

    a. Place the cursor in the empty line under the heading *THE SUAREZ MARKETING BELIEF SYSTEM*.

    b. Click the **Insert** tab.

    c. In the *Tables* group, click the **Table** button and select a **2 × 1 (two columns and one row)** table.

d. Type the information below into the table. Press (Tab ⇥) to move forward from cell to cell. Press (Tab ⇥) at the end of a row to insert a new row.

Commitment	Putting the needs of the client first
Communication	Seek first to listen
Trust	Begins with open communication
Integrity	Doing the right thing
Customers	Always come first
Teamwork	Working together for success
Creativity	Ideas and know-how
Win-Win	Is always the goal
Success	Results with integrity

11. Insert a row.

   a. Place the cursor in the first row of the table.

   b. Click the **Table Tools Layout** tab.

   c. In the *Rows & Columns* group, click the **Insert Above** button.

   d. Type: **Suarez Marketing Beliefs**

   e. Apply the following formatting to the text:

      i. Font: **Calibri**

      ii. Size: **14 pt**

      iii. Color: **Ice Blue, Accent 1, Darker 50%**. It is the fifth option in the last row under *Theme Colors* in the color palette.

12. Merge cells in a table.

   a. Select the first row in the table.

   b. Click the **Table Tools Layout** tab.

   c. In the *Merge* group, click the **Merge Cells** button.

13. Change the height of rows in a table.

   a. Select the table.

   b. On the *Table Tools Layout* tab, in the *Cell Size* group, type **.25"** in the *Height* box.

14. Apply a Quick Style to the table.

   a. Click the **Table Tools Design** tab.

   b. In *Table Style Options* group, click the **First Column** check box so it is deselected.

   c. In the *Table Styles* group, click the **More** button.

   d. In the *List Tables* section, select the **Grid Table Light 1** Quick Style. It is the first option in the *Grid* section of the gallery.

15. Select a border style.

   a. On the *Table Tools Design* tab, in the *Borders* group, click the **Border Styles** button.

   b. Select the **Single solid line, ½ point** border style (it is the first option in the second row of the gallery).

16. Apply a border to the table
    a. Verify the table is selected.
    b. In the *Borders* group, click the **Borders** button.
    c. Select **Outside Border**.

17. Insert a logo from a location on your computer.
    a. Navigate to the beginning of the document and place the cursor in the blank line above the *Experience* heading.
    b. Click the **Insert** tab.
    c. In the *Illustrations* group, click the **Pictures** button.
    d. In the *Insert Picture* dialog, browse to your student data file location, select the **Suarez logo** file, and click the **Insert** button.

18. Position the logo on the page.
    a. On the *Picture Tools Format* tab, in the *Arrange* group, click the **Position** button.
    b. Select the **Position in Top Left with Square Text Wrapping** option (it is the first option under *With Text Wrapping*).
    c. Delete the blank line above the *Experience* heading.

19. Add alt text to the picture.
    a. Right-click the image of the logo and select **Edit Alt Text**.
    b. In the *Alt Text* task pane, type **Suarez Marketing logo**.
    c. Click the **X** in the upper right corner of the task pane to close it.

20. Save and close the document.

skill review **4.2**

In this project you will be editing a document for the Tri-State Book Festival. You will add graphic elements to the document including WordArt, an icon, a shape, and pictures. You will add alt text to a picture. You will adjust the look of images by adding Quick Styles and resizing them. You will organize data in a table and create and modify a chart of information.

Skills needed to complete this project:

- Adding WordArt to Documents (Skill 4.12)
- Changing Picture Layouts (Skill 4.6)
- Adding Icons (Skill 4.9)
- Moving Pictures (Skill 4.7)
- Adding Alt Text to Pictures (Skill 4.3)
- Inserting a Shape (Skill 4.11)
- Resizing Pictures (Skill 4.5)
- Applying Quick Styles to Pictures (Skill 4.8)
- Creating a Chart (Skill 4.22)
- Modifying a Chart (Skill 4.23)
- Working with Tables (Skill 4.14)
- Deleting Columns, Rows, and Cells (Skill 4.16)
- Merging and Splitting Cells (Skill 4.18)

- Inserting Rows and Columns (Skill 4.15)
- Sorting Data in Tables (Skill 4.19)
- Applying Table Quick Styles (Skill 4.20)

1. Open the start file **WD2019-SkillReview-4-2** and resave the file as: `[your initials]WD-SkillReview-4-2`

2. If the document opens in Protected View, click the **Enable Editing** button in the Message Bar at the top of the document so you can modify the document.

3. Add WordArt to a document.

   a. Place the cursor at the top of the document.

   b. Click the **Insert** tab.

   c. In the *Text* group, click the **WordArt** button.

   d. Select the **Fill: Green, Accent color 1, Shadow** WordArt style (the second option in the first row of the gallery).

   e. Type **The Tri-State Book Festival** and drag the WordArt object to the top of the document.

   f. Select the text you typed.

   g. Click the **Home** tab. In the *Font* group, click the **Font Size** arrow, and select **26**.

4. Change the layout of the WordArt.

   a. Click the **Layout Options** button. If you don't see the *Layout Options* button, select the WordArt object to display it.

   b. Select the **In Line with Text** option.

   c. Click outside the *Layout Options* box to hide it.

5. Insert an icon.

   a. Click the **Insert** tab.

   b. In the *Illustrations* group, click the **Icons** button.

   c. Navigate to the *Education* section and select **3 stacked books** option.

   d. Click the **Insert** button.

6. Modify the icon.

   a. On the *Graphics Tools Format* tab, apply **Colored Fill – Accent 1, Dark 1 Outline** style to the icon. It is the second option in the third row of the gallery.

   b. Click the **Layout Options** button and select the **Square** option.

7. Move the icon using alignment guides.

   a. If necessary, select the icon you inserted.

   b. Click and drag the icon so it is aligned vertically with the WordArt text and the right side of the icon is aligned with the right side of the paragraph text. See Figure WD 4.43.

The Tri-State Book Festival

The Tri-State Book festival will take place this year from September 6-8 at the Westfield Hotel & Spa in Davidsonville, Virginia. This year looks to be one of the best festivals yet; there will be authors from a wide range of genres (both fiction and nonfiction) reading from their latest works and answering questions from audience members. Over 40 publishing houses will be exhibiting their top offerings along with great giveaways for attendees.

FIGURE WD 4.43

word 365 chapter 4 Working with Pictures, Tables, and Charts

8. Add alt text to an image.

   a. Right-click the icon and select **Edit Alt Text**.

   b. In the *Alt Text* task pane, if there is a text description, delete it. Type `line drawing of three stacked books` as the alt text for the icon.

9. Insert a shape.

   a. Navigate to the *Authors* section of the document.

   b. In the *Illustrations* group, click the **Shapes** button and select **Star: 5 Points** option in the *Stars and Banners* section.

   c. The cursor changes to a crosshair cursor.

   d. Click to the right of the text *Authors* to add the star shape.

10. Apply a Quick Style to a shape.

    a. Verify the star shape is selected.

    b. On the *Drawing Tools Format* tab, in the *Shape Styles* group, click the **More** button.

    c. In the *Shape Quick Styles* gallery, select **Subtle Effect - Green, Accent 1** (it is the second option in the fourth row under *Theme Styles*).

11. Change the size, layout options, and location of the shape.

    a. Verify the star shape is selected.

    b. On the *Drawing Tools Format* tab, click in the *Height* box and type **.7"**. Click in the *Width* box and type **.7"** and press Enter.

    c. Click the **Layout Options** button and select the **Square** option.

    d. Click and drag the icon so it is aligned vertically with the heading text and the left side of the shape is aligned with the left side of the *Fiction* list. See Figure WD 4.44.

FIGURE WD 4.44

12. Add a chart to the document.

    a. Place the cursor in the empty line below the line *The following chart shows the breakdown of authors by genre:*.

    b. Click the **Insert** tab.

    c. In the *Illustrations* group, click the **Chart** button.

    d. In the *Insert Chart* dialog, click the **Pie** category on the left.

    e. Click the **3-D Pie** option (the second option) is selected.

    f. Click **OK**.

g. In the *Chart in Microsoft Word* dialog, change the data in the chart to match the table below:

	Authors
Fiction General	4
Crime Fiction	2
Non-Fiction General	2
Lifestyle	3

h. Click the **Close** button in the *Chart in Microsoft Word* dialog.

13. Modify the look of the chart.

    a. On the *Chart Design* tab, in the *Chart Styles* group, click the **More** tab.

    b. Scroll the list of chart styles and rest your mouse over each style to see the name of the style. Select the **Style 8** option.

    c. Click outside the chart to deselect it.

14. Delete rows from tables.

    a. Navigate to the *Agenda* section.

    b. In the first table, select the row with the text *Thursday September 6*.

    c. Click the **Table Tools Layout** tab.

    d. In the *Rows & Columns* group, click the **Delete** button.

    e. Click **Delete Rows**.

    f. Repeat these steps to delete the first row of the other two tables in this section.

15. Merge cells in a table.

    a. In the *Thursday September 6* table, select the **Book signing and dinner cell** and the **two empty cells** to the right.

    b. On the *Table Tools Layout* tab, in the *Merge* group, click the **Merge Cells** button.

16. Insert a row to a table.

    a. In the *Thursday September 6* table, place the cursor in the *3:00-4:00 cell*.

    b. Move the cursor to the left until you see the *Insert Row* button above the cell.

    c. Click the **Insert Row** button to add a new blank row.

    d. In the blank cell under *Time*, type: **1:30-3:00**

    e. In the blank cell under *The Washington Theater*, type: **Welcome and Keynote**.

17. Sort data in a table.

    a. In the *Friday September 7* table, select all the rows except the first row.

    b. On the *Table Tools Layout* tab, in the *Data* group, click the **Sort** button.

    c. Verify the column will sort in ascending order, by **Column 1**, using the text in the paragraphs.

    d. Click **OK**.

18. Apply Quick Styles to tables.

    a. Select the **Thursday September 6** table.

    b. Click the **Table Tools Design** tab.

    c. In the *Table Style Options* group, uncheck the **Banded Rows** option. *Header Row* and *First Column* should be the only options selected.

d. In the *Table Styles* group, click the **More** button.

e. In the *Grid Tables* section, click the **Grid Table 1 Light - Accent 1**. It is the second option in the *Grid* section of the gallery.

f. Apply this table Quick Style to the other two tables in the *Agenda*. Be sure to uncheck the **Banded Row** option in the *Table Style Options* group before applying the Quick Style.

19. Save and close the document.

challenge yourself **4.3**

In this project you will be editing a document from Greenscapes landscaping company. You will add an icon and resize and position the icon in the document. You will add a SmartArt diagram and a picture from your computer to the document. Finally, you will organize information in a table and then format the table by applying Quick Styles and borders.

Skills needed to complete this project:

- Adding Icons (Skill 4.9)
- Resizing Pictures (Skill 4.5)
- Changing Picture Layouts (Skill 4.6)
- Moving Pictures (Skill 4.7)
- Inserting SmartArt (Skill 4.10)
- Inserting a Picture (Skill 4.1)
- Positioning Pictures (Skill 4.2)
- Creating a Table (Skill 4.13)
- Working with Tables (Skill 4.14)
- Sorting Data in Tables (Skill 4.19)
- Inserting Rows and Columns (Skill 4.15)
- Merging and Splitting Cells (Skill 4.18)
- Sizing Tables, Columns, and Rows (Skill 4.17)
- Applying Table Quick Styles (Skill 4.20)
- Adding Borders to a Table (Skill 4.21)

1. Open the start file **WD2019-ChallengeYourself-4-3** and resave the file as: [your initials]WD-ChallengeYourself-4-3

2. If the document opens in Protected View, click the **Enable Editing** button in the Message Bar at the top of the document so you can modify the document.

3. Place the cursor before the *Our Way of Life* heading and insert an icon of a **watering can**. *Hint*: It is in the *Home* section of the dialog.

4. Change the height of the icon to be **.75"** and the width of the icon to be **.75"**.

5. Apply the **Colored Fill – Accent 1, Dark 1 Outline** style option to the icon. It is the second option in the third row of the gallery.

6. Apply the **Tight** layout option to the icon.

7. Move the icon so it is aligned under the *Our Way of Life* heading with the paragraph text displayed to the right. Use the guides so the top of the icon is aligned with the top of the paragraph text and the left side of the icon is aligned with the left side of the heading text. See Figure WD 4.45.

Our Way of Life

Greenscapes uses only natural, organic techniques. Not only do we not use chemical fertilizers or pesticides, but we focus on using composting materials found in the natural lifecycle of the ecosystem. In addition to our organic lawn care system, Greenscapes is dedicated to creating natural, organic landscapes using all native species. Every effort has been made to reduce our carbon footprint, including using all electric and solar powered motors in our mowers, trimmers, and leaf blowers.

FIGURE WD 4.45

8. Insert a *SmartArt* diagram.

   a. Place the cursor in the empty line after the first paragraph in the *Leaf and Debris Removal* section.

   b. Insert a **Chevron Accent Process** SmartArt diagram.

   c. Enter `Blow and Rake` in the first box.

   d. Enter `Gather and Haul Away` in the second box.

   e. Enter `Compost` in the third box.

9. Navigate to the *What We Provide* section of the document. Place the cursor before the *Lawn Care Plans* heading. Insert the **greenscapes_logo** picture from your student data file location.

10. Change the position of the logo so it appears **centered at the of the page with square wrapping**.

11. Resize the logo to be **.6"** tall and **4.55"** wide.

12. Place the cursor at the end of the document. Insert a table with the following information:

Lawn Maintenance	Fertilization, Insect and Disease Control	$150.00 per treatment
Shrub and Tree Maintenance	Pruning, Fertilization, Insect and Disease Control	$75.00 per hour
Leaf Removal	Composting Included	$25.00 per hour
Lawn Care	Mowing, Edging, Weed-eating	$20.00 per service (weekly) $30.00 per service (bi-weekly)
All Four Services	10% Customer Discount	
Specialty Services	As Requested	Call for a quote

13. Select the first four rows of the table. Sort the text in the selected row in ascending order based on the first column.

14. Insert a new row above the first row in the table. Type `Our Services and Pricing` in the first cell.

15. Change the font of the text to be **Candara, 14 pt**.

16. Merge the three cells in the first row of the table.

17. Change the height of the first row in the table to be **0.4"** tall.

18. Change the table Quick Styles to show styles without the first column formatted. Apply the **Grid Table 4 Dark - Accent 1** Quick Style to the table. It is in the *Grid Styles* section of the gallery.

19. Change the border style to **Single Solid Line, 1 1/2 pt, Accent 1** option. It is the second option in the second row of the gallery.

20. Apply **all borders** to the entire table.

21. Save and close the document.

challenge yourself **4.4**

In this project you will be editing a document from the Winter Springs community. You will add WordArt and pictures to the document. You will add alt text to a picture. You will modify the size and position of pictures and apply a Quick Style to a picture. Finally, you will create a table and add data to the table and then display the data as a chart.

Skills needed to complete this project:

- Adding WordArt to Documents (Skill 4.12)
- Changing Picture Layouts (Skill 4.6)
- Creating a Chart (Skill 4.22)
- Modifying a Chart (Skill 4.23)
- Working with Tables (Skill 4.14)
- Inserting Rows and Columns (Skill 4.15)
- Deleting Columns, Rows, and Cells (Skill 4.16)
- Sorting Data in Tables (Skill 4.19)
- Applying Table Quick Styles (Skill 4.20)
- Inserting a Picture (Skill 4.1)
- Adding Alt Text to Pictures (Skill 4.3)
- Resizing Pictures (Skill 4.5)
- Positioning Pictures (Skill 4.2)
- Applying Quick Styles to Pictures (Skill 4.8)

1. Open the start file **WD2019-ChallengeYourself-4-4** and resave the file as: `[your initials]WD-ChallengeYourself-4-4`

2. If the document opens in Protected View, click the **Enable Editing** button in the Message Bar at the top of the document so you can modify the document.

3. Add WordArt to a document.
   a. Place the cursor at the top of the document (not in the header).
   b. Insert WordArt using the **Fill: Black, Text color 1; Shadow** style.
   c. Change the WordArt text to: `Winter Springs Community News`

4. Change the layout of the WordArt to be in line with the text.

5. Add a chart to the document.
   a. Place the cursor on the blank line after the first paragraph in the *Most Targeted Electronic Devices* section.
   b. Insert a **Clustered Bar** chart.
   c. Change the data in the chart to match the table below.

	Month 1	Month 2	Month 3
GPS Devices	7	10	9
Laptop Computers	12	14	13
Smartphones	18	21	19
Tablet Computers	13	15	12

6. Modify the look of the chart.

   a. Apply the **Style 6** Quick Style to the chart.

   b. Hide the chart title on the chart.

7. Add a column and a row to a table.

   a. Place the cursor in the first cell in the table under the *Upcoming Safety Improvements* section.

   b. Add a column to the right of the existing column.

   c. Place the cursor in the first cell again and insert a row above the first row in the table.

8. Enter data in a table.

   a. In the first cell of the new row, type: **Improvement**

   b. In the second cell of the new row, type: **Approval Status**

   c. Add the status for each modification as shown in the table below.

Improvement	Approval Status
New security gates	**Approved**
Motion sensing security cameras	**Waiting for Approval**
App for reporting incidents	**Denied**
Electric security vehicles	**Approved**
Smartphone entrance for all garages	**Finished**
Reinforcements to perimeter fence	**Approved**
Weekly security meetings with staff	**Approved**

9. Delete the fourth row in the table (the row with the *Denied* status).

10. Apply a Quick Style to the table.

    a. Change the table *Quick Styles* to show styles without the first column formatted.

    b. Apply the **Grid Table 4 – Accent 2** style to the table. It is in the *Grid Styles* section of the gallery.

    c. Apply the same table style to the table in the *Security Meeting Schedule* section. Be sure to deselect the *First Column* option.

11. Sort data in a table.

    a. Select the table in the *Security Meeting Schedule* section.

    b. Sort the table in ascending order based on the **date** in the first column.

12. Insert a picture from a location on your computer.

    a. Place the cursor at the end of the first paragraph in the *Security Staff* section.

    b. Insert the **security-badge** picture from your student data file location.

13. Add the following description as alt text for the picture of the badge: **Security Enforcement Officer badge**

14. Resize the picture so the height is **1.75"** and the width is **1.99"**.

15. Position the picture using the **Position in Bottom Right with Square Text Wrapping** option.

16. Apply the **Drop Shadow Rectangle** Quick Style to the picture. It is the fourth option in the gallery.

17. Save and close the document.

In this project you will be editing a paper on a behavior change project. You will add and modify pictures in the document. You will display information in a table and then display that information in a chart.

Skills needed to complete this project:

- Inserting Online Pictures (Skill 4.4)
- Adding Alt Text to Pictures (Skill 4.3)
- Resizing Pictures (Skill 4.5)
- Changing Picture Layouts (Skill 4.6)
- Moving Pictures (Skill 4.7)
- Applying Quick Styles to Pictures (Skill 4.8)
- Creating a Table (Skill 4.13)
- Working with Tables (Skill 4.14)
- Inserting Rows and Columns (Skill 4.15)
- Merging and Splitting Cells (Skill 4.18)
- Sorting Data in Tables (Skill 4.19)
- Applying Table Quick Styles (Skill 4.20)
- Creating a Chart (Skill 4.22)
- Modifying a Chart (Skill 4.23)

1. Open the start file **WD2019-OnYourOwn-4-5** and resave the file as: `[your initials]WD-OnYourOwn-4-5`

2. If the document opens in Protected View, click the **Enable Editing** button in the Message Bar at the top of the document so you can modify the document.

3. From the *Online Pictures* dialog, use *Bing* to search for pictures of students raising their hands. Insert a picture of your choice.

4. Add an appropriate alt text description to the picture.

5. Resize the picture so it fits well in the document.

6. Change the layout options on the picture to wrap with the text.

7. Move the picture so it appears to the right of the first paragraph of the document.

8. Apply a Quick Style of your choice to the picture.

9. Place the cursor in the blank line above the *Totals* line in the *Observation Phase* section. Insert a table for the four columns of data in the section and move the text from the section into the table. When you are finished, delete any extra blank lines.

10. Place the cursor in the blank line above the *Totals* line in the *Implementation Phase* section. Insert a table for the four columns of data in the section and move the text from the section into the table. When you are finished, delete any extra blank lines.

11. Sort the data in the *Implementation Phase* table so the dates appear in ascending order.

12. Insert a new row to the top of the *Implementation Phase* table. In the first cell of the new row, type **Date**. In the second cell of the new row, type **Raises Hand**. In the third cell of the new row, type **Does Not Raise Hand**. In the fourth cell of the new row, type **Percentage**.

13. Format the information in the *Implementation Phase* table so it matches the formatting in the *Observation Phase* table.

14. Insert a new row to the top of the *Observation Phase* table. Cut the text **Observation Phase** and paste it into the first cell of the new table. Merge the cells in the new row.

15. Insert a new row to the top of the *Implementation Phase* table. Cut the text **Implementation Phase** and paste it into the first cell of the new table. Merge the cells in the new row.

16. Apply a Quick Style of your choice to the **Observation Phase** table.

17. Apply the same Quick Style to the **Implementation Phase** table.

18. Place the cursor in the blank line below the *Totals* line in the *Observation Phase* section. Add a **pie chart** of your choice using the information in the *Totals* rows.

19. Place the cursor in the blank line below the *Totals* line in the *Implementation Phase* section. Add the same **pie chart** type as the previous step using the information in the *Totals* rows.

20. Change the style of each of the charts to one of your choice.

21. Modify the charts so the titles do not appear on the chart.

22. Save and close the document.

fix it 4.6

In this project you will be correcting a marketing brochure from Suarez Marketing. You will fix problems with pictures, including resizing and positioning pictures for a better layout and editing the alt text of a picture. You will replace a shape with an icon and then format that icon. You will display information in a SmartArt diagram and modify the structure and appearance of a table.

Skills needed to complete this project:
- Positioning Pictures (Skill 4.2)
- Adding Alt Text to Pictures (Skill 4.3)
- Adding Icons (Skill 4.9)
- Inserting SmartArt (Skill 4.10)
- Resizing Pictures (Skill 4.5)
- Changing Picture Layouts (Skill 4.6)
- Moving Pictures (Skill 4.7)
- Applying Quick Styles to Pictures (Skill 4.8)
- Working with Tables (Skill 4.14)
- Inserting Rows and Columns (Skill 4.15)
- Deleting Columns, Rows, and Cells (Skill 4.16)
- Sizing Tables, Columns, and Rows (Skill 4.17)
- Merging and Splitting Cells (Skill 4.18)
- Sorting Data in Tables (Skill 4.19)
- Applying Table Quick Styles (Skill 4.20)
- Adding Borders to a Table (Skill 4.21)

1. Open the start file **WD2019-FixIt-4-6** and resave the file as: [your initials]WD-FixIt-4-6

2. If the document opens in Protected View, click the **Enable Editing** button in the Message Bar at the top of the document so you can modify the document.

word 365   chapter 4 Working with Pictures, Tables, and Charts

3. Select the **Suarez Marketing** logo in the middle of the first page. Position the picture to be in the upper left corner of the page with square wrapping.

4. Edit the alt text of the logo to read **Suarez Marketing logo**.

5. Delete the explosion shape next to the *Our Goal* heading.

6. Insert an icon of a **target with an arrow**. *Hint*: It is in the *Analytics* section of the dialog.

7. Change the height of the icon to be **.6"** and the width of the icon to be **.6"**.

8. Apply the **Colored Fill – Accent 6, No Outline** style option to the icon. It is the last option in the second row of the gallery.

9. Navigate to *Our Process* section and place the cursor in the blank line above the bulleted list. Insert a **Circle Process** diagram.

10. Cut and paste the items from the bulleted list into the segments of the diagram. Remove any extra blank lines.

11. Select the large picture of the people with the talking bubbles. Change the size of the picture to be **1.5"** tall and **2.94"** wide.

12. Change the layout option of the picture to use the **Tight** text wrapping option.

13. Move the picture to the left side of the document using guides to align the picture with the left edge of the text. Have the top of the picture align with the top of the first quote in the *Client Quotes* section. See Figure WD 4.46.

FIGURE WD 4.46

14 Apply the **Drop Shadow Rectangle** Quick Style to the picture. It is the fourth option in the gallery.

15. Navigate to the table on the first page of the document. Insert a new row at the bottom of the table.

16. Cut and paste the **Success** text into the first cell of the new row. Cut and paste the **Results with Integrity** text into the second cell of the new row. Delete any extra blank lines under the table.

17. This table includes a duplicate row of information. Find the duplicated information and delete the second duplicate row.

18. Use the **AutoFit** command to resize the table columns to fit the window.

19. **Merge** the two cells in the first row of the table.

20. Apply the **Grid Table 1 Light** Quick Style to the table (it is the first option in the *Grid Tables* section). Be sure the *First Column Table Style Option* is not part of the design.

21. Apply an **outside border** to the table using the **Double solid lines, 1/2 pt** border style.

22. Save and close the document.

Source of screenshots: Microsoft Office 365: Word, Excel, Access, and PowerPoint.

Foot spa: Comstock/Mediabakery
Manicure: Valua Vitaly/Shutterstock

chapter **5**

Working with Reports and Collaborating with Others

In this chapter, you will learn the following skills:

skills

introduction

In this chapter you will learn the skills to create reports and collaborate with others. First you will learn to create a new document from a template and to use some of Word's valuable tools for writing documents, including AutoCorrect and the Thesaurus. You will add a number of reference elements to a report, including a table of contents, footnotes, and captions. You will learn about the *Researcher* feature, reference styles, and citations. You will then create a bibliography from citations you have added. You will mark entries and create an index for a document from those entries. You will learn how to turn on track changes and work with changes you have received, including adding comments.

Skill 5.1 Creating a New Document Using a Template

A **template** is a document with predefined settings that you can use as a pattern to create a new file of your own. Using a template makes creating a fully formatted and designed new file easy, saving you time and effort. There are templates available for letters, memos, résumés, newsletters, and almost any other type of document you can imagine.

To create a new document from a template:

1. Click the **File** tab to open Backstage view.
2. Click **New**. Word displays your recently used templates in addition to a set of default templates, so your screen may look different from the one in Figure WD 5.1.
3. Click each template preview picture for a brief description of the template.
4. When you find the template you want to use, click the **Create** button.
5. A new document opens, prepopulated with all of the template elements.

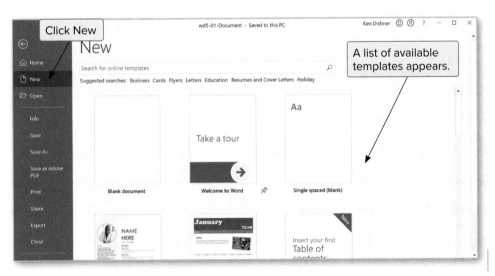

FIGURE WD 5.1

You can search for more document templates online. (You must have an active Internet connection.)

1. Near the top of the *New* page, in the *Search for online templates* box, type a keyword or phrase that describes the template you want.

2. Click the **Start searching** button (the magnifying glass image at the end of the *Search for online templates* box).

3. The search results display previews of the templates that match the keyword or phrase you entered. To further narrow the results, click one of the categories listed in the *Filter by pane* at the right side of the window. Notice that each category lists the number of templates available.

4. When you find the template you want, click it to display the larger preview with detailed information about the template, and then click **Create**.

FIGURE WD 5.2

tell me **more**

Some templates include fully formed documents with sample text for you to replace with your own information. Other templates are empty shells based on a certain design. The template includes the proper styles applied to document elements to help you get started in creating well-formatted documents using proper desktop publishing rules.

let me **try**

Open the student data file **wd5-01-Document1** and try this skill on your own:

1. Display the **New** page in Backstage view.

2. Search for a template of a **cover letter**.

3. Create a new document based on a cover letter of your choice.

4. Save the file as directed by your instructor and close it. Close the original file you opened but do not save it.

Skill 5.2 Using the Thesaurus

When writing documents, you may find you are reusing a certain word over and over again and would like to use a different word that has the same meaning. Microsoft Word's **Thesaurus** tool provides you with a list of synonyms (words with the same meaning) and antonyms (words with the opposite meaning).

To replace a word using the Thesaurus:

1. Place the cursor in the word you want to replace.

2. Click the **Review** tab.

3. In the *Proofing* group, click the **Thesaurus** button.

4. The selected word appears in the *Search for* box of the *Thesaurus* task pane with a list of possible meanings below it. Each possible meaning has a list of synonyms (and, in some cases, antonyms).

5. Point to a synonym (or antonym) and click the arrow that appears to display a menu of options.

6. Click **Insert** on the menu to replace the original word with the one you selected.

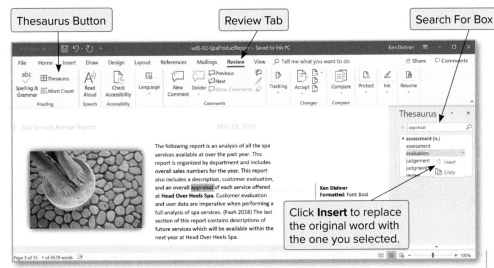

FIGURE WD 5.3

tips & tricks

You can look up and replace words with synonyms without opening the *Thesaurus* task pane. Right-click the word you want to replace and point to *Synonyms*. Word lists a number of possible synonyms on the submenu. Click a synonym to replace the original word with the synonym.

another **method**

To look up a word using the Thesaurus, you can also:

❯ Right-click the word, point to *Synonyms*, and select **Thesaurus...**

❯ With the cursor in the word you want to look up, press ⬆Shift + F7 on the keyboard.

let me try

Open the student data file **wd5-02-SpaProductReport** and try this skill on your own:

1. Select the word **appraisal** in the third sentence of the first paragraph of the document.

2. Using the Thesaurus, replace the word with the synonym **evaluation**.

3. If you will be moving on to the next skill in this chapter, leave the document open to continue working. If not, save the file as directed by your instructor and close it.

Skill 5.3 Using AutoCorrect

While you are typing, Word's **AutoCorrect** feature analyzes each word as it is entered. Each word you type is compared to a list of common misspellings, symbols, and abbreviations. If a match is found, AutoCorrect automatically replaces the text in your document with the matching replacement entry. For example, if you type "teh," AutoCorrect will replace the text with "the."

You can create your own AutoCorrect entries, as well as modify pre-existing ones. AutoCorrect also allows you to check for common capitalization errors. If you find yourself making spelling errors that AutoCorrect does not recognize, you can add your own entries to the AutoCorrect replacement list.

To add a new entry to the AutoCorrect list:

1. Click the **File** tab.
2. Click the **Options** button.
3. In the *Word Options* dialog, click the **Proofing** button.
4. Click the **AutoCorrect Options...** button.

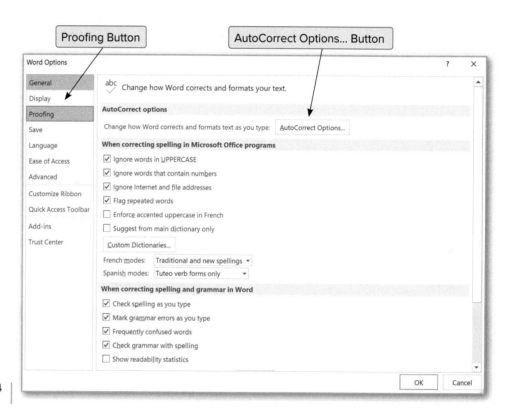

FIGURE WD 5.4

5. Type your commonly made mistake in the *Replace* box.
6. Type the correct spelling in the *With* box.
7. Click **OK** in the *AutoCorrect* dialog.
8. Click **OK** in the *Word Options* dialog.

The next time you type the error, Word will automatically correct it for you.

Type your commonly made mistake in the *Replace* box.

Type the correct spelling in the *With* box.

FIGURE WD 5.5

tips & tricks

If you find yourself typing certain long phrases over and over again, you can use the AutoCorrect feature to replace short abbreviations with long strings of text that you don't want to type. For example, you could replace the text *hhspa* with *Head Over Heels Spa*. This will not only save you time when typing, but more important, it will ensure accuracy in your documents.

tell me **more**

AutoCorrect does more than just fix spelling errors. From the *AutoCorrect* dialog you can set options to:

❭ Correct accidental use of the Caps Lock key.

❭ Automatically capitalize the first letter in a sentence or the names of days.

❭ Automatically apply character formatting such as bold and italic, and format lists and tables.

Explore the *AutoCorrect* dialog on your own to discover all the options available.

let me try

If you do not have the data file from the previous skill open, open the student data file **wd5-03-SpaProductReport** and try this skill on your own:

1. Open the **Word Options** dialog.
2. Open the **AutoCorrect** dialog.
3. Create an AutoCorrect entry to change **hhspa** to **Head Over Heels Spa** when typed.
4. Return to the document and navigate to the first paragraph in the document. Place the cursor before the word *over* in the first sentence of the first paragraph on the page.
5. Type **hhspa** and press the spacebar. Notice Word replaces the text with the entry you created.
6. If you will be moving on to the next skill in this chapter, leave the document open to continue working. If not, save the file as directed by your instructor and close it.

Skill 5.4 Inserting a Table of Contents

If you have a long document with many sections and headings, it is a good idea to include a table of contents at the beginning of the document. A **table of contents** lists the topics and associated page numbers, so your reader can easily locate information. The table of contents is created from heading styles in the document. If you want your document's section titles to display in the table of contents, be sure to apply heading styles to that text.

To insert a table of contents:

1. Verify the insertion point is at the beginning of the document.
2. Click the **References** tab.
3. In the *Table of Contents* group, click the **Table of Contents** button and select an option from the gallery.
4. The table of contents is added to the beginning of the document.

FIGURE WD 5.6

If you make changes to your document after you have inserted a table of contents, you should be sure to update the table of contents to keep the information accurate. To update the table of contents, click the **Update Table** button in the *Table of Contents* group. You can also update the table of contents by clicking on the table of contents and clicking the **Update Table...** button at the top of the control.

To remove a table of contents, click the **Table of Contents** button and select **Remove Table of Contents** at the bottom of the gallery.

FIGURE WD 5.7

tips & tricks

If you want to add your own customized table of contents, click **Custom Table of Contents...** at the bottom of the gallery. The *Table of Contents* dialog opens. Here you can choose different options for the table of contents, including tab leaders, formats, and page number formatting.

tell me **more**

❭ A table of contents is typically based on heading styles, but you can create a table of contents based on custom styles or from marked entries.

❭ A table of contents is a building block that is added to the document. When you select the building block, extra controls appear at the top, including the *Table of Contents* and the *Update Table...* buttons.

let me **try**

If you do not have the data file from the previous skill open, open the student data file **wd5-04-SpaProductReport** and try this skill on your own:

1. Place the cursor on the blank page between the cover page and the beginning of the document.

2. Insert a table of contents based on the **Automatic Table 2** format.

3. If you will be moving on to the next skill in this chapter, leave the document open to continue working. If not, save the file as directed by your instructor and close it.

Skill 5.5 Adding Tab Leaders

Adding **tab leaders** can make data even easier to read. Tab leaders fill in the space between tabs with solid, dotted, or dashed lines. Using tab leaders helps associate columns of text by leading the reader's eye from left to right.

To add tab leaders:

1. Select the text to which you want to add the leader.
2. On the *Home* tab, in the *Paragraph* group, click the **dialog launcher**.
3. In the *Paragraph* dialog, click the **Tabs...** button.
4. In the *Tab stop position* section, select the tab you want to add the leader to, or create a new tab.
5. In the *Leader* section, select the leader option you want.
6. Click **OK**.

FIGURE WD 5.8

tips & tricks

When creating a table of contents for your document, use tab leaders to visually link section headings with page numbers.

another **method**

To open the *Tabs* dialog, you can double-click a tab stop on the ruler.

let me try

If you do not have the data file from the previous skill open, open the student data file **wd5-05-SpaProductReport** and try this skill on your own:

1. Select the list of services and dates in the *Future Products* section on the second to last page of the document.
2. Open the **Tabs** dialog.
3. Add a **dotted tab leader** to the text (option **2** in the *Leader* section of the *Tabs* dialog).
4. If you will be moving on to the next skill in this chapter, leave the document open to continue working. If not, save the file as directed by your instructor and close it.

Skill 5.6 Adding a Caption

A **caption** is a brief description of an illustration, chart, equation, or table. Captions can appear above or below the image, and typically begin with a label followed by a number and the description of the image. Captions are helpful when referring to images and tables within paragraphs of text (for example, see *Table 1: Manicure and Pedicure Annual Sales*).

To add a caption to a figure or table:

1. Select the figure or table you want to add the caption to.
2. Click the **References** tab.
3. In the *Captions* group, click the **Insert Caption** button.
4. The *Caption* dialog opens.
5. Click the **Label** arrow and select a figure type.
6. Click the **Position** arrow and select where you want the caption to appear.
7. Type any additional text, such as a description of the figure, in the *Caption* box.
8. Click **OK** to close the dialog and add the caption.

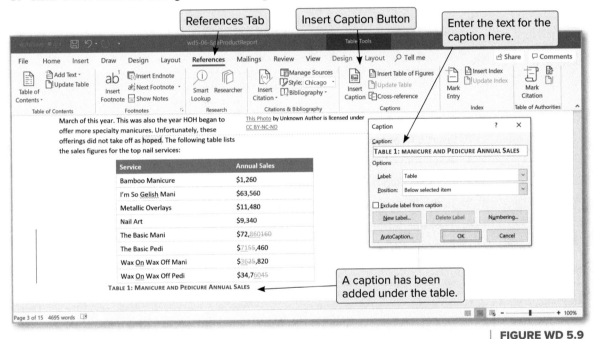

FIGURE WD 5.9

tips & tricks

Word automatically numbers the figures and tables in your document based on the label type. For example, if you have several tables that use the "table" label, those captions will be numbered sequentially. If you have other figures labeled as "figures," those images will be numbered sequentially. If you go back and add a new caption or change the label of an existing caption, Word will renumber the existing captions for you.

let me try

If you do not have the data file from the previous skill open, open the student data file **wd5-06-SpaProductReport** and try this skill on your own:

1. Place the cursor in the *sales figures table* in the *Manicures and Pedicures* section.
2. Add a caption to display below the table. The caption should read: **Table 1: Manicure and Pedicure Annual Sales**
3. If you will be moving on to the next skill in this chapter, leave the document open to continue working. If not, save the file as directed by your instructor and close it.

Skill 5.7 Inserting Footnotes and Endnotes

Footnotes and **endnotes** provide your reader with further information on a topic in a document. They are often used for source references. Footnotes and endnotes are composed of two parts: a **reference mark** (a superscript character placed next to the text) and the associated text. Footnotes appear at the bottom of a page, whereas endnotes are placed at the end of the document.

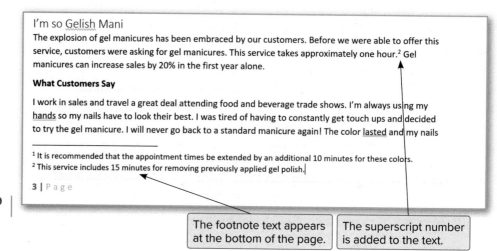

FIGURE WD 5.10

The footnote text appears at the bottom of the page.

The superscript number is added to the text.

To insert a footnote:

1. Place your cursor where you want the footnote to appear.
2. Click the **References** tab.
3. In the *Footnotes* group, click the **Insert Footnote** button.
4. The superscript number is added next to the text, and the cursor is moved to the footnote area at the bottom of the page.
5. Type the text for your footnote. When you are finished, return to your document by clicking anywhere in the main document area.

FIGURE WD 5.11

Insert Endnote Button

References Tab

Insert Footnote Button

Dialog Launcher

To insert an endnote:

1. Place your cursor where you want the endnote to appear.
2. Click the **References** tab.
3. In the *Footnotes* group, click the **Insert Endnote** button.
4. The superscript number is added next to the text, and the cursor is moved to the endnote area at the end of the document.
5. Type the text for your endnote.

To convert footnotes to endnotes or vice versa:

1. Click the **dialog launcher** in the *Footnotes* group.

2. In the *Footnote and Endnote* dialog, click the **Convert...** button and choose an option.

3. Click **OK**.

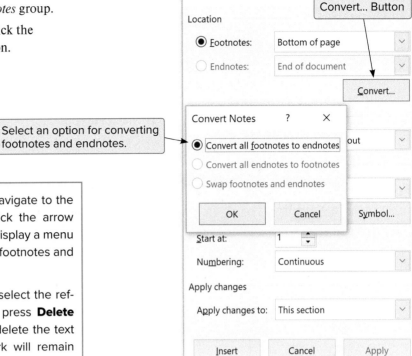

FIGURE WD 5.12

tips & tricks

〉 Click the **Next Footnote** button to navigate to the next footnote in the document. Click the arrow next to the *Next Footnote* button to display a menu allowing you to navigate to previous footnotes and between endnotes in the document.

〉 To delete a footnote, you must first select the reference mark in the document and press **Delete** on the keyboard. If you select and delete the text of the footnote, the reference mark will remain and the footnote will not be removed from the document.

tell me **more**

Once you have inserted and formatted your first footnote or endnote, Word automatically numbers all subsequent notes in your document for you. If you add a new footnote between two existing footnotes, Word will renumber all the footnotes in the document, keeping them in sequential order.

another **method**

To insert a footnote, you can also click the **dialog launcher** in the *Footnotes* group. In the *Footnote and Endnote* dialog, verify that the *Footnote* radio button is selected and click **Insert**.

let me **try**

If you do not have the data file from the previous skill open, open the student data file **wd5-07-SpaProductReport** and try this skill on your own:

1. Place the cursor at the end third sentence in the first paragraph in the *I'm So Gelish Mani* section (the sentence ending *approximately one hour*).

2. Add a footnote that reads: `This service includes 15 minutes for removing previously applied gel polish.`

3. Convert the footnotes in the document into endnotes.

4. Convert the endnotes back to footnotes.

5. If you will be moving on to the next skill in this chapter, leave the document open to continue working. If not, save the file as directed by your instructor and close it.

Skill 5.8 Using Researcher

If you are writing a research paper, a quick way to add sources to your document is to use Word's **Researcher** feature. The *Researcher* uses Microsoft's Bing search to find topics on the Internet and then allows you to quickly add a citation for any source you use.

To use *Researcher* to look up information and add a citation:

1. Click the **References** tab.
2. In the *Research* group, click the **Researcher** button.

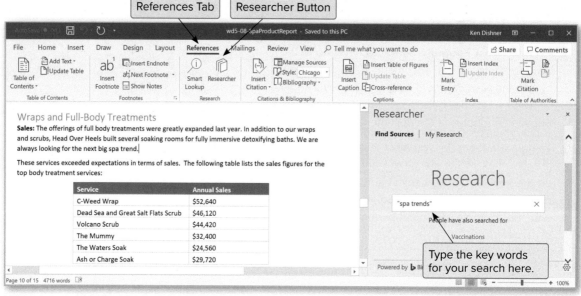

FIGURE WD 5.13

3. The *Researcher* task pane opens.
4. Type the key words for your search in the text box.
5. Click the **Search** button.
6. A list of results appears.
7. When you have added text from a source, click the **Add this source as a citation** button in the upper right corner of the source in the task pane.

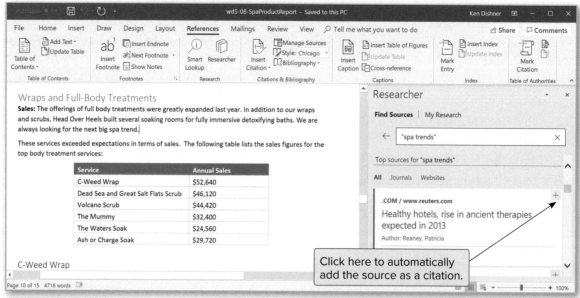

FIGURE WD 5.14

word 365 chapter 5 Working with Reports and Collaborating with Others

let me **try**

If you do not have the data file from the previous skill open, open the student data file **wd5-08-SpaProductReport** and try this skill on your own:

1. Place the cursor before the period at the end of the first paragraph in the *Wraps and Full-Body Treatments* section (the sentence ending *next big spa trend*).
2. Open the *Researcher* task pane and type **"spa trends"** in the search box. *NOTE*: If you do not have the *Researcher* feature in your version of Microsoft Word, skip to step 5.
3. Type a sentence based on the research you completed.
4. From the *Researcher* task pane, add a citation to the source you used.
5. If you will be moving on to the next skill in this chapter, leave the document open to continue working. If not, save the file as directed by your instructor and close it.

from the perspective of . . .

GRADUATE STUDENT

When I wrote my first term paper, my professor rejected it informing me that it wasn't formatted correctly and I was using the wrong reference style. I didn't understand. I had typed everything very carefully, but apparently I was supposed to use the APA style and not the Chicago style. After that, I started using the reference tools built into Word. Now I can generate a table of contents from headings in my paper, mark entries for my index as I write, and auto-generate the index. Most important, I can set my reference style to use the APA style, add my sources, and create a bibliography in the correct style. When I resubmitted my paper, my professor was impressed with how well it was formatted. I got an A!

Rubberball/Getty Images

Skill 5.9 Selecting a Reference Style

A **reference style** is a set of rules used to display references in a bibliography. These rules include the order of information, when and how punctuation is used, and the use of character formatting, such as italic and bold. The three most common reference styles in use today are *APA*, *MLA*, and *Chicago*; however, there are a number of other reference styles you can choose from. It is important that you use the correct reference style for the subject of your document.

When creating a bibliography, it is important to use a consistent reference style for your citations. Word makes this easy by allowing you to set the reference style for the entire document at once.

To change the reference style for a document:

1. Click the **References** tab.

2. In the *Citations & Bibliography* group, click the arrow next to *Style* and select a style from the list.

FIGURE WD 5.15

The following table lists the available styles in Word and when they are most commonly used.

STYLE ABBREVIATION	FULL NAME	PURPOSE
APA Sixth Edition	American Psychological Association	Education, psychology, and social sciences
Chicago Sixteenth Edition	The Chicago Manual of Style	Books, magazines, and newspapers
GB7714 2005	NA	Used in China
GOST—Name Sort	Russian State Standard	Used in Russia
GOST—Title Sort	Russian State Standard	Used in Russia
Harvard—Anglia 2008	Harvard reference style	For the specification at Anglia Ruskin University
IEEE 2006	IEEE Citation Reference	Research papers in technical fields
ISO 690—First Element and Date	International Standards Organization	Patents and industry (both print and nonprint works)
ISO 690—Numerical Reference	International Standards Organization	Patents and industry (both print and nonprint works)
MLA Seventh Edition	Modern Language Association	Arts and humanities
SIST02	NA	Used in Asia
Turabian Sixth Edition	Turabian	All subjects (designed for college students)

tips & tricks

When you change the reference style for a document, all citations are automatically updated to use the new style.

tell me more

To see a preview of the source style, click the **Manage Sources** button in the *Citations & Bibliography* group. The preview box at the bottom of the *Manage Sources* dialog shows how the selected reference will appear as a citation and in the bibliography.

let me try

If you do not have the data file from the previous skill open, open the student data file **wd5-09-SpaProductReport** and try this skill on your own:

1. Navigate to the first paragraph of the document. Notice the format of the reference *(Faah 2018)* in the first sentence.
2. Change the reference style for the document to use the **APA Sixth Edition** style.
3. Notice how the reference has changed to *(Faah, 2018)*.
4. If you will be moving on to the next skill in this chapter, leave the document open to continue working. If not, save the file as directed by your instructor and close it.

Skill 5.10 Adding Citations to Documents

When you use materials in a document from other sources, such as a book or a journal article, you need to give credit to the original source material. A **citation** is a reference to such source material. Citations include information such as the author, title, publisher, and the publication date.

To add a citation to a document, you must first create the source:

1. Place the cursor where you want to add the citation.
2. Click the **References** tab.
3. In the *Citations & Bibliography* group, click the **Insert Citation** button and select **Add New Source...**

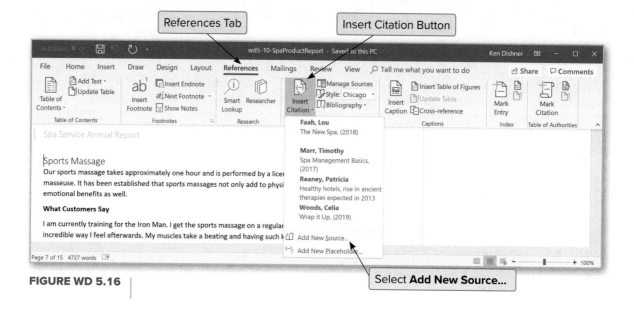

References Tab

Insert Citation Button

Select **Add New Source...**

FIGURE WD 5.16

4. In the *Create Source* dialog, click the arrow next to *Type of Source* and select an option.
5. In the *Author* box, type the name of the author.
6. In the *Title* box, type the title of the book or article.
7. In the *Year* box, type the year the book or article was published.
8. Add other information about the source to the appropriate fields.
9. When you are finished, click **OK** to add the citation to the document.

Choose the type of source.

Type the name of the author.

Type the title of the book or article.

Type the publication date information.

FIGURE WD 5.17

After you have added a new source, it appears on the *Insert Citation* menu. To add the same source to another part of the document, click the **Insert Citation** button and select the source for the citation.

Click a source from the menu to add the citation.

FIGURE WD 5.18

tips & tricks

Citations appear in the document as a control. When you click the control, you will see an arrow on the right side. Click the arrow to display a menu for editing the source and the citation. In the *Edit Source* dialog, you can change the information you added when you created the source. In the *Edit Citation* dialog, you can change information specific to the citation, such as page numbers.

tell me **more**

When you add a citation, the citation appears inside parentheses at the place where you inserted it. A citation includes basic information from the source, including the author and year. A bibliography lists all the citations in a document and includes more of the source information than the citation does.

let me **try**

If you do not have the data file from the previous skill open, open the student data file **wd5-10-SpaProductReport** and try this skill on your own:

1. Navigate to the *Sports Massage* section and place the cursor before the period at the end of the first paragraph.

2. Add a new source with the following information:

Type of Source	Journal Article
Author	Neil Patella
Title	Multipurpose Massage Therapy
Journal Name	Sports Physio Journal
Year	2019
Pages	42

3. Navigate to the *Doggie and Me Massage* section and place the cursor before the period at the end of the first paragraph (after *a great seller*).

4. Add a citation that references the **Lou Faah** source.

5. If you will be moving on to the next skill in this chapter, leave the document open to continue working. If not, save the file as directed by your instructor and close it.

Skill 5.11 Using the Source Manager

When you add a new source to a document, it is available to add throughout that document. But what if you want to add a source to multiple documents? The **Source Manager** allows you to save source information to a master list. When you open or create new documents, you can add the sources in the master list to the document, so there is no need to re-enter the same source information.

To add and save sources using the Source Manager:

1. Click the **References** tab.
2. In the *Citations & Bibliography* group, click the **Manage Sources** button.

FIGURE WD 5.19

3. The box on the left displays the sources that have been saved to the master list. Select a source and click the **Copy ->** button to add the source for use in the current document.

4. The box on the right displays the sources that are part of the current document. Select a source and click the **<- Copy** button to add the source to the master list.

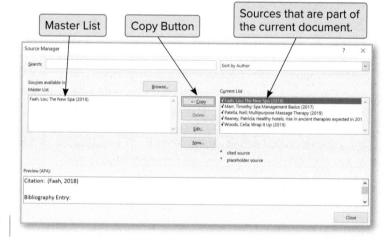

FIGURE WD 5.20

tips & tricks

To delete a source, click the source you want to delete and click the **Delete** button. To edit a source, select the source and click the **Edit...** button. Make the changes in the *Edit Source* dialog and click **OK**. To add a new source, click the **New...** button. Make the changes in the *Create Source* dialog and click **OK**.

let me try

If you do not have the data file from the previous skill open, open the student data file **wd5-11-SpaProductReport** and try this skill on your own:

1. Open the **Source Manager**.
2. Add a source from the master list to the document. If you do not have any sources in the master list, you may skip this step.
3. Add the **Lou Faah** source to the master list of sources.
4. If you will be moving on to the next skill in this chapter, leave the document open to continue working. If not, save the file as directed by your instructor and close it.

word 365   chapter 5 Working with Reports and Collaborating with Others

Skill 5.12 Creating a Bibliography

A **bibliography** is a compiled list of sources you referenced in your document. Typically, bibliographies appear at the end of a document and list all the sources you marked throughout the document. Word comes with a number of prebuilt bibliography building blocks for you to use. When you select one of these building blocks, Word will search the document and compile all the sources from your document and format them according to the style you chose.

To add a bibliography to a document:

1. Place the cursor at the end of the document.

2. Click the **References** tab.

3. In the *Citations & Bibliography* group, click the **Bibliography** button and select one of the bibliography building blocks.

4. The bibliography is added to the end of the document, listing all the sources referenced in the document.

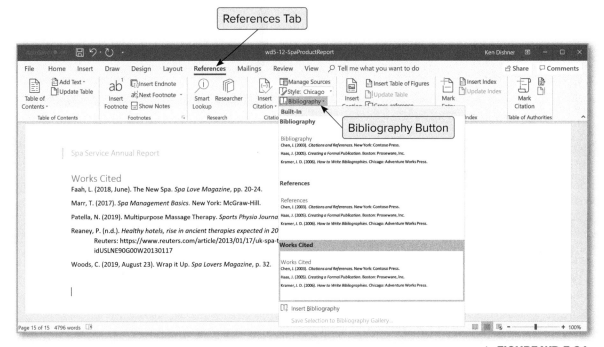

FIGURE WD 5.21

another **method**

To add a simple bibliography, click the **Insert Bibliography** command at the bottom of the *Bibliography* gallery.

let me **try**

If you do not have the data file from the previous skill open, open the student data file **wd5-12-SpaProductReport** and try this skill on your own:

1. Navigate to the end of the document. Place the cursor at the top of the blank page.

2. Add a bibliography using the **Works Cited** style.

3. If you will be moving on to the next skill in this chapter, leave the document open to continue working. If not, save the file as directed by your instructor and close it.

Skill 5.13 Marking Entries

When creating long documents, you may want to add an index to the document to help your readers quickly locate specific information. To create an index, you must first mark the topics you want to include, and then create the index. When formatting marks are hidden, marked entries look no different from other text in the document. However, when the index is created, Word finds all the marked entries and adds them to the index.

To mark entries:

1. Select the word or phrase you want to add to the index.
2. Click the **References** tab.
3. In the *Index* group, click the **Mark Entry** button.
4. The word or phrase appears in the *Main entry* box. Click the **Mark** button to mark the entry.
5. Click the **Close** button to close the *Mark Index Entry* dialog.

After you mark an entry, Word adds the *XE (Index Entry)* formatting mark to the word and displays all formatting marks in the document, so you can double-check your page layout. Click the **Show/Hide** button on the *Home* tab to hide the formatting marks.

FIGURE WD 5.22

tips & tricks

To add a reference to every instance of a word to the index, click the **Mark All** button in the *Mark Index Entry* dialog.

another method

To open the *Mark Index Entry* dialog, you can also click the **Insert Index** button in the *Index* group. In the *Index* dialog, click the **Mark Entry** button.

let me try

If you do not have the data file from the previous skill open, open the student data file **wd5-13-SpaProductReport** and try this skill on your own:

1. Select the text **manicures** in the first sentence of the *Manicures and Pedicures* section.
2. Mark the text as an entry to use in the index.
3. Close the *Mark Index Entry* dialog and hide the formatting marks in the document.
4. If you will be moving on to the next skill in this chapter, leave the document open to continue working. If not, save the file as directed by your instructor and close it.

Skill 5.14 Creating an Index

An **index** is a list of topics and associated page numbers that typically appears at the end of a document. Adding an index to your document can help your readers find information quickly. An index entry can reference a single word, a phrase, or a topic spanning several pages.

To add an index to a document:

1. Place the cursor at the end of the document.
2. Click the **References** button. In the *Index* group, click the **Insert Index** button.
3. The *Index* dialog opens. Click the **Formats** arrow and select a format.
4. Modify the other options until the preview looks the way you want.
5. Click **OK** to insert the index into your document.

FIGURE WD 5.23

tips & tricks

To add new entries to an index, do not type directly in the index. Instead, mark the entries and then update the index. Any entries typed directly into the index will be deleted when the index is updated. To update an index, first select the index and then click the **Update Index** button in the *Index* group.

tell me **more**

A cross-reference is an index entry that refers to another entry in the index rather than to a page in the document. Cross-references are often used to direct readers from an uncommon entry to a more frequently used one.

let me try

If you do not have the data file from the previous skill open, open the student data file **wd5-14-SpaProductReport** and try this skill on your own:

1. Navigate to the end of the document. Place the cursor below the bibliography.
2. Insert an index based on the **Classic** format. The entries should display in two columns.
3. If you will be moving on to the next skill in this chapter, leave the document open to continue working. If not, save the file as directed by your instructor and close it.

Skill 5.15 Using Track Changes

The **Track Changes** feature in Word marks any changes made to a document by reviewers. Such changes include any deletions, insertions, or formatting. Word displays some changes directly in the document and other changes in balloons displayed in the margin. When the *Track Changes* feature is active, the *Track Changes* button appears in its active state.

To track changes to a document:

1. Click the **Review** tab.

2. In the *Tracking* group, click the **Track Changes** button.

3. When changes are made to the document, they display either in-line (for insertions and deletions) or in the margin (for comments and formatting changes).

4. Click the **Track Changes** button again to turn off the feature.

FIGURE WD 5.24

tell me **more**

The **Reviewing pane** displays all the changes in a document. It shows a summary of the revisions in a document, including the number of insertions, deletions, moves, formatting changes, and comments. To display the *Reviewing* pane, click the **Reviewing Pane** button in the *Tracking* group on the *Review* tab.

another **method**

To turn on the *Track Changes* feature, you can also click the bottom half of the **Track Changes** button and select *Track Changes* from the menu.

let me try

If you do not have the data file from the previous skill open, open the student data file **wd5-15-SpaProductReport** and try this skill on your own:

1. Turn on the **Track Changes** feature.
2. Select the text **basic manicure** in the first sentence of the first paragraph in *The Basic Mani* section at the top of page 3.
3. Change the selected text to **Basic Mani**.
4. Turn off the **Track Changes** feature.
5. If you will be moving on to the next skill in this chapter, leave the document open to continue working. If not, save the file as directed by your instructor and close it.

Skill 5.16 Working with Comments

A **comment** is a note you add to a document that is not meant to be part of the document. When you add a comment, it appears in the margin of the document. Comments are useful when you are reviewing a document and want to add messages about changes or errors.

To insert a comment:

1. Place the cursor where you want to add the comment.
2. Click the **Review** tab.
3. In the *Comments* group, click the **New Comment** button.
4. The comment balloon appears in the margin of the document. The cursor appears in the comment.
5. Type your comment.
6. Click outside the balloon to deselect the comment and continue working.

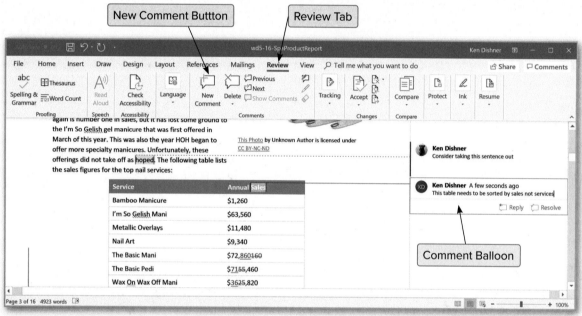

FIGURE WD 5.25

There are a number of ways you can work with comments. If your document has multiple comments, click the **Next Comment** and **Previous Comment** buttons to move between comments in a document.

FIGURE WD 5.26

Replying to a comment allows you to directly respond to comments in a document. The comments appear within the same bubble, so it is obvious the comments are related.

To reply to a comment:

1. Roll your mouse over the comment balloon and click the **Reply** button at the bottom of the balloon.

2. Another comment appears inside the original comment. Type your reply and click outside.

If you are done with a comment, you can resolve it or delete the comment. Resolving a comment changes the comment so it appears faded. It can still be read but you can no longer interact with it. If you no longer need to see or interact with the comment, you can delete the comment.

❭ To resolve a comment, roll your mouse over the comment balloon and click the **Resolve** button.

❭ To delete a comment, select the comment you want to delete. In the *Comments* group on the *Review* tab, click the **Delete Comment** button.

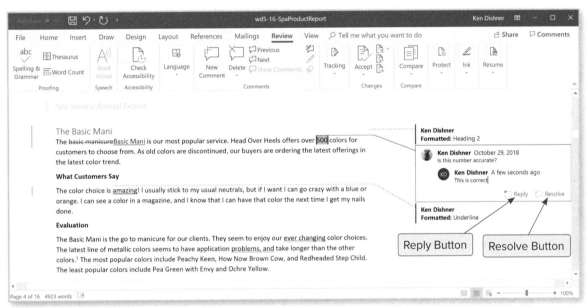

FIGURE WD 5.27

tips & tricks

❭ After you have resolved a comment, the button changes to **Reopen**. Click **Reopen** to make the comment active again.

❭ To delete all comments in the document, on the *Review* tab, in the *Comments* group, click the **Delete** button arrow and select **Delete All Comments in Document**.

another **method**

❭ To add a comment, you can also right-click the area you want to add a comment to and select **New Comment** from the shortcut menu.

❭ To work with comments, you can also right-click the comment and select a command—**Reply to Comment**, **Delete Comment**, or **Resolve Comment**.

let me **try**

from the perspective of . . .

MEDIA ASSISTANT

In my job, I am often working with long scripts that I have to proofread with several other employees. When I work through a script, I like to use the Side to Side view to be able to flip through the pages. Thanks to *Track Changes*, I can share a file with several colleagues, review their input, and decide which changes I want to accept or reject. I can even add a password preventing others from accidentally turning off the feature. The result is a document worth reading!

Photodisc/Getty Images

Skill 5.17 Hiding and Showing Changes in a Document

When you activate the *Track Changes* feature in Word, all changes are displayed by default. This includes any comments, deletions, insertions, or formatting changes. Word displays some changes directly in the document and other changes in balloons displayed in the margin. If your document has gone through some major revisions, it may be difficult to differentiate between all the tracked changes. You can show and hide the various changes from the *Tracking* group on the *Review* tab.

To show and hide the different types of tracked changes in a document:

1. Click the **Review** tab.
2. In the *Tracking* group, click the **Show Markup** button.
3. If a change type appears with a checkmark next to it, it is currently displayed in the document. If a change type appears without a checkmark next to it, it is currently hidden in the document.
4. Click an option on the menu to hide that type of change in the document.
5. Click the same option again to display the hidden changes.

From the *Show Markup* button, you can show or hide comments, ink notations, insertions and deletions, and formatting changes.

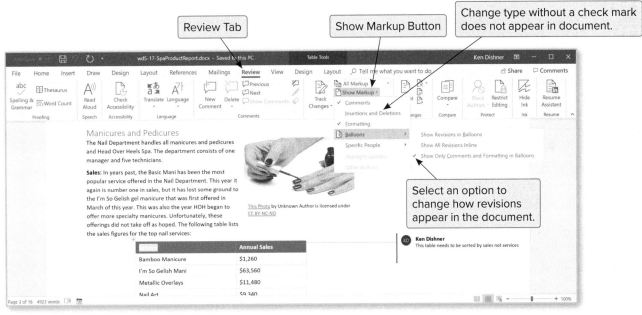

FIGURE WD 5.28

You can choose to have all revisions display in balloons or all revisions display in-line. By default, revisions are displayed in-line and comments and formatting changes are displayed in balloons.

To change what displays in balloons:

1. On the *Review* tab, in the *Tracking* group, click the **Show Markup** button.
2. Point to *Balloons* and select an option.

The *Display for Review* menu allows you to display the document in a number of states, including the final version with simplified markup for changes, the final version with all markup for the changes, the final version with no markup for changes, and the original document without any markup.

To change the display of tracked changes in a document:

1. On the *Review* tab, in the *Tracking* group, click the **Display for Review** drop-down arrow.
2. Select a display option.

FIGURE WD 5.29

tips & tricks

You can choose to review all changes by all reviewers or specify the type of changes you want to review and by which reviewer. To modify which reviewer's comments are displayed, click the **Show Markup** button in the *Tracking* group, point to *Specific People*, and select the reviewer(s) you want.

let me try

If you do not have the data file from the previous skill open, open the student data file **wd5-17-SpaProductReport** and try this skill on your own:

1. Navigate to the *Manicures and Pedicures* section where you can see the tracked changes.
2. Hide **insertions and deletions** in the document.
3. Show **insertions and deletions** again.
4. Change the formatting so revisions are shown in balloons in the margin.
5. Change the formatting so only comments and formatting are displayed in balloons in the margin.
6. Change the track changes option to show **no markup** in the document.
7. Change the track changes option to show **all markup** in the document.
8. If you will be moving on to the next skill in this chapter, leave the document open to continue working. If not, save the file as directed by your instructor and close it.

Skill 5.18 Accepting and Rejecting Changes in a Document

When you send a document for review with *Track Changes* on, the document you receive will show all the changes made by reviewers. To finalize the document, you need to accept or reject each change suggested.

There are a number of ways you can accept and reject changes:

Accept or Reject Change and Move to Next—Accepts or rejects the change and automatically moves to the next change in the document.

Accept or Reject Change—Accepts or rejects the change and does not move to the next change in the document.

Accept or Reject All Changes Shown—Accepts or rejects only the currently displayed changes.

Accept or Reject All Changes in Document—Accepts or rejects both visible and hidden changes in the document.

To accept or reject changes in a document:

1. Click the **Review** tab.

2. In the *Changes* group, click the **Next Change** button to navigate to the first change in the document.

3. To accept the selected change and move to the next change, click the **Accept and Move to Next** button.

4. To reject the selected change and move on to the next change, click the **Reject and Move to Next** button.

FIGURE WD 5.30

tips & tricks

To navigate between changes in a document, click the **Previous Change** and **Next Change** buttons.

tell me **more**

If you have sent the document to multiple reviewers, each reviewer's comments and changes will be displayed in a specific color. To see which reviewer is represented by which color, in the *Tracking* group, click the **Show Markup** button and point to *Reviewers*. Each reviewer is listed in the menu by color. If a checkmark appears next to the reviewer's name, that reviewer's comments and changes are visible. If there is no checkmark next to the reviewer's name, that reviewer's comments and changes have been hidden. Click a reviewer's name on the menu to hide or show comments and changes from that reviewer.

another **method**

❭ To accept a change and automatically move to the next change, you can click the **Accept and Move to Next** button arrow and select the **Accept and Move to Next** command from the menu.

❭ To reject a change and automatically move to the next change, you can click the **Reject and Move to Next** button arrow and select the **Reject and Move to Next** command from the menu.

let me **try**

If you do not have the data file from the previous skill open, open the student data file **wd5-18-SpaProductReport** and try this skill on your own:

1. Place the cursor at the beginning of the document.
2. Move to the first change in the document.
3. The first change found is the formatting of **Head Over Heels Spa**. Reject the formatting change and move to the next change.
4. The next change found is the insertion of the word **five**. Accept this change and move to the next change.
5. The next change found is a comment. Move to the next change.
6. The next changes found are the deletion of **160** and the insertion of **860**. Reject both these changes and move to the next change.
7. At this point, all remaining changes are correct. With one command, accept all the remaining changes in the document.
8. If you will be moving on to the next skill in this chapter, leave the document open to continue working. If not, save the file as directed by your instructor and close it.

Skill 5.19 Locking Track Changes

When you send out your documents for review with *Track Changes* on, you may want to prevent your reviewers from turning off the feature. This will ensure that any changes made by reviewers will be marked and gives you the ability to review and then accept or reject all changes made to the document. Use the **Lock Tracking** feature to add a password to a document that will be required to be entered in order to disable *Track Changes*.

To lock Track Changes:

1. Click the **Review** tab.
2. In the *Tracking* group, click the bottom half of the **Track Changes** button.
3. Select **Lock Tracking**.

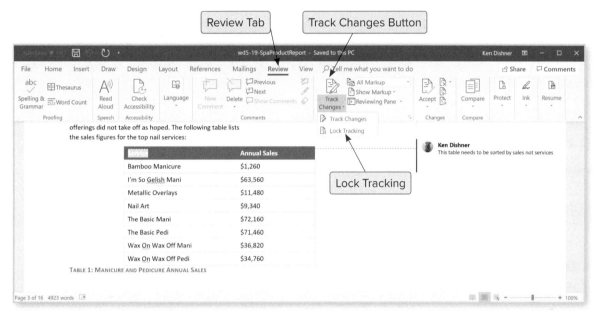

FIGURE WD 5.31

4. In the *Lock Tracking* dialog, type a password that will be required to be entered to unlock *Track Changes* in the **Enter Password (optional)** box.
5. Retype the password in the **Reenter to confirm** box.
6. Click **OK**.

FIGURE WD 5.32

To unlock Track Changes:

1. In the *Tracking* group, click the bottom half of the **Track Changes** button again and select **Lock Tracking**.

2. In the *Unlock Tracking* dialog, type the password in the **Password** box.

3. Click **OK**.

Type the password to unlock Track Changes.

FIGURE WD 5.33

tips & tricks

You do not have to require a password to unlock *Track Changes*. In the *Lock Tracking* dialog, click **OK** without entering a password. *Track Changes* will still be locked, but in order to unlock *Track Changes*, reviewers will only need to select the option from the *Track Changes* menu.

tell me **more**

Adding a password for locking *Track Changes* is not a security feature. It only unlocks the ability to accept and reject changes and turn off the *Track Changes* feature. It does not require a password for your users to open and modify the document. However, any changes made to the document will be tracked.

let me **try**

If you do not have the data file from the previous skill open, open the student data file **wd5-19-SpaProductReport** and try this skill on your own:

1. Lock tracking in the document so readers will not be able to turn off *Track Changes*.

2. Add the password: **hhspa789**

3. Unlock the tracking in the document using the password: **hhspa789**

4. Turn off the **Track Changes** feature.

5. If you will be moving on to the next skill in this chapter, leave the document open to continue working. If not, save the file as directed by your instructor and close it.

Skill 5.20 Using Read Mode

Today more and more documents are read on devices such as tablets and smartphones. Word includes a view that is designed for reading documents in electronic format called **Read Mode**. In Read Mode, documents are displayed as screens rather than pages.

To display a document in Read Mode:

1. Click the **Read Mode** button on the status bar.
2. Click the **Next** button to navigate to the next screen.
3. Click the **Back** button to navigate to the previous screen.

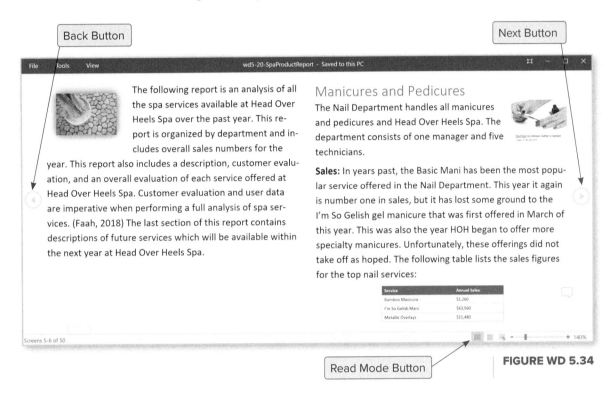

FIGURE WD 5.34

Read Mode comes with specific tools to modify the look of the document as you read. When reading documents electronically, some people prefer a softer screen appearance than black text on a white background, while others prefer reading white text on a black background. Read Mode comes with specific tools to modify the look of the document as you read, including changing the page color.

To change the page color in Read Mode:

1. Click the **View** menu.
2. Point to *Page Color* and select an option:
   - **None**–Displays black text on a white background
   - **Sepia**–Displays black text on a light brown tone background
   - **Inverse**–Displays white text on a black background

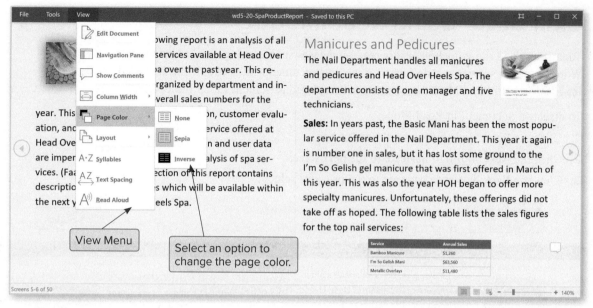

FIGURE WD 5.35

tell me **more**

If you resize the Read Mode window, the text will automatically resize to fit the window. If you make the window smaller, you will notice the number of screens to display increases. If you make the window larger, the number of screens to display decreases.

another **method**

To navigate through pages of a document in Read Mode, you can also use the horizontal scrollbar along the bottom of the window.

let me **try**

If you do not have the data file from the previous skill open, open the student data file **wd5-20-SpaProductReport** and try this skill on your own:

1. Navigate to the beginning of the document.
2. Switch to **Read Mode**.
3. Navigate to the next screen in the document.
4. Navigate to the previous screen in the document.
5. Change the color of the page to **Sepia**.
6. Switch to **Print Layout** view.
7. If you will be moving on to the next skill in this chapter, leave the document open to continue working. If not, save the file as directed by your instructor and close it.

Skill 5.21 Changing How Pages Scroll

Documents are typically displayed in a vertical fashion with one page displayed above or below another page. To navigate between pages, you use the vertical scrollbar, moving it up to move to navigate to an earlier place in the document and moving it down to move to a later place in the document. Word's default display is still this **vertical layout**, but you can also choose to use Word's **side to side layout** to navigate a document. In the side to side layout, pages are displayed next to each other and you navigate by flipping between pages, just as you would in a book.

To change how pages scroll:

1. Click the **View** tab.
2. In the *Page Movement* group, click a scrolling option:
   - **Vertical**—scrolls the document vertically using a vertical scrollbar
   - **Side to Side**—scrolls the document horizontally, one page at a time, using a horizontal scrollbar

FIGURE WD 5.36

tips & tricks

When you are scrolling a document using the *Side to Side* option, the *Thumbnails* button appears in the *Zoom* group and the other *Zoom* options are no longer available. Click the **Thumbnails** button to display each page in the document as a large thumbnail that provides a quick overview of the page structure of the document and allows you to navigate quickly to the page you want.

tell me **more**

Side to side layout is helpful when using a touch screen or tablet. Swiping left or right with your finger will flip between the pages.

let me **try**

If you do not have the data file from the previous skill open, open the student data file **wd5-21-SpaProductReport** and try this skill on your own:

1. Change the scrolling of the document to **Side to Side**.
2. Change the scrolling of the document back to **Vertical**.
3. Save the file as directed by your instructor and close it.

key terms

Template
Thesaurus
AutoCorrect
Table of contents
Tab leaders
Caption
Footnotes
Endnotes
Reference mark
Researcher
Reference style

Citation
Source Manager
Bibliography
Index
Track Changes
Reviewing pane
Comment
Lock Tracking
Read Mode
Vertical layout
Side to side layout

concept review

1. What would you use to look up a synonym for a word?

a. grammar check

b. Thesaurus

c. Dictionary

d. translate tool

2. If you often mistype a word, use Word's _____ to automatically replace the misspelling with the correct spelling as you type.

a. Find and Replace commands

b. spelling checker

c. grammar checker

d. AutoCorrect

3. When you add a table of contents to a document, the entries created are based on _____.

a. marked entries

b. headings

c. custom styles

d. all of the above

4. Which of the following fills in the space between tabs with solid, dotted, or dashed lines?

a. border

b. tab leader

c. tab marker

d. none of the above

5. You can add a caption for both figures and tables.

a. true

b. false

6. Which of the following appears at the bottom of a page and is composed of two parts: a reference mark (a superscript character placed next to the text) and the associated text?

    a. footnote

    b. endnote

    c. marked entry

    d. citation

7. What is the set of rules used to display references in a bibliography known as?

    a. source

    b. reference style

    c. template

    d. citation

8. When *Track Changes* is active, all insertions, deletions, and formatting changes are marked.

    a. true

    b. false

9. Which of the following are notes you add to a document that are not intended to be part of the final document?

    a. tracked changes

    b. balloons

    c. ink notations

    d. comments

10. Which view should you use to view documents optimally on an electronic device, such as a tablet?

    a. Read Mode

    b. Print Layout view

    c. Web Layout view

    d. Draft view

Data files for projects can be found by logging into
your SIMnet account and going to the *Library* section.

projects

skill review 5.1

In this project you will be working on a research paper about alternate assessments for students. First you will work with track changes by accepting and rejecting changes that have been made. You will also add and reply to comments. You will find a synonym for a word using the Thesaurus. You will add a table of contents. You will add an endnote and then convert the endnote to a footnote. You will change the reference style for the paper to APA, add a new source, and add a citation to the document. You will mark an entry for the index and then add the index along with a bibliography.

Skills needed to complete this project:

- Using Track Changes (Skill 5.15)
- Working with Comments (Skill 5.16)
- Accepting and Rejecting Changes in a Document (Skill 5.18)
- Using the Thesaurus (Skill 5.2)
- Using AutoCorrect (Skill 5.3)
- Inserting a Table of Contents (Skill 5.4)
- Inserting Footnotes and Endnotes (Skill 5.7)
- Selecting a Reference Style (Skill 5.9)
- Adding Citations to Documents (Skill 5.10)
- Creating a Bibliography (Skill 5.12)
- Marking Entries (Skill 5.13)
- Creating an Index (Skill 5.14)

1. Open the start file **WD2019-SkillReview-5-1** and resave the file as: `[your initials]WD-SkillReview-5-1`

2. If the document opens in Protected View, click the **Enable Editing** button in the Message Bar at the top of the document so you can modify the document.

3. Use *Track Changes*.

   a. Click the **Review** tab.

   b. In the *Tracking* group, click the **Track Changes** button.

4. Select the first sentence in the first paragraph of *What is an Alternate Assessment* section (the sentence beginning with *All of this brings us to*). Press the **Delete** key to delete the sentence.

5. Accept and reject changes in a document.

   a. Press **Ctrl+Home** to navigate to the beginning of the document.

   b. On the *Review* tab, in the *Changes* group, click the **Next Change** button.

   c. In the *Changes* group, click the **Accept and Move to Next** button to accept the deletion of the text *particular tasks*.

   d. Click the **Accept and Move to Next** button to accept the insertion of the word *tasks*.

   e. Click the **Accept and Move to Next** button to accept the formatting change.

f. Click the **Accept and Move to Next** button to accept the deletion you just made.

g. Click the **Reject and Move to Next** button to reject the formatting change.

h. Click the **Reject and Move to Next** button to reject the deletion.

i. Click the **Reject and Move to Next** button to reject the insertion.

j. Click the **Accept** button arrow and select **Accept All Changes** to accept the remaining changes in the document.

k. Turn *Track Changes* off by clicking the **Track Changes** button.

6. Reply to a comment and resolve the comment.

a. Click the **Reply** button in the first comment in the document.

b. Type the following reply: `This has been fixed`

c. Click the **Resolve** comment button to resolve the comment

7. Add a comment to a document.

a. Place the cursor at the end of the *Introduction* heading at the beginning of the document.

b. On the *Review* tab, in the *Comments* group, click the **New Comment** button.

c. Type the following comment: `Review one more time looking for mistakes`

8. Use the Thesaurus to look up synonyms of a word.

a. In the first paragraph under *Introduction*, select the word **pick** in the second sentence.

b. On the *Review* tab, in the *Proofing* group, click the **Thesaurus** button.

c. Scroll the list of synonyms, in the *select (v.)* section, point to the first option **select** and click the **arrow**.

d. Click **Insert** on the menu.

e. Close the *Thesaurus* task pane.

9. Add an AutoCorrect entry and type the text to see the correction.

a. Click the **File** tab.

b. Click **Options**.

c. In the *Word Options* dialog, click **Proofing**.

d. Click the **AutoCorrect Options...** button.

e. In the *Replace* box, type `acomodations`. In the *With* box, type `accommodations`.

f. Click the **Add** button.

g. Click **OK** in the *AutoCorrect* dialog. Click **OK** in the *Word Options* dialog.

h. Place the cursor between the words *of* and *that* in the first sentence of the first paragraph of the document.

i. Type `acomodations` then press the spacebar. Notice Word replaces the misspelled word with the correct spelling you added.

10. Insert a table of contents.

a. Place the cursor before the *Introduction* heading.

b. Click the **Layout** tab.

c. In the *Page Setup* group, click the **Breaks** button and select **Page**.

d. Place the cursor at the beginning of the empty line on the newly inserted page.

e. Click the **References** tab.

f. In the *Table of Contents* group, click the **Table of Contents** button and select **Automatic Table 2**.

11. Insert a footnote.

    a. Navigate to the *No Child Left Behind* section of the document. Place the cursor after the word *state* in the first sentence.

    b. On the *References* tab, in the *Footnotes* group, click the **Insert Footnote** button.

    c. Type the following text for the footnote: `The Ohio state standards have been used in this project.`

12. Add a new source.

    a. In the *Modified Achievement Standards* section, place the cursor before the period in the second sentence of the last paragraph of the section. This is the sentence ending with *scheduling, presentation format or response format.*

    b. On the *References* tab, in the *Citations & Bibliography* group, click the **Insert Citation** button.

    c. Select **Add New Source...**

    d. In the *Create Source* dialog, select **Journal Article** as the type of source. Enter `Pamela Johnson` as the author. Enter `The Benefits of Administration of Alternate Assessments` as the title. Enter `New Horizons` as the journal name.

    e. Enter `2016` for the year.

    f. Enter `32-33` for the pages.

    g. Click **OK** to create the source.

13. Insert a citation.

    a. Navigate to the *Who Will Benefit* section. Place the cursor before the last period at the end of the second paragraph in the section. This is the sentence ending with *validity of the alternate assessment.*

    b. On the *References* tab, in the *Citations & Bibliography* group, click the **Insert Citation** button and select the **Johnson, Pamela** citation.

14. Change the reference style for the document.

    a. On the *References* tab, in the *Citations & Bibliography* group, click the **Style** arrow.

    b. Select **APA Sixth Edition**.

15. Mark an entry for the index.

    a. Navigate to the *No Child Left Behind* section. Select **No Child Left Behind Act (NCLB)** in the first sentence of the first paragraph.

    b. On the *References* tab, in the *Index* group, click the **Mark Entry** button.

    c. In the *Mark Index Entry* dialog, click the **Mark** button.

    d. Click the **Close** button.

16. Hide the formatting marks in the document.

    a. Click the **Home** tab.

    b. In the *Paragraph* group, click the **Show/Hide** button to hide formatting marks in the document.

17. Add a bibliography to the document.

    a. Place the cursor at the end of the document.

    b. Click the **Layout** tab.

    c. In the *Page Setup* group, click the **Breaks** button and select **Page**.

    d. Click the **References** tab.

    e. In the *Citations & Bibliography* group, click the **Bibliography** button and select **Bibliography**.

18. Create an index for the document.

    a. Verify the cursor is on the empty line under the *Bibliography* section.

    b. Click the **Layout** tab.

    c. In the *Page Setup* group, click the **Breaks** button and select **Page**.

    d. Click the **References** tab.

    e. In the *Index* group, click the **Insert Index** button.

    f. Click the **Formats** arrow and select **Modern**.

    g. Click **OK** to add the index.

19. Save and close the document.

skill review **5.2**

In this project, you will be reviewing the document for the Tri-State Book Festival. You will be making changes, accepting and rejecting other changes, and working with comments. You will also use the Thesaurus to replace a word with a synonym. Finally, you will add a footnote and tab leaders to text in the document and a caption to a chart.

Skills needed to complete this project:

- Using Track Changes (Skill 5.15)
- Accepting and Rejecting Changes in a Document (Skill 5.18)
- Working with Comments (Skill 5.16)
- Hiding and Showing Changes in a Document (Skill 5.17)
- Using AutoCorrect (Skill 5.3)
- Using the Thesaurus (Skill 5.2)
- Adding a Caption (Skill 5.6)
- Adding Tab Leaders (Skill 5.5)
- Inserting Footnotes and Endnotes (Skill 5.7)

1. Open the start file **WD2019-SkillReview-5-2** and resave the file as: `[your initials]WD-SkillReview-5-2`

2. If the document opens in Protected View, click the **Enable Editing** button in the Message Bar at the top of the document so you can modify the document.

3. Use *Track Changes*.

    a. Click the **Review** tab.

    b. In the *Tracking* group, click the **Track Changes** button to turn the feature on.

    c. In the first sentence of the first paragraph select the text **October 10-12**. Press the **Delete** key to delete the sentence.

    d. Type **September 6-8**.

4. Change the display of tracked changes in a document.

    a. On the *Review* tab, in the *Tracking* group, click the **Show Markup** button.

    b. Point to *Balloons* and select **Show Revisions in Balloons**.

5. Accept and reject changes in a document.

    a. Place the cursor at the beginning of the first paragraph of the document.

    b. On the *Review* tab, in the *Changes* group, click the **Next Change** button.

    c. The first item found is a comment. Click **Next Change** again to move to the first change in the document

d. Click the **Accept and Move to Next** button to accept the deletion you just made.

e. Click the **Accept and Move to Next** button to accept the insertion you just made.

f. In the *Changes* group, click the **Accept and Move to Next** button to accept the deletion of the text *95*.

g. Click the **Accept and Move to Next** button to accept the insertion of the text *75*.

h. Click the **Accept and Move to Next** button to accept the formatting change.

i. Click the **Accept and Move to Next** button to accept the formatting change.

j. Click the **Reject and Move to Next** button to reject the formatting change.

k. Click the **Reject and Move to Next** button to reject the deletion.

6. Accept all changes in the document.

   a. In the *Tracking* group, click the **Accept** button arrow.

   b. Select **Accept All Changes** to accept the remaining changes in the document.

7. Turn *Track Changes* off by clicking the **Track Changes** button.

8. Reply to a comment.

   a. Click the **Reply** button in the comment on page 1.

   b. Type the following reply: `This has been updated`

9. Click the **Resolve** button in the comment balloon to resolve the comment.

10. Add a comment to a document.

    a. Place the cursor at the end of the *Book signing and dinner* text in the last row of the table in the *September 6* section

    b. On the *Review* tab, in the *Comments* group, click the **New Comment** button.

    c. Type the following comment: `Be sure to confirm with authors`

11. Change the review display of the document.

    a. On the *Review* tab, in the *Tracking* group, click the **Display for Review** drop-down arrow.

    b. Select **No Markup**.

12. Use the Thesaurus.

    a. In the second sentence of the first paragraph, select the word **kinds**.

    b. On the *Review* tab, in the *Proofing* group, click the **Thesaurus** button.

    c. Point to *genres* in the list of synonyms, click the arrow, and click **Insert**.

13. Insert a footnote.

    a. Place the cursor after the period in the second to last sentence in the second paragraph (after *written by one of our authors.*).

    b. Click the **References** tab.

    c. In the *Footnotes* group, click the **Insert Footnote** button.

    d. Type the following text for the footnote: `Prizes will be awarded to the attendees who solve the crime the fastest`

14. Adding tab leaders.

    a. Navigate to the *Authors* section and select the list of authors (both *Fiction* and *Nonfiction*).

    b. Click the **Home** tab.

    c. In the *Paragraph* group, click the **dialog launcher**.

    d. In the *Paragraph* dialog, click the **Tabs...** button.

    e. In the *Tab stop position* box, type **2.5"**.

f. In the *Leader* section, select the **second option**.

g. Click **OK**.

h. Delete the space between *Max Wallace* and *Featured Work* and press the ⌨Tab⇥ key.

i. Repeat this step for all the authors in the *Fiction* and *Nonfiction* sections.

15. Add a caption.

a. Navigate to the end of the document and select the chart.

b. Click the **References** tab.

c. In the *Captions* group, click the **Insert Caption** button.

d. Change the text in the *Caption* text box to read: `Figure 1: Authors by Genre`

e. Click **OK**.

16. Save and close the document.

challenge yourself 5.3

In this project you will be working on a safety report from the Winter Springs Community. First, you will work with track changes by accepting and rejecting changes that have been made. You will also add and reply to comments. You will create an AutoCorrect entry and then use the Thesaurus to find synonyms of words. You will add a caption to a chart. You will add tab leaders to text, a table of contents, and a footnote. You will then mark an entry for the index and add an index to the document.

Skills needed to complete this project:

- Using Track Changes (Skill 5.15)
- Accepting and Rejecting Changes in a Document (Skill 5.18)
- Working with Comments (Skill 5.16)
- Using AutoCorrect (Skill 5.3)
- Using the Thesaurus (Skill 5.2)
- Adding a Caption (Skill 5.6)
- Adding Tab Leaders (Skill 5.5)
- Inserting a Table of Contents (Skill 5.4)
- Inserting Footnotes and Endnotes (Skill 5.7)
- Marking Entries (Skill 5.13)
- Creating an Index (Skill 5.14)

1. Open the start file **WD2019-ChallengeYourself-5-3** and resave the file as: `[your initials]WD-ChallengeYourself-5-3`

2. If the document opens in Protected View, enable editing so you can make changes to the document.

3. Review the document from the beginning and make the following changes:

a. Accept the formatting on the title of the document.

b. Reject the deletion of the word **neighborhood**.

c. Accept the insertion of the word **electronic**.

d. Reject the deletion of the word **Never** and reject the insertion of the word **Rarely**.

e. Accept all the remaining tracked changes in the document.

4. Add a comment to the *Most Targeted Electronic Devices* heading that reads: `Be sure to check these numbers`

5. Navigate to the comment in the *Security Staff* section and type `This took effect 3 months ago` as a reply to the comment.

6. Resolve the comment.

7. Change the display of the document to show no markup.

8. Navigate to the beginning of the document and place the cursor at the beginning of the *Introduction* heading.

9. Create an AutoCorrect entry that will change the letters **wsc** to **Winter Springs Community** when typed.

10. Place the cursor between the words *The* and *currently* in the first sentence of the *Security Staff* section. Type `wsc` and press the spacebar. Notice Word changes the text to the entry you just created.

11. Select the word **neighborhood** in the first sentence of the first paragraph of the document (*secure, gated neighborhood*). Use the Thesaurus to replace the word **neighborhood** with the synonym **community**.

12. Select the word **robberies** in the second sentence of the first paragraph. Use the Thesaurus to replace the word **robberies** with the synonym **thefts**.

13. Select the chart in the document. Add a caption that reads **Figure 1: Most Targeted Electronics**. Have the figure appear below the chart.

14. Select the list of round the clock officers in the *Security Staff* section. Open the *Tabs* dialog, add a **right tab** at the **5"** mark. Include a **dotted tab leader (option 2)**.

15. For each item in the bulleted list, place the cursor between the name and the number of years. Remove the space and press **Tab**.

16. Repeat steps 14–15 for the list of day shift officers.

17. Place the cursor at the end of the document title *Winter Springs Community News* (at the beginning of the document) and press Enter. Add a table of contents based on the **Automatic Table 2** style. Delete the extra blank line.

18. Place the cursor at the end of the heading *Guidelines for Staying Safe*. Insert a footnote that reads: **Adapted from Sylvester Bryant's safety presentation**.

19. Select the text *monthly security meetings* in the first sentence of the first paragraph in the *Security Meeting Schedule* section. Mark the text for use in an index. Close the *Mark Index Entry* dialog.

20. Place the cursor in the blank line below the table at the end of the document and add a page break. Insert an index based on the **Classic** format. Have the index display in one column.

21. Hide the formatting marks in the document when you are done.

22. Save and close the document.

challenge yourself 5.4

In this project, you will be reviewing a paper on behavioral change. You will be replacing words by looking up synonyms in the Thesaurus. You will add a footnote to the document. Next, you will be working with tracked changes. You will be accepting and rejecting changes, changing the markup display, and locking track changes. Next, you will add captions to charts. Finally, you will work with comments including adding a comment, replying to a comment, and resolving a comment.

Skills needed to complete this project:

- Using the Thesaurus (Skill 5.2)
- Inserting Footnotes and Endnotes (Skill 5.7)
- Hiding and Showing Changes in a Document (Skill 5.17)
- Using Track Changes (Skill 5.15)
- Accepting and Rejecting Changes in a Document (Skill 5.18)
- Adding a Caption (Skill 5.6)
- Working with Comments (Skill 5.16)
- Locking Track Changes (Skill 5.19)
- Changing How Pages Scroll (Skill 5.21)

1. Open the start file **WD2019-ChallengeYourself-5-4** and resave the file as: `[your initials]WD-ChallengeYourself-5-4`

2. If the document opens in Protected View, enable editing so you can make changes to the document.

3. Use the Thesaurus to change the word **pupil** to **student** in the last sentence of the first paragraph of the document.

4. Add a footnote at the end of the second sentence of the first paragraph (the sentence ending with *time period*). The footnote should read `Observed the student over five days in both phases`.

5. Change the display of the tracked changes to show all revisions in balloons.

6. Review the document from the beginning and make the following changes:

   a. Reject the insertion of the word **absolutely**.

   b. Reject the formatting of **Language Arts**.

   c. Accept the deletion of **observation** and the insertion of **implementation**.

7. Accept all the remaining tracked changes in the document.

8. Select the first chart in the document and add a caption that appears below the chart. Have the caption read `Figure 1: Observation Phase`.

9. Select the second chart in the document and add a caption that appears below the chart. Have the caption read `Figure 2: Implementation Phase`.

10. Reply to the first comment in the document with: `This has been completed`

11. Resolve the comment.

12. Add a comment to the *Techniques* heading that reads: `Can this section be deleted?`.

13. Change the display of the document to show no markup.

14. Lock tracking on the document.

15. Switch to the **Side to Side** page movement view.

16. Switch back to the **Vertical** page movement view.

17. Save and close the document.

on your own 5.5

In this project, you will be reviewing a memo from the Trade Winds Food company. You will finish out the document by adding a caption, replacing a word using the Thesaurus, and adding tab leaders to the document. You will work with tracked changes and comments, including locking tracking. Finally, you will create an AutoCorrect entry and view the document using Read Mode.

Skills needed to complete this project:
- Adding a Caption (Skill 5.6)
- Using the Thesaurus (Skill 5.2)
- Adding Tab Leaders (Skill 5.5)
- Using Track Changes (Skill 5.15)
- Hiding and Showing Changes in a Document (Skill 5.17)
- Accepting and Rejecting Changes in a Document (Skill 5.18)
- Working with Comments (Skill 5.16)
- Locking Track Changes (Skill 5.19)
- Using AutoCorrect (Skill 5.3)
- Using Read Mode (Skill 5.20)

1. Open the start file **WD2019-OnYourOwn-5-5** and resave the file as: `[your initials]WD-OnYourOwn-5-5`
2. If the document opens in Protected View, click the **Enable Editing** button in the Message Bar at the top of the document so you can modify the document.
3. Add a caption to the chart on the second page of the document.
4. Use the Thesaurus to replace the word **rival** in the second paragraph with a word of your choice.
5. Add a tab stop at the 4.5″ mark with a tab leader of your choice to the last line of the document. Insert a tab between *Marketing Strategies* and *Trade Wind Foods*.
6. Turn on **Track Changes**.
7. Change the display of the markup in the document.
8. Change the color of the **Trade Winds Food Committee Memo** text to a color of your choice.
9. Accept the formatting change you made.
10. Review the document and accept and reject the tracked changes as you see fit.
11. Add a comment directing others to review a specific part of the document.
12. Reply to and resolve the comments in the document.
13. Lock tracking in the document.
14. Add an AutoCorrect entry to be able to quickly enter the company name **Trade Wind Foods**.
15. Change the display of the document so comments will be hidden.
16. Switch to **Read Mode** and then back to **Print Layout** view.
17. Save and close the document.

fix it 5.6

In this project you will be working on a research paper about alternate assessments for students. You will be fixing a number of errors in the paper. First you will work with track changes by accepting and rejecting changes that have been made. You will also reply to and resolve a comment. You will find a synonym for a word using the Thesaurus. You will change the reference style for the paper to APA and then correct a citation error. You will add a bibliography. You will replace the hand-typed table of contents with one that is autogenerated. You will remove a manually entered note and replace it with a footnote. You will mark an entry for the index and then replace the hand-typed index with an autogenerated one.

Skills needed to complete this project:

- Using Track Changes (Skill 5.15)
- Accepting and Rejecting Changes in a Document (Skill 5.18)
- Using the Thesaurus (Skill 5.2)
- Selecting a Reference Style (Skill 5.9)
- Adding Citations to Documents (Skill 5.10)
- Creating a Bibliography (Skill 5.12)
- Inserting Footnotes and Endnotes (Skill 5.7)
- Marking Entries (Skill 5.13)
- Creating an Index (Skill 5.14)
- Inserting a Table of Contents (Skill 5.4)
- Working with Comments (Skill 5.16)

1. Open the start file **WD2019-FixIt-5-6** and resave the file as:
   `[your initials]WD-FixIt-5-6`

2. If the document opens in Protected View, click the **Enable Editing** button in the Message Bar at the top of the document so you can modify the document.

3. Navigate to the first heading in the document (*Introduction*), and review the tracked changes in the document, making the following changes:

   a. Accept the first change of **accommodations** to **modifications**.

   b. Accept the second change of **accommodations** to **modifications**.

   c. Reject the deletion of the word **fundamental**.

   d. Reject the deletion of the word **educational**.

   e. The remaining changes are formatting changes to headings. Accept the remaining changes in the document.

4. In the second sentence in the first paragraph under *What is an Alternate Assessment*, use the *Thesaurus* to replace the word **duties** with **responsibilities**.

5. Change the reference style for the document to **APA Sixth Edition**.

6. Place the cursor before the period in the second to last sentence of the first paragraph in the *Modified Achievement Standards* section (the sentence ending with *demonstrate adequate proficiency.*). Insert a citation to the **Pamela Johnson** source.

7. In the first paragraph of the *No Child Left Behind* section, the citations have been manually entered. Create a new source based on the following information:

   a. Type of Source: **Journal Article**

   b. Author: **Elliot, Stephen; Kettler, Ryan**

   c. Title: **Assessments Based on Modified Standards**

   d. Journal Name: **Exceptional Children**

   e. Year: **2017**

   f. Pages: **44-46**

8. Replace the three manually entered citations in the first paragraph of the *No Child Left Behind* section with the source you just created.

9. The bibliography at the end of the document has been entered in manually. Delete the existing bibliography.

10. Replace the bibliography you deleted with one generated by Word based on the **Bibliography** style.

11. In the *No Child Left Behind* section of the document, a note has been added manually. Delete the superscript number next to the word **state** and the note at the end of the *No Child Left Behind* section (the line beginning with ^{1} *In this project, the*).

12. Place the cursor after the word *state* in the first sentence of the first paragraph in the *No Child Left Behind* section and add a footnote that reads: `In this project, the Ohio state standards were applied.`

13. Navigate to the *Who Will Benefit* section. In the first sentence of the second paragraph mark the words **determining eligibility** for use in the index.

14. Hide the formatting marks in the document.

15. Navigate to the end of the document and delete the index that was entered in manually.

16. Replace the index you deleted with one generated by Word using the **Classic** format in a two-column layout.

17. The table of contents at the beginning of the document has been manually entered. Delete the table of contents.

18. Replace the table of contents you deleted with one generated by Word using the **Automatic Table 1** option.

19. Click the **Reply** button in the comment on the title page and type the following reply: `These have been corrected`

20. Click the **Resolve** comment button to resolve the comment.

21. Save and close the document.

Source of screenshots: Microsoft Office 365: Word, Excel, Access, and PowerPoint.

Foot spa: Comstock/Mediabakery
Manicure: Valua Vitaly/Shutterstock

excel 365

chapter 1

Getting Started with Excel

In this chapter, you will learn the following skills:

❯ Identify the elements of a Microsoft Excel workbook

❯ Navigate a workbook

❯ Enter and format text, numbers, and dates in cells

❯ Understand the concept of charts

❯ Use the Recommended Charts feature

❯ Enter simple formulas

❯ Understand relative and absolute cell references

❯ Understand the concept of a function

❯ Use AutoSum and the Quick Analysis tool to add totals

❯ Use the status bar to display totals and other values

❯ Change the zoom level to view more or less of the worksheet

❯ Create a new workbook from a template

❯ Arrange multiple workbook windows

❯ Spell check a worksheet

❯ Preview and print a worksheet

skills

introduction

This chapter provides you with the basic skills necessary to start working with Excel. The first step is to become familiar with the Excel interface and learn how to navigate a workbook. Next, you'll learn how to enter data and apply simple number and date formats. You will learn about charts and how to use the Recommended Charts feature to add a chart quickly. This chapter introduces the concepts of formulas, functions, and absolute and relative references. Pay close attention to the skill *Understanding Absolute and Relative References*. These concepts are used throughout Excel. You will add totals to worksheet data using the SUM function with a variety of methods including AutoSum and the Quick Analysis tool. To help you start using Excel for your own purposes, you will learn how to create a new workbook from a template and how to manage multiple workbooks at the same time. Finally, the chapter covers how to check a worksheet for spelling errors and how to preview and print.

Skill 1.1 Introduction to Excel

Microsoft Excel is a spreadsheet program in which you enter, manipulate, calculate, and chart numerical and text data. An Excel file is referred to as a **workbook**, which is a collection of worksheets. Each worksheet (also called a "sheet") is made up of rows and columns of data on which you can perform calculations. It's these calculations that make Excel such a powerful tool. Some of the basic elements of a Microsoft Excel workbook include:

❯ **Worksheet**—an electronic ledger in which you enter data. The worksheet appears as a grid where you can enter and then manipulate data using functions, formulas, and formatting. Excel workbooks have one worksheet by default named *Sheet1*. You can rename, add, and delete worksheets as necessary.

❯ **Row**—a horizontal group of cells. Rows are identified by numbers. For example, the third row is labeled with the number *3*.

❯ **Column**—a vertical group of cells. Columns are identified by letters. For example, the fourth column is labeled with the letter *D*.

❯ **Cell**—the intersection of a column and a row. A cell is identified by the **cell address**—its column and row position. For example, the cell at the intersection of column D and row 3 has a cell address of *D3*.

❯ **Cell range**—a contiguous group of cells. A cell range is identified by the address of the cell in the upper left corner of the range, followed by a colon, and then the address of the cell in the lower right corner of the range. The cell range *B3:B5* includes cells B3, B4, and B5. A cell range can incorporate multiple columns and rows as long as the cells are all contiguous. The range *B3:D5* includes cells B3, B4, B5, C3, C4, C5, D3, D4, and D5.

❯ **Formula bar**—data entry area directly below the Ribbon and above the worksheet grid. Although you can type any data in the formula bar, the *Insert Function* button at the left side of the formula bar was designed to make it easier to create complex formulas.

❯ **Name box**—appears at the left side of the formula bar and displays the address of the selected cell. If a group of cells is selected, the *Name* box displays the address of the first cell in the group.

❭ **Status bar**–appears at the bottom of the worksheet grid and can display information about the selected data, including the number of cells selected that contain data (count) and the average and sum (total) of the selected values.

You can use Excel for a wide variety of purposes, from calculating payments for a personal loan, to creating a budget, to tracking cash flow for your business. Excel is not limited to numerical calculations.

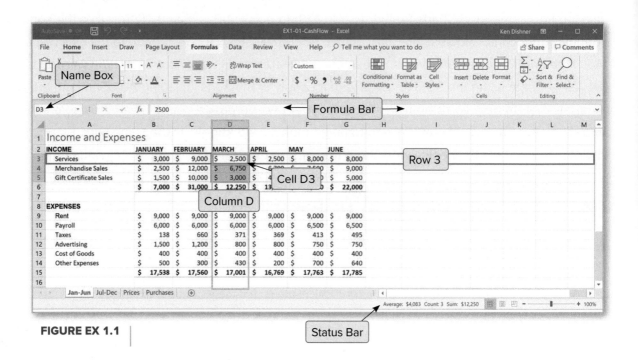

FIGURE EX 1.1

let me try

Open the student data file **EX1-01-CashFlow** and explore the Excel workbook on your own:

1. If necessary, click the **Jan-Jun** worksheet tab at the bottom of the workbook.
2. Click anywhere in **column D**.
3. Click anywhere in **row 3**.
4. Click cell **D3**.
5. Click the **formula bar**.
6. Click the **Name box**.
7. Click the **status bar**.
8. If you will be moving on to the next skill in this chapter, leave the workbook open to continue working. If not, save the file as directed by your instructor and close it.

Skill 1.2 Navigating a Workbook

An Excel worksheet can include more than one million rows and more than sixteen thousand columns. That's a lot of potential data to navigate! Luckily, most spreadsheets are not quite that large. However, you may encounter workbooks with multiple worksheets and hundreds of rows and columns of data.

The Excel window includes both a **vertical scroll bar** (at the right side of the window) and a **horizontal scroll bar** (at the bottom of the window). Click the arrows at the ends of the scroll bars to move up and down or left and right to see more cells in an individual worksheet. You can also click and drag the scroll box to reposition your view of the spreadsheet. Notice that when you use the scroll bars, the selected cell does not change. Using the scroll bars changes only your view of the worksheet.

The most obvious way to select a cell in a worksheet is to click it with the mouse. Notice that Excel highlights the appropriate column letter and row number to identify the selected cell. When you select a single cell, the cell address appears in the *Name* box in the upper left corner of the spreadsheet, and the cell content appears in the formula bar (immediately below the Ribbon).

To navigate to another worksheet in the workbook, click the appropriate tab at the bottom of the worksheet grid. If the worksheet tab is not visible, use the navigation arrows located at the left side of the first sheet tab to show one worksheet at a time to the left or the right. These arrows are active only when there are worksheets not visible in your current view.

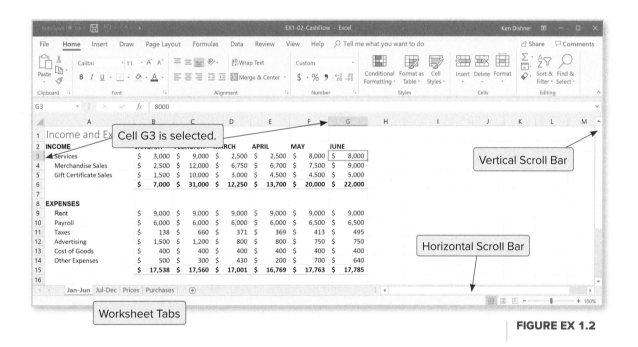

FIGURE EX 1.2

To navigate from cell to cell, use the mouse to click the cell you want to go to. You can also use keyboard shortcuts to navigate around or between worksheets.

↑	Move up one cell
↓	Move down one cell
→	Move one cell to the right
←	Move one cell to the left
Home	Move to the first cell in the row
Ctrl + Home	Go to cell A1
Ctrl + Page down	Move one worksheet to the right
Ctrl + Page up	Move one worksheet to the left

To select a range of cells, click the first cell in the range and drag the mouse until the cells you want are selected. Release the mouse button. You can also click the first cell in the range, press ↑ Shift, and then click the last cell in the range.

To select an entire row, point to the **row selector** (the box with the row number at the left side of the worksheet grid). When the mouse pointer changes to an arrow, click the left mouse button.

To select an entire column, point to the **column selector** (the box with the column letter at the top of the worksheet grid). When the mouse pointer changes to an arrow, click the left mouse button.

FIGURE EX 1.3

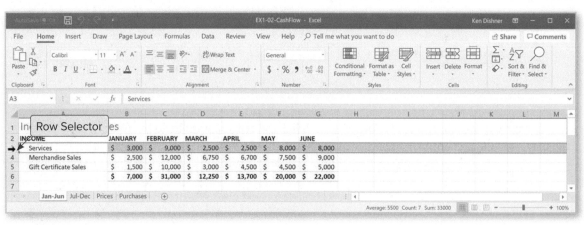

FIGURE EX 1.4

tips & tricks

To make more worksheets visible at one time, adjust the size of the horizontal scroll bar by clicking the dotted line that appears immediately to the left of the scroll bar. Notice that the cursor shape changes to a double-sided arrow. Click and drag to the right to make the horizontal scroll bar shorter and reveal more worksheet tabs.

tell me **more**

Another way to navigate to a specific cell location is to type the cell address in the *Name* box, and then press **Enter**.

Use the *Go To* dialog to navigate to a specific cell. On the *Home* tab, in the *Editing* group, click the **Find & Select** button and select *Go To* from the menu. In the *Reference* box, type the cell address and then click *OK*.

let me **try**

If you do not have the data file from the previous skill open, open the student data file **EX1-02-CashFlow** and try this skill on your own:

1. On the *Jan-Jun* worksheet, select cell **G3**.
2. Select column **G**.
3. Select row **3**.
4. Navigate to the **Jul-Dec** worksheet.
5. Select cells **B3:G5**.
6. If you will be moving on to the next skill in this chapter, leave the workbook open to continue working. If not, save the file as directed by your instructor and close it.

from the perspective of. . .

SPORTS CLINIC OFFICE MANAGER

I couldn't do my job without Microsoft Excel. All the clinic financial data are kept in Excel spreadsheets, and I use Excel's analysis and formatting tools to visualize our cash flow. Any problem areas are easy to find. We sell rehab equipment directly to our patients, and I also use Excel to track the progress of our orders and sales.

Ryan McVay/Getty Images

Skill 1.3 Working in Protected View

When you download a workbook from a location that Excel considers potentially unsafe, it opens automatically in Protected View. **Protected View** provides a read-only format that protects your computer from becoming infected by a virus or other malware. Potentially unsafe locations include the Internet, e-mail messages, or a network location. Files that are opened in Protected View display a warning in the **Message Bar** at the top of the window, below the Ribbon.

To disable Protected View, click the **Enable Editing** button in the Message Bar.

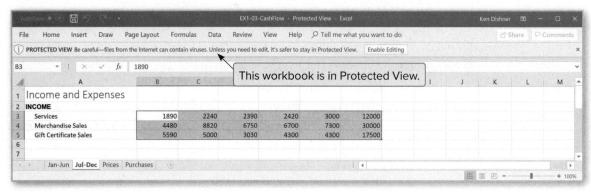

FIGURE EX 1.5

You can also enable editing from the Info page in Backstage view.

1. Click the **File** tab to open Backstage view.

2. If necessary, click **Info**.

3. The *Info* page provides more information about the file. If you are sure you want to remove it from Protected View, click the **Enable Editing** button.

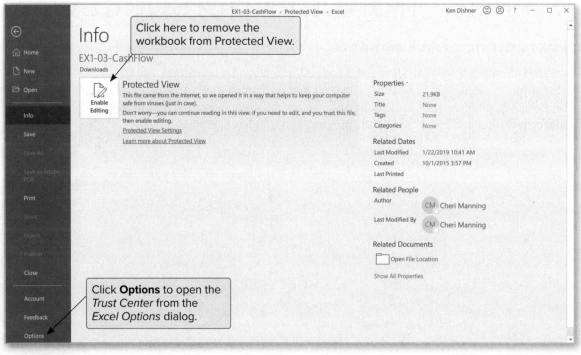

FIGURE EX 1.6

excel 365   chapter 1 Getting Started with Excel

Once you enable editing for a file, it is added to the **Trusted Documents** list and will not appear in Protected View again unless you clear the *Trusted Documents* list.

To remove all files from the *Trusted Documents* list:

1. Click the **File** tab, and then click the **Options** button to open the *Excel Options* dialog.
2. Click **Trust Center**, and then click the **Trust Center Settings...** button to open the *Trust Center* dialog.
3. If necessary, click **Trusted Documents** at the left side of the *Trust Center* dialog.
4. Click the **Clear** button to clear all Trusted Documents so that they are no longer trusted.
5. Click **Yes**.
6. Click **OK** to close the *Trusted Locations* dialog.
7. Click **OK** again to close the *Excel Options* dialog.
8. The next time you open a file that was trusted previously, it will once again appear in Protected View.

tell me **more**

You can modify the Trust Center settings to control which files open in Protected View.

If you are currently in Protected View, the Info page will include a link to go to the Protected View settings. If you are not currently in Protected View, open the Trust Center from the *Excel Options* dialog.

1. Click the **File** tab, and then click the **Options** button to open the *Excel Options* dialog.
2. Click **Trust Center**, and then click the **Trust Center Settings...** button.
3. If necessary, click **Protected View** at the left side of the *Trust Center* dialog. Notice that all the options for Protected View are checked by default. We do not recommend changing any of these default settings.
4. To exempt a specific location from Protected View, click **Trusted Locations**, and add the location you trust (such as a secure network folder).
5. Click **OK** to save your changes and close the *Trusted Locations* dialog.
6. Click **OK** again to close the *Excel Options* dialog.

let me **try**

If you do not have the data file from the previous skill open, open the student data file **EX1-03-CashFlow** and try this skill on your own:

1. This workbook came from a trusted source. If the workbook opens in Protected View, disable Protected View and allow editing.
2. Open the *Trust Center* dialog and review the settings.
3. Close the *Trust Center* and *Excel Options* dialogs without making any changes.
4. If you will be moving on to the next skill in this chapter, leave the workbook open to continue working. If not, save the file as directed by your instructor and close it.

Skill 1.4 Entering and Editing Text and Numbers in Cells

The most basic task in Excel is entering data in your workbook. Entering numerical data is as easy as typing a number in a cell. Numbers can be displayed as dates, currency values, percentages, or other formats. (Later skills discuss number formatting and using functions and formulas to automate numerical calculations.)

Excel is not just about numbers, though. Without text headers, descriptions, and instructions, your workbook would consist of numbers and formulas without any structure. Adding text headers to your rows and columns creates the structure for you to enter data into your workbook.

To enter data in a cell:

1. Click the cell where you want the data to appear.

2. Type the number or text.

3. Press ⏎ Enter or Tab ⭾.

Pressing ⏎ Enter after entering text will move the cursor down one cell.
Pressing Tab ⭾ will move the cursor to the right one cell.

Excel gives you different ways to edit the data in your worksheet. If you want to change the contents of the entire cell, use **Ready mode**. If you want to change only part of the cell data, use **Edit mode**. The status bar, located at the lower left corner of the Excel window, displays which mode you are in—Ready or Edit.

To use Ready mode to change text:

1. Click the cell you want to change.

2. Type the new contents for the cell.

3. Press ⏎ Enter or Tab ⭾ when you are finished.

4. The old contents are completely removed and replaced with what you've typed.

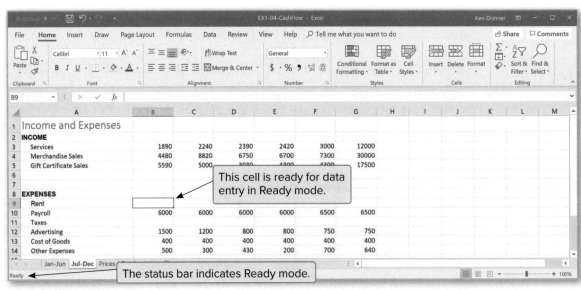

FIGURE EX 1.7

To use Edit mode to change text:

1. Double-click the cell you want to change.

2. You should now see a blinking cursor in the cell.

3. Use → and ← to move the cursor within the cell. Type the changes you want. Use ← Backspace to delete characters to the left of the cursor. Use Delete to delete characters to the right of the cursor. You can also click and drag your mouse to select a section of text to delete.

4. Press ← Enter or Tab ⇥ when you are finished making your changes.

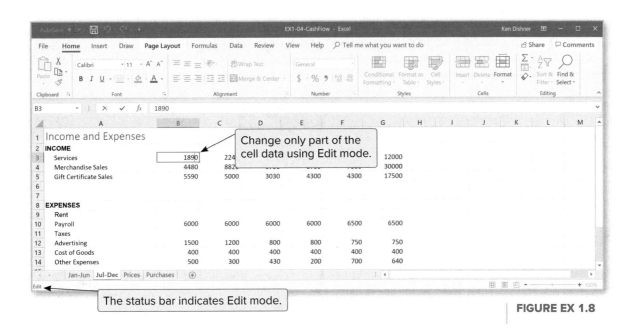

Change only part of the cell data using Edit mode.

The status bar indicates Edit mode.

FIGURE EX 1.8

tips & tricks

To add a line break within the cell, press Alt while pressing ← Enter.

another method

As you type in a cell, the entry is displayed in the formula bar as well as in the active cell. Clicking the **Enter Formula** button ✓ next to the formula bar accepts your entry. Clicking the **Cancel** button ✗ next to the formula bar removes your entry.

let me try

If you do not have the data file from the previous skill open, open the student data file **EX1-04-CashFlow** and try this skill on your own:

1. On the *Jul-Dec* worksheet, add the number **9500** to cell **B9**.

2. Add the word **JULY** to cell **B2**.

3. Change the value in cell **B3** to **1870**. You can use Ready mode or Edit mode.

4. If you will be moving on to the next skill in this chapter, leave the workbook open to continue working. If not, save the file as directed by your instructor and close it.

Skill 1.5 Applying Number Formats

When you first type numbers in a worksheet, Excel applies the **General number format** automatically. The General format right-aligns numbers in the cells but does not maintain a consistent number of decimal places (43.00 will appear as 43, while 42.25 appears as 42.25) and does not display commas (so 1,123,456 appears as 1123456). For consistency, and to make your worksheet easier to read, you should apply the specific number format that is most appropriate for your data. Excel provides several number formats for you to choose from.

Figure EX 1.9 shows common Excel number formats. All numbers in row 2 contain the number 0.567. All numbers in row 3 contain the number 1234. Formatting numbers changes the appearance of the data in your worksheet but doesn't change the numerical values. The formatted number is displayed in the cell, and the actual value is displayed in the formula bar.

Formula bar displays the full number 0.567 while cell B2 formatted using the Number Style format display 0.57

	A	B	C	D	E	F
1	General	Number Style	Comma Style	Currency Style	Accounting Number Format	Percent Style
2	0.567	0.57	0.57	$0.57	$ 0.57	57%
3	1234	1234.00	1,234.00	$1,234.00	$ 1,234.00	123400%
4						

FIGURE EX 1.9

To apply the most common number formats, go to the *Home* tab, *Number* group, and click one of the following buttons:

$ ·	Click the **Accounting Number Format** button to apply formatting appropriate for monetary values. The **Accounting Number Format** aligns the $ at the left side of the cell, displays two places after the decimal, and aligns all numbers at the decimal point. Zero values are displayed as dashes (–).
%	Click the **Percent Style** button to have your numbers appear as %. For example, the number .02 will appear as 2%. By default, **Percent Style format** displays zero places to the right of the decimal point.
,	Click the **Comma Style** button to apply the same format as the Accounting Number Format but without the currency symbol. **Comma Style format** is a good number format to use if your worksheet includes many rows of numbers, summed in a total row (like a budget or cash flow projection), where too many $ symbols could be distracting. Use Comma Style formatting for all numbers except the total row. Use Accounting Number Format for the total row.

Increase Decimal   Decrease Decimal

General

$ · % ,   .00 .00

Number

FIGURE EX 1.10

Use *Increase Decimal* and *Decrease Decimal* to increase or decrease the number of digits that appear to the right of the decimal point. For example, if a cell contains the number 1.234 and you click the **Decrease Decimal** button twice, the cell will display 1.2. The formula bar will still display 1.234 because that is the number stored in the worksheet.

For other common number formats, click the **Number Format** arrow above the buttons in the *Number* group to display the *Number Format* menu.

Number—The default **Number format** shows two decimal places by default so 1,234 displays as 1234.00 but does not include commas.

Currency—With the **Currency format**, columns of numbers do not align at the $ and at the decimal as they do with Accounting Number Format. Instead, the Currency format places the $ immediately to the left of the number.

Percentage—The *Percentage* option on the *Number Format* menu does not apply the same Percent Style format as clicking the *Percent Style* button. The *Percentage* option from the *Number Format* menu displays two digits to the right of the decimal.

More Number Formats...—This option opens the *Format Cells* dialog to the Number tab, where you can select from even more number formats and customize any format, including adding color, specifying the number of decimal places to display, and setting whether or not negative numbers should be enclosed in parentheses.

tips & tricks

If you type $ before a number, Excel automatically applies the Currency number format.

tell me **more**

On the *Home* tab, in the *Styles* group, click the **Cell Styles** button to expand the *Styles* gallery. At the bottom of the gallery are five number styles. Applying one of these cell styles is the same as applying a number format. However, be aware that applying the Currency cell style actually applies the Accounting Number Format, not the Currency format.

❯ **Comma**—applies the default Comma Style format, with two digits to the right of the decimal.

❯ **Comma [0]**—applies the Comma Style format, but with no digits to the right of the decimal.

❯ **Currency**—applies the default Accounting Number Format, with two digits to the right of the decimal.

❯ **Currency [0]**—applies the Accounting Number Format, but with no digits to the right of the decimal.

❯ **Percent**—applies the default Percent Style format.

ⓛ 123	**General** No specific format
12	**Number**
▭	**Currency**
▦	**Accounting**
▭	**Short Date**
▭	**Long Date**
ⓛ	**Time**
%⃞	**Percentage**
½	**Fraction**
10^2	**Scientific**
ab	**Text**

More Number Formats...

FIGURE EX 1.11
Number Format Menu

another **method**

When you right-click a cell, these formats are available from the Mini toolbar: Accounting Number Format, Percent style, and Comma style.

The *Increase Decimal* and *Decrease Decimal* buttons are also available from the Mini toolbar.

To apply the Percent Style, you can use the keyboard shortcut (Ctrl) + (↑ Shift) + (5).

let me **try**

If you do not have the data file from the previous skill open, open the student data file **EX1-05-CashFlow** and try this skill on your own:

1. On the *Jul-Dec* worksheet, select cells **B3:G5**.
2. Apply the **Accounting Number Format**.
3. Modify the number format so no decimal places are visible after the decimal point.
4. Go to the *Prices* worksheet and select cells **C2:C10**.
5. Apply the **Currency** number format.
6. If you will be moving on to the next skill in this chapter, leave the workbook open to continue working. If not, save the file as directed by your instructor and close it.

Skill 1.6 Entering Dates and Applying Date Formats

When you enter numbers in a date format such as 6/30/2019 or June 30, 2019, Excel detects that you are entering a date and automatically applies one of the date formats. Excel treats dates as a special type of number, so cells formatted as dates can be used in calculations. There are many types of date formats available, but the underlying number for the date will always be the same.

There are two number formats available from the *Number Format* menu. To apply one of these formats, from the *Home* tab, click the **Number Format** arrow above the buttons in the *Number* group, and then click the format you want:

❭ **Short Date format**—Applies a simple format displaying the one- or two-digit number representing the month, followed by the one- or two-digit number representing the day, followed by the four-digit year: 6/30/2019.

❭ **Long Date format**—Applies a longer format displaying the day of the week, and then the name of the month, the two-digit date, and the four-digit year: Sunday, June 30, 2019.

FIGURE EX 1.12

If you would like to use a different date format:

1. Select **More Number Formats...** from the *Number Format* list.

2. In the *Format Cells* dialog, from the *Number* tab, if necessary, click **Date** in the *Category* list. Excel offers a variety of prebuilt date formats to choose from.

3. Notice that as you click each format in the *Type* list, the *Sample* box shows how the active cell will display with the selected format.

4. Click the date format you would like and click **OK**.

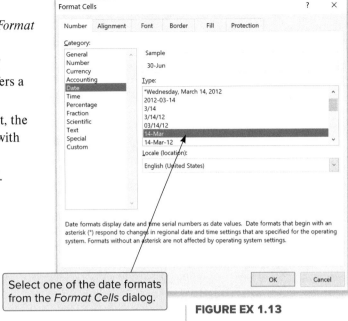

Select one of the date formats from the *Format Cells* dialog.

FIGURE EX 1.13

tips & tricks

Only dates from January 1, 1900, through December 31, 9999, are stored as numbers. Dates prior to January 1, 1900 are stored as text and cannot be used in calculations. To see the serial number for a date, change the cell format from Date to *General* or *Number*. The date will be converted to a "regular" number. For example, December 31, 2009, is the number 40178.

tell me more

Every date format can be expressed as a code. The code for the Short Date format is **m/d/yyyy**. The code for the Long Date format is more complicated: **[$ -x-sysdate]dddd, mmmm dd, yyyy**. If Excel does not offer the exact date format you want to use, you can modify the date code using the Custom number option.

1. Select **More Number Formats...** from the *Number* list.

2. In the *Format Cells* dialog, from the *Number* tab, click **Custom** in the *Category* list.

3. The *Custom* list includes the code for every number format offered. Click the code for the format closest to the format you want, and then make adjustments to the code in the *Type* box. The *Sample* box shows how the number format will look in your worksheet.

4. Click **OK** to apply your new custom number format.

let me try

If you do not have the data file from the previous skill open, open the student data file **EX1-06-CashFlow** and try this skill on your own:

1. On the *Purchases* worksheet, review the date formats used in column A.

2. Select column A, and apply the **Long Date** format.

3. With column A still selected, apply the **Short Date** format.

4. With column A still selected, apply the format to display dates in the format similar to **14-Mar**.

5. If you will be moving on to the next skill in this chapter, leave the workbook open to continue working. If not, save the file as directed by your instructor and close it.

Skill 1.7 Inserting Data Using AutoFill

Use the **AutoFill** feature to fill a group of cells with the same data or to extend a data series.

With AutoFill, you can copy the same value or formula to a group of cells at once. This is much more efficient than using copy and paste over and over again.

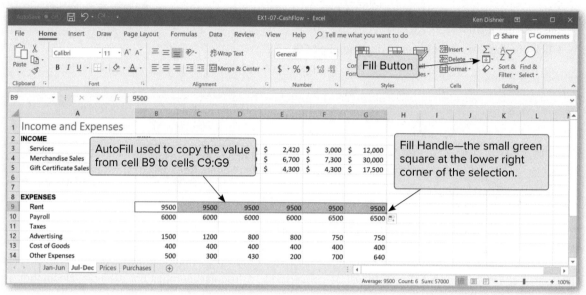

FIGURE EX 1.14

The easiest way to use AutoFill is to use the **Fill Handle** to fill data up or down in a column or to the left or right in a row.

To use the Fill Handle:

1. Select the cell(s) that contain(s) the data you want to use in the AutoFill.

2. Click and drag the **Fill Handle** in the direction you want to fill the data. The Fill Handle is the very small green square at the lower right corner of the cell(s) you selected. As you drag the Fill Handle, a tool tip appears displaying the suggested value for each highlighted cell.

3. Release the mouse button when you have highlighted the last cell you want to fill.

If you have a difficult time using the Fill Handle, use the *Fill* command from the Ribbon instead:

1. Select the entire range you want to fill, beginning with the cell(s) containing the data.

2. On the *Home* tab, in the *Editing* group, click the **Fill** button and select the type of fill you want. The options available will vary depending on the data you selected to use as the source for the fill.

If you have a group of cells with similar data in a series, AutoFill can extend the series automatically. A **data series** is any sequence of cells with a recognizable pattern like those shown in Figure EX 1.15.

Excel attempts to detect automatically if the data appear to be a series. Sometimes, however, the series doesn't fill with the data you expect or want. To change the type of data AutoFill inserts, click the **AutoFill Options** button and select a different option. From the *AutoFill Options* button, you can choose to copy the cells or fill the series. By default, Excel includes formatting when copying or filling a series; however, you can choose to copy only the cell formatting or to fill or copy the data series without formatting.

	A	B	C	D
1		**Numeric Patterns**		
2	1	2	3	4
3	3	5	7	9
4	Student 1	Student 2	Student 3	Student 4
5				
6		**Date Patterns**		
7	January	February	March	April
8	1/1/2020	2/1/2020	3/1/2020	4/1/2020
9	1/1/2020	1/1/2021	1/1/2022	1/1/2023
10				

FIGURE EX 1.15

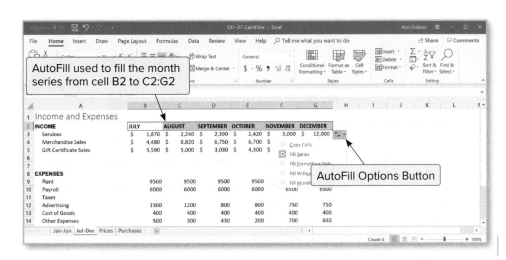

FIGURE EX 1.16

tips & tricks

Use AutoFill to enter repetitive data in your worksheet to avoid errors from entering data manually.

tell me **more**

The Fill Handle tool can be used to fill a series of dates by month as well as year. For example, if you start the series with Jan-2019 and Feb-2019, the Fill Handle will fill in the next cells with Mar-2019, Apr-2019, May-2019, and so on. When the series reaches Dec-2019, the next cell will be filled in with Jan-2020. If you are filling a series of dates, the *AutoFill Options* button will give you the options to fill by day, weekday, month, or year.

another **method**

1. Pressing (Ctrl) + (D) will fill the selected cell(s) with the value from the cell above it.

2. Pressing (Ctrl) + (R) will fill the selected cell(s) with the value from the cell to the left of it.

let me try

If you do not have the data file from the previous skill open, open the student data file **EX1-07-CashFlow** and try this skill on your own:

1. On the *Jul-Dec* worksheet, select cell **B9** (the rent value for July).

2. Use AutoFill to copy the value of cells **C9:G9**.

3. Select cell **B2** (JULY) and use AutoFill to complete the month series through cell **G2**.

4. If you will be moving on to the next skill in this chapter, leave the workbook open to continue working. If not, save the file as directed by your instructor and close it.

Skill 1.8 Exploring Charts

A **chart** is a graphic that represents numeric data visually. In a chart, the values selected in the worksheet, the **data points**, are transformed into graphic **data markers**. Data markers can be columns, bars, pie pieces, lines, or other visual elements. Related data points, usually in the same row or column, are grouped into a **data series**. Some chart types allow you to plot multiple data series.

Figure EX 1.17 shows a column chart with a single data series—*Services - Individual*. You can tell at a glance that the FEB column is the shortest and, therefore, that February has the fewest sales for individual services.

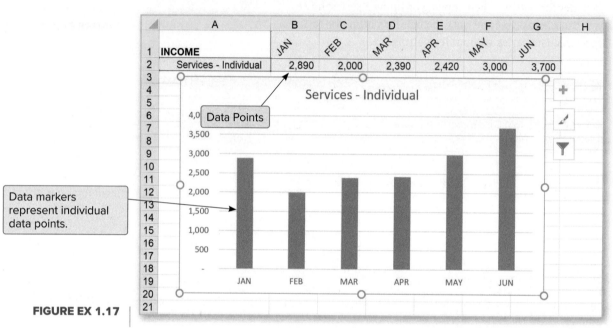

FIGURE EX 1.17

Figure EX 1.18 is a pie chart using the same data as Figure EX 1.17. Each individual data point is represented by a piece of the pie. In this chart, it is not as obvious that FEB is the smallest data point.

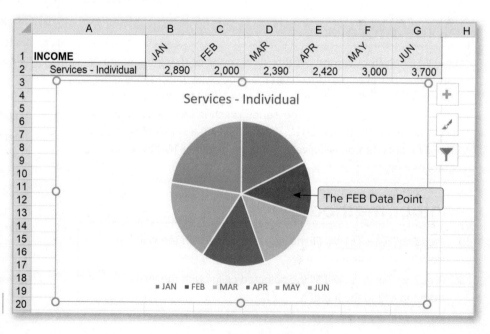

FIGURE EX 1.18

Most charts plot data along two axes. The **y axis** goes from bottom to top. It is the vertical axis. The **x axis** goes from left to right. It is the horizontal axis. Typically, but not always, values are plotted against the y axis and categories are listed along the x axis. In Figure EX 1.19, the y axis shows a range of values from 0 to 4,000. The x axis lists the months. For each category (month), the top of the column reaches the appropriate value on the y axis.

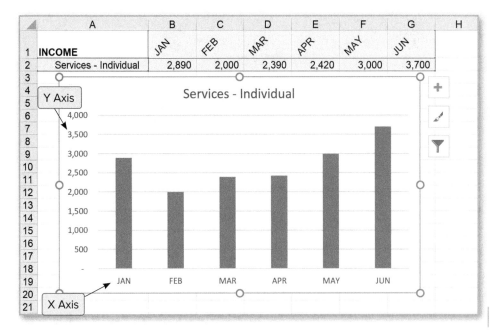

FIGURE EX 1.19

When working with charts, there are a few other common chart elements you should be familiar with:

❭ The **plot area** is the area where the data series are plotted.

❭ The **chart area** is the area that encompasses the entire chart including the plot area and optional layout elements, such as title and legend.

❭ The **chart title** is a text box above or overlaying the chart.

❭ The **legend** tells you which data point or data series is represented by each color in the chart.

When a chart is selected, two contextual tabs are available: the *Chart Tools Design* tab and the *Chart Tools Format* tab. On the *Chart Tools Format* tab, in the *Current Selection* group, the *Chart Elements* box displays the name of the chart element that is currently selected. This can be helpful if you need to ensure that you have selected the chart area, the plot area, or another chart element. To select a specific chart element, expand the **Chart Elements** list and select the chart element you want to select.

FIGURE EX 1.20

tips & tricks

Because charts make it easier to see trends and relationships, they are an important tool for analyzing data. However, the chart type and formatting can influence how others perceive the data. Be careful that the chart does not present the data in a way that may be misleading.

tell me **more**

If the chart is located on the same worksheet as its data, Excel will highlight that data when you select certain chart elements. For example, select the chart area or the plot area, and Excel highlights the cells containing the data point values in blue, the data series labels in red, and the category labels in purple. If you select a single data series, only those data will be highlighted.

let me **try**

Open the student data file **EX1-08-ChartSamples** and try this skill on your own:

1. Begin with the *Column Chart* sheet. Click any of the data markers to select the entire data series. Use the *Chart Elements* box to verify that you have selected the data series. Observe how the worksheet data are represented by the column data markers.

2. Go to the *Pie Chart* sheet. Select the chart legend. Use the legend to match the pie pieces to the data point values.

3. Go to the *Line Chart* sheet. Select the line representing the *Merchandise* data series. Observe that when the *Merchandise* series is selected, cells B4:G4 (the data points) are highlighted in blue.

4. Select the x axis.

5. Select the y axis. Use the *Chart Elements* list if necessary.

6. Close the file without saving any changes you may have made accidentally.

Skill 1.9 Using the Recommended Charts Feature

One trick to working with charts is to select the correct chart type. Excel makes this easier by recommending specific chart types based on the data you have selected in the worksheet. The recommended charts are available from both the Quick Analysis tool and the *Chart Options* dialog.

To add a recommended chart to a worksheet using the Quick Analysis tool:

1. Select the data you want to visualize as a chart.

2. The *Quick Analysis tool* button appears near the lower right corner of the selected range. Click the **Quick Analysis tool** button, and then click the **Charts** tab in the Quick Analysis tool.

3. Hover the mouse cursor over each chart type to see a live preview of the chart. Click the button for the chart type you want. Recommended charts may include multiple versions of the same chart type. Check the live preview carefully to ensure that the data display exactly as you want.

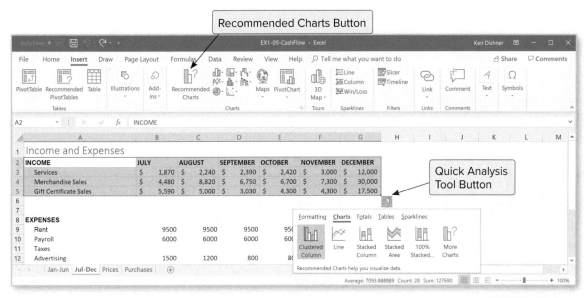

FIGURE EX 1.21

If none of the recommended charts presented in the Quick Analysis tool are precisely what you want, use the *Recommended Charts* button to open the *Insert Chart* dialog:

1. Select the data for the chart.

2. On the *Insert* tab, in the *Charts* group, click the **Recommended Charts** button.

3. The first tab in the *Insert Chart* dialog, *Recommended Charts*, displays the same chart options as the *Charts* tab in the Quick Analysis tool, plus a few more. When you select a chart type, a preview of the chart appears in the right pane of the dialog.

4. Click **OK** to insert the selected chart into the worksheet.

FIGURE EX 1.22

When you insert a new chart, there is a title placeholder that displays *Chart Title*. To change the title text, click the **Chart Title** box once to select it and type the new title. The default text is overwritten once you begin typing. You can also type new text in the formula bar and then press ⟨← Enter⟩.

To edit the chart title, click the **Chart Title** box once to select it and then click it again to enter Edit mode. Edit the text directly in the *Chart Title* box.

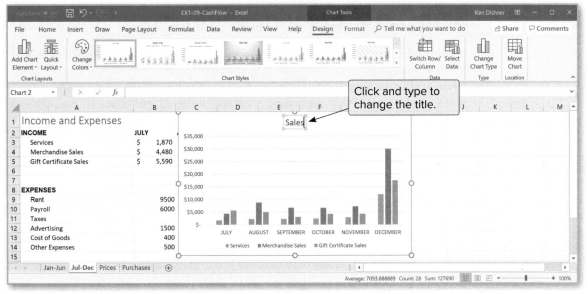

FIGURE EX 1.23

To delete a chart, click the chart once to select it, and then press ⬅ Backspace or Delete.

tips & tricks

The Quick Analysis tool is available only if the data selected for the chart are in contiguous cells—a group of cells that are all next to one another without any cells left out of the group. To create a chart from a noncontiguous group of cells, you must use the *Insert Chart* dialog or one of the insert chart buttons from the *Insert* tab, *Charts* group.

tell me **more**

To create a chart that is not listed as a recommended chart, you can use one of the insert chart buttons from the *Insert* tab, *Charts* group or the *All Charts* tab in the *Insert Chart* dialog. To learn about creating these charts, refer to the skills *Inserting a Column Chart or Bar Chart*, *Inserting a Pie Chart*, and *Inserting a Line Chart*. There are also advanced skills on creating other charts such as hierarchy charts, statistical charts, and waterfall charts.

another **method**

You can open the *Insert Chart* dialog from the *Quick Analysis tool* button:

1. Select the data for the chart.
2. Click the **Quick Analysis tool** button.
3. Click the **Charts** tab, and then click the **More Charts** button to open the *Insert Chart* dialog.

let me **try**

Open the student data file **EX1-09-CashFlow** and try this skill on your own:

1. If necessary, go to the *Jul-Dec* worksheet, and select cells **A2:G5**.
2. Insert a **Clustered Column** chart based on the first recommended chart type.
3. Change the title to: **Sales**
4. If you will be moving on to the next skill in this chapter, leave the workbook open to continue working. If not, save the file as directed by your instructor and close it.

Skill 1.10 Entering Simple Formulas

A **formula** is an equation used to calculate a value. A formula can perform a mathematical calculation, such as displaying the sum of $35 + 47$, or a formula can calculate a value using cell references, such as displaying a value equal to the value of another cell ($= \mathbf{B15}$) or calculating an equation based on values in multiple cells ($= \mathbf{B17} + \mathbf{B18} - \mathbf{B19}$).

In Figure EX 1.24, cell B19 contains the formula $= \mathbf{B15}$. This formula directs Excel to make the value of cell B19 equal to the value of cell B15. If the value in cell B15 changes, the value displayed in cell B19 will update accordingly.

Notice that when the cell is selected, the result of the formula is displayed in the cell, while the formula is displayed in the formula bar.

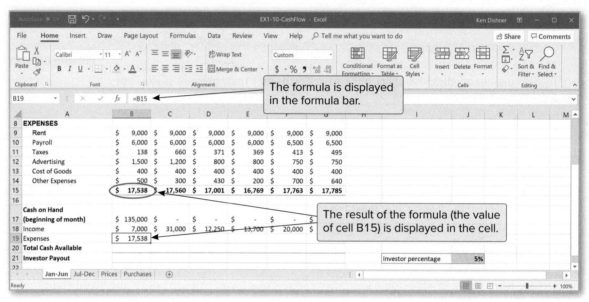

FIGURE EX 1.24

To enter a formula:

1. Click the cell in which you want to enter the formula.

2. Press ⬚= and begin typing the formula. The ⬚= tells Excel that you are entering a formula, not standard text or numeric data.

3. Use the following symbols for mathematical operations:

Addition	+
Subtraction	−
Multiplication	*
Division	/

4. To add a cell reference to a formula, you can type the cell address or click the cell. If you are in the middle of typing a formula and you click another cell in the worksheet, Excel knows to add that cell reference to the formula instead of moving to it.

5. Press ⬚(← Enter) or click the **Enter** button ✓ to the left of the formula bar when you are finished entering the formula.

When you edit the formula in the cell or the formula bar, any referenced cells are highlighted in the same color as the cell reference in the formula. When you have a formula with multiple cell references, such as the one in Figure EX 1.25, the colors make it easier to troubleshoot any errors.

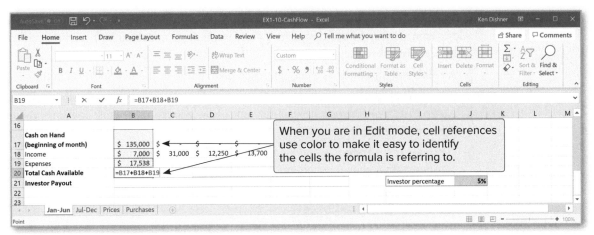

FIGURE EX 1.25

tell me **more**

When you enter a formula with more than one mathematical operation, the formula is not necessarily calculated from left to right. Excel calculations follow the mathematical rules called the **order of operations** (also called **precedence**).

The rules state that mathematical operations in a formula are calculated in this order:

1. Exponents and roots
2. Multiplication and division
3. Addition and subtraction

Adding parentheses around part of a formula will override the order of operations, forcing Excel to perform the calculation within the parentheses first.

$4 + (5 * 2) = 14$—Excel calculates $5 * 2$ first (10), and then adds 4.

$(4 + 5) * 2 = 18$—Excel calculates $4 + 5$ first (9), and then multiples by 2.

$4 + 5 \wedge 2 = 29$—Excel calculates 5 to the 2nd power first (25), and then adds 4.

$(4 + 5) \wedge 2 = 81$—Excel calculates $4 + 5$ first (9), and then raises that number to the 2nd power.

If you have trouble remembering the order of operations, use the phrase "**P**lease **E**xcuse **M**y **D**ear **A**unt **S**ally." PEMDAS = **P**arentheses, **E**xponents, **M**ultiplication, **D**ivision, **A**ddition, **S**ubtraction

let me **try**

If you do not have the data file from the previous skill open, open the student data file **EX1-10-CashFlow** and try this skill on your own:

1. On the *Jan-Jun* worksheet, enter a formula in cell **B19** to display the value of cell **B15** (the total expenses for January).

2. In cell B20, enter a formula to calculate the cash balance for the month: the cash available at the beginning of the month (cell **B17**) + income for the month (cell **B18**) – expenses for the month (cell **B19**).

3. On the *Jul-Dec* worksheet, enter a formula in cell **B11** to calculate taxes by multiplying the value of merchandise sales (cell **B4**) by **5.5%**.

4. If you will be moving on to the next skill in this chapter, leave the workbook open to continue working. If not, save the file as directed by your instructor and close it.

Skill 1.11 Understanding Absolute and Relative References

A cell's address, its position in the workbook, is referred to as a **cell reference** when it is used in a formula. In Excel, the $ character before a letter or number in the cell address means that part of the cell's address is *absolute* (nonchanging). Cell references can be relative, absolute, or mixed.

> A **relative reference** is a cell reference that adjusts to the new location in the worksheet when the formula is copied.

> An **absolute reference** is a cell reference whose location remains constant when the formula is copied.

> A **mixed reference** is a combination cell reference with a row position that stays constant with a changing column position (or vice versa).

Relative reference—A1

Absolute reference—$A$1

Mixed reference with absolute row—A$1

Mixed reference with absolute column—$A1

Here's how relative and absolute references work:

When you type a formula into a cell, it uses *relative* references by default. Excel notes the position of the referenced cell *relative* to the active cell. For example, if cell B19 is the active cell and you type the formula **=B15**, Excel displays the value of the cell that is up four rows from the active cell.

> If you change the structure of the worksheet by adding or removing rows or columns, Excel will automatically update all relative cell references. In this example, Excel will update the formula to reflect the new address of the cell that is up four rows from the cell containing the formula.

> If you copy the formula **=B15** from cell B19 and paste it into cell C19, the pasted formula will update automatically to **=C15** to reflect the cell address that is up four rows from the pasted formula.

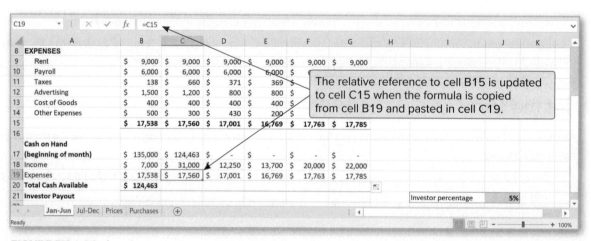

FIGURE EX 1.26

excel 365   chapter 1 Getting Started with Excel

But what if you don't want the cell reference to adjust? For example, in Figure EX 1.27 cell J21 contains a value that you want to use in calculations for multiple cells in a row. If you were to copy the formula **=B20*J21** from cell B21 to cell C21, the formula would update to **=C20*K21** (not what you intended) because both of the cell references are relative. Instead, you want the reference to cell J21 to be *absolute*, so it does not update when you copy it. If you use the formula **=B20*$J$21** instead and copy it from cell B21 to cell C21, the pasted formula will update only the relative reference **B20**. The absolute reference **$J$21** will remain constant. The formula in cell C21 will be **=C20*$J$21**.

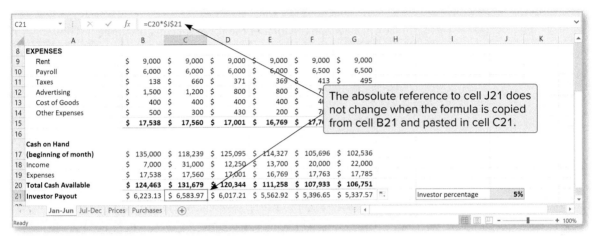

FIGURE EX 1.27

tips & tricks

If you cut and paste a formula, Excel assumes that you want the formula to maintain its previous value and treats the formula as if it had included absolute references, pasting the formula exactly as it was in the original cell.

another **method**

Another way to change the cell reference type is to select the cell reference in the formula bar, and then press `F4` to cycle through the various reference types until you find the one you want (absolute, mixed with absolute row, mixed with absolute column, and then back to relative).

let me try

If you do not have the data file from the previous skill open, open the student data file **EX1-11-CashFlow** and try this skill on your own:

1. On the *Jan-Jun* worksheet, use AutoFill to copy the formula from cell **B19** to cells **C19:G19**. Click cell **G19** to observe the updated cell reference. Now copy the formula in cell **B20** to cells **C20:G20**. Note how the relative reference in the formulas update.

2. In cell **B21**, enter a formula to calculate the investor payout for the month: the cash balance (cell **B20**) multiplied by the investor percentage (cell **J21**). Be sure to use an absolute reference for cell J21.

3. Use AutoFill to copy the formula in cell **B21** to cells **C21:G21**. Click cell **G21** to observe the copied formula with the absolute reference to cell *J21*. If you entered the formula in B21 correctly, the cell reference to J21 will remain constant.

4. On the *Jul-Dec* worksheet, use AutoFill to copy the formula in cell **B11** to cells **C11:G11**. Observe that the relative reference updates as the formula is copied across the row. Delete the chart if it is in the way.

5. If you will be moving on to the next skill in this chapter, leave the workbook open to continue working. If not, save the file as directed by your instructor and close it.

skill 1.11   Understanding Absolute and Relative References

Skill 1.12 Using Functions in Formulas

Functions are preprogrammed shortcuts for calculating equations. Functions can simplify a straightforward computation such as figuring the total of a list of values. They can also calculate the answer to a complicated equation such as figuring the monthly payment amount for a loan.

Most functions require you to provide input called the **arguments**. For example, when writing a formula using the SUM function to calculate the total of a list of values, each value or range of values to be included in the calculation is an argument. Multiple arguments are separated by commas (,).

This formula will calculate the total of the values in cells B9 through B14:

SUM(B9, B10, B11, B12, B13, B14)

In this example, each cell reference is an argument.

An easier way to write the arguments for this formula is:

SUM(B9:B14)

In the second example, the function requires only one argument—the cell range containing the values. Both formulas will return the same total value.

The easiest way to enter a formula using a simple function like SUM is to type the formula directly in the cell or the formula bar. Begin the formula by typing (=), and then type the function name. After the function name, type (() followed by the function arguments, separated by commas, and then ()). Press (←Enter) to complete the formula.

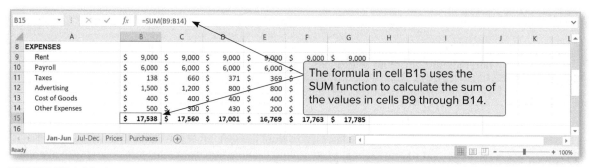

FIGURE EX 1.28

The formula in cell B15 uses the SUM function to calculate the sum of the values in cells B9 through B14.

tell me **more**

You can also enter functions in formulas using AutoSum, Formula AutoComplete, and the *Function Arguments* dialog. These methods are covered in later skills.

let me **try**

If you do not have the data file from the previous skill open, open the student data file **EX1-12-CashFlow** and try this skill on your own:

1. On the *Jan-Jun* worksheet, review the formulas in rows **6** and **15**.

2. On the *Jul-Dec* worksheet, in cell **B6**, enter the formula using the SUM function to calculate the total of cells **B3** through **B5**.

3. If you will be moving on to the next skill in this chapter, leave the workbook open to continue working. If not, save the file as directed by your instructor and close it.

excel 365   chapter 1 Getting Started with Excel

Skill 1.13 Using AutoSum to Insert a SUM Function

If your spreadsheet includes numerical data organized in rows or columns, **AutoSum** can enter totals for you. When you use AutoSum, Excel enters the SUM function arguments using the most likely range of cells based on the structure of your worksheet. For example, if you use AutoSum at the bottom of a column of values, Excel will assume that you want to use the values in the column as the function arguments. If you use AutoSum at the end of a row of values, Excel will use the values in the row. To insert a SUM function using AutoSum:

1. Select the cell in which you want to enter the function.

2. On the *Home* tab, in the *Editing* group, click the **AutoSum** button.

3. Excel automatically inserts a formula with the SUM function, using the range of cells contiguous to (next to) the selected cell as the arguments for the function. You can increase or decrease the range of cells selected by clicking and dragging the corner of the highlighted cell range.

4. Press ⏎ Enter to accept the formula.

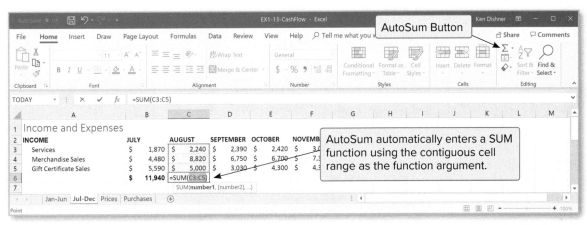

FIGURE EX 1.29

another **method**

❭ AutoSum is also available on the *Formulas* tab, in the *Function Library* group.

❭ You can also click the **AutoSum** button arrow and select **SUM** from the list.

❭ Another way to use the AutoSum function is to select a range of cells, and then click the **AutoSum** button. Excel will insert the SUM function in the next available (empty) cell.

let me **try**

If you do not have the data file from the previous skill open, open the student data file **EX1-13-CashFlow** and try this skill on your own:

1. On the *Jul-Dec* worksheet, select cell **C6**.

2. Use AutoSum to enter a formula to calculate the total of cells **C3:C5**.

3. If you will be moving on to the next skill in this chapter, leave the workbook open to continue working. If not, save the file as directed by your instructor and close it.

Skill 1.14 Calculating Totals with the Quick Analysis Tool

When you have a range of cells selected, you can use the **Quick Analysis tool** to calculate totals down entire columns or across entire rows at once. The Quick Analysis tool includes five types of calculations:

❭ **Sum**–calculates the total of the values in each row or column.

❭ **Average**–calculates the average of the values in each row or column.

❭ **Count**–counts the number of cells that contain values in each row or column.

❭ **% Total**–calculates the percentage of the overall total for the total of each row or column: the sum of values in the row or column divided by the sum of the values in the entire selection.

❭ **Running Total**–calculates a total for each row or column that includes the values in the row or column plus the values in all the previous rows or columns. Notice that the formula for the running total uses an absolute reference for the first cell in the range and a relative reference for the last cell in the range.

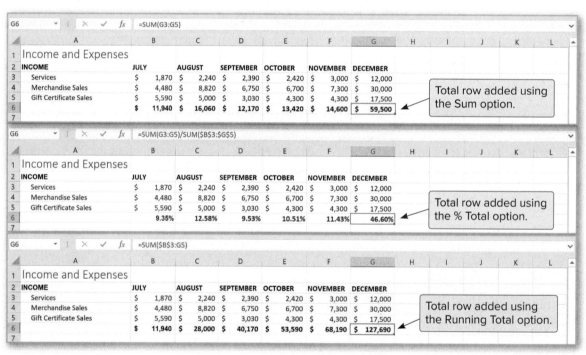

FIGURE EX 1.30

To use the Quick Analysis tool to calculate totals:

1. Select the range of cells. Totals can be inserted below or to the right of the selected cells.

2. The *Quick Analysis tool* button appears near the lower right corner of the selected range. Click the **Quick Analysis tool** button, and then click the **Totals** tab.

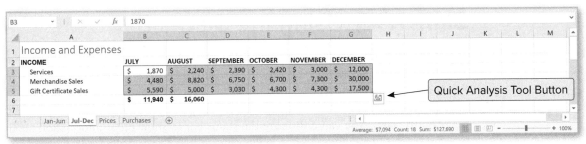

FIGURE EX 1.31

3. Notice that Excel displays a preview of the formulas as you hover the mouse pointer over each option. As shown in Figure EX 1.32, the images in the Quick Analysis tool show where the formulas will be inserted. The first set of buttons shows a blue highlight along the bottom, indicating that the formulas will be inserted below the selected range. The second set of buttons shows a yellow highlight along the right side, indicating that the formulas will be inserted to the right of the selected range.

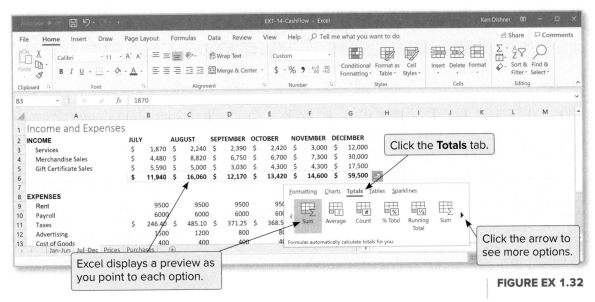

FIGURE EX 1.32

4. Click the button that represents the type of calculation you want to insert.

5. If there are data in any of the cells where the total formulas will be inserted, Excel asks if you want to replace them. Click **OK**.

tips & tricks

If the *Quick Analysis tool* button is not visible, move your mouse cursor over the selected cell range, without clicking. This action should make the button appear.

let me try

If you do not have the data file from the previous skill open, open the student data file **EX1-14-CashFlow** and try this skill on your own:

1. On the *Jul-Dec* worksheet, select the cell range **B3:G5**.

2. Click the **Quick Analysis tool** button, and then click the **Totals** tab.

3. Click the first **Sum** button to insert totals in the row beneath the selected cell range.

4. If Excel asks if you want to replace the existing data, click **OK**.

5. If you will be moving on to the next skill in this chapter, leave the workbook open to continue working. If not, save the file as directed by your instructor and close it.

skill 1.14   Calculating Totals with the Quick Analysis Tool

Skill 1.15 Using the Status Bar

The **status bar** appears at the bottom of the Excel window and displays information about the current worksheet. By default, the status bar displays whether you are in Ready or Edit mode and information about the selected cells (such as the number of cells selected, the sum of the values in the selected cells, or the average of the values in the selected cells). You can customize the status bar to show other information about the worksheet, the minimum or maximum value in the selected cells, and whether Caps Lock is on or off.

To change the information shown on the status bar:

1. Right-click anywhere on the status bar.
2. The *Customize Status Bar* menu appears. Options with checkmarks next to them are currently active. Options without a checkmark are not currently active.
3. Click an item on the menu to add it to or remove it from the status bar display.

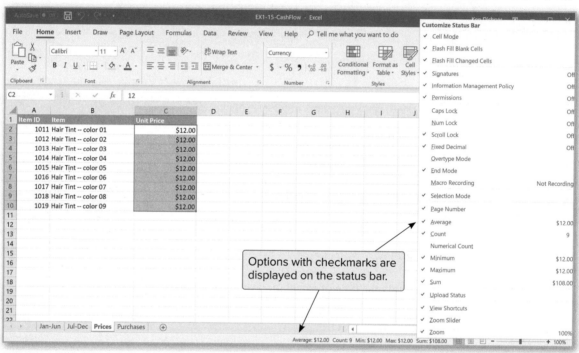

Options with checkmarks are displayed on the status bar.

FIGURE EX 1.33

let me try

If you do not have the data file from the previous skill open, open the student data file **EX1-15-CashFlow** and try this skill on your own:

1. On the *Prices* worksheet, select cells **C2:C10** and observe the calculations displayed on the status bar. You should see the average, count, and sum of the selected cells.
2. Add the minimum and maximum values to the status bar.
3. Observe the changes, and then remove the minimum and maximum values from the status bar so it is back to its original state.
4. If you will be moving on to the next skill in this chapter, leave the workbook open to continue working. If not, save the file as directed by your instructor and close it.

excel 365   chapter 1 Getting Started with Excel

Skill 1.16 Changing the Zoom Level

If you are working with a large spreadsheet, you may find that you need to see more of the spreadsheet at one time or that you would like a closer look at a cell or group of cells. You can use the **zoom slider** in the lower right corner of the window to zoom in and out of a worksheet, changing the size of text and images on screen. As you move the slider, the zoom level displays the percentage the worksheet has been zoomed in or zoomed out. Zooming a worksheet affects only how the worksheet appears on-screen. It does not affect how the worksheet will print.

FIGURE EX 1.34

To zoom in on a worksheet, making the text and graphics appear larger:

❭ Click and drag the zoom slider to the right.

❭ Click the **Zoom In** button on the slider.

To zoom out of a worksheet, making the text and graphics appear smaller:

❭ Click and drag the zoom slider to the left.

❭ Click the **Zoom Out** button on the slider.

FIGURE EX 1.35

On the *View* tab, the *Zoom* group includes buttons for two of the most common zoom options:

❭ Click the **Zoom to Selection** button to zoom in as close as possible on the currently selected cell(s).

❭ Click the **100%** button to return the worksheet back to 100% of the normal size.

You can also change the zoom level through the *Zoom* dialog.

1. On the *View* tab, in the *Zoom* group, click the **Zoom** button.

2. In the *Zoom* dialog, click the radio button for the zoom option you want, and then click **OK**.

FIGURE EX 1.36

tips & tricks

another **method**

You can also open *Zoom* dialog by clicking the zoom level number that appears at the right side of the zoom slider.

let me **try**

If you do not have the data file from the previous skill open, open the student data file **EX1-16-CashFlow** and try this skill on your own:

1. Change the zoom level to **110%**.
2. Change the zoom level back to **100%**.
3. Change the zoom level to **90%**.
4. If you will be moving on to the next skill in this chapter, leave the workbook open to continue working. If not, save the file as directed by your instructor and close it.

from the perspective of. . .

ACCOUNTING FIRM INTERN

My boss works on two 24″ monitors. She always has her files set at 150% or higher because she has the room to spread the worksheet across two large monitors. I work on a laptop with a 15″ screen. When I open her files, I can see only part of the worksheet until I set the zoom level back to 100%. It is harder to see details when the zoom level is set lower, but for me, it's more important to see the whole worksheet without having to scroll.

Brand X Pictures/Stockbyte/Getty Images

Skill 1.17 Creating a New Workbook Using a Template

A **template** is a file with predefined settings that you can use as a starting point for your workbook. Using an Excel template makes creating a new workbook easy and results in a professional appearance. Many templates use advanced techniques that you may not have learned yet—but you can take advantage of them in a template where someone else has created the workbook framework for you. Templates are available for every imaginable task: from creating budgets to tracking exercise to calculating your grade point average.

To create a new workbook using a template:

1. Click the **File** tab to open Backstage view.
2. Click **New**. Excel includes a variety of templates that are copied to your computer when you install the application. These templates are always available from the *New* page. Additional templates that you download are also displayed on the *New* page, so your screen may look different than the one in Figure EX 1.37.

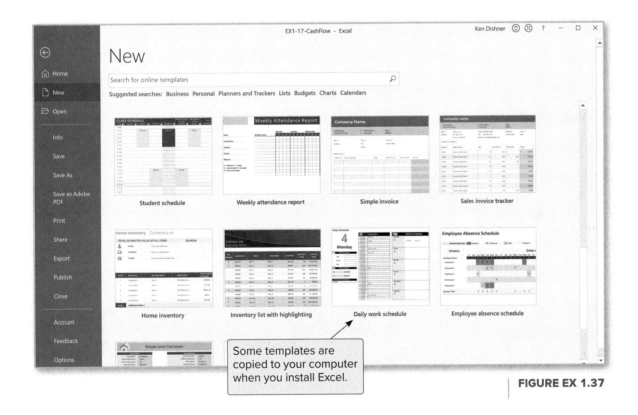

Some templates are copied to your computer when you install Excel.

FIGURE EX 1.37

3. Click a template picture to open the template preview including a brief description of the template.
4. You can cycle through the template previews by clicking the arrows that appear on either side of the preview.

5. When you find the template you want to use, click the **Create** button.

6. A new workbook opens, prepopulated with all of the template elements and sample data. Work through the template, replacing the sample data with your own.

7. Don't forget to save the file.

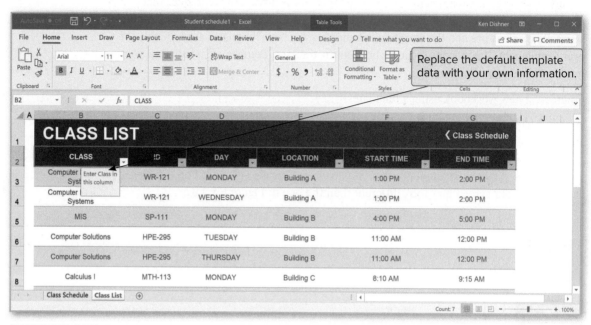

FIGURE EX 1.38

You can search for additional workbook templates online. (You must have an active Internet connection.)

1. Near the top of the *New* page, in the *Search online templates* box, type a keyword or phrase that describes the template you want.

2. Click the **Start searching** button (the magnifying glass image at the end of the *Search online templates* box).

3. The search results display previews of the templates that match the keyword or phrase you entered. To further narrow the results, click one of the categories listed in the *Filter by* pane at the right side of the window. Notice that each category lists the number of templates available.

4. When you find the template you want, click it to display the larger preview with detailed information about the template, and then click **Create**.

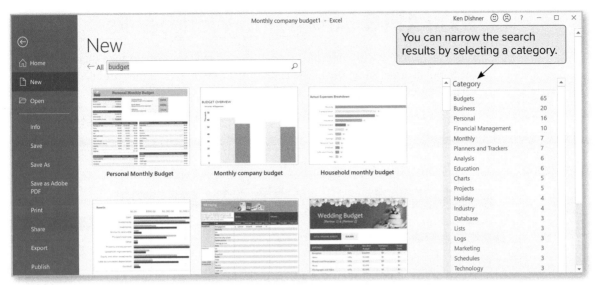

> You can narrow the search results by selecting a category.

FIGURE EX 1.39

tips & tricks

Many Excel templates have a special worksheet labeled Settings, Instructions, or something similar. Be sure to read all of the instructions before entering data.

let me try

If you do not have the data file from the previous skill open, open the student data file **EX1-17-CashFlow** and try this skill on your own:

1. Create a new file based on the **Student schedule** template. If this template does not appear on your *New* page, search for it using the *Search online templates* feature. You may find more than one template named Student schedule. Select one that appeals to you.

2. Create another new file by searching for a template based on the word **budget**. Use the **Simple monthly budget** template or another budget template that appeals to you.

3. If you will be moving on to the next skill in this chapter, leave the workbooks open to continue working. If not, save the files as directed by your instructor and close them.

from the perspective of. . .

COLLEGE STUDENT

I thought Excel was only for business. It's not! I found some really useful templates—one for tracking my day-to-day expenses and another one to help me budget my expenses for the semester. And even though some of the templates look fancy and complicated, I find that I can use them easily by reading the instructions and taking a little bit of time to personalize the data with my own information.

michaeljung/123RF

Skill 1.18 Arranging Workbooks

If you are working with multiple workbooks, you may want to arrange them so you can see them all at the same time. You can arrange workbooks so they are tiled, horizontal, vertical, or cascading windows.

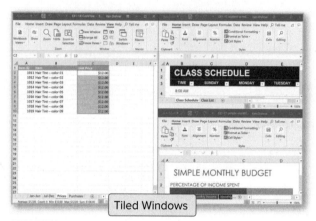

Tiled Windows

FIGURE EX 1.40

Vertical Windows

FIGURE EX 1.42

Horizontal Windows

FIGURE EX 1.41

Cascading Windows

FIGURE EX 1.43

To change the arrangement of workbooks:

1. On the *View* tab, in the *Window* group, click the **Arrange All** button.
2. In the *Arrange Windows* dialog, select an arrangement option:
   - **Tiled**—places the windows in a grid pattern.
   - **Horizontal**—places the windows in a stack one on top of the other.
   - **Vertical**—places the windows in a row next to each other.
   - **Cascade**—places the windows in a staggered, overlapping, diagonal arrangement.
3. Click **OK**.

Maximize Button

Arrange All Button

Switch Windows Button

FIGURE EX 1.44

To switch between workbooks, you can:

❭ Click anywhere in the workbook you want to make active.

❭ On the *View* tab, in the *Window* group, click the **Switch Windows** button, then click the name of the workbook you want.

To undo the arrangement and put the workbooks back into separate windows, maximize any of the workbooks by clicking the **Maximize** button on the title bar.

tell me **more**

If you have two workbooks with similar data, you may want to compare their data row by row. Excel's *Compare Side by Side* feature allows you to compare two workbooks at the same time. When you compare workbooks, the *Synchronous Scrolling* feature is on by default. This feature allows you to scroll both workbooks at once. If you scroll the active workbook, the other workbook will scroll at the same time, allowing you to carefully compare data row by row.

1. Open the workbooks you want to compare.

2. On the *View* tab, in the *Window* group, click the **View Side by Side** button.

3. The two workbooks are displayed one on top of the other.

4. Scroll the active window to scroll both workbooks at once.

5. Click the **View Side by Side** button again to restore the windows to their previous positions.

let me **try**

If you do not have the data files from the previous skill open, open the student data file **EX1-18-CashFlow** and a few other Excel files to try this skill on your own:

1. Arrange the Excel windows so they are in a staggered arrangement.

2. Arrange the Excel windows so they are in a row next to each other.

3. If you will be moving on to the next skill in this chapter, close all of the workbooks except the *CashFlow* workbook. If not, save the files as directed by your instructor and close them.

Skill 1.19 Checking Spelling

In Excel, the *Spelling* command analyzes the current worksheet for spelling errors. The *Spelling* dialog cycles through each spelling error, allowing you to make decisions about how to handle each one.

To check a worksheet for spelling errors:

1. On the *Review* tab, in the *Proofing* group, click the **Spelling** button or use the keyboard shortcut (F7).

2. The first spelling error appears in the *Spelling* dialog.

3. Review the spelling suggestion and then select an action:

    - Click **Ignore Once** to make no changes to this instance of the word.
    - Click **Ignore All** to make no changes to all instances of the word.
    - Click **Add to Dictionary** to make no changes to this instance of the word and add it to the spelling checker dictionary, so future uses of this word will not show up as misspellings.
    - Click the correct spelling in the *Suggestions* list, and click **Change** to correct just this instance of the misspelling in your worksheet.
    - Click the correct spelling in the *Suggestions* list, and click **Change All** to correct all instances of the misspelling in your worksheet.

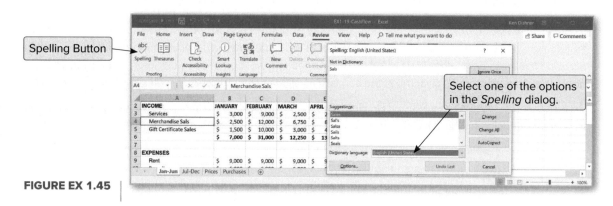

FIGURE EX 1.45

4. After you select an action, the spelling checker automatically advances to the next suspected spelling error.

5. When the spelling checker finds no more errors, it displays a message telling you the check is complete. Click **OK** to close the dialog and return to your worksheet.

tips & tricks

Whether or not you use the Spelling tool, you should always proofread your files. Spelling checkers are not infallible, especially if you misuse a word yet spell it correctly—for instance, writing "bored" instead of "board."

let me try

If you do not have the data file from the previous skill open, open the student data file **EX1-19-CashFlow** and try this skill on your own:

1. Spell check the *Jan-Jun* worksheet and correct any errors you find.

2. If you will be moving on to the next skill in this chapter, leave the workbook open to continue working. If not, save the file as directed by your instructor and close it.

Skill 1.20 Previewing and Printing a Worksheet

In Excel, all the print settings are combined in a single page along with a preview of how the printed file will look. As you change print settings, the preview updates. To preview and print the current worksheet:

1. Click the **File** tab to open Backstage view.

2. Click **Print**.

3. At the right side of the page is a preview of how the printed file will look. Beneath the preview there is a page count. If there are multiple pages, use the *Next* and *Previous* arrows to preview all the pages in the file. You can also use the scroll bar to the right to scroll through the preview pages.

4. Set the number of copies to print by changing the number in the *Copies* box.

5. Click the **Print** button to send the file to your default printer.

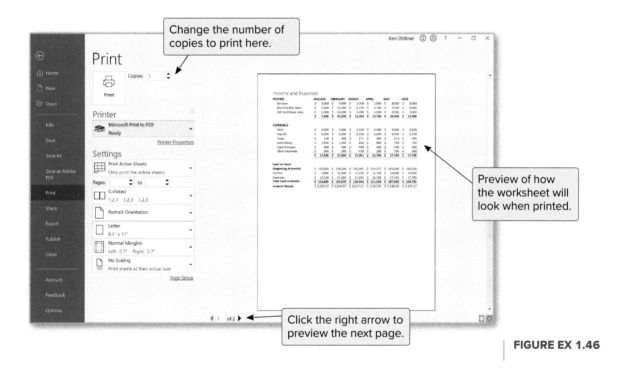

FIGURE EX 1.46

tips & tricks

Add the *Quick Print* command to the Quick Access Toolbar so you can print with a single mouse click. If you do not need to change the default print settings, you can click the *Quick Print* button instead of going through the *Print* tab in Backstage view.

tell me more

To open the *Print* page in Backstage view, you can use the keyboard shortcut [Ctrl] + [P].

let me try

If you do not have the data file from the previous skill open, open the student data file **EX1-20-CashFlow** and try this skill on your own:

1. Preview how the worksheet will look when printed.

2. If you can, print the worksheet and compare the printed page to the preview.

3. Save the file as directed by your instructor and close it.

key terms

Workbook
Worksheet
Row
Column
Cell
Cell address
Cell range
Formula bar
Name box
Status bar
Vertical scroll bar
Horizontal scroll bar
Row selector
Column selector
Protected View
Message Bar
Trusted Document
Ready mode
Edit mode
General number format
Accounting Number Format
Percent Style format
Comma Style format
Number format
Currency format
Short Date format
Long Date format
AutoFill
Fill Handle tool

Data series
Chart
Data points
Data markers
Data series (chart)
Y axis
X axis
Plot area
Chart area
Chart title
Legend
Formula
Order of Operations (precedence)
Cell reference
Relative reference
Absolute reference
Mixed reference
Function
Argument
AutoSum
Quick Analysis tool
Status bar
Zoom slider
Template
Tiled window arrangement
Horizontal window arrangement
Vertical window arrangement
Cascade window arrangement

concept review

1. How many worksheets does a new Excel 2019 workbook have?

a. None

b. one

c. two

d. four

2. The cell C4 refers to the cell at _____.

a. the intersection of row C and column 4

b. the first cell on the C4 worksheet

c. the intersection of column C and row 4

d. none of the above

3. Which of these dates uses the Long Date format?

    a. Saturday, January 1, 2020

    b. 1/1/2020

    c. January 1, 2020

    d. 01/01/2020

4. Data markers are graphic representations of the values of data points in a chart.

    a. true

    b. false

5. Formulas begin with which character?

    a. $

    b. @

    c. ^

    d. =

6. Which of these cell references is an absolute reference?

    a. C9

    b. C$9

    c. $C$9

    d. none of the above

7. AutoSum is located _____.

    a. on the *Home* tab, in the *Formulas* group

    b. on the *Home* tab, in the *Editing* group

    c. on the *Insert* tab, in the *Formulas* group

    d. on the *Insert* tab, in the *Tables* group

8. The zoom slider is located _____.

    a. on the Ribbon

    b. on the *View* tab, in the *Zoom* group

    c. in the *Zoom* dialog

    d. at the lower right corner of the status bar

9. The keyboard shortcut to begin the spelling checker is _____.

    a. F4

    b. F5

    c. F7

    d. F9

10. Which of these tasks can you perform in Backstage view?

    a. Enable Editing when a workbook is in Protected View.

    b. Preview how a workbook will look when printed.

    c. Create a new workbook from a template.

    d. All of the above.

skill review **1.1**

The workbook for this project generates client bills from staff hours in multiple worksheets. In this project, you will complete the worksheet for staff member Swinson to calculate the daily bill, the total billable hours per week, and the total weekly bill. The worksheet for staff member Stevens has been completed. You may use it for reference as necessary.

Skills needed to complete this project:

- Working in Protected View (Skill 1.3)
- Navigating a Workbook (Skill 1.2)
- Exploring Charts (Skill 1.8)
- Entering and Editing Text and Numbers in Cells (Skill 1.4)
- Applying Number Formats (Skill 1.5)
- Entering Dates and Applying Date Formats (Skill 1.6)
- Inserting Data Using AutoFill (Skill 1.7)
- Understanding Absolute and Relative References (Skill 1.11)
- Entering Simple Formulas (Skill 1.10)
- Calculating Totals with the Quick Analysis Tool (Skill 1.14)
- Using the Recommended Charts Feature (Skill 1.9)
- Previewing and Printing a Worksheet (Skill 1.20)

1. Open the start file **EX2019-SkillReview-1-1** and resave the file as: `[your initials]EX-SkillReview-1-1`

2. If the workbook opens in Protected View, click the **Enable Editing** button in the Message Bar at the top of the workbook so you can modify the workbook.

3. Explore the workbook. If you accidentally make changes while exploring, press `Ctrl` + `Z` to undo the change.

   a. Click the worksheet tab labeled *Stevens Hours.*

   b. If necessary, use the vertical scroll bar to scroll down so you can see both weeks of billable hours. (If necessary, use the vertical scroll bar again to return to the top of the worksheet.)

   c. Click cell **B2** (the cell displaying the staff member's last name, Stevens). This is the cell at the intersection of column B and row 2.

   i. Note that the column B and row 2 selector boxes highlight.

   ii. Note that the status bar displays Ready, indicating that you are in Ready mode.

   iii. On the *Home* tab, in the *Number* group, look at the *Number Format* box at the top of the group. Note that the format for this cell is *General.*

   iv. Double-click cell **B2** to switch to Edit mode. Note that the status bar now displays *Edit*, and the blinking cursor appears within the cell. If you needed to, you could edit the text directly in the cell.

d. Press (Esc) to exit Edit mode and return to Ready mode.

e. Press (← Enter) twice to move to cell **B4** (the cell displaying the staff member's billable rate). This cell is formatted with the Accounting Number Format number format.

   i. Look in the *Number Format* box and note that the format for this cell is *Accounting*.

   ii. On the *Home* tab, in the *Styles* group, look in the *Cell Styles* gallery, and note that the cell style *Currency* is highlighted. (If the *Cell Styles* gallery is collapsed on your Ribbon, click the **Cell Styles** button to display it.)

f. Click cell **B8** (the cell displaying the number of hours for Monday, August 5). This cell is formatted with the Comma cell style.

   i. Look in the *Number Format* box and note that the format for this cell is also *Accounting*.

   ii. On the *Home* tab, in the *Styles* group, look in the *Cell Styles* gallery, and note that the cell style *Comma* is highlighted for this cell. (If the *Cell Styles* gallery is collapsed on your Ribbon, click the **Cell Styles** button to display it.)

   iii. Note the style differences between cell **B4** (Accounting Number Format, Currency style) and cell **B8** (Accounting Number Format, Comma style).

g. Click cell **B7** (the cell displaying the date 8/5/2019). This cell is formatted using the Short Date format. Note that the *Number Format* box displays *Date*.

h. Double-click cell **B14**.

   i. Note that the status bar now displays *Edit*, indicating that you are in Edit mode.

   ii. This cell contains a formula to calculate the daily bill for Monday, August 5: **=B12*$B$4**

   iii. Note that cells B12 and B4 are highlighted with colors matching the cell references in the formula.

   iv. Note that the reference to cell B4 is an absolute reference ($B$4).

i. Press (Esc) to exit Edit mode.

j. Double-click cell **B12**.

   i. Note that once again the status bar displays *Edit*, indicating that you are in Edit mode.

   ii. This cell contains a formula using the SUM function to calculate the total billable hours for Monday, August 5: **=SUM(B8:B11)**

   iii. In this case, the SUM function uses a single argument **B8:B11** to indicate the range of cells to total.

   iv. Note that the cell range **B8:B11** is highlighted with the color matching the argument in the SUM function formula.

   v. Note that the reference to the cell range **B8:B11** uses relative references.

k. Press (Esc) to exit Edit mode.

l. Press (Tab ⇄) to move to cell **C12**. Look in the formula bar and note that this cell contains a similar formula to the one in cell **B12**: **=SUM(C8:C11)**

m. Press (→) to move through cells **D12 through H12**. Note the formula in the formula bar for each cell.

n. Did you notice that the cell references in the formulas in cells **C12 through H12** all use relative references?

4. The *Stevens Hours* worksheet contains a stacked column chart. Review the chart so you can re-create it on the *Swinson Hours* worksheet.

    a. The stacked column chart to the right of the hours for the week of August 5 represents the hours worked for each client each day.

    b. The column height for each day represents the total hours worked. Each column is divided into segments representing the hours worked for each client.

    c. The number of hours worked is represented on the y axis. The dates are represented along the x axis.

    d. The chart title has been changed to: **Week of 8/5/19**

5. Now you are ready to complete the worksheet for David Swinson. Navigate to the *Swinson Hours* worksheet by clicking the **Swinson Hours** worksheet tab.

6. The staff member's last name is spelled incorrectly. Navigate to cell **B2** and edit the text so the last name is spelled correctly (Swinson—with an *i* instead of an *a*). Use Edit mode.

    a. Double-click cell **B2**.

    b. Edit the text to: Swinson

    c. Press ⏎ Enter to accept your changes.

7. The billable rate amount is missing. Navigate to cell **B4** and enter the rate. Use Ready mode.

    a. Click cell **B4**.

    b. Type: **180**

    c. Press ⏎ Enter.

8. Modify the billable rate to use the Accounting Number Format.

    a. Press the ↑ to return to cell **B4**.

    b. On the *Home* tab, in the *Number* group, click the **Accounting Number Format** button.

9. The dates are missing from the timesheet. Enter the first date, August 5, 2019.

    a. Click cell **B7**.

    b. Type: **8/5/2019**

    c. Press ⏎ Enter.

10. Use Autofill to complete the dates in the timesheet.

    a. Click cell **B7**.

    b. Click the **Fill Handle**, and drag to cell **H7**. Release the mouse button.

11. Change the date format to the 8/5/2019 format.

    a. The cell range **B7:H7** should still be selected. If not, click cell **B7**, press and hold ⇧ Shift, click cell **H7**, and then release the ⇧ Shift key.

    b. On the *Home* tab, in the *Number* group, expand the *Number Format* list, and click **Short Date**.

12. Use the Quick Analysis tool to enter total hours for each day.

    a. Select cells **B8:H11**. Click cell **B8**, hold down the left mouse button, and drag the mouse to cell **H11**. Release the mouse button. The cell range B8 through H11 should now appear selected.

    b. The *Quick Analysis tool* button should appear near the lower right corner of the selected cell range. (If the *Quick Analysis tool* button is not visible, move your mouse cursor over the selected cell range again, without clicking. This action should make the button appear.)

    c. Click the **Quick Analysis tool** button, and then click **Totals**.

    d. Click **Sum** (the first option).

13. Format the hours billed section to use the Comma Style number format. Be sure to include the total row.

    a. Select cells **B8:H12**. Try another method: Click cell **B8**, press and hold `⇧ Shift`, click cell **H12**, and release the `⇧ Shift` key.

    b. On the *Home* tab, in the *Number* group, click the **Comma Style** button.

14. Enter a formula in cell **B14** to calculate the daily bill for Monday, August 5. The formula should calculate the total billable hours for the day (cell B12) times the billable rate (B4).

    a. Click cell **B14**.

    b. Type: **=**

    c. Click cell **B12**.

    d. Type: *****

    e. Click cell **B4**.

    f. Press `F4` to change the cell reference **B4** to an absolute reference **($B$4)**.

    g. Press `← Enter`.

    h. The formula should look like this: **=B12*$B$4**

15. Use AutoFill to copy the formula to the remaining days in the timesheet.

    a. Click cell **B14** again.

    b. Click the **AutoFill handle**. Hold down the left mouse button and drag to cell **H14**. Release the mouse button.

    c. The formulas in cells B14 through H14 should look like this.

	B	C	D	E	F	G	H
14	=B12*$B$4	=C12*$B$4	=D12*$B$4	=E12*$B$4	=F12*$B$4	=G12*$B$4	=H12*$B$4

Notice that when the AutoFill copied the formula, it updated the relative reference (B12) to reflect the new column position, but it did not change the absolute reference ($B$4).

16. Now you can calculate the bill total for the week by summing the daily bill amounts. Enter a formula using the SUM function with the cell range **B14:H14** as the argument.

    a. Click cell **B15**.

    b. Type: **=SUM(B14:H14)**

    c. Press `← Enter`.

17. Use the Recommended Charts feature to insert a **stacked column chart** representing hours worked for each day for the week of August 5.

    a. Select cells **A7:H11**. Click cell **A7**, hold down the left mouse button, and drag the mouse to cell **H11**. Release the mouse button. The cell range A7 through H11 should now appear selected.

Projects   www.simnetkeepitsimple.com | EX-47

b. The *Quick Analysis tool* button should appear near the lower right corner of the selected cell range. (If the *Quick Analysis tool* button is not visible, move your mouse cursor over the selected cell range again, without clicking. This action should make the button appear.)

c. Click the **Quick Analysis tool** button, and then click **Charts**.

d. Click **Stacked Column** to insert a stacked column chart.

18. Change the chart title.

a. Click the **Chart Title** placeholder once to select it.

b. Type: **Week of August 5, 2019**

c. Press ⏎ Enter.

19. Preview how the worksheet will look when printed.

a. Click cell **A1** to deselect the chart.

b. Click the **File** tab to open Backstage view.

c. Click **Print** to display the print preview.

d. Click the left arrow to close the Backstage view.

20. Save and close the workbook.

skill review **1.2**

In this project you will create a new workbook to track the cost of books for your college classes. For each book, you will enter the purchase price, the potential sell-back price, and the cost difference. You will calculate totals using AutoSum. You will then create a new workbook from a template, and practice changing the zoom level and arranging the workbooks.

Skills needed to complete this project:

- Entering and Editing Text and Numbers in Cells (Skill 1.4)
- Navigating a Workbook (Skill 1.2)
- Inserting Data Using AutoFill (Skill 1.7)
- Applying Number Formats (Skill 1.5)
- Using the Status Bar (Skill 1.15)
- Using AutoSum to Insert a SUM Function (Skill 1.13)
- Entering Simple Formulas (Skill 1.10)
- Using the Recommended Charts Feature (Skill 1.9)
- Exploring Charts (Skill 1.8)
- Creating a New Workbook Using a Template (Skill 1.17)
- Checking Spelling (Skill 1.19)
- Arranging Workbooks (Skill 1.18)
- Changing the Zoom Level (Skill 1.16)

1. Start a new blank Excel workbook. Save the file as: **[your initials] EX-SkillReview-1-2**

2. The new workbook opens with one sheet (*Sheet1*). Cell A1 is selected.

3. In cell A1, type the title for the worksheet: **Textbooks**

4. Enter data in the worksheet as follows:

	A	B	C	D
1	Textbooks			
2				
3	Book	Cost	Value	Difference
4	Book1	85	45	
5	Book2	100	80	
6	Book3	250	125	
7	Book4	80.95	24.25	

5. Use AutoFill to add two additional books to the list.

    a. Click cell **A4**, hold down the left mouse button and drag the mouse to cell **A7**. Release the mouse button. The cell range A4 through A7 should now appear selected.

    b. Click the **Fill Handle** (located at the lower right corner of the selected cell range).

    c. Drag down to cell **A9**, and release the mouse button.

    d. Excel adds Book 5 and Book 6 to the list.

6. Book 5 cost **$125.00** and can be sold for **$75.00**. Book 6 cost **$175.00** and can be sold for **$100.00**. Add these data to the worksheet.

    a. Click cell **B8** and type: **125**

    b. Press (Tab ⇆) and type: **75**

    c. Click cell **B9** and type: **175**

    d. Press (Tab ⇆) and type: **100**

    e. Press (← Enter).

7. Modify the **status bar** to display the minimum value.

    a. Right-click anywhere on the **status bar**.

    b. Click **Minimum** to add a checkmark.

    c. Click anywhere to dismiss the menu.

8. Use the status bar to check the total value of the books and the minimum value.

    a. Click cell **C4**. Press and hold (↑ Shift) and click cell **C9**. Release the (↑ Shift) key.

    b. Look at the status bar and find the *Sum* value (**449.25**).

    c. Look at the status bar and find the *Min* value (**24.25**).

9. Use AutoSum to calculate total cost and total value. The totals should be placed in cells **B10** and **C10**.

    a. Click cell **A10** and type: **Total**

    b. Press (Tab ⇆).

    c. Cell **B10** should be selected. Press and hold (↑ Shift) and click cell **C10**. Release the (↑ Shift) key.

    d. On the *Home* tab, in the *Editing* group, click the **AutoSum** button.

10. Change the number format for the cost and value numbers to the Accounting Number Format.

    a. Click cell **B4**. Press and hold (↑ Shift). Click cell **C10**. Release (↑ Shift).

    b. On the *Home* tab, in the *Number* group, click the **Accounting Number Format** button.

11. Enter a formula in cell **D4** to calculate the difference between the cost and the value for Book1. The formula will use only relative references because in the next step, you will use AutoFill to copy the formula down the column.

    a. Click cell **D4**.

    b. Type: =

    c. Click cell **B4**.

    d. Type: −

    e. Click cell **C4**.

    f. Press ⎗ Enter .

12. Use AutoFill to copy the formula to calculate the difference for books 2 through 6 and the total.

    a. Click cell **D4**.

    b. Click the **AutoFill handle**. Hold down the left mouse button and drag to cell **D10**. Release the mouse button.

13. Use the Quick Analysis tool to insert a **pie chart** representing the cost of books.

    a. Select cells **A3:B9**. Click cell **A3**, hold down the left mouse button, and drag the mouse to cell **B9**. Release the mouse button. The cell range A3 through B9 should now appear selected.

    b. The *Quick Analysis tool* button should appear near the lower right corner of the selected cell range. (If the *Quick Analysis tool* button is not visible, move your mouse cursor over the selected cell range again, without clicking. This action should make the button appear.)

    c. Click the **Quick Analysis tool** button, and then click **Charts**.

    d. Click **Pie** to insert a pie chart.

    e. Observe how each book is assigned a color in the chart legend.

    f. The size of each pie piece represents the cost of each book relative to the total cost of all the books. Book 3 is the most expensive book and is represented by the largest piece of the pie.

14. Change the chart title.

    a. Click the **Cost** chart title once to select it.

    b. Type: `Comparative Cost of Books`

    c. Press ⎗ Enter .

15. Save the workbook. Do not close it or exit Excel.

16. Create a new file from a template called *Personal Monthly Budget*.

    a. Click the **File** tab to open Backstage view.

    b. Click **New**.

    c. Open a new file based on the *Personal Monthly Budget* template. (This step may require an active Internet connection.)

       i. The *Personal Monthly Budget* template may appear in the list of templates automatically. If it does not, you will need to search for it. In the *Search online templates* box, type: `personal monthly budget`

       ii. Click the template preview.

       iii. Click **Create**.

17. The new workbook based on the *Personal Monthly Budget* template opens. This is a complex workbook using many advanced techniques. The good news is that you don't have to understand how this workbook was created in order to use it.

a. Click the **Personal Monthly Budget** worksheet tab to begin working.

b. Scroll through the worksheet to review all the budget income and expenses. Edit category names and values to reflect your personal budget.

c. If you think you might like to come back to this workbook later for your personal use, this is a good point to save it. Be sure not to close the file. Use the file name: `[Your Initials]Personal Monthly Budget`

18. You should still have two workbooks open: the textbooks workbook from the beginning of the project and the *Personal Monthly Budget* workbook based on the template. Arrange the workbooks so you can see both at the same time.

a. On the *View* tab, in the *Window* group, click the **Arrange All** button.

b. In the *Arrange Windows* dialog, click the **Vertical** radio button. Click **OK**.

19. The *Personal Monthly Budget* workbook should be active. If not, click the title bar for that window. Review the *Personal Monthly Budget* sheet and change the zoom level to 50% so you can see more of the data at once.

a. If necessary, click the **Personal Monthly Budget** tab.

b. On the *View* tab, in the *Zoom* group, click the **Zoom** button.

c. In the *Zoom* dialog, click the **50%** radio button for the zoom option you want. Click **OK**.

20. Close both workbooks. If you made changes to the *Personal Monthly Budget* workbook and you plan to continue using it, be sure to save the changes.

challenge yourself 1.3

In this project, you will complete a timesheet for David Swinson, similar to the one you worked on in Skill Review 1.1. You will need to enter and format missing dates, correct a data entry mistake, apply number formatting, and enter formulas to calculate the total billable hours per day, the daily total for each day, and the bill total for the week.

Skills needed to complete this project:

- Working in Protected View (Skill 1.3)
- Navigating a Workbook (Skill 1.2)
- Entering and Editing Text and Numbers in Cells (Skill 1.4)
- Inserting Data Using AutoFill (Skill 1.7)
- Entering Dates and Applying Date Formats (Skill 1.6)
- Calculating Totals with the Quick Analysis Tool (Skill 1.14)
- Applying Number Formats (Skill 1.5)
- Understanding Absolute and Relative References (Skill 1.11)
- Entering Simple Formulas (Skill 1.10)
- Using the Recommended Charts Feature (Skill 1.9)
- Exploring Charts (Skill 1.8)
- Previewing and Printing a Worksheet (Skill 1.20)

1. Open the start file **EX2019-ChallengeYourself-1-3** and resave the file as: `[your initials]EX-ChallengeYourself-1-3`

2. If the workbook opens in Protected View, enable editing so you can make changes to the workbook.

3. If necessary, scroll to the bottom of the worksheet so you can see the empty timesheet beginning on row 17.

4. The dates are missing from the timesheet. Enter the date **7/29/2019** in cell **B18**.

5. Use AutoFill to complete the dates in cells **C18:H18**.

6. Change the date format for **B18:H18** to the date format similar to **14-Mar**.

7. The hours reported for the Proctor client on Friday (cell F22) are incorrect. Change the number in cell **F22** to: **4**

8. Use the Quick Analysis tool to enter total hours for each day. Use the cell range **B19:H22**. The daily totals should be inserted into the range **B23:H23**.

9. Format the hours billed section (cells **B19:H23**) to use the Comma Style number format. Be sure to include the total row.

10. Enter a formula in cell **B25** to calculate the daily bill for Monday, July 29. The formula should calculate the total billable hours for the day (cell **B23**) times the billable rate (**B4**). Be sure to use an absolute cell reference for the billable rate.

11. Use AutoFill to copy the formula to the remaining days in the timesheet (cells **C25:H25**).

12. Calculate the bill total for the week by summing the daily bill amounts. In cell **B26**, enter a formula using the SUM function. The function argument should be the range of cells representing the daily bill totals (**B25:H25**).

13. Apply the **Currency** number format to cells **B25:H25** and cell **B26**.

14. Use the Recommended Charts feature to insert a **line chart** representing hours worked for each day for the week of July 29. Select cells **A18:H22** for the chart data.

15. Change the chart title to: `Week of July 29`

16. Preview how the worksheet will look when printed. If the print preview shows only the chart, return to the worksheet and click anywhere to deselect the chart. Now the print preview should show the entire worksheet.

17. Save and close the workbook.

challenge yourself 1.4

In this project you will work with a college budget spreadsheet. You will change a few values in the budget, modify number formats, and calculate totals and the difference between expected income and expenses. You will then create a new budget workbook from a template, and practice changing the zoom level and arranging the workbooks.

Skills needed to complete this project:

- Working in Protected View (Skill 1.3)
- Entering and Editing Text and Numbers in Cells (Skill 1.4)
- Navigating a Workbook (Skill 1.2)
- Using AutoSum to Insert a SUM Function (Skill 1.13)
- Calculating Totals with the Quick Analysis Tool (Skill 1.14)
- Using the Status Bar (Skill 1.15)
- Applying Number Formats (Skill 1.5)
- Understanding Absolute and Relative References (Skill 1.11)
- Entering Simple Formulas (Skill 1.10)

excel 365   chapter 1 Getting Started with Excel

- Checking Spelling (Skill 1.19)
- Using the Recommended Charts Feature (Skill 1.9)
- Exploring Charts (Skill 1.8)
- Creating a New Workbook Using a Template (Skill 1.17)
- Arranging Workbooks (Skill 1.18)
- Changing the Zoom Level (Skill 1.16)

1. Open the start file **EX2019-ChallengeYourself-1-4** and resave the file as:
   `[your initials]EX-ChallengeYourself-1-4`

2. If the workbook opens in Protected View, enable editing so you can make changes to the workbook.

3. Make the following changes to the *Budget* worksheet:
   a. Change the *Electric* item to `Utilities` (cell **A12**).
   b. Change the Insurance value from *90* to **125** (cell **B19**).
   c. Update the text in cell **D6** to: `Quarter expenses`

4. The worksheet is missing formulas to calculate totals. Enter formulas using the **SUM** function to calculate the following totals. Use any of the methods you learned in this chapter.
   a. Enter a formula in cell **B7** to calculate the total monthly income.
   b. Enter a formula in cell **B24** to calculate the total monthly expenses.
   c. Enter a formula in cell **E16** to calculate the total quarter expenses.
   d. Use the **status bar** to verify that the formula is calculating the correct total for each cell range.

5. Cell **E18** displays the number of months in the quarter. Change the number format in this cell to the **Number** format with no numbers showing after the decimal (so the number appears as **3** instead of **$3.00**).

6. The number format in the *Quarter Expenses* section does not match the number format in the other sections of the worksheet. Change the number format for cells **E11:E16** to the **Accounting Number Format**.

7. Review the formulas in the *Discretionary Income* section.
   a. Cells **E4:E6** should contain references to the cells where you just entered the formulas to calculate totals. Add the appropriate formula to cell **E6** to reference the value in cell **E16** (the total quarter expenses).
   b. The quarter is three months long, so the formulas in cells **E4** and **E5** should multiply the total monthly income and total monthly expenses by three. Correct the formulas in cells **E4** and **E5**. Use an absolute reference to the value in cell **E18** (the number of months in the quarter).

8. Use spelling checker to find and correct any spelling errors in the *Budget* worksheet. (*Hint*: There is one spelling error on this worksheet.)

9. Use the Recommended Charts feature to insert a **clustered bar chart** representing the monthly expenses. Select cells **A10:B23** for the chart data.

10. Change the chart title to: `Monthly Expenses`

11. Save the workbook. Do not close it or exit Excel.

12. Create a new file from a template called *Personal Expenses Calculator*. If you do not see this template, search for it using the search phrase *personal expenses*.

13. Explore the worksheets in this workbook.

14. If you think you might like to come back to this workbook later for your personal use, this is a good point to save it. Be sure not to close the file. Use the file name: [Your Initials]PersonalExpenses

15. You should still have two workbooks open: the college budget workbook from the beginning of the project and the personal expenses workbook based on the template. Arrange the workbooks so you can see both at the same time.

    a. Try different arrangements until you find the one that works best for you.

    b. Practice moving back and forth between the two workbooks.

16. Make the personal budget workbook active and navigate to the Dashboard worksheet. Modify the zoom to **80%**.

17. Close both workbooks. If you made changes to the personal budget workbook and you plan to continue using it, be sure to save the changes.

on your own **1.5**

For Spring Break, you've decided to take a seven-day road trip. Use this Excel workbook to calculate the number of miles you will drive each day and the gas cost for each day. Use the techniques you've learned in this chapter to calculate the total miles and the total gas cost. Don't forget to end the trip at the same location you started! You may want to use the Internet to look up mileage, MPG (miles per gallon), and gas price information.

Skills needed to complete this project:

- Navigating a Workbook (Skill 1.2)
- Working in Protected View (Skill 1.3)
- Entering and Editing Text and Numbers in Cells (Skill 1.4)
- Entering Dates and Applying Date Formats (Skill 1.6)
- Inserting Data Using AutoFill (Skill 1.7)
- Understanding Absolute and Relative References (Skill 1.11)
- Entering Simple Formulas (Skill 1.10)
- Calculating Totals with the Quick Analysis Tool (Skill 1.14)
- Using AutoSum to Insert a SUM Function (Skill 1.13)
- Applying Number Formats (Skill 1.5)
- Using the Recommended Charts Feature (Skill 1.9)
- Exploring Charts (Skill 1.8)
- Checking Spelling (Skill 1.19)

1. Open the start file **EX2019-OnYourOwn-1-5** and resave the file as: [your initials]EX-OnYourOwn-1-5

2. If the workbook opens in Protected View, click the **Enable Editing** button in the Message Bar at the top of the workbook so you can modify the workbook.

3. Complete the *Trip Details* section of the *Spring Break* worksheet:

    a. Enter the dates of your road trip. Use a date format that includes the day of the week.

    b. Enter a start and end location for each day. Remember—the starting location for each day should be the same as the end location for the previous day. If you use a formula with a relative reference rather than retyping the location name for each start location, you can use AutoFill to complete the start location column. Consider using a formula to ensure that the final end location is the same as the first start location.

   c. Look up and enter the miles between each location. Use an appropriate number format for the *Number of Miles* column. (Hint: Use *mapquest.com* or *maps.google.com* to look up the mileage between locations.)

4. Enter your car information including the MPG (miles per gallon). If you don't know your MPG, the government website *www.fueleconomy.gov* has excellent information on average MPG for a variety of car makes, models, and years.

5. Enter the average gas price in your area (or the area of your road trip). Again, the *www.fueleconomy.gov* website has links to this type of information.

6. Enter a formula to calculate the gas cost per mile for your car (gas price per gallon/your car's MPG).

7. Now that you have the gas cost per mile for your car, you can figure the cost of the road trip. Enter a formula to figure the gas cost per day (the number of miles * your gas cost per mile) for the first day of the trip. Be sure to use absolute and relative references as appropriate, so you can use AutoFill to copy the formula to the rest of the cells in the *Gas Cost per Day* column.

8. Apply appropriate number formats to all the cells in the workbook that display costs. *Hint*: The Accounting Number Format is best for costs that appear in a column. For costs that appear on their own, you may want to use the Currency Style format.

9. Use the Recommended Charts feature to insert a chart representing the number of miles driven per day. Change the chart title.

10. Don't forget to spell check the workbook.

11. Save and close the workbook.

fix it **1.6**

The workbook for this project tracks how many miles you walked each day for the week of October 6, 2019, through October 12, 2019. Your goal for each day is to walk at least four miles. Use the skills learned in this chapter to fix the workbook.

Skills needed to complete this project:

- Navigating a Workbook (Skill 1.2)
- Working in Protected View (Skill 1.3)
- Entering and Editing Text and Numbers in Cells (Skill 1.4)
- Entering Dates and Applying Date Formats (Skill 1.6)
- Inserting Data Using AutoFill (Skill 1.7)
- Applying Number Formats (Skill 1.5)
- Understanding Absolute and Relative References (Skill 1.11)
- Entering Simple Formulas (Skill 1.10)
- Calculating Totals with the Quick Analysis Tool (Skill 1.14)
- Using AutoSum to Insert a SUM Function (Skill 1.13)
- Using the Recommended Charts Feature (Skill 1.9)
- Exploring Charts (Skill 1.8)
- Checking Spelling (Skill 1.19)

1. Open the start file **EX2019-FixIt-1-6** and resave the file as: **[your initials] EX-FixIt-1-6**

2. If the workbook opens in Protected View, click the **Enable Editing** button in the Message Bar at the top of the workbook so you can modify the workbook.

3. The worksheet is missing a title. Type this title in cell A1: **My Exercise Log**

4. The daily goal should be 3, not 30. Correct the value in cell **D2**.

5. The dates are missing from cells **A6:A11**. Use AutoFill to complete the dates for the rest of the week.

6. The exercise log would be more useful if the date showed the day of the week in addition to the date. Change the date format for cells **A5:A11** so the date displays in this format: **Sunday, October 6, 2019**

7. The mileage for each day should use the Comma Style number format. Correct the number format in cells **C5:C11**.

8. Use one of the skills you learned in this chapter to enter formulas using the **SUM** function in cells **C12** and **D12** to calculate the weekly total minutes and miles.

9. The formulas in the *Under/Over Goal* column are not quite right. Fix the formula in cell **D5** to use an absolute reference where appropriate, and then use AutoFill to replace the formulas in cells **D6:D11**.

10. The worksheet is missing a chart. Use the Recommended Charts feature to insert a clustered column chart representing how many minutes you walked each day. Title the chart: **Minutes Walked per Day**

11. There may be spelling errors. Be sure to use spelling checker before you finish the project.

12. Preview how the worksheet will look when printed.

13. Save and close the workbook.

Source of screenshots: Microsoft Office 365: Word, Excel, Access, and PowerPoint.

chapter 2

Formatting Cells

In this chapter, you will learn the following skills:

> Move and copy cell contents using cut, copy, and paste

> Insert, delete, and merge cells

> Work with text and font attributes

> Apply borders and shading

> Format cells using cell styles

> Copy formatting using Format Painter

> Format cells using conditional formatting

> Modify cell data using find and replace

> Work with the print area

skills

introduction

This chapter focuses on skills for working with cells and cell ranges. You will learn to move data and to insert, delete, and merge cells to create a worksheet structure that fits your data. This chapter also covers the essential skills for formatting cells, including in-depth coverage of conditional formatting. Formatting not only enhances a workbook's appearance, but when used properly, it can make the data easier to understand.

Skill 2.1 Cutting, Copying, and Pasting Cell Content

While you may be familiar with cut, copy, and paste functionality from other applications, keep in mind that in Excel you are working with the cell contents—not the cells themselves. **Cut** removes the content from the selected cell, **Copy** duplicates the content from the selected cell, and **Paste** replaces the cell content with whatever was cut or copied.

When using *Copy/Paste* or *Cut/Paste* commands in Excel, watch out for cells containing formulas. If you *copy* and paste a cell containing a formula with relative references, Excel will update the references to reflect the new position in the workbook. However, if you *cut* and paste instead, Excel will treat the formula as if it contained absolute references and will not update the cell references in the formula.

FIGURE EX 2.1

FIGURE EX 2.2

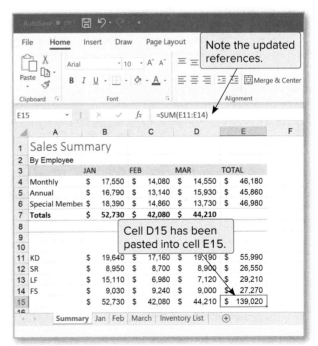

FIGURE EX 2.3

Use the *Cut*, *Copy*, and *Paste* commands to move or duplicate cell content from one location to another:

1. Select the cell, cell range, row, or column that contains the data you want to move or copy.
2. On the *Home* tab, in the *Clipboard* group, click the **Cut** or **Copy** button.
3. The selection appears with a flashing dotted line around it, and the contents of the cells are stored temporarily in the computer's memory.
4. Click the cell where you want to paste the content. If you selected a range of cells to cut or copy, click the cell in the upper left corner of the area where you want to paste.
5. Click the **Paste** button to paste the cell content and formatting. Notice that if you use the *Cut* command, Excel does not remove the content from its original location until the *Paste* command is used.

tips & tricks

A quick way to move cell content from one location to another is to click and drag with the mouse. Select the cell(s) containing the content you want to move. Place the mouse pointer at the edge of the selection. When the pointer changes to the move pointer ⌖, click and drag to the new location, and then release the mouse button.

You can use the same technique to copy cell contents to another location. Press and hold (Ctrl) to change the move pointer to the copy pointer ⌖, drag to the new location, and then release the mouse button.

tell me **more**

If you paste into a cell that contains data, the original cell data will be overwritten. To paste without overwriting existing cells, use the *Insert Copied Cells* or *Insert Cut Cells* command instead.

1. Copy or cut the cells you want to insert.
2. Select the cell where you want to insert.
3. On the *Home* tab, in the *Cells* group, click the **Insert** button arrow and select **Insert Copied Cells** or **Insert Cut Cells**.

Refer to the skill *Inserting and Deleting Cells* for information about formatting options when using the *Insert* command.

another **method**

To apply the *Cut*, *Copy*, or *Paste* command, you can also use the following shortcuts:

❯ **Cut**: Press (Ctrl) + (X), or right-click and select **Cut**.

❯ **Copy**: Press (Ctrl) + (C), or right-click and select **Copy**.

❯ **Paste**: Press (Ctrl), + (V), or right-click and select **Paste**.

let me **try**

Open the student data file **EX2-01-Sales** and try this skill on your own:

1. On the *Summary* worksheet, copy cell **D15**, and paste to cell **E15**. Note that the formula updated to reflect the new cell range E11:E14.
2. Use the *Cut* and *Paste* commands to move the content in cell **A2** to cell **A10**.
3. If you will be moving on to the next skill in this chapter, leave the workbook open to continue working. If not, save the file as directed by your instructor and close it.

Skill 2.2 Using Paste Options

When you copy and paste data in Excel, you can use the default *Paste* command to paste the copied data (including formulas and formatting) into the selected cell, or you can select from the paste options to control more precisely what is pasted.

	Paste—The default paste command that pastes all of the source content and formatting.
	Formulas—Pastes the formulas but none of the formatting. The pasted content will use the cell and number formatting of the cell into which it was pasted.
	Formulas & Number Formatting—Pastes the formulas and number formatting but none of the cell formatting such as font size, borders, and shading.
	Keep Source Formatting—Pastes the content, including formulas, and all formatting from the source.
	No Borders—Pastes the content, including formulas, and all formatting except borders.
	Keep Source Column Widths—Pastes the copied cell, including formulas and all number and cell formatting. Also adjusts the column width to match the width of the source column.
	Transpose—Pastes the rows from the source into columns, and the columns from the source into rows.

When your source includes formulas, you have the option to paste the calculated cell values without pasting the underlying formulas.

	Values—Pastes only the values, not the underlying formula or cell formatting.
	Values & Number Formatting—Pastes only the values, not the underlying formulas. Includes number formatting but not other cell formatting such as borders and shading.
	Values & Source Formatting—Pastes only the values, not the underlying formulas. Includes all formatting from the source.

The final group of paste options provides alternatives to pasting the actual contents of one cell into another.

	Formatting—Pastes only the cell and number formatting, not the formula or cell value from the source.
	Paste Link—Pastes a formula that references the source cell rather than pasting the contents of the source itself. When the source cell is updated, the linked cell displays the update automatically.
	Picture—Pastes an image of the source cell rather than the actual cell contents. The pasted cell looks like any other cell in the worksheet, except it cannot be edited, and when you select the cell, nothing appears in the formula bar.
	Linked Picture—Pastes an image, like the Picture paste option, but updates when the source cell is updated.

FIGURE EX 2.4

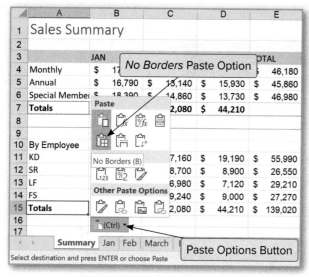

FIGURE EX 2.5

To use paste options from the *Paste* button on the Ribbon:

1. Copy the content you want to paste and then navigate to the location where you want to paste.

2. On the *Home* tab, in the *Clipboard* group, click the bottom part of the **Paste** button (the **Paste** button arrow) to expand the *Paste Options* menu.

3. Move your mouse over the icon for each paste option to see a live preview of how the paste would look, and then click the paste option you want.

To use the *Paste Options* button:

1. Copy the content you want to paste.

2. Use the standard *Paste* command to paste the content where you want it.

3. The source content is pasted using the default *Paste* option, and the *Paste Options* button appears at the lower right corner of the pasted content.

4. Click the **Paste Options** button or press Ctrl to display the *Paste Options* menu. This is the same menu that is available from the *Paste* button on the Ribbon, but moving your mouse over the icons does not show a preview of how the paste would look.

5. Click the paste option you want.

tell me **more**

Additional paste options are available from the *Paste Special* dialog. To open the *Paste Special* dialog, select **Paste Special...** from the bottom of the paste options from the *Paste* button on the Ribbon or from the right-click menu.

another **method**

You can also access the paste options from the right-click menu. Six of the paste options appear on the right-click menu (*Paste, Values, Formulas, Transpose, Formatting,* and *Paste Link*). To select an option from the full *Paste Options* menu, point to **Paste Special...**, and then click the paste option you want.

tips & tricks

A useful paste option is *Keep Source Column Widths*. Often, when you paste data into a new worksheet, the default column width is too narrow to display the data. Use the *Keep Source Column Widths* paste option to maintain any column width adjustments you made in the source worksheet.

let me try

If you do not have the data file from the previous skill open, open the student data file **EX2-02-Sales** and try this skill on your own:

1. On the *Summary* worksheet, copy cell **E6** and paste only the formula to cell **E7**. Do not paste the original cell formatting.

2. Copy cell **A7** and paste the cell value and formatting without borders into cell **A15**.

3. If you will be moving on to the next skill in this chapter, leave the workbook open to continue working. If not, save the file as directed by your instructor and close it.

excel 365   chapter 2 Formatting Cells

Skill 2.3 Inserting and Deleting Cells

Use the *Insert* command to insert an empty cell, group of cells, row, or column into your worksheet.

To insert an empty cell range, select the range where you want to insert the new cells.

❭ If you have a vertical cell range selected, on the *Home* tab, in the *Cells* group, click the **Insert** button and Excel will automatically shift existing cells to the right to make room for the new cells.

❭ If you have a single cell or a horizontal cell range selected, on the *Home* tab, in the *Cells* group, click the **Insert** button and Excel will automatically shift existing cells down to make room for the new cells.

If you want more control over whether cells are shifted to the right or down, use the *Insert* dialog.

1. Select the cell or cell range where you want to insert the new cell(s).
2. On the *Home* tab, in the *Cells* group, click the **Insert** button arrow.
3. Click **Insert Cells...** to open the *Insert* dialog.
4. Select the option you want and then click **OK**.

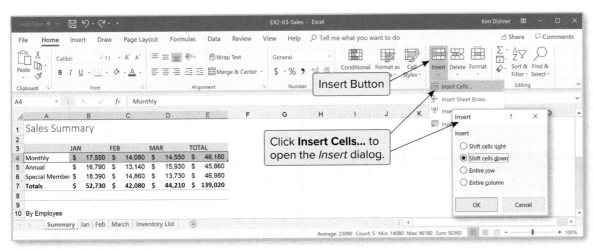

FIGURE EX 2.6

Recall that in Excel, pasting cell content that has been cut or copied will overwrite the content of the cell where it is pasted. If you want to insert the content instead, use the *Insert* command.

1. Cut or copy the cell content and then click the cell where you want to insert the new content.
2. On the *Home* tab, in the *Cells* group, click the **Insert** button arrow.

3. Instead of the *Insert Cells...* option, you now have *Insert Cut Cells* or *Insert Copied Cells*. Select this option to insert new cells with the cut or copied content. These commands are only available immediately after using the *Cut* or *Copy* command.

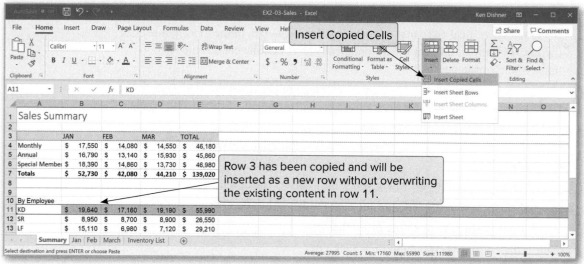

FIGURE EX 2.7

When you insert new cells, the cells will use the same formatting as the cells above (if you shifted cells down) or to the left (if you shifted cells to the right). If you want to use formatting from the cells below or to the right instead, or to insert the cells with no formatting, click the **Insert Options** button that appears at the lower right of the insertion and make a selection from the menu options.

FIGURE EX 2.8

Of course, you can also delete cells. Deleting cells not only deletes the information and formatting in the cell, but also shifts the layout of the worksheet. Even if you delete an empty cell, you shift all the surrounding cells into new positions.

1. If you have a vertical cell range selected, click the **Delete** button and Excel will automatically shift existing cells to the left.

2. If you have a single cell or a horizontal cell range selected, click the button and Excel will automatically shift existing cells up.

If you want more control over how the remaining cells are shifted, use the *Delete* dialog.

1. On the *Home* tab, in the *Cells* group, click the **Delete** button arrow.
2. Click **Delete Cells...** to open the *Delete* dialog.
3. Select the option you want and then click **OK**.

FIGURE EX 2.9

tips & tricks

Be careful not to delete cells that are referenced in formulas. Even though a new value may shift into the original cell's position, the formula will still be looking for the original cell (now deleted), causing an invalid cell reference error.

another **method**

Both *Insert...* and *Delete...* commands are available from the right-click menu.

Pressing (Delete) will delete the contents of the cell but not the cell itself.

let me try

If you do not have the data file from the previous skill open, open the student data file **EX2-03-Sales** and try this skill on your own:

1. On the *Summary* worksheet, select cells **A4:E4**.
2. Insert cells so the remaining cells shift down.
3. Display the *Insert Options* menu and select the option to format the new cells the same as those below.
4. Delete cells **A4:E4**, shifting the remaining cells up.
5. Copy row **3** and insert a copy above row **11**.
6. If you will be moving on to the next skill in this chapter, leave the workbook open to continue working. If not, save the file as directed by your instructor and close it.

Skill 2.4 Wrapping Text in Cells

When you type text in a cell, the text will appear to continue to the right as far as it can until there is another cell that contains data. At that point, the text will appear to be cut off. You could increase the width of the cell to show all the text, but do you really want the entire column to be that wide? If your worksheet includes cells with more text than will comfortably fit in the cell, you should use the wrap text feature. When wrap text is enabled for a cell, the text in the cell will automatically wrap to multiple lines, just as a paragraph would.

To wrap text in a cell:

> On the *Home* tab, in the *Alignment* group, click the **Wrap Text** button. Notice the button appears selected when text wrapping is active for the cell.

FIGURE EX 2.10

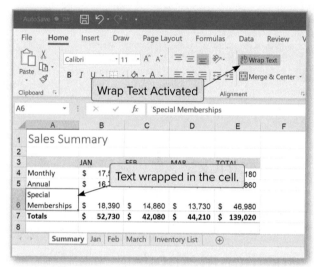

FIGURE EX 2.11

To turn off text wrapping in a cell, click the **Wrap Text** button again to deselect it.

tips & tricks

The text wrapping feature works only for cells that contain text. If a column is too narrow to display its numerical data, Excel will not wrap it. Instead, the cell will show a series of # symbols, indicating that the cell contains numerical data, but the column is too narrow to display it.

another **method**

You can also turn on the text wrapping feature from the *Format Cells* dialog.

1. On the *Home* tab, in the *Alignment* group, click the **Alignment Settings dialog launcher** to open the *Format Cells* dialog.

2. In the *Text control* section, click the **Wrap text** check box.

3. Click **OK**.

let me **try**

If you do not have the data file from the previous skill open, open the student data file **EX2-04-Sales** and try this skill on your own:

1. On the *Summary* worksheet, activate text wrapping for cell **A6**.

2. If you will be moving on to the next skill in this chapter, leave the workbook open to continue working. If not, save the file as directed by your instructor and close it.

Skill 2.5 Using Undo and Redo

If you make a mistake when working, the **Undo** command allows you to reverse the last action you performed. The **Redo** command allows you to reverse the *Undo* command and restore the file to its previous state. The Quick Access Toolbar gives you immediate access to both these commands.

To undo the last action taken, click the **Undo** button on the Quick Access Toolbar.

To redo the last action taken, click the **Redo** button on the Quick Access Toolbar.

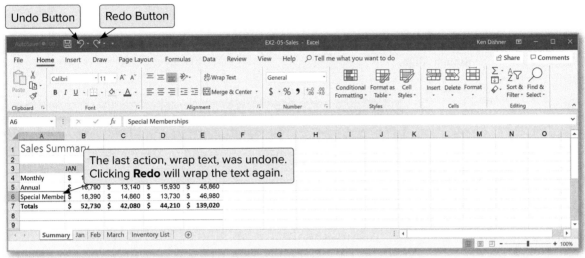

FIGURE EX 2.12

To undo multiple actions at the same time:

1. Click the **Undo** button arrow to expand the list of your most recent actions.

2. Click an action in the list.

3. The action you click will be undone, along with all the actions completed after that. In other words, your workbook will revert to the state it was in before that action.

tips & tricks

Be careful when using the *Undo* and *Redo* commands in Excel. In other Office applications, undo and redo actions are confined to the file you are currently working on—even if you have multiple files open. However, in Excel, the undo-redo list of actions includes all the open workbooks. This means that if you are working on multiple Excel files at the same time, using the *Undo* command can actually undo an action in one of the other open workbooks.

another **method**

❭ To undo an action, you can also press (Ctrl) + (Z).

❭ To redo an action, you can also press (Ctrl) + (Y).

let me try

If you do not have the data file from the previous skill open, open the student data file **EX2-05-Sales** and try this skill on your own:

1. Undo the last action.

2. Redo the last action.

3. If you will be moving on to the next skill in this chapter, leave the workbook open to continue working. If not, save the file as directed by your instructor and close it.

Skill 2.6 Aligning Cells

Alignment refers to how text and numbers are positioned within the cell both horizontally and vertically. By default, cells use the **General horizontal alignment**. When cells are formatted using the General horizontal alignment, Excel detects the type of content in the cell. Cells that contain text are aligned to the left, and cells that contain numbers are aligned to the right.

To change the horizontal alignment of a cell, click one of the horizontal alignment buttons located on the *Home* tab, in the *Alignment* group: **Align Left**, **Center**, or **Align Right**.

To change the vertical alignment of a cell, click one of the vertical alignment buttons located on the *Home* tab, in the *Alignment* group: **Top Align**, **Middle Align**, or **Bottom Align**.

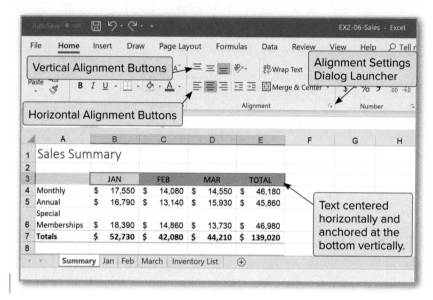

FIGURE EX 2.13

You can also change the angle at which the content displays. On the *Home* tab, in the *Alignment* group, click the **Orientation** button and select one of the options.

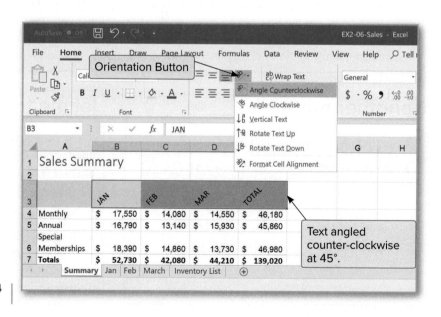

FIGURE EX 2.14

The alignment and orientation options are also available from the *Format Cells* dialog, *Alignment* tab. To change alignment using the *Format Cells* dialog:

1. Click the **Alignment Settings dialog launcher** at the lower right corner of the *Alignment* group.

2. The *Format Cells* dialog opens to the *Alignment* tab.

3. In the *Text alignment* section, select the options you want from the **Horizontal** and **Vertical** drop-down lists.

4. In the *Orientation* section, change the angle of rotation by clicking one of the dots on the *Orientation* dial, by clicking and dragging the *Orientation* dial to the position you want, or by entering the specific degree of rotation in the *Degrees* box.

5. Click **OK**.

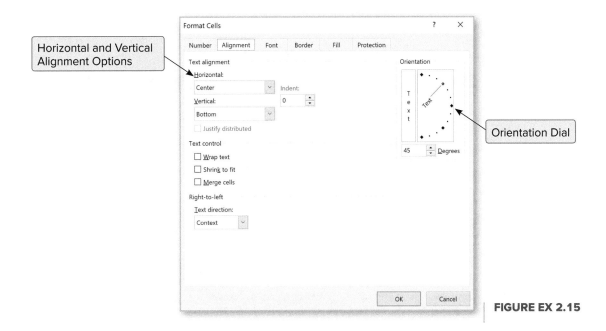

FIGURE EX 2.15

tips & tricks

If you have narrow columns of data with descriptive headers, try using one of the orientation options to angle the cells containing the header text.

let me try

If you do not have the data file from the previous skill open, open the student data file **EX2-06-Sales** and try this skill on your own:

1. On the *Summary* worksheet, select cells **B3:E3**.

2. Center the content in each cell horizontally.

3. Change the angle of rotation for these cells to counterclockwise at 45°.

4. If you will be moving on to the next skill in this chapter, leave the workbook open to continue working. If not, save the file as directed by your instructor and close it.

Skill 2.7 Merging Cells and Splitting Merged Cells

Merging cells is one way to control the appearance of your worksheet. You can merge cells to create a header cell across multiple columns of data or center a title across your worksheet. The *Merge & Center* button automatically merges the selected cells and then centers the data from the first cell across the entire merged area. When you merge cells together, Excel will keep only the data in the uppermost left cell. All other data will be lost.

To merge cells and center their content:

1. Select the cells you want to merge, making sure the text you want to keep is in the uppermost left cell.

2. On the *Home* tab, in the *Alignment* group, click the **Merge & Center** button.

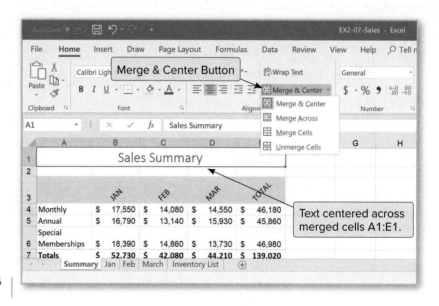

FIGURE EX 2.16

Click the *Merge & Center* button arrow for additional merge commands:

Merge Across—lets you merge cells in multiple rows without merging the rows together. The cells in each row are merged together, keeping the data in the leftmost cell in each row, while still keeping each row separate.

Merge Cells—lets you merge cells together without centering the data. Like the *Merge & Center* command, *Merge Cells* combines all the selected cells into one cell, keeping only the data in the uppermost left cell.

Unmerge Cells—splits a merged cell back into its original cells.

You can also merge and center cells from the *Format Cells* dialog:

1. On the *Home* tab, in the *Alignment* group, click the **Alignment Settings dialog launcher** to open the *Format Cells* dialog.

2. On the *Alignment* tab, in the *Text alignment* section, click the **Horizontal** arrow and select **Center** from the dropdown list. (You can also select **Center Across Selection**. When you merge the cells, it does not matter if the horizontal alignment is *Center* or *Center Across Selection*.)

3. In the *Text control* section, click the **Merge cells** check box.

4. Click **OK**.

Select **Center** as the horizontal alignment option.

Check the **Merge cells** check box.

FIGURE EX 2.17

To unmerge a merged cell, use one of these methods:

❯ On the *Home* tab, in the *Alignment* group, click the **Merge & Center** button. When the selected cell is a merged cell, clicking the *Merge & Center* button will undo the merge and reset the horizontal alignment to *General*.

❯ On the *Home* tab, in the *Alignment* group, click the **Merge & Center** button arrow and select **Unmerge Cells**.

❯ In the *Format Cells* dialog, on the *Alignment* tab, in the *Text alignment* section, the *Text control* section, click the **Merge cells** check box to uncheck it.

tips & tricks

You cannot split cells in Excel. You can unmerge a merged cell back into its original cells, but you cannot split a single cell into two new columns or two new rows (like you can with a table in Word or PowerPoint). However, if you have a column of data that you would like to split across multiple cells, you can use the *Text to Columns* command (on the *Data* tab, in the *Data Tools* group).

let me try

If you do not have the data file from the previous skill open, open the student data file **EX2-07-Sales** and try this skill on your own:

1. On the *Summary* worksheet, select cells **A1:E1**.

2. Merge the cells so the text appears centered across the merged cells.

3. On the *Jan* worksheet, cells **A1:D1** have been merged and centered. Unmerge them.

4. If you will be moving on to the next skill in this chapter, leave the workbook open to continue working. If not, save the file as instructed by your instructor and close it.

Skill 2.8 Applying Bold, Italic, and Underline

You may be familiar with using bold, italic, and underline formatting to emphasize text in a Word document or a PowerPoint presentation. You can use these same techniques in Excel to emphasize cells in your workbook.

To apply bold, italic, and underline formatting:

1. Select a cell or cell range to apply the formatting to all the content in the cell(s). To apply formatting to only part of the content in a cell, double-click the cell to enter Edit mode, and then select the text you want to apply the formatting to.

2. On the *Home* tab, in the *Font* group, click the appropriate button to apply formatting to the selected cell(s).

FIGURE EX 2.18

When a cell includes bold, italic, or underline formatting, the applicable buttons appear highlighted on the Ribbon. To remove the formatting, click the highlighted button.

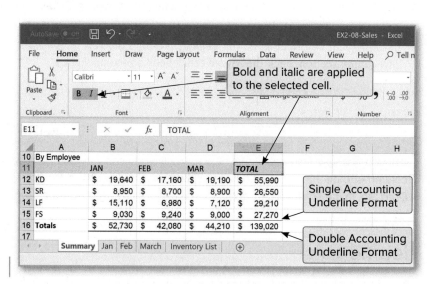

FIGURE EX 2.19

Underline styles used in accounting spreadsheets are slightly different from "regular" underline styles. If you need to apply the accounting style of underline or double underline, do not use the *Underline* button on the Ribbon. Instead, use one of the accounting underline options from the *Format Cells* dialog:

1. On the *Home* tab, in the *Font* group, click the **Font Settings dialog launcher** to open the *Format Cells* dialog.

2. On the *Font* tab, in the *Underline* section, expand the **Underline** list and select **Single Accounting** or **Double Accounting**.

3. Click **OK**.

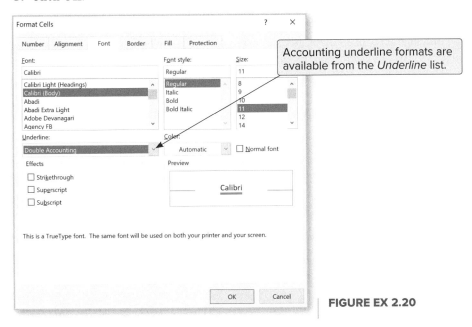

FIGURE EX 2.20

The single and double underline options available when you click the *Underline* button arrow will apply the accounting underline styles only if you recently selected those formats from the *Format Cells* dialog.

tips & tricks

The cell underline formats underline only the content in the cell. The underline does not extend from one edge of the cell to the other. If you want to create an underline that extends across a range of cells without a break in between, use a border instead. (For more information about borders, refer to the skill *Adding Borders*.)

another **method**

When you right-click a cell, the *Bold* and *Italic* buttons are available on the Mini toolbar.

Bold, italic, and underline font styles are available from the *Format Cells* dialog, *Font* tab. You can also use the keyboard shortcuts:

❯ Bold: Ctrl + B

❯ Italic: Ctrl + I

❯ Underline: Ctrl + U

let me try

If you do not have the data file from the previous skill open, open the student data file **EX2-08-Sales** and try this skill on your own:

1. On the *Summary* worksheet, select cell **E11** and apply **bold** and **italic** formatting.

2. Remove just the **bold** formatting.

3. Select cells **B15:E15** and apply the **Single Accounting** underline format.

4. Select cells **B16:E16** and apply the **Double Accounting** underline format.

5. If you will be moving on to the next skill in this chapter, leave the workbook open to continue working. If not, save the file as directed by your instructor and close it.

Skill 2.9 Changing Fonts, Font Size, and Font Color

A **font**, or typeface, refers to a set of characters of a certain design. The font is the shape of a character or number as it appears on-screen or when printed. Use the commands from the *Home* tab, *Font* group to change font attributes such as font family, font size, and font color.

> To change the font, click the **Font** box arrow to expand the list of available fonts, and then select the font you want.

> To change the font size, click the **Font Size** box arrow and select the size you want.

> To change the font color, click the **Font Color** button arrow to expand the color palette, and then select the color you want.

FIGURE EX 2.21

The font color palette is divided into three parts:

1. The top part shows the *Automatic* color choice (black or white, depending on the color of the background).

2. The middle part shows the *Theme Colors* included in the theme that is applied to the workbook. These colors are designed to work together.

3. The bottom part of the palette shows the *Standard Colors* (dark red, red, orange, etc.). These colors are always available, no matter what theme is in use.

FIGURE EX 2.22

You can also change the font, font size, and font color from the *Format Cells* dialog:

1. On the *Home* tab, in the *Font* group, click the **Font Settings dialog launcher** to open the *Format Cells* dialog.

2. On the *Font* tab, make the font and size selections you want.

3. In the *Color* section, click the arrow to expand the color palette, and then click a color. The color palette from the Ribbon and in the *Format Cells* dialog is the same.

4. Review the sample text in the *Preview* box to see how your choices will look.

5. Click **OK** to apply the changes.

FIGURE EX 2.23

tell me **more**

You can pick a custom color by clicking **More Colors...** from the bottom of the font color palette.

another **method**

You can also change the font, font size, or font color by right-clicking and making the font, font size, and font color selections you want from the Mini toolbar.

let me **try**

If you do not have the data file from the previous skill open, open the student data file **EX2-09-Sales** and try this skill on your own:

1. On the *Summary* worksheet, select cells **A4:A6**.

2. Change the font to **Arial**.

3. Change the font size to **10**.

4. Change the font color to **Dark Blue** (in the row of standard colors, the second color from the right).

5. If you will be moving on to the next skill in this chapter, leave the workbook open to continue working. If not, save the file as directed by your instructor and close it.

skill 2.9   Changing Fonts, Font Size, and Font Color

Skill 2.10 Adding Borders

Add borders to your workbook to emphasize a cell or group of cells. Use borders to make your workbook look more like a desktop publishing form or to show separation between a column of values and the total row.

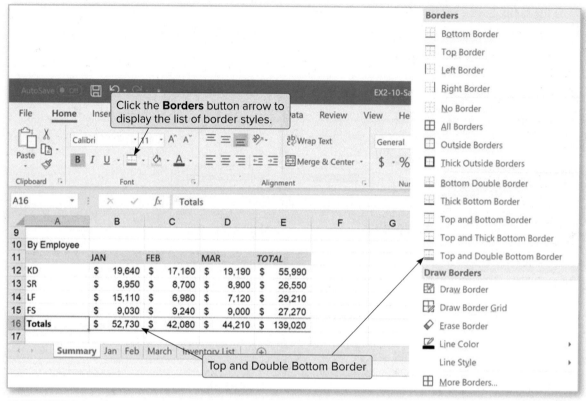

FIGURE EX 2.24

To add borders to your workbook:

1. Select the cell(s) you want to add a border to.
2. On the *Home* tab, in the *Font* group, click the **Borders** button arrow and select the border style you want.

To remove borders:

1. Select the cell(s) you want to remove the borders from.
2. On the *Home* tab, in the *Font* group, click the **Borders** button arrow and select **No Border** from the list of border styles.

For more control over the look of cell borders, select **More Borders...** from the *Borders* menu to open the *Format Cells* dialog. From the *Border* tab, you can specify the line style and color for the border. You can also see a preview of how the border will look.

1. On the *Home* tab, in the *Font* group, click the **Borders** button arrow and select **More Borders...** from the list of border styles.
2. Select a line style from the *Style* section.
3. Expand the **Color** palette and select a color.
4. To add borders around the outside or inside the selected cells, click the appropriate button(s) in the *Presets* section.

5. In the *Border* section, add a border line by clicking the button representing the location of the border or by clicking directly in the area of the preview image where you want the border to appear.

6. Click **OK**.

FIGURE EX 2.25

tips & tricks

A properly formatted spreadsheet for accounting purposes should use the cell underline formatting instead of borders on total rows. However, most non-accountant Excel users favor borders above and below total rows instead of using cell underlining.

another **method**

The *Borders* button displays the most recently used border style. If you want to reuse this style, you can just click the button. You do not need to reselect the border style from the menu again.

The *Borders* button is also available from the Mini toolbar when you right-click a cell.

let me **try**

If you do not have the data file from the previous skill open, open the student data file **EX2-10-Sales** and try this skill on your own:

1. On the *Summary* worksheet, select cells **A9:E9** and remove the borders.

2. If necessary, remove the underline formatting from cells **B15:E16**.

3. Apply the **Top and Double Bottom Border** to cells **A16:E16**.

4. Add a **Dark Blue** (in the row of standard colors, the second color from the right) top border to cells **A10:E10**. Use the thickest single line style available.

5. If you will be moving on to the next skill in this chapter, leave the workbook open to continue working. If not, save the file as directed by your instructor and close it.

Skill 2.11 Adding Shading with Fill Color

Another way to emphasize cells in your workbook is to use a **fill color** to change the background color of cells. Fill colors are available in a variety of shades to make it easy to read the cell content. Shading is often used to differentiate alternating rows in a large table or to make the heading row stand out. To add shading to your workbook:

1. Select the cell(s) you want to add shading to.

2. On the *Home* tab, in the *Font* group, click the **Fill Color** button arrow to display the color palette. The color palette includes colors from the workbook theme as well as a row of standard colors along the bottom. Notice that as you hold the mouse over each color in the palette, a tool tip appears displaying the color name.

3. Click the color you want.

FIGURE EX 2.26

To remove shading:

1. Select the cell(s) you want to remove shading from.

2. On the *Home* tab, in the *Font* group, click the **Fill Color** button arrow to display the color palette.

3. Click **No Fill** to remove the fill color from the selected cells.

tips & tricks

❱ Avoid overusing shading and using too many colors in your workbook. Shading should be used for emphasis and to make the workbook easier to read, not to make the workbook more colorful.

❱ If you use a dark color for shading, change the font color to white or another light color.

tell me **more**

In the *Format Cells* dialog, options for fill effects and pattern styles are available under the *Fill* tab.

another **method**

Like the *Borders* button, the *Fill Color* button displays the most recently used shading color. If you want to reuse this color, just click the button. You do not need to reselect the color from the Fill Color palette.

The *Fill Color* button is also available from the Mini toolbar when you right-click a cell.

let me **try**

If you do not have the data file from the previous skill open, open the student data file **EX2-11-Sales** and try this skill on your own:

1. On the *Summary* worksheet, select cells **A11:E11** and remove the fill color.

2. On the *Jan* worksheet, select cells **A2:D2** and apply the **Orange, Accent 2, Lighter 60%** fill color (in the third row of theme colors, the fifth color from the right).

3. If you will be moving on to the next skill in this chapter, leave the workbook open to continue working. If not, save the file as directed by your instructor and close it.

from the perspective of . . .

HEALTH CLUB OFFICE MANAGER

I use Excel to prepare financial reports for the club owners and their accountant. Proper formatting makes it easier for the owners to read the reports. I would never submit a report without checking for text that appears cut off or titles that aren't centered across columns. And I always use the accounting underline formats instead of borders in my financial reports. Our accountant insists on it!

Rubberball Productions /Getty Images

Skill 2.12 Applying Cell Styles

A **cell style** is a combination of effects that can be applied at one time. Styles can include formatting such as borders, fill color, font size, and number formatting.

Excel includes an extensive gallery of prebuilt cell styles. You can use these styles to help visualize your data by consistently applying them to your worksheet. Use text styles such as *Title* for the title of your worksheet and *Calculation* and *Input* to highlight cells used in formulas. The *Total* style applies borders and font formatting appropriate for a total row in a table.

To apply a cell style:

1. Select the cell(s) you want to apply the style to.
2. On the *Home* tab, in the *Styles* group, click the **Cell Styles** button.
3. Click the style you want to apply to your cell(s).

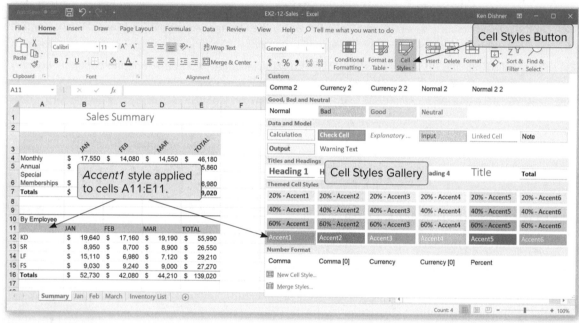

FIGURE EX 2.27

tips & tricks

If you have Live Preview enabled, you can move your mouse over each style in the *Cell Styles* gallery to see a preview of how that style would look applied to your worksheet.

let me try

If you do not have the data file from the previous skill open, open the student data file **EX2-12-Sales** and try this skill on your own:

1. On the *Summary* worksheet, select cells **A11:E11** and apply the **Accent1** cell style.
2. Select cells **A16:E16** and apply the **Total** style.
3. If you will be moving on to the next skill in this chapter, leave the workbook open to continue working. If not, save the file as directed by your instructor and close it.

Skill 2.13 Using Format Painter

A professional, well-organized workbook uses consistent formatting. Use the **Format Painter** tool to copy formatting from one part of your worksheet to another, rather than trying to re-create the exact combination of font color and size, number formatting, borders, and shading to reuse.

To use *Format Painter*:

1. Begin with a cell that has the formatting you want.

2. On the *Home* tab, in the *Clipboard* group, click the **Format Painter** button to copy the cell formatting.

3. Notice that your mouse pointer changes to the Format Painter shape ⊹🖌. Click a cell to apply the formatting or click and drag to apply the formatting to a range of cells.

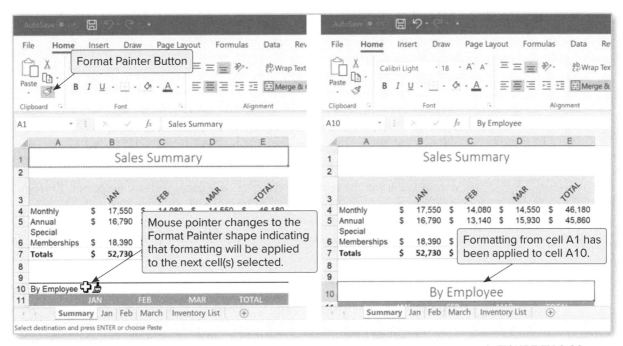

FIGURE EX 2.28

tell me **more**

If you want to apply the formatting to different parts of a worksheet or workbook, double-click the **Format Painter** button when you select it. It will stay on until you click the **Format Painter** button again or press **Esc** to deselect it.

another **method**

To activate *Format Painter*, you can also right-click the cell with formatting you want to copy and click the **Format Painter** button on the Mini toolbar.

let me try

If you do not have the data file from the previous skill open, open the student data file **EX2-13-Sales** and try this skill on your own:

1. On the *Summary* worksheet, use **Format Painter** to copy the formatting from cell **A1** and apply it to cell **A10**.

2. If you will be moving on to the next skill in this chapter, leave the workbook open to continue working. If not, save the file as directed by your instructor and close it.

Skill 2.14 Applying Conditional Formatting Using the Quick Analysis Tool

Conditional formatting provides a visual analysis of data by applying formatting to cells based on their values. Excel offers a wide variety of conditional formatting options from the *Conditional Formatting* menu (available on the *Home* tab, in the *Styles* group).

> Data bars, color scales, and icon sets display a visual representation comparing all cell values in the selection.

> *Highlight Cells Rules* highlight only cells that meet specific criteria (conditions).

> *Top/Bottom Rules* highlight cells that have the highest or lowest values compared to other cells in the selection.

If you're not sure which conditional formatting option is best for the selected data, use the Quick Analysis tool. The Quick Analysis tool detects whether you've selected numerical or text data and displays only the conditional formatting options appropriate for each type of data. From the Quick Analysis tool, you can also preview conditional formatting before applying it to your data.

To apply conditional formatting with the Quick Analysis tool:

1. Select the cells to which you want to apply conditional formatting.

2. Click the **Quick Analysis tool** button at the lower right corner of the selection.

3. Notice that Live Preview displays the effect of the conditional formatting on your data as you hover the mouse pointer over each of the formatting options. Review each formatting option before making your selection.

4. Click the button for the type of conditional formatting you want to apply.

FIGURE EX 2.29

tips & tricks

You should resist the temptation to overuse conditional formatting. Conditional formatting should be used to highlight important data or data trends, not to colorize the entire worksheet.

tell me **more**

Some types of conditional formatting apply formatting to all the cells in the selection and are applied automatically when you click the button in the Quick Analysis tool. Other types require a comparison value and will open a dialog where you can specify the value for the rule and select formatting options.

another **method**

You can press Ctrl + Q to open the Quick Analysis tool instead of clicking the **Quick Analysis tool** button.

let me **try**

If you do not have the data file from the previous skill open, open the student data file **EX2-14-Sales** and try this skill on your own:

1. On the *Inventory List* worksheet, select cells **D2:D11** and apply the **Data Bars** conditional formatting option from the Quick Analysis tool.

2. If you will be moving on to the next skill in this chapter, leave the workbook open to continue working. If not, save the file as directed by your instructor and close it.

from the perspective of . . .

HELP DESK COORDINATOR

I love conditional formatting! Every week, each department sends me a spreadsheet of all the help desk calls for each software package we support. I use color scales to identify the software packages with the highest volume of calls. In my spreadsheet that combines the weekly data, I use icon sets to indicate whether the number of calls went up or down for each software package on a week-by-week basis.

Ryan McVay/Getty Images

Skill 2.15 Applying Conditional Formatting with Data Bars, Color Scales, and Icon Sets

Data bars, color scales, and icon sets can be used to visually represent the value of each cell relative to the other cells in the data selection. These types of conditional formatting apply formatting to all the selected cells.

Data Bars—Display a color bar (gradient or solid) representing the cell value in comparison to other values (cells with higher values have longer data bars).

FIGURE EX 2.30

Color Scales—Color the cells according to one of the color scales (e.g., red to green [bad/low to good/high] or blue to red [cold/low to hot/high]).

FIGURE EX 2.31

Icon Sets—Display a graphic in the cell representing the cell value in relation to other values.

3 Arrows (Colored) icon set applied to cells B3:D12.

FIGURE EX 2.32

To apply conditional formatting using data bars, color scales, or icon sets:

1. Select the data you want to apply conditional formatting to.

2. On the *Home* tab, in the *Styles* group, click the **Conditional Formatting** button.

3. From the menu, point to **Data Bars**, **Colors Scales**, or **Icon Sets**, and then click the specific style of formatting you want. Notice that Live Preview displays the effect of the conditional formatting on your data as you hover the mouse pointer over each of the formatting options.

let me try

If you do not have the data file from the previous skill open, open the student data file **EX2-15-Sales** and try this skill on your own:

1. On the *Jan* worksheet, select cells **B3:D12** and apply conditional formatting using the **orange gradient fill data bar**.

2. On the *Feb* worksheet, select cells **B3:D12** and apply conditional formatting using the **Red-White-Blue color scale**.

3. On the *March* worksheet, select cells **B3:D12** and apply conditional formatting using the **3 Arrows (Colored)** icon set (the first icon set in the *Directional* section).

4. If you will be moving on to the next skill in this chapter, leave the workbook open to continue working. If not, save the file as directed by your instructor and close it.

---

skill 2.15   Applying Conditional Formatting with Data Bars, Color Scales, and Icon Sets

Skill 2.16 Applying Conditional Formatting with Highlight Cells Rules

Conditional formatting with **Highlight Cells Rules** allows you to define formatting for cells that meet specific numerical or text criteria (e.g., greater than a specific value or containing a specific text string). Use this type of conditional formatting when you want to highlight cells based on criteria you define.

To apply *Highlight Cells Rules*:

1. Select the data you want to apply conditional formatting to.
2. On the *Home* tab, in the *Styles* group, click the **Conditional Formatting** button.
3. From the menu, point to **Highlight Cells Rules**, and click the option you want.
4. Each option opens a dialog where you can enter a value or date to which the value of each cell will be compared. The default formatting is light red fill with dark red text. To change the formatting, expand the dropdown list in the dialog and select another option.
5. Click **OK** to apply the conditional formatting.

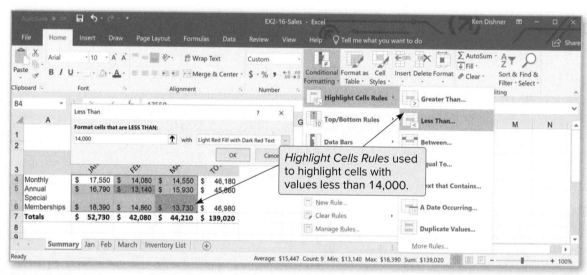

Highlight Cells Rules used to highlight cells with values less than 14,000.

FIGURE EX 2.33

tips & tricks

The *Highlight Cells Rules* menu includes an option to highlight duplicate values. This option can be especially helpful when you are trying to find a potential data entry error in a long list of values.

let me try

If you do not have the data file from the previous skill open, open the student data file **EX2-16-Sales** and try this skill on your own:

1. On the *Summary* worksheet, select cells **B4:D6** and apply conditional formatting so cells with a value **less than 14,000** are formatted using a light red fill with dark red text.
2. If you will be moving on to the next skill in this chapter, leave the workbook open to continue working. If not, save the file as directed by your instructor and close it.

Skill 2.17 Applying Conditional Formatting with Top/Bottom Rules

One way to analyze worksheet data is to compare cell values to other cell values. When analyzing a worksheet, you may want to highlight the highest or lowest values or values that are above or below the average. In these cases, use conditional formatting **Top/Bottom Rules**. When you use *Top/Bottom Rules*, Excel automatically finds the highest, lowest, and average values to compare values to, rather than asking you to enter criteria (as you do when using *Highlight Cells Rules*).

To highlight cells with conditional formatting *Top/Bottom Rules*:

1. Select the data you want to apply conditional formatting to.

2. On the *Home* tab, in the *Styles* group, click the **Conditional Formatting** button.

3. From the menu, point to **Top/Bottom Rules**, and click the option you want.

4. Each option opens a dialog where you can select the formatting to apply when cells meet the condition. The top and bottom options allow you to modify the threshold to a value other than 10 (top/bottom 10 items and top/bottom 10%).

5. Click **OK** to apply the conditional formatting.

Top/Bottom Rules used to highlight cells with values greater than the average.

FIGURE EX 2.34

let me try

If you do not have the data file from the previous skill open, open the student data file **EX2-17-Sales** and try this skill on your own:

1. On the *Summary* worksheet, select cells **B12:D15** and apply conditional formatting so cells with a value **greater than the average** are formatted using a green fill with dark green text.

2. If you will be moving on to the next skill in this chapter, leave the workbook open to continue working. If not, save the file as directed by your instructor and close it.

Skill 2.18 Removing Conditional Formatting

You cannot remove conditional formatting from cells by clearing the data or pressing Delete or ← Backspace. Instead, you must remove the conditional formatting rule from the cells.

To remove conditional formatting:

1. On the *Home* tab, in the *Styles* group, click the **Conditional Formatting** button.

2. Point to **Clear Rules**, and click the option you want from the menu: **Clear Rules from Selected Cells**, **Clear Rules from Entire Sheet**, **Clear Rules from This Table** (available if the selected cells are part of a table), or **Clear Rules from This PivotTable** (available if the selected cells are part of a PivotTable).

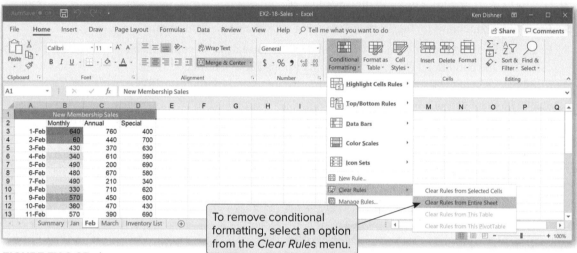

FIGURE EX 2.35

tell me **more**

Through the Conditional Formatting Rules Manager, you can view all of your conditional formatting rules at one time and add, modify, or delete rules. Open the Conditional Formatting Rules Manager from the *Manage Rules...* option at the bottom of the *Conditional Formatting* menu.

another **method**

You can also clear conditional formatting from the Quick Analysis tool:

1. Select the cells from which you want to remove conditional formatting.

2. Click the **Quick Analysis tool** button at the lower right corner of the selection, and click the **Clear Format** button.

let me **try**

If you do not have the data file from the previous skill open, open the student data file **EX2-18-Sales** and try this skill on your own:

1. Go to the *Feb* worksheet and clear the conditional formatting rules from this worksheet.

2. If you will be moving on to the next skill in this chapter, leave the workbook open to continue working. If not, save the file as directed by your instructor and close it.

excel 365   chapter 2 Formatting Cells

Skill 2.19 Clearing Cell Content

To remove the contents of a cell without removing the cell from the structure of your workbook, on the *Home* tab, in the *Editing* group, click the **Clear** button and select one of the *Clear* menu options. You can remove everything from the cell—contents, formats, comments, and hyperlinks, or remove contents or formatting only.

Clear Button

FIGURE EX 2.36

Figure EX 2.37 shows the original content and formatting in cells A3:E3.

FIGURE EX 2.37

Clear All—clears all cell contents and formatting and deletes any comments or hyperlinks attached to the cell.

	A	B	C	D	E
3					
4	Monthly	$ 17,550	$ 14,080	$ 14,550	$ 46,180
5	Annual	$ 16,790	$ 13,140	$ 15,930	$ 45,860

FIGURE EX 2.38

Clear Formats—clears only the cell formatting and leaves the cell contents, comments, and hyperlinks. The *Clear Formats command* does not remove conditional formatting.

	A	B	C	D	E
3		JAN	FEB	MAR	TOTAL
4	Monthly	$ 17,550	$ 14,080	$ 14,550	$ 46,180
5	Annual	$ 16,790	$ 13,140	$ 15,930	$ 45,860

FIGURE EX 2.39

Clear Contents—clears only the contents (including hyperlinks) and leaves the cell formatting and comments. Figure EX 2.40 has sample text added to cell B3 to illustrate the cell formatting.

	A	B	C	D	E
3		abc			
4	Monthly	$ 17,550	$ 14,080	$ 14,550	$ 46,180

FIGURE EX 2.40

tell me **more**

There are two additional options available from the Clear menu:

Clear Comments—deletes any comments attached to the cell while leaving the cell contents, formatting, and hyperlinks intact.

Clear Hyperlinks—removes the hyperlink action from the cell without removing the content or the hyperlink style of formatting.

another **method**

To clear the contents of a cell, you can:

❯ Right-click the cell and select **Clear Contents** from the menu. Using the right-click method, there are no options to clear formats or comments.

❯ Select the cell and then press (Delete) or (← Backspace) to clear the cell contents but not the cell formatting.

NOTE: These methods leave the cell formatting intact.

let me **try**

If you do not have the data file from the previous skill open, open the student data file **EX2-19-Sales** and try this skill on your own:

1. On the *Summary* worksheet, select cells **A3:E3** and clear the formatting only (leaving the content).
2. Select cells **A11:D11** and clear only the content (leaving the formatting).
3. Select cell **A10** and use a single command to clear everything (content and formatting).
4. If you will be moving on to the next skill in this chapter, leave the workbook open to continue working. If not, save the file as directed by your instructor and close it.

Skill 2.20 Using Find and Replace

All of the Microsoft Office applications include **Find** and **Replace** commands that allow you to search for and replace data in your file. In Excel, these commands can be used to find and replace not only text but also numbers in values and formulas in a single worksheet or across an entire workbook.

Before using the *Replace* command, you should use *Find* to make sure the data you are about to replace are what you expect:

1. On the *Home* tab, in the *Editing* group at the far right side of the Ribbon, click the **Find & Select** button.

2. From the *Find & Select* menu, click **Find...**

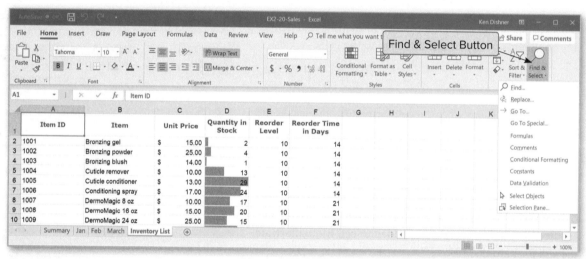

FIGURE EX 2.41

3. The *Find and Replace* dialog opens, with the *Find* tab selected.

4. Type the word, phrase, or number you want to find in the *Find what* box.

    a. To go to just the first instance, click the **Find Next** button.

    b. To find all instances, click the **Find All** button. When you click *Find All*, Excel displays a list detailing every instance of the data—workbook file name, worksheet name, cell name, cell address, the value of the cell, and the formula (if there is one).

Find All results show details about every cell that matches.

FIGURE EX 2.42

Once you have verified the data you want to replace, switch to the *Replace* tab in the *Find and Replace* dialog:

1. Click the **Replace** tab.
2. Excel keeps the data you typed in the *Find what* box.
3. Now type the replacement text or values in the *Replace with* box.
   a. Click the **Replace** button to replace one instance of the data at a time.
   b. Click the **Replace All** button to replace all instances at once.
4. If you select *Replace All*, Excel displays a message telling you how many replacements were made. Click **OK** to dismiss the message. The results now display details about every cell that was updated with the *Replace* command.
5. Click **Close** to close the *Find and Replace* dialog.

FIGURE EX 2.43

tell me **more**

By default, Excel searches for the data both in cell values and within formulas. If you want to limit the search to only cell values, first click the **Options >>** button in the *Find and Replace* dialog to display the find and replace optional settings. Next, expand the *Look in* list by clicking the arrow, and select **Values**.

another **method**

Use the keyboard shortcut (Ctrl) + (F) to open the *Find and Replace* dialog with the *Find* tab selected.

Use the keyboard shortcut (Ctrl) + (H) to open the *Find and Replace* dialog with the *Replace* tab selected.

let me **try**

If you do not have the data file from the previous skill open, open the student data file **EX2-20-Sales** and try this skill on your own:

1. On the *Inventory* worksheet, find all instances of the word **oz**.
2. Replace all instances of the word **oz** with **ounce**.
3. If you will be moving on to the next skill in this chapter, leave the workbook open to continue working. If not, save the file as directed by your instructor and close it.

skill 2.20   Using Find and Replace

Skill 2.21 Replacing Formatting

The *Find and Replace* commands allow you to find and replace formatting as well as data. This feature is especially helpful when replacing number formats throughout a workbook.

To find and replace formatting:

1. On the *Home* tab, in the *Editing* group, click the **Find & Select** button and select **Replace...** to open the *Find and Replace* dialog.

2. If necessary, click the **Options >>** button to display the find and replace optional settings. Notice that next to the *Find what* and *Replace with* boxes, the *Preview* box displays *No Format Set*.

FIGURE EX 2.44

3. If you want to find specific data, enter it in the *Find what* box. If the *Find what* box is empty, Excel will find all cells with the formatting defined in the next step.

4. Click the **Format...** button next to the *Find what* box to open the *Find Format* dialog where you can define the formatting you want to find. The *Find Format* dialog includes all the tabs and formatting options available in the *Format Cells* dialog. Set the formatting to find just as you would set formatting to apply to cells.

FIGURE EX 2.45

5. The *Preview* box next to the *Find what* box displays the word *Preview* using the formatting you defined. If you included number formatting, *Preview* will appear with an * after it (because the word *Preview* cannot display number formatting).

6. Now repeat the same steps to define the replacement formatting.

7. If you want to replace data as well as formatting, enter the replacement data in the *Replace with* box. If you do not enter anything, Excel will modify the formatting and leave the data in each cell unchanged.

8. Click the **Format...** button next to the *Replace with* box and repeat the same process to define the new format you want to use.

9. The *Preview* box next to the *Replace with* box displays the word *Preview* using the formatting you defined. If you included number formatting, *Preview* will appear with an * after it (because the word *Preview* cannot display number formatting).

10. Click **Replace All**.

11. Click **OK** in the message that appears.

12. Click **Close** to close the *Find and Replace* dialog.

FIGURE EX 2.46

another **method**

You can also define the formatting styles to find and replace by picking cells that are already formatted with those attributes.

1. In the *Find and Replace* dialog, click the **Format** button arrow next to the *Find what* box and select **Choose Format from Cell...**

2. The cursor changes to a picker shape ⊕✎.

3. Click a cell with the formatting attributes you want to find.

4. Click the **Format** button arrow next to the *Replace with* box and select **Choose Format from Cell...**

5. Click a cell with the formatting attributes you want to apply.

6. Click **Replace All**.

7. Click **OK**.

8. Click **Close** to close the *Find and Replace* dialog.

let me **try**

If you do not have the data file from the previous skill open, open the student data file **EX2-21-Sales** and try this skill on your own:

1. On the *Inventory List* worksheet, using the *Replace* command, find and replace all cells formatted with the **Accounting Number Format** with the **Currency** format.

2. If you will be moving on to the next skill in this chapter, leave the workbook open to continue working. If not, save the file as directed by your instructor and close it.

Skill 2.22 Setting and Clearing the Print Area

By default, Excel will print the entire active worksheet as shown in Figure EX 2.47.

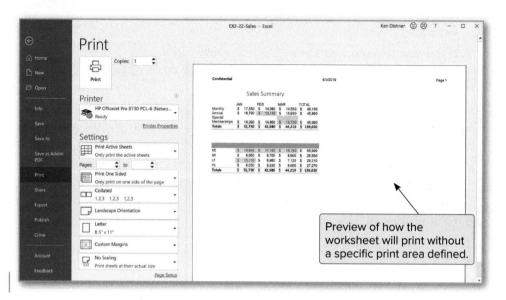

If you do not want to print your entire worksheet, you can set a print area. The **print area** is a range of cells that you designate as the default print selection. If you have defined a print area for your worksheet, it will be the only part of the worksheet that prints.

To set a print area:

1. Select the area you want to print.
2. On the *Page Layout* tab, in the *Page Setup* group, click the **Print Area** button.
3. Click **Set Print Area**.

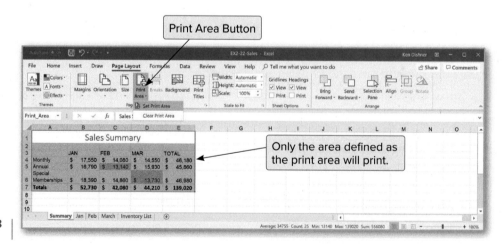

FIGURE EX 2.48

Now only the defined print area will print.

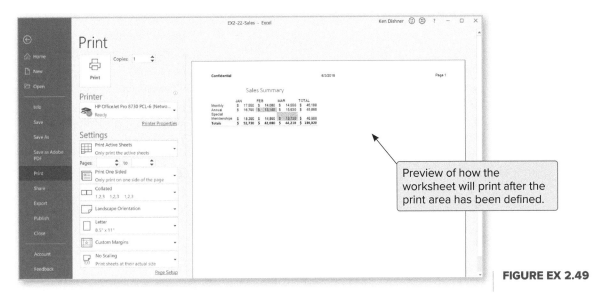

FIGURE EX 2.49

When you save the worksheet, the print area is saved as well. To clear a print area:

1. On the *Page Layout* tab, in the *Page Setup* group, click the **Print Area** button.

2. Click **Clear Print Area**.

tips & tricks

Notice that when the print area is selected, the *Name* box to the left of the address bar displays *Print_Area*. When you define a print area, Excel automatically creates a named range called *Print_Area*.

tell me **more**

You can define more than one print area per worksheet. Select the cells you want in the first print area, and then press (Ctrl) and drag the mouse to select the range of cells for the second print area. Each print area will print on a separate page.

let me **try**

If you do not have the data file from the previous skill open, open the student data file **EX2-22-Sales** and try this skill on your own:

1. Go to the *Summary* worksheet and preview how the worksheet will look when printed.

2. Set the print area so only cells **A1:E7** will print.

3. Preview how the worksheet will look when printed after the new print area has been set.

4. Save the file as directed by your instructor and close it.

key terms

Cut	Format Painter
Copy	Conditional formatting
Paste	Data bars
Undo	Color scales
Redo	Icon sets
Alignment	Highlight Cells Rules
General horizontal alignment	Top/Bottom Rules
Font	Find
Fill color	Replace
Cell style	Print area

concept review

1. When you cut and paste a cell containing a formula with relative references, Excel _____.

   a. updates the cell references to the new location

   b. does not update the cell references to the new location

   c. treats the formulas as if it contained absolute references

   d. b and c

2. Which paste option pastes formulas and number formatting but none of the cell formatting?

   a. Keep Source Formatting

   b. Values

   c. Formulas

   d. Formulas & Number Formatting

3. To split a cell into two cells _____.

   a. in the *Format Cells* dialog, on the *Alignment* tab, in the *Text Control* section, click the **Merge cells** box to uncheck it

   b. on the *Home* tab, in the *Alignment* group, click the **Merge & Center** button and select **Unmerge Cells**

   c. on the *Data* tab, in the *Data Tools* group, click the **Text to Columns** button

   d. you cannot split a cell into two cells; you can only unmerge merged cells

4. To apply the *Double Accounting* underline format _____.

   a. press $\boxed{\text{Ctrl}}$ + $\boxed{\text{U}}$

   b. in the *Font* dialog, on the *Font* tab, expand the **Underline** list and select **Double Accounting**

   c. on the *Home* tab, in the *Font* group, click the **Underline** button

   d. on the *Home* tab, in the *Font* group, click the **Underline** button arrow and select **Double Underline**

5. Clicking the **Borders** button on the Ribbon applies which border style?

   a. none

   b. outline

   c. bottom border only

   d. the most recently used border style

6. The keyboard shortcut to open the Quick Analysis tool is _____.

    a. Ctrl + A

    b. Ctrl + Q

    c. F7

    d. F10

7. To highlight cells with values in the top 10% of the select range, use _____ conditional formatting.

    a. *Highlight Cells Rules*

    b. *Top/Bottom Rules*

    c. data bars

    d. icon sets

8. You can remove conditional formatting using the _____.

    a. *Clear All* command

    b. Ctrl + X keyboard shortcut

    c. Delete keyboard shortcut

    d. *Clear Rules from Selected Cells* command

9. Selecting a cell and pressing Delete clears _____.

    a. cell content only

    b. cell content and formatting

    c. cell content, formatting, and formulas

    d. cell formatting only

10. Where is the *Set Print Area* command located?

    a. on the *Page Layout* tab, in the *Page Setup* group

    b. in the *Page Layout* dialog

    c. in the *Print* dialog

    d. on the *Home* tab, in the *Print* group

skill review **2.1**

In this project you will add formatting to a daily vitamin and supplement plan to make the spreadsheet more attractive and easier to read. Throughout the project, use the *Undo* command ($\boxed{\text{Ctrl}} + \boxed{\text{z}}$) if you make a mistake.

Skills needed to complete this project:

- Using Undo and Redo (Skill 2.5)
- Merging Cells and Splitting Merged Cells (Skill 2.7)
- Applying Cell Styles (Skill 2.12)
- Inserting and Deleting Cells (Skill 2.3)
- Aligning Cells (Skill 2.6)
- Changing Fonts, Font Size, and Font Color (Skill 2.9)
- Using Format Painter (Skill 2.13)
- Adding Borders (Skill 2.10)
- Cutting, Copying, and Pasting Cell Content (Skill 2.1)
- Wrapping Text in Cells (Skill 2.4)
- Applying Conditional Formatting Using the Quick Analysis Tool (Skill 2.14)
- Applying Conditional Formatting with Data Bars, Color Scales, and Icon Sets (Skill 2.15)
- Applying Conditional Formatting with Highlight Cells Rules (Skill 2.16)
- Removing Conditional Formatting (Skill 2.18)
- Applying Conditional Formatting with Top/Bottom Rules (Skill 2.17)
- Replacing Formatting (Skill 2.21)

1. Open the start file **EX2019-SkillReview-2-1** and resave the file as: **[your initials] EX-SkillReview-2-1**

2. If the workbook opens in Protected View, click the **Enable Editing** button in the Message Bar at the top of the workbook so you can modify the workbook.

3. Merge and center the worksheet title across cells A1:H1 and cells A2:H2.

   a. Select cells **A1:H1**.

   b. On the *Home* tab, in the *Alignment* group, click the **Merge & Center** button.

   c. Select cells **A2:H2**.

   d. On the *Home* tab, in the *Alignment* group, click the **Merge & Center** button.

4. Apply the Title style to the main worksheet title.

   a. Select the merged cells **A1:H1**.

   b. On the *Home* tab, in the *Styles* group, click the **Cell Styles** button.

   c. Click the **Title** style.

5. Apply the Accent5 style to the worksheet subtitle.

    a. Select the merged cells **A2:H2**.

    b. On the *Home* tab, in the *Styles* group, click the **Cell Styles** button.

    c. Click the **Accent5** style.

6. There are extra cells to the left of the patient name and daily cost. Delete them.

    a. Select cells **B3:B4**.

    b. On the *Home* tab, in the *Cells* group, click the **Delete** button.

7. The patient name would look better aligned at the right side of the cell.

    a. Select cell **B3**.

    b. On the *Home* tab, in the *Alignment* group, click the **Align Right** button.

8. Format the *Patient Name* and *Daily Cost* labels with bolding and the Blue, Accent 5 font color.

    a. Select cells **A3:A4**.

    b. On the *Home* tab, in the *Font* group, click the **Bold** button.

    c. On the *Home* tab, in the *Font* group, click the **Font Color** button arrow, and select the **Blue, Accent 5** color. It is the second to last color in the first row under *Theme Colors*.

9. Use *Format Painter* to apply the label formatting to the data table header row (cells A6:H6).

    a. If necessary, click cell **A3** or **A4**.

    b. On the *Home* tab, in the *Clipboard* group, click the **Format Painter** button.

    c. Click cell **A6** and drag to cell **H6** to apply the formatting.

10. Add a border beneath the data table header row to separate the titles from the data. The border should be the same color as the font.

    a. If necessary, select cells **A6:H6**.

    b. On the *Home* tab, in the *Font* group, click the **Borders** button arrow, and select **More Borders…**

    c. In the *Format Cells* dialog, on the *Border* tab, expand the **Color** palette, and select the **Blue, Accent 5** color from the first row of the theme colors.

    d. Click the bottom border area of the preview diagram to add the border.

    e. Click **OK**.

11. The data in row 14 are misplaced and belong in the data table. Cut it and insert the cut cells above row 9.

    a. Select cells **A14:H14**.

    b. On the *Home* tab, in the *Clipboard* group, click the **Cut** button.

    c. Click cell **A9**.

    d. On the *Home* tab, in the *Cells* group, click the **Insert** button arrow, and select **Insert Cut Cells**.

12. Apply the Note cell style to the note in cell A13.

    a. Select cell **A13**.

    b. On the *Home* tab, in the *Styles* group, click the **Cell Styles** button.

    c. Click the **Note** style.

13. The note text is much longer than the width of cell A13, and it looks odd with the cell style applied. Apply text wrapping so all the text is visible within the cell formatted with the *Note* style.

    a. If necessary, select cell **A13**.

    b. On the *Home* tab, in the *Alignment* group, click the **Wrap Text** button.

14. Apply conditional formatting using solid blue data bars to cells H7:H11 to represent the relative daily cost of each supplement.

    a. Select cells **H7:H11**.

    b. Click the **Quick Analysis tool** button.

    c. Click the **Data Bars** button.

15. Apply conditional formatting using Highlight Cells Rules to the cost per bottle data (cells F7:F11) to format cells with a value greater than 20 with yellow fill with dark yellow text.

    a. Select cells **F7:F11**.

    b. On the *Home* tab, in the *Styles* group, click the **Conditional Formatting** button.

    c. Point to **Highlight Cells Rules**, and select **Greater Than…**

    d. In the *Greater Than* dialog, type **20** in the **Format cells that are GREATER THAN** box.

    e. Click the *with* drop-down arrow and select **Yellow Fill with Dark Yellow Text**.

    f. Click **OK**.

16. There might be too much conditional formatting in this worksheet. Remove the conditional formatting from cells G7:G11.

    a. Select cells **G7:G11**.

    b. On the *Home* tab, in the *Styles* group, click the **Conditional Formatting** button.

    c. Point to *Clear Rules*, and select **Clear Rules from Selected Cells**.

17. You would still like to highlight the least expensive cost per pill. Apply conditional formatting to cells **G7:G11** using **Top/Bottom Rules** to format only the lowest value with green fill with dark green text.

    a. Select cells **G7:G11**.

    b. On the *Home* tab, in the *Styles* group, click the **Conditional Formatting** button.

    c. Point to **Top/Bottom Rules**, and select **Bottom 10 Items…**

    d. In the *Bottom 10 Items* dialog, type **1** in the **Format cells that rank in the BOTTOM** box.

    e. Expand the formatting list and select **Green Fill with Dark Green Text**.

    f. Click **OK**.

18. Click cell **G12** so the cost per pill data is no longer selected.

19. Find all of the values that use the Accounting Number Format with four digits after the decimal and change the formatting to the Accounting Number Format with two digits after the decimal.

    a. On the *Home* tab, in the *Editing* group, click the **Find & Select** button, and select **Replace…**

    b. In the *Find and Replace* dialog, ensure that there are no values in the *Find what* and *Replace with* boxes.

    c. If necessary, click the **Options >>** button to display the *Find and Replace* options.

    d. Click the **Format…** button next to the *Find What* box.

    e. In the *Find Format* dialog, on the *Number* tab, click **Accounting** in the *Category* list. If necessary, change the *Decimal places* value to **4**. Verify that the *Symbol* value is $.

    f. Click **OK**.

    g. Click the **Format…** button next to the *Replace with* box.

    h. In the *Replace Format* dialog, on the *Number* tab, click **Accounting** in the *Category* list. If necessary, change the *Decimal* places value to **2**. Verify that the *Symbol* value is $.

i. Click **OK**.

j. Click **Replace All**.

k. Excel should make nine replacements. Click **OK**.

l. Click **Close**.

20. Save and close the workbook.

skill review **2.2**

You want to share your recipe for Greek yogurt with friends, but the spreadsheet is a little rough. Use the formatting skills you learned in this chapter to make the recipe look as good as it tastes.

Throughout the project, use the *Undo* command ($Ctrl + Z$) if you make a mistake.

Skills needed to complete this project:

- Using Undo and Redo (Skill 2.5)
- Merging Cells and Splitting Merged Cells (Skill 2.7)
- Applying Cell Styles (Skill 2.12)
- Inserting and Deleting Cells (Skill 2.3)
- Using Format Painter (Skill 2.13)
- Changing Fonts, Font Size, and Font Color (Skill 2.9)
- Applying Bold, Italic, and Underline (Skill 2.8)
- Adding Borders (Skill 2.10)
- Using Find and Replace (Skill 2.20)
- Cutting, Copying, and Pasting Cell Content (Skill 2.1)
- Using Paste Options (Skill 2.2)
- Setting and Clearing the Print Area (Skill 2.22)
- Replacing Formatting (Skill 2.21)

1. Open the start file **EX2019-SkillReview-2-2** and resave the file as:
   `[your initials]EX-SkillReview-2-2`

2. If the workbook opens in Protected View, click the **Enable Editing** button in the Message Bar at the top of the workbook so you can modify it.

3. Center and merge the recipe title across cells **A1:D1**.

   a. Select cells **A1:D1**.

   b. On the *Home* tab, in the *Alignment* group, click the **Merge & Center** button.

4. Format the title using the *Accent 2* themed cell style.

   a. If necessary, select the merged cells **A1:D1**.

   b. On the *Home* tab, in the *Styles* group, click the **Cell Styles** button.

   c. In the *Themed Cell Styles* section of the gallery, click the **Accent 2** style.

5. Delete cell **B2**, shifting other cells to the left.

   a. Select cell **B2**.

   b. On the *Home* tab, in the *Cells* group, click the **Delete** button arrow and select **Delete Cells...**

   c. Click the **Shift cells left** radio button.

   d. Click **OK**.

6. Use *Format Painter* to copy formatting from the title and apply it to the Ingredients (**A5**) and Directions (**A10**) headers.

    a. Select the merged cells **A1:D1**.

    b. On the *Home* tab, in the *Clipboard* group, double-click the **Format Painter** button.

    c. Click cell **A5**. Notice that *Format Painter* merged cells **A5:D5** and centered the text across the merged cells.

    d. Click cell **A10**. Notice that *Format Painter* merged cells **A10:D10** and centered the text across the merged cells.

    e. On the *Home* tab, in the *Clipboard* group, click the **Format Painter** button again to disable it.

7. The worksheet title should be more prominent than the section headers. Increase the font size to 16 and bold the text.

    a. Select the merged cells **A1:D1**.

    b. On the *Home* tab, in the *Font* group, click the **Font Size** button arrow, and select **16**.

    c. On the *Home* tab, in the *Font* group, click the **Bold** button.

8. Add a bottom border to cells **B6:D6** to separate the headings from the data.

    a. Select cells **B6:D6**.

    b. On the *Home* tab, in the *Font* group, click the **Borders** button arrow and select **Thick Bottom Border**.

9. This recipe is better using whole milk. Find and replace all instances of *non fat* with *whole*.

    a. On the *Home* tab, in the *Editing* group, click the **Find & Select** button and select **Replace...**

    b. If necessary, display the find and replace options and clear any formats.

       i. Click the **Options >>** button.

       ii. If the button next to the *Find what* box does not display *No Format Set*, click the **Format** button arrow and select **Clear Find Format**.

       iii. If the button next to the *Replace with* box does not display *No Format Set*, click the **Format** button arrow and select **Clear Replace Format**.

       iv. Click the **Options >>** button to hide the find and replace options.

    c. Type **non fat** in the *Find what* box.

    d. Type **whole** in the *Replace with* box.

    e. Click the **Replace All** button.

    f. Excel should make three replacements. Click **OK**.

    g. Click **Close**.

10. Apply thick outside borders around the entire recipe (cells **A1:D20**).

    a. Select cells **A1:D20**.

    b. On the *Home* tab, in the *Font* group, click the **Borders** button arrow and select **Thick Outside Borders**.

11. Now that your recipe is formatted, make a copy of it and change the number of servings to **5**. Be sure to retain formulas and column widths.

    a. If necessary, select cells **A1:D20**.

    b. On the *Home* tab, in the *Clipboard* group, click the **Copy** button.

    c. Click cell **F1**.

    d. On the *Home* tab, in the *Clipboard* group, click the **Paste** button arrow.

    e. Select **Keep Source Column Widths**.

12. Change the value in cell **G2** to **5**.

13. Set the print area so only the original version of the recipe will print. Be sure to preview the printed worksheet.

    a. Select cells **A1:D20**.

    b. On the *Page Layout* tab, it the *Page Setup* group, click the **Print Area** button and select **Set Print Area**.

    c. Click the **File** tab.

    d. Click **Print**.

14. Save and close the workbook.

challenge yourself 2.3

In this project, you will format a blood pressure report to make it look less like a spreadsheet and more like a form. You will use conditional formatting to highlight important data.

Skills needed to complete this project:

- Using Undo and Redo (Skill 2.5)
- Adding Shading with Fill Color (Skill 2.11)
- Merging Cells and Splitting Merged Cells (Skill 2.7)
- Applying Cell Styles (Skill 2.12)
- Changing Fonts, Font Size, and Font Color (Skill 2.9)
- Aligning Cells (Skill 2.6)
- Adding Borders (Skill 2.10)
- Using Format Painter (Skill 2.13)
- Applying Bold, Italic, and Underline (Skill 2.8)
- Applying Conditional Formatting with Data Bars, Color Scales, and Icon Sets (Skill 2.15)
- Applying Conditional Formatting with Top/Bottom Rules (Skill 2.17)
- Setting and Clearing the Print Area (Skill 2.22)

1. Open the start file **EX2019-ChallengeYourself-2-3** and resave the file as: `[your initials]EX-ChallengeYourself-2-3`

2. If the workbook opens in Protected View, click the **Enable Editing** button in the Message Bar at the top of the workbook so you can modify it.

3. Select cells **A1:F26** and apply the **White, Background 1** fill color. It is the first option in the first row under *Theme Colors*.

4. Merge and center the title across cells **A1:F1**.

5. Apply the **Title** cell style to the merged cells.

6. Apply the **Tan, Accent 6, Lighter 80%** fill color to the merged cells. It is the last option in the second row under *Theme Colors*.

7. Change the font color to **Dark Purple, Accent 5**. It is the second to last color in the first row under *Theme Colors*.

8. Merge cells **C2:D2** and right-align the content in the cell.

9. Apply the default **Outside Borders** border style to the merged cells **C2:D2**.

10. Apply the **40% - Accent5** cell style to cells **C4:D4**.

11. Apply the same formatting to cells **C7:D7**.

12. Apply the default **Outside Borders** border style to cells **C4:D5** and cells **C7:D8**.

13. Bold cells **B2**, **B5**, **B8**, and **B10**.
14. Merge cells **C10:D10** and right-align the content in the cell.
15. Apply the default **Outside Borders** border style to the merged cells.
16. Apply the **Dark Green, Accent 4, Lighter 60%** fill color to cells **A12:F12**. It is the eighth color in the third row under *Theme Colors*.
17. Left-align the content in cells **A13:A26**.
18. Apply the default **All Borders** border style to cells **A13:F26**.
19. Add conditional formatting to cells **E13:E26** using the **Red to Black** icon set.
20. Add conditional formatting to cells **C13:C26** to format values **greater than 136** with **light red fill with dark red text**.
21. Add conditional formatting to cells **C13:C26** to format values **between 120 and 136** with **yellow fill with dark yellow text**.
22. Add conditional formatting to cells **D13:D26** to format values **greater than 82** with **light red fill with dark red text**.
23. Add conditional formatting to cells **D13:D26** to format values **between 80 and 82** with **yellow fill with dark yellow text**.
24. Add conditional formatting to cells **D13:D26** to format values **less than 80** with **green fill with dark green text**.
25. Apply the default **Thick Outside Borders** border style around cells **A1:F26**.
26. Set cells **A1:F26** as the print area.
27. Preview how the worksheet will look when printed.
28. Save and close the workbook.

challenge yourself **2.4**

In this project you will add formatting to a college budget spreadsheet and rearrange items that are in the wrong categories.

Skills needed to complete this project:

- Using Undo and Redo (Skill 2.5)
- Merging Cells and Splitting Merged Cells (Skill 2.7)
- Applying Cell Styles (Skill 2.12)
- Adding Shading with Fill Color (Skill 2.11)
- Applying Bold, Italic, and Underline (Skill 2.8)
- Cutting, Copying, and Pasting Cell Content (Skill 2.1)
- Using Paste Options (Skill 2.2)
- Inserting and Deleting Cells (Skill 2.3)
- Using Format Painter (Skill 2.13)
- Applying Conditional Formatting with Data Bars, Color Scales, and Icon Sets (Skill 2.15)
- Wrapping Text in Cells (Skill 2.4)
- Adding Borders (Skill 2.10)

1. Open the start file **EX2019-ChallengeYourself-2-4** and resave the file as:
   `[your initials]EX-ChallengeYourself-2-4`

2. If the workbook opens in Protected View, click the **Enable Editing** button in the Message Bar at the top of the workbook so you can modify it.

3. Center and merge the title across cells **A1:E1**.

4. Apply the **Heading 1** cell style to the merged cells.

5. Merge and center the four section titles across the appropriate cells (**Monthly Income**, **Discretionary Income**, **Monthly Expenses**, and **Semester Expenses**).

6. Apply cell styles to the section titles as follows:

    a. Monthly Income—**20% - Accent5**

    b. Discretionary Income—**20% - Accent2**

    c. Monthly Expenses—**20% - Accent6**

    d. Semester Expenses—**20% - Accent1**

7. Add the **Gray, Accent 6, Lighter 80%** fill color to cells **A3:B3**. It is the last color in the second row under *Theme Colors*.

8. Bold cells **A3:B3**.

9. Copy only the formatting of cells **A3:B3** to the headers in the other sections (cells **A10:B10**, **D3:E3**, and **D10:E10**).

10. The line item for lab fees (cells **A21:B21**) is in the wrong category. Cut the cells and insert them into cells **D12:E12**, shifting the other cells down. Do not overwrite the existing data.

11. Delete the empty cells **A21:B21**, shifting the other cells up.

12. Cell **E6** has the wrong number format applied. Copy the formatting from cell **E5** and apply it to cell **E6**.

13. Apply conditional formatting to cells **B11:B23** to display a red gradient data bar in each cell.

14. The text in cell **A21** appears cutoff. Apply text wrapping to the cell.

15. Apply the default **All Borders** border style to the following cell ranges: **A3:B7**, **D3:E7**, **A10:B24**, and **D10:E16**.

16. Save and close the workbook.

on your own 2.5

In this project, you will add your own data to a worksheet that tracks the original cost and current resell value for textbooks. As you format the worksheet, keep in mind that you want the worksheet to be visually appealing, but you don't want it to look like a circus! Try a variety of formatting options and keep using the Undo command until you find the formats you like best.

Skills needed to complete this project:

- Using Undo and Redo (Skill 2.5)
- Adding Shading with Fill Color (Skill 2.11)
- Merging Cells and Splitting Merged Cells (Skill 2.7)
- Applying Cell Styles (Skill 2.12)
- Inserting and Deleting Cells (Skill 2.3)
- Aligning Cells (Skill 2.6)
- Changing Fonts, Font Size, and Font Color (Skill 2.9)
- Using Format Painter (Skill 2.13)
- Adding Borders (Skill 2.10)
- Cutting, Copying, and Pasting Cell Content (Skill 2.1)

- Applying Conditional Formatting Using the Quick Analysis Tool (Skill 2.14)
- Applying Conditional Formatting with Data Bars, Color Scales, and Icon Sets (Skill 2.15)
- Replacing Formatting (Skill 2.21)
- Wrapping Text in Cells (Skill 2.4)
- Applying Bold, Italic, and Underline (Skill 2.8)
- Applying Conditional Formatting with Highlight Cells Rules (Skill 2.16)
- Applying Conditional Formatting with Top/Bottom Rules (Skill 2.17)

1. Open the start file **EX2019-OnYourOwn-2-5** and resave the file as: `[your initials]EX-OnYourOwn-2-5`

2. If the workbook opens in Protected View, click the **Enable Editing** button in the Message Bar at the top of the workbook so you can modify it.

3. Update the data in the workbook with an inventory of textbooks you own. Include the purchase price and estimated resell value for each title.

4. Add and delete cells as necessary.

5. Wrap text if any of your book titles are too long to fit in the cell.

6. Format the worksheet title and data table using cell styles, borders, and fill color. Change fonts, font color, and font size as appropriate.

7. Remember to use *Format Painter* to copy formatting from one part of the worksheet to another.

8. You can also use the *Replace* command if you want to change formatting from one style to another in multiple cells at the same time.

9. Apply conditional formatting to identify the most expensive books and the ones with the highest resell values. Use any type of conditional formatting you'd like.

10. Apply conditional formatting to identify the book with the best resell value and the book with the worst resell value.

11. When you are satisfied with the appearance of the worksheet, save and close the workbook.

fix it 2.6

In this project, you will fix a rather unattractive worksheet that was intended for recording walking/running miles and times.

Skills needed to complete this project:

- Using Undo and Redo (Skill 2.5)
- Adding Shading with Fill Color (Skill 2.11)
- Merging Cells and Splitting Merged Cells (Skill 2.7)
- Applying Cell Styles (Skill 2.12)
- Inserting and Deleting Cells (Skill 2.3)
- Changing Fonts, Font Size, and Font Color (Skill 2.9)
- Using Format Painter (Skill 2.13)
- Adding Borders (Skill 2.10)
- Wrapping Text in Cells (Skill 2.4)
- Applying Conditional Formatting Using the Quick Analysis Tool (Skill 2.14)

- Applying Conditional Formatting with Data Bars, Color Scales, and Icon Sets (Skill 2.15)
- Using Find and Replace (Skill 2.20)
- Applying Bold, Italic, and Underline (Skill 2.8)

1. Open the start file **EX2019-FixIt-2-6** and resave the file as:
   `[your initials]EX-FixIt-2-6`

2. If the workbook opens in Protected View, click the **Enable Editing** button in the Message Bar at the top of the workbook so you can modify it.

3. Begin by removing all the fill color, font colors, and borders from the worksheet. This worksheet has so many different formats, it is probably easier to start from a clean slate.

   Hint: Do not use the *Clear Formats* command. Using this command will remove all numbering formats to the General number format.

4. All fonts in the worksheet should be set to **Calibri**, **12** point size.

5. Merge cells **A1:D1** and center the title across the merged cells.

6. Apply appropriate formatting for the title. Use the **Title** cell style.

7. Apply the **Blue, Accent 1, lighter 80%** fill color to cells **B4:D9** to make the data table stand out. It is the fifth color in the second row under *Theme Colors*.

8. Apply a dotted border to the inside of cells **A4:D9**. *Hint*: Use the *Format Cells* dialog, and select the second border style in the list after *None*. In the *Presets* section, apply the **Inside** option.

9. Apply a border around cells **A3:D9** using the **Thick Outside Borders** option.

10. Apply a border to cells **A3:D3** using the **Bottom Double Border** option.

11. Apply bold to cells **B3:D3** and **A4:A9** to make row and column headers stand out from the data.

12. Apply text wrapping in cell **D3**.

13. An entry for October 9 is missing. You walked for 45 minutes that day and went 3.7 miles. Insert the data in the appropriate place. (You can copy the formula to calculate miles per hour from one of the other cells).

    NOTE: You must complete step 13 correctly in order to be able to receive points for completing the next steps. Check your work carefully.

14. Apply conditional formatting using data bars to visually compare the distance jogged each day.

15. Ensure that all entries for miles and miles per hour display using the Number format with two digits after the decimal.

16. Ensure that all average calculations display using the Number format with two digits after the decimal.

17. Find all instances of *walk* and replace with *jog*.

    NOTE: If you receive the warning message "We couldn't find anything to replace. Click options for more ways to search," clear replace format options.

18. Save and close the workbook.

Source of screenshots: Microsoft Office 365: Word, Excel, Access, and PowerPoint.

Using Formulas and Functions

skills

Introduction

It is time to go beyond simple formulas. In this chapter you will learn to use the functions built into Excel to compute statistics, insert dates, modify text, work with logical expressions, compute loan payments, and perform table lookups. Also, you will create formulas that reference named ranges and other worksheets for fast replication. Finally, you will learn skills necessary for troubleshooting formulas.

Skill 3.1 Using the Function Arguments Dialog to Enter Functions

Previously, you learned to enter functions three ways:

1. **Typing the formula directly in the cell or the formula bar**. This method is easiest for simple functions.

2. **Using the *AutoSum* button**. This method works well when your spreadsheet includes numerical data organized in rows or columns. Functions available via AutoSum are limited to simple math and statistical functions (SUM, AVERAGE, COUNT, MIN, and MAX).

3. **Using the Quick Analysis tool**. This method is the easiest way to enter totals for multiple rows or columns of data at once. Like AutoSum, the Quick Analysis tool offers a limited number of functions (SUM, AVERAGE, and COUNT). It has the advantage of including options not available from AutoSum (calculating running totals and calculating the percentage of the overall total for each row or column) and showing a live preview of the totals before you make a selection.

Every function can be entered using its *Function Arguments* dialog. This dialog is different for each function. There are two primary methods for opening the *Function Arguments* dialog.

1. **Select the function from the *Formulas* tab, *Function Library* group**. Each button in this Ribbon group represents a category of functions. Clicking a button displays a menu of functions in that category. Selecting a function opens its *Insert Function* dialog.

FIGURE EX 3.1

skill 3.1   Using the Function Arguments Dialog to Enter Functions

Select a function category.

Select a function to see the
function arguments and a brief
description of the function.

SUM(number1,number2,...)
Adds all the numbers in a range of cells

Click **OK** to open *Function
Argumnets* dialog for
the selected fuction.

FIGURE EX 3.2

2. **Select the function from the *Insert Function* dialog**. To
   open the *Insert Function* dialog, on the *Formulas* tab,
   in the *Function Library* group, click the **Insert Function**
   button. You can also click the **Insert Function** button to
   the left of the formula bar.

To use the *Insert Function* dialog:

1. Functions in the *Insert Function* dialog are organized in
   the same categories as the *Function Library* group. By
   default, the category list will default to the category you
   last used or it will show the *Most Recently Used* list. To
   select another category, expand the **Or select a category**
   list and select the function category you want.

2. Click a function in the *Select a function* box to see a brief
   description of what it does and the arguments it takes.

3. Click **OK** to open the *Function Arguments* dialog for the
   selected function.

To use the *Function Arguments* dialog:

1. Enter values or cell references in each of the argument boxes as needed by typing
   or by clicking the cell or cell range in the worksheet. As you click each argument
   box, a brief description of the argument appears near the bottom of the dialog.
   The *Function Arguments* dialog also displays a preview of the result of the
   calculation. This value updates as you add arguments.

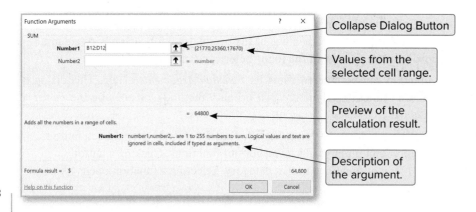

Collapse Dialog Button

Values from the
selected cell range.

Preview of the
calculation result.

Description of
the argument.

FIGURE EX 3.3

2. If the position of the *Function Arguments* dialog makes it difficult to click the cell
   you want, click the **Collapse Dialog** button next to the argument box. As shown in
   Figure EX 3.4, the *Function Arguments* dialog collapses to show only the function
   argument box you are working with. Click the cell(s) to add the reference to the dialog.

3. Click the **Expand Dialog** button to return the *Function Arguments* dialog to its
   full size.

4. When you are finished entering arguments, click **OK**.

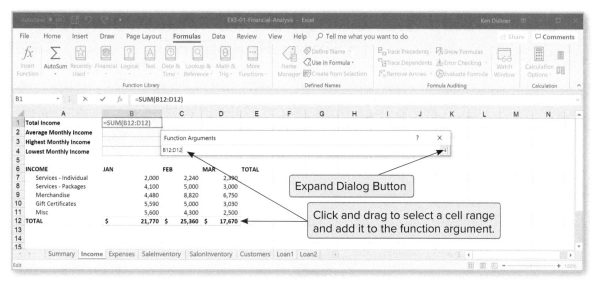

tips & tricks

The *SUM Function Arguments* dialog shown in Figure EX 3.3 includes an extra argument box. For functions that calculate a value based on a series of cells, Excel adds a blank argument box each time you enter an argument (up to 256 arguments). Enter values or cell references only in the argument boxes you need.

tell me **more**

If you're not sure of the name of the function you want, open the *Insert Function* dialog and type keywords describing the function in the *Search for a function* box, and then click the **Go** button. The *Or select a category* box changes to *Recommended*, and the *Select a function* box now displays a list of functions that match the keywords you typed.

let me **try**

Open the student data file **EX3-01-Financial-Analysis** and try this skill on your own:

1. On the *Income* worksheet, enter a SUM function in cell **B1** to calculate the total of cells **B12:D12**. Open the *Function Arguments* dialog from the *Formulas* tab, *Function Library* group, *Math & Trig* button. You will have to scroll down the list to find SUM.

2. Enter a SUM function in cell **E7** to calculate the total of cells **B7:D7**. Use the *Insert Function* dialog. If the SUM function is not listed in the *Select a Function* box, expand the **Or select a category list**, and select either **Math & Trig** or **Most Recently Used**. Again, Excel enters the adjacent cell range as the function arguments for you.

3. If you will be moving on to the next skill in this chapter, leave the workbook open to continue working. If not, save the file as directed by your instructor and close it.

Skill 3.2 Using Formula AutoComplete to Enter Functions

Formula AutoComplete is a shortcut for entering functions. When you type = and then a letter, Formula AutoComplete displays a list of potential matches (functions and other valid reference names). This is a good method to use if you prefer typing the function arguments, but you need a reminder of what the arguments are or the order in which they should be entered.

FIGURE EX 3.5

1. Type = in the cell or the formula bar to begin the formula. Formula AutoComplete displays the list of potential matches.

2. Type more letters to shorten the Formula AutoComplete list.

3. Double-click a function name to enter it in your formula.

4. Enter the expected arguments by typing values or selecting a cell or cell range.

5. Press (←Enter) to complete the formula. Excel enters the closing) for you.

	A	B	C	D	E	F	G	H	I	J	K
6	INCOME	JAN	FEB	MAR	TOTAL						
7	Services - Individual	2,000	2,240	2,390	6,630						
8	Services - Packages	4,100	5,000	3,000							
9	Merchandise	4,480	8,820	6,750							
10	Gift Certificates	5,590	5,000	3,030							
11	Misc	5,600	4,300	2,500							
12	TOTAL	$ 21,770	$ 25,360	$ 17,670	=SUM(B12:D12						
13					SUM(**number1**, [number2], ...)						
14											
15											

Excel displays the function argument below the formula as you complete it.

FIGURE EX 3.6

tips & tricks

When you use Formula AutoComplete, you can click the function name in the ScreenTip to open the Excel help topic for that function.

let me try

If you do not have the data file from the previous skill open, open the student data file **EX3-02-Financial-Analysis** and try this skill on your own:

1. On the *Income* worksheet, use Formula AutoComplete to enter a SUM function in cell **E12** to calculate the total of cells **B12:D12**.

2. If you will be moving on to the next skill in this chapter, leave the workbook open to continue working. If not, save the file as directed by your instructor and close it.

Skill 3.3 Calculating Averages

The **AVERAGE** statistical function is used to calculate the average value of a group of values. Average is calculated by adding the values, and then dividing the sum by the number of values.

A formula using the AVERAGE function looks like this:

=AVERAGE(B12:D12)

The result of this formula is the sum of the values in cells B12:D12 divided by the number of values in that cell range.

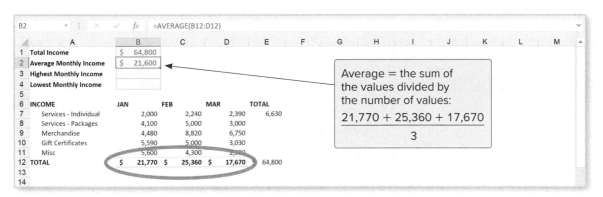

FIGURE EX 3.7

To create a formula with the AVERAGE function, use any of these methods:

❭ If you prefer typing in the cell or the formula bar, try using Formula AutoComplete.

❭ If the data are organized in rows or columns, you can use AutoSum. On the *Home* tab, *Editing* group or on the *Formula* tab, *Function Library* group, click the **AutoSum** button arrow and select **Average**.

❭ If you want to calculate the average for multiple rows or columns at once, use one of the average options in the Quick Analysis tool, *Totals* tab.

❭ If you prefer using the *Function Arguments* dialog, on the *Formulas* tab, in the *Function Library* group, click the **More Functions** button, point to **Statistical**, and click **AVERAGE**.

tips & tricks

When calculating an average, Excel will ignore empty cells. If you want to include those cells in your average calculations, make sure they have a value of zero.

tell me **more**

What you might think of as the "average" is actually the statistical mean. *Average* is a general term in statistics that includes **mean** (the sum of a group of values divided by the number of values in the group), **median** (the middle value of a set of values), and **mode** (the value that appears most often in a group of values). In Excel, the AVERAGE function calculates the mean value. Most people say *average* when they really want to calculate the mean value.

let me **try**

If you do not have the data file from the previous skill open, open the student data file **EX3-03-Financial-Analysis** and try this skill on your own:

1. On the *Income* worksheet, enter a formula in cell **B2** to calculate the average value of cells **B12:D12**. Use any method you like.

2. If you will be moving on to the next skill in this chapter, leave the workbook open to continue working. If not, save the file as directed by your instructor and close it.

Skill 3.4 Finding Minimum and Maximum Values

In addition to AVERAGE, there are a few other statistical functions you may find useful in working with day-to-day spreadsheets.

The **MAX** (maximum) statistical function will give you the largest value in a range of values. A formula using the MAX function looks like this: **=MAX(A3:A6)**

The **MIN** (minimum) statistical function will give you the smallest value in a range of values. A formula using the MIN function looks like this: **=MIN(A3:A6)**

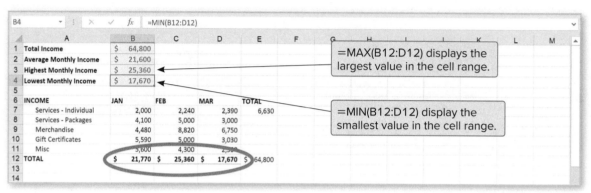

FIGURE EX 3.8

To create a formula with the MAX or MIN function, use any of these methods:

〉 If you prefer typing in the cell or the formula bar, try using Formula AutoComplete.

〉 If the data are organized in rows or columns, you can use AutoSum. On the *Home* tab, *Editing* group or on the *Formula* tab, *Function Library* group, click the **AutoSum** button arrow and select **MAX** or **MIN**.

〉 If you prefer using the *Function Arguments* dialog, on the *Formulas* tab, in the *Function Library* group, click the **More Functions** button, point to **Statistical**, and click **MAX** or **MIN**.

let me **try**

If you do not have the data file from the previous skill open, open the student data file **EX3-04-Financial-Analysis** and try this skill on your own:

1. On the *Income* worksheet, in cell **B3**, enter a formula to find the highest (maximum) monthly income total (cells **B12:D12**).

2. On the *Income* worksheet, in cell **B4**, enter a formula to find the lowest (minimum) monthly income total (cells **B12:D12**).

3. If you will be moving on to the next skill in this chapter, leave the workbook open to continue working. If not, save the file as directed by your instructor and close it.

Skill 3.5 Using Date and Time Functions

Excel includes two functions that insert the current date or date and time. The **NOW** function inserts the current date and time. The **TODAY** function inserts only the current date. Both of these functions are **volatile**—that is, they are not constant. They update with the current date or date and time each time the workbook is opened.

A formula using the NOW function looks like this:

=NOW()

A formula using the TODAY function looks like this:

=TODAY()

Notice that both of these functions include parentheses, but there are no arguments inside them. These functions do not require arguments.

To create a formula with NOW or TODAY, use either of these methods:

❭ If you prefer typing in the cell or the formula bar, try using Formula AutoComplete.

❭ If you prefer using the *Function Arguments* dialog, on the *Formulas* tab, in the *Function Library* group, click the **Date & Time** button and click **NOW** or **TODAY**.

FIGURE EX 3.9

tips & tricks

Both NOW and TODAY use the date and time from your computer's clock. If your computer's clock is wrong, the date and time displayed in your workbook will be wrong as well.

tell me **more**

If the cell is formatted to use a date format that does not display the time, the result of the NOW and TODAY functions will appear the same. However, the underlying value will be different. If you change the formatting of the cell to display the time, a cell using the TODAY function will always display a time of 12:00 AM, whereas a cell using the NOW function will display the correct time.

let me **try**

If you do not have the data file from the previous skill open, open the student data file **EX3-05-Financial-Analysis** and try this skill on your own:

1. On the *Summary* worksheet, enter a formula in cell **B1** to display only the current date.

2. On the *Summary* worksheet, enter a formula in cell **B2** to display the current date and time.

3. If you will be moving on to the next skill in this chapter, leave the workbook open to continue working. If not, save the file as directed by your instructor and close it.

Skill 3.6 Creating Formulas Using Counting Functions

The counting functions are useful when you need to know how many numbers or items are in a list or how many rows are missing data for a particular column.

COUNT—Counts the number of cells that contain numbers within a specified range of cells. A formula using the COUNT function looks like this:

=COUNT(A7:A20)

The result of this formula is the number of cells in **A7** through **A20** that contain numerical values. If you want to include cells that contain text, use COUNTA instead.

To count numbers, you have two additional options:

> If the data are organized in rows or columns, you can use AutoSum to enter the COUNT function. On the *Home* tab, *Editing* group or on the *Formula* tab, *Function Library* group, click the **AutoSum** button arrow and select **Count Numbers**.

> If you want to count the numbers in multiple rows or columns at once, use one of the *Count* options from the Quick Analysis tool, *Totals* tab.

COUNTA—Counts the number of cells that are not blank within a specified range of cells. Use COUNTA if your cell range includes text data or a mix of text and numbers. A formula using the COUNTA function looks like this:

=COUNTA(B7:B20)

The result of this formula is the number of cells in **B7** through **B20** that contain any data (numerical or text).

FIGURE EX 3.10

COUNTBLANK—Counts the number of empty (blank) cells within a specified range of cells. Cells that contain a zero (0) or a formula that results in zero are not considered blank. Use COUNTBLANK to find the number of rows missing values in a column. A formula using the COUNTBLANK function looks like this:

=COUNTBLANK(E7:E20)

The result of this formula is the number of cells in **E7** through **E20** that are empty.

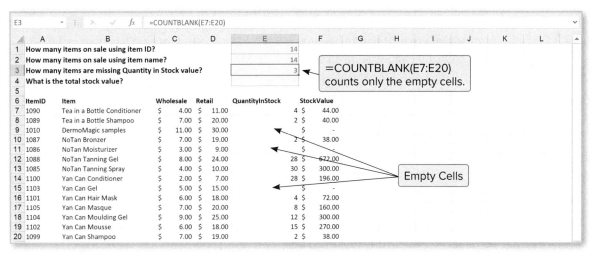

FIGURE EX 3.11

To create a formula with COUNT, COUNTA, or COUNTBLANK, use either of these methods:

❯ If you prefer typing in the cell or the formula bar, try using Formula AutoComplete.

❯ If you prefer using the *Function Arguments* dialog, on the *Formulas* tab, in the *Function Library* group, click the **More Functions** button, point to **Statistical**, and click **COUNT**, **COUNTA**, or **COUNTBLANK**.

tips & tricks

The COUNT and COUNTA functions can take multiple arguments.

COUNTBLANK accepts only a single argument. If you want to count blanks across a non-contiguous range of cells, you will need to create a formula adding together the results of multiple functions.

=COUNTBLANK(A1:C1)+COUNTBLANK(B10:C15)

let me try

If you do not have the data file from the previous skill open, open the student data file **EX3-06-Financial-Analysis** and try this skill on your own:

1. On the *SaleInventory* worksheet, in cell **E1**, enter a formula using a counting function to count the number of items on sale. Count the numerical values in the *ItemID* column (cells **A7:A20**).

2. On the *SaleInventory* worksheet, in cell **E2**, enter a formula using a counting function to count the number of items on sale. Count the values in the *Item* column (cells **B7:B20**).

3. In cell **E3**, enter a formula using a counting function to count the number of blank cells in the *QuantityInStock* column (cells **E7:E20**).

4. If you will be moving on to the next skill in this chapter, leave the workbook open to continue working. If not, save the file as directed by your instructor and close it.

Skill 3.7 Formatting Text Using Functions

Functions can do more than perform calculations. Excel includes a special group of functions to modify text. These text functions are useful for ensuring that text data have a consistent appearance. In functions, text is referred to as a **string** or **text string**.

Commonly used text functions are:

PROPER—Converts the text string to proper case (the first letter in each word is capitalized). A formula using the PROPER function looks like this:

=PROPER(D2)

UPPER—Converts the text string to all uppercase letters. A formula using the UPPER function looks like this:

=UPPER(F2)

LOWER—Converts the text string to all lowercase letters. A formula using the LOWER function looks like this:

=LOWER(H2)

FIGURE EX 3.12

To create a formula with PROPER, UPPER, or LOWER, use either of these methods:

❭ If you prefer typing in the cell or the formula bar, try using Formula AutoComplete.

❭ If you prefer using the *Function Arguments* dialog, on the *Formulas* tab, in the *Function Library* group, click the **Text** button and click **PROPER**, **UPPER**, or **LOWER**.

tips & tricks

Typically, when you use one of the text functions, you are left with two groups of cells containing the same data: One group has the original incorrectly formatted text; the second group contains the formulas and displays correctly formatted text. There are two options for managing this:

❭ Hide the columns or rows that contain the original text. For information on hiding rows and columns, refer to the skill *Hiding and Unhiding Rows and Columns*.

❭ Copy the cells containing the text formulas; use one of the *Paste Values* options to paste just the values of the text formulas over the original cells, then delete the cells containing the text formulas. For information on using the *Paste Values* commands, refer to the skill *Using Paste Options*.

let me try

If you do not have the data file from the previous skill open, open the student data file **EX3-07-Financial-Analysis** and try this skill on your own:

1. On the *Customers* worksheet, enter a formula in cell **D3** to display the text from cell **D2** so the first letter in each word is capitalized.

2. On the *Customers* worksheet, enter a formula in cell **F3** to display the text from cell **F2** so all the letters display in uppercase.

3. On the *Customers* worksheet, enter a formula in cell **H3** to display the text from cell **H2** so all the letters display in lowercase.

4. If you will be moving on to the next skill in this chapter, leave the workbook open to continue working. If not, save the file as directed by your instructor and close it.

Skill 3.8 Using CONCAT to Combine Text

To **concatenate** means to link items together. You can use the **CONCAT** function to combine the text values of cells or cell ranges. CONCAT replaces the old CONCATENATE function. In Figure EX 3.13, the customer name in cell B3 is created by concatenating the values in column B (first name) and column C (last name). The formula looks like this:

=CONCAT(B2," ",C2)

The argument in the middle (" ") places a one-space text string between the values of cells B2 and C2.

If you are building a long string from multiple cells, you may want to use the *Function Arguments* dialog until you become familiar with this function. Of course, you can always type directly in the cell or formula bar and use Formula AutoComplete.

1. On the *Formulas* tab, in the *Function Library* group, click the **Text** button.

2. Click **CONCAT**.

3. In the *Function Arguments* dialog, enter each cell reference or text string you want to combine in its own argument. If one of the arguments is a blank space, enter " " in the argument box.

4. Click **OK**.

FIGURE EX 3.13

FIGURE EX 3.14

tips & tricks

For sorting purposes, you may want to keep the cells that you concatenate. If you do not want them to display in your worksheet, hide the columns or rows that contain the original text. For information on hiding rows and columns, refer to the skill *Hiding and Unhiding Rows and Columns*.

let me try

If you do not have the data file from the previous skill open, open the student data file **EX3-08-Financial-Analysis** and try this skill on your own:

1. On the *Customers* worksheet, enter a formula in cell **B3** to combine the text from cells **B2** and **C2** to display the customer name in the format *Maxwell Arch*. Don't forget the argument for the space.

2. If you will be moving on to the next skill in this chapter, leave the workbook open to continue working. If not, save the file as directed by your instructor and close it.

Skill 3.9 Using TEXTJOIN to Combine Text

Another way to combine text is to use the **TEXTJOIN** function. TEXTJOIN concatenates cells using a **delimiter** character to separate values in the new text string. In Figure EX 3.15, the customer name in cell B4 is created by combining the values in A2 (title), B2 (first name), and C2 (last name) and separating each text value with a space. The formula looks like this:

FIGURE EX 3.15

FIGURE EX 3.16

=TEXTJOIN(" ",TRUE,A2:C2)

To combine text using TEXTJOIN:

1. On the *Formulas* tab, in the *Function Library* group, click the **Text** button.
2. Click **TEXTJOIN**.
3. Enter the **Delimiter** argument. This argument defines the character to use between each text item.
4. Enter the **Ignore_empty** argument. If set to TRUE, the function will skip blank cells. If set to FALSE, the function will include the blank cells, resulting in two of the delimiter characters together.
5. Enter the **Text1** argument. This argument is the first text string, cell, or cell range to combine. If you use a cell range, the delimiter character will be added between the values from each cell in the range.
6. Continue adding **Text** arguments as necessary.
7. Click **OK**.

tips & tricks

When using a space as the delimiter in a TEXTJOIN formula, if you type the formula directly in the cell or address bar, you must enclose the space in quotation marks. If you use the *Function Arguments* dialog, you can just type the space in the *Delimiter* argument box. Excel will add the quotation marks for you.

let me try

If you do not have the data file from the previous skill open, open the student data file **EX3-09-Financial-Analysis** and try this skill on your own:

1. On the *Customers* worksheet, enter a formula in cell **B4** to combine the text from cells **A2:C2** to display the customer name in the format *Mr. Maxwell Arch*. Use a space as the delimiter. Ignore blank cells. Use a cell range as the *Text1* argument.
2. If you will be moving on to the next skill in this chapter, leave the workbook open to continue working. If not, save the file as directed by your instructor and close it.

Skill 3.10 Creating Formulas Referencing Data from Other Worksheets

Cell references are not limited to cells within the same worksheet. To specify a cell location in another worksheet, begin the reference with the name of the worksheet followed by an exclamation point ! and then the cell reference. This feature is useful when you want to create summary sheets or perform analysis on data from multiple sheets at once.

The formula shown in Figure EX 3.17 displays the value of cell E8 from the *Expenses* worksheet:

=Expenses!E8

To include a reference to a cell from another sheet in your workbook:

1. Click the cell where you want the formula.

2. Type: =

3. Navigate to the cell you want to reference by clicking the sheet tab and then clicking the cell. Notice Excel adds the worksheet name to the cell reference for you.

4. Press (← Enter) to complete the formula.

You can also refer to cells in other worksheets within formulas as shown in Figure EX 3.18.

=Income!B1−Expenses!E8

To include a reference to another worksheet in a formula:

1. Begin entering the formula as normal.

2. When you want to add a reference to a cell in another sheet, click the sheet tab, then click the cell(s) you want to add to the formula or click and drag to select a cell range.

3. When you are finished with the formula, Press (← Enter).

FIGURE EX 3.17

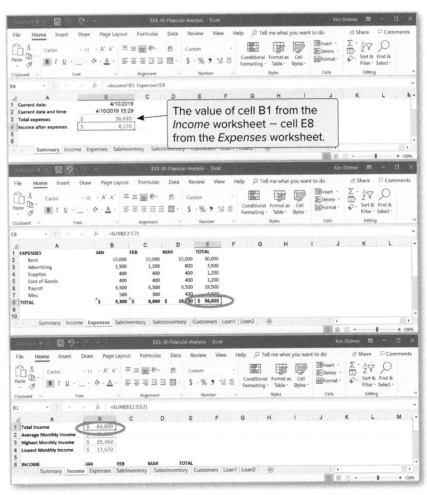

FIGURE EX 3.18

skill 3.10   Creating Formulas Referencing Data from Other Worksheets

tips & tricks

If your workbook includes multiple sheets with the same data structure, you can create a formula that references the same cell(s) on multiple sheets. This is called a **3-D reference**. A formula with a 3-D reference looks like this:

=SUM(ExpensesQ1:ExpensesQ4!A4:A7)

The result of this formula is the sum of the values in cells A4 through A7 on all worksheets from *ExpensesQ1* through the worksheet named *ExpensesQ4*.

To add a 3-D reference to a formula:

1. Begin entering the formula as you would normally.

2. Then, when you want to add the 3-D reference, instead of clicking a cell on a single worksheet, first select the sheet tabs for all the sheets you want included, and then click the specific cell(s) you want on the first worksheet.

3. Press ⏎ Enter .

tell me **more**

You can use the same techniques taught in this skill to reference cells in other workbooks. When you reference a cell in another workbook, you create a link between the two workbooks.

let me **try**

If you do not have the data file from the previous skill open, open the student data file **EX3-10-Financial-Analysis** and try this skill on your own:

1. On the *Summary* sheet, in cell **B3**, enter a formula to display the value of cell **E8** from the *Expenses* worksheet.

2. On the *Summary* sheet, in cell **B4**, enter a formula to calculate the value of cell **B1** from the *Income* worksheet **minus** cell **E8** from the *Expenses* worksheet.

3. If you will be moving on to the next skill in this chapter, leave the workbook open to continue working. If not, save the file as directed by your instructor and close it.

Skill 3.11   Naming Ranges of Cells

Cell references like A4 and F7:F20 do not provide much information about what data the cells contain—they just tell you where the cells are located in the worksheet. However, you can assign names to cells or ranges of cells to give your cell references names that are more user-friendly. These **names** (also called **range names** or **named ranges**) act as a list of shortcuts to the cell locations.

To create a named range:

1. Select the cell or range of cells to which you want to assign a name.
2. Type the name in the *Name* box to the left of the formula bar.
3. Press ⬅ Enter to apply the name to the cell(s).

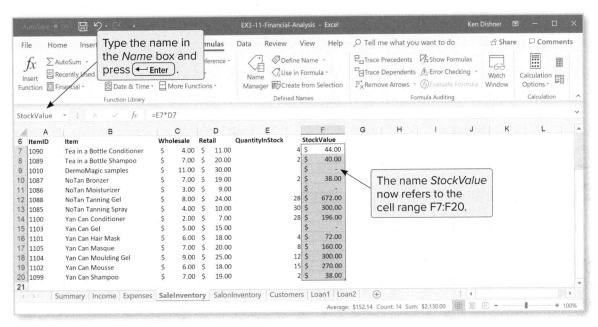

FIGURE EX 3.19

If your worksheet is organized in a table format, with column or row labels, you can automatically create named ranges for each column or row using the labels as names:

1. Select the range of cells you want to name including the labels.
2. On the *Formulas* tab, in the *Defined Names* group, click the **Create from Selection** button.
3. In the *Create Names from Selection* dialog, click the check box to indicate where the names are (*Top row*, *Left column*, *Bottom row*, or *Right column*).
4. Click **OK**.

Excel automatically creates named ranges for the cell range associated with each label. The named ranges will not include the labels. The *Create Names from Selection* command in Figure EX 3.20 will create the following named ranges:

Name:	ItemID	Item	Wholesale	QuantityInStock	ReorderLevel
Refers to cell range:	A5:A20	B5:B20	C5:C20	D5:D20	E5:E20

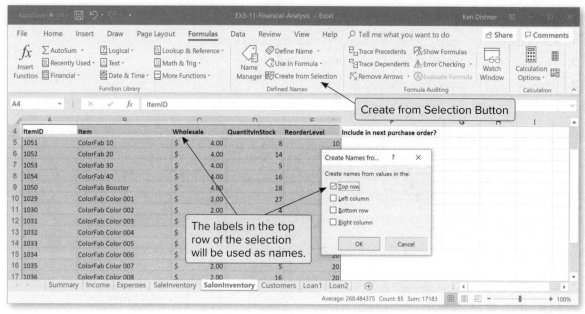

FIGURE EX 3.20

tips & tricks

Remember, names may not include spaces. If you use the *Create Names from Selection* command and the values for your names include spaces, Excel will replace the spaces with underscore _ characters.

Also, you cannot use numbers as names. When using *Create Names from Selection*, be sure to check that the text in the row or column containing labels is valid for names.

another **method**

You can also create new names through the *New Name* dialog.

1. On the *Formulas* tab, in the *Defined Names* group, click the **Define Name** button.

2. The selected cell(s) is (are) entered in the *Refers to* box.

3. Type the name you want in the *Name* box. If the cell to the immediate left or immediately above the selected cell appears to include a label, Excel will prepopulate the *Name* box with that text.

4. Click **OK**.

let me **try**

If you do not have the data file from the previous skill open, open the student data file **EX3-11-Financial-Analysis** and try this skill on your own:

1. On the *SaleInventory* worksheet, select cells **F7:F20**, and name them as follows: **StockValue**

2. Go to the *SalonInventory* worksheet, select cells **A4:E20** and use the *Create from Selection* command to create named ranges for the data table **A5:E20** using the labels in row **4** as the basis for the names.

3. If you will be moving on to the next skill in this chapter, leave the workbook open to continue working. If not, save the file as directed by your instructor and close it.

Skill 3.12 Working with Named Ranges

Rather than using a range of cells in your formulas, you can use a named range. The name will always refer to the cells, even if their position in the worksheet changes. Using named ranges in your formulas also makes it easier for others to use your workbook. Which formula is easier to understand: **=SUM(F7:F20)** or **=SUM(StockValue)**?

Formula AutoComplete lists named ranges as well as functions. Named ranges are identified by the label icon next to the name ⊟. Using the AutoComplete list is a good way to avoid typographical errors and ensure that you enter the name correctly.

To use a named range in a formula:

1. Click the cell where you want to enter the new formula.
2. Type the formula, substituting the range name for the cell references.
3. As you type alphabetical characters, Formula AutoComplete will offer name suggestions. If you see the name you want, double-click it and Excel will insert the name into the formula.
4. Press ⏎ Enter to accept the formula.

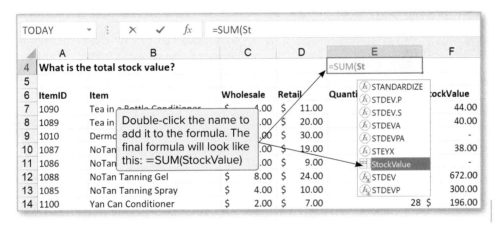

FIGURE EX 3.21

tips & tricks

❭ When you copy and paste a formula containing a named range, the name does not change with the new position in the workbook (similar to using an absolute reference).

❭ If you move a named cell, the name updates with the new cell location automatically.

another **method**

❭ On the *Formulas* tab, in the *Defined Names* group, click the **Use in Formula** button to display a list of names in your workbook, and then click one of the names to insert it into your formula.

❭ You can also click **Paste Names...** from the bottom of the *Use in Formula* list. The *Paste Names* dialog opens and lists all of the names in your workbook. Click a name and then click **OK** to add it to your formula.

let me **try**

If you do not have the data file from the previous skill open, open the student data file **EX3-12-Financial-Analysis** and try this skill on your own:

1. On the *SaleInventory* worksheet, in cell **E4**, enter a formula to calculate the total stock value. Use the **SUM** function and use the range name **StockValue** as the function argument.

2. If you will be moving on to the next skill in this chapter, leave the workbook open to continue working. If not, save the file as directed by your instructor and close it.

Skill 3.13 Updating Named Ranges with the Name Manager

The **Name Manager** lists all the named ranges used in your workbook, the current value for each, the cells to which the name refers (including the sheet name), the scope of the name (whether it is limited to a specific worksheet or applies to the entire workbook), and comments (if there are any).

To open the Name Manager, on the *Formulas* tab, in the *Defined Names* group, click the **Name Manager** button.

FIGURE EX 3.22 | Name Manager Button

FIGURE EX 3.23

To change the cell or range of cells to which a name refers:

1. Open the Name Manager and select the name you want to modify.

2. Edit the cell references in the *Refers to* box. You can also click the **Collapse Dialog** button to hide the Name Manager, and then click and drag to select the new cell range. When you are finished, click the **Expand Dialog** button to display the Name Manager again.

3. Click the checkmark icon to the left of the *Refers to* box to accept the change.

4. Click **Close** to close the Name Manager. If you forgot to save your change, Excel will ask if you want to save the change you made to the cell reference. Click **Yes**.

let me try

If you do not have the data file from the previous skill open, open the student data file **EX3-13-Financial-Analysis** and try this skill on your own:

1. Open the Name Manager.

2. Edit the workbook **Inventory** name so it refers to cells **A5:F20** on the *SalonInventory* worksheet. Be sure to modify the second *Inventory* name, not the one that is limited in scope to just the *SaleInventory* worksheet.

3. Close the Name Manager.

4. If you will be moving on to the next skill in this chapter, leave the workbook open to continue working. If not, save the file as directed by your instructor and close it.

Skill 3.14 Editing and Deleting Names with the Name Manager

When you copy data, you may find that some of the names in your workbook are repeated. Remember that names must be unique—but only within their scopes. You can have more than one named range with the same name, but only one can belong to the entire workbook. The others are specific to the worksheet in which they are defined.

In Figure EX 3.24, there are two *Inventory* names. The first is limited in scope to the *SaleInventory* worksheet. If you refer to the name *Inventory* in a formula in any other sheet in the workbook, it will refer to the second *Inventory* named range.

FIGURE EX 3.24

Duplicate names can be confusing. A good practice is to rename duplicates to make them easier to identify and use.

To change a name:

1. Open the Name Manager.
2. Click the name you want to modify, and then click the **Edit...** button.
3. The *Edit Name* dialog opens.
4. Type the new name in the *Name* box.
5. Click **OK** to save your changes.
6. Click the **Close** button to close the Name Manager.

When you change a name, Excel updates the name in any formulas that reference that name.

FIGURE EX 3.25

If your workbook includes names you no longer need, you should delete them.

To delete a name:

1. On the *Formulas* tab, in the *Defined Names* group, click the **Name Manager** button.
2. Click the name you want to delete, and then click the **Delete** button.
3. Excel displays a message asking if you are sure you want to delete the name. Click **OK**.

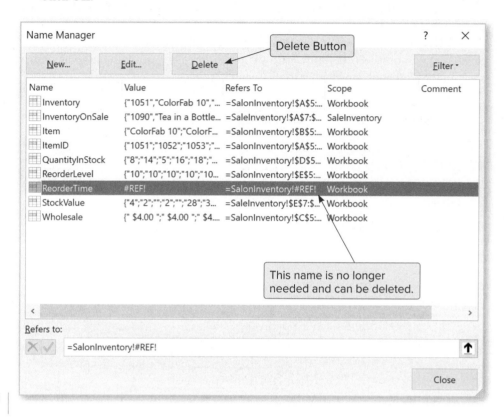

FIGURE EX 3.26

tips & tricks

❭ There are two types of names identified in the Name Manager. **Defined names** are the names you created and names that Excel creates automatically when you define a print area or print titles. Table names are names created automatically when you define a data range as a table. By default, tables are named Table1, Table2, Table3, and so on. To make table names easier to use, consider renaming them through the Name Manager.

❭ If your workbook includes many named ranges, you may find it useful to filter the list of names in the Name Manager. Click the **Filter** button in the upper right corner of the Name Manager and filter the list to show only names with errors or only names limited in scope to a worksheet.

let me try

If you do not have the data file from the previous skill open, open the student data file **EX3-14-Financial-Analysis** and try this skill on your own:

1. Open the Name Manager.
2. There are two *Inventory* names. Rename the one that is limited in scope to the *SaleInventory* worksheet to: **InventoryOnSale**
3. In the Name Manager, review the information about the *ReorderTime* name. The name results in an error—probably because the data to which it referred were deleted. Delete the **ReorderTime** name.
4. Close the Name Manager.
5. If you will be moving on to the next skill in this chapter, leave the workbook open to continue working. If not, save the file as directed by your instructor and close it.

Skill 3.15 Using the Logical Function IF

The **IF** logical function returns one value if a condition is true and another value if the condition is false. The IF function can return a numerical value or display a text string.

The formula in Figure EX 3.27 uses the IF function to determine whether or not an item should be ordered. If the value of cell D2 (the quantity in stock) is greater than the value of cell E2 (the reorder level), the formula will return "do not order". If the value of cell D2 is not greater than the value of cell E2, the formula will return "order". The formula looks like this:

=IF(D5>E5,"do not order","order")

In Figure EX 3.27, the value of cell D5 is *not* greater than the value of cell E5, so the IF function returns the *Value_if_false* argument displaying the word *order*. In the next row in the worksheet, the value of cell D6 *is* greater than the value of cell E6, so the IF function returns the *Value_if_true* argument displaying the phrase *do not order*.

FIGURE EX 3.27

To create a formula using the IF function:

1. Select the cell where you want to enter the formula.

2. On the *Formulas* tab, in the *Function Library* group, click the **Logical** button.

3. Select **IF** to open the *Function Arguments* dialog. IF functions take three arguments as shown in the *Function Arguments* dialog in Figure EX 3.28.

4. Enter the **Logical_test** argument. This argument states the condition you want to test for. The *Logical_test* always includes a comparison operator (=, >, <, etc.).

5. Enter the **Value_if_true** argument. This argument is the text string or value that will be displayed or the formula that will be calculated if the *Logical_test* argument is true.

6. Enter the **Value_if_false** argument. This argument is the text string or value that will be displayed or the formula that will be calculated if the *Logical_test* argument is false.

7. Click **OK**.

Function Arguments

IF

Logical_test   D5>E5 ←   ↑   =   The IF function evaluates this statement as TRUE or FALSE and displays the value from the appropriate argument.

Value_if_true   "do not order"   ↑   =   "do not order"

Value_if_false   "order"   ↑   =   "order"

=   "order"

Checks whether a condition is met, and returns one value if TRUE, and another value if FALSE.

Value_if_false   is the value that is returned if Logical_test is FALSE. If omitted, FALSE is returned.

Formula result = order

Help on this function   [OK]   [Cancel]

FIGURE EX 3.28

tips & tricks

If you use the *Function Arguments* dialog to enter text as the *Value_if_true* or the *Value_if_false* argument, you do not need to include the quotation marks. Excel will add them for you. However, if you type the formula directly in the cell or the formula bar, you must include quotation marks around the text.

let me try

If you do not have the data file from the previous skill open, open the student data file **EX3-15-Financial-Analysis** and try this skill on your own:

1. On the *SalonInventory* worksheet, enter a formula in cell **F5** using the logical function IF to display **do not order** if the quantity in stock (cell **D5**) is greater than the reorder level (cell **E5**) and **order** if it is not.

2. Copy the formula to cells **F6:F20** and review the results for each row.

3. If you will be moving on to the next skill in this chapter, leave the workbook open to continue working. If not, save the file as directed by your instructor and close it.

from the perspective of. . .

INSTRUCTOR

I use a spreadsheet to keep a grid of class attendance by student and by day. Using formulas and functions for grading gives me the flexibility to add scores, calculate averages, and provide feedback to my students.

Comstock/SuperStock

Skill 3.16 Calculating Loan Payments Using the PMT Function

One of the most useful financial functions in Excel is **PMT** (payment), which you can use to calculate loan payments. The PMT function is based on constant payments and a constant interest rate. To calculate a payment using PMT, you need three pieces of information: the interest rate (the *Rate* argument), the number of payments (the *Nper* argument), and the amount of the loan (the *Pv* argument).

=PMT(Rate,Nper,Pv)

Because the result of the formula is a payment (money going out), it is expressed as a negative number. If you want the result expressed as a positive number instead, add a negative symbol before the loan amount (the *Pv* argument).

When working with complex functions like PMT, use cell references as arguments rather than entering values directly. This way you can change values in your spreadsheet and see the results instantly without opening the *Function Arguments* dialog again.

Using cell references, the PMT function in Figure EX 3.29 looks like this:

=PMT(B4/12,B5,−B3)

In this example, the ***annual*** interest rate in cell B4 is 4%. To calculate ***monthly*** payments, the interest rate must be divided by the number of payments per year (12).

FIGURE EX 3.29

To use the PMT function:

1. Select the cell where you want to enter the formula.

2. On the *Formulas* tab, in the *Function Library* group, click the **Financial** button.

3. Select **PMT** from the list to open the *Function Arguments* dialog. PMT takes three required arguments and two optional arguments as shown in Figure EX 3.30.

4. Enter the **Rate** argument. This argument is the interest rate. Usually, interest rate is expressed as an annual rate. If the loan requires a monthly payment, the annual percentage rate (APR) should be divided by 12.

5. Enter the **Nper** argument. This argument is the total number of payments over the life of the loan.

6. Enter the **Pv** argument. This argument is the present value of the loan—how much you owe now (the loan principal).

7. (Optional) The **Fv** argument is future value of the loan. Excel assumes a value of 0 unless you include the argument and specify a different value. If you will make payments on the loan until it is completely paid off, you can leave this argument blank or enter 0.

8. (Optional) The **Type** argument represents when payments will be made during each loan period. Enter 1 if the payment is at the beginning of the period. If you omit this argument, Excel assumes a value of 0 (meaning each payment is at the end of the period).

9. Click **OK**.

FIGURE EX 3.30

tips & tricks

It can be helpful to name the cells containing data for the function arguments with the same name as the argument. For example, name the cell with the interest rate **Rate**. Then when you build the PMT function, the cell names match the argument names. It makes creating the function easy.

let me try

If you do not have the data file from the previous skill open, open the student data file **EX3-16-Financial-Analysis** and try this skill on your own:

1. On the *Loan1* worksheet, enter a formula in cell **B7** using the PMT function to calculate the monthly loan payment. Use cell references as the function arguments. Remember, payments will be monthly, so divide the annual interest rate by 12. Use a negative number for the **Pv** argument. Do not include the optional arguments.

2. If you will be moving on to the next skill in this chapter, leave the workbook open to continue working. If not, save the file as directed by your instructor and close it.

Skill 3.17 Finding Data Using the VLOOKUP Function

Excel includes a group of functions that can be used to look up matching values in a cell range. The **VLOOKUP** function finds a value or cell reference in a cell range and returns another value from the same row. VLOOKUP requires you to specify the value you want to find, the cell range that contains the data, and the column that contains the value you want the function to return.

> **=VLOOKUP(Lookup_value,Table_array,Col_index_num,Range_lookup)**

The formula in Figure EX 3.31 finds the value from cell **B2** in the cell range named **Inventory** and then returns the value from the second column of the range. In other words, VLOOKUP finds the item ID and returns the item name.

> **=VLOOKUP(B2,Inventory,2,FALSE)**

FIGURE EX 3.31

To use the VLOOKUP function:

1. Select the cell where you want to enter the formula.

2. On the *Formulas* tab, in the *Function Library* group, click the **Lookup & Reference** button.

3. Select **VLOOKUP** from the list to open the *Function Arguments* dialog. VLOOKUP takes three required arguments and one optional argument as shown in Figure EX 3.32.

4. Enter the **Lookup_value** argument. Enter the cell reference for which you want to find a corresponding value, in other words, the value you want to look up. The *Lookup_value* must be located in the first column of the cell range defined in the *Table_array* argument.

5. Enter the **Table_array** argument. Enter the range of cells (or the range name) that contains the lookup data. If your data include a header row, do not include it in the range used for the *Table_array* argument.

6. Enter the **Col_index_num** argument. This argument is the position of the column in the *Table_array* from which the function should return a matching value. Enter the column number, not the letter or the column heading.

7. (Optional) Enter the **Range_lookup** argument. Type FALSE if you want to find only an exact match for the value entered in the *Lookup_value* box. If you omit this argument, Excel assumes a value of **TRUE** and will return the value for the closest match in the first column.

8. Click **OK**.

FIGURE EX 3.32

tips & tricks

If you do not specify *False* for the *Range_lookup* argument, be aware that the formula will return the first close match it finds. You may see unexpected results.

tell me **more**

The examples here all use the VLOOKUP function to find corresponding values in different columns within the same row (a *vertical* lookup). The **HLOOKUP** function works similarly, except you use it to find corresponding values in different rows within the same column (a *horizontal* lookup).

Use HLOOKUP when your worksheet uses a horizontal layout—few rows with many columns.

Use VLOOKUP when your worksheet uses a vertical layout—few columns with many rows.

let me **try**

If you do not have the data file from the previous skill open, open the student data file **EX3-17-Financial-Analysis** and try this skill on your own:

1. On the *SalonInventory* worksheet, enter a formula in cell **B2** using the VLOOKUP function to find the item name for the item number listed in cell **B1**. Use the name **Inventory** for the lookup table. The item names are located in column **2** of the lookup table. Require an exact match.

2. If you will be moving on to the next skill in this chapter, leave the workbook open to continue working. If not, save the file as directed by your instructor and close it.

Skill 3.18 Checking Formulas for Errors

Some worksheet errors are easily identifiable—such as divide by zero errors, which look like this in your worksheet: **#DIV/0!** (because Excel cannot calculate a value to display). Other potential errors, like formulas that leave out part of a cell range, are harder to find yourself. You can use Excel's error checking features to review your worksheet for errors.

Cells that include potential errors are marked with a green triangle in the upper-left corner of the cell. When you click the cell, Excel displays a **Smart Tag** to help you resolve the error.

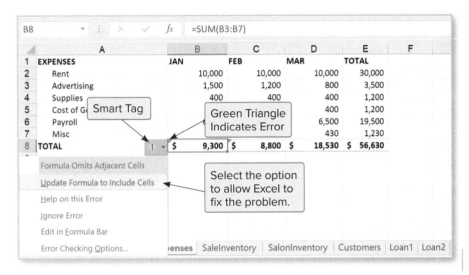

FIGURE EX 3.33

To use Smart Tags to resolve errors in formulas:

1. When a Smart Tag appears, move your mouse over the icon to display a tool tip describing the possible error.

2. Click the **Smart Tag** to display the possible error resolutions.

3. If you want to keep the formula as it is, select **Ignore Error**.

4. If you want to resolve the error, select one of the options:

   - The first option is usually a suggestion of how to resolve the error. Click it to accept Excel's suggestion.
   - Select **Help on this error** to open Microsoft Office Help.
   - Select **Ignore Error** to leave the cell unchanged.
   - Select **Edit in Formula Bar** to manually edit the formula.
   - Select **Error Checking Options...** to open the *Options* dialog and modify the way that Excel checks for errors.

5. Once you have made a selection from the Smart Tag options, the Smart Tag is dismissed.

Error checking is also available from the *Formulas* tab, *Formula Auditing* group. The *Error Checking* dialog displays each error it finds, allowing you to resolve or ignore each error in turn.

To use error checking to find errors in your worksheet:

1. On the *Formulas* tab in the *Formula Auditing* group, click the **Error Checking** button.

2. The *Error Checking* dialog displays information about the first error. The buttons available in the dialog will differ, depending on the type of error found.

   - If Excel is able to offer a solution to the error, the dialog will include a button to accept the suggested fix.
   - Click the **Help on this error** button to open Microsoft Office Help.

- Click **Ignore Error** to dismiss the error. Excel will ignore this error until you manually reset ignored errors through Excel *Options.*
- Click **Edit in Formula Bar** to fix the error manually.

3. Click the **Next** button to see the next error in your worksheet.

4. When you have reviewed all errors, Excel displays a message that the error check is complete. Click **OK** to dismiss the message box.

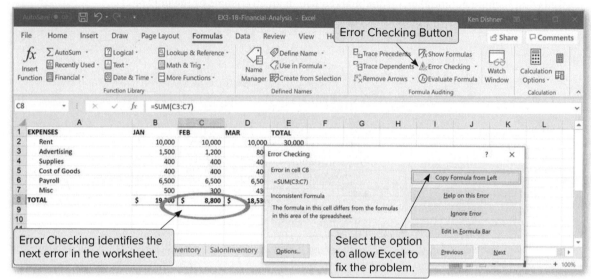

FIGURE EX 3.34

tips & tricks

You can make changes to your worksheet without closing the *Error Checking* dialog. When you click away from the dialog, one of the buttons changes to a *Resume* button and none of the other buttons in the dialog are available. When you are ready to return to error checking, click the **Resume** button.

tell me more

If the error is part of a complex formula, Excel may include a *Show Calculation Steps...* button in the *Error Checking* dialog. This button launches the *Evaluate Formula* dialog where you can walk through the formula step by step to try to find the cause of the error.

If the error is related to a reference to another cell, Excel will offer a *Trace Error* button to display precedent and dependent arrows showing dependencies between formulas in your worksheet.

another **method**

You can also start the Error Checking feature by clicking the **Error Checking** button arrow and selecting **Error Checking...**

let me **try**

If you do not have the data file from the previous skill open, open the student data file **EX3-18-Financial-Analysis** and try this skill on your own:

1. On the *Expenses* worksheet, cell **B8** has an error. Display the **Smart Tag** and accept Excel's suggestion for fixing the error.

2. On the *Formulas* tab, in the *Formula Auditing* group, open the *Error Checking* dialog and check the rest of the worksheet for errors.

3. Review the information about the next error and select the option to edit the error in the formula bar.

4. Correct the error and resume error checking until Excel reports that the error check is complete.

5. If you will be moving on to the next skill in this chapter, leave the workbook open to continue working. If not, save the file as directed by your instructor and close it.

Skill 3.19 Finding Errors Using Trace Precedents and Trace Dependents

In a complex worksheet where formulas often reference each other, an error in one formula can cause a ripple effect of errors throughout the entire workbook. However, finding and fixing the formula that is the root cause of the errors can be difficult. One way to review your workbook for errors is to display the dependencies between formulas.

There are two types of dependencies: precedents and dependents. A **precedent** is the cell containing the formula or value the selected cell refers to. A **dependent** is the cell containing a formula that references the value or formula in the selected cell. On the *Formulas* tab, the *Formula Auditing* group includes commands for displaying and hiding arrows tracing dependencies.

Tracer arrows normally appear blue. If the tracer arrow points to a cell that contains an error, the tracer arrow will appear red. If the tracer arrow points to a cell that references a cell in another worksheet or workbook, the arrow will appear black and include a small worksheet icon. Double-click the tracer arrow to open the *Go To* dialog to navigate to the worksheet or workbook that contains the referenced cell.

Figure EX 3.35 shows both precedent tracer arrows for cell B8. You can see that the precedent arrow changes from blue to red at cell B6. The formula in that cell is the first error. (However, the error itself is not necessarily in that cell. It could be in another cell that B6 refers to.)

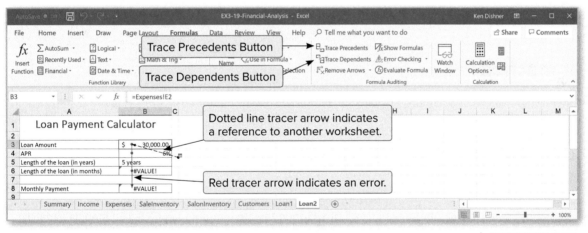

FIGURE EX 3.35

To trace precedents:

1. Select the cell containing the formula for which you want to trace precedents.

2. On the *Formulas* tab, in the *Formula Auditing* group, click the **Trace Precedents** button.

3. Tracer arrows appear pointing to the selected cell from precedent cells.

To trace dependents:

1. Select the cell containing the formula for which you want to trace dependents.

2. On the *Formulas* tab, in the *Formula Auditing* group, click the **Trace Dependents** button.

3. Tracer arrows appear pointing from the selected cell to dependent cells.

To remove the tracer arrows from your worksheet, on the *Formulas* tab, in the *Formula Auditing* group, click the **Remove Arrows** button arrow and select the option you want:

❯ To remove the precedent tracer arrows, select **Remove Precedent Arrows**.

❯ To remove the dependent tracer arrows, select **Remove Dependent Arrows**.

❯ To remove all tracer arrows at once, select **Remove Arrows**. Clicking the *Remove Arrows* button instead of the button arrow will also remove all the tracer arrows.

tips & tricks

Tracer arrows cannot identify cells with incorrect values or values of the wrong type (for example, a text value where a number is expected). However, using the tracer arrows may help you find those errors yourself.

tell me **more**

There may be multiple layers of dependencies in your workbook. Clicking the **Trace Precedents** button or the **Trace Dependents** button once displays only the immediate dependencies. To display tracer arrows from the precedent and dependent cells to their precedents and dependents, click the appropriate button again. Continue clicking the **Trace Precedents** button or the **Trace Dependents** button until you reach the end of the trail.

Selecting **Remove Precedent Arrows** and **Remove Dependent Arrows** removes the tracer arrows one level at a time.

another **method**

If the selected cell contains an error, you can display tracer arrows by clicking the **Error Checking** button arrow and selecting **Trace Error.**

let me **try**

If you do not have the data file from the previous skill open, open the student data file **EX3-19-Financial-Analysis** and try this skill on your own:

1. On the *Loan2* worksheet, show the dependent arrows for cell **B6**.

2. Show the precedent arrows for cell **B8**.

3. Show the next level of precedent arrows. Note that cell B3 refers to a cell in another worksheet.

4. Change the value in cell **B5** to: **5** Note that the arrows change color from red to blue.

5. Hide all of the arrows at once.

6. If you will be moving on to the next skill in this chapter, leave the workbook open to continue working. If not, save the file as directed by your instructor and close it.

Skill 3.20 Displaying and Printing Formulas

How do you troubleshoot a worksheet that is displaying unexpected values? When you look at a worksheet, you see only the results of formulas—cells display the values, not the formulas themselves. When you click a cell, the formula is displayed in the formula bar. But what if you want to view all of the formulas in your worksheet at once?

To display the formulas in the current worksheet instead of values:

On the *Formulas* tab in the *Formula Auditing* group, click the **Show Formulas** button.

To hide the formulas and display calculated values:

Click the **Show Formulas** button again.

FIGURE EX 3.36

tips & tricks

When you show formulas in your worksheet, Excel automatically adjusts the column sizes so the formulas are visible.

another method

The keyboard shortcut to display (or hide) formulas is [Ctrl] + [`] (the [`] key is directly to the left of [1] at the top of the keyboard).

let me try

If you do not have the data file from the previous skill open, open the student data file **EX3-20-Financial-Analysis** and try this skill on your own:

1. On the *Loan2* worksheet, display the formulas in this worksheet.
2. Preview how the worksheet will look when printed.
3. Save the file as directed by your instructor and close it.

key terms

Formula AutoComplete	Concatenate
AVERAGE	CONCAT
Mean	TEXTJOIN
Median	Delimiter (TEXTJOIN)
Mode	3-D Reference
MAX	Name
MIN	Range name
NOW	Named range
TODAY	Name Manager
Volatile	Defined name
COUNT	IF
COUNTA	PMT
COUNTBLANK	VLOOKUP
String	HLOOKUP
Text String	Smart Tag
PROPER	Precedent
UPPER	Dependent
LOWER	

concept review

1. Which of these methods can you use to enter a formula using the AVERAGE function?

   a. Formula AutoComplete

   b. AutoSum

   c. Function Arguments dialog

   d. all of the above

2. Which of these functions returns the current date and time?

   a. TIME

   b. DATE

   c. TODAY

   d. NOW

3. To count the number of cells that contain text or numerical values, but not blanks, use which function?

   a. COUNT

   b. COUNTALL

   c. COUNTA

   d. COUNTBLANK

4. What is the definition of *concatenate*?

   a. to convert text to proper case

   b. to link items together

   c. to look up a value

   d. a logical comparison

5. A formula to display the value of cell A5 on the Inventory worksheet looks like this:

    a. =Inventory(A5)

    b. =Inventory!A5

    c. =A5,Inventory!

    d. =Inventory,A5

6. Which of these is *not* an acceptable name for a named range?

    a. CURRENTINVENTORY

    b. Current Inventory

    c. CurrentInventory

    d. Current_Inventory

7. Identify the *Value_if_true* argument in this formula: =IF(A2>100,"high","low")

    a. A2

    b. 100

    c. high

    d. low

8. Identify the *Pv* argument in this formula: =PMT(B1/12,B2,-B3)

    a. B1

    b. B1/12

    c. B2

    d. −B3

9. In a PMT function, what is the *Pv* argument?

    a. the number of payments

    b. the present value of the loan

    c. the interest rate

    d. the value of the loan at the end of the loan period

10. A(n) _____ is the cell containing a formula that references the value or formula in the selected cell.

    a. argument

    b. precedent

    c. dependent

    d. 3-D reference

skill review **3.1**

In this project you will complete a staff billing workbook similar to the one you worked on in Chapter 1. This worksheet is more complicated and uses a variety of formulas to calculate information about each staff member's weekly billing and to generate client bills from the staff hours. As you work on the *Marshall Hours* worksheet, you can use the *Lutz Hours* or *Stevens Hours* worksheet as a guide. This is a long project. Be sure to save your work often!

Skills needed to complete this project:

- Naming Ranges of Cells (Skill 3.11)
- Using CONCAT to Combine Text (Skill 3.8)
- Creating Formulas Referencing Data from Other Worksheets (Skill 3.10)
- Finding Data Using the VLOOKUP Function (Skill 3.17)
- Working with Named Ranges (Skill 3.12)
- Using the Function Arguments Dialog to Enter Functions (Skill 3.1)
- Creating Formulas Using Counting Functions (Skill 3.6)
- Using Formula AutoComplete to Enter Functions (Skill 3.2)
- Calculating Averages (Skill 3.3)
- Finding Minimum and Maximum Values (Skill 3.4)
- Using the Logical Function IF (Skill 3.15)
- Displaying and Printing Formulas (Skill 3.20)
- Using Date and Time Functions (Skill 3.5)
- Checking Formulas for Errors (Skill 3.18)
- Finding Errors Using Trace Precedents and Trace Dependents (Skill 3.19)
- Updating Named Ranges with the Name Manager (Skill 3.13)
- Editing and Deleting Names with the Name Manager (Skill 3.14)
- Calculating Loan Payments Using the PMT Function (Skill 3.16)

1. Open the start file **EX2019-SkillReview-3-1** and resave the file as:
   `[your initials]EX-SkillReview-3-1`

2. If the workbook opens in Protected View, click the **Enable Editing** button in the Message Bar at the top of the workbook so you can modify it.

3. The *Lutz Hours* and *Stevens Hours* worksheets are completed, but they contain errors. You'll need to fix the errors before working on the *Marshall Hours* worksheet.

   a. Click the **Lutz Hours** sheet tab.

   b. Click cell **C4**.

   c. Notice the #NAME? error. Move your mouse over the **Smart Tag** icon to display a tool tip describing the possible error—*The formula contains unrecognized text.*

d. The formula =VLOOKUP(C3,BillableRates,4,FALSE) references the named range BillableRates. That name has not yet been defined. That's what is causing the error.

4. Billable rates are kept in the *Rates* worksheet. Create the name **BillableRates** to use in formulas throughout the workbook.

   a. Click the **Rates** sheet tab.

   b. Select cells **A3:D5**.

   c. Type **BillableRates** in the *Name* box.

   d. Press ⏎ Enter .

   e. Return to the *Lutz Hours* worksheet. Notice all the errors have been fixed. Now you can move on to completing the *Marshall Hours* sheet.

5. Use a formula to display Marshall's full name in the format *Bob Smith*. Staff names are kept in the *Rates* worksheet.

   a. Click the **Marshall Hours** sheet tab, and click cell **C2**.

   b. On the *Formulas* tab, in the *Function Library* group, click the **Text** button, and select **CONCAT**.

   c. Click the **Rates** sheet tab. If necessary, position the *Function Arguments* dialog so you can click the sheet tabs.

   d. Click cell **C4** to enter the cell reference in the *Text1* argument box.

   e. Press Tab ⇄ to move to the *Text2* argument box.

   f. Type **" "** to place a space between the first and last names.

   g. Press Tab ⇄ to move to the *Text3* argument box.

   h. Click the **Rates** tab again.

   i. Click cell **B4** to enter the text reference in the *Text3* argument box.

   j. Click **OK**. The completed formula should look like this:
   =CONCAT(Rates!C4," ",Rates!B4)

6. Use a formula to look up Marshall's current billable rate. Use the employee number as the lookup value.

   a. Click cell **C4**.

   b. On the *Formulas* tab, in the *Function Library* group, click the **Lookup & Reference** button, and select **VLOOKUP**.

   c. Click cell **C3** to enter it in the *Lookup_value* argument box.

   d. Type **BillableRates** in the *Table_array* argument box.

   e. The rates are located in the fourth column of the lookup table. Type **4** in the *Col_index_num* argument box.

   f. Ensure that the function will return only an exact match. Type **false** in the *Range_lookup* argument box.

   g. Click **OK**. The completed formula should look like this:
   =VLOOKUP(C3,BillableRates,4,FALSE)

7. Enter formulas to calculate the number of clients served each day.

   a. Click cell **B16**.

   b. Type **=COU**

   c. Double-click **COUNT** in the Formula AutoComplete list.

   d. Click cell **B8** and drag to cell **B11**.

   e. Press ⏎ Enter . The completed formula should look like this:
   =COUNT(B8:B11)

   f. Copy the formula in cell **B16** to cells **C16:H16**. Use any method you want.

8. Use a formula to calculate the average daily billable hours.

   a. Click cell **H18**.

   b. Type **=AV** and then double-click **AVERAGE** in the Formula AutoComplete list.

   c. Click cell **B12** and drag to cell **H12**.

   d. Press ⏎ Enter . The completed formula should look like this:
     =AVERAGE(B12:H12)

9. Use a formula to calculate the total billable hours for the week.

   a. Click cell **H19**.

   b. Type **=SU** and then double-click **SUM** in the Formula AutoComplete list.

   c. Click cell **B12** and drag to cell **H12**.

   d. Press ⏎ Enter . The completed formula should look like this: **=SUM(B12:H12)**

10. Use a formula to calculate the lowest daily bill for the week.

   a. Click cell **H21**.

   b. Type **=MIN(** and then click cell **B14** and drag to cell **H14**.

   c. Press ⏎ Enter . The completed formula should look like this: **=MIN(B14:H14)**

11. Use a formula to calculate the highest daily bill for the week.

   a. Click cell **H22**.

   b. Type **=MAX(** and then click cell **B14** and drag to cell **H14**.

   c. Press ⏎ Enter . The completed formula should look like this: **=MAX(B14:H14)**

12. Each staff member is required to log a minimum number of billable hours per week. Enter a formula using an IF statement to display "yes" if the total billable hours for the week are greater than or equal to the required hours and "no" if they are not.

   a. Click cell **H3**.

   b. On the *Formulas* tab, in the *Function Library* group, click **Logical**.

   c. Click **IF**.

   d. If necessary, move the *Function Arguments* dialog to the side so you can see the worksheet data.

   e. In the *Logical_test* argument box, type: **H19>=H2**

   f. In the *Value_if_true* argument box, type: **yes**

   g. In the *Value_if_false* argument box, type: **no**

   h. Click **OK**. The completed formula should look like this:
     =IF(H19>=H2,"yes","no")

13. Display your formulas temporarily to check for accuracy.

   a. On the *Formulas* tab, in the *Formula Auditing* group, click the **Show Formulas** button.

   b. When you are ready to continue, hide the formulas and display formula values by clicking the **Show Formulas** button again.

14. Now that the worksheet for Marshall is complete, you can generate a bill for the Smith client for the week. All bills are due 60 days from the date the bill was created. Calculate the bill due date using the TODAY function.

   a. Click the **Smith Bill** sheet tab.

   b. Double-click cell **C2**.

   c. Type the formula: **=TODAY( )+60**

   d. Press ⏎ Enter .

15. Enter formulas to reference the number of hours each staff member billed for Smith.

   a. Click cell **B5** and type **=** to begin the formula.

   b. Click the **Lutz Hours** sheet, and click cell **J11**.

   c. Press ⬅ Enter . The completed formula should look like this:
      ='Lutz Hours'!J11

   d. Type **=** to begin the next formula in cell B6.

   e. Click the **Marshall Hours** sheet, and click cell **J11**.

   f. Press ⬅ Enter . The completed formula should look like this:
      ='Marshall Hours'!J11

   g. Type **=** to begin the next formula in cell B7.

   h. Click the **Stevens Hours** sheet, and click cell **J11**.

   i. Press ⬅ Enter . The completed formula should look like this:
      ='Stevens Hours'!J11

16. There are errors in the *Rate* and *Bill Amount* columns in the *Smith Bill* worksheet. Use your error checking skills to track down the cause of the error.

   a. On the *Formulas* tab, in the *Formula Auditing* group, click the **Error Checking** button to open the *Error Checking* dialog.

   b. After you've reviewed the first error, click the **Next** button to go to the next error. Continue reviewing each error and clicking **Next** until you receive the message that the error check is complete for the entire sheet. Click **OK**.

17. Did you notice that every error in the worksheet is a "value not available" error? You probably need to dig deeper to find the root cause of the problem.

   a. Click cell **D5** and look at the formula in the formula bar: **=B5*C5**

   b. Display the Trace Precedent and Trace Dependent arrows for this cell. On the *Formulas* tab, in the *Formula Auditing* group, click both the **Trace Precedents** button and the **Trace Dependents** button.

   c. You can see that the problem appears to start in the precedent cell C5. Hide the arrows for cell **D5** by clicking the **Remove Arrows** button, and then click cell **C5** and click the **Trace Precedents** button.

   d. Notice that one of the precedent arrows for cell C5 refers to another worksheet. Double-click the dashed precedent arrow line.

   e. In the *Go To* dialog, click the worksheet reference and then click the **OK** button.

18. The link takes you to the *Rates* sheet where cells A2:D5 are selected. Notice that the *Name* box displays the name *ClientRates*. (Depending on your screen resolution, the name may be slightly cut off.) The formula in cell C5 is a lookup formula that uses the named range *ClientRates* as the *Table_array* argument. There are two problems with the definition of the named range: It includes the label row (A2:D2), and it includes the employee number data (A2:A5).

   a. On the *Formulas* tab, in the *Defined Names* group, click the **Name Manager** button.

   b. Click the **ClientRates** name and review the cell range in the *Refers to* box. The range is incorrect. The *ClientRates* name should refer to cells **B3:D5** on the *Rates* sheet.

   c. Click in the *Refers to* box and then click and drag to select the cell range **B3:D5**. The reference in the *Refers to* box should update to:
      =Rates!$B$3:$D$5

d. Click the **Close** button to close the Name Manager.

e. When Excel asks if you want to save the changes to the name reference, click **Yes**.

19. Now that the total bill amount is computing correctly, you can create a formula to give the client the option of a monthly payment plan. You are authorized to offer a 9-month payment plan at a 4% annual percentage rate. Use cell references in the formula.

a. If necessary, click the **Smith Bill** sheet.

b. Click cell **D12**.

c. On the *Formulas* tab, in the *Function Library* group, click the **Financial** button.

d. Scroll down the list, and click **PMT**.

e. In the *Function Arguments* dialog, enter the *Rate* argument: **D11/12**

f. Click in the **Nper** argument box, and then click cell **D10** (the number of payments).

g. Click in the **Pv** argument box, type − and then click cell **D8** (the present value of the loan). You want to use a negative value for the *Pv* argument so the result of the formula will appear as a positive number.

h. In the *Function Arguments* dialog, click **OK**. The completed formula should look like this: **=PMT(D11/12,D10,−D8)**

20. Save and close the workbook.

skill review 3.2

In this project you will edit a worksheet to compute student grades and grade statistics. Be sure to save your work often!

Skills needed to complete this project:

- Using Date and Time Functions (Skill 3.5)
- Using CONCAT to Combine Text (Skill 3.8)
- Formatting Text Using Functions (Skill 3.7)
- Creating Formulas Using Counting Functions (Skill 3.6)
- Using Formula AutoComplete to Enter Functions (Skill 3.2)
- Displaying and Printing Formulas (Skill 3.20)
- Naming Ranges of Cells (Skill 3.11)
- Using the Logical Function IF (Skill 3.15)
- Using the Function Arguments Dialog to Enter Functions (Skill 3.1)
- Working with Named Ranges (Skill 3.12)
- Finding Minimum and Maximum Values (Skill 3.4)
- Calculating Averages (Skill 3.3)
- Finding Data Using the VLOOKUP Function (Skill 3.17)
- Checking Formulas for Errors (Skill 3.18)

1. Open the start file **EX2019-SkillReview-3-2** and resave the file as: `[your initials]EX-SkillReview-3-2`

2. If the workbook opens in Protected View, click the **Enable Editing** button in the Message Bar at the top of the workbook so you can modify it.

3. Take a look at the two sheets. The first sheet contains the students' names and their scores. The second sheet will be used to look up the letter grade for each student.

4. On the *Scores* worksheet, enter a function in cell **B3** to display the current date and time.

   a. If necessary, click the **Scores** worksheet tab. Click cell **B3**.

   b. On the *Formulas* tab, in the *Function Library* group, click the **Date &Time** button.

   c. Click **NOW**.

   d. Click **OK**.

5. The first column should display the full student name. Use CONCAT to combine the values from the *First Name* and *Last Name* columns.

   a. Click cell **A10**.

   b. On the *Formulas* tab, in the *Function Library* group, click the **Text** button, and select **CONCAT**.

   c. Click cell **C10** to enter the cell reference in the *Text1* argument box.

   d. Press (Tab ⇥) to move to the *Text2* argument box.

   e. Type **" "** to place a space between the first and last names.

   f. Press (Tab ⇥) to move to the *Text3* argument box.

   g. Click cell **B10** to enter the text reference in the *Text3* argument box.

   h. Click **OK**. The completed formula should look like this:
      =CONCAT(C10," ",B10)

6. Add the PROPER function to the formula so student names do not appear in all uppercase.

   a. Double-click cell **A10** to edit the formula.

   b. Create a nested formula by typing **PROPER(** between the = symbol and CONCAT.

   c. Type another **)** at the end of the formula.

   d. Press (← Enter). The completed formula should look like this:
      =PROPER(CONCAT(C10," ",B10))

   e. Copy the formula from cell **A10** to **A11:A26** to fill the list of student names. Use any method you want.

7. Count the number of students to calculate the class size.

   a. Click cell **B2**.

   b. Type **=COU**

   c. Double-click **COUNTA** in the Formula AutoComplete list.

   d. Click cell **A10** and drag to cell **A26**.

   e. Press (← Enter). The completed formula should look like this:
      =COUNTA(A10:A26)

8. Display your formulas to check for accuracy.

   a. On the *Formulas* tab, in the *Formula Auditing* group, click the **Show Formulas** button.

   b. When you are ready to continue, hide the formulas and display formula values by clicking the **Show Formulas** button again.

9. Define a named range for the total possible points up to the class drop cut-off point.

   a. Select cells **D7:R7**.

   b. In the *Name* box, type: **PossiblePtsMid**

   c. Press (← Enter).

10. Find out which students have a grade below C at the cut-off point for dropping the class. Enter an IF function in cell **S10** to check if the student's total points divided by the total possible points through the midterm is less than 70% (the lowest percentage for a C grade). Use SUM functions within the IF function. Be sure to use the range name you just defined for possible points. If the student is below a C grade, display **Warning!** in the cell; otherwise leave the cell blank.

   a. Click cell **S10**.

   b. On the *Formulas* tab, in the *Function Library* group, click **Logical**.

   c. Click **IF**.

   d. If necessary, move the *Function Arguments* dialog so you can see the worksheet data.

   e. In the *Logical_test* argument box, type:
`SUM(D10:R10)/SUM(PossiblePtsMid)<70%`

   f. In the *Value_if_true* argument box, type: `Warning!`

   g. In the *Value_if_false* argument box, type: `" "`

   h. Click **OK**. The completed formula should look like this:
=IF(SUM(D10:R10)/SUM(PossiblePtsMid)<70%,"Warning!"," ")

   i. Fill the IF function in cell **S10** down for all students. Use any method you want. There should be three students with **Warning!** in the *Class Drop Cut-Off Point* column.

11. Find the highest score for each assignment.

   a. Click cell **D4**.

   b. Type `=MAX(` and then click cell **D10** and drag to cell **D26**.

   c. Press `← Enter`. The completed formula should look like this: **=MAX(D10:D26)**

   d. Copy the formula across the row to cell **AB4**. Use any method you want. Be sure to leave cell S4 blank.

12. Find the lowest score for each assignment.

   a. Click cell **D5**.

   b. Type `=MIN(` and then click cell **D10** and drag to cell **D26**.

   c. Press `← Enter`. The completed formula should look like this: **=MIN(D10:D26)**

   d. Copy the formula across the row to cell **AB5**. Use any method you want. Be sure to leave cell S5 blank.

13. Calculate the average score for each assignment.

   a. Click cell **D6**.

   b. Type `=AV` and then double-click **AVERAGE** in the Formula AutoComplete list.

   c. Click cell **D10** and drag to cell **D26**.

   d. Press `← Enter`. The completed formula should look like this:
=AVERAGE(D10:D26)

   e. Copy the formula across the row to cell **AB6**. Use any method you want. Be sure to leave cell S6 blank.

14. Compute the students' total points. Enter a SUM function in cell **AC10** to add all the points across for the first student.

   a. Click cell **AC10**.

   b. Type `=SU` and then double-click **SUM** in the Formula AutoComplete list.

   c. Click cell **D10** and drag to cell **AB10**.

   d. Press `← Enter`. The completed formula should look like this: **=SUM(D10:AB10)**

   e. Copy the formula from **AC10** through cell **AC26**. Use any method you want.

15. Enter a formula to compute the percentage for the first student. Divide the student's total points by the total possible points. You will be copying this formula, so make sure the reference to the total possible points uses an absolute reference.

   a. In cell **AD10,** enter the following formula to calculate the percentage: **=AC10/$AC$7**

   b. Copy the formula from **AD10** through **AD26**. Use any method you want.

16. The grade scale is stored in the *Grades* worksheet. Before calculating students' final grades, create a named range to use in the formula.

   a. Click the **Grades** sheet tab.

   b. Select cells **B4:C8**.

   c. Type `GradeScale` in the *Name* box.

   d. Press ⏎ Enter .

17. Now you are ready to create a lookup formula to display each student's final letter grade.

   a. Return to the *Scores* sheet, and click cell **AE10**.

   b. On the *Formulas* tab, in the *Function Library* group, click the **Lookup & Reference** button, and select **VLOOKUP**.

   c. Click cell **AD10** to enter it in the *Lookup_value* argument box.

   d. Type `GradeScale` in the *Table_array* argument box.

   e. The rates are located in the second column of the lookup table. Type **2** in the *Col_index_num* argument box.

   f. In this case, you do not want to specify an exact match, as the percentage grades do not match the grade scale percentages exactly. An approximate match will return the correct letter grade.

   g. Click **OK**. The completed formula should look like this: **=VLOOKUP(AD10,GradeScale,2)**

   h. Fill down for all students. Use any method you want.

18. Before closing the project, check your workbook for errors.

   a. On the *Formulas* tab, in the *Formula Auditing* group, click the **Error Checking** button.

   b. If errors are found, use the error checking skills learned in this chapter to find and fix the errors.

   c. When Excel displays a message that the error check is complete, click **OK**.

19. Save and close the workbook.

challenge yourself **3.3**

In this project you will complete a vehicle shopping workbook to compare the purchase of several vehicles. After completing the project, you can make a copy of the file and use it to compare vehicle purchases you are considering for yourself. Be sure to save your work often!

Skills needed to complete this project:

- Naming Ranges of Cells (Skill 3.11)
- Calculating Averages (Skill 3.3)

- Finding Data Using the VLOOKUP Function (Skill 3.17)
- Working with Named Ranges (Skill 3.12)
- Using the Function Arguments Dialog to Enter Functions (Skill 3.1)
- Using the Logical Function IF (Skill 3.15)
- Calculating Loan Payments Using the PMT Function (Skill 3.16)
- Creating Formulas Referencing Data from Other Worksheets (Skill 3.10)
- Displaying and Printing Formulas (Skill 3.20)
- Finding Errors Using Trace Precedents and Trace Dependents (Skill 3.19)
- Finding Minimum and Maximum Values (Skill 3.4)
- Using Formula AutoComplete to Enter Functions (Skill 3.2)
- Updating Named Ranges with the Name Manager (Skill 3.13)
- Editing and Deleting Names with the Name Manager (Skill 3.14)
- Checking Formulas for Errors (Skill 3.18)

1. Open the start file **EX2019-ChallengeYourself-3-3** and resave the file as: `[your initials]EX-ChallengeYourself-3-3`

2. If the workbook opens in Protected View, click the **Enable Editing** button in the Message Bar at the top of the workbook so you can modify it.

3. The registration fee information in cells **B11:C17** on the *Data* sheet will be used in lookup formulas later in this project. Name the range `RegistrationFees` to make it easier to use later.

4. Return to the *Purchase* worksheet.

5. Calculate the average MPG for each vehicle.

    a. Enter a formula in cell **C10** using the AVERAGE function to calculate the average value of **C8:C9**. Use only one argument.

    b. Copy the formula to the appropriate cells for the other vehicles.

    c. Excel will detect a possible error with these formulas. Use the **SmartTag** to ignore the error. *Hint*: Use the **SmartTag** while cells **C10:F10** are selected and the error will be ignored for all the selected cells.

6. Calculate the registration fee for each vehicle.

    a. Enter a formula in cell **C13** to look up the registration fee for the first vehicle. Use the vehicle type in cell **C4** as the *Lookup_value* argument. Use the **RegistrationFees** named range as the *Table_array* argument. The registration fees are located in column **2** of the data table. Require an exact match.

    b. Copy the formula to the appropriate cells for the other vehicles.

7. Determine whether or not you will need a loan for each potential purchase.

    a. In cell **C15**, enter a formula using an IF function to determine if you need a loan. Your available cash is located on the *Data* sheet in cell **A3**. If the price of the car is less than or equal to your available cash, display **"no"**. If the price of the car is more than your available, cash, display **"yes"**. Use absolute references where appropriate—you will be copying this formula across the row.

    b. Copy the formula to the appropriate cells for the other vehicles.

8. Calculate how much you would need to borrow for each purchase.

    a. In cell **C16**, enter a formula to calculate the price of the vehicle minus your available cash (from cell **A3** in the *Data* worksheet). Use absolute references where appropriate—you will be copying this formula across the row.

    b. Copy the formula to the appropriate cells for the other vehicles.

9. Calculate the monthly payment amount for each loan.

    a. In cell **C20**, enter a formula using the PMT function to calculate the monthly loan payment for the first vehicle.

        ▪ *Hint*: Divide the interest rate by 12 in the *Rate* argument to reflect monthly payments.

        ▪ *Hint*: Multiply the number of years by 12 in the *Nper* argument to reflect the number of monthly payments during the life of the loan.

        ▪ *Hint*: Use a negative value for the loan amount in the *Pv* argument so the payment amount is expressed as a positive number.

    b. Copy the formula to the appropriate cells for the other vehicles.

10. Compute the monthly cost of gas.

    a. In cell **C21**, enter a formula to calculate the number of miles you expect to drive each month. Divide the value of number of miles (cell **A5** from the *Data* sheet) by the average MPG for the vehicle multiplied by the price of a gallon of gas (cell **A6** from the *Data* sheet).

    b. Copy the formula to the appropriate cells for the other vehicles.

    c. If cells **D21:F21** display an error or a value of 0, display formulas and check for errors.

    d. If you still can't find the error, try displaying the precedent arrows.

    e. *Hint*: The references to the cells on the *Data* sheet should use absolute references. If they do not, the formula will update incorrectly when you copy it across the row.

11. Compute the monthly cost of maintenance.

    a. In cell **C22**, enter a formula to calculate the monthly maintenance cost: Divide cell **C12** by 12.

    b. Copy the formula to the appropriate cells for the other vehicles.

12. Compute the monthly cost of insurance.

    a. In cell **C23**, enter a formula to calculate the monthly insurance cost: Divide cell **C14** by 12.

    b. Copy the formula to the appropriate cells for the other vehicles.

13. In cells **C24:F24**, compute the total the monthly cost for each vehicle.

14. Determine which vehicles are affordable.

    a. In cell **C26**, enter a formula using the IF function to display **"yes"** if the total monthly cost (cell **C24**) is less than or equal to the total monthly amount available for vehicle expenses (*Data* sheet, cell **A4**). Display **"no"** if the total monthly cost is not less than or equal to the total monthly amount available.

    b. Copy the formula to the appropriate cells for the other vehicles.

    c. Display formulas and use the error checking skills learned in this lesson to track down and fix any errors.

15. Complete the Analysis section using formulas with statistical functions. Use named ranges instead of cell references in the formulas.

    a. *Hint*: Select cells **B7:F24** and use Excel's **Create from Selection** command to create named ranges for each row using the labels at the left side of the range as the names.

b. *Hint*: Open the **Name Manager** and review the names Excel created. Notice that any spaces or special characters in the label names are converted to _ characters in the names.

c. *Hint*: To avoid typos as you create each formula, try using Formula AutoComplete to select the correct range name.

16. Before finishing the project, check the worksheet for errors.

17. Save and close the workbook.

challenge yourself 3.4

In this project, you will record data about your completed and planned college courses. You will compute your GPA, college course costs, and various statistics. You will compute your expected college loan payment and count down the days to graduation and paying off the loan. Be sure to save your work often!

Skills needed to complete this project:

- Finding Errors Using Trace Precedents and Trace Dependents (Skill 3.19)
- Finding Data Using the VLOOKUP Function (Skill 3.17)
- Using the Function Arguments Dialog to Enter Functions (Skill 3.1)
- Checking Formulas for Errors (Skill 3.18)
- Creating Formulas Referencing Data from Other Worksheets (Skill 3.10)
- Calculating Loan Payments Using the PMT Function (Skill 3.16)
- Using Date and Time Functions (Skill 3.5)
- Finding Minimum and Maximum Values (Skill 3.4)
- Using Formula AutoComplete to Enter Functions (Skill 3.2)
- Calculating Averages (Skill 3.3)
- Using the Logical Function IF (Skill 3.15)

1. Open the start file **EX2019-ChallengeYourself-3-4** and resave the file as: `[your initials]EX-ChallengeYourself-3-4`

2. If the workbook opens in Protected View, click the **Enable Editing** button in the Message Bar at the top of the workbook so you can modify it.

3. There are three sheets. Start with the *GPA* sheet.

4. There is at least one error on this sheet. Click the cell that displays an error and use the precedent arrows to find the cause of the error. If the error is caused by missing values in other cells in the worksheet, you will probably fix the error by the end of this project. Hide the arrows before continuing.

5. Enter the formulas for the *GPA* worksheet as follows.

a. In cell **B14** compute the cost for the first course by multiplying the unit cost (cell **C11**) by the number of units for the course (cell **G14**). Use absolute references where appropriate.

b. Fill and copy to compute the cost for each course, both semesters (cells **B15:B16** and **B19:B22**).

6. Look up the grade points for each letter grade as follows:

   a. In cell **I14**, enter a formula using the VLOOKUP function. Use the cell range **J3:K7** as the *Table_array* argument. The grade points are located in column **2** of this table. Use absolute references where appropriate.

   b. Fill and copy to look up the grade points for each course, both semesters (cells **I15:I16** and **I19:I22**).

7. Multiply the grade points by the units to calculate the quality points for each course, for both semesters.

   a. In cell **J14**, enter a formula to multiply **I14** (the grade points) * cell **G14** (the units).

   b. Copy the formula to cells **J15:J16** and **J19:J22**.

8. Use AutoSum to calculate totals for cost (cells **B17** and **B23**), units (cells **G17** and **G23**), and quality points (cells **J17** and **J23**) for each semester.

9. In cell **K17**, compute the GPA for the first semester by dividing the total quality points by the total units (**J17/G17**).

10. In cell **K23**, compute the GPA for the second semester using the same formula.

11. Check the worksheet for errors. Is the error you found in step 4 fixed now? (It should be!)

12. Next go to the *Loan* worksheet.

13. In cell **B3**, enter a formula to display the total cost shown in cell **B9** on the *GPA* sheet.

14. Enter a formula in cell **B7** to look up the number of years to pay based on the loan amount shown in cell **B3**. Use the data table in cells **G6:H11** as the *Table_array* argument. Do not require an exact match.

15. Now that you have the loan amount and the number of payments, enter a formula using the PMT function in cell **B8** to calculate the payment amount. Allow the payment to display as a negative number.

16. In cell **B10**, enter a formula to display the current date (just the date, not the date and time).

17. Enter a formula in cell **B16** to estimate the date of the last loan payment. Take the number of years to pay (cell **B7**) times **365.3** and add that to the date of the first loan payment (cell **B15**).

18. Enter a formula in cell **B17** to estimate the number of days until the loan is paid off.

19. Complete the *Summary* sheet information.

20. On the *Summary* sheet, in cell **B5**, enter a simple formula to reference the *Cumulative GPA* number from the *GPA* worksheet (***GPA* worksheet, cell B5**).

21. Do the same for Total Units (cell **B6**), Total Cost (cell **B9**), and Total Debt (cell **B3**). For Total Debt, reference the Amount Owed number from the *Loan* sheet.

22. Compute the Average Cost Per Unit by dividing the Total Cost (cell **B8**) by the Total Units (cell **B6**).

23. Compute Average Debt Per Unit in the same way.

24. In cell **B14**, enter a formula using a statistical function to calculate the most paid for any semester. Reference cells **B17** and **B23** in the *GPA* sheet. *Hint*: You will need two arguments.

25. In cell **B16**, enter a formula to calculate the average semester cost. Reference cells **B17** and **B23** in the *GPA* sheet. *Hint*: You will need two arguments.

26. In cell **F1**, enter a formula using the IF function to determine if the student met her GPA goal. Display **"yes"** if the goal was met and **"no"** if it was not.

27. In cell **F2**, enter a formula using the IF function to determine if the student met her unit goal. Display **"yes"** if the goal was met and **"no"** if it was not.

28. Before finishing the project, check each worksheet for errors.

29. Save and close the workbook.

on your own 3.5

In this project you will complete a dental plan workbook. Be sure to save your work often!

Skills needed to complete this project:

- Updating Named Ranges with the Name Manager (Skill 3.13)
- Editing and Deleting Names with the Name Manager (Skill 3.14)
- Naming Ranges of Cells (Skill 3.11)
- Working with Named Ranges (Skill 3.12)
- Finding Data Using the VLOOKUP Function (Skill 3.17)
- Using the Function Arguments Dialog to Enter Functions (Skill 3.1)
- Calculating Averages (Skill 3.3)
- Finding Minimum and Maximum Values (Skill 3.4)
- Using Formula AutoComplete to Enter Functions (Skill 3.2)
- Creating Formulas Using Counting Functions (Skill 3.6)
- Using CONCAT to Combine Text (Skill 3.8)
- Creating Formulas Referencing Data from Other Worksheets (Skill 3.10)
- Formatting Text Using Functions (Skill 3.7)
- Using Date and Time Functions (Skill 3.5)
- Using the Logical Function IF (Skill 3.15)
- Calculating Loan Payments Using the PMT Function (Skill 3.16)
- Checking Formulas for Errors (Skill 3.18)
- Finding Errors Using Trace Precedents and Trace Dependents (Skill 3.19)
- Displaying and Printing Formulas (Skill 3.20)

1. Open the start file **EX2019-OnYourOwn-3-5** and resave the file as: `[your initials]EX-OnYourOwn-3-5`

2. If the workbook opens in Protected View, click the **Enable Editing** button in the Message Bar at the top of the workbook so you can modify it.

3. Start with the *Pocket Chart* worksheet. This dental chart is designed to be used to record measurements of the depth of gum pockets around the teeth. Each tooth is identified by number and name. The teeth of the upper and lower jaws are arranged across the worksheet from the patient's right side to the left. Pocket depth measurements have been entered.

4. Enter your name as the patient's name and enter the date of the examination. Do not use a function for the date. (You don't want the value to update every time you open the workbook.)

5. Review the information in the *Look Up* worksheet and assign names as necessary to each of the lookup tables to use in formulas in other worksheets. One of the lookup tables already has a name assigned.

6. Return to the *Pocket Chart* worksheet and complete the patient data.

    a. Use VLOOKUP functions to determine the severity level for each tooth.

    b. Use statistical functions to calculate the smallest pocket depth, the largest pocket depth, and the average pocket depth for the upper and lower teeth sections. Use similar formulas in **O2:O4** to calculate the overall statistical information for the patient (the average, minimum, and maximum pocket depths for both upper and lower teeth).

    c. Count the number of cells missing pocket depth information (blank cells). *Hint*: Remember, the COUNTBLANK function accepts only one argument, so you will need to count the blank cells for the upper teeth and the lower teeth and then add those values together.

7. Now switch to the *Treatment Plan* worksheet and fix any errors. *Hint*: Display formulas and then use the **Name Manager** to review names and create missing names as needed. Delete any duplicate names you may have accidentally created.

8. Create a formula to display the patient name in the format Bob Smith. Reference the patient name cells from the *Pocket Chart* sheet. Be sure to include a space between the first and last names.

9. Modify the formula that displays the patient name so the name appears in all uppercase.

10. Enter a formula to display today's date in cell **I1**.

11. Cells B7:C9 summarize the number of teeth with each severity level. Use this data table to complete the treatment plan. For each treatment, display **"yes"** if the patient meets the requirement below and **"no"** if he does not.

    a. Sonic Toothbrush: Recommend only if the patient has more than five mild pockets.

    b. Scaling & Planing: Recommend only if the patient has more than seven moderate pockets.

    c. Surgery: Recommend only if the patient has more than three severe pockets.

12. Complete the billing information.

    a. Look up the cost of each treatment.

    b. Compute the amount the insurance company will cover for each treatment. Multiply the treatment cost by the insurance company rate. *Hint*: Use the HLOOKUP function to find the insurance company rate.

    c. Compute the billable amount for each treatment. If the treatment is recommended, compute the billable amount by subtracting the amount insurance will cover from the cost of the treatment. If the treatment is not recommended, display **"N/A"** instead.

    d. Enter a formula to calculate the total bill for the patient.

13. Enter a formula to compute the monthly payment for the payment plan option. Be sure to display the number as a positive value.

14. Display your formulas and check for errors. Use the error checking skills you learned in this chapter as needed.

15. Save and close the workbook.

In this project, you will correct function mistakes and other formula errors in a workbook designed for planning a large party or event. Be sure to save your work often!

Skills needed to complete this project:

- Checking Formulas for Errors (Skill 3.18)
- Finding Errors Using Trace Precedents and Trace Dependents (Skill 3.19)
- Displaying and Printing Formulas (Skill 3.20)
- Creating Formulas Using Counting Functions (Skill 3.6)
- Finding Minimum and Maximum Values (Skill 3.4)
- Formatting Text Using Functions (Skill 3.7)
- Using CONCAT to Combine Text (Skill 3.8)
- Finding Data Using the VLOOKUP Function (Skill 3.17)
- Using the Function Arguments Dialog to Enter Functions (Skill 3.1)
- Using Formula AutoComplete to Enter Functions (Skill 3.2)
- Calculating Averages (Skill 3.3)
- Naming Ranges of Cells (Skill 3.11)
- Working with Named Ranges (Skill 3.12)
- Updating Named Ranges with the Name Manager (Skill 3.13)
- Editing and Deleting Names with the Name Manager (Skill 3.14)
- Using Date and Time Functions (Skill 3.5)
- Using the Logical Function IF (Skill 3.15)
- Creating Formulas Referencing Data from Other Worksheets (Skill 3.10)
- Calculating Loan Payments Using the PMT Function (Skill 3.16)

1. Open the start file **EX2019-FixIt-3-6** and resave the file as:
   `[your initials]EX-FixIt-3-6`

2. If the workbook opens in Protected View, click the **Enable Editing** button in the Message Bar at the top of the workbook so you can modify the workbook.

3. On the *GuestList* sheet, check all the formulas. Cells to check are filled with the light purple color. Most of them need to be corrected. Use error checking as needed and/or display the formulas on-screen for easy viewing.

   a. In the *Name Tag* column, modify the formula to display the guest name in this format: **BILL SMITH** *Hint*: There are multiple errors in this formula. Fix the formula in cell **D10** and then copy it to the other cells in the column.

   b. Correct the function used in cell **A3** to calculate the sum of the values in the *NumAttending* column.

   c. Correct the function used in cell **A4** to count the number of values in the *Street* column.

   d. Correct the function used in cell **A5** to count the number of blank cells in the *NumAttending* column.

   e. Correct the function used in cell **A6** to display the largest value in the *NumAttending* column.

   f. Correct the function used in cell **A7** to display the average value in the *NumAttending* column.

4. On the *Shopping List* sheet, check all the formulas. Cells to check are filled with the light purple color. Most of them need to be corrected. Many of the problems on this worksheet can be solved by creating named ranges or using a name that already exists.

   a. The formula in cell **B2** uses the wrong function.

   b. The formulas in cells **A9:A23** reference a named range that doesn't exist. There is more than one correct way to fix this problem using the cell range **A5:H18** on the *Places to Shop* worksheet. You can create the named range referenced in the formulas, or you can change the function arguments to reference the cell range instead.

   c. The formula in cell **H9** results in the correct value. However, the workbook author copied this formula to the remaining cells in the column and those values are definitely not correct! Fix the formula in cell **H9** and copy it to cells **H10:H23**. *Hint*: Notice that cell **H8** is named *Tax*.

5. If you've fixed the formulas in cells **H9:H23** correctly, the formulas in cells **I9:I23** and **G5** should calculate properly now. However, the formulas in cells **G2:G4** still have errors that need to be fixed. *Hint*: Use error checking as needed and/or display the formulas on-screen for easy viewing.

   a. Correct the function used in cell **G2** to average value of the *Cost* column.

   b. Correct the function used in cell **G3** to display the largest value in the *Cost* column.

   c. Correct the function used in cell **G4** to display the smallest value in the *Cost* column.

6. On the *Summary* sheet, you will be entering all the formulas. Cells to complete are filled with the light purple color. *Hint*: Use error checking as needed and/or display the formulas on-screen for easy viewing.

   a. Cell **B2** should use a function that will update the date to the current date every time the workbook is opened.

   b. Cell **B4** references a named range that doesn't exist. It should reference cell **A4** on the *Guest List* sheet. You can create the named range or edit the formula to reference the cell instead.

   c. Cell **B5** references a named range that doesn't exist. It should reference cell **A3** on the *Guest List* sheet. You can create the named range or edit the formula to reference the cell instead.

   d. Cell **B8** is missing the formula to calculate whether or not the total *Cost* with tax on the *Shopping List* sheet + the total *Cost* for purchasing and mailing invitations on the *Guest List* sheet is greater than the available cash. The cell should display *yes* or *no*.

   e. Add a formula to cell **B9** to calculate the amount to borrow (total *Cost* with tax on the *Shopping List* sheet + the total *Cost* for purchasing and mailing invitations on the *Guest List* sheet – the cash available) if the value in cell **B8** is *yes*. If the value in cell **B8** is not *yes*, the cell should display 0.

   f. Add a formula to cell **B12** to calculate the monthly loan payment based on the information in cells **B9:B11**. Use a negative number for the *Pv* argument.

7. Save and close the workbook.

chapter **4**

Formatting Worksheets and Managing the Workbook

In this chapter, you will learn the following skills:

❭ Insert, delete, and format worksheets

❭ Apply themes

❭ Insert, delete, and modify rows and columns

❭ Modify the worksheet view

❭ Manage how the worksheet prints

skills

introduction

As Excel projects get bigger and more complicated, more formatting skills are required. In this chapter, you will learn how to manage the organization and appearance of worksheets for the optimal display of data both on-screen and when printed.

Skill 4.1 Inserting Worksheets

When you create a new workbook, it contains a single worksheet named *Sheet1*. If you need more than one worksheet, you can add more. It is a good practice to keep all related information in the same workbook by adding more worksheets, rather than starting a new workbook.

❭ To add a new worksheet to the right of the active worksheet, click the **New sheet** button to the right of the last worksheet tab ⊕.

❭ To add a worksheet to the left of the active worksheet, on the *Home* tab, in the *Cells* group, click the **Insert** button arrow, and select **Insert Sheet**.

Click the **New Sheet** button to add a worksheet to the right of the active worksheet.

Select **Insert Sheet** to add a worksheet to the left of the active worksheet.

FIGURE EX 4.1

The new sheet is given the name Sheet# (where # is the next number available–for example, if your workbook contains *Sheet1* and *Sheet2*, the next sheet inserted will be named *Sheet3*).

another **method**

To add a worksheet, you can also:

1. Right-click on a sheet tab and select **Insert...** on the shortcut menu.
   - To insert a blank worksheet, click the **Worksheet** icon in the dialog.
   - To insert a formatted worksheet, click the **Spreadsheet Solutions** tab, and click any of the template icons.
2. Click **OK**.

let me **try**

Open the student data file **EX4-01-PurchaseOrders** and try this skill on your own:

1. Add a new worksheet to the right of the *July* sheet.

2. Add another new worksheet to the left of the worksheet you just added.

3. If you will be moving on to the next skill in this chapter, leave the workbook open to continue working. If not, save the file as directed by your instructor and close it.

Skill 4.2 Naming Worksheets

When you create a new workbook, Excel automatically includes a worksheet named *Sheet1*. Additional worksheets that you insert are automatically named *Sheet2*, *Sheet3*, and so forth. It is a good idea to rename your worksheets to something more descriptive. Giving your worksheets descriptive names can help organize multiple worksheets, making it easier for you to find and use information.

To rename a worksheet:

1. Double-click the sheet tab or right-click the worksheet tab and select **Rename**.
2. Excel highlights the sheet name, allowing you to replace it as you type.
3. Type the new sheet name, and press ⏎ Enter.

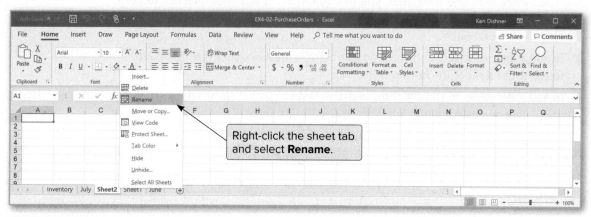

FIGURE EX 4.2

another **method**

You can also use the Ribbon to rename a worksheet.

1. Click the sheet tab you want to rename.
2. On the *Home* tab, in the *Cells* group, click the **Format** button.
3. Select **Rename Sheet**.
4. Type the new sheet name, and press ⏎ Enter.

let me **try**

If you do not have the data file from the previous skill open, open the student data file **EX4-02-PurchaseOrders** and try this skill on your own:

1. Rename *Sheet1*: **August**
2. Rename *Sheet2*: **Orders**
3. If you will be moving on to the next skill in this chapter, leave the workbook open to continue working. If not, save the file as directed by your instructor and close it.

Skill 4.3 Changing the Color of Sheet Tabs

By default, all the worksheet tabs in Excel are white. If you have many sheets in your workbook, changing the tab colors can help you organize your data.

To change a worksheet tab color:

1. Right-click the sheet tab and point to **Tab Color** to display the color palette.
2. Hover the mouse pointer over each color to preview how the color will look when the worksheet is active.
3. Click the color you want.

Right-click the sheet tab, point to **Tab Color**, and click the color you want to apply to the tab.

Preview of color applied to the sheet tab.

FIGURE EX 4.3

tips & tricks

❯ The color palette used for worksheet tab color is the same color palette used for font color, fill color, and border color. The colors available change depending on the theme applied to the workbook.

❯ If you have sheets that contain related data, color them using different shades of the same color.

another **method**

1. Click the sheet tab you want to color.
2. On the *Home* tab, in the *Cells* group, click the **Format** button.
3. Point to **Tab Color** to display the color palette.
4. Click the color you want.

let me try

If you do not have the data file from the previous skill open, open the student data file **EX4-03-PurchaseOrders** and try this skill on your own:

1. Change the color of the sheet tab for the *July* worksheet to the standard **Blue** color (the third color from the right in the row of standard colors).
2. If you will be moving on to the next skill in this chapter, leave the workbook open to continue working. If not, save the file as directed by your instructor and close it.

Skill 4.4 Moving and Copying Worksheets

You can move worksheets around in a workbook, rearranging them into the most logical order.

To move a worksheet within a workbook:

1. Click the worksheet tab and hold down the mouse button.

2. Notice that the mouse pointer changes to the ⬚ shape.

3. Drag the mouse cursor to the position where you want to move the sheet, and release the mouse button. Excel places a small black triangle ▼ to let you know where the sheet will be placed.

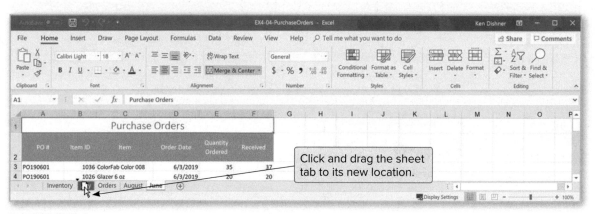

Click and drag the sheet tab to its new location.

FIGURE EX 4.4

If you want to experiment with worksheet layouts or formulas, you can create a copy of the worksheet in case you want to go back to the original version.

To create a copy of a worksheet:

1. Click the worksheet tab, hold down the mouse button, and press and hold Ctrl.

2. Notice that the mouse pointer changes to the ⬚ shape.

3. Drag the mouse cursor to the position where you want to insert a copy of the selected sheet, and release the mouse button.

To move or copy a worksheet to another workbook or to a new workbook:

1. Right-click the sheet tab, and select **Move or Copy...** to open the *Move or Copy* dialog.

2. In the *Move or Copy* dialog, expand the **To book** list at the top of the dialog. The *To book* list shows all the Excel workbooks you have open. Click the workbook you want. To move or copy the sheet to a new blank workbook, select **(new book)**.

3. The list of sheets in the *Before sheet* box will update to show the sheets available in the workbook you selected. Click the name of the sheet you want to move the selected sheet before. If you want to move the sheet to the end of the workbook, select **(move to end)** in the *Before sheet* box.

4. If you want to create a copy of the selected sheet, instead of moving the original, click the **Create a copy** check box.

5. Click **OK**.

Select **Move or Copy...** to open the *Move or Copy* dialog.

Be sure to remember to click the **Create a copy** check box if you want to copy instead of move the worksheet.

You can use this same method to move or copy worksheets within a workbook by not changing the workbook listed in the *To book* list in the *Move or Copy* dialog.

tips & tricks

Moving a worksheet from one workbook to another deletes the worksheet from the original workbook. Consider copying the worksheet to the second workbook first, and then, once you are confident that formulas work as you intend, delete the worksheet from the original workbook.

tell me **more**

To move or copy more than one worksheet, press ⬆ Shift and click the worksheets you want to move or copy. If the worksheets are not consecutive, then press Ctrl instead.

another **method**

You can also open the *Move or Copy* dialog from the Ribbon. On the *Home* tab, in the *Cells* group, click the **Format** button, and select **Move or Copy Sheet...**

let me **try**

If you do not have the data file from the previous skill open, open the student data file **EX4-04-PurchaseOrders** and try this skill on your own:

1. Move the **June** worksheet so it is positioned before the *July* worksheet.
2. Copy the **Inventory** worksheet to a new workbook.
3. Save the new workbook with the name **InventoryCopy** and close it.
4. If you will be moving on to the next skill in this chapter, leave the *PurchaseOrders* workbook open to continue working. If not, save the file as directed by your instructor and close it.

Skill 4.5 Deleting Worksheets

It is always a good practice to delete any unnecessary worksheets in your workbook.

To delete a worksheet:

1. Select the sheet you want to delete by clicking the worksheet tab.

2. On the *Home* tab, in the *Cells* group, click the **Delete** button arrow, and select **Delete Sheet**.

3. If you try to delete a sheet that contains data, Excel will display a warning that the sheet may contain data and ask if you are sure you want to permanently remove it from your workbook. Click the **Delete** button to continue and delete the worksheet.

Be careful—you cannot undo the *Delete Sheet* command.

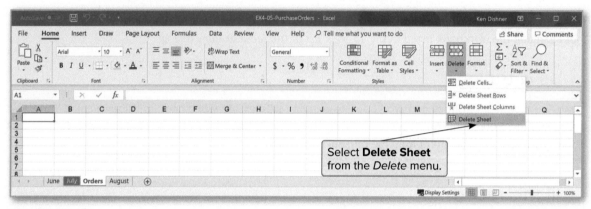

Select **Delete Sheet** from the *Delete* menu.

FIGURE EX 4.6

tips & tricks

If you have multiple copies of the same worksheet in a workbook, be sure to delete the versions you no longer need.

tell me **more**

You can delete multiple worksheets at the same time. First, select all the sheet tabs you want to remove, and then invoke the *Delete Sheet* command.

another **method**

To delete a worksheet, right-click on a sheet tab and then select **Delete** from the shortcut menu.

let me **try**

If you do not have the data file from the previous skill open, open the student data file **EX4-05-PurchaseOrders** and try this skill on your own:

1. Delete the **Orders** worksheet.

2. If you will be moving on to the next skill in this chapter, leave the workbook open to continue working. If not, save the file as directed by your instructor and close it.

Skill 4.6 Grouping Worksheets

If you have multiple worksheets with the same structure, you can make changes to all of the worksheets at the same time by **grouping** them. This is convenient when you are setting up a series of worksheets with the same row or column headings. When sheets are grouped together, you can also change column widths and formatting, add formulas such as totals, or add headers and footers. Using grouping saves time and ensures that the sheets share a consistent format.

To group worksheets:

1. Click the first worksheet tab.

2. Hold down (↑ Shift) and click the tab for the last worksheet you want included in the group. If you want to select noncontiguous worksheets (sheets that are not next to each other), press (Ctrl) instead, and then click each sheet tab.

3. Notice that the title bar now includes *Group* after the file name.

4. Make the change you want to the sheet. The change will be made to all sheets in the group.

5. To ungroup, click any sheet tab that is not part of the group.

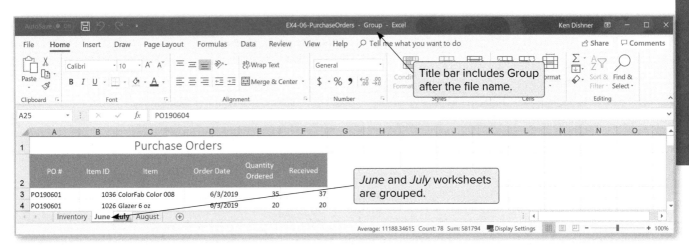

FIGURE EX 4.7

tell me **more**

To group together all the sheets in your workbook, right-click any sheet tab and then click **Select All Sheets**.

To ungroup sheets, right-click one of the grouped sheet tabs and then click **Ungroup**. If all of the sheets in your workbook are grouped together, clicking any sheet will ungroup them all.

let me **try**

If you do not have the data file from the previous skill open, open the student data file **EX4-06-PurchaseOrders** and try this skill on your own:

1. Group sheets **June** and **July**.

2. Change the text in cell **E2** to: **Ordered**

3. Review cell **E2** in sheets *June* and *July* to ensure that the change was made to both sheets. Notice that the sheets remain grouped as you click back and forth between them.

4. Ungroup the worksheets.

5. If you will be moving on to the next skill in this chapter, leave the workbook open to continue working. If not, save the file as directed by your instructor and close it.

Skill 4.7 Inserting and Deleting Rows and Columns

You may find you need to add rows or columns of new information into the middle of your workbook. Adding a new row will shift down other rows; adding a new column will shift other columns to the right.

To insert a column:

1. Place your cursor in a cell in the column to the right of where you want the new column.
2. On the *Home* tab, in the *Cells* group, click the **Insert** button arrow and select **Insert Sheet Columns**.
3. The new column will appear to the left of the selected cell.

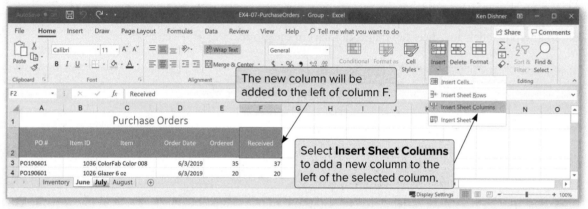

FIGURE EX 4.8

To insert a row:

1. Place your cursor in a cell in the row below where you want the new row.
2. On the *Home* tab, in the *Cells* group, click the **Insert** button arrow and select **Insert Sheet Rows**.
3. The new row will appear above the selected cell.

Of course, you can also delete rows and columns. Deleting a row will shift other rows up; deleting a column will shift the remaining columns to the left.

To delete a row:

1. Place your cursor in a cell in the row you want to delete.
2. On the *Home* tab, in the *Cells* group, click the **Delete** button arrow and select **Delete Sheet Rows**.
3. The row will be deleted and the rows below it will shift up.

To delete a column:

1. Place your cursor in a cell in the column you want to delete.
2. On the *Home* tab, in the *Cells* group, click the **Delete** button arrow and select **Delete Sheet Columns**.
3. The column will be deleted, and columns to the right of the deleted column will shift left.

tips & tricks

Depending on whether you have a cell, a range of cells, a row, or a column selected, the behavior of the *Insert* and *Delete* commands will change. If you have a single cell selected and click the **Insert** button instead of the button arrow, Excel will insert a single cell, automatically moving cells down. However, if you select the entire column first, and then click the **Insert** button, Excel will automatically insert a column.

tell me **more**

When you insert a row or column, a Smart Tag will appear. Click the **Smart Tag** to choose formatting options for the new row or column—**Format Same as Above**, **Format Same as Below**, or **Clear Formatting** for rows and **Format Same as Left**, **Format Same as Right**, or **Clear Formatting** for columns. The Smart Tag formatting options are not available if you are inserting a row or column in two or more grouped worksheets.

another **method**

To insert or delete rows and columns:

1. Right-click in a cell, then select **Insert...** or **Delete...**
2. In the dialog, select **Entire row** or **Entire column**.
3. Click **OK**.

You can also insert or delete an entire row or column by right-clicking the row or column selector and selecting **Insert** or **Delete** from the menu. Because you have already selected an entire row or column, Excel will not ask you to specify what you want to insert or delete.

let me **try**

If you do not have the data file from the previous skill open, open the student data file **EX4-07-PurchaseOrders** and try this skill on your own:

1. On the *June* worksheet, insert a new column to the left of column **F**.
2. Delete row **3**.
3. Verify that the changes were made to both worksheets.
4. If you will be moving on to the next skill in this chapter, leave the workbook open to continue working. If not, save the file as directed by your instructor and close it.

Skill 4.8 Applying Themes

A **theme** is a unified color, font, and effects scheme. When you apply a theme to the workbook, you ensure that all visual elements work well together, giving the workbook a polished, professional look. When you create a new blank workbook in Excel, the Office theme is applied by default.

FIGURE EX 4.10

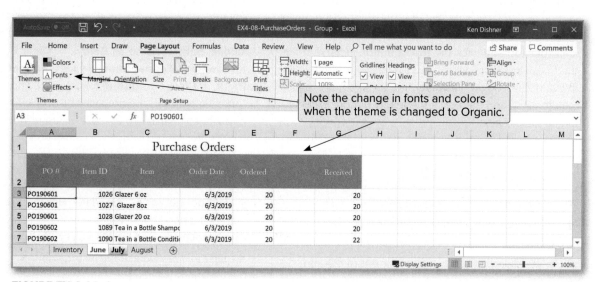

FIGURE EX 4.11

To apply a theme to a workbook:

1. On the *Page Layout* tab, in the *Themes* group, click the **Themes** button to expand the gallery.

2. Roll your mouse over each theme in the gallery to preview the formatting changes.

3. Click one of the themes to apply it to your workbook.

From the *Themes* group, you can apply specific aspects of a theme by making a selection from the *Theme Colors*, *Theme Fonts*, or *Theme Effects* gallery. Applying one aspect of a theme (for example, colors) will not change the other aspects (fonts and effects).

Theme Colors—Limits the colors available from the color palette for fonts, borders, and cell shading. Notice that when you change themes, the colors in the color palette change.

Theme Fonts—Affects the fonts used for cell styles (including titles and headings). Changing the theme fonts does not limit the fonts available to you from the *Font* group on the Ribbon.

Theme Effects—Controls the way graphic elements in your worksheet appear. Chart styles change according to the theme color and effects.

FIGURE EX 4.12

tips & tricks

Changing the theme affects all the worksheets in the workbook.

When you change the workbook theme, the look of the built-in cell styles changes. Be careful, as the change in style may increase the font size, causing some of your data to be too wide for the columns. If you change themes, you may need to adjust some of your column widths or row heights.

let me try

If you do not have the data file from the previous skill open, open the student data file **EX4-08-PurchaseOrders** and try this skill on your own:

1. If necessary, click the **June** sheet tab.

2. Expand the **Themes** gallery and preview how each theme would affect the workbook.

3. Apply the **Organic** theme and note the changes to the workbook.

4. Reapply the **Office** theme.

5. If you will be moving on to the next skill in this chapter, leave the workbook open to continue working. If not, save the file as directed by your instructor and close it.

Skill 4.9 Modifying Column Widths and Row Heights

Some columns in your spreadsheet may be too narrow to display the data properly. If a cell contains text data, the text appears cut off. (If the cell to the right is empty, however, the text appears to extend into the empty cell.) If the cell contains numerical data, Excel displays a series of pound signs (#) when the cell is too narrow to display the entire number. You should adjust the column widths so the spreadsheet is easy to read.

Excel offers an easy way to automatically set columns to the width to best fit the data in the column:

To make the column automatically fit the contents:

1. Move your mouse over the right column boundary.
2. The cursor will change to a ↔ shape.
3. Double-click the right column border.

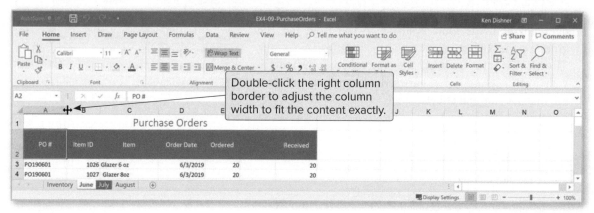

FIGURE EX 4.13

You can also modify column widths manually:

1. Move your mouse over the right column boundary.
2. The cursor will change to a ↔ shape.
3. Click and drag until the column is the size you want, and then release the mouse button.

To specify an exact column width for multiple columns:

1. Select the columns you want to modify. Click the column selector for the first column, press and hold (↑ Shift), and click the column selector for the last column.
2. On the *Home* tab, in the *Cells* group, click the **Format** button.
3. Select **Column Width...**
4. Enter the value you want in the *Column Width* dialog.
5. Click **OK**.

FIGURE EX 4.14

Rows in Excel are automatically sized to fit the font size. However, if you change the font size or apply a new theme, you may need to modify row heights. Use the same techniques you use for resizing columns:

〉 To make the row automatically fit the contents, double-click the bottom row boundary.

〉 To modify row heights manually, click and drag the bottom row boundary up or down.

〉 To specify an exact row height, select the row(s) you want to modify and then from the *Format* button menu, select **Row Height...** to enter the row height value in the *Row Height* dialog.

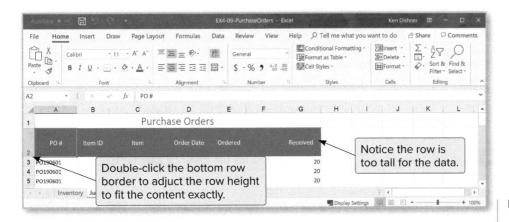

FIGURE EX 4.15

let me try

If you do not have the data file from the previous skill open, open the student data file **EX4-09-PurchaseOrders** and try this skill on your own:

1. If necessary, click the **June** worksheet tab.
2. Autofit column **A** to best fit the data.
3. Select columns **E:G** and change the column width to **11**.
4. Autofit row **2** to best fit the data.
5. If you will be moving on to the next skill in this chapter, leave the workbook open to continue working. If not, save the file as directed by your instructor and close it.

Skill 4.10 Freezing and Unfreezing Rows and Columns

If you have a large spreadsheet, you may want to **freeze** part of the worksheet so it is always visible. By doing this, you can keep column headings and row labels visible as you scroll through your data.

To freeze part of the worksheet:

1. Arrange the worksheet so the row you want to be visible is the top row or the column you want is the first column visible at the left.

2. On the *View* tab, in the *Window* group, click the **Freeze Panes** button.

   ❭ If you want the first row to always be visible, click **Freeze Top Row**.

   ❭ If you want the first column to always be visible, click **Freeze First Column**.

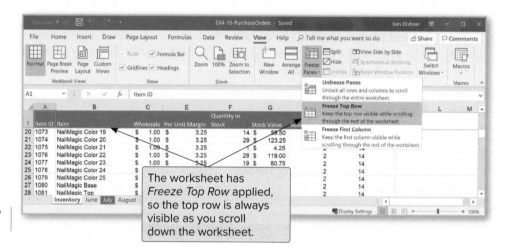

FIGURE EX 4.16

If your worksheet has both a header row and a column of labels in the first column, use the *Freeze Panes* option to freeze the worksheet at the selected cell, so the rows above the cell and the columns to the left of the cell are always visible.

1. Select the cell immediately below the header row and immediately to the right of the label column (usually cell B2).

2. On the *View* tab, in the *Window* group, click the **Freeze Panes** button, and select **Freeze Panes**.

To return your worksheet to normal, click the **Freeze Panes** button and select **Unfreeze Panes**.

let me try

If you do not have the data file from the previous skill open, open the student data file **EX4-10-PurchaseOrders** and try this skill on your own:

1. Verify that the *Inventory* sheet is selected and the header row (row 1) is visible at the top of the worksheet.

2. Apply the **Freeze Panes** command so the top row will remain visible as you scroll down the worksheet.

3. If you will be moving on to the next skill in this chapter, leave the workbook open to continue working. If not, save the file as directed by your instructor and close it.

Skill 4.11 Hiding and Unhiding Rows and Columns

When you hide a row or column, the data still remain in your workbook, but they are no longer displayed onscreen and are not part of the printed workbook. Hiding rows can be helpful when you want to print a copy of your workbook for others but do not want to share all the information contained in your workbook.

To hide a row or column:

1. Select any cell in the row or column you want to hide.
2. On the *Home* tab, in the *Cells* group, click the **Format** button.
3. Point to **Hide & Unhide**, and click **Hide Rows** or **Hide Columns**.

To unhide a row or column:

1. Select the rows or columns on either side of the row or column you want to unhide.
2. On the *Home* tab, in the *Cells* group, click the **Format** button.
3. Point to **Hide & Unhide**, and click **Unhide Rows** or **Unhide Columns**.

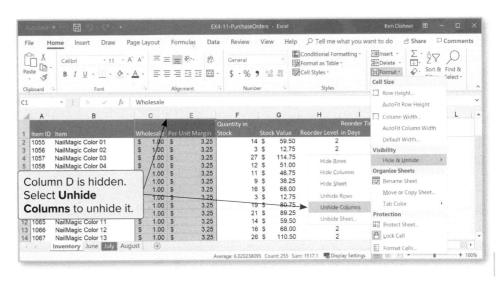

FIGURE EX 4.17

another **method**

The *Hide* and *Unhide* commands are also available from the right-click menu when columns or rows are selected.

let me try

If you do not have the data file from the previous skill open, open the student data file **EX4-11-PurchaseOrders** and try this skill on your own:

1. Verify that the *Inventory* sheet is selected.
2. Unhide column **D**.
3. Hide column **G** (*Stock Value*).
4. If you will be moving on to the next skill in this chapter, leave the workbook open to continue working. If not, save the file as directed by your instructor and close it.

Skill 4.12 Hiding and Unhiding Worksheets

Just as you can hide rows and columns in a worksheet, you can also hide entire worksheets. When you hide a worksheet, the sheet is hidden from view, but it is not deleted from the workbook. Hiding worksheets can be helpful when you have several worksheets in a large workbook, but only need to be working in a few sheets at once.

To hide a worksheet:

1. On the *Home* tab, in the *Cells* group, click the **Format** button.
2. Point to **Hide & Unhide** and click **Hide Sheet**.

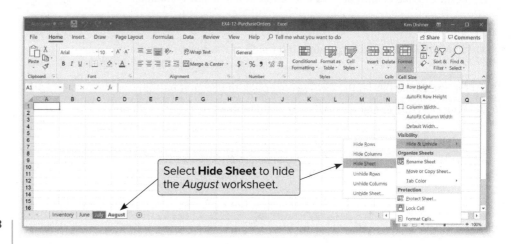

Select **Hide Sheet** to hide the *August* worksheet.

FIGURE EX 4.18

To unhide a worksheet:

1. On the *Home* tab, in the *Cells* group, click the **Format** button.
2. Point to **Hide & Unhide** and click **Unhide Sheet**.
3. In the *Unhide* dialog, if necessary, select the worksheet to unhide, and click **OK**.

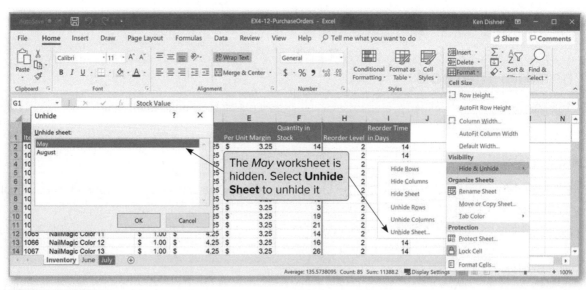

The *May* worksheet is hidden. Select **Unhide Sheet** to unhide it

FIGURE EX 4.19

tips & tricks

Be careful when hiding worksheets. Sometimes you may forget that a worksheet is hidden, or other people using the workbook may not know that there are hidden worksheets.

tell me **more**

If there is only one worksheet in the workbook, the *Hide* command is unavailable.

another **method**

To hide a worksheet, right-click the sheet tab and select **Hide**.

let me **try**

If you do not have the data file from the previous skill open, open the student data file **EX4-12-PurchaseOrders** and try this skill on your own:

1. Hide the **August** worksheet.

2. Unhide the **May** worksheet

3. If you will be moving on to the next skill in this chapter, leave the workbook open to continue working. If not, save the file as directed by your instructor and close it.

from the perspective of. . .

PROJECT MANAGER

I was troubleshooting a budget spreadsheet for another department when I realized some formulas were referencing values in a worksheet that didn't appear to be in the workbook. I couldn't figure out where that worksheet was. Then I realized it was hidden! Now I use the same trick and hide unfinished worksheets or worksheets that contain data used for calculations only.

Comstock/SuperStock

Skill 4.13 Splitting Workbooks

In Excel, you can split the worksheet view into two or four panes. Each pane scrolls independently of the other(s), so you can see two (or four) different areas of the worksheet at the same time. This can be especially helpful if you want to compare data in multiple parts of the worksheet at the same time.

To split the worksheet view:

1. Click the cell in the worksheet where you would like to split the view. You can select an entire row or column as the split point.

   ❭ If you want to split the worksheet into two horizontal panes, click a cell in column **A**.

   ❭ If you want to split the worksheet into two vertical panes, click a cell in row **1**.

   ❭ If you want to split the worksheet into four panes, click any cell in the worksheet. The cell you selected will be the top left cell in the pane in the lower-right quadrant.

2. On the *View* tab, in the *Window* group, click the **Split** button.

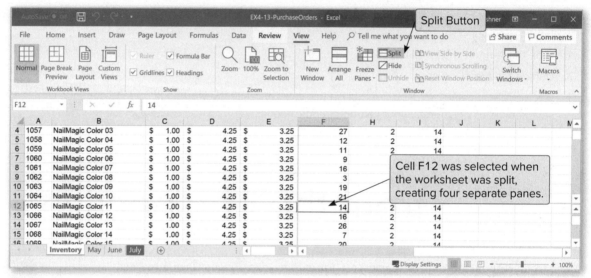

FIGURE EX 4.20

To undo the split and return the worksheet to a single view, click the **Split** button again.

tips & tricks

Splitting your worksheet will undo the *Freeze Panes* command.

tell me **more**

To adjust the size of a pane, click and drag the pane border.

let me **try**

If you do not have the data file from the previous skill open, open the student data file **EX4-13-PurchaseOrders** and try this skill on your own:

1. Select the **Inventory** worksheet.

2. Select cell **F12**, and then split the worksheet into four panes. Observe how using the scroll bars affects the view in each of the panes.

3. Remove the split and return the worksheet to a single view. *Hint:* The *Undo* command will not undo the *Split* command.

4. If you will be moving on to the next skill in this chapter, leave the workbook open to continue working. If not, save the file as directed by your instructor and close it.

Skill 4.14 Changing the Worksheet View

Excel offers three ways to view a worksheet.

Just as the name implies, **Normal view** is the typical working view. In Normal view, Excel shows the aspects of the worksheet that are visible only on-screen. Elements that are visible only when printed (like headers and footers) are hidden.

Page Layout view shows all the worksheet elements as they will print, including page margins and headers and footers as shown in Figure EX 4.21. You will work with Page Layout view when you learn about headers and footers.

Page Break Preview view allows you to manipulate where page breaks occur when the worksheet is printed. You will work with Page Break Preview view when you learn about inserting page breaks.

To switch between worksheet views, click the appropriate button in the status bar at the bottom of the Excel window, or on the *View* tab, in the *Workbook Views* group, click the button for the view you want.

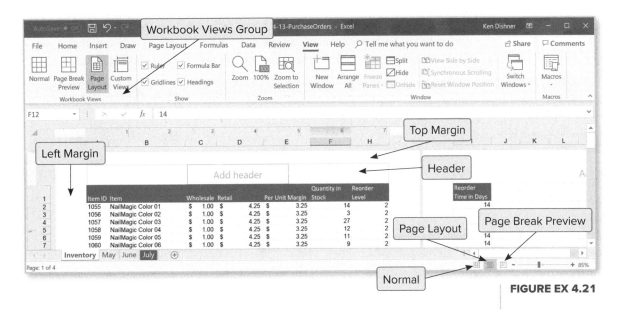

FIGURE EX 4.21

tips & tricks

Page Layout view is not compatible with *Freeze Panes*. If you have *Freeze Panes* applied to your worksheet, Excel will warn you before switching to Page Layout view. Click **OK** in the message box to continue to *Page Layout* view and undo *Freeze Panes*.

let me try

If you do not have the data file from the previous skill open, open the student data file **EX4-14-PurchaseOrders** and try this skill on your own:

1. Select the **Inventory** worksheet.

2. Switch to **Page Break Preview** view.

3. Switch to **Page Layout** view. If Excel warns you that Page Layout view is not compatible with *Freeze Panes,* click **OK**.

4. If you will be moving on to the next skill in this chapter, leave the workbook open in Page Layout view to continue working. If not, save the file as directed by your instructor and close it.

Skill 4.15 Adding Headers and Footers

A **header** is text that appears at the top of every page, just below the top margin; a **footer** is text that appears at the bottom of every page, just above the bottom margin. Typically, headers and footers display information such as dates, page numbers, sheet names, file names, and authors' names.

To add a header or footer to a worksheet from Page Layout view:

1. Switch to Page Layout view by clicking the **Page Layout** button on the status bar.
2. The header area has three sections with the text *Add header* in the center section. If you do not see the *Add header* text, move the mouse pointer to the area just above row 1 to make the header area visible. Click the header section where you want to add information (left, center, or right).
3. The *Header & Footer Tools Design* tab appears.
4. In the *Header & Footer* group, click the **Header** button and select one of the predefined headers, or click a button in the *Header & Footer Elements* group to add a specific header element such as the sheet name or the current date. Excel inserts the code for the header element as show in Figure EX 4.22. Once you click away from the header, you will see the actual header text as shown in Figure EX 4.23.

FIGURE EX 4.22

FIGURE EX 4.23

5. To switch to the footer, on the *Header & Footer Tools Design* tab, in the *Navigation* group, click the **Go to Footer** button. Add footer elements the same way you add header elements.
6. Another way to add a header or footer is to select an option from the *Header & Footer Tools Design* tab, *Header & Footer* group. Click the **Header** or **Footer** button, and then select from the list. Be aware that this method will completely replace the entire header or footer, not just add an element to the selected section.
7. When you are finished adding your header and footer elements, click anywhere in the worksheet and then switch back to Normal view to continue working.

excel 365   chapter 4 Formatting Worksheets and Managing the Workbook

Another method for adding headers and footers uses the *Page Setup* dialog. This method will be familiar to users who have worked with older versions of Excel. When the *Header & Footer Tools Design* tab is active, you cannot use this method.

To add a header or footer to a worksheet using the *Page Setup* dialog:

1. On the *Page Layout* tab, in the *Page Setup* group, click the **Page Setup Dialog Launcher** to open the *Page Setup* dialog.

FIGURE EX 4.24

2. Click the **Header/Footer** tab.
3. Click the arrow beneath the *Header* or *Footer* area to expand the list of predefined header/footer options. Click the option you want to use.
4. Click **OK**.

FIGURE EX 4.25

tell me **more**

If the predefined header/footer options in the *Page Setup* dialog do not meet your needs, you can customize the header or footer by clicking the **Custom Header...** or **Custom Footer...** button and adding elements through the *Header* or *Footer* dialog. In the *Header* or *Footer* dialog, click the section you want, and then click one of the header/footer element buttons.

another **method**

Another way to add a header or footer to your worksheet is to click the **Insert** tab. In the *Text* group, click the **Header & Footer** button. The worksheet will automatically switch to Page Layout view when you click the **Header & Footer** button.

let me **try**

If you do not have the data file from the previous skill open, open the student data file **EX4-15-PurchaseOrders** and try this skill on your own:

1. If necessary, select the **Inventory** sheet and switch to Page Layout view.
2. From the *Header & Footer Tools Design* tab, add a header that displays the sheet name in the center section.
3. Add a footer that displays the word *Page* and then the page number in the center section.
4. Click anywhere in the worksheet grid, and then switch back to Normal view.
5. Preview how the worksheet will look when printed and note the header and footer.
6. If you will be moving on to the next skill in this chapter, leave the workbook open to continue working. If not, save the file as directed by your instructor and close it.

Skill 4.16 Inserting Page Breaks

Excel automatically inserts page breaks so columns and rows are not split across pages when you print. However, you may want to control where page breaks happen so your worksheet prints in a more logical order. When the worksheet is in Normal view, page breaks appear as faint dotted lines. To view the page breaks more clearly, switch to Page Break Preview view.

To manually insert a new page break:

1. From Normal view or Page Break Preview view, begin by selecting the cell below and/or to the right of where you want the new page break.

2. On the *Page Layout* tab, in the *Page Setup* group, click the **Breaks** button.

3. Click **Insert Page Break**.

4. A new page break is inserted to the left of the selected column or above the selected row.

When the worksheet is in Page Break Preview view, automatic page breaks appear as blue dotted lines and manually inserted page breaks appear as solid blue lines. You can manually move a page break by clicking the page break line, and then dragging to the right or left or up or down. Release the mouse button when the line appears where you want the break. Notice that if you move an automatic page break, the line changes from dotted to solid.

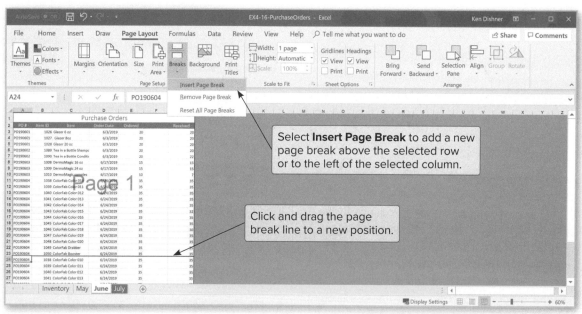

FIGURE EX 4.26

To remove a manual page break, select any cell adjacent to (to the right of or below) the break, then on the *Page Layout* tab, in the *Page Setup* group, click the **Breaks** button, and click **Remove Page Break**.

excel 365   chapter 4 Formatting Worksheets and Managing the Workbook

tips & tricks

If you insert a page break but nothing seems to happen, check to see if you have the scaling option set for printing. For example, if you have the worksheet set to print all columns on a single page, inserting a new page break between columns will not appear to have any effect on the worksheet. However, if you remove the scaling option, the new manual page break will appear.

tell me **more**

To remove all the manual page breaks at once, on the *Page Layout* tab, in the *Page Setup* group, click the **Breaks** button, and click **Reset All Page Breaks**.

let me try

If you do not have the data file from the previous skill open, open the student data file **EX4-16-PurchaseOrders** and try this skill on your own:

1. Select the **June** worksheet.
2. Switch to Page Break Preview view and observe the page breaks.
3. Insert a page break immediately above cell **A23**.
4. If you will be moving on to the next skill in this chapter, leave the workbook open to continue working. If not, save the file as directed by your instructor and close it.

from the perspective of. . .

WAREHOUSE LOGISTICS SUPERVISOR

Part of our company's "green" initiative is to minimize paper usage for printing. Using Excel's page break controls and layout controls like scaling, page orientation, and margins, we make sure that the reports we *have* to print use as little paper as possible.

Rubberball/Getty Images

Skill 4.17 Showing and Hiding Worksheet Elements

Gridlines are the lines that appear on the worksheet defining the rows and columns. Gridlines make it easy to see the individual cells in your worksheet. By default, gridlines are visible on-screen when you are working in Excel, but they do not print.

    Headings are the numbers at the left of rows and the letters at the top of columns. By default, Excel displays the row and column headings on-screen to make it easy to identify cell references but they do not print.

To hide gridlines or headings on-screen for the active worksheet:
> On the *Page Layout* tab, in the *Sheet Options* group, click the **View** check box under **Gridlines** or **Headings** to remove the checkmark.

To print the gridlines and headings when you print the worksheet:
> On the *Page Layout* tab, in the *Sheet Options* group, click the **Print** check box under **Gridlines** or **Headings**.

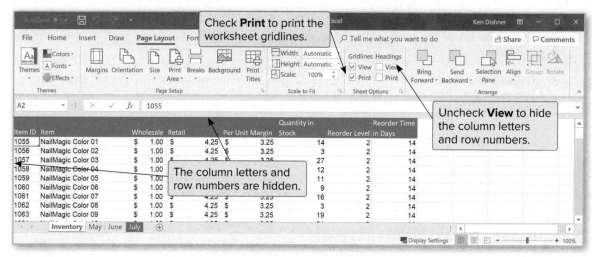

FIGURE EX 4.27

another **method**

> Set gridlines to print from the *Page Setup* dialog. On the *Page Layout* tab, in the *Page Setup* group, click the **Page Setup Dialog Launcher**. In the *Page Setup* dialog, click the **Sheet** tab. In the *Print* section, click the **Gridlines** check box. Click **OK**.

> To show or hide gridlines and headings onscreen, you can also check or uncheck the appropriate boxes on the *View* tab, in the *Show* group.

let me **try**

If you do not have the data file from the previous skill open, open the student data file **EX4-17-PurchaseOrders** and try this skill on your own:

1. Go to the *Inventory* worksheet and switch to Normal view if necessary.
2. Modify the **Inventory** worksheet so gridlines will print.
3. Modify the **Inventory** worksheet so headings are hidden on-screen.
4. If you will be moving on to the next skill in this chapter, leave the workbook open to continue working. If not, save the file as directed by your instructor and close it.

Skill 4.18 Changing Worksheet Orientation

Orientation refers to the direction the worksheet prints. It doesn't affect the way the worksheet looks on your computer screen. The default print setting is for **portrait orientation**—when the height of the page is greater than the width (like a portrait hanging on a wall). If your workbook is wide, you may want to use **landscape orientation** instead, where the width of the page is greater than the height.

You can set the worksheet orientation from the *Page Layout* tab on the Ribbon:

1. On the *Page Layout* tab, in the *Page Setup* group, click the **Orientation** button.
2. Click the **Portrait** or **Landscape** option.

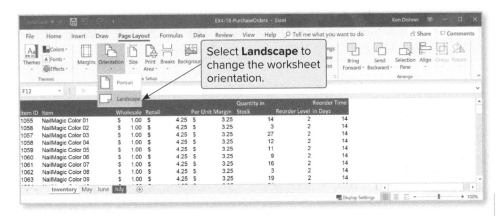

FIGURE EX 4.28

You can also change the worksheet orientation when you print:

1. Click the **File** tab to open Backstage view.
2. Click **Print**.
3. In the *Settings* section, click the button displaying the current orientation setting, and then click the orientation setting you want.

tips & tricks

Changing the *Orientation* setting affects only the active worksheet.

another **method**

On the *Page Layout* tab, in the *Page Setup* group, click the **Page Setup Dialog Launcher**. In the *Page Setup* dialog, click the **Page** tab. Click the **Portrait** or **Landscape** radio button. Click **OK**.

let me **try**

If you do not have the data file from the previous skill open, open the student data file **EX4-18-PurchaseOrders** and try this skill on your own:

1. Verify that the *Inventory* worksheet is active. Note the page break line between the *Reorder Level* and *Reorder Time in Days* columns.
2. Change the worksheet orientation to **Landscape**.
3. Note that the page is wider now and all the columns fit on one page.
4. If you will be moving on to the next skill in this chapter, switch back to **Portrait** orientation, and leave the workbook open to continue working. If not, save the file as directed by your instructor and close it.

Skill 4.19 Setting Up Margins for Printing

Margins are the blank spaces at the top, bottom, left, and right of a printed page. You may need to adjust the margins individually for each worksheet in your workbook to ensure they print exactly as you intend. Excel provides three margin settings:

〉 **Normal**—Uses Excel's default margins: 0.75 inch for the top and 0.7 bottom and inch for the left and right.

〉 **Wide**—Adds more space at the top, bottom, left, and right sides.

〉 **Narrow**—Reduces the amount of space at the top, bottom, left, and right sides, so more of your worksheet fits on each printed page.

If none of the automatic margins options is exactly what you want, the *Custom Margins...* option opens the *Page Setup* dialog where you can specify exact margins.

To change the margins, on the *Page Layout* tab, in the *Page Setup* group, click the **Margins** button, and click one of the preset margins options: **Normal**, **Wide**, or **Narrow**, or click **Custom Margins...** to specify your own values.

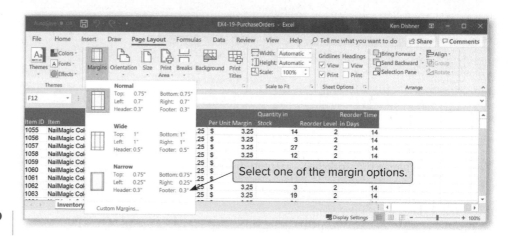

FIGURE EX 4.29

Because you will often want to adjust margins once you are ready to print, Excel allows you to adjust the margins directly from Backstage view.

1. Click the **File** tab to open Backstage view.

2. Click **Print**.

3. In the *Settings* section, click the button displaying the current margins setting, and then select the option you want.

let me **try**

If you do not have the data file from the previous skill open, open the student data file **EX4-19-PurchaseOrders** and try this skill on your own:

1. Verify that the *Inventory* worksheet is active. If necessary, set the orientation back to **portrait**. Note the page break line between the *Reorder Level* and *Reorder Time in Days* columns.

2. Change the worksheet margins to the **Narrow** option.

3. Note the printable area has become larger and all the columns fit on one page now.

4. If you will be moving on to the next skill in this chapter, switch back to **Normal** margins and leave the workbook open to continue working. If not, save the file as directed by your instructor and close it.

Skill 4.20 Scaling Worksheets for Printing

When printing your worksheet, you can set the **scale** and specify that the worksheet prints at a percentage of the original size or at a maximum number of pages wide and/ or tall. Each worksheet in the workbook has its own scale settings.

On the *Page Layout* tab, in the *Scale to Fit* group, select the option(s) you want.

❯ Click the **Width** arrow and select the maximum number of pages you want the worksheet to print across.

❯ Click the **Height** arrow and select the maximum number of pages you want the worksheet to print vertically.

❯ Click the **Scale** box and enter a percentage to grow or shrink the worksheet when printed.

When *Width* is set to *1 page*, all the worksheet columns will print on one page.

FIGURE EX 4.30

Because you often need to adjust scaling once you are ready to print, Excel has included scaling options on the *Print* page in Backstage view:

1. Click the **File** tab to open Backstage view.

2. Click **Print**.

3. In the *Settings* section, click the button displaying the current scaling setting and select the setting you want to use.

tips & tricks

When scaling your worksheet, be careful not to make the worksheet too small to read.

let me try

If you do not have the data file from the previous skill open, open the student data file **EX4-20-PurchaseOrders** and try this skill on your own:

1. Verify that the *Inventory* worksheet is active. If necessary, switch the orientation back to **portrait** and the margins to **Normal**.

2. Set the scaling options so all the columns will print on one page across.

3. If you will be moving on to the next skill in this chapter, leave the workbook open to continue working. If not, save the file as directed by your instructor and close it.

Skill 4.21 Printing Titles

If your worksheet includes a large table of data that prints on more than one page, you should ensure that the column or row labels print on every page.

To repeat rows and columns on every printed page:

1. On the *Page Layout* tab, in the *Page Setup* group, click the **Print Titles** button.
2. In the *Page Setup* dialog, on the *Sheet* tab, click in the **Rows to repeat at top** box, and then click and drag to select the rows to repeat. You can also type the row reference(s) using the format $1:$1. This example would repeat the first row only.
3. Click in the **Columns to repeat at left** box, and then click and drag to select the columns to repeat. You can also type the column reference(s) using the format $A:$A. This example would repeat the first column only. $A:$B would repeat columns A and B on every printed page.
4. Click **OK**.

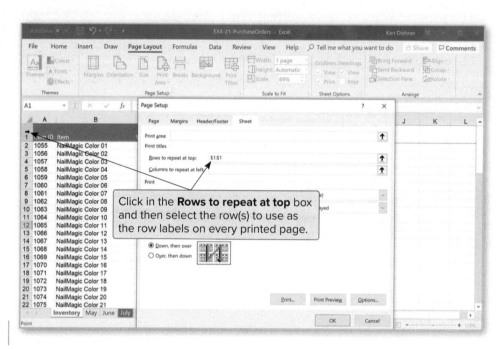

FIGURE EX 4.31

let me try

If you do not have the data file from the previous skill open, open the student data file **EX4-21-PurchaseOrders** and try this skill on your own:

1. Verify that the *Inventory* worksheet is active. If necessary, check the worksheet **Headings View** option so the column letters and row numbers are visible. This will make it easier to understand which row is set to print on every page.

2. Set row **1** to print on every page.

3. Go to Backstage view and preview how the worksheet will look when printed. Verify that the titles from row 1 are included at the top of every page.

4. If you will be moving on to the next skill in this chapter, leave the workbook open to continue working. If not, save the file as directed by your instructor and close it.

Skill 4.22 Printing Selections, Worksheets, and Workbooks

By default, Excel will print the current, active worksheet. You can change the printing options, however, to print only part of a worksheet or the entire workbook at once.

1. Click the **File** tab to open Backstage view.

2. Click **Print**.

3. In the *Settings* section, the first button displays which part of the workbook will print. By default, **Print Active Sheets** is selected. To change the print selection, click the button, and then click one of the other options:

   》 **Print Entire Workbook**—Prints all the sheets in the workbook.

   》 **Print Selection**—Prints only the selected cells in the active worksheet, overriding any print area definitions in the active worksheet.

   》 **Print Selected Table**—Prints the table only (available only if the current selection is within a defined table).

4. If you want to ignore the defined print area, click **Ignore Print Area** at the bottom of the list.

5. Click the **Print** button to print.

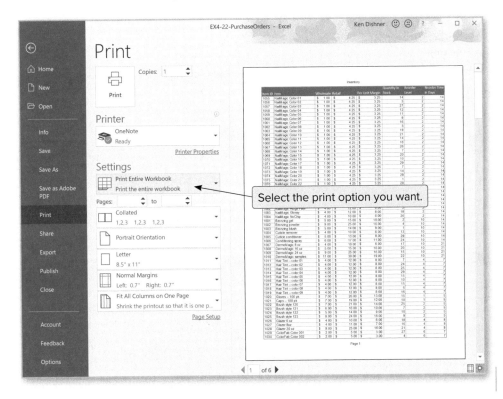

FIGURE EX 4.32

let me try

If you do not have the data file from the previous skill open, open the student data file **EX4-22-PurchaseOrders** and try this skill on your own:

1. Change the print option to print the entire workbook.

2. Verify that all the worksheets in the workbook are included in the print preview.

3. Save the file as directed by your instructor and close it.

key terms

Group
Theme
Theme Colors
Theme Fonts
Theme Effects
Freeze
Normal view
Page Layout view
Page Break Preview view

Header
Footer
Gridlines
Headings
Orientation
Portrait orientation
Landscape orientation
Margins
Scale

concept review

1. If you delete a worksheet, you can undo the action.

    a. true

    b. false

2. To group worksheets that are not next to each other, select the first worksheet and press the _____ key, and then click the other sheet tabs you want included in the group.

    a. Ctrl

    b. ↑ Shift

    c. Alt

    d. None of the above

3. A _____ is a unified color, font, and effects scheme you apply to a workbook.

    a. style

    b. conditional format

    c. theme

    d. cell format

4. To keep column headings as you scroll through a large spreadsheet, you should use the _____ command.

    a. *Freeze First Column*

    b. *Freeze Top Row*

    c. *Split*

    d. *View Headings*

5. When you hide a row or column, the data remain in your workbook. They are no longer displayed on-screen but will be part of the printed workbook.

    a. true

    b. false

6. To display a worksheet in two or four panes, you should _____ the worksheet.

    a. merge

    b. freeze

    c. group

    d. split

7. A _____ is text that appears at the bottom of every page just above the margin.

   a. title

   b. header

   c. footer

   d. sheet tab

8. _____ are the numbers at the left of rows and the letters at the top of columns.

   a. Headings

   b. Gridlines

   c. Headers

   d. Footers

9. If your worksheet is wide, you may want to use portrait orientation where the height of the page is greater than the width.

   a. true

   b. false

10. If you want more or less white space around your worksheet area when printing, you should adjust the _____.

   a. orientation

   b. scaling

   c. margins

   d. page size

Data files for projects can be found by logging into your SIMnet account and going to the *Library* section.

projects

skill review 4.1

In this project, you will work on an attendance log for a 16-week college course. For one section of the course, you will set up the sheet to print as an attendance sign-in sheet. For another section, you will set up the sheet to print as an attendance report for the administration office. This is a long project. Be sure to save often!

Skills needed to complete this project:

- Naming Worksheets (Skill 4.2)
- Changing the Color of Sheet Tabs (Skill 4.3)
- Moving and Copying Worksheets (Skill 4.4)
- Grouping Worksheets (Skill 4.6)
- Modifying Column Widths and Row Heights (Skill 4.9)
- Changing the Worksheet View (Skill 4.14)
- Adding Headers and Footers (Skill 4.15)
- Applying Themes (Skill 4.8)

- Splitting Workbooks (Skill 4.13)
- Inserting and Deleting Rows and Columns (Skill 4.7)
- Hiding and Unhiding Worksheets (Skill 4.12)
- Freezing and Unfreezing Rows and Columns (Skill 4.10)
- Hiding and Unhiding Rows and Columns (Skill 4.11)
- Changing Worksheet Orientation (Skill 4.18)
- Setting Up Margins for Printing (Skill 4.19)
- Scaling Worksheets for Printing (Skill 4.20)
- Showing and Hiding Worksheet Elements (Skill 4.17)
- Printing Selections, Worksheets, and Workbooks (Skill 4.22)
- Printing Titles (Skill 4.21)
- Inserting Page Breaks (Skill 4.16)

1. Open the start file **EX2019-SkillReview-4-1** and resave the file as: `[your initials]EX-SkillReview-4-1`

2. If the workbook opens in Protected View, click the **Enable Editing** button in the Message Bar at the top of the workbook so you can modify the workbook.

3. Rename *Sheet1* and change the color of the sheet tab.

   a. Right-click on the *Sheet1* tab, choose **Rename**, and type: `WF300`

   b. Press `← Enter`.

   c. Right-click the sheet tab again, point to **Tab Color**, and select **Blue, Accent 1** (the fifth color in the first row of theme colors).

4. Make a copy of the *WF300* sheet.

   a. Right-click the sheet tab and select **Move or Copy...** to open the *Move or Copy* dialog.

   b. In the *Before sheet* box, select **Sheet2**.

   c. Check the **Create a copy** check box.

   d. Click **OK**.

5. Name the new sheet **WF301** and change the tab color.

   a. Right-click the new *WF300 (2)* sheet tab, choose **Rename**, and type: `WF301`

   b. Press `← Enter`.

   c. Right-click the sheet tab again, point to **Tab Color**, and select **Green, Accent 6** (the last color in the first row of theme colors).

6. Group sheets *WF300* and *WF301* so you can apply formatting changes to both sheets at once.

   a. Click the **WF300** sheet tab, press and hold `Ctrl`, and click the **WF301** sheet tab. Now any changes made to one of the sheets will be made to both sheets.

   b. Verify that *Group* appears in the title bar, indicating that the selected sheets are grouped.

7. Resize **column A** in both worksheets at once to best fit the data by double-clicking the right border of the column heading.

8. Add a header and footer to both worksheets at once.

   a. Switch to Page Layout view by clicking the **Page Layout** button on the status bar.

   b. Click in the center section of the header.

c. On the *Header & Footer Tools Design* tab, in the *Header & Footer Elements* group, click the **File Name** button. The code **&[File]** will be entered in the center section of the header. Once you click somewhere else, this will display the name of your file.

d. Click in the right section of the header and type your own name.

e. On the *Header & Footer Tools Design* tab, in the *Navigation* group, click the **Go to Footer** button.

f. Click in the center section of the footer.

g. On the *Header & Footer Tools Design* tab, in the *Header & Footer Elements* group, click the **Sheet Name** button. The code **&[Tab]** will be entered. Once you click somewhere else, this will display the name of the sheet.

h. Click in the right section of the footer.

i. On the *Header & Footer Tools Design* tab, in the *Header & Footer Elements* group, click the **Current Date** button. Once you click somewhere else, this will display the current date.

j. Click in any cell of the worksheet and click the **Normal** button on the status bar.

9. Ungroup the sheets by clicking **Sheet2**. Verify that the same formatting was applied to both sheets and that they are now ungrouped.

10. Apply the **Gallery** theme to the workbook.

   a. On the *Page Layout* tab, in the *Themes* group, click the **Themes** button to display the *Themes* gallery.

   b. Notice that as you hover the mouse pointer over each option in the *Themes* gallery, Excel updates the worksheet to display a live preview of how the theme would affect the worksheet.

   c. Click the **Gallery** option.

11. Select the **WF300** sheet. It can be difficult to work with such a wide worksheet. Scroll to the right to see the end of the semester, and you can no longer see the student names. Split the screen into two views of different parts of this worksheet.

   a. Click cell **D1**. On the *View* tab, in the *Window* group, click the **Split** button. Now you can scroll each pane separately, but it is all still the same worksheet. You can drag the split bar to the right or left as needed.

   b. Scroll to show the student names and the last few weeks of the semester on your screen.

   c. Click the **Split** button again to return to normal.

12. Insert a new row to add a new student to the list.

   a. Right-click on the row heading for row number **9** and select **Insert**.

   b. Click the **Insert Options** button that appears immediately below where you right-clicked, and select **Format Same As Below**.

   c. Enter the new student name: **Abrams, Maria**

   d. Enter her student ID #: **1350417**

13. Select the **WF301** sheet. Because this sheet was copied from the WF300 class worksheet, the student names and ID numbers are not those of the students in WF301 class. Copy the student data from *Sheet2*, and then hide *Sheet2* when it is no longer needed.

   a. On sheet *WF301*, select cells **A9:B29**. Press **Delete** to delete the content.

   b. Go to *Sheet2* and copy the student names and ID numbers from cells **A2:B20**.

c. Paste the copied names and ID numbers to cell **A9** in the *WF301* sheet.

d. Hide *Sheet2* by right-clicking on the sheet name and selecting **Hide**.

14. Mary Wahl has decided to drop the class. Remove her from the WF301 class roster.

a. On worksheet *WF301*, delete the entire row for Mary by right-clicking on the row heading for row number **25** and selecting **Delete**.

15. Use the *Freeze Panes* option to keep rows 1:8 and columns A:B visible at all times.

a. Verify that the *WF301* sheet is selected, and click cell **C9**.

b. On the *View* tab, in the *Window* group, click the **Freeze Panes** button, then click the **Freeze Panes** option.

c. Verify that you selected the correct point at which to freeze panes. Scroll down and to the right. Are rows 1:8 and columns A:B visible regardless where you scroll?

16. There is an extra blank worksheet in the workbook. Right-click **Sheet3** and select **Delete**.

Modify sheet *WF301* to print as an attendance sign-in sheet.

17. First, hide the student ID numbers by right-clicking on the **column B** heading and selecting **Hide**.

18. Set the page layout options.

a. On the *Page Layout* tab, in the *Page Setup* group, click the **Orientation** button, and select **Landscape**.

b. On the *Page Layout* tab, in the *Page Setup* group, click the **Margins** button, and select **Narrow**.

c. On the *Page Layout* tab, in the *Scale to Fit* group, expand the **Width** list and select **1 page**, and expand the **Height** list and select **1 page**.

d. On the *Page Layout* tab, in the *Sheet Options* group, click the **Print** check box under **Gridlines**.

19. Print only the part of the worksheet to use as the attendance sign-in sheet.

a. Select the appropriate cells to print as an attendance sign-in by selecting cells **A1:C26**.

b. Click the **File** tab to open Backstage view, and then click **Print** to display the *Print* page.

c. Under *Settings*, click the **Print Active Sheets** button to expand the options, and select **Print Selection**.

d. If your instructor has directed you to print the attendance sign-in list, click the **Print** button.

e. Click the **Back** arrow to exit Backstage view.

At the end of the semester you will need to print all the attendance records to turn in to the administration office. Let's set this up for the *WF300* class worksheet.

20. Select the **WF300** worksheet, and hide the attendance sign-in column by right-clicking the **column C** heading and selecting **Hide**.

21. Modify the worksheet so column A and rows 1 through 8 will print on every page.

a. On the *Page Layout* tab, in the *Page Setup* group, click the **Print Titles** button.

b. Click in the **Rows to repeat at top** box, and then click and drag with the mouse to select rows **1:8**. When you release the mouse button, you should see $1:$8 in the box.

c. Click in the **Columns to repeat at left** box, and then click with the mouse to select column **A**. When you release the mouse button, you should see $A:$A in the box.

d. Click **OK**.

22. Preview how the worksheet will look when printed and make adjustments from the *Print* page to keep the report to four or fewer pages.

a. Click the **File** tab to open Backstage view, and then click **Print**.

b. If necessary, click the **Print Selection** under *Settings* and select **Print Active Sheets**. Click the **Show Print Preview** button.

c. Note that the current settings will cause the worksheet to print on five pages.

d. Under *Settings*, click the **Portrait Orientation** button and switch to **Landscape Orientation** instead.

e. Under *Settings*, click the **Normal Margins** button, and select **Custom Margins...** to set your own margins.

f. In the *Page Setup* dialog, on the *Margins* tab, change the **Top**, **Bottom**, **Left**, and **Right** values to **0.5 inches**. Click **OK**.

g. Under *Settings*, click the **No Scaling** button, and select **Fit All Rows on One Page**.

h. Click the **Back** arrow to exit Backstage.

23. Modify the worksheet page breaks so weeks 1-8 print on the first page and weeks 9-16 print on the second page.

a. If necessary, scroll to the right so columns T:V are visible. Note that the current page break occurs between columns U and V (after week 9).

b. Click cell **T1**.

c. On the *Page Layout* tab, in the *Page Setup* group, click the **Breaks** button, and select **Insert Page Break**. This inserts a page break to the left of the selected cell (after week 8).

d. Click the **File** tab to open Backstage view, and then click **Print** to preview how the change will affect the printed pages.

e. If your instructor has directed you to print the worksheet, click the **Print** button.

f. Click the **Back** arrow to exit Backstage view.

24. Save and close the workbook.

skill review 4.2

In this project, you will be working with a workbook designed to plan employees' or volunteers' work schedules.

Skills needed to complete this project:

- Naming Worksheets (Skill 4.2)
- Changing the Color of Sheet Tabs (Skill 4.3)
- Deleting Worksheets (Skill 4.5)
- Applying Themes (Skill 4.8)
- Grouping Worksheets (Skill 4.6)
- Modifying Column Widths and Row Heights (Skill 4.9)
- Splitting Workbooks (Skill 4.13)

- Freezing and Unfreezing Rows and Columns (Skill 4.10)
- Moving and Copying Worksheets (Skill 4.4)
- Hiding and Unhiding Rows and Columns (Skill 4.11)
- Showing and Hiding Worksheet Elements (Skill 4.17)
- Changing the Worksheet View (Skill 4.14)
- Adding Headers and Footers (Skill 4.15)
- Changing Worksheet Orientation (Skill 4.18)
- Setting Up Margins for Printing (Skill 4.19)
- Scaling Worksheets for Printing (Skill 4.20)
- Inserting Page Breaks (Skill 4.16)
- Printing Titles (Skill 4.21)
- Printing Selections, Worksheets, and Workbooks (Skill 4.22)

1. Open the start file **EX2019-SkillReview-4-2** and resave the file as: `[your initials]EX-SkillReview-4-2`

2. If the workbook opens in Protected View, click the **Enable Editing** button in the Message Bar at the top of the workbook so you can modify the workbook.

3. Look at the various worksheets. The monthly schedule worksheets need to be named and color coded.

   a. Double-click the tab for **Sheet 1**, type **January** and press `← Enter`.

   b. Right-click the tab, point to **Tab Color**, and select **Blue, Accent 5** (the second color from the right in the top row of theme colors).

   c. Double-click the tab for **Sheet 2**, type **February** and press `← Enter`.

   d. Right-click the tab, point to **Tab Color**, and select **Orange, Accent 2** (the fifth color from the right in the top row of theme colors).

   e. Double-click the tab for **Sheet 3**, type **March** and press `← Enter`.

   f. Right-click the tab, point to **Tab Color**, and select **Gold, Accent 4** (the third color from the right in the top row of theme colors).

4. The *Sheet 4* worksheet is unnecessary. Delete it.

   a. Click the **Sheet 4** tab.

   b. On the *Home* tab, in the *Cells* group, click the **Delete** button arrow and select **Delete Sheet**.

   c. Click the **Delete** button when prompted.

5. Apply a new theme to the workbook.

   a. On the *Page Layout* tab, in the *Themes* group, click the **Themes** button. Slide the mouse over different themes and notice the preview of the theme appearance on the worksheet.

   b. Choose the **Ion** theme.

6. The monthly schedule sheets all need formatting. Group them and then format them all at once.

   a. Click the **January** sheet tab, hold down `↑ Shift`, click the **March** sheet tab, and then release `↑ Shift`. Notice the three sheet tabs' appearance has changed to indicate that the three are selected. The *Regular Schedule* tab is not selected.

   b. Verify that the title bar displays *Group*. Any changes you make to the current sheet will be made to all three of the selected sheets, so be very careful.

excel 365   chapter 4 Formatting Worksheets and Managing the Workbook

7. Adjust column widths and row heights to fit the contents and to make the worksheet more readable.

    a. Look in column **A**. If you see ########## it means that the cell content is too wide for the column. Double-click the right column border to autofit the column to the data.

    b. Select all the time columns (**B:U**). Locate the columns that are too narrow to display both the *From* time and the *To* time. Double-click the right column border to best fit the column width to the content. All the selected columns will size to match.

    c. Select all the rows (**5:35**).

    d. On the *Home* tab, in the *Cells* group click the **Format** button, and select **Row Height**. In the *Row Height* dialog, change the height value to **20** to make each row a little roomier.

    e. Click **OK**.

8. Ungroup the sheets by clicking the **Regular Schedule** sheet.

    a. Look at the *January*, *February*, and *March* sheets; they should all have been formatted.

    b. Verify that the sheets are now ungrouped.

9. Select just the **Regular Schedule** sheet. It is hard to work with such a wide worksheet. Scroll to the right to see the night shift and you can no longer see the dates. Split the screen into two views of different parts of this worksheet.

    a. Click cell **G1**. On the *View* tab, in the *Window* group, click the **Split** button. Now you can scroll each pane separately, but it is all still the same worksheet. You can drag the split bar to the right or left as needed.

    b. Scroll to show the morning and night shifts on your screen.

    c. Click the **Split** button again to return to normal.

10. Another way to deal with large worksheets is to freeze panes.

    a. Select any one of the month worksheets.

    b. Select cell **B5**. On the *View* tab, in the *Window* group, click **Freeze Panes**, and select **Freeze Panes**.

    c. Now you can scroll up or down and everything above and to the left of B5 remains visibly frozen on the screen.

    d. Freeze panes must be set on each of the month sheets separately. Grouping does not work for freeze panes. Repeat the freeze panes process for each of the month worksheets.

11. Drag the sheet tab for **Regular Schedule** before the sheet tab for **January** so that *Regular Schedule* is the first worksheet in the workbook.

12. Look closely at the *Regular Schedule* sheet. There are two row numbers missing.

    a. Select the rows before and after the missing rows. Select the entire rows by dragging over the row heading numbers at the far left.

    b. With both rows selected, right-click on the selection, and select **Unhide** to reveal the rows for Tuesdays and Wednesdays.

13. Ensure that the worksheet gridlines will print with the worksheet.

    a. On the *Page Layout* tab, in the *Sheet Options* group, click the **Print** check box under *Gridlines*.

    b. Repeat this process for the *January*, *February*, and *March* worksheets. (If you group the sheets first, be sure to ungroup them when you are finished.)

14. Prepare to print your worksheets by adding headers and footers. You will need to use the *Page Setup* dialog instead of Page Layout view because your worksheets have *Freeze Panes* applied.

  a. Group all the worksheets to save time. This way the headers and footers may be added to all the sheets at once. Verify that all the sheets are selected.

  b. On the *Page Layout* tab, in the *Page Setup* group, click the **Page Setup dialog launcher** button.

  c. In the *Page Setup* dialog, click the **Header/Footer** tab.

  d. Click the **Custom Header...** button.

  e. Click in the **Center section** and then click the **Insert File Name** button.

  f. Click **OK**.

  g. Click the **Custom Footer...** button.

  h. Click in the **Center section** and then click the **Insert Sheet Name** button.

  i. Click **OK**.

  j. Click **OK** again to close the *Page Setup* dialog.

  k. Ungroup the sheets. Right-click on any sheet tab and choose **Ungroup Sheets**.

15. Set up printing options for the *Regular Schedule* sheet.

  a. Select the **Regular Schedule** sheet. Click the **File** tab, and then click **Print**.

  b. Scroll down to see all the pages for your worksheet. Scroll back up to the first page.

  c. Click the **Portrait Orientation** button and select **Landscape**.

  d. Click the **Normal Margins** button and select **Narrow**.

  e. Click the **No Scaling** button, and select **Fit Sheet on One Page**.

16. The monthly schedules would be easier to read if the morning, afternoon, and night shifts each printed on a separate page in a reasonably large font size.

  a. Click the **Back** arrow to return to the worksheet.

  b. Group sheets **January:March**.

  c. On the *Page Layout* tab, in the *Page Setup* group, click the **Orientation** button, and select **Landscape**.

  d. On the *Page Layout* tab, in the *Page Setup* group, click the **Margins** button, and select **Narrow**.

  e. Review the current page break. Switch to Page Break Preview view if you want by clicking the **Page Break Preview** button at the lower right corner of the status bar.

  f. Notice that the schedule just barely requires two pages vertically. On the *Page Layout* tab, in the *Scale to Fit* group, click the **Height** box arrow and select **1 Page**.

  g. Click cell **I1**. On the *Page Layout* tab, in the *Page Setup* group, click the **Breaks** button. Select **Insert Page Break**. (Note that you cannot drag the page break lines when the worksheets are grouped. You must use the Ribbon method to insert manual page breaks.)

  h. Click in cell **N1**. On the *Page Layout* tab, in the *Page Setup* group, click the **Breaks** button. Select **Insert Page Break**.

  i. Click the **Normal** button to return to Normal view.

17. The days will show only on the first sheet, so the second and third sheets will make no sense. Set the worksheets so column A will print on every page. You must ungroup the sheets first.

   a. Click the **Regular Schedule** sheet to ungroup the sheets, and then click the **January** sheet tab again.

   b. On the *Page Layout* tab, in the *Page Setup* group, click **Print Titles** button.

   c. In the *Columns to repeat at left* box enter $A:$A or click in the box and then click anywhere in column **A**.

   d. Click **OK** in the *Page Setup* dialog.

   e. Repeat this process with the *February* and *March* worksheets.

18. Preview how the entire workbook will print. Be sure to verify that column A will print at the left side of the *January*, *February*, and *March* worksheets.

   a. Click the **File** tab to open Backstage view.

   b. Click **Print**.

   c. Click the **Print Active Sheets** button and select **Print Entire Workbook**.

   d. Use the **Next Page** button below the print preview to review how every printed page will look. There should be 10 pages. Note the worksheet name in the footer area at the bottom of each page.

19. Save and close the workbook.

challenge yourself 4.3

In this project, you will be working with a workbook used to analyze loan payments.

Skills needed to complete this project:

- Naming Worksheets (Skill 4.2)
- Applying Themes (Skill 4.8)
- Changing the Color of Sheet Tabs (Skill 4.3)
- Changing the Worksheet View (Skill 4.14)
- Adding Headers and Footers (Skill 4.15)
- Freezing and Unfreezing Rows and Columns (Skill 4.10)
- Moving and Copying Worksheets (Skill 4.4)
- Inserting and Deleting Rows and Columns (Skill 4.7)
- Grouping Worksheets (Skill 4.6)
- Modifying Column Widths and Row Heights (Skill 4.9)
- Hiding and Unhiding Rows and Columns (Skill 4.11)
- Showing and Hiding Worksheet Elements (Skill 4.17)
- Hiding and Unhiding Worksheets (Skill 4.12)
- Deleting Worksheets (Skill 4.5)
- Changing Worksheet Orientation (Skill 4.18)
- Printing Titles (Skill 4.21)
- Scaling Worksheets for Printing (Skill 4.20)
- Printing Selections, Worksheets, and Workbooks (Skill 4.22)

1. Open the start file **EX2019-ChallengeYourself-4-3** and resave the file as: `[your initials]EX-ChallengeYourself-4-3`

2. If the workbook opens in Protected View, click the **Enable Editing** button in the Message Bar at the top of the workbook so you can modify the workbook.

3. Change the name of *Sheet1* to: `NewHybrid`

4. Apply the **Retrospect** theme.

5. Change the *NewHybrid* sheet tab color to **Orange, Accent 1** (the fifth color from the left in the top row of theme colors).

6. Add header and footer information to the *NewHybrid* worksheet.

   a. Set the center header section to display the sheet name.

   b. Add the page number to the left footer section.

   c. Set the right footer section to display the current date.

7. Freeze panes so rows **1:8** and columns **A:B** remain in place when you scroll through the worksheets.

8. Make a copy of the *NewHybrid* sheet, placing before the *Working* worksheet.

9. Change the name of the new sheet to: `Option2`

10. Change the *Option2* sheet tab color to **Green, Accent 6** (the first color from the right in the top row of theme colors).

11. Change the values in the *Option2* worksheet.

    a. Change the amount borrowed (cell **B3**) to: **14,000**

    b. Change the APR (cell **B5**) to: **1.9%**

12. Delete any extra rows at the bottom of the worksheet where the payment due is 0 (row **41**).

13. Group the *NewHybrid* and *Option2* worksheets. Make the following changes to both sheets at once.

    a. Change the width of the *Payment Date* column (column **C**) to exactly **19**.

    b. Delete the extra column (column **H**).

    c. Unhide column **G**.

    d. Hide the gridlines so they do not appear onscreen.

    e. Ungroup the worksheets.

14. Hide the *Working* worksheet.

15. Delete the *Sheet2* worksheet.

16. Change the page orientation for the *NewHybrid* sheet to **Landscape**.

17. Modify the *NewHybrid* sheet so row **8** will repeat at the top of every printed page.

18. Scale the *Option2* sheet so all columns will fit on one page and all rows will fit on one page.

19. Print preview the entire workbook.

20. Save and close the workbook.

challenge yourself 4.4

In this project, you will be working with data about automobile emissions and fuel economy. These green car data were downloaded from the website fueleconomy.gov. The SmartWay scores range from 0 to 10, where 10 is best. The vehicles with the best scores

excel 365 chapter 4 Formatting Worksheets and Managing the Workbook

on both air pollution and greenhouse gas receive the Elite designation. More information about the SmartWay program can be found at http://www3.epa.gov/greenvehicles/you/smartway.htm.

Skills needed to complete this project:

- Naming Worksheets (Skill 4.2)
- Applying Themes (Skill 4.8)
- Changing the Color of Sheet Tabs (Skill 4.3)
- Changing the Worksheet View (Skill 4.14)
- Adding Headers and Footers (Skill 4.15)
- Moving and Copying Worksheets (Skill 4.4)
- Inserting and Deleting Rows and Columns (Skill 4.7)
- Grouping Worksheets (Skill 4.6)
- Modifying Column Widths and Row Heights (Skill 4.9)
- Hiding and Unhiding Rows and Columns (Skill 4.11)
- Showing and Hiding Worksheet Elements (Skill 4.17)
- Setting Up Margins for Printing (Skill 4.19)
- Changing Worksheet Orientation (Skill 4.18)
- Scaling Worksheets for Printing (Skill 4.20)
- Printing Titles (Skill 4.21)
- Freezing and Unfreezing Rows and Columns (Skill 4.10)
- Inserting Page Breaks (Skill 4.16)
- Printing Selections, Worksheets, and Workbooks (Skill 4.22)

1. Open the start file **EX2019-ChallengeYourself-4-4** and resave the file as: `[your initials]EX-ChallengeYourself-4-4`

2. If the workbook opens in Protected View, click the **Enable Editing** button in the Message Bar at the top of the workbook so you can modify the workbook.

3. Rename the *all_alpha_10* worksheet: `Raw Data`

4. Apply the **Facet** workbook theme.

5. Color the *Raw Data* worksheet tab **Green, Accent 1** (the sixth color from the right in the first row of theme colors).

6. Review the worksheet header and footer.

   a. Delete the text in the left footer section and replace it with: `Source: fueleconomy.gov`

   b. Add the sheet name to the footer center section. *Hint*: Do not type the sheet name in the footer. Insert a code so Excel will display the name of the current worksheet.

7. Copy the *Raw Data* worksheet. Place the new worksheet at the end of the workbook.

8. Rename the new worksheet: `Nissan`

9. Color the *Nissan* worksheet tab **Dark Green, Accent 2** (the fifth color from the right in the first row of theme colors).

10. In the *Nissan* worksheet, delete rows **2:233** and then delete rows **22:92** so only the 20 Nissan models remain.

11. Group the *Raw Data* and *Nissan* worksheets.

    a. Autofit column **K** to best fit the data.

    b. Set the column width for columns **L:Q** to: **6**

    c. Set the row height for row **1** to: **70**

    d. Hide the **Underhood ID** and **Stnd Description** columns.

    e. Set the worksheet gridlines to print.

    f. Set **Wide** margins.

    g. Set the worksheet orientation to **Landscape**.

    h. Scale the worksheets so all columns will print on one page.

    i. Ungroup the sheets.

12. Set the worksheet options so row **1** will print on every page. You will need to do this individually for each worksheet.

13. Review the page breaks in the *Raw Data* worksheet. Move the page break between pages 2 and 3 to after row **53** so the fourth page begins with the first Ford model.

14. Apply **Freeze Panes** to the *Raw Data* worksheet so the first row is always visible as you scroll down the worksheet.

15. Preview how the entire workbook will print.

16. Save and close the workbook.

on your own 4.5

In this project you will work with data from the United States Census Bureau. The data were downloaded from https://www.census.gov/data/tables/time-series/demo/popest/2010s-state-total.html.

Skills needed to complete this project:

- Moving and Copying Worksheets (Skill 4.4)
- Naming Worksheets (Skill 4.2)
- Applying Themes (Skill 4.8)
- Changing the Color of Sheet Tabs (Skill 4.3)
- Inserting and Deleting Rows and Columns (Skill 4.7)
- Modifying Column Widths and Row Heights (Skill 4.9)
- Changing the Worksheet View (Skill 4.14)
- Adding Headers and Footers (Skill 4.15)
- Freezing and Unfreezing Rows and Columns (Skill 4.10)
- Changing Worksheet Orientation (Skill 4.18)
- Setting Up Margins for Printing (Skill 4.19)
- Scaling Worksheets for Printing (Skill 4.20)
- Showing and Hiding Worksheet Elements (Skill 4.17)
- Inserting Page Breaks (Skill 4.16)
- Printing Selections, Worksheets, and Workbooks (Skill 4.22)

1. Open the start file **EX2019-OnYourOwn-4-5** and resave the file as: `[your initials]EX-OnYourOwn-4-5`

2. If the workbook opens in Protected View, click the **Enable Editing** button in the Message Bar at the top of the workbook so you can modify the workbook.

3. The workbook includes one worksheet with census data for regions and individual states. Create one or more copies of the original worksheet and modify the data in each so each worksheet has a unique set of data.

4. Delete any rows you do not want to include in each worksheet. *Hint*: The Note near the bottom of the original worksheet is very long and will print across multiple pages. You may want to delete it or move it to a cell with *Wrap Text* applied.

5. Rename each worksheet.

6. Apply a theme of your choice to the workbook.

7. Apply a color to the tab of each worksheet.

8. Add header and footer elements of your choice to all the worksheets at once. *Hint*: You may want to move the suggested citation from the last rows in the worksheet into the worksheet footer.

9. Add a row at the top of each sheet and enter an appropriate title.

10. Adjust column widths to best fit the data (all worksheets individually).

11. Apply cell styles and cell formatting to make the data easier to read.

12. As appropriate, apply *Freeze Panes* to make it easier to work with each worksheet.

13. Make an attractive readable printout of each worksheet. Each should fit neatly on one page or have logical page breaks and print titles when more than one page is required. Print the worksheets only if directed to do so by your instructor.

   a. Set the worksheets' orientation appropriately.

   b. Set appropriate margins.

   c. Scale the worksheets appropriately.

   d. Add manual page breaks if necessary.

   e. Set at least one of the sheets to print with gridlines and at least one to print without gridlines.

   f. For worksheets that print on more than one page, ensure that the label row will be included on every page.

   g. For one worksheet, adjust the print settings to print a useful selection of just some cells that will fit all on one page.

14. Save and close the workbook.

fix it 4.6

In this project, you will correct errors in a party planning workbook.

Skills needed to complete this project:
- Changing the Worksheet View (Skill 4.14)
- Applying Themes (Skill 4.8)
- Deleting Worksheets (Skill 4.5)
- Adding Headers and Footers (Skill 4.15)
- Showing and Hiding Worksheet Elements (Skill 4.17)
- Naming Worksheets (Skill 4.2)
- Moving and Copying Worksheets (Skill 4.4)
- Modifying Column Widths and Row Heights (Skill 4.9)
- Inserting and Deleting Rows and Columns (Skill 4.7)

- Hiding and Unhiding Rows and Columns (Skill 4.11)
- Changing Worksheet Orientation (Skill 4.18)
- Setting Up Margins for Printing (Skill 4.19)
- Scaling Worksheets for Printing (Skill 4.20)
- Freezing and Unfreezing Rows and Columns (Skill 4.10)
- Printing Titles (Skill 4.21)
- Inserting Page Breaks (Skill 4.16)

1. Open the start file **EX2019-FixIt-4-6** and resave the file as: **[your initials] EX-FixIt-4-6**

2. If the workbook opens in Protected View, click the **Enable Editing** button in the Message Bar at the top of the workbook so you can modify the workbook.

3. The workbook was last saved in Page Break Preview view. Switch it back to **Normal** view.

4. The workbook uses a very unattractive theme. Change the theme to **Office**.

5. The copy of the *Shopping List* worksheet is incomplete. Delete it. Be careful to delete the copy, not the original.

6. Both worksheets should include the sheet name in the header center section.

7. Both worksheets should include the gridlines when printed.

8. Correct the following errors in the *Shopping List* worksheet:

   a. The *Shopping List* worksheet should be first in the workbook.

   b. One of the columns is not wide enough to display the data. Autofit that column.

   c. There is an extra row between the label row and the shopping data. Delete the extra row.

9. Correct the following errors in the *Guest List* worksheet:

   a. The worksheet tab is misspelled. Correct the spelling of *Gest*.

   b. Column **D** should not be visible.

   c. Row **3** is too tall. Autofit the row to fit the content.

   d. Page orientation should be **Portrait**.

   e. Margins should be set to the **Narrow** option.

   f. All columns should fit on one page when printed.

   g. The right footer section should include the page number.

   h. Rows **1:3** should always be visible as you scroll down the worksheet. *Hint*: Select the entire row where you want to apply the *Freeze Panes* command.

   i. Rows **1:3** should also print on every page.

   j. The page break should be between rows **56** and **57** so the guests who have not yet RSVP'd are grouped together on the second page.

   k. If you were working in Page Layout view or Page Break Preview view, be sure to switch back to **Normal** view.

10. Review your work by previewing how each worksheet will print and then save and close the workbook.

Source of screenshots: Microsoft Office 365: Word, Excel, Access, and PowerPoint.

chapter 5

Adding Charts and Analyzing Data

In this chapter, you will learn the following skills:

❯ Create and format charts

❯ Create and format tables

❯ Sort and filter data

❯ Create PivotTables and PivotCharts

❯ Conduct what-if analysis using Goal Seek and data tables

skills

introduction

This chapter introduces data analysis. You will learn to use charts to visualize data; to use tables and PivotTables to quickly sort, filter, and summarize data; and to conduct what-if analyses using data tables and Goal Seek.

Skill 5.1 Inserting a Column Chart or a Bar Chart

Column charts work best with data that are organized into rows and columns like a table. Data point values are transformed into vertical columns, with the values plotted along the vertical (y) axis. Each row in the table is grouped as a data series. Excel uses the column labels as the categories along the horizontal (x) axis.

In the **clustered column chart** shown in Figure EX 5.1, each column represents a single data point. The data points are grouped (clustered) together by category. Each data series is represented by a single color as shown in the legend below the chart.

To insert a column chart:

1. Select the data you want to include in the column chart.
2. On the *Insert* tab, in the *Charts* group, click the **Insert Column or Bar Chart** button.
3. Click the chart type you want to insert the chart into the worksheet.

FIGURE EX 5.1

FIGURE EX 5.2

Bar charts are like column charts turned on their side. The categories are displayed on the vertical axis, and the data point values are plotted along the horizontal axis.

The clustered bar chart in Figure EX 5.3 displays the same data as Figure EX 5.2. Each bar represents a single data point. However, in this bar chart, the sales values are plotted along the horizontal axis, grouped into data series by membership type, and the months are displayed along the vertical axis.

To insert a bar chart:

1. Select the data you want to include in the bar chart.

2. On the *Insert* tab, in the *Charts* group, click the **Insert Column or Bar Chart** button.

3. Click the chart type you want to insert the chart into the worksheet.

FIGURE EX 5.3

If you don't like the way Excel grouped the data series, you can switch them, making the categories the data series and the data series the categories. On the *Chart Tools Design* tab, in the *Data* group, click the **Switch Row/Column** button. Figure EX 5.4 charts the same data as Figure EX 5.3 with the rows and columns switched, so the data points are organized into data series by column instead of by row.

excel 365   chapter 5 Adding Charts and Analyzing Data

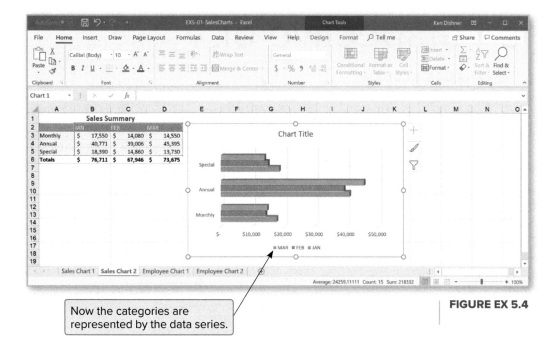

Now the categories are represented by the data series.

FIGURE EX 5.4

tips & tricks

In previous versions of Excel, column charts and bar charts had separate buttons on the *Insert* tab, *Charts* group.

tell me **more**

A **stacked column chart** displays each data series as a single vertical column divided into sections representing each data point. A **stacked bar chart** is similar—combining the data points of each data series into a single horizontal bar. Stacked charts are useful for comparing parts of a whole or showing how parts of a whole change over time.

another **method**

You can also insert a column chart or a bar chart from the *Insert Chart* dialog, *All Charts* tab.

let me **try**

Open the student data file **EX5-01-SalesCharts** and try this skill on your own:

1. If necessary, go to the *Sales Chart 2* worksheet, and select cells **A2:D5**.

2. Insert a **3-D Clustered Bar** chart (the first chart type in the *3-D Bar* section of the *Insert Column or Bar Chart* menu).

3. Switch the rows and columns in the chart, so the data points are grouped into data series by column.

4. If you will be moving on to the next skill in this chapter, leave the workbook open to continue working. If not, save the file as directed by your instructor and close it.

From the Perspective of. . .

Lane Oatey/Getty Images

COLLEGE STUDENT

I use Excel to track my monthly budget. Before I started using charts, the spreadsheets were just numbers. I knew how much money was going out each month, but I didn't really understand how much of my money I was spending on unnecessary expenses. Once I started using charts, it was obvious that I was spending more on lattes than on transportation! I bought a coffee maker, and now I have a little extra cash each month to put away for a rainy day.

Skill 5.2 Inserting a Pie Chart

Pie charts represent data as parts of a whole. They do not have x and y axes like column charts. Instead, each value is a visual "slice" of the pie. Pie charts work best when you want to evaluate values as they relate to a total value—for example, departmental budgets in relation to the entire budget, or each employee's bonus in relation to the entire bonus pool.

In Figure EX 5.5, the total sales for each salesperson is represented by a slice of the pie.

To add a pie chart:

1. Select the data you want to include in the pie chart.
2. On the *Insert* tab, in the *Charts* group, click the **Insert Pie Chart** button.
3. Click the chart type you want to insert the chart into the worksheet.

FIGURE EX 5.5

tips & tricks

In an "exploded" pie chart, each slice is slightly separated from the whole. You can explode a single slice by clicking it and dragging it away from the rest of the slices. Exploding a single slice of data gives it emphasis.

tell me **more**

Doughnut charts are similar to pie charts, but they can display more than one series. Each series is represented by a ring around the doughnut. Each data point in the series is represented by a piece of the ring proportional to the total. Doughnut charts can be confusing and are not commonly used.

another **method**

You can also insert a pie chart from the *Insert Chart* dialog, *All Charts* tab.

let me try

If you do not have the data file from the previous skill open, open the student data file **EX5-02-SalesCharts** and try this skill on your own:

1. If necessary, go to the *Employee Chart 1* worksheet, and select cells **A3:A6** (the row labels) and cells **E3:E6** (the row totals). *Hint*: Remember to press Ctrl to select noncontiguous cells.
2. Insert a **3-D Pie** chart.
3. If you will be moving on to the next skill in this chapter, leave the workbook open to continue working. If not, save the file as directed by your instructor and close it.

Skill 5.3 Inserting a Line Chart

Line charts feature a line connecting each data point—showing the movement of values over time. Line charts work best when data trends over time are important.

The line chart in Figure EX 5.6 shows sales over a three-month period. Each data series represents sales for a specific employee. This type of line chart, called a **line with markers**, includes dots along the line for each data point.

To add a line chart:

1. Select the data you want to include in the line chart. Be sure to include both values and the related cells that represent time segments (dates, calendar quarters, etc.).

2. On the *Insert* tab, in the *Charts* group, click the **Insert Line Chart** button.

3. Click the chart type you want to insert the chart into the worksheet.

4. If Excel does not display the time categories along the x axis, switch the data series and the categories. On the *Chart Tools Design* tab, in the *Data* group, click the **Switch Row/Column** button.

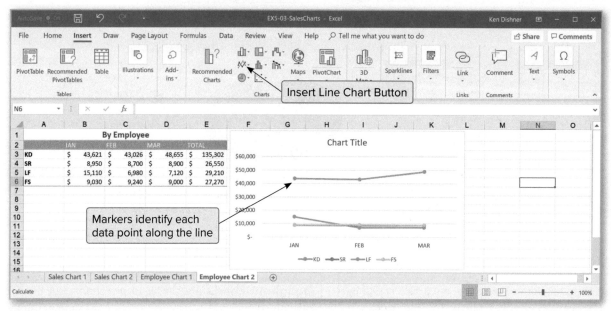

FIGURE EX 5.6

tips & tricks

While line charts are a good choice if the data set has many data points, use a line chart with markers only if there are relatively few data points.

another **method**

You can also insert a line chart from the *Insert Chart* dialog, *All Charts* tab.

let me **try**

If you do not have the data file from the previous skill open, open the student data file **EX5-03-SalesCharts** and try this skill on your own:

1. If necessary, go to the *Employee Chart 2* worksheet, and select cells **A2:D6**.

2. Insert a **Line with Markers** chart (the fourth chart type in the *Insert Line Chart* menu).

3. If necessary, switch the rows and columns in the chart to list the months along the x axis.

4. If you will be moving on to the next skill in this chapter, leave the workbook open to continue working. If not, save the file as directed by your instructor and close it.

Skill 5.4 Resizing and Moving Charts

When you first create a chart, Excel places the chart in the middle of the worksheet. Often, you will need to resize and move the chart so it doesn't cover the worksheet data.

With the chart selected, resize the chart using the resize handles located at the four corners and the middle of each side of the chart area. Click and drag toward the center of the chart to make it smaller or outward to make it larger.

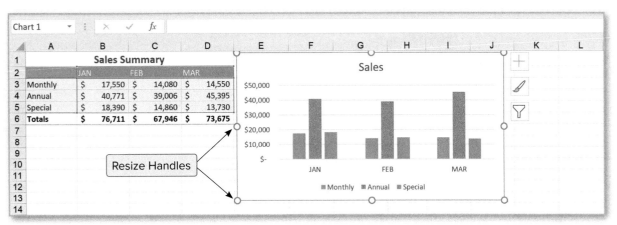

FIGURE EX 5.7

To move a chart to a new position on the worksheet:

1. Select the chart. Be careful not to click in the plot area or you will move just the plot area instead of the entire chart. Your mouse cursor will change to the move cursor.

2. With your left mouse button depressed, drag the chart to the new location on the worksheet, and then release the mouse button to "drop" the chart at the new location.

If your chart is large or complex, you may want the chart to appear on its own worksheet. To move a chart to a new sheet:

1. If necessary, select the chart. If you just created the chart, it will still be selected.

2. On the *Chart Tools Design* tab, in the *Location* group, click the **Move Chart** button.

3. In the *Move Chart* dialog, click the **New sheet** radio button to move the chart to its own worksheet. If you want to specify a name for the new sheet, type it in the *New sheet* box. To move the chart to an existing worksheet, click the **Object in** radio button, and then select the name of the sheet you want to move the chart to.

4. Click **OK**.

FIGURE EX 5.8

When you use the *Move Chart* dialog to move a chart to its own sheet, Excel creates a special type of worksheet called a **chart sheet**. The chart sheet does not include the columns, rows, and cells you are used to seeing in Excel; it contains only the chart object. The new chart sheet automatically changes the zoom level so the entire chart is visible.

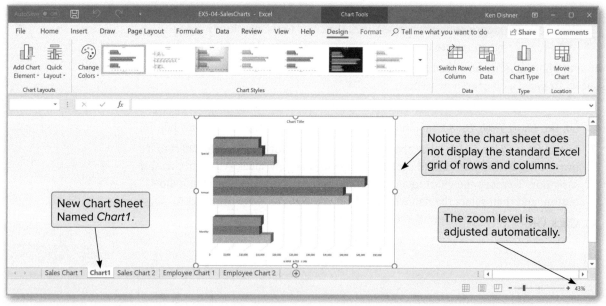

FIGURE EX 5.9

tips & tricks

You cannot resize a chart in a chart sheet.

another **method**

❯ Right-click an empty area of the chart and select **Move Chart...** to open the *Move Chart* dialog.

❯ Use the *Cut*, *Copy*, and *Paste* commands to move a chart from one sheet to another.

let me try

If you do not have the data file from the previous skill open, open the student data file **EX5-04-SalesCharts** and try this skill on your own:

1. If necessary, go to the *Sales Chart 1* worksheet and select the chart.

2. Resize the chart so it is approximately 13 rows tall.

3. Move the chart to the empty area of the worksheet to the right of the data.

4. Go to the *Sales Chart 2* worksheet and move the chart to a new worksheet.

5. If you will be moving on to the next skill in this chapter, leave the workbook open to continue working. If not, save the file as directed by your instructor and close it.

Skill 5.5 Applying Quick Layouts to Charts

When you insert a chart, Excel displays the *Chart Tools Design* contextual tab. From this tab, you can change the chart layout. **Quick Layouts** apply combinations of data labels, titles, and data tables.

Data labels—Display data values for each data marker.

Data table—Displays a table of the data point values below the chart.

FIGURE EX 5.10

To apply a Quick Layout to a chart:

1. Select the chart.

2. On the *Chart Tools Design* tab, in the *Chart Layouts* group, click the **Quick Layout** button.

3. Notice that as you move over each Quick Layout option, Excel shows a preview of the layout. Click the layout you want to apply it to the chart.

let me try

If you do not have the data file from the previous skill open, open the student data file **EX5-05-SalesCharts** and try this skill on your own:

1. Go to the *Sales Chart 1* worksheet and select the chart.

2. Apply the **Layout 2** Quick Layout to the chart.

3. If you will be moving on to the next skill in this chapter, leave the workbook open to continue working. If not, save the file as directed by your instructor and close it.

Skill 5.6 Showing and Hiding Chart Elements

If there is not a Quick Layout with exactly the look you want, you can hide or show chart elements individually. Showing and hiding chart elements such as the chart title, axes, and gridlines can make a chart easier to read.

To hide or show chart elements:

1. Click any empty area of the chart area to select the chart.
2. Click the **Chart Elements** button that appears near the upper right corner of the chart.
3. Click the check boxes to show or hide chart elements.
4. To select a specific option for a chart element, click the arrow that appears at the right side of the element name, and then click an option.

FIGURE EX 5.11

another **method**

You can hide or show chart elements and control their appearance and position from the *Chart Tools Design* tab, *Chart Layouts* group. Click the **Add Chart Elements** button, point to the chart element you want, and click an option.

let me try

If you do not have the data file from the previous skill open, open the student data file **EX5-06-SalesCharts** and try this skill on your own:

1. If necessary, select the chart on the *Chart1* worksheet.
2. Hide the chart title.
3. Hide the primary horizontal axis.
4. Display the data table, including the legend keys.
5. Display the data labels.
6. If you will be moving on to the next skill in this chapter, leave the workbook open to continue working. If not, save the file as directed by your instructor and close it.

Skill 5.7 Applying Quick Styles and Colors to Charts

You can change the style of a chart using the predefined Quick Styles. **Quick Styles** apply combinations of fonts, line styles, fills, and shape effects. You can also change the color scheme from a preset list of colors that coordinate with the workbook theme.

To change the chart style:

1. Select the chart.
2. On the *Chart Tools Design* tab, in the *Chart Styles* group, click the style you want to use, or click the **More** button to see all of the Quick Styles available.
3. To change the color scheme, on the *Chart Tools Design* tab, in the *Chart Styles* group, click the **Change Colors** button and select the color scheme you want.

FIGURE EX 5.12

another **method**

Quick Styles and color schemes are also available from the *Chart Styles* button that appears near the upper right corner of the chart when it is selected.

let me **try**

If you do not have the data file from the previous skill open, open the student data file **EX5-07-SalesCharts** and try this skill on your own:

1. If necessary, select the chart on the *Sales Chart 1* worksheet.
2. Apply the **Style 3** Quick Style.
3. Apply the **Color 3** color scheme from the *Colorful* section.
4. If you will be moving on to the next skill in this chapter, leave the workbook open to continue working. If not, save the file as directed by your instructor and close it.

Skill 5.8 Changing the Chart Type

If you find that your initial chart selection wasn't quite right, you can change the chart type from the *Change Chart Type* dialog without having to delete and re-create the chart.

To change the chart type:

1. On the *Chart Tools Design* tab, in the *Type* group, click the **Change Chart Type** button.

Change Chart Type Button

FIGURE EX 5.13

2. In the *Change Chart Type* dialog, click a chart type category to display that category in the right pane.

3. Click one of the chart types along the top of the right pane to see previews of the options available, and then click the chart type you want.

4. Click **OK**.

The chart type you select affects the story your chart tells. A **clustered column chart** would show a separate column for sales of each membership type per month, but it doesn't depict the total sales for all memberships. By changing the chart type to a **stacked column chart** as shown in the preview in Figure EX 5.14, each column will represent the total sales for the month, and individual sales for each membership type are represented by a piece of that column. Using this chart type makes it easier to compare total sales as well as sales for each individual type of membership.

FIGURE EX 5.14

another **method**

To change the chart type, you can also right-click in the chart area and select **Change Chart Type...**

let me try

If you do not have the data file from the previous skill open, open the student data file **EX5-08-SalesCharts** and try this skill on your own:

1. If necessary, select the chart on the *Sales Chart 1* worksheet.

2. Change the chart type to the first stacked column option.

3. If you will be moving on to the next skill in this chapter, leave the workbook open to continue working. If not, save the file as directed by your instructor and close it.

Skill 5.9 Filtering Chart Data

Excel includes a feature that allows you to hide and show data in a chart without having to modify the chart data source.

To filter chart data:

1. Select the chart.

2. Click the **Chart Filters** button that appears near the upper right corner of the chart.

3. Notice that when you hover the mouse pointer over the chart filter options, the live preview does not take into account the options that are checked or unchecked. The preview shows only what the chart would look like if the highlighted option were the only one checked. All other series or categories are dimmed in the preview. In Figure EX 5.15, the *Annual* series is highlighted, so the chart preview shows the *Annual* series in full color and the other series faded.

4. Click the check boxes to add or remove data series or categories from the chart. Note that the live preview does not update to reflect these changes.

5. Click the **Apply** button to apply the changes.

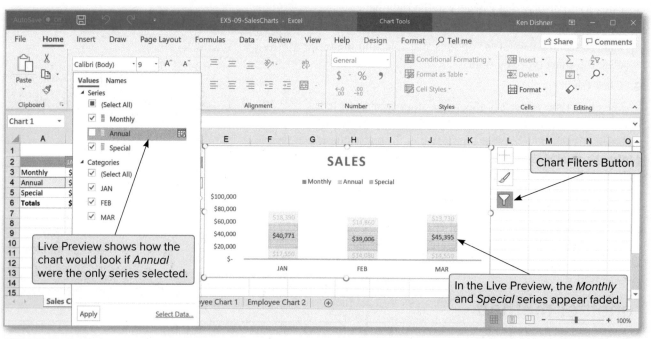

FIGURE EX 5.15

The chart in Figure EX 5.16 shows the chart after the *Annual* series has been hidden. Only the data for the *Monthly* and *Special* series remain. Observe that the chart data still shows the *Annual* row. Filtering the chart affects only the chart display, not the data in the spreadsheet.

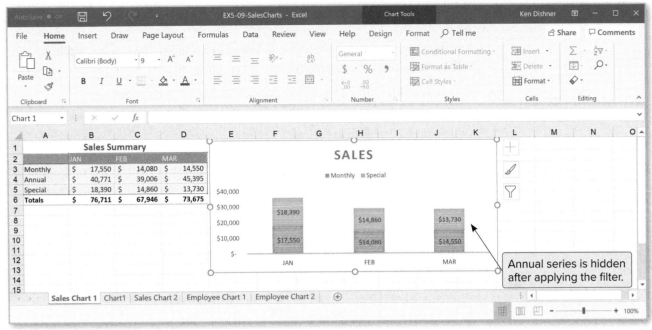

FIGURE EX 5.16

tips & tricks

When a chart is selected, the filter options on the *Data* tab, *Sort & Filter* group are unavailable. If you want to filter the underlying chart data, you must deselect the chart first.

tell me **more**

If you apply a filter to the underlying chart data, the chart will update automatically to reflect the data change.

let me **try**

If you do not have the data file from the previous skill open, open the student data file **EX5-09-SalesCharts** and try this skill on your own:

1. If necessary, select the chart on the *Sales Chart 1* worksheet.
2. Without changing the data source, filter the chart so the **Annual** series is hidden.
3. If you will be moving on to the next skill in this chapter, leave the workbook open to continue working. If not, save the file as directed by your instructor and close it.

Skill 5.10 Inserting Sparklines

Sparklines represent a series of data values as an individual graphic within a single cell. As you update the underlying data series, the Sparklines update immediately.

To add Sparklines to your worksheet using the Quick Analysis tool:

1. Select the data you want to visualize as Sparklines. If you want the Sparklines to appear in empty cells, ensure that there are empty cells to the right of your selection.

2. The Quick Analysis Tool button appears near the lower right corner of the selected range. Click the **Quick Analysis Tool** button, and then click the **Sparklines** tab.

3. Click the button for the Sparkline type you want.

FIGURE EX 5.17

If you do not want Excel to place the Sparklines automatically, or if you are adding Sparklines in a situation where the Quick Analysis tool is not available, use the *Create Sparklines* dialog to specify their location:

1. Select the data range with the data points for the Sparklines.

2. On the *Insert* tab, in the *Sparklines* group, click the button for the type of Sparkline you want to insert: **Line**, **Column**, or **Win/Loss**.

3. The *Create Sparklines* dialog opens with the selected range added to the *Data Range* box.

4. In the *Location Range* box, enter the cell range where you want the Sparklines to appear. You can type the cell range or click and drag in the worksheet to select the cells.

5. Click **OK** to insert the Sparklines.

FIGURE EX 5.18

When cells containing Sparklines are selected, the *Sparkline Tools Design* contextual tab becomes active. From this tab you can customize the look of the Sparklines including emphasizing high or low points, changing the type of Sparkline used, and changing colors.

To remove Sparklines, you must select the cells containing the Sparklines, and then on the *Sparkline Tools Design* tab, in the *Group* group, click the **Clear** button.

FIGURE EX 5.19

tips & tricks

Sparklines are not actually chart objects—they are charts in the background of the cells. You can add text and other data to the cells that contain Sparklines. You can also extend the Sparklines over multiple cells using the *Merge & Center* commands.

let me try

If you do not have the data file from the previous skill open, open the student data file **EX5-10-SalesCharts** and try this skill on your own:

1. Go to the *Sales Chart 2* worksheet and select cells **B3:D5** as the data range for the Sparklines.

2. Insert column Sparklines in cells **E3:E5**.

3. Go to the *Sales Chart 3* worksheet and clear the Sparklines.

4. Save the file as directed by your instructor and close it.

skill 5.10   Inserting Sparklines

Skill 5.11 Converting Data into Tables

In Excel, you can define a series of adjacent cells as a **table**. When you define data as a table, Excel provides a robust tool set for formatting and analyzing the data. In the table, the header row automatically includes filtering and sorting. When you add data to the right of the table, Excel includes the new column in the table automatically.

To define data as a table:

1. Click any cell in the data range. You do not need to select the entire range.
2. On the *Home* tab, in the *Styles* group, click the **Format as Table** button to display the *Table Styles* gallery.
3. Click the style you want to use for your table.

FIGURE EX 5.20

FIGURE EX 5.21

Check if data range includes a header row.

4. Excel will automatically populate the *Format As Table* dialog with the entire data range. If the data range is not correct, you can manually enter the cell range in the dialog.
5. Be sure to check the **My table has headers** check box if appropriate.
6. Click **OK** to create the table.

FIGURE EX 5.22

tips & tricks

You cannot create a table in a shared workbook. If your workbook contains a table, you will need to convert the table back to a normal cell range before sharing the workbook.

tell me more

One of the most useful features of tables is the ability to reference table column names in formulas. When you enter a formula in a table, you can reference column names by enclosing the column header text in brackets. For example, to add a new column to the table in Figure EX 5.22 to calculate the cost of each inventory record, you would enter the formula [Wholesale]*[Quantity in Stock] in the first row of the new column. Excel will copy the formula to the remaining cells in the table column automatically.

another method

To insert a table without specifying the table formatting:

1. Select any cell in the data range for the table.
2. On the *Insert* tab, in the *Tables* group, click the **Table** button.
3. Excel will populate the *Insert Table* dialog automatically with the appropriate data range.
4. Be sure to check the **My table has headers** check box if appropriate.
5. Click **OK** to create the table. Excel will format the table with the most recent table style used.

let me try

Open the student data file **EX5-11-PurchaseOrders** and try this skill on your own:

1. On the *Inventory* worksheet, click any cell in the range **A1:F18**.
2. Convert the cell range to a table using table style **Green, Table Style Light 14**. The data range contains a header row.
3. If you will be moving on to the next skill in this chapter, leave the workbook open to continue working. If not, save the file as directed by your instructor and close it.

Skill 5.12 Applying Quick Styles to Tables

When you are working with a table, use the *Table Tools Design* tab to apply formatting. This contextual tab is available when you select any cell in the table. From the *Table Styles* gallery, you can select a **Quick Style** to apply a combination of font colors, fill colors, and banding options. **Banding** applies a fill color to alternating rows or columns, making the table easier to read.

To apply a table Quick Style:

1. Click anywhere in the table.

2. On the *Table Tools Design* tab, in the *Table Styles* group, click the **Quick Styles** button to display the full *Table Styles* gallery. Depending on the width of your Excel window, you may see part of the *Quick Styles* gallery displayed in the Ribbon. In this case, click the **More** button ⟱ to expand the entire gallery.

3. Click a style to apply it to the table.

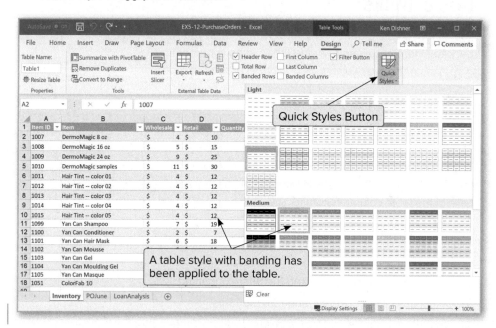

FIGURE EX 5.23

tips & tricks

If your table includes a header row like the one in Figure EX 5.23, select a style that includes formatting for the first row to help it stand out from the rest of the table.

tell me **more**

Use the check boxes in the *Table Style Options* group to customize the table formatting by adding or removing banding for rows or columns.

let me **try**

If you do not have the data file from the previous skill open, open the student data file **EX5-12-PurchaseOrders** and try this skill on your own:

1. On the *Inventory* worksheet, if necessary, click any cell in the table.

2. Apply the **Blue, Table Style Medium 2** Quick Style.

3. If you will be moving on to the next skill in this chapter, leave the workbook open to continue working. If not, save the file as directed by your instructor and close it.

Skill 5.13 Adding Total Rows to Tables

If you have data formatted as a table, you can add a **Total row** to quickly calculate an aggregate function such as the sum, average, minimum, or maximum of all the values in the column.

To add a Total row to a table:

1. On the *Table Tools Design* tab, in the *Table Style Options* group, click the **Total Row** check box.

2. In the Total row at the bottom of the table, click the cell where you want to add the calculation.

3. Click the arrow, and select a function. Excel inserts the formula for you.

FIGURE EX 5.24

tips & tricks

The *Count* option can be useful when filtering records in a table. Count tells you how many records are included in the filtered table. The Count option from the Total row uses the COUNTA function.

tell me **more**

When you enable the Total row, the first cell in the Total row displays the word "Total" automatically and the last cell in the Total row calculates the sum of the values in that column (if the column contains numbers).

another **method**

To add the Total row to the table, right-click any cell in the table, point to **Table**, and click **Total Row**.

let me **try**

If you do not have the data file from the previous skill open, open the student data file **EX5-13-PurchaseOrders** and try this skill on your own:

1. On the *Inventory* worksheet, if necessary, click any cell in the table.

2. Add a Total row to the table.

3. In the Total row, display the **average** value for the **Wholesale** column.

4. In the Total row, display the **maximum** value for the **Quantity in Stock** column.

5. If you will be moving on to the next skill in this chapter, leave the workbook open to continue working. If not, save the file as directed by your instructor and close it.

Skill 5.14 Removing Duplicate Rows from Tables

If you have a large table, it may be difficult to identify rows with duplicate data. Excel includes a tool to find and remove duplicate rows. A "duplicate" can be an exact match, where every cell in the row contains the same data, or you can specify matching data for certain columns only.

To remove duplicate rows from a table:

1. Select any cell in the table.
2. On *Table Tools Design* tab, in the *Tools* group, click the **Remove Duplicates** button.
3. By default, all the columns are selected in the *Remove Duplicates* dialog and Excel will remove duplicates only where the data in the rows are 100 percent identical. To identify duplicate rows where only some of the columns have duplicate data, click the check boxes to uncheck column names. Now Excel will identify rows as duplicates only when the checked columns have the same data.
4. Click **OK** to remove duplicate rows from the table.
5. Excel displays a message box, telling you how many duplicate rows were found and removed and how many unique values remain in the table. Click **OK** to dismiss the message box.

FIGURE EX 5.25

another **method**

If the data are not formatted as an Excel table, you can access the *Remove Duplicates* command from the *Data* tab, *Data Tools* group.

let me **try**

If you do not have the data file from the previous skill open, open the student data file **EX5-14-PurchaseOrders** and try this skill on your own:

1. If necessary, click any cell in the table on the *POJune* worksheet.
2. Remove duplicate rows where data in all the columns are identical. Excel should remove one duplicate row, leaving 15 unique values.
3. If you will be moving on to the next skill in this chapter, leave the workbook open to continue working. If not, save the file as directed by your instructor and close it.

Skill 5.15 Sorting Data

Sorting rearranges the rows in your worksheet by the data in a column or columns. You can **sort** alphabetically by text, by date, or by values. Sorting works the same whether or not the data have been formatted as a table.

To sort data:

1. Click any cell in the column you want to sort by.

2. On the *Data* tab, in the *Sort & Filter* group, click the button for the sort order you want:

   > $\begin{smallmatrix}A\\Z\end{smallmatrix}\downarrow$ sorts text in alphabetical order from A to Z, numbers from smallest to largest, and dates from oldest to newest.

   > $\begin{smallmatrix}Z\\A\end{smallmatrix}\downarrow$ sorts text in reverse alphabetical order from Z to A, numbers from largest to smallest, and dates from newest to oldest.

If the data are formatted as a table, you can click the arrow at the top of any column and select the sort order you want from the options available.

When a table column has been sorted, the column header displays an arrow indicating which way the column has been sorted. An arrow pointing up indicates an A–Z sort order; an arrow pointing down indicates a Z–A sort order.

| FIGURE EX 5.26

another **method**

Sort options are also available from the *Home* tab, *Editing* group. Click the **Sort & Filter** button and then select the option you want.

You can also right-click any cell in the column you want to sort by. Point to **Sort**, and select the option you want.

let me **try**

If you do not have the data file from the previous skill open, open the student data file **EX5-15-PurchaseOrders** and try this skill on your own:

1. Verify that the *Inventory* worksheet is active.

2. Sort the **Item** column in alphabetical order from A to Z.

3. Go to the *POJune* worksheet, and sort the **Order Cost** column so the largest numbers are listed first.

4. If you will be moving on to the next skill in this chapter, leave the workbook open to continue working. If not, save the file as directed by your instructor and close it.

Skill 5.16 Filtering Data

If your worksheet has many rows of data, you may want to **filter** the data to show only rows that meet criteria you specify. If your data are formatted as a table, filtering is enabled automatically. If your data are not formatted as a table, you must first enable filtering:

1. On the *Home* tab, in the *Editing* group, click the **Sort & Filter** button.

2. Click the **Filter** button to enable filtering. An arrow will appear in each cell of the heading row just as if the data were formatted as a table.

Once filtering is enabled, it works the same whether or not the data have been formatted as a table.

To filter data:

1. Click the arrow at the top of the column that contains the data you want to filter for.

2. At first, all the filter options are checked. Click the **(Select All)** check box to remove all the checkmarks.

3. Click the check box or check boxes in front of the values you want to filter by.

4. Click **OK**. Excel displays only the rows that include the values you specified.

FIGURE EX 5.27

When a filter has been applied to a column, the column header will display a funnel icon.

To clear the filter, on the *Data* tab, in the *Sort & Filter* group, click the **Clear** button. You can also click the funnel icon at the top of the filtered column and select **Clear Filter From "Name of Column"**.

FIGURE EX 5.28

If the column values are dates, Excel will group the dates in the filter list if possible. You can filter for an entire grouping such as a year or month or for a specific date. Use the + and - buttons in front of each date grouping to expand or collapse the group.

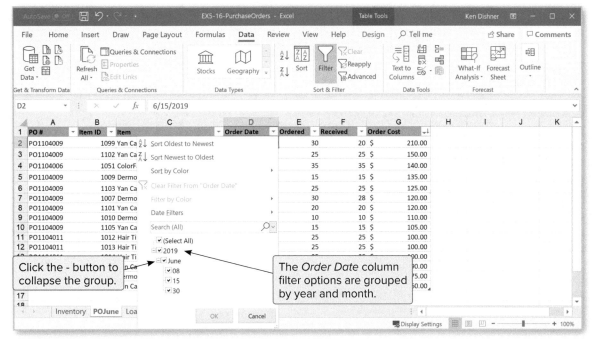

FIGURE EX 5.29

another **method**

❯ When filtering is enabled, you can clear the filter and disable filtering from the *Data* tab, *Sort & Filter* group, by clicking the **Filter** button again.

❯ You can also enable or clear filtering from the *Home* tab, *Editing* group, by clicking the **Sort & Filter** button and then making the appropriate choice from the menu.

let me **try**

If you do not have the data file from the previous skill open, open the student data file **EX5-16-PurchaseOrders** and try this skill on your own:

1. If necessary, go to the *Inventory* worksheet.

2. If necessary, enable filtering.

3. Filter the **Quantity in Stock** column so only rows with the blanks are shown. *Hint*: Scroll to the bottom of the filter list to find the *(Blanks)* option.

4. If you will be moving on to the next skill in this chapter, leave the workbook open to continue working. If not, save the file as directed by your instructor and close it.

Skill 5.17 Filtering Table Data with Slicers

A **slicer** is a visual representation of filtering options. You can display multiple slicers and filter the table by multiple values from each. Slicers are available only when the data have been formatted as a table.

To add a slicer:

1. Click anywhere in the table to activate the *Table Tools Design* tab.
2. On the *Table Tools Design* tab, in the *Tools* group, click the **Insert Slicer** button.
3. In the *Insert Slicers* dialog, click the check boxes for the column(s) you want in the slicers.
4. Click **OK**.

FIGURE EX 5.30

> In the slicer, click the option you want to use as the data filter. If you click another option in the slicer, the first option you selected will toggle off and the new selection will be used as the filter.

> To use more than one filtering option in a slicer, click the **Multi-Select** button at the upper right corner of the slicer box. When you enabled multi-select, all the slicer options remain *on* by default. Click the options you do *not* want included in the filter to turn them off.

> Notice that as you make selections in one slicer, options in the other slicer may become unavailable—indicating that there are no data available for that option under the current filtering conditions.

The table in Figure EX 5.31 has been filtered to show only rows with **PO1104009** in the *PO #* column and **20** and **25** in the *Ordered* column. Notice that the PO1104008 and PO1104011 options in the PO # slicer are disabled—indicating that they do not include rows with 20 or 25 in the *Ordered* column. Also, in the Ordered slicer, the 35 option is disabled—indicating that PO1104009 does not include any rows with the value 35 in the *Ordered* column.

FIGURE EX 5.31

To remove filtering, click the **Clear Filter** button in the upper right corner of the slicer.

To remove a slicer from the table, click the slicer and then press (Delete). Removing a slicer does not clear the filtering from the table.

tell me **more**

❭ To move a slicer, move your mouse pointer over the slicer. When the cursor changes to the move cursor, click and drag the slicer to a new position on the worksheet.

❭ When a slicer is selected, the *Slicer Tools Options* tab becomes available. From this tab, you can apply a style to the slicer and control slicer settings.

let me try

If you do not have the data file from the previous skill open, open the student data file **EX5-17-PurchaseOrders** and try this skill on your own:

1. If necessary, select the *POJune* sheet and click any cell in the table.

2. Add slicers for **PO #** and **Ordered**.

3. Using the slicers, filter the table to show only rows where the PO # is **PO1104009**.

4. Filter the data further to display only records where the value in the *Ordered* column is **20** or **25**.
   Hint: Enable the **Multi-Select** button to apply more than one filter option in the **Ordered** slicer.

5. If you will be moving on to the next skill in this chapter, leave the workbook open to continue working. If not, save the file as directed by your instructor and close it.

Skill 5.18 Converting Tables to Ranges

Although Excel tables are extremely useful, there are times when you do not want your data formatted as a table. Certain data analysis tools, including creating subtotals and grouping outlines, are not available if data are formatted as a table.

To convert a table to a normal range:

1. On the *Table Tools Design* tab, in the *Tools* group, click the **Convert to Range** button.
2. Excel displays a message box asking if you want to convert the table to a normal range. Click **Yes**.

FIGURE EX 5.32

As shown in Figure EX 5.33, when you convert from a table to a normal range, Excel removes any filtering that may have been applied. Any table formatting such as banding and the Total row are still applied to the range.

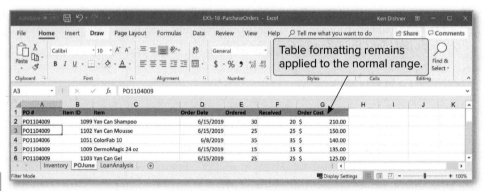

FIGURE EX 5.33

tips & tricks

If you want to use one of the table styles but do not want the data formatted as a table, begin by formatting the range as a table, applying the table style you want, and then convert the table back to a normal range.

another **method**

You can also right-click anywhere in the table, point to **Table**, and select **Convert to Range**.

let me try

If you do not have the data file from the previous skill open, open the student data file **EX5-18-PurchaseOrders** and try this skill on your own:

1. If necessary, click any cell in the table on the *POJune* sheet.
2. Convert the table to a normal range.
3. If you will be moving on to the next skill in this chapter, leave the workbook open to continue working. If not, save the file as directed by your instructor and close it.

excel 365   chapter 5 Adding Charts and Analyzing Data

Skill 5.19 Creating PivotTables Using Recommended PivotTables

A **PivotTable** is a special report view that summarizes data and calculates the intersecting totals. PivotTables do not contain any data themselves–they summarize data from a cell range or a table in another part of your workbook.

The easiest way to begin a new PivotTable is to use one of the recommended PivotTables:

1. Select any cell within the table or cell range you want to use for your PivotTable.

2. On the *Insert* tab, in the *Tables* group, click the **Recommended PivotTables** button.

3. Preview each of the options in the *Recommended PivotTables* dialog. Click the one that is closest to how you want your final PivotTable to look.

4. Click **OK** to create the PivotTable in a new worksheet.

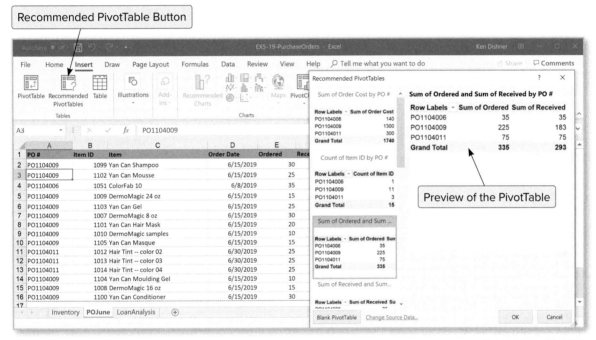

FIGURE EX 5.34

Use the *PivotTable Fields* pane to review and modify the structure of the PivotTable. The top part of the *PivotTable Fields* pane shows you the list of available fields–the columns from the PivotTable's data source. The bottom part of the *PivotTable Fields* pane allows you to build or modify the PivotTable by adding field data to one of four areas: *Filters*, *Columns*, *Rows*, or *Values*. In Figure EX 5.35, the recommended PivotTable added the *PO #* field to the *Rows* section and the *Ordered* and *Received* fields to the *Values* section. The PivotTable summarizes values in the *Ordered* and *Received* fields for each value in the *PO #* field.

FIGURE EX 5.35

In the *PivotTable Fields* pane, check the boxes in front of each column name to add or remove fields from the PivotTable.

> Fields that contain text or date data are added to the *Rows* section automatically. If there are multiple rows, Excel will attempt to group them in a logical way.

> Fields that contain numeric data are added to the *Values* section automatically. For each row in the PivotTable, Excel summarizes the values in each of the fields listed in the *Values* section. In Figure EX 5.36, adding the *Order Cost* field to the PivotTable adds it to the *Values* section and calculates the total value ordered for each PO #.

FIGURE EX 5.36

Excel summarizes numerical data in the PivotTable using the SUM function by default. You can choose another calculation type such as count or average.

To change the calculation type for a field:

1. Click anywhere in the field you want to change.
2. On the *PivotTable Tools Analyze* tab, in the *Active Field* group, click the **Field Settings** button.
3. In the *Value Field Settings* dialog, *Summarize Values By* tab, select the function for the type of calculation you want.
4. Click **OK**.

FIGURE EX 5.37

The PivotTable now displays the average order cost for each PO #.

FIGURE EX 5.38

tips & tricks

❯ Click and drag the field names in the *PivotTable Fields* pane to move them between the *Filters*, *Columns*, *Rows*, or *Values* boxes.

❯ Click and drag fields in the *Rows* and *Values* boxes in the *PivotTable Fields* pane to reorder them in the PivotTable.

another method

❯ If you have the data range for the PivotTable selected, the recommended PivotTables are also available from the *Tables* tab in the Quick Analysis tool.

❯ You can also open the *Value Field Settings* dialog by clicking the arrow next to the field name in the *Values* box, and then selecting **Value Field Settings...**

let me try

If you do not have the data file from the previous skill open, open the student data file **EX5-19-PurchaseOrders** and try this skill on your own:

1. Verify that the *POJune* sheet is active and one of the cells in the data range is selected.
2. Insert a recommended PivotTable using the **Sum of Ordered and Sum of Received by PO #** option.
3. Add the **Order Cost** field to the PivotTable.
4. Modify the **Order Cost** field to use the **Average** function instead of the Sum function.
5. If you will be moving on to the next skill in this chapter, leave the workbook open to continue working. If not, save the file as directed by your instructor and close it.

skill 5.19   Creating PivotTables Using Recommended PivotTables

Skill 5.20 Creating a PivotChart from a PivotTable

A **PivotChart** is a graphic representation of a PivotTable. In a column chart, the category fields are represented along the x (horizontal) axis while the data values are represented along the y (vertical) axis.

To create a PivotChart from a PivotTable:

1. Select any cell in the PivotTable.
2. On the *PivotTable Tools Analyze* tab, in the *Tools* group, click the **PivotChart** button.

FIGURE EX 5.39

3. Select a chart type from the *Insert Chart* dialog.
4. Click **OK**.

The *Insert Chart* dialog used when creating a PivotChart is very similar to the one used when creating regular charts. Click a chart type at the left side of the dialog, and then click an option from the examples along the top of the right-hand pane. Excel displays a preview of the chart. There are no recommended charts for PivotCharts.

FIGURE EX 5.40

If you need more room to display the PivotChart, you may want to hide the *Pivot-Table Fields* pane. On the *PivotChart Tools Analyze* tab, in the *Show/Hide* group, click the **Field List** button to hide or display the *PivotTable Fields* pane.

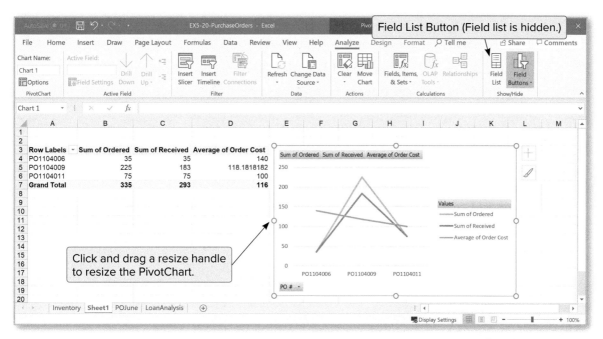

FIGURE EX 5.41

PivotCharts include all the formatting options that regular charts do. You can apply Quick Styles and hide or show chart elements from the *PivotChart Tools Design* tab. You can also resize the PivotChart or move it to its own sheet.

tell me **more**

To sort or filter the category data in the PivotChart, click the button in the lower left corner of the PivotChart with the name of the field you want to sort or filter. If your PivotTable used multiple row labels, you will see a button for each.

let me try

If you do not have the data file from the previous skill open, open the student data file **EX5-20-PurchaseOrders** and try this skill on your own:

1. If necessary, click anywhere in the PivotTable. If your workbook does not include a PivotTable, complete the Let Me Try exercise from *Creating PivotTables Using Recommended PivotTables* before continuing.

2. Insert a PivotChart using the first line chart type.

3. If you will be moving on to the next skill in this chapter, leave the workbook open to continue working. If not, save the file as directed by your instructor and close it.

skill 5.20   Creating a PivotChart from a PivotTable

Skill 5.21 Analyzing Data with Data Tables

Data tables provide a quick what-if analysis of the effects of changing one or two variables within a formula. The **data table** is organized with a series of values for the variable(s) in a column or a row or both.

To create a one-variable data table with a column input format:

1. In a column, type the series of values you want to substitute for the variable in your formula.
2. In the cell above and to the right of the first value, type the formula that references the cell you want to replace with the new values.
3. Select the cell range for the data table, beginning with the empty cell above the first value you entered.
4. On the *Data* tab, in the *Forecast* group, click the **What-If Analysis** button, and click **Data Table...**
5. In the *Data Table* dialog, the input cell is the cell that contains the original value for which you want to substitute the data table values. In this data table, the output values will be listed in a column, so enter the cell reference in the *Column input cell* box.
6. Click **OK**.

In the one-variable data table in Figure EX 5.42, the formula in cell **B9** references the loan amount in cell **B2**—the *pv* argument for the PMT function. This is the **column input cell** for the data table. The substitute values for cell B2 are listed in cells **A10:A14**.

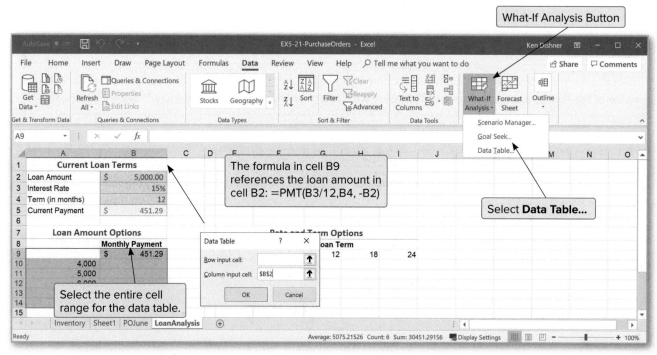

FIGURE EX 5.42

Excel completes the values in the table, using the substitute values in the formula as shown in Figure EX 5.43.

A two-variable data table works the same way as a one-variable data table, using inputs for both a column and a row variable. In a two-variable data table, the formula is located in the cell above the column input values and to the left of the row input values.

In the two-variable data table in Figure EX 5.44, the formula in cell E9 references the loan term in cell **B4**—the *nper* argument for the PMT function. This is the **row input cell** for the data table. The substitute values for cell B4 are listed in cells **F9:I9**.

The formula also references the second variable used in the data table, the interest rate in cell **B3**—the *rate* argument for the PMT function. This is the column input cell for the data table. The substitute values for cell B3 are listed in cells **E10:E14**.

FIGURE EX 5.43

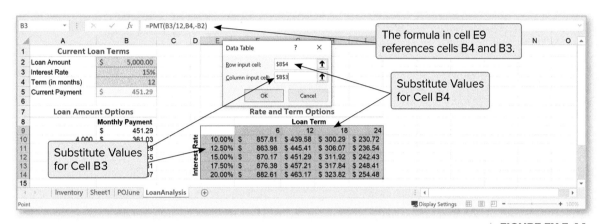

FIGURE EX 5.44

In a **two-variable data table**, you may want to hide the data table formula by changing the cell font color to match the worksheet background. The data table is easier to follow if the cell in the upper left corner of the data table appears blank as shown in cell E9 in Figure EX 5.44. Of course, you can still see the formula in the formula bar.

tips & tricks

Use Goal Seek if the result you are looking for is a specific value in a single cell. Use data tables when you want to see multiple possible outcomes based on multiple input options.

let me try

If you do not have the data file from the previous skill open, open the student data file **EX5-21-PurchaseOrders** and try this skill on your own:

1. Go to the *LoanAnalysis* worksheet.

2. Insert a one-variable data table in cells **A9:B14** to calculate the monthly loan payment for the loan amounts listed in cells A10:A14. The formula has been entered for you in cell B9. It references the original loan amount in cell **B2**.

3. Insert a two-variable data table in cells **E9:I14** to calculate the monthly loan payments for various interest rates and loan terms. The formula in cell E9 has been formatted using the white font color so it appears hidden. It references the original interest rate in cell **B3** and the loan term in cell **B4**.

4. If you will be moving on to the next skill in this chapter, leave the workbook open to continue working. If not, save the file as directed by your instructor and close it.

Skill 5.22 Analyzing Data with Goal Seek

Excel's **Goal Seek** function lets you enter a desired value (outcome) for a formula and specify an input cell that can be modified in order to reach that goal. Goal Seek changes the value of the input cell incrementally until the target outcome is reached. In Figure EX 5.45, the outcome cell is cell **B5**, the loan payment; the desired outcome value is 750; and the input cell is cell **B2**, the loan amount.

FIGURE EX 5.45

To find a value using Goal Seek:

1. On the *Data* tab, in the *Forecast* group, click the **What-If Analysis** button, and then click **Goal Seek...**

2. Enter the outcome cell in the *Set cell* box. This cell must contain a formula.

3. Enter the outcome value you want in the *To value* box.

4. Enter the input cell (the cell that contains the value to be changed) in the *By changing cell* box. This cell must be referenced in the formula in the outcome cell either directly or indirectly and must contain a value, not a formula.

5. Click **OK**.

6. The *Goal Seek Status* box appears, letting you know if Goal Seek was able to find a solution. Click **OK** to accept the solution and change the value in the input cell or click **Cancel** to return the input cell to its original value.

FIGURE EX 5.46

tips & tricks

Goal Seek works best in situations where there is only one variable, such as:

> Finding the loan amount to result in a specific loan payment when the loan rate and terms are inflexible.

> Finding the required number of units to sell to reach a sales goal when the price is inflexible.

let me try

If you do not have the data file from the previous skill open, open the student data file **EX5-22-PurchaseOrders** and try this skill on your own:

1. On the *LoanAnalysis* worksheet, use Goal Seek to find the amount of loan you can afford (cell **B2**) that will result in a payment of **750** in cell **B5**.

2. If Goal Seek is able to find a solution, accept it.

3. Save the file as directed by your instructor and close it.

key terms

Column chart
Clustered column chart
Bar chart
Stacked column chart
Stacked bar chart
Pie chart
Doughnut chart
Line chart
Line with markers
Chart sheet
Quick Layout
Data labels
Data table (chart)
Quick Style

Sparklines
Table
Banding
Total row
Sort
Filter
Slicer
PivotTable
PivotChart
Data table (what-if analysis)
Column input cell
Row input cell
Two-variable data table
Goal Seek

concept review

1. Data markers are graphic representations of the values of data points in a chart.

   a. true

   b. false

2. _____ charts represent data as parts of a whole.

   a. Column

   b. Bar

   c. Line

   d. Pie

3. _____ apply combinations of fonts, line styles, fills, and shape effects to charts.

   a. Quick Layouts

   b. Quick Styles

   c. Chart Effects

   d. Chart Templates

4. _____ represent each data series as an individual graphic within a single cell.

   a. Charts

   b. Sparklines

   c. Tables

   d. PivotCharts

5. A Total row can be used to quickly calculate the _____ of all the values in a column.

   a. sum

   b. average

   c. both a and b

   d. neither a nor b

6. When you format data as a table, the header row automatically includes filtering and sorting.

    a. true

    b. false

7. _____ rearranges the rows in your worksheet by the data in a column or columns.

    a. Grouping

    b. Filtering

    c. Sorting

    d. Formatting

8. _____ is a special report view that summarizes data and calculates the intersecting totals.

    a. Table

    b. Chart

    c. PivotTable

    d. Scenario

9. The _____ command provides a quick what-if analysis of the effects of changing one or two variables within a formula.

    a. *Scenario*

    b. *Consolidate*

    c. *Data Table*

    d. *Goal Seek*

10. The _____ command lets you enter a designated value for a formula and specify an input cell that can be modified in order to reach that goal.

    a. *Scenario*

    b. *Consolidate*

    c. *Data Table*

    d. *Goal Seek*

skill review **5.1**

In this project, you will analyze data for an event planning company.

Skills needed to complete this project:

- Converting Data into Tables (Skill 5.11)
- Adding Total Rows to Tables (Skill 5.13)
- Sorting Data (Skill 5.15)
- Filtering Data (Skill 5.16)
- Analyzing Data with Data Tables (Skill 5.21)
- Inserting a Column Chart or a Bar Chart (Skill 5.1)
- Changing the Chart Type (Skill 5.8)
- Applying Quick Styles and Colors to Charts (Skill 5.7)
- Showing and Hiding Chart Elements (Skill 5.6)
- Resizing and Moving Charts (Skill 5.4)
- Analyzing Data with Goal Seek (Skill 5.22)
- Inserting a Pie Chart (Skill 5.2)
- Applying Quick Layouts to Charts (Skill 5.5)
- Creating PivotTables Using Recommended PivotTables (Skill 5.19)
- Creating a PivotChart from a PivotTable (Skill 5.20)

1. Open the start file **EX2019-SkillReview-5-1** and resave the file as:
   `[your initials]EX-SkillReview-5-1`

2. If the workbook opens in Protected View, click the **Enable Editing** button in the Message Bar at the top of the workbook so you can modify the workbook.

3. Format the data on the *Table* worksheet into a table using one of the table Quick Styles.

   a. Select all the data including the headings, being careful not to select any blank rows or columns.

   b. On the *Home* tab, in the *Styles* group, click the **Format as Table** button to display the *Table Styles* gallery.

   c. Click the **Orange, Table Style Medium 3** Quick Style. It is the third option in the *Medium* section of the gallery.

   d. Verify that the correct cells will be used. Check the **My table has headers** check box. Click **OK**.

4. Add a Total row to the table to count the number of invitations sent.

   a. On the *Table Tools Design* tab, in the *Table Style Options* group, click the **Total Row** check box.

   b. In the Total row at the bottom of the table, note the total count of guests attending.

   c. In the Total row at the bottom of the table, click in the **City** column, click the arrow, and select the **Count** function to count the invitations sent.

5. Sort the table by city in alphabetical order:

   a. Click anywhere in the **City** column.

   b. On the *Data* tab, in the *Sort & Filter* group, click the **A-Z** button.

6. Filter the data in the table to show only guests from the city of Auburn.

   a. Click the arrow in the **City** column header.

   b. Click the **(Select All)** check box to remove all of the checkmarks.

   c. Click the check box in front of **Auburn** to filter for only guests from Auburn.

   d. Click **OK**. Excel displays only the rows for invitations sent to Auburn.

7. Switch to work with the *Data Table* worksheet and use a data table to estimate costs for different numbers of attendees. Cell C18 contains a formula that sums the costs in cells **C3:C15**. The formulas in those cells all refer to the number of guests in cell **C1**.

   a. Select cells **B18:C25** to use as the data table.

   b. On the *Data* tab, in the *Forecast* group, click the **What-If Analysis** button, and click **Data Table…**

   c. In the *Column input cell* box, type **C1** and then click **OK**.

   d. Review the data table results computing the party costs for the various numbers of guests.

8. Create a column chart to compare the cost of various size parties.

   a. Select cells **B17:C25**.

   b. Click the **Insert** tab.

   c. In the *Charts* group, click the **dialog launcher** to open the *Insert Chart* dialog.

   d. Click the **All Charts** tab and, if necessary, select the **Column** chart category.

   e. Click the second option under *Clustered Column*. It is the one with the number of guests displayed on the x axis.

   f. Click **OK**.

9. Change the chart to a line chart.

   a. If necessary, click to select the chart.

   b. On the *Chart Tools Design* tab, in the *Type* group, click the **Change Chart Type** button.

   c. In the *Change Chart Type* dialog, click **Line**, and click the first line chart type.

   d. Click **OK**.

10. Format the chart using a Quick Style. On the *Chart Tools Design* tab, in the *Chart Styles* group, click **Style 3**.

11. Display the chart gridlines and hide the data labels.

   a. Click the **Chart Elements** button that appears near the upper right corner of the chart.

   b. Click the **Gridlines** check box to add a checkmark.

   c. Click the **Data Labels** check box to add a checkmark.

12. Move the chart to its own sheet in the workbook.

   a. On the *Chart Tools Design* tab, in the *Location* group, click the **Move Chart** button.

   b. In the *Move Chart* dialog, click the **New sheet** radio button.

   c. In the *New sheet* box, type: **Data Table Chart**

   d. Click **OK**.

13. Use Goal Seek to determine the most you can afford for dinner per person on a total $14,000 budget for 130 guests assuming all other per guest costs remain the same.

    a. Switch to the *Goal Seek* sheet.

    b. Select the outcome cell **C18** and review the formula.

    c. On the *Data* tab, in the *Forecast* group, click the **What-If Analysis** button and click **Goal Seek...**

    d. Verify that the outcome cell **C18** is referenced in the *Set cell* box.

    e. Enter the outcome value of **14000** in the *To value* box.

    f. Enter the input cell **A4** in the *By changing cell* box.

    g. Click **OK** to run Goal Seek.

    h. Click **OK** again to accept the Goal Seek solution.

14. Insert a 3-D pie chart to show the breakdown of the per guest costs.

    a. Select cells **B3:C11**.

    b. On the *Insert* tab, in the *Charts* group, click the **Pie** button, and click the **Pie** option.

    c. If necessary, move the chart to the right so it does not cover the worksheet data.

    d. On the *Chart Tools Design* tab, click the **Quick Layout** button and select **Layout 6**.

    e. Change the chart title to: **Per Guest Costs**

15. Create a PivotTable listing the number attending from each city.

    a. Return to the *Table* worksheet.

    b. Click anywhere in the table.

    c. On the *Insert* tab, in the *Tables* group, click the **Recommended PivotTables** button.

    d. Select the option **Sum of NumAttending by City**.

    e. Click **OK**.

16. Modify the PivotTable to calculate the average number of attendees per city instead of the total.

    a. Click anywhere in the **Sum of NumAttending** field.

    b. On the *PivotTable Tools Analyze* tab, in the *Active Field* group, click the **Field Settings** button.

    c. In the *Value Field Settings* dialog, *Summarize Values By* tab, select **Average** to change the calculation from SUM to AVERAGE.

    d. Click **OK**.

17. Create a PivotChart from the PivotTable.

    a. Select any cell in the PivotTable.

    b. On the *PivotTable Tools Analyze* tab, in the *Tools* group, click the **PivotChart** button.

    c. Verify that the Clustered Column chart type is selected in the *Insert Chart* dialog.

    d. Click **OK**.

    e. Click the title and change it to read: **Number of Guests Attending from Each City**

    f. Hide the legend by clicking the **Chart Elements** button that appears near the upper right corner of the PivotChart and clicking the **Legend** check box to remove the checkmark.

    g. If necessary, move the PivotChart to the right so it does not cover the PivotTable.

18. Save and close the workbook.

skill review **5.2**

In this project you will analyze real estate data.

Skills needed to complete this project:

- Converting Data into Tables (Skill 5.11)
- Adding Total Rows to Tables (Skill 5.13)
- Sorting Data (Skill 5.15)
- Filtering Data (Skill 5.16)
- Inserting a Line Chart (Skill 5.3)
- Resizing and Moving Charts (Skill 5.4)
- Showing and Hiding Chart Elements (Skill 5.6)
- Applying Quick Styles and Colors to Charts (Skill 5.7)
- Creating PivotTables Using Recommended PivotTables (Skill 5.19)
- Inserting Sparklines (Skill 5.10)
- Creating a PivotChart from a PivotTable (Skill 5.20)
- Analyzing Data with Data Tables (Skill 5.21)
- Analyzing Data with Goal Seek (Skill 5.22)

1. Open the start file **EX2019-SkillReview-5-2** and resave the file as: **[your initials] EX-SkillReview-5-2**

2. If the workbook opens in Protected View, click the **Enable Editing** button in the Message Bar at the top of the workbook so you can modify the workbook.

3. Format the data on the *Sales Data* worksheet as a table using the **Blue, Table Style Medium 2** table style:

   a. Select any cell in the data.

   b. On the *Home* tab, in the *Styles* group, click the **Format as Table** button to display the *Table Styles* gallery.

   c. Click the **Blue, Table Style Medium 2** Quick Style. It is the second option in the *Medium* section of the gallery.

   d. Verify that the **My table has headers** check box is checked and that the correct data range is selected.

   e. Click **OK**.

4. Add a Total row to the table to display the number of buyers; the average number of bedrooms and bathrooms for each sale; and the average purchase price, interest rate, and mortgage length.

   a. On the *Table Tools Design* tab, in the *Table Style Options* group, click the **Total Row** check box.

   b. In the Total row at the bottom of the table, click in the **Buyers** column, click the arrow, and select the **Count** function.

   c. In the Total row at the bottom of the table, click in the **Bedrooms** column, click the arrow, and select the **Average** function.

   d. In the Total row at the bottom of the table, click in the **Bathrooms** column, click the arrow, and select the **Average** function.

   e. In the Total row at the bottom of the table, click in the **Purchase Price** column, click the arrow, and select the **Average** function.

f. In the Total row at the bottom of the table, click in the **Rate** column, click the arrow, and select the **Average** function.

g. In the Total row at the bottom of the table, click in the **Mortgage Years** column, click the arrow, and select the **Average** function.

5. Sort the data so the newest purchases appear at the top.

a. Click anywhere in the **Date of Purchase** column.

b. On the *Data* tab, in the *Sort & Filter* group, click the **Z-A** button.

6. Filter the data to show only houses sold by owner with three or four bedrooms.

a. Click the arrow at the top of the **Agent** column.

b. Click the **(Select All)** check box to remove all of the checkmarks.

c. Click the check box in front of **By Owner**.

d. Click **OK**.

e. Click the arrow at the top of the **Bedrooms** column.

f. Click the **(Select All)** check box to remove all of the checkmarks.

g. Click the check boxes in front of **3** and **4**.

h. Click **OK**.

7. Create a line chart showing the purchase prices for houses by date.

a. Select the **Date of Purchase** data cells. Be careful not to include the column heading. Press and hold Ctrl and click and drag to select the **Purchase Price** data cells, again being careful not to include the column heading.

b. On the *Insert* tab, in the *Charts* group, click the **Insert Line or Area Chart** button.

c. Select the first line chart type shown.

d. Click **OK**.

8. Move the chart to its own sheet named *Purchase Prices*.

a. If necessary, select the chart. On the *Chart Tools Design* tab, in the *Location* group, click the **Move Chart** button.

b. In the *Move Chart* dialog, click the **New sheet** radio button.

c. In the box type: `Purchase Prices`

d. Click **OK**.

9. Update the chart title and display the data labels as callouts.

a. Change the chart title to: `Homes For Sale By Owner`

b. Click the **Chart Elements** button near the upper right corner of the chart.

c. Click the **Data Labels** check box to add a checkmark.

d. Point to **Data Labels**, click the arrow that appears at the right side, and click **Data Callout**.

10. Apply the **Style 2** Quick Style to the chart.

a. Click the **Chart Styles** button that appears near the upper right corner of the chart.

b. Click **Style 2**.

11. Create a PivotTable to summarize the average purchase price of different house types for each agent.

a. Return to the *Sales Data* worksheet and click anywhere in the table.

b. Click the **Insert** tab. In the *Tables* group, click the **Recommended PivotTables** button.

c. Verify that the first recommended PivotTable is **Sum of Purchase Price by Agent**.

d. Click **OK**.

e. Select any cell in the **Sum of Purchase Price** column.

f. On the *PivotTable Tools Analyze* tab, in the *Active Field* group, click the **Field Settings** button.

g. In the *Summarize value field by* box, select **Average**.

h. Click **OK**.

i. Add the **House Type** field to the PivotTable by clicking the check box in the *Fields List* pane. Excel automatically places the *House Type* field in the Rows box and displays the house type data as a subgroup of rows below each agent.

j. To summarize the house type data for each agent, use the *House Type* field as columns in the PivotTable. Click and drag the **House Type** field from the Rows box to the Columns box in the *PivotTable Fields* pane.

12. Add column Sparklines to the right of the PivotTable.

a. Select cells **B5:E9** to use as the data for the Sparklines. You do not want to include the grand total column or row.

b. On the *Insert* tab, in the *Sparklines* group, click the **Column** button.

c. In the *Create Sparklines* dialog, verify that the cell range **B5:E9** is listed in the *Data Range* box.

d. Add the range **G5:G9** to the *Location Range* box either by typing the cell range or by clicking and dragging to select it in the worksheet.

e. Click **OK**.

13. Create a PivotChart from the PivotTable.

a. Select any cell in the PivotTable.

b. On the *PivotTable Tools Analyze* tab, in the *Tools* group, click the **PivotChart** button.

c. Select the first bar chart type from the *Insert Chart* dialog. Click **OK**.

d. If necessary, move the PivotChart to another part of the worksheet so it does not cover the PivotTable data.

14. Use the data in the *Loan Worksheet* sheet to run a what-if scenario for a client to show loan payments for a variety of interest rates and loan lengths. This what-if scenario requires a two-variable data table.

a. Go to the *Loan Worksheet* sheet and familiarize yourself with the formula in cell **B5**. Pay close attention to the cell references.

b. Select cells **B5:E25** to use the payment formula in B5 and the various years and rates as the data table.

c. On the *Data* tab, in the *Forecast* group, click the **What-If Analysis** button, and click **Data Table**.

d. In the *Row input cell* box, enter the cell reference for the length of the loan–the *nper* argument from the formula in cell B5: **C2**

e. In the *Column input cell* box, enter the cell reference for the loan interest rate– the *interest* argument from the formula in cell B5: **A2**

f. Click **OK**.

15. Use Goal Seek to determine the most you can afford to borrow, on a $950 per month budget:

a. On the *Loan Worksheet* sheet, select the outcome formula cell, **H4**.

b. On the *Data* tab, in the *Forecast* group, click the **What-If Analysis** button and click **Goal Seek...**

c. Verify that the outcome cell **H4** is referenced in the *Set cell* box.

d. Enter the outcome value of **950** in the *To value* box.

e. Enter the input cell **H9** in the *By changing cell* box.

f. Click **OK**.

g. Click **OK** again to accept the Goal Seek solution.

h. Notice the loan payment changed to $950 and the amount to borrow was computed to be $206,395.

16. Save and close the workbook.

challenge yourself **5.3**

In this project, you will analyze shoe sales data and use what-if analysis to determine your commission potential and your sales goal.

Skills needed to complete this project:

- Converting Data into Tables (Skill 5.11)
- Adding Total Rows to Tables (Skill 5.13)
- Removing Duplicate Rows from Tables (Skill 5.14)
- Filtering Data (Skill 5.16)
- Sorting Data (Skill 5.15)
- Inserting a Line Chart (Skill 5.3)
- Filtering Chart Data (Skill 5.9)
- Resizing and Moving Charts (Skill 5.4)
- Filtering Table Data with Slicers (Skill 5.17)
- Creating PivotTables Using Recommended PivotTables (Skill 5.19)
- Creating a PivotChart from a PivotTable (Skill 5.20)
- Showing and Hiding Chart Elements (Skill 5.6)
- Inserting Sparklines (Skill 5.10)
- Analyzing Data with Data Tables (Skill 5.21)
- Analyzing Data with Goal Seek (Skill 5.22)

1. Open the start file **EX2019-ChallengeYourself-5-3** and resave the file as: **[your initials]EX-ChallengeYourself-5-3**

2. If the workbook opens in Protected View, click the **Enable Editing** button in the Message Bar at the top of the workbook so you can modify the workbook.

3. Convert the shoe sales data in the *Sales* worksheet into a table.

a. Use the **Orange, Table Style Medium 3** table style. It is the third option in the *Medium* section of the gallery.

b. Add a Total row to the table to display the total for the *Total Sale* column.

c. In the Total row, display the average for the *# of Pairs* and the *Price Per Pair* columns.

d. Delete any rows in the table that have duplicate data in all the columns. There are four.

4. Filter to show just the sales for the **Washington** region.

5. Sort the table by order date with the newest orders first.

6. Insert a line chart to show the total sale amount for each order by order date.

   a. Create the line chart using just the data from the *Order Date* and *Total Sale* columns. Be sure to include the header row when selecting the data for the chart.

   b. There was an ordering glitch on August 31 that caused a spike in sales. Apply a filter to the chart to hide orders from that date.

   c. If necessary, move the chart so it does not cover the table data.

7. Add a slicer to the table so you can filter by shoe name. Use the slicer to display data for the **Sperry** shoe only. Notice the effect on the chart.

8. Create a PivotTable from the data in the *Sales* worksheet. Use the **Sum of Price Per Pair by Region** recommended PivotTable.

   a. Modify the PivotTable so the *Price Per Pair* data are averaged, not totaled.

   b. Add the **Shoe** field to the PivotTable. It should appear in the *Rows* section below the *Region* field.

   c. Format all the values in the PivotTable using the **Accounting Number Format**.

9. Create a clustered column PivotChart based on the PivotTable data. Use the first recommended column chart type.

   a. Hide the chart title and legend.

   b. If necessary, move the PivotChart on the worksheet so it does not cover the PivotChart data.

10. Go to the *By Region* worksheet and add Column Sparklines in **F3:F7** for data in columns **B3:E7**.

11. On the *By Region* worksheet, create a pie chart to display the sales by region for the Sperry shoe.

    a. Display the data labels as data callouts.

    b. Hide the chart legend.

    c. If necessary, move the chart so it does not cover the table data.

12. You have been told that you will receive a commission between 5 and 10 percent. On the *Commission* sheet, make a one-variable data table using cells **A4:B14** to determine how much that commission may be based on $17,000 in sales. The column input cell is **A4**.

13. You owe $9,000 in student loans and would like to pay it all off with your commissions. Use Goal Seek to determine the amount you must sell (cell **G5**) in order for cell **G3** (your commission) to equal $9,000 so you can fully pay off your student loans. Accept the Goal Seek solution.

14. Save and close the workbook.

challenge yourself 5.4

In this project, the local library has received a significant collection of DVDs as a donation and has asked you to provide an analysis of the titles. It needs to decide whether it should keep the collection or sell it to raise money for a new computer.

Skills needed to complete this project:

- Converting Data into Tables (Skill 5.11)
- Adding Total Rows to Tables (Skill 5.13)
- Removing Duplicate Rows from Tables (Skill 5.14)
- Applying Quick Styles to Tables (Skill 5.12)

- Sorting Data (Skill 5.15)
- Filtering Data (Skill 5.16)
- Filtering Table Data with Slicers (Skill 5.17)
- Creating PivotTables Using Recommended PivotTables (Skill 5.19)
- Creating a PivotChart from a PivotTable (Skill 5.20)
- Showing and Hiding Chart Elements (Skill 5.6)
- Analyzing Data with Data Tables (Skill 5.21)
- Analyzing Data with Goal Seek (Skill 5.22)

1. Open the start file **EX2019-ChallengeYourself-5-4** and resave the file as: `[your initials]EX-ChallengeYourself-5-4`

2. If the workbook opens in Protected View, click the **Enable Editing** button in the Message Bar at the top of the workbook so you can modify the workbook.

3. Convert the data on the *Videos* sheet into a table using the style **Red, Table Style Medium 3**. It is the third option in the *Medium* section of the gallery.

   a. Add a Total row to the table and count the number of movie titles and the average price.

   b. Delete all the duplicate rows. Be careful, there may be duplicate rows with the same movie title, but different data in the other columns. When you are finished, there should be 294 unique titles in the collection.

   c. Change the table style to use the **Purple, Table Style Medium 5** Quick Style. It is the fifth option in the *Medium* section of the gallery.

4. Sort the data in the table alphabetically by category.

5. Filter the table to show only **Horror** and **Sci Fi** movies that are rated **PG-13**.

6. Create a PivotTable from the table data using the **Sum of Price by Rating** recommended PivotTable.

7. Create a pie PivotChart from the PivotTable.

   a. Display the data labels using the **Inside End** option.

   b. Hide the chart title.

8. On the *Data Table* worksheet, create a one-variable data table to determine the amount of money that would be raised if 150 DVDs were sold at the various prices listed. Review the formula in cell **C7** to identify the appropriate cell to use as the input cell for the data table.

9. How many DVDs would the library need to sell at $1.50 each to raise $500? Use Goal Seek to find a value for cell **F9** that will result in a value of 500 for cell **F7**.

10. Save and close the workbook.

on your own 5.5

In this project, you will be working with data about automobile emissions and fuel economy. These green car data were downloaded from the website fueleconomy.gov. The SmartWay scores range from 0 to 10, where 10 is best. The vehicles with the best scores on both air pollution and greenhouse gas receive the Elite designation. More information about the SmartWay program can be found at http://www3.epa.gov/greenvehicles/you/smartway.htm.

Skills needed to complete this project:

- Converting Data into Tables (Skill 5.11)
- Filtering Data (Skill 5.16)
- Filtering Table Data with Slicers (Skill 5.17)
- Sorting Data (Skill 5.15)
- Inserting a Column Chart or a Bar Chart (Skill 5.1)
- Showing and Hiding Chart Elements (Skill 5.6)
- Applying Quick Styles and Colors to Charts (Skill 5.7)
- Changing the Chart Type (Skill 5.8)
- Creating PivotTables Using Recommended PivotTables (Skill 5.19)
- Creating a PivotChart from a PivotTable (Skill 5.20)
- Analyzing Data with Data Tables (Skill 5.21)
- Analyzing Data with Goal Seek (Skill 5.22)

1. Open the start file **EX2019-OnYourOwn-5-5** and resave the file as: **[your initials]EX-OnYourOwn-5-5**

2. If the workbook opens in Protected View, click the **Enable Editing** button in the Message Bar at the top of the workbook so you can modify the workbook.

3. The *Green Cars* worksheet contains almost 500 rows. That's a lot of data! Use filtering techniques to find the subset of cars that meet the following criteria:

   a. Display only cars with the **Elite** Smartway designation. *Hint*: The *Smartway* column is at the far right side of the data. You may need to scroll to find it.

   b. Include only cars in the **midsize car** class (use the *Veh Class* column).

   c. Include only cars with **Gasoline** as the fuel (use the *Fuel* column).

   d. You should end up with three records visible.

4. Sort the data so the cars with the best combination MPG (*Cmb MPG* column) appear at the top.

5. Create a chart comparing the **City MPG**, **Hwy MPG**, and **Cmb MPG** for the cars shown.

   a. Add and remove chart elements as necessary to make the chart clear and easy to read.

   b. Apply one of the chart Quick Styles.

   c. Try changing the chart to another chart type. Is there another chart type available that's appropriate for the data?

6. Create a PivotTable from the car data. Use one of the recommended PivotTables or create one from scratch. Add at least two fields to the *Values* section. Change the function used for at least one of the value fields. Name the worksheet: **Pivot**

7. Create a PivotChart from the PivotTable data.

8. On the *Commuting Costs* worksheet, create a two-variable data table to calculate the daily cost of gas for a variety of gas prices and a variety of miles driven per day. If you have a daily commute to school or work, use variations on your actual commuting miles in the data table.

   a. The formula to calculate the cost of your daily commute is: Commuting miles/your car's MPG*price of gas per gallon

   b. In the data table formula, you can use the MPG in cell B3 or change the value to your car's estimated MPG.

c. Find a way to hide the data table formula.

d. Add formatting as appropriate.

9. You're in the market for a new car, and you'd like to reduce your monthly gas costs to around $30. What's the minimum gas mileage you should look for in your new car? Can you use Goal Seek with the data on this worksheet to find an answer?

10. Save and close the workbook.

fix it 5.6

The staff members of a private college preparatory school have been trying to analyze student data and create what-if scenarios regarding investment decisions. Unfortunately, they've made a mess of this workbook. Can you help them fix it?

Skills needed to complete this project:

- Sorting Data (Skill 5.15)
- Converting Data into Tables (Skill 5.11)
- Filtering Table Data with Slicers (Skill 5.17)
- Removing Duplicate Rows from Tables (Skill 5.14)
- Adding Total Rows to Tables (Skill 5.13)
- Creating PivotTables Using Recommended PivotTables (Skill 5.19)
- Inserting a Pie Chart (Skill 5.2)
- Changing the Chart Type (Skill 5.8)
- Analyzing Data with Data Tables (Skill 5.21)

1. Open the start file **EX2019-FixIt-5-6** and resave the file as: **[your initials] EX-FixIt-5-6**

2. If the workbook opens in Protected View, click the **Enable Editing** button in the Message Bar at the top of the workbook so you can modify the workbook.

3. The data in the *Student Test Data* worksheet has a couple of problems to fix:

    a. The data should be organized alphabetically by student.

    b. Format the data so the school faculty can use slicers to filter data. Use any style you want.

    c. Display slicers so data can be filtered by month, by subject, or by student or by any combination of the three. Go ahead and display the slicers, but you don't need to apply any filtering.

    d. Find and delete the duplicate records. There should be 90 unique records.

    e. The data should include a Total row to calculate the average score.

4. The PivotTable on the *Student Pivot* sheet should summarize the average scores for each subject for each student by month. However, the *Score* field data have been added to the wrong section of the PivotTable.

    a. Move the *Score* field to the correct section of the PivotTable.

    b. Modify the calculation to display the average score instead of the total score.

5. The PivotChart on the *Faculty Pivot* sheet should show the size of each department as a proportional part of a whole. A line chart was the wrong choice.

    a. Change the chart type to a better choice.

    b. Display Data Labels using the **Data Callout** format.

6. The school finance committee has determined that a $30,000 facilities upgrade will be needed in 12 years. An alumnus has donated $24,000. If invested, will it grow to be enough? That depends on the rate of return. On the *Data Table* worksheet, an attempt has been made to use Excel's data table feature to determine the value of the investment after 12 years at different rates of return. The formula in cell D6 is correct, but something went wrong with the data table. Delete the zeros in cells **D7:D30** and try again. Even if you're not familiar with the FV formula used in cell D6, you should be able to figure this out.

7. Save and close the workbook.

access 365

chapter 1

Getting Started with Access

In this chapter, you will learn the following skills:

❯ Identify the elements of a Microsoft Access database

❯ Use the Navigation Pane to open, organize, and view database objects

❯ Understand and view table relationships

❯ Understand database object views

❯ Navigate records in tables and forms

❯ Create new records, enter, edit, find, sort, and move data in tables and forms

❯ Delete records in tables and forms

❯ Rename and delete database objects

❯ Preview and print database objects

❯ Perform a backup

❯ Start a new database

❯ Use the Compact and Repair tool

skills

introduction

This chapter is an introduction to working with a relational database. You will learn about the database objects that make up an Access database and how they relate to one another. As a database user, you will learn to navigate, create, edit, delete, sort, and search records in tables and forms. You also will learn the importance of database maintenance operations such as creating a backup and using the *Compact and Repair* utility. Once you are comfortable as a database user, you will learn how to create a new Access database of your own.

Skill 1.1 Introduction to Access

In the simplest terms, a **database** is a collection of data. An effective database allows you to enter, store, organize, and retrieve large amounts of related data. Access is different from other Microsoft Office applications you may have used. Although you create and work with a single Access database file, inside the file, there are multiple objects. Within each Access database, you create, edit, and save (and delete) objects. The types of objects in an Access database are:

> **Tables**—Store all the database data. They are the essential building blocks of the database. A table looks similar to a spreadsheet. Each row in the table contains all the data for a single **record**. Each column in the table represents a specific data value called a **field**. All records in a table have the same fields.

> Figure AC 1.1 shows the *Appointments* table, which stores the data for each customer appointment.

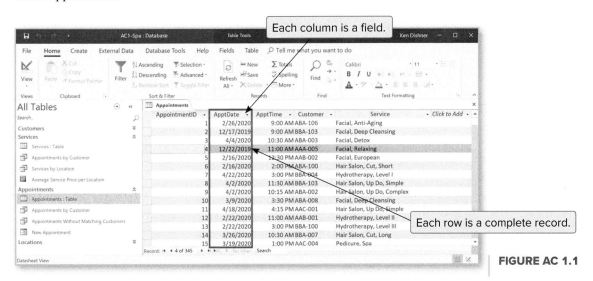

FIGURE AC 1.1

Because Access allows you to relate tables to one another, it is often referred to as a **relational database**. A relational database is a group of tables related to one another by common fields.

> **Forms**—Allow users to input data through a friendly interface. Entering data through a form is easier than entering it directly into a table. All the data entered into a form are stored in the underlying database table(s).

> Figure AC 1.2 shows the *New Appointment* form, which allows a data-entry operator to enter new appointments. When a new appointment is created using this form, a new record is added to the *Appointments* table.

FIGURE AC 1.2

Each data-entry box in the form corresponds to a field in the *Appointments* table.

Queries—Extract data from a table or related tables. Queries can also perform actions on tables such as updating data values or deleting data. Query results may look like a table, but they do not store data permanently. The query results are updated dynamically each time the query is run—retrieving data fresh from the table(s) upon which the query is based.

The query in Figure AC 1.3 returns a list of all the appointments for each customer. The query combines data from three tables: *Appointments*, *Customers*, and *Services*.

The appointment date is stored in the *Appointments* table.

The customer name and address information is stored in the *Customers* table.

The service name is stored in the *Services* table.

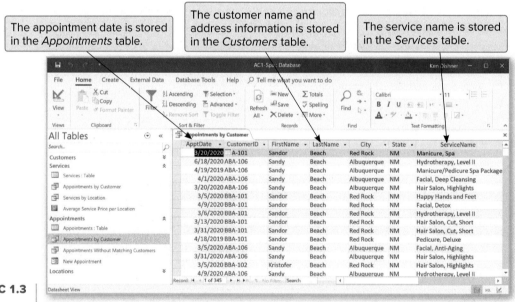

FIGURE AC 1.3

Reports—Display database information for printing or viewing onscreen. Reports do not allow data entry; they are read-only.

The report in Figure AC 1.4, *Average Service Price per Location*, displays a printable list of services available for each location. This report displays the results of the *Services by Location* query in a format suitable for printing.

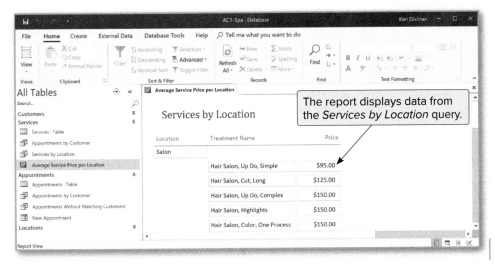

The report displays data from the *Services by Location* query.

FIGURE AC 1.4

All the database objects are organized in the **Navigation Pane**, which is docked at the left side of the screen. Each database object in the Navigation Pane has a name and an icon representing the type of object.

The Navigation Pane is usually expanded when you open an Access database. If you need more room to work, you can collapse the Navigation Pane by clicking the **Shutter Bar Open/Close** button. To expand the Navigation Pane again, click the **Shutter Bar Open/Close** button.

To open a database object, double-click the object name in the Navigation Pane. The object will appear as a new tab within the Access work area unless it is specifically designed to open in a window format. You can have multiple database objects open at the same time. To navigate from one object to another, click the object tab.

To close an object, click the **X** at the far right side of the object. Be careful not to click the X in the upper right corner of the database window—that will close the database!

Shutter Bar Open/ Close Button

Report

Table

Query

Form

FIGURE AC 1.5

tell me **more**

A fourth type of database object called a **macro** is a collection of programming code usually used within forms and reports to create buttons and other user interface elements. You will not work with macros until you are a more experienced Access user.

another **method**

You can also close an open database object by right-clicking the object tab and selecting **Close**.

let me **try**

Open the student data file **AC1-Spa** and try this skill on your own:

1. Open the *Appointments* table. (If the Navigation Pane is not open, open it.)
2. Open the *New Appointment* form.
3. Close the Navigation Pane.
4. Click the tabs to move back and forth between the *Appointments* table and the *New Appointment* form.
5. Close the *New Appointment* form.
6. Close the *Appointments* table.
7. Open the Navigation Pane.

Skill 1.2 Working with Security Warnings

When you open a database for the first time, Access may display a security warning in the **Message Bar** at the top of the window, below the Ribbon. Access disables active content such as ActiveX controls and VBA macros to protect your computer from becoming infected by a virus or other malware.

If you trust the source of the database, click the **Enable Content** button in the Message Bar. When you enable active content for a database, Access remembers the setting and you will not see the security warning message the next time you open the database.

FIGURE AC 1.6

tips & tricks

To learn more about the security settings in Access, open the Trust Center and review the options. We do not recommend changing any of the default Trust Center settings.

another **method**

You can also enable active content from the *Info* page in Backstage view.

1. Click the **File** tab to open Backstage view.
2. Click **Info**.
3. The *Info* page provides more information about the database. If you are sure you want to allow active content, click the **Enable Editing** button.

let me **try**

If you do not have the data file from the previous skill open, open the student data file **AC1-Spa** and try this skill on your own:

1. Open the database and enable active content. Once you have done this for the database, you will not see the warning again. If you do not see the warning, you may have enabled active content previously.
2. Close the database and reopen it to confirm that the warning does not appear again.

Skill 1.3 Understanding and Viewing Table Relationships

Access is a relational database. Objects in the database are related to one another through relationships defined by common fields between tables. Before working with a database, you should understand the underlying database structure—how the tables are related.

For example, a table of customer data might include fields for customer ID, title, first name, last name, and address information. Another table for tracking customer appointments might have fields for appointment ID, appointment date, appointment time, customer, and service. The two tables are related by the data in the *CustomerID* and *Customer* fields, so the database can generate reports combining information from the two tables.

There are three types of relationships: one-to-many, one-to-one, and many-to-many. One-to-many relationships are the most common. In a **one-to-many relationship**, the main table contains a **primary key** field that is included as a field (the **foreign key**) in the secondary table. Thus, one record in the first table can relate to many records in the second table. In Figure AC 1.7, the *CustomerID* field in the *Customers* table is the primary key. Records in the *Appointments* table are related to the *Customers* table through the *Customer* field (the foreign key in the relationship).

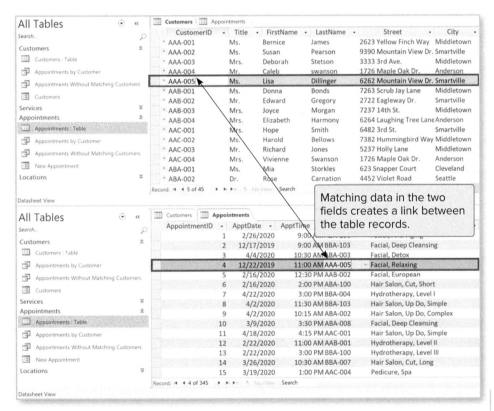

FIGURE AC 1.7

The relationships between primary and foreign key fields are fundamental to understanding and working with any relational database. You will learn more about primary key fields in other skills.

The **Relationships window** provides a visual representation of the relationships in your database.

To open the Relationships window, on the *Database Tools* tab, in the *Relationships* group, click the **Relationships** button.

Relationships Button

FIGURE AC 1.8

In the Relationships window, each table is represented by a box listing all the fields in the table. Primary key fields are identified with a key icon next to the field name. Lines representing the type of relationship connect related fields. In a one-to-many relationship, the one field in the main table that relates to many records in the secondary table is represented by a 1. The corresponding field in the secondary table is represented by an infinity symbol ∞.

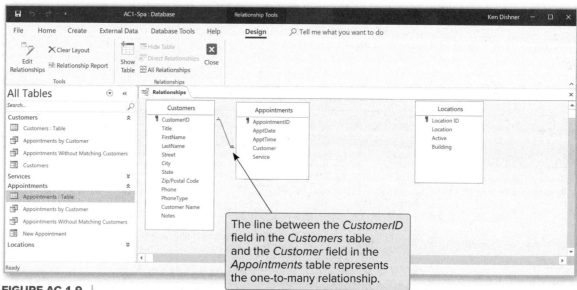

The line between the *CustomerID* field in the *Customers* table and the *Customer* field in the *Appointments* table represents the one-to-many relationship.

FIGURE AC 1.9

To display a table that isn't already showing in the Relationships window:

1. On the *Relationship Tools Design* tab, in the *Relationships* group, click the **Show Table** button to open the *Show Table* dialog.

2. Double-click the table you want to add to the Relationships window. You can also select the table name and then click the **Add** button in the *Show Table* dialog.

3. When you are finished adding tables to the Relationships window, click the **Close** button to close the *Show Table* dialog.

Figure AC 1.10 shows the effect of adding the *Services* table to the Relationships window. Notice the new lines representing the relationships between the *Appointments* table and the *Services* table and between the *Services* table and the *Locations* table.

FIGURE AC 1.10

On the *Relationship Tools Design* tab, in the *Relationships* group, click the **Close** button to close the Relationships window.

If you have made changes to the layout of the Relationships window, Access will ask if you want to save the changes. Click **Yes**.

tips & tricks

You can display all the database relationships at once by clicking the **All Relationships** button on the *Relationship Tools Design* tab.

tell me more

To hide a table in the Relationships window:

1. Select the table by clicking it in the Relationships window.
2. On the *Relationship Tools Design* tab, in the *Relationships* group, click the **Hide Table** button.
3. Select the table by clicking it in the Relationships window.

another method

To open the *Show Table* dialog, right-click anywhere in the Relationships window and select **Show Table...** from the shortcut menu.

let me try

If you do not have the data file from the previous skill open, open the student data file **AC1-Spa** and try this skill on your own:

1. Open the Relationships window.
2. Open the *Show Table* dialog.
3. Show the *Services* table.
4. Close the *Show Table* dialog.
5. Close the Relationships window, saving the layout changes.

Skill 1.4 Organizing Objects in the Navigation Pane

As you have learned, the Navigation Pane lists all the objects in the database. By default, the Navigation Pane displays objects organized by the *Tables and Related Views* category. This category creates a group for each table in the database. The first object listed in the group is the table. Beneath the table, Access lists the other database objects that are dependent on that table. For example, in Figure AC 1.11, the *Customers* group includes the *Customers* table and the queries and form that use the data stored in that table.

The *Customers* table is listed first in the group.

The database objects dependent on the *Customers* table are listed below it.

Customers Group

Collapse Group Button

Expand Group Button

FIGURE AC 1.11

If you are working with the database objects in a single group, it may be helpful to collapse the other groups:

❭ To collapse a group in the Navigation Pane so only the group name is visible, click the **Collapse Group** button ⌃ located at the right side of the group name.

❭ To expand a group, click the **Expand Group** button ⌄.

If you would rather group the database objects by object type, you can change the category by which the Navigation Pane is grouped:

1. Click the top of the Navigation Pane to display the category and group list.

2. In the *Navigate To Category* section, select **Object Type**.

Now the Navigation Pane groups all the tables together in one group, all the queries together in another, all the forms together in another, and all the reports together in the final group.

FIGURE AC 1.12

You can also group database objects by date:

1. Click the top of the Navigation Pane to display the category and group list.
2. In the *Navigate To Category* section:
   - Select **Created Date** to group database objects by the date they were created.
   - Select **Modified Date** to group database objects by the date they were last changed.

tips & tricks

If you have a custom group defined in your Navigation Pane, select the **Custom** option from the Navigation Pane category and group list to group objects into those you have assigned to the custom group and those that are unassigned.

tell me more

You can also apply a filter to the Navigation Pane to display only a specific group within the category. Click the top of the Navigation Pane, and click an option in the *Filter By Group* section. The groups available vary, depending on the category and the actual objects in your database.

To remove the group filter, click the top of the Navigation Pane again, and select the last option (*All Access Objects*, *Show All*, *All Dates*, or *All Tables*) in the *Filter By Group* section.

let me try

If you do not have the data file from the previous skill open, open the student data file **AC1-Spa** and try this skill on your own:

1. Change the Navigation Pane grouping option to **Object Type**.
2. Change the Navigation Pane grouping option back to **Tables and Related Views**.

Skill 1.5 Switching between Database Object Views

When you open a database object from the Navigation Pane, it opens in the default view for that object. For examples of each of the default object views, review the figures in the skill *Introduction to Access*.

❯ Tables open in **Datasheet view** where you can enter, sort, and filter data. From Datasheet view you can also add new fields and modify some field properties.

❯ Forms open in **Form view** which provides a user-friendly interface for entering data. If the form is formatted similar to a table, it will open in a special form Datasheet view. You cannot change the form layout or formatting from these views.

❯ Queries open in Datasheet view showing the record set that matches the query criteria. Datasheet view for a query does not allow you to modify fields.

❯ Reports open in **Report view** which shows a static view of the report. You cannot change the layout or formatting of the report from Report view.

If you want to work on the structure of a database object, you will need to switch to another view. On the *Home* tab, in the *Views* group, click the **View** button arrow, and select the view you want.

You can also switch views from the buttons at the far right side of the status bar. The button representing the current view appears highlighted. The name of the current view appears at the left side of the status bar.

Design view is used to modify the structure of the database object. When you are working with an object in Design view, you see only the structural elements of the object, not the data. Figure AC 1.13 shows the *Average Service Price per Location* report in Design view.

FIGURE AC 1.13

For queries, Design view provides a visual grid to create the underlying programming code that defines the parameters and criteria used to generate the resulting dataset. Queries also offer **SQL view** where advanced users can write code directly to build the query.

Forms and reports also offer **Layout view** where you can modify some (but not all) structural elements. The benefit of Layout view is that you can see live data in the object while you work on the object layout. Figure AC 1.14 shows the *Average Service Price per Location* report in Layout view. Observe the differences between Design view in Figure AC 1.13 and Layout view in Figure AC 1.14.

FIGURE AC 1.14

Reports include **Print Preview**, which shows how the report will look when printed. When you are in Print Preview view, only the *Print Preview* tab is available. From this tab, you can adjust print settings and export the report to another file format.

tips & tricks

Table data and query results in Datasheet view are sometimes referred to as **datasheets**.

another method

To switch views you can also right-click the object tab and select the view you want.

let me try

If you do not have the data file from the previous skill open, open the student data file **AC1-Spa** and try this skill on your own:

1. Open the *Average Service Price per Location* report located in the *Locations* group in the Navigation Pane. Alternatively, you may need to expand the *Services* group or the *Reports* group to find the report. It will open in *Report* view.
2. Switch to **Design** view.
3. Switch to **Layout** view.
4. Close the report.

Skill 1.6 Navigating Records

Tables, forms, and query results often contain many records and can be difficult to navigate. At the bottom of the datasheet or form window, you'll find navigation buttons to help you move quickly to the beginning or end of the dataset. You can jump to a specific record number or advance through records one at a time.

To navigate among records in a table, form, or query results:

❭ Move to the next record by clicking the **Next Record** button.

❭ Move to the previous record by clicking the **Previous Record** button.

❭ Move to the first record in the dataset by clicking the **First Record** button.

❭ Move to the last record in the dataset by clicking the **Last Record** button.

❭ Move to a specific record number by typing the number in the **Current Record** box, then pressing **Enter**.

Figure AC 1.15 shows the *Customers* form and the *Customers* table. Both database objects have the same navigation tools even though the form displays only one record at a time while the table datasheet shows all the records.

FIGURE AC 1.15

You can use the arrow keys on your keyboard to navigate through fields in a record or between records.

❭ Press ⭢ to go to the next field in the record.

❭ Press ⭠ to go to the previous field in the record.

❭ Press ⭣ to go to the next record.

❭ Press ⭡ to go to the previous record.

❯ Press ⌃Ctrl + ⬆ to go to the first record.

❯ Press ⌃Ctrl + ⬇ to go to the last record.

You can use ⭾Tab to navigate from field to field and from record to record:

❯ Pressing ⭾Tab moves you from field to field within a record.

❯ Pressing ⭾Tab from the last field in the record will move you to the first field in the next record.

❯ If you are on the last record in the dataset, pressing ⭾Tab will create a new blank record (if creating a new record is allowed).

another **method**

The record navigation commands are also available from the *Home* tab, in the *Find* group. Click the **Go To** button, and then click one of the navigation options from the menu.

let me **try**

If you do not have the data file from the previous skill open, open the student data file **AC1-Spa** and try this skill on your own:

1. If necessary, open the *Customers* table in *Datasheet* view.
2. Go to the **last** record.
3. Go to the **previous** record.
4. Go to the **first** record.
5. Go to the **next** record.
6. Go to record number **22**.
7. Keep the table open if you are moving on to the next skill; close it if you are finished working with these skills.

From the Perspective of. . .

PROJECT MANAGER

I inherited a database from the person who had my job before me. I am not a database expert, so before I attempted any data entry, I made sure I understood the structure of the database. I used the Relationships window to see how the tables relate to one another. I also switched the Navigation Pane organization to show the tables and related views, so I could see which forms and reports go with which tables. After spending some time exploring the database objects, I felt much more comfortable about using the database. I'm really glad I didn't jump in and start making changes right away.

Comstock/SuperStock

Skill 1.7 Creating a New Record in a Table and Entering Data

Data are entered in records—through tables or forms. When entering records in a table, you must use Datasheet view. When you enter data in a table, Access commits the data (saves them) each time you move to a new field or begin a new record.

To enter data in a new record in a table:

1. Open the table in Datasheet view.

2. If the last row of the table is visible, you can enter data by typing in the first field in the next row available for data entry indicated by an asterisk * in the row selector.

3. If the last row of the table is not visible, insert a new record by clicking the **New (blank) record** button at the bottom of the table, or on the *Home* tab, in the *Records* group, click the **New** button.

FIGURE AC 1.16

4. Enter the data in the first field of the blank record. Notice that when you begin entering data, the * changes to a pencil icon 🖉 to indicate you are writing data to the record.

5. Press (Tab) or (← Enter) to move to the next field.

6. When you've entered all the data for the new record, press (Tab) or (← Enter) to start another new record.

Not all fields allow you to enter data by typing.

❭ If a field uses the *AutoNumber* format, you will not be able to type in that cell of the datasheet. Instead, move to the next cell to begin entering data. Access will populate the *AutoNumber* field automatically with the next number in sequence.

❭ Some fields (called lookup fields) have lists from which you choose values. Click the arrow in the field to display the list of available values and click the value you want.

FIGURE AC 1.17

❭ Some fields require a specific input format (called an input mask). When you enter data in a field that has an input mask, Access will display placeholder characters such as underscores to guide you as you enter data. Access will not let you enter characters that violate the input mask rules (for example, entering a number when a letter is required). The input mask in the *Phone* field in Figure AC 1.18 requires three numbers for the area code followed by three numbers and then four numbers. The periods separating the parts of the phone number are entered automatically as part of the input mask.

FIGURE AC 1.18

another **method**

Here are other ways to add a new blank record to the table:

❭ On the *Home* tab, in the *Find* group, click the **Go To** button, and select **New**.

❭ Right-click any of the row selector buttons and select **New Record** from the menu.

❭ Use the keyboard shortcut (Ctrl) + (+).

let me **try**

If you do not have the data file from the previous skill open, open the student data file **AC1-Spa** and try this skill on your own:

1. If necessary, open the *Customers* table in *Datasheet* view. You may want to collapse the Navigation Pane to give yourself more room to work with the table data.

2. Begin a new record.

3. Enter the customer ID: **BBA-200**

4. Select **Ms.** as the title from the lookup list in the next field.

5. Enter **Margo** as the first name and **Manning** as the last name.

6. Enter data for the remaining fields in the table using an address and phone number of your choice.

7. Keep the table open if you are moving on to the next skill; close it if you are finished working with these skills.

Skill 1.8 Sorting Records in a Datasheet

You can control the order in which records appear in a table, query, or form by using the *Sort* feature. Sorting records in Access is similar to sorting data in Excel.

To sort records in a table:

1. Open the table in Datasheet view.

2. Click anywhere in the field you want to sort.

3. On the *Home* tab, in the *Sort & Filter* group, click the button for the sort order you want to apply: **Ascending** or **Descending**. Ascending and descending have different meanings for different data types.

   - *Text* and *Hyperlink* fields sort alphabetically from A to Z (ascending) or Z to A (descending).

   - *Number*, *Currency*, and *AutoNumber* fields sort on their numeric values from smallest to largest (ascending) or largest to smallest (descending)

   - *Date/Time* fields sort by time from oldest to newest (ascending) or newest to oldest (descending).

   - *Yes/No* fields are often displayed as check boxes and sort from selected to cleared (ascending) or cleared to selected (descending). A checkmark or "yes" value is the "selected" state.

4. Save the database object if you want to save the sorting.

   To clear all sorting from the database object, on the *Home* tab, in the *Sort & Filter* group, click the **Remove Sort** button.

FIGURE AC 1.19

You can create multiple levels of sorting by applying the sort command to the fields in the ***opposite*** order in which you want the sort to appear. For example, if you want records sorted by appointment date and then by appointment time for each date, you would sort by appointment time first, and then sort by appointment date. The first sort level is called the **outermost sort**. The last sort level is called the **innermost sort**. This may seem completely counterintuitive, but when applying the sort commands, sort the innermost sort first and the outermost sort last. You can have as many sort levels as you want, but remember to begin with the innermost sort and work your way out.

To create the sort shown in Figure AC 1.20, first apply an ascending sort to the *ApptTime* field, and then apply a descending sort to the *ApptDate* field. The records in the table display sorted first by dates in the *ApptDate* field with the newest dates at the top. This is the outermost sort. Within each date, the records are then sorted by the *ApptTime* field from oldest to newest. This is the innermost sort.

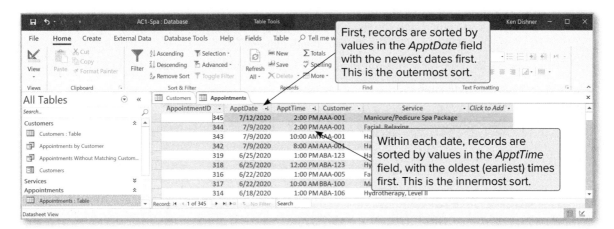

FIGURE AC 1.20

tips & tricks

The sort order you apply to a database object is saved when you save the object.

another **method**

> If the database object is in datasheet format, you can click the arrow at the top of the column you want to sort and select a sort option.

> You can also right-click a field and select a sort option.

let me **try**

If you do not have the data file from the previous skill open, open the student data file **AC1-Spa** and try this skill on your own:

1. If necessary, open the *Customers* table in *Datasheet* view.
2. Sort the records by values in the *LastName* field, from A to Z.
3. Clear the sort.
4. Open the *Appointments* table in *Datasheet* view.
5. Sort the records so the results are sorted by date, with the newest date first, and then by time within each date, with the oldest time first. *Hint*: Remember, in a multilevel sort, apply the innermost sort first.
6. Save and close the *Appointments* table.
7. Keep the *Customers* table open if you are moving on to the next skill; close it if you are finished working with these skills.

Skill 1.9 Adjusting Table Column Widths

When you insert a new field, it is created with the standard width, which may not be wide enough to display all your data. Adjusting column widths in Datasheet view is similar to working with column widths in Excel.

To use the *Column Width* dialog to change the column size:

1. On the *Home* tab, in the *Records* group, click the **More** button, and select **Field Width** to open the *Column Width* dialog.
2. Type the width you want in the **Column Width** box, or click the **Best Fit** button.
3. Click **OK.**

FIGURE AC 1.21

Select **Field Width** to open the *Column Width* dialog.

Double-click right column border to resize for best fit.

FIGURE AC 1.22

To use the mouse to change the column size:

1. Move the mouse to the right border of the field header.
2. The cursor changes to a ✛ shape.
3. Click and drag to resize the column width, or double-click the right column border to automatically resize the column to best fit the data.

tips & tricks

Do not confuse field size with field width. *Field size* refers to the number of characters the field can hold in the database. *Field width* or *column width* refers to the number of characters that are visible onscreen. This can be a little confusing because Access uses the terms *field width* and *column width* interchangeably.

Refer to the skill *Modifying the Field Size Property* for more information about working with the Field Size property.

another **method**

You can also open the *Column Width* dialog by right-clicking the field column header and selecting **Field Width**.

let me **try**

If you do not have the data file from the previous skill open, open the student data file **AC1-Spa** and try this skill on your own:

1. If necessary, open the *Customers* table in *Datasheet* view.
2. Modify the width of the *CustomerID* column to exactly **12**.
3. Modify the width of the *Street* column to best fit the data.
4. Save and close the table.

Skill 1.10 Creating a New Record in a Form and Entering Data

When you use a form to enter data, you are actually adding data to the underlying table. The form is a more convenient and user-friendly format for entering and editing records. When you enter or edit data in a form, Access commits the data (saves it) each time you move to a new field or begin a new record.

To enter data in a new record in a form:

1. Open the form in Form view.

2. Some forms are designed to automatically open to a new record where you can immediately begin entering data. If necessary, you can start a new blank record by clicking the **New (blank) record** button at the bottom of the form window. Or, on the *Home* tab, in the *Records* group, click the **New** button.

FIGURE AC 1.23

3. Type or select the data in the first field of the record. Notice that when you begin entering data, the * in the record selector changes to a pencil icon to indicate that you are writing data to the record.

4. Press (Tab) or (← Enter) to move to the next field. The form design determines the tab order—that is, the order in which (Tab) moves from field to field in the form.

5. When you've entered all the data for the new record, press (Tab) or (← Enter) to start another new record.

Access offers database designers a wide variety of tools for creating forms, so no two forms may look or behave exactly alike. Some forms are designed for entering new records only and do not allow you to view or edit existing records; other forms are designed for editing existing records and do not allow you to create new ones.

If a field uses the *AutoNumber* format, you will not be able to enter a value in the form. Access will add a number automatically when you begin entering data in the form. *Date* fields may include a Date Picker control which provides a calendar interface for selecting a date. For more information about data entry, refer to the skill *Creating a New Record in a Table and Entering Data*.

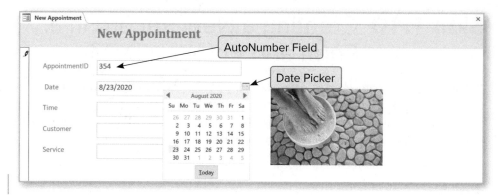

FIGURE AC 1.24

tips & tricks

If one of the fields is a *Long Text* field, you won't be able to use ⏎Enter to move to the next field. Pressing ⏎Enter will just keep adding blank lines to the text. Use Tab⇄ or the mouse to move to the next field.

another **method**

Here are other ways to enter a new blank record in a form:

❭ On the *Home* tab, in the *Find* group, click the **Go To** button, and select **New**.

❭ Right-click any of the row selector buttons and select **New Record** from the menu.

❭ Use the keyboard shortcut Ctrl + +.

let me **try**

If you do not have the data file from the previous skill open, open the student data file **AC1-Spa** and try this skill on your own:

1. Open the *New Appointment* form.

2. Begin a new blank record.

3. Notice that you cannot enter data in the *AppointmentID* field. When you begin entering data in the next field in the form, Access will add the next sequential appointment number to this field automatically.

4. Enter the date **8/23/20** and time **1:00 PM** for the appointment.

5. Select the customer **Dr. Rose Carnation** and the service **Hair Salon, Cut, Short** from the lists for those fields.

6. Keep the *New Appointment* form open if you are moving on to the next skill; close it if you are finished working with these skills.

Skill 1.11 Using Undo and Redo

If you make a mistake when working, the **Undo** command allows you to reverse the last action you performed. The **Redo** command allows you to reverse the *Undo* command and restore the file to its previous state. The Quick Access Toolbar gives you immediate access to both these commands.

To undo the last action taken, click the **Undo** button on the Quick Access Toolbar, or click the **Undo** button arrow and select the action to undo.

If you are working on data entry in Datasheet view or Form view, the *Undo* command is applied to the entire record, not each individual field within the record. If you made multiple changes to the record at the same time, the *Undo* command will reverse all the changes at once. In addition, the *Undo* command can be applied only to the last modified record. If you made changes to multiple records, you are out of luck.

FIGURE AC 1.25

To redo the last action taken, click the **Redo** button on the Quick Access Toolbar.

The *Redo* command is useful mostly when you are working with formatting design elements in forms and reports. It is not available for data entry tasks.

tips & tricks

If you are familiar with using *Undo* and *Redo* in other Office applications, be very careful in Access. There are many actions that cannot be undone. Usually, but not always, Access will warn you before you do something that can't be undone.

another method

Use the keyboard shortcuts:

❯ Undo = `Ctrl` + `Z`

❯ Redo = `Ctrl` + `Y`

let me try

If you do not have the data file from the previous skill open, open the student data file **AC1-Spa** and try this skill on your own:

1. If necessary, open the *New Appointment* form in *Form* view.

2. Enter data for a new appointment. Do not continue to another new record.

3. Undo the data entry. Notice that the data entry for the entire record is undone at once.

4. Close the form.

Skill 1.12 Finding and Replacing Data

Access provides a number of ways to search for information in your database. For a simple search in a table, form, or query, you can use the *Search* box next to the navigation buttons at the bottom of the datasheet or form.

1. In the *Search* box, begin typing the letters, numbers, or symbols you want to find.

2. As you type, Access highlights the first field in the first record that matches what you have typed so far.

3. As you continue typing, Access dynamically updates the search result.

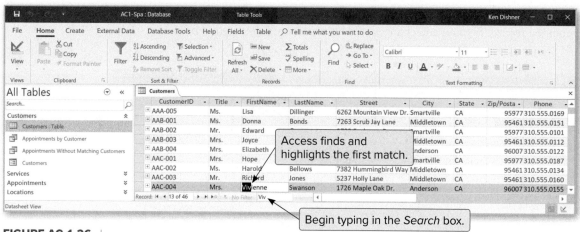

FIGURE AC 1.26

If you need to find multiple records that match your search parameters, not just the first one, use the *Find* command. If you have used other Microsoft Office applications, the *Find and Replace* dialog will be familiar to you.

To search for specific records using the *Find* command:

1. Open the database object you want to search. The *Find* command is available for any object in Datasheet view, Form view, Report view, or Layout view.

2. On the *Home* tab, in the *Find* group, click the **Find** button to open the *Find and Replace* dialog.

3. Type the data you want to search for in the *Find What* box.

4. Click **Find Next** to go to the first record that matches the search criteria. Continue clicking **Find Next** until Access displays a message that there are no more records that meet your search criteria.

5. Click the **X** in the upper right corner of the dialog to close it.

To narrow the search parameters in the *Find and Replace* dialog:

❭ Use the *Look In* list to specify whether to search only in the currently selected field or throughout the entire document (the open database object).

❭ Use the *Match* list to specify a match for any part of the field, the whole field, or only the beginning of the field.

❭ Use the *Search* list to search only up or down from the current record or to search all the records.

❭ Use the *Match Case* check box to find only records that match the case of your find text. This check box is available even if you are searching for numerical data.

FIGURE AC 1.27

To find and replace data:

1. On the *Home* tab, in the *Find* group, click the **Replace** button. If the *Find and Replace* dialog is already open, click the **Replace** tab.

2. Enter the data to find in the *Find What* box.

3. Enter the data to replace it with in the *Replace With* box.

4. Click the **Replace** button to find and replace just the first instance, or click the **Replace All** button to replace all instances at once. Unlike other Office applications, Access will not tell you how many replacements were made.

5. Access warns you that you will not be able to undo this operation. Click **Yes** to continue.

6. Click the X in the upper right corner of the *Find and Replace* dialog to close it.

tips & tricks

Use wildcards in the *Find and Replace* dialog if you are not sure of the exact data you want to find.

❱ Use an asterisk * in place of text or numbers of any length. For example, if you know the word or phrase begins with B, using B* will find records for Ben, Bob, and Betty.

❱ Use question marks ? in place of specific letters or numbers where each ? represents one character or digit. For example, B?? will find records that start with B followed by two characters such as Ben and Bob but not Betty.

let me try

If you do not have the data file from the previous skill open, open the student data file **AC1-Spa** and try this skill on your own:

1. Open the *Customers* table in *Datasheet* view.

2. Use the *Search* box to begin searching for a customer with the first name beginning with *Vivi*. Notice that as you type **V** and then **i**, Access first highlights a record with the word *View* in the *Street* field. Once you finish entering **Viv** in the *Search* box, Access finds the record with **Vivienne** in the *FirstName* field.

3. Use the *Find and Replace* dialog to find the record with the text **swanson**, matching the case exactly.

4. Replace all instances of **swanson** with **Swanson**. Be sure to match the case exactly.

5. Close the table.

Skill 1.13 Deleting Records

You can delete records. However, if your database has a complex structure, deleting records may not be as simple as the procedures listed below because records in one table may be linked to records in another table. Access will prevent you from deleting records if the deletion would violate the integrity of the database. *You cannot undo a record deletion*.

To delete a record in Datasheet view:

1. Click the record selector so the record you want to delete is selected.
2. On the *Home* tab, in the *Records* group, click the **Delete** button.
3. Access warns you that you cannot undo the deletion. Click **Yes** to continue.

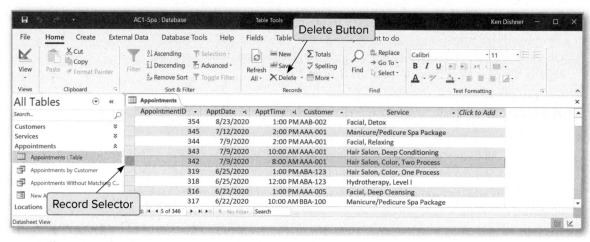

FIGURE AC 1.28

Deleting a record in a form will delete the record in the underlying table. To delete a record in Form view:

1. Navigate to the record you want to delete.
2. On the *Home* tab, in the *Records* group, click the **Delete** button arrow, and select **Delete Record**.
3. Access warns you that you cannot undo the deletion. Click **Yes** to continue.

another **method**

1. Right-click the record selector and select **Delete Record**.
2. Select the record, and press **Delete**.
3. Select the record and use the keyboard shortcut (Ctrl) + (-).

let me **try**

If you do not have the data file from the previous skill open, open the student data file **AC1-Spa** and try this skill on your own:

1. Open the *Appointment* table in *Datasheet* view.
2. Delete the appointment with the Appointment ID **342**. It should be the third record in the table.
3. Close the table.

Skill 1.14 Deleting and Renaming Database Objects

When you are in the process of designing your database, you may find that you have database objects you no longer need or that you want to use different names for objects. Access allows you to delete and rename forms, reports, and other database objects.

To delete a database object:

1. Right-click the object name in the Navigation Pane and select **Delete**.

2. Access displays a confirmation message asking if you want to delete the object. Click **Yes** to delete it or **No** to cancel the delete command.

Be careful! Once you delete a database object, you cannot undo the deletion.

To rename a database object:

1. Right-click the object name in the Navigation Pane and select **Rename**.

2. Type the new object name, and press ⏎ Enter.

Changing the name of a table may have unexpected consequences. Forms and reports based on the table will update automatically to use the new table name. However, queries may not update properly, causing errors not only in the query, but in the forms and reports that use the query as well.

FIGURE AC 1.29

FIGURE AC 1.30

tips & tricks

Access will warn you if you try to delete a table that would invalidate relationships. If you are sure you want to delete the table, Access will automatically delete the relationships, and then delete the table. If you do not allow Access to delete the relationships, Access will not delete the table.

another method

You can delete a database object by selecting it in the Navigation Pane, and then on the *Home* tab, in the *Records* group, click the **Delete** button.

let me try

If you do not have the data file from the previous skill open, open the student data file **AC1-Spa** and try this skill on your own:

1. If necessary, open the Navigation Pane.

2. If necessary, change the Navigation Pane category to **Tables and Related Views**.

3. If there are open database objects, close them all.

4. In the *Customers* group, delete the query **Appointments Without Matching Customers**.

5. In the *Customers* group, rename the form Customers to: **Master Customer Form**

Skill 1.15 Previewing and Printing Database Objects

Normally in Access, reports are the only database objects printed. However, there may be times when you want to print a table, form, or the results of a query. Although these database objects do not have a Print Preview view like reports do, you can still print and preview them from Backstage view. From Backstage view, Print Preview shows you a reduced version of the active database object as it will appear when printed. Save time and paper by always checking your page layout in Print Preview view before you print. To preview a database object for printing:

1. Click the **File** tab to open Backstage view.
2. Click **Print**.
3. On the *Print* page, click the **Print Preview** button.

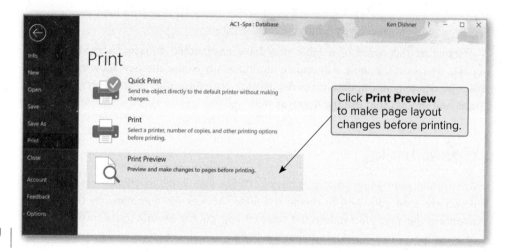

Click **Print Preview** to make page layout changes before printing.

FIGURE AC 1.31

4. Access switches to Print Preview view.
5. Before printing, you should ensure that the data fit on the printed page the way you want.
   - On the *Print Preview* tab, in the *Zoom* group, click the **Two Pages** button or click the **More Pages** button and select **Four Pages**, **Eight Pages**, or **Twelve Pages**. This lets you preview how the printed data will break across pages.
   - If the object you are printing has many columns or is wider than 8.5 inches, switch the page orientation from portrait to landscape. On the *Print Preview* tab, in the *Page Layout* group, click the **Landscape** button.
6. To print, click the **Print** button located at the far left side of the *Print Preview* tab.
7. The *Print* dialog opens. From the *Print* dialog, you can set a range of pages to print, enter the number of copies to print, and choose to print to any printer connected to your computer.
8. Click **OK** in the dialog to print the database object.
9. Click the **Close Print Preview** button at the far right side of the Ribbon to return to your regular Access view.

FIGURE AC 1.32

tips & tricks

Access is the only Office application that uses a dedicated Print Preview page. Word, Excel, and PowerPoint incorporate a Print Preview directly into Backstage view. However, keep in mind that the print options for table, form, and query are not saved once the object is closed.

tell me **more**

The *Quick Print* command prints database objects using all the default print settings.

1. Click the **File** tab.
2. Click **Print**.
3. On the *Print* page, click the **Quick Print** button.

another **method**

To print the current database object using the default print settings, you can also press $Ctrl$ + P. The *Print* dialog will open. Click **OK** to print the database object.

let me **try**

If you do not have the data file from the previous skill open, open the student data file **AC1-Spa** and try this skill on your own:

1. In the Navigation Pane, double-click the **Appointments by Customer** query to view the query results in Datasheet view.
2. Preview how the *Appointments by Customer* query would look if it were printed.
3. Change the orientation to **Landscape**.
4. Change the view to show two pages at once.
5. Close Print Preview.

Skill 1.16 Backing Up a Database

Remember that the *Undo* function is very limited in Access. If you are about to add a significant amount of data that you may not want to keep, or if you are experimenting with the design of the database, you should create a backup first. By backing up your database, you create a copy of it and preserve the data at a certain point. At any time you can open the backup and restore your data from an earlier stage. Be sure to create a backup of your database before making any major changes to the database structure.

To create a backup of your database:

1. Close and save any open objects.
2. Click the **File** tab.
3. Click **Save As**.
4. Click **Back Up Database** in the *Save Database As* section at the right side of the page.
5. Click the **Save As** button.

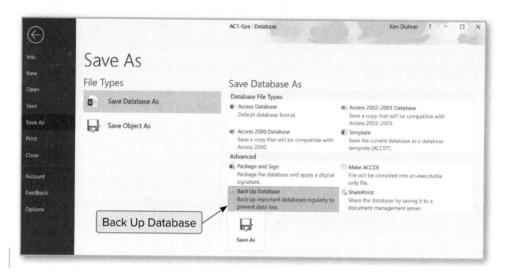

FIGURE AC 1.33

6. The *Save As* dialog opens.

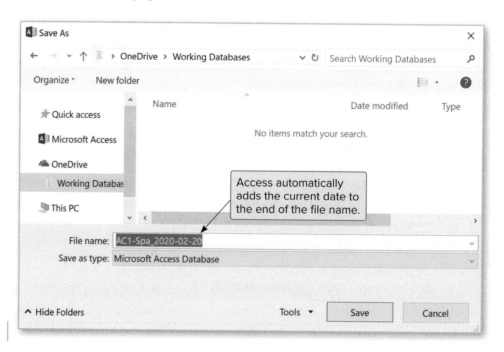

Access automatically adds the current date to the end of the file name.

FIGURE AC 1.34

7. If necessary, navigate to the location where you want to save the backup file. Access automatically creates a new file name for the backup using the original file name with the current date.

8. Click **Save** to create the backup file.

To make a copy of the database to experiment with, but not necessarily keep as a backup:

1. Follow the same steps as you would to create a backup, but in the *Save As* page, select **Access Database** in the *Save Database As* section.

2. If necessary, navigate to the location where you want to save the copy. In the *File name* box, enter a name for the database copy.

3. Click **Save** to create the copy.

   You are now working on a copy of the database, and any further changes you make will not affect the original.

tips & tricks

To save a copy of the database, you must close all open database objects. If you have any database objects open when you invoke the *Save As* command, Access will offer to close them for you. If any of the open objects have not been saved, Access will also offer to save them for you.

tell me **more**

If you find that you need to restore a database object (such as a table, query, form, or report) from a backup copy, click the *External Data* tab. In the *Import & Link* group, click the **Import Access Database** button to find and restore the database object you want.

If you want to completely replace a database with a backup copy, delete the database file you no longer want and then rename the backup so it has the original file name.

let me **try**

If you do not have the data file from the previous skill open, open the student data file **AC1-Spa** and try this skill on your own:

1. Save a copy of the database to use as a backup.

2. Accept the file name suggested by Access.

Skill 1.17 Creating a Database from a Template

A **template** is a file with predefined settings that you can use as a base to create a new database of your own. Using a template makes creating a fully formatted and designed database easy, saving you time and effort. Access templates include databases to manage contacts, track projects, and create a sales pipeline. When the database opens, you'll have an empty database structure complete with tables, forms, and reports, ready for you to enter data.

To create a new database from a template:

1. If you already have a database open, click the **File** tab to open Backstage view, and click **New**.
2. The *New* page displays templates included when you installed Access.
3. Click a template icon for a detailed description of the template.
4. To download the template, type a meaningful name in the *File Name* box to replace the default database name.
5. If necessary, change the location by clicking the folder icon and navigate to the location where you want to save the new database.
6. Click the **Create** button to create the new database from the template.

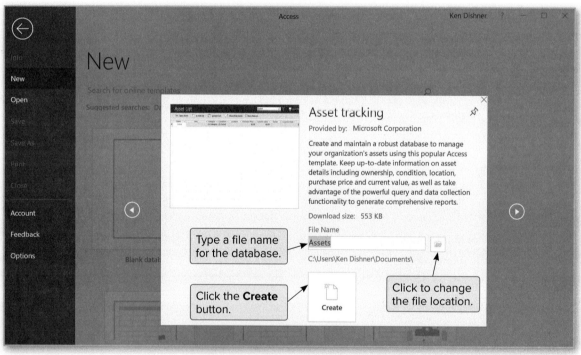

FIGURE AC 1.35

7. A new database opens, prepopulated with all the template objects.

8. If the database template you selected includes macros or other active content, the Message Bar will show a security warning. Click the **Enable Content** button to allow the active content to run.

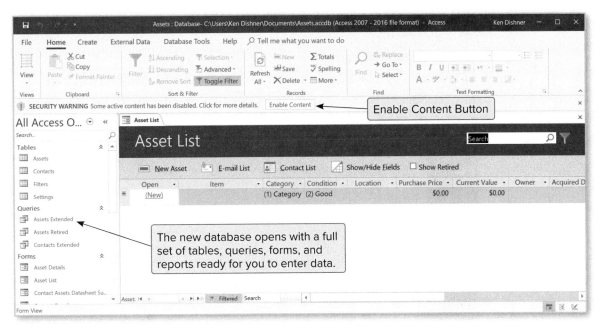

tips & tricks

Some of the database templates can be complicated, with many related tables. Before entering data, take some time to review the tables and table relationships. You may remove any unnecessary fields, but be careful not to remove a field that is part of a relationship.

tell me **more**

If the installed templates listed on the *New* page do not meet your needs, try searching for one online. At the top of the *New* page, type a keyword in the *Search for online templates* box or click one of the suggested terms listed below the search box. Access returns a list of templates that match the search. Note that searching for online templates requires an active Internet connection.

another **method**

If you are opening the Access application directly, you begin at the *Start* page. Templates are listed at the right side of the page just as they are in the *New* page.

let me **try**

If a database is not already open, open Access and try this skill on your own:

1. Create a new database from the **Asset tracking** template.

2. Name the database: **Assets**

Skill 1.18 Creating a New Blank Database

To begin a new Access database from scratch, you must first create the database file. You cannot begin creating tables, forms, and other database objects until the database has been saved.

To create a new blank database:

1. If you already have a database open, click the **File** tab to open Backstage view.
2. Click **New**.
3. Click the **Blank database** icon.

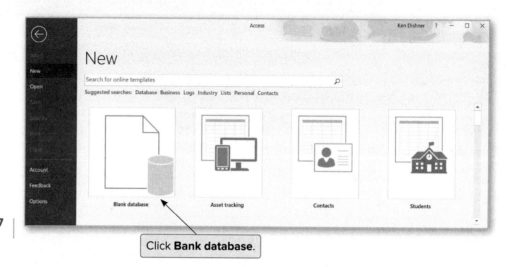

FIGURE AC 1.37

Click **Bank database**.

4. Enter a file name for the new database in the *File Name* box. If you want to create the file in a different location, click the folder icon and navigate to the location you want.
5. Click the **Create** button to create the new blank database.

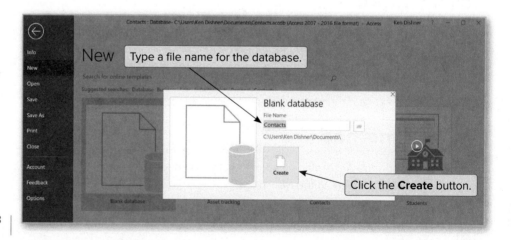

Type a file name for the database.

Click the **Create** button.

FIGURE AC 1.38

If you began with another database open, Access will close it and open the new blank database.

Access begins the new database with a temporary table, *Table1*, open in Datasheet view where you can begin adding data. As with any new table in Datasheet view, the first field is an *AutoNumber* field named *ID*. When you close the table, Access will prompt you to save the table with a new name. If you close the table and choose not to save it, Access will remove it from the Navigation Pane.

FIGURE AC 1.39

tips & tricks

Unlike other Microsoft Office applications, Access does not create a new blank database when you open the application. Instead, Access opens to Backstage view where you can select an existing database to open or begin a new one.

tell me more

For more information about working with new tables, refer to these skills:

❭ *Creating and Saving a Table in Datasheet View*

❭ *Renaming Fields*

❭ *Adding Fields in Datasheet View*

❭ *Using Quick Start to Add Related Fields*

let me try

If a database is not already open, open Access and try this skill on your own:

1. Create a new blank database and name it: **Contacts**

2. Close the default table without saving it.

3. Keep the *Contacts* database open if you are moving on to the next skill; close it if you are finished working with these skills.

Skill 1.19 Using Quick Start Application Parts

Beginning a new blank database can be intimidating. **Quick Start application parts** provide a table template that you can use to start building a database. Most also include forms for data entry. There are five Quick Start application parts available:

Comments—Contains a single table. Good for maintaining a running list of changes to the database.

Contacts—Contains one table, one query, three forms, and four reports. Good for storing names, addresses, and phone numbers for customers, vendors, students, employees, or any similar group of people.

Issues—Contains one table and two forms for data entry. Good for tracking technical support issues or project-related problems.

Tasks—Contains one table and two forms for data entry. Good for a to-do list or parts of a larger project.

Users—Contains one table and two forms for data entry. Good for tracking e-mail addresses and login information for website or network users.

To use a Quick Start application part:

1. On the *Create* tab, in the *Templates* group, click the **Application Parts** button to expand the gallery.

2. In the *Quick Start* section, click the option you want to add.

FIGURE AC 1.40

3. If you have any objects open, Access will ask to close them. Click **Yes**.

4. If your database has other tables, Access will ask if you want to establish a relationship between the new table added by the application part and another table in your database.

   • To continue without adding any table relationships, select the **There is no relationship** radio button and then click the **Create** button.

   • To create a one-to-many relationship between the tables, select the radio button for the relationship you want to create and then follow the prompts to create the new field for the "many" side of the relationship.

5. Access automatically adds the objects in the application part you selected to your database.

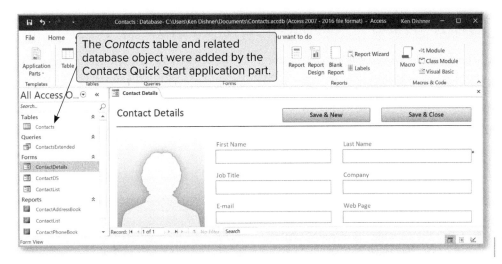

FIGURE AC 1.41

tell me more

If you have a table and related database objects that you use often, you can save the group as a custom application part.

1. Delete any database objects you don't want to include in the application part. (Be sure to make a copy of the database first!)
2. Click the **File** tab and then click **Save As**.
3. In the list of database file types, select **Template**, and then click the **Save As** button.
4. In the *Create New Template from this Database* dialog, enter a name for the application part and a description.
5. Click the **Application Part** check box.
6. Click **OK**.

The new application part is now available from the *User Templates* section at the bottom of the *Application Parts* gallery.

let me try

If the *Contacts* database is not already open, open the data file **Contacts** and try this skill on your own:

1. Add database objects from the *Contacts* Quick Start application part.
2. If Access displays the security warning, click the **Enable Content** button.
3. Open the **ContactDetails** form and enter information for a few records. Use the **Save & New** and **Save & Close** buttons.
4. Open the other database objects and observe how the database objects work together.
5. Close all open database objects without saving any changes you may have made.
6. Keep the *Contacts* database open if you are moving on to the next skill; close it if you are finished working with these skills.

Skill 1.20 Using Compact and Repair

When you delete records from an Access database, the database maintains space for the deleted data until you compact the database by removing unnecessary file space. Access also creates hidden, temporary database objects that take up database space unnecessarily. The longer your database is in use, the more of these unnecessary temporary objects there are. The **Compact and Repair Database command** eliminates these unnecessary database objects for optimum efficiency.

To use *Compact and Repair*:

1. Click the **File** tab.
2. Backstage view opens to the *Info* page automatically.
3. Click the **Compact & Repair Database** button.

FIGURE AC 1.42

If you need to interrupt the compact and repair process for any reason, press and hold **Esc**.

tips & tricks

To help your database run as efficiently as possible, it is a good practice to run *Compact and Repair* on a regular basis.

tell me more

You can set your database to compact automatically when you close it by changing the database options:

1. Click the **File** tab.
2. Click the **Options** button.
3. Click **Current Database** at the left side of the *Access Options* dialog.
4. Click the check box in front of *Compact on Close*.
5. Click **OK**.

another method

The *Compact & Repair Database* button is also available on the *Database Tools* tab, in the *Tools* group.

let me try

If the *Contacts* database is not already open, open the data file Contacts and try this skill on your own:

1. Run **Compact and Repair**.
2. Close the database if you are finished working with these skills.

Database
Table
Record
Field
Relational database
Forms
Queries
Reports
Navigation Pane
Macro
Message Bar
One-to-many relationship
Primary key
Foreign key
Relationships window
Datasheet view

Form view
Report view
Design view
SQL view
Layout view
Print Preview
Datasheets
Outermost sort
Innermost sort
Undo
Redo
Template
Quick Start application parts
Compact and Repair Database
command

concept review

1. _____ are the basic building blocks of a database.

   a. Tables

   b. Forms

   c. Queries

   d. Reports

2. Each row in a table contains all the data for a single _____.

   a. field

   b. form

   c. record

   d. query

3. Each column in a table represents a specific data value called a _____.

   a. field

   b. form

   c. record

   d. query

4. All data entered into a form are stored in the underlying _____.

   a. form

   b. table

   c. all of the above

   d. none of the above

5. You must manually save the record each time you enter data in a table or form.

   a. true

   b. false

6. When you are entering data in a new record in a form, the Undo command will _____.

   a. undo only the most recently entered field

   b. undo the entire record at once

   c. undo only formatting and layout changes to the record

   d. do nothing. The Undo command does not work in forms.

7. You can undo a record deletion.

   a. true

   b. false

8. To rename a database object, double-click the name in the Navigation Pane and type the new name.

   a. true

   b. false

9. When sorting a datasheet on more than one field, apply the _____ first.

   a. innermost sort

   b. outermost sort

   c. primary key sort

   d. foreign key sort

10. Creating a backup of the database removes unnecessary file space and hidden, temporary objects from your database.

    a. true

    b. false

projects

Data files for projects can be found by logging into your SIMnet account and going to the *Library* section.

skill review 1.1

In this project, you will review a database created for the Computer Science department of a local college. The school would like your assistance in using Access to keep track of which employees have borrowed items from the department. Become comfortable with the department's database by completing the steps below.

Skills needed to complete this project:

- Introduction to Access (Skill 1.1)
- Working with Security Warnings (Skill 1.2)
- Backing Up a Database (Skill 1.16)
- Organizing Objects in the Navigation Pane (Skill 1.4)
- Switching between Database Object Views (Skill 1.5)
- Navigating Records (Skill 1.6)
- Creating a New Record in a Table and Entering Data (Skill 1.7)

- Finding and Replacing Data (Skill 1.12)
- Deleting Records (Skill 1.13)
- Adjusting Table Column Widths (Skill 1.9)
- Sorting Records in a Datasheet (Skill 1.8)
- Deleting and Renaming Database Objects (Skill 1.14)
- Creating a New Record in a Form and Entering Data (Skill 1.10)
- Understanding and Viewing Table Relationships (Skill 1.3)
- Using Compact and Repair (Skill 1.20)

1. Open the **AC2019-SkillReview-1-1** document.

2. If necessary, enable active content by clicking the **Enable Content** button in the Message Bar.

3. Save a copy of the file to work on.

   a. Click the **File** tab.

   b. Click **Save As**.

   c. Verify that *Access Database* is selected in the *Save Database As* section.

   d. Click **Save As**.

   e. If necessary, navigate to the location where you save your personal project files.

   f. In the *File name* box, change the file name to: `[your initials]`
   `AC-SkillReview-1-1`

   g. Click **Save**.

   h. Enable active content in the new database by clicking the **Enable Content** button in the Message Bar.

4. Use the Navigation Pane.

   a. By default, the Navigation Pane displays the *Tables and Related Views* category. All tables and related objects are visible.

   b. Click the top of the Navigation Pane and select the **Object Type** category.

   c. Observe that now all database objects are visible in the Navigation Pane, grouped by object type.

5. Open the *Items* table.

   a. In the Navigation Pane, double-click the table object named **Items**.

   b. Review the fields in this table: *ItemID*, *ItemName*, *Description*, *Category*, and *Cost*.

   c. If necessary, use the horizontal scroll bar to view all the fields.

6. Switch views for the *Items* table.

   a. Note the state of the *View* button (on the *Home* tab, in the *Views* group). When you are in Datasheet view, the *Views* button displays Design view.

   b. On the *Home* tab, in the *Views* group, click the **View** button.

   c. Observe that the *View* button has switched to Datasheet view to indicate that clicking the button will return you to Datasheet view.

   d. Review the field names in Design view.

   e. Go back to Datasheet view by clicking the **View** button again.

7. Navigate records in a table.

   a. Observe the record navigation buttons at the bottom of the table. Move your mouse over the different arrow buttons and observe the ScreenTips.

b. Observe which record in the table becomes highlighted as you click the following record navigation buttons: **Last record**, **First record**, **Next record**, **Previous record**.

c. Find the *Current Record* box, which indicates the current record number and the total number of records. Click to select the number in the *Current Record* box. Type the number **7** in this box and press ⏎ Enter. The *Current Record* box should now display **7 of 21** and the seventh record in the table should be highlighted.

d. Click in any record in the table. Use the following shortcut keys on your keyboard and observe which field/record becomes highlighted: Tab ⇆, ↑, ↓, ←, →. In addition, try holding **Ctrl** while pressing the ↑, or ↓.

8. Enter a new record in the *Items* table.

a. Click the **New (blank) record** button at the bottom of the table.

b. Enter the following record into your table, using Tab ⇆ to move from one field to the next. When you reach the *Category* field, observe that it is a lookup field. Use the **drop-down arrow** to view and select from the available values.

ItemID	ItemName	Description	Category	Cost
ACC1	AccountingPro 2.0	Accounting software for professionals	Software	$175.00

9. Find the record with an item ID of **GRA1** and edit the content.

a. Type **GRA1** in the *Search* box at the bottom of the table.

b. Edit the content in the *ItemName* field to: `Graphics Studio 14`

10. Delete the **UFD1** item record.

a. Type **UFD1** in the *Search* box at the bottom of the table.

b. Click the record selector box at the left side of that row to highlight the entire record.

c. On the *Home* tab, in the *Records* group, click the **Delete** button.

d. Click **Yes** to verify that you want to delete the record.

11. AutoFit the width of the *Description* column so all the descriptions are visible by double-clicking the right border of the top of the **Description** column.

12. Sort the items in the table so they are sorted alphabetically by category and then by item name within each category.

a. Click anywhere in the *ItemName* field.

b. On the *Home* tab, in the *Sort & Filter* group, click the **Ascending** button.

c. Click anywhere in the *Category* field.

d. On the *Home* tab, in the *Sort & Filter* group, click the **Ascending** button.

e. Save the table by clicking the **Save** button on the Quick Access Toolbar at the upper left corner of the Access window.

13. Close the *Items* table by clicking the **X** at the upper right corner of the table. Be careful not to close the Access database instead.

14. Rename the *Items* form.

a. In the Navigation Pane, right-click the **Items** form and select **Rename**. Be careful not to rename the *Items* table.

b. Type: `Enter Items`

c. Press ⏎ Enter.

15. Enter a new record in a form.

   a. In the Navigation Pane, double-click the form object named **Enter Items**.

   b. Observe the record navigation buttons at the bottom of the form and note that they are the same as those in the table.

   c. Click the **New (blank) record** button at the bottom of the form.

16. Enter the following record into your form, using (Tab ⇄) to move from one field to the next.

ItemID	ItemName	Description	Category	Cost
TAB1	Tablet	High res tablet	Equipment	$649.00

17. Find and edit the record with the item ID **LAP1**.

   a. On the *Home* tab, in the *Find* group, click the **Find** button.

   b. Type **LAP1** in the *Find What* box.

   c. Click the **Find Next** button.

   d. Close the *Find and Replace* dialog by clicking the **X** in the upper right corner of the dialog.

   e. The form should now display the *Laptop 1000* item.

   f. Click in the **Cost** field and change the value from **$550** to **$799**.

18. Find and delete the record with the item ID **PB03**.

   a. On the *Home* tab, in the *Find* group, click the **Find** button.

   b. Type **PB03** in the *Find What* box.

   c. Click the **Find Next** button.

   d. Close the *Find and Replace* dialog by clicking the **X** in the upper right corner of the dialog.

   e. The form should now display the *Presentation Basics* item.

   f. On the *Home* tab, in the *Records* group, click the **Delete** button arrow, and select **Delete Record**.

   g. Click **Yes** to verify that you want to delete the record.

19. Close the *Enter Items* form.

20. Open the *Items* table again.

   a. In the Navigation Pane, double-click the table object named **Items**.

   b. Observe that the *TAB1* item record you entered in the form was added to the table. It should be listed as the eighth item in the table.

   c. Click the **Last record** button at the bottom of the table.

   d. Close the *Items* table.

21. Review the table relationships.

   a. On the *Database Tools* tab, in the *Relationships* group, click the **Relationships** button.

   b. Verify that all table relationships are shown. On the *Relationship Tools Design* tab, in the *Relationships* group, click the **All Relationships** button.

   c. Save the changes to the relationship window layout by clicking the **Save** button on the Quick Access Toolbar.

   d. Close the Relationships window. On the *Relationship Tools Design* tab, in the *Relationships* group, click the **Close** button.

22. Use the *Compact and Repair Databases* command.

    a. Minimize the Access window and navigate to the folder where you saved this database. Observe the file size.

    b. Return to Access and click the **File** tab.

    c. Click the **Compact & Repair Database** button.

    d. Minimize Access and look at your database file again. How much did the file size decrease?

23. Back up the database.

    a. If necessary, maximize Access and click the **File** tab.

    b. Click **Save As**.

    c. In the *Save Database As* section, under *Advanced*, click **Back Up Database**, and click the **Save As** button.

    d. If necessary, navigate to the location where you save your personal project files. Click the **Save** button.

24. Close the database and exit Access.

Skill Review **1.2**

You have just been hired by a small health insurance company. One of your duties is using Access to manage the company's list of in-network doctors and covered procedures. Become comfortable with the company's database by completing the steps below.

Skills needed to complete this project:

- Introduction to Access (Skill 1.1)
- Working with Security Warnings (Skill 1.2)
- Backing Up a Database (Skill 1.16)
- Organizing Objects in the Navigation Pane (Skill 1.4)
- Understanding and Viewing Table Relationships (Skill 1.3)
- Navigating Records (Skill 1.6)
- Deleting Records (Skill 1.13)
- Sorting Records in a Datasheet (Skill 1.8)
- Creating a New Record in a Table and Entering Data (Skill 1.7)
- Adjusting Table Column Widths (Skill 1.9)
- Previewing and Printing Database Objects (Skill 1.15)
- Switching between Database Object Views (Skill 1.5)
- Creating a New Record in a Form and Entering Data (Skill 1.10)
- Finding and Replacing Data (Skill 1.12)
- Using Quick Start Application Parts (Skill 1.19)
- Using Compact and Repair (Skill 1.20)

1. Open the **AC2019-SkillReview-1-2** document.

2. If necessary, enable active content by clicking the **Enable Content** button in the Message Bar.

3. Save a copy of the file to work on.

    a. Click the **File** tab.

    b. Click **Save As**.

    c. Verify that *Access Database* is selected in the *Save Database As* section.

    d. Click **Save As**.

    e. If necessary, navigate to the location where you save your personal project files.

    f. In the *File name* box, change the file name to: `[your initials] AC-SkillReview-1-2`

    g. Click **Save**.

    h. If necessary, enable active content in the new database by clicking the **Enable Content** button in the Message Bar.

4. The Navigation Pane is organized using the *Object Type* category. Switch to use the *Tables and Related Views* category instead.

    a. Observe the organization of objects in the Navigation Pane.

    b. Click the top of the Navigation Pane and select the **Tables and Related Views** category.

    c. Observe the changes in the Navigation Pane.

5. Review the table relationships.

    a. On the *Database Tools* tab, in the *Relationships* group, click the **Relationships** button.

    b. Add the *Orders* table to the Relationships window. On the *Relationship Tools Design* tab, in the *Relationships* group, click the **Show Table** button.

    c. In the *Show Table* dialog, double-click **Orders**.

    d. Click the **Close** button to close the *Show Table* dialog.

    e. Save the changes to the relationship window layout by clicking the **Save** button on the Quick Access Toolbar.

    f. Close the Relationships window. On the *Relationship Tools Design* tab, in the *Relationships* group, click the **Close** button.

6. Navigate records in a table.

    a. In the Navigation Pane, double-click the object labeled **Physicians : Table**.

    b. Go to the last record in the table. Click the **Last Record** navigation button at the bottom of the table.

7. Delete the record.

    a. Click the record selector box on the left side of that row to highlight the entire record. Verify that you have selected the record with the physician ID **TW01**.

    b. On the *Home* tab, in the *Records* group, click the **Delete** button.

    c. Click **Yes** to verify that you want to delete the record.

8. Sort the records in the *Physicians* table alphabetically by last name.

    a. Click anywhere in the **LastName** field.

    b. On the *Home* tab, in the *Sort & Filter* group, click the **Ascending** button.

9. Enter a new record in the *Physicians* table.

    a. Click the **New (blank) record** button at the bottom of the table.

    b. Enter the following record into your table, using Tab or → to move from one field to the next. When you reach the *City* field, observe that it is a lookup field. Use the drop-down arrow to view and select from the available values.

PhysicianID	FirstName	LastName	StreetAddress	City	ZipCode	Phone	MemberCount
JB02	Mary	Frank	4455 Main Street	Miami	33143	(305) 555-2122	21

10. Resize the width of the *ZipCode* column to exactly 9.

    a. Click anywhere in the **ZipCode** field.

    b. On the *Home* tab, in the *Records* group, click the **More** button, and select **Field Width**.

    c. In the *Column Width* dialog, type: **9**

    d. Click **OK**.

    e. Save the table by clicking the **Save** button on the Quick Access Toolbar at the upper left corner of the Access window.

11. Preview how the *Physicians* table would look if it were printed from Access.

    a. Click the **File** tab.

    b. Click **Print**.

    c. Click **Print Preview**.

    d. Change the zoom to two pages. On the *Print Preview* tab, in the *Zoom* group, click the **Two Pages** button.

    e. Observe that in portrait orientation, the last two columns print on a second page.

    f. Change the orientation to landscape. On the *Print Preview* tab, in the *Page Layout* group, click the **Landscape** button.

    g. Observe that the printed table will now fit on a single page.

    h. Close the print preview by clicking the **Close Print Preview** button at the far right side of the Ribbon.

12. Close the *Physicians* table. Click the **X** at the upper right corner of the table. Be careful not to close the Access database instead.

13. Switch views for a form.

    a. In the Navigation Pane, double-click the **Physicians** form.

    b. Note the state of the *View* button (on the *Home* tab, in the *Views* group). When you are in Form view, the *View* button displays Layout view.

    c. Switch to Layout view. On the *Home* tab, in the *Views* group, click the **View** button.

    d. Observe that the *View* button has switched to Form view to indicate that clicking the button will return you to Form view.

    e. Review the form design in Layout view. Observe that while you can see live data, you cannot edit data in the record. Review the features available on the *Form Layout Tools* tabs.

    f. Switch back to Form view by clicking the **View** button again.

14. Add a new record in a form

    a. Observe the record navigation buttons at the bottom of the form and note that they are the same as those in the table.

    b. Click the **New (blank) record** button at the bottom of the form.

    c. Enter the following record into your form, using ⌨Tab or → to move from one field to the next.

PhysicianID	FirstName	LastName	StreetAddress	City	ZipCode	Phone	MemberCount
KS01	Emile	Swann	837 Franklin Street	Miami	33155	(305) 555-9832	18

15. Edit a record in a form.

    a. Find the record with a physician ID of **SD01**. Type **SD01** in the *Search* box at the bottom of the form.

    b. Click inside the *ZipCode* field and change the number from **33304** to **33305**.

    c. Close the *Physicians* form by clicking the **X** at the top right of the form.

16. Rename the *Physicians* form.

    a. In the Navigation Pane, right-click the **Physicians** form and select **Rename**. Be careful not to rename the *Physicians* table.

    b. Type: **PhysiciansForm**

    c. Press **Enter**.

17. Use the *Comments* Quick Start application part to add a new table to the database.

    a. On the *Create* tab, in the *Templates* group, click the **Application Parts** button.

    b. In the *Quick Start* section, click **Comments**. It may take Access a few seconds to create the *Comments* table.

    c. Click the **There is no relationship**. radio button.

    d. Click the **Create** button.

18. Use the *Compact and Repair Database* command.

    a. Minimize the Access window and navigate to the folder where you saved this database. Observe the file size.

    b. Return to Access and click the **File** tab.

    c. Click the **Compact & Repair Database** button.

    d. Minimize Access and look at your database file again. How much did the file size decrease?

19. Back up the database.

    a. If necessary, maximize Access and click the **File** tab.

    b. Click **Save As**.

    c. In the *Save Database As* area, under *Advanced*, click **Back Up Database**, and click the **Save As** button.

    d. If necessary, navigate to the location where you save your personal project files.

    e. Click the **Save** button.

20. Close the database and exit Access.

challenge yourself **1.3**

In this project, you will work on a database for a greenhouse. The database contains records of the plants in the greenhouse and the employees who assist with maintenance duties.

Skills needed to complete this project:

- Introduction to Access (Skill 1.1)
- Working with Security Warnings (Skill 1.2)
- Adjusting Table Column Widths (Skill 1.9)
- Creating a New Record in a Table and Entering Data (Skill 1.7)
- Sorting Records in a Datasheet (Skill 1.8)

- Finding and Replacing Data (Skill 1.12)
- Deleting Records (Skill 1.13)
- Organizing Objects in the Navigation Pane (Skill 1.4)
- Creating a New Record in a Form and Entering Data (Skill 1.10)
- Understanding and Viewing Table Relationships (Skill 1.3)
- Previewing and Printing Database Objects (Skill 1.15)
- Deleting and Renaming Database Objects (Skill 1.14)
- Using Compact and Repair (Skill 1.20)
- Backing Up a Database (Skill 1.16)

1. Open the **AC2019-ChallengeYourself-1-3**.

2. If necessary, enable active content by clicking the **Enable Content** button in the Message Bar.

3. Save a copy of the file to work on. Name the file:
   [your initials] AC-ChallengeYourself-1-3

   If necessary, enable active content in the new database by clicking the **Enable Content** button in the Message Bar.

4. Open the *Employees* table and change the width of the *Position* column to exactly **20**.

5. Enter the following record in the *Employees* table. Keep the table open when you are finished.

EmployeeID	FirstName	LastName	Position	WeeklyHours
5937845	Nathan	Marr	Greenhouse Tech 1	35

6. Sort the records in the table alphabetically from A to Z by values in the *LastName* field.

7. Find and edit the record with a *LastName* value of **Rojas**. Change the *WeeklyHours* value from 35 to: **28**

8. Delete the record with an *EmployeeID* of **98335487**.

9. Save and close the *Employees* table.

10. By default, the Navigation Pane displays the *Tables and Related Views* category. Change the Navigation Pane so database objects are grouped by object type instead.

11. Add the following record to the *EmployeesForm*. Close the form when you are finished.

EmployeeID	FirstName	LastName	Position	WeeklyHours
77338147	Tom	Morris	Greenhouse Tech 2	15

12. Open the Relationships window and add the *MaintenanceLog* table to the layout. Review the table relationships, save the changes, and then close the Relationships window.

13. Open the *Plants* table and find and replace all instances of **Violet** in the *FlowerColor* field with: **Purple**

14. AutoFit the width of the *ScientificName* column so all the names are visible.

15. Sort the items in the table so they are sorted by values in the *DatePlanted* field with the newest dates at the top and then by values in the *CommonName* field alphabetically from A to Z. *Hint*: Remember to sort the innermost sort first. Save the table.

16. Preview how the *Plants* table will look when printed. Change the zoom view to see if all the columns will fit on one page when printed in portrait view. If they will not, change to layout orientation. Close the table when you are finished.

17. Open the *Purchases* table, observe that there are no records, and then close the table.

18. Delete the *Purchases* table.

19. Observe the file size of your database. Use the *Compact and Repair Database* command and check the file again. How much did the file size decrease?

20. Create a backup of this database using the default name chosen by Access.

21. Close the database and exit Access.

challenge yourself 1.4

In this project, you will work with a database for a volunteer organization that ships and administers vaccines to various relief centers all over the world. The database must maintain a list of all approved vaccines and keep track of all shipments made to the relief centers.

Skills needed to complete this project:

- Introduction to Access (Skill 1.1)
- Working with Security Warnings (Skill 1.2)
- Organizing Objects in the Navigation Pane (Skill 1.4)
- Understanding and Viewing Table Relationships (Skill 1.3)
- Navigating Records (Skill 1.6)
- Creating a New Record in a Table and Entering Data (Skill 1.7)
- Finding and Replacing Data (Skill 1.12)
- Deleting Records (Skill 1.13)
- Adjusting Table Column Widths (Skill 1.9)
- Sorting Records in a Datasheet (Skill 1.8)
- Creating a New Record in a Form and Entering Data (Skill 1.10)
- Deleting and Renaming Database Objects (Skill 1.14)
- Using Compact and Repair (Skill 1.20)

1. Open the start file **AC2019-ChallengeYourself-1-4**.

2. If necessary, enable active content by clicking the **Enable Content** button in the Message Bar.

3. Save a copy of the file to work on. Name the file: **[your initials] AC-ChallengeYourself-1-4**

   If necessary, enable active content by clicking the **Enable Content** button in the Message Bar.

4. Change the organization of the Navigation Pane to use the *Tables and Related Views* category.

5. Open the Relationships window and show the *Vaccines* table. Save the changes to the layout, and then close the Relationships window.

6. Open the *Vaccines* table and browse the records using the record navigation buttons and keyboard shortcuts.

7. Enter the following record into the table. Note that the *TargetAudience* field is a lookup field.

VaccineID	VaccineName	TargetAudience
TYPH	Typhoid Fever	At-risk persons

8. Find the record with the value **TD** in the *VaccineID* field and change the value of the *TargetAudience* field from *Adults* to **Teenagers**.

9. Find and delete the record with a *VaccineID* of **JE**.

10. Change the width of the *VaccineName* column to exactly **28**.

11. Sort the records in the table alphabetically from A to Z by values in the *VaccineName* field.

12. Save and close the table.

13. Open the *VaccinesForm* form and enter the following as a new record:

VaccineID	VaccineName	TargetAudience
MAL	Malaria	At-risk persons

14. Close the *VaccinesForm* form.

15. Open the *Locations* table and use the *Replace* command to replace all instances of **Angola** with: `Republic of Angola`

16. AutoFit the width of the *Country* column so all the names are visible.

17. AutoFit the width of the *City* column so all the names are visible.

18. Sort the records so they are sorted by values in the *Country* field alphabetically from A to Z and then by values in the *City* field alphabetically from A to Z. *Hint*: Remember to sort the innermost sort first.

19. Save and close the table.

20. In the Navigation Pane, rename the *Shipments* form to: `ShipmentsForm`

21. Observe the file size of your database. Use the *Compact and Repair Database* command and check the file again. How much did the file size decrease?

22. Close the database and exit Access.

on your own 1.5

Find an Access template. Demonstrate your basic understanding of Access by working with this database.

Skills needed to complete this project:

- Creating a Database from a Template (Skill 1.17)
- Working with Security Warnings (Skill 1.2)
- Introduction to Access (Skill 1.1)
- Understanding and Viewing Table Relationships (Skill 1.3)
- Creating a New Record in a Table and Entering Data (Skill 1.7)
- Creating a New Record in a Form and Entering Data (Skill 1.10)
- Using Undo and Redo (Skill 1.11)
- Previewing and Printing Database Objects (Skill 1.15)
- Backing Up a Database (Skill 1.16)

1. Open Access and start a new database from one of the templates. Select a template that will be useful to you such as the *Home Inventory* template which is great for keeping track of items for insurance.

2. Save the file with the name: `[your initials] AC-OnYourOwn-1-5`

   If necessary, enable active content by clicking the **Enable Content** button in the Message Bar.

3. If necessary, change the Navigation Pane so objects are organized by the *Object Type* or *Tables and Related Views* category.

4. Spend some time exploring the structure of the database. Identify the database objects and how they are related to one another. Open and explore the different database objects.

5. Open one of the tables and enter a few records.

6. Preview how the table would print.

7. Open a related form and enter a few more records. Did you find it easier to enter records in the form?

8. Create a backup of the database.

9. Close all open database objects, and then close the database and exit Access.

fix it 1.6

A local pet store has hired you to fix its database, which keeps track of inventory, customers, and store sales.

Skills needed to complete this project:

- Introduction to Access (Skill 1.1)
- Working with Security Warnings (Skill 1.2)
- Organizing Objects in the Navigation Pane (Skill 1.4)
- Understanding and Viewing Table Relationships (Skill 1.3)
- Navigating Records (Skill 1.6)
- Adjusting Table Column Widths (Skill 1.9)
- Finding and Replacing Data (Skill 1.12)
- Deleting Records (Skill 1.13)
- Deleting and Renaming Database Objects (Skill 1.14)
- Sorting Records in a Datasheet (Skill 1.8)
- Previewing and Printing Database Objects (Skill 1.15)
- Using Compact and Repair (Skill 1.20)
- Backing Up a Database (Skill 1.16)

1. Open the start file **AC2019-FixIt-1-6**.

2. If necessary, enable active content by clicking the **Enable Content** button in the Message Bar.

3. Save a copy of the file to work on. Name the file: `[your initials] AC-FixIt-1-6`

   If necessary, enable active content by clicking the **Enable Content** button in the Message Bar.

4. The employees cannot see their forms and reports in the Navigation Pane. Please help them by organizing the Navigation Pane using the *Tables and Related Views* category.

5. Spend some time exploring the structure of the database. Identify the database objects and how they are related to one another. Verify that all the table relationships are visible in the Relationships window.

6. The owner tells you that a former employee would often make data entry errors, and he wants your help in finding and correcting errors in the *Pets* table.

   a. Change the width of the *Breed* column to AutoFit the data. This will make it easier to review the data.

   b. Find and replace all instances of **Lab** with **Labrador Retriever** in the *Breed* field.

   c. One of the records has the data in the *Breed* and the *MainColor* fields swapped. Find the record and fix it. *Hint*: Find the record with **White** in the *Breed* field.

   d. There is also a duplicate record. Delete the record with the pet ID **1446011**.

   e. Save and close the table.

7. The *CustomersReport* report is poorly formatted. Delete it for now. You will need to re-create it at another time.

8. The records in the *Customers* table should be sorted by customer last names not cities. Remove the sort and re-sort the records alphabetically by last name. Save and close the table.

9. The owner plans on printing the *Customers* table. Make sure it will fit on one page when printed.

10. The owner wonders why the database file size is so large. Help him reduce the file size.

11. Create a backup of the database so you can easily fix the data if these problems crop up again.

12. Close any open database objects and save changes if necessary.

13. Close the database and exit Access.

Source of screenshots: Microsoft Office 365: Word, Excel, Access, and PowerPoint.

Foot spa: Comstock/Mediabakery

Working with Tables

skills

introduction

In this chapter you will learn the skills essential for creating well-designed tables. You will learn to create tables from scratch in both Datasheet view and Design view. You will add and rename fields, set field formats, and modify field properties. In Design view, you will add primary keys and apply an input mask to control formatting. Finally, you will create lookup fields and create relationships between tables.

Skill 2.1 Designing a Table

Remember that Access is a relational database—objects in your database are related to one another through relationships defined by common fields between tables. Take advantage of these relationships, and design your database so information is stored in one table only. For example, a database of customer appointments need not include every detail about each customer. The appointments table should include fields required for the appointment only. Details about customers and services should be kept in separate, related tables.

The customer details are stored in the *Customers* table, not in the *Appointments* table.

FIGURE AC 2.1

Storing each unique piece of data in a single table helps prevent data entry errors. There is only one record for each customer, so every time a new appointment record is created you need to reference only the related field (in this case the *CustomerID* field) rather than entering all the customer information again.

Another key to an efficient database design is ensuring that each field is assigned the appropriate data type. For example, you can't run calculations on a field with the *Short Text* data type, and you can't sort a date field efficiently unless you use the *Date/Time* data type. Carefully consider the type of data you will include in each field before you decide on the data type.

To check to see what data type is applied to a field, click anywhere in the field. The data type is displayed on the *Table Tools Fields* tab, in the *Formatting* group, in the *Data Type* box.

FIGURE AC 2.2

AutoNumber—An *AutoNumber* field is automatically assigned its value by Access. The value in this field for each new record is incremented by one from the previous record. Database users cannot edit or enter data in an *AutoNumber* field. *AutoNumber* fields are often used as a primary key if no other unique field exists in the table. In Figure AC 2.2, the *AppointmentID* field uses the *AutoNumber* data type.

Short Text—A *Short Text* field can hold up to 255 characters. *Short Text* fields are used for short text data or numbers that should be treated as text. In Figure AC 2.2, both the *Customer* and *Service* fields use the *Short Text* data type.

Long Text—A *Long Text* field holds text and numbers like a *Short Text* field, except you can enter up to 65,535 characters in a *Long Text* field. Text in *Long Text* fields can be formatted using Rich Text Formatting.

Number—A *Number* field holds a numerical value. The default number is described as a long integer, a number between $-2,147,483,648$ and $2,147,483,647$.

Large Number—A *Large Number* field holds a very large numerical value. Use the *Large Number* data type for compatibility with the SQL_BIGINT data type in ODBC. This data type is not compatible with Access databases prior to Access 2016. Do not use this data type unless you know you need it for compatibility with other databases.

Date/Time—A *Date/Time* field stores a numerical value that is displayed as a date and time. The format in which the date and/or time displays is controlled by the Format property. Using the *Date/Time* data type allows you to sort the field by date. In Figure AC 2.2, both the *ApptDate* and *ApptTime* fields use the *Date/Time* data type. The data in the *ApptDate* field have the *Medium Date* format applied. The data in the *ApptTime* field have the *Short Time* format applied.

Currency—A *Currency* field stores a numerical value with a high degree of accuracy (up to four decimal places to the right of the decimal). Access will not round the values stored in currency fields, regardless of the format in which the value displays.

Yes/No—A *Yes/No* field stores a true/false value as a -1 for yes and 0 for no. Yes/No fields can display the words *Yes/No* or *True/False* or a checkbox.

OLE Object—An *OLE Object* field stores OLE files such as Word documents or Excel spreadsheets. Unless you need backward compatibility with a legacy database, use the newer and more flexible *Attachment* data type instead.

Hyperlink—A *Hyperlink* field stores a web address or email address. Fields with the *Hyperlink* data type can be active and set to open the computer's default email program or web browser populated with the data from the *Hyperlink* field.

Attachment—An *Attachment* field stores files as attachments to records. Attachments can be images, Word documents, or almost any other type of data file. *Attachment* fields allow multiple files as attachments to a single record.

Calculated Field—A *Calculated* field uses an expression (a formula) to calculate a value.

tips & tricks

Keeping repeated data in separate tables where they are stored only once keeps the database file size down, allowing the database to operate more efficiently.

tell me **more**

Tables in the sample database are related to one another via one-to-many relationships where the main table contains a primary key field that is included as a field (the foreign key) in the secondary table. Refer to the skill *Understanding and Viewing Table Relationships* for more information.

let me **try**

If the database is not already open, open the data file **AC02-01-Spa** and try this skill on your own:

1. Open the *Appointments* table and explore the fields in the table.
2. Click the field that uses the *AutoNumber* data type.
3. Click one of the fields that uses the *Date/Time* data type.
4. Click one of the fields that uses the *Short Text* data type.
5. Open the *Customers* table and explore the fields in the table. Observe how the *CustomerID* field relates to the *Customer* field in the *Appointments* table. Identify the data type for each field.
6. Close all open database objects. Do not save any changes you may have made accidentally.

Skill 2.2 Creating and Saving a Table in Datasheet View

One way to create a new table is to add a blank table and add fields directly in Datasheet view.

1. On the *Create* tab, in the *Tables* group, click the **Table** button to insert a new table.

Click to create a new blank table in Datasheet view.

FIGURE AC 2.3

2. The new table opens in Datasheet view. Access adds the first field automatically as the primary key with the data type *AutoNumber* and the name *ID*.

3. To add a new field, begin typing data for the first record. Access names the first field *Field1*. Access will apply a data type based on what you type. For example, if you type a date, Access will automatically apply the *Date/Time* data type to the field.

4. Press `Tab` or `Enter` to enter data for the next field.

5. Repeat steps 3 and 4 to enter all the data for the first record.

6. Save the table by clicking the **Save** button on the Quick Access Toolbar.

7. In the *Save As* dialog, type the table name in the *Table Name* box and click **OK**.

Save Button

AutoNumber field named *ID*.

Field1 created by entering data.

FIGURE AC 2.4

another **method**

To save a database object, you can use the keyboard shortcut Ctrl + S.

let me **try**

If the database is not already open, open the data file **AC02-02-Spa** and try this skill on your own:

1. Create a new table in Datasheet view.

2. Allow Access to create the first *AutoNumber* field named *ID*.

3. Enter data for the second field: **Bob's Mud Shop**

4. Save the table with the name: **Suppliers** Keep the *Suppliers* table open if you are moving on to the next skill; close it if you are finished working with these skills.

Skill 2.3 Renaming Fields

When you create a new, blank table in Datasheet view, Access names the fields *Field1*, *Field2*, and so forth by default. The **field name** is the name by which other database objects reference the field. This is the name you use when you build a query or add fields to a form or report. You should rename fields to something short, but descriptive.

We recommend ***not*** using spaces in field names because this can cause complications when working in code such as SQL or VBA. Instead, use the field **Caption property** to store the field name with spaces. The *Caption* property is the field name as it will appear in labels and column headings.

Change the field name and add a caption by modifying the field properties:

1. Click anywhere in the field to select it.
2. On the *Table Tools Fields* tab, in the *Properties* group, click the **Name & Caption** button to open the *Enter Field Properties* dialog.
3. In the *Name* box, type the new field name.
4. In the *Caption* box, type the field name as it should appear in labels and column headings.
5. In the *Description* box, type additional information about the field (if necessary).
6. Click **OK**.

FIGURE AC 2.5

tips & tricks

In forms and reports, if a field does not include a caption, Access will use the field name for the label. If you want your form and report labels to include spaces (such as *First Name* instead of *FirstName*), be sure to add captions to your table fields.

another **method**

To rename a field:

❯ Right-click the field name at the top of the column in Datasheet view and select **Rename Field**. When the field name appears highlighted, type the new name, and press ⏎ Enter .

❯ Double-click the column header to highlight the field name. Type the new field name and then press ⏎ Enter .

You can also modify the field *Caption* property from the Field Properties pane in Design view.

let me **try**

If the database is not already open, open the data file **AC02-03-Spa** and try this skill on your own:

1. If necessary, open the *Suppliers* table in Datasheet view.
2. Rename the *ID* field to: **SupplierID**
3. Use the *Enter Field Properties* dialog to rename the *Field1* field to **CompanyName** and change the *Caption* property to **Company Name**. Do not add a description.
4. Save the table.
5. Keep the *Suppliers* table open if you are moving on to the next skill; close it if you are finished working with these skills.

Skill 2.4 Adding Fields in Datasheet View

You can always add a new field to a table by typing data in the blank cell at the end of a record, but what if you want to set up the table without entering data?

To add a new field:

1. On the *Table Tools Fields* tab, in the *Add & Delete* group, click the button for the data type you want to add. If there isn't a button for the data type you want, click the **More Fields** button to expand the *Data Type* gallery and make a selection from the gallery.

2. Access adds the new field to the right of the active field.

3. Type the new field name and then press ⏎ Enter.

Note that when you use the buttons in the *Add & Delete* group, the field is inserted to the right of whatever field was active.

To add the new field at the end of the table, click the arrow in the *Click to Add* column at the far right side of the table and select the field type you want to add.

FIGURE AC 2.6

another **method**

You can also insert a new field by right-clicking any field name and selecting **Insert Field**. A new blank text field is inserted to the *left* of the field you selected.

let me **try**

If the database is not already open, open the data file **AC02-04-Spa** and try this skill on your own:

1. If necessary, open the *Suppliers* table in Datasheet view.

2. Add a new *Yes/No* field to the far right side of the table.

3. Name the field: **Favorite**

4. Keep the *Suppliers* table open if you are moving on to the next skill; close it if you are finished working with these skills.

Skill 2.5 Using Quick Start to Add Related Fields

As you work with more databases, you will find there are certain fields that are usually grouped together such as first and last names; home, work, and fax numbers; and street address, city, state, and zip. The last section in the *Field Types* gallery, **Quick Start fields**, provides an easy way to add a group of related fields with a single command.

To add a *Quick Start* group of fields:

Quick Start Section of the *Field Types* Gallery

FIGURE AC 2.7

1. The *Quick Start* fields will be inserted to the **left** of the selected field. To add them to the far right of the table, click anywhere in the *Click To Add* column.
2. On the *Table Tools Design* tab, in the *Add & Delete* group, click the **More Fields** button.
3. Scroll to the bottom of the *Field Types* gallery to the *Quick Start* section.
4. Click the *Quick Start* option you want.
5. Access inserts the fields.

FIGURE AC 2.8

let me try

If the database is not already open, open the data file **AC02-05-Spa** and try this skill on your own:

1. If necessary, open the *Suppliers* table in Datasheet view.
2. Add the **Phone** *Quick Start* fields to the end of the table.
3. Keep the *Suppliers* table open if you are moving on to the next skill; close it if you are finished working with these skills.

Skill 2.6 Deleting Fields in Datasheet View

When you delete a field, you delete all the data in that field, and the action cannot be undone.

To delete a field in Datasheet view:

1. Click anywhere in the field you want to delete.
2. On the *Table Tools Fields* tab, in the *Add & Delete* group, click the **Delete** button.
3. When Access asks if you if you want to permanently delete the field, click **Yes**.

FIGURE AC 2.9

another **method**

❭ In Datasheet view, right-click the field name at the top of the column and select **Delete Field**.

❭ In Datasheet view, select the field by clicking the column heading, and then on the *Home* tab, in the *Records* group, click the **Delete** button.

let me **try**

If the database is not already open, open the data file **AC02-06-Spa** and try this skill on your own:

1. If necessary, open the *Suppliers* table in Datasheet view.
2. Delete the **Fax Number** field.
3. Keep the *Suppliers* table open if you are moving on to the next skill. Close it if you are finished working with these skills.

Skill 2.7 Moving Fields in Datasheet View

When you add new fields in Design view it can be tricky to remember whether the field will be added to the right or left of the active field. If you add a field to the wrong place in the datasheet, you can always move it.

To move a field in Datasheet view:

1. Select the column by moving the mouse pointer over the column header and clicking when the mouse pointer changes to an arrow ↓.

2. Access highlights the entire column to indicate that it is selected. Hold down the mouse button and drag to the new position in the datasheet. As you drag, the mouse pointer changes to the move shape ↳ and Access displays a thick black line to show you where the column will be placed.

3. Release the mouse button to finish moving the field.

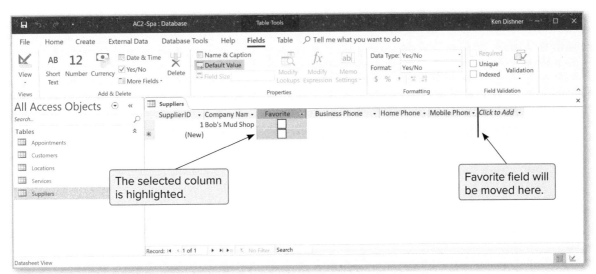

FIGURE AC 2.10

tips & tricks

It is important to understand that you are rearranging the fields in Datasheet view only. The underlying table design has not been changed. You can learn more in the skill *Inserting, Deleting, and Moving Fields in Design View*.

let me try

If the database is not already open, open the data file **AC02-07-Spa** and try this skill on your own:

1. If necessary, open the *Suppliers* table in Datasheet view.

2. Move the **Favorite** field so it is the last field in the table.

3. Close the table.

Skill 2.8 Creating a Table in Design View and Setting the Primary Key

Another way to create a new table is in Design view. In Design view, you create the fields without entering data. You must specify the field name and data type for each field. Notice that the Design view window is divided into two panes. The top pane lists the table fields. The bottom pane is the **Field Properties pane**. It displays details about the selected field. You will learn more about using the Field Properties pane in other skills.

To create a table in Design view:

1. On the *Create* tab, in the *Tables* group, click the **Table Design** button.

FIGURE AC 2.11

Table Design Button

2. Type the name of the first field. Press (Tab ⇥).
3. Expand the list of data types, and select the data type you want. Press (Tab ⇥) again.
4. Optional: Type a useful description of the field. Press (Tab ⇥) to go to the next field.
5. Repeat steps 2–4 to enter all the fields for the table.

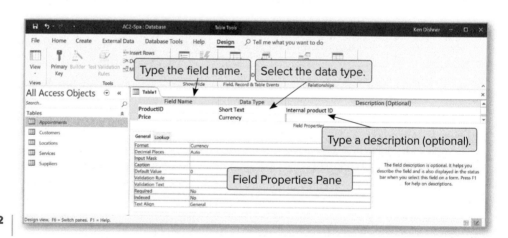

FIGURE AC 2.12

Type the field name.   Select the data type.

Type a description (optional).

Field Properties Pane

Before saving the table, you should set the **primary key** field. Because the data contained in the primary key field must be unique for each record, primary keys are often IDs—product IDs, employee IDs, or record IDs.

❭ If your data does not already contain a field that is unique for each record, you can add a new field that uses the *AutoNumber* data type. Using an *AutoNumber* field ensures that each record has a unique numerical ID.

❭ If your table contains a field that you know is unique for each record (such as a previously established product ID, employee ID, or part number), you can set this field as the primary key.

To set the primary key in a table:

1. In Design view, click the field that is going to be the primary key.

2. On the *Table Tools Design* tab, in the *Tools* group, click the **Primary Key** button.

Notice that on the *Table Tools Design* tab, in the *Tools* group, the *Primary Key* button is highlighted to indicate that the selected field is the primary key and a key icon appears in the row selector at the left side of the field. In the Field Properties pane, the *Indexed* property is set to *Yes (No Duplicates)* because values in the primary key field must be unique.

FIGURE AC 2.13

tips & tricks

Once you establish a field as the primary key, Access automatically sets the *Required* property to *Yes* to ensure that each record has a unique primary key.

another **method**

In Design view, right-click the row selector and select **Primary Key**.

let me **try**

If the database is not already open, open the data file **AC02-08-Spa** and try this skill on your own:

1. Add a new table in Design view.

2. Name the first field **ProductID** and set the data type to **Short Text**.

3. Add the description **Internal product ID** and press (Tab ⇆) or (← Enter) to add another field.

4. Name the next field **Price** and set the data type to **Currency**. Do not add a description for this field.

5. Set the **ProductID** field as the primary key field.

6. Save the table with the name: **Products**

7. Keep the *Products* table open if you are moving on to the next skill; close it if you are finished working with these skills.

Skill 2.9 Inserting, Deleting, and Moving Fields in Design View

If you are working in Design view, you can always add new fields to the end of the field list by typing a new field name and selecting a data type. You can also insert fields between existing fields.

To insert a new field in Design view:

1. Click the field below where you want to insert the new field.
2. On the *Table Tools Design* tab, in the *Tools* group, click the **Insert Rows** button.
3. Enter the field name and select the data type. Enter a description if you want.
4. When you are finished, save the table.

FIGURE AC 2.14

To delete a field in Design view:

1. Click anywhere in the field you want to delete.
2. On the *Table Tools Design* tab, in the *Tools* group, click the **Delete Rows** button.
3. When Access asks if you want to permanently delete the field, click **Yes**.

FIGURE AC 2.15

To change the order of fields in Design view:

1. Select the row by moving the mouse pointer over the row selector when the mouse pointer changes to an arrow ➡.
2. Access highlights the entire row to indicate that it is selected. Hold down the mouse button and drag to the new position. As you drag, the mouse pointer changes to the move shape ⬚ and Access displays a thick black line to show you where the field will be placed.
3. Release the mouse button to finish moving the field.

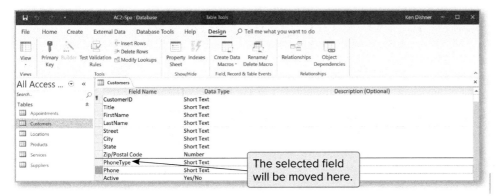

FIGURE AC 2.16

tips & tricks

When you move a field column in Datasheet view, the new position is reflected in Datasheet view *only*. It does not affect the actual design of the table. However, when you move a field in Design view, you are changing the design of the table, so the new field position is reflected in Datasheet view as well.

another **method**

❭ To insert a field in Design view, right-click the row selector at the left side of the field and select **Insert Rows** to insert a new field row above the selected field.

❭ To delete a field in Design view, right-click the row selector to the left of the field name, and select **Delete Rows**.

let me **try**

If the database is not already open, open the data file **AC02-09-Spa** and try this skill on your own:

1. If necessary, open the *Products* table in Design view.
2. From Design view, insert a new field between the *ProductID* and *Price* fields.
3. Name the field **ProductName** and set the data type to **Short Text**. Do not add a description for this field.
4. Save and close the table.
5. Open the *Locations* table in Design view.
6. Delete the *Building* field.
7. Save and close the table.
8. Open the *Customers* table in Design view.
9. Move the **Phone** field so it is immediately above the *PhoneType* field.
10. Save and close the table.

Skill 2.10 Changing Data Type

After you have created your database tables, you may find that you want to change the data type for a field. Before changing the data type, carefully consider the characteristics of any data you've already entered in the table. Will changing the data type invalidate current data? For example, if you change the data type from *Short Text* to *Number*, Access will delete all non-numeric data.

To change the data type for a field from Datasheet view:

1. Click anywhere in the field you want to change.

2. On the *Table Tools Fields* tab, in the *Formatting* group, expand the **Data Type** list, and select the data type you want.

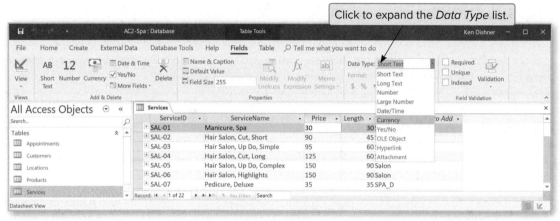

FIGURE AC 2.17

3. Access will warn you that some data may be lost. If you are sure you want to continue, click **Yes**. If the change will require Access to remove data from the table, Access will show a second warning telling you how many records will lose data. You will only see the second warning if the change will delete data.

   Once you click **Yes**, the data type change is made and you cannot undo it.

FIGURE AC 2.18

FIGURE AC 2.19

tips & tricks

Changing data type could have unexpected consequences. It's best to plan carefully and create the tables before entering data. However, if you need to change the data type after values are entered, make a backup copy of the database before proceeding.

tell me **more**

If the field you are changing is the primary or foreign key in a relationship, Access may require you to delete the relationship before changing the data type. You can reestablish the relationship after the change is made.

another **method**

You can also change data type from Design view, but we do not recommend it. When you change a field's data type from Design view, Access does not warn you that you may lose data. You could potentially remove all the data from a field if you change from one data type to another data type that is incompatible with the data already entered.

let me **try**

If the database is not already open, open the data file **AC02-10-Spa** and try this skill on your own:

1. If it is not already open, open the *Services* table in Datasheet view.
2. Change the data type for the *Price* field to **Currency**.
3. Close the table.

from the perspective of . . .

SMALL BUSINESS OWNER

I use an Access database to keep track of business contacts, inventory, sales, and customers. When I first set up the database, I included all the customer information with every record in the sales table. Later, when I tried to analyze my sales records to find repeat customers, I realized my mistake. There were multiple records for the same customer, but with the customer information entered slightly differently in each. I know that Cindy Williams and Cynthia Williams are the same person, but Access doesn't. I had to bring in a temp to pull out the customer information into a separate table and make sure the sales records were referencing the correct customers. If I had designed the tables the right way in the first place, I could have saved a lot of time and money. Now my sales table uses a lookup field to add customer data. No more mistakes!

Rubberball/Getty Images

Skill 2.11 Formatting Fields

When designing a table, you specify what type of data can be entered in each field by selecting the data type. You can also define specific formatting options to control the appearance of data by changing the **Format field property**. Changing this property does not affect the data stored in the table; it controls only the way the data are displayed to the end user.

To make changes to the *Format* field property from Datasheet view:

1. Click anywhere in the field you want to format.

2. On the *Table Tools Fields* tab, in the *Formatting* group, expand the **Format** list, and select the format you want. Not all formats are available for all field data types. Figure AC 2.20 shows the *Format* options available for fields with the *Date/Time* data type.

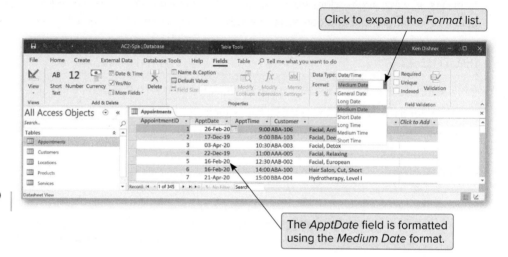

Click to expand the *Format* list.

The *ApptDate* field is formatted using the *Medium Date* format.

FIGURE AC 2.20

From Datasheet view, you can quickly apply the *Currency*, *Percent*, or *Comma* number formats by clicking the appropriate button in the *Formatting* group. These formats can be used with *AutoNumber*, *Number*, and *Currency* data types.

❭ The **Currency format** displays a $ symbol before the number and two digits to the right of the decimal place. The *Currency* format is applied automatically when the field uses the *Currency* data type, although you can apply the *Currency* format without using the *Currency* data type.

❭ The **Percent format** displays the number as a percentage, so .05 displays as 5, and 5 displays as 500.

❭ The **Comma Style format** displays the , symbol within the number and two digits to the right of the decimal. This is the same as selecting **Standard** from the *Format* list.

FIGURE AC 2.21

Click these buttons to apply *Currency*, *Percent*, or *Comma Style* formatting.

To modify the *Format* field property from Design view:

1. Click anywhere in the field you want to format.
2. In the Field Properties pane, click in the **Format** property box.
3. Click the arrow at the right end of the box to expand the list of available formats, and select the format you want.
4. If you want this property change to affect all other database objects that use this field, click the **Property Update Options** button and select **Update Format everywhere [field name] is used**.
5. Save the table.

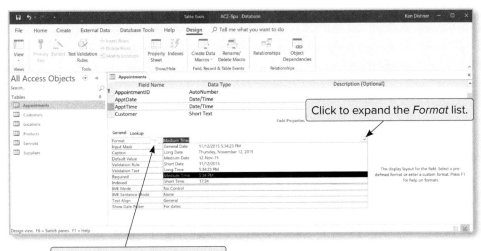

Click to expand the *Format* list.

Property Update Options Button

FIGURE AC 2.22

tips & tricks

When you make data type, format, and other property changes to fields in Datasheet view, Access applies the change immediately and it is not necessary to save the table to save the changes. However, when you make these changes in Design view, you must save the table to commit the changes.

tell me **more**

To increase or decrease the number of digits that appear to the right of the decimal in your *AutoNumber*, *Number*, and *Currency* fields, on the *Table Tools Fields* tab, in the *Formatting* group, click the **Increase Decimals** or **Decrease Decimals** button.

let me **try**

If the database is not already open, open the data file **AC02-11-Spa** and try this skill on your own:

1. If necessary, open the *Appointments* table in Datasheet view.
2. Apply the **Short Date** format to the *ApptDate* field. *Hint:* Verify that the data type is *Date/Time* before applying the format.
3. Switch to Design view.
4. Apply the **Medium Time** format to the *ApptTime* field.
5. Save and close the table.

Skill 2.12 Setting the Default Value Property

The **Default Value property** adds a preset value to the field. Entering a value in the *Default Value* property can save time during data entry. For example, if most of your employees live in California, use CA as the default value for the *State* field. As shown in Figure AC 2.23, when a field has a default value set, the *Default Value* button appears highlighted. Whenever a new record is created, the default value is entered into this field automatically.

FIGURE AC 2.23

To add a default value in Datasheet view:

1. Select the field to which you want to add a default value.

2. On the *Table Tools Fields* tab, in the *Properties* group, click the **Default Value** button to open the *Expression Builder*.

FIGURE AC 2.24

3. In the *Expression Builder*, enter the numerical value, text, or formula you want to use as the default value for the field. The default value expression always begins with the = sign, which Access adds for you. If the default value is a text string with a space or other special character in it, you must enclose it in quotation marks. If the text is something simple, such as *CA*, you do not need to type the quotation marks. Access will add them for you.

4. Click **OK**.

You can also set the default value from Design view:

1. Select the field.

2. In the Field Properties pane, click in the **Default Value** box and type the numerical value, text, or formula you want to use as the default value.

FIGURE AC 2.25

3. If you want to use the *Expression Builder*, click the **Build…** button at the right side of the *Default Value* box.

4. Save the table.

tips & tricks

Changing a field to a lookup field removes any values in the *Default Value* property. If you want the field to have a default value, you will need to set the property again after you change the data type.

let me try

If the database is not already open, open the data file **AC02-12-Spa** and try this skill on your own:

1. If necessary, open the *Customers* table in Datasheet view.

2. Set the **Default Value** property for the *State* field to **CA**.

3. Keep the *Customers* table open if you are moving on to the skill; close it if you are finished working with these skills.

Skill 2.13 Modifying the Field Size Property

The **Field Size property** limits the number of characters that can be entered in a text field. The default size for a *Short Text* field is 255 (the maximum size for a *Short Text* field). Limiting the field size can ensure that data are entered properly. For example, if you want entries in the *State* field to always use the two-letter state abbreviation, limit the field size to 2.

To modify the Field Size property in Datasheet view:

1. Select the field.

2. On the *Table Tools Fields* tab, in the *Properties* group, type the new field size in the **Field Size** box and press ⏎ Enter .

3. If you are making the field size smaller, Access will warn you that the smaller size may result in data loss, as Access will delete any data in the field that exceeds the new field size limit. Click **Yes** to continue with the change.

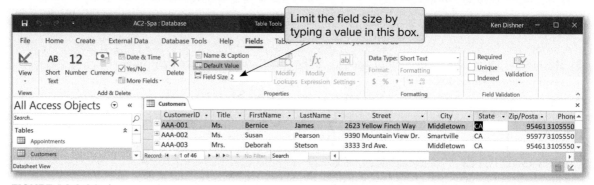

FIGURE AC 2.26

To modify the Field Size property in Design view, select the field and then enter the new field size value in the **Field Size** box in the Field Properties pane. If you change the property in Design view, be sure to save the table.

tips & tricks

You cannot limit the size of *Long Text* fields.

tell me **more**

If the selected field is a *Long Text* field, the *Memo Settings* button controls two properties exclusive to *Long Text* fields:

❭ *Rich Text Formatting* allows you to add text formatting.

❭ *Append Only* saves a history of changes made to the text in the field.

let me **try**

If the database is not already open, open the data file **AC02-13-Spa** and try this skill on your own:

1. If necessary, open the *Customers* table in Datasheet view.

2. Change the **Field Size** property for the *State* field to: **2**

3. Keep the *Customers* table open if you are moving on to the skill; close it if you are finished working with these skills.

Skill 2.14 Applying an Input Mask

One of the keys to an effective database is consistent data entry. An **input mask** forces users to enter data in a consistent format. Input masks are only available from the Design view Field Properties pane. The *Input Mask Wizard* offers a variety of common input masks including phone number and date and time formats.

In Figure AC 2.27, the *Phone* field uses the *Phone Number* input mask. The input mask adds the parentheses and dashes to the phone number format automatically. It also forces users to input the correct number of digits for the phone number.

FIGURE AC 2.27

The *Phone* field has the *Phone Number* input mask applied.

Access has many predefined input masks built into the program. To apply one of the predefined input masks to a field:

1. With the table open in Design view, click the field you want to apply the input mask to.
2. Click the **Input Mask** box in the Field Properties pane.
3. Click the **Build...** button to open the *Input Mask Wizard*.

Click in the **Input Mask** box and then click the **Build...** button to start the *Input Mask Wizard*.

FIGURE AC 2.28

Input Mask Wizard

Which input mask matches how you want data to look?

To see how a selected mask works, use the Try It box.

To change the Input Mask list, click the Edit List button.

Input Mask:	Data Look:
Phone Number	(206) 555-1212
Social Security Number	831-86-7180
Zip Code	98052-6399
Extension	63215
Password	*******
Long Time	1:12:00 PM

Try It: (703) 555-1234

Type sample data here to see how the selected input mask works.

Edit List   Cancel   < Back   Next >   Finish

FIGURE AC 2.29

4. Click **Yes** if Access prompts you to save the table.
5. Click the input mask format you want.
6. To test the format, click in the **Try It** box, and type a sample to see how the input mask will affect data entry as shown in Figure AC 2.29. You must enter all the required characters in the *Try It* box.
7. Click **Next**.

Input Mask Wizard

Do you want to change the input mask?

Input Mask Code

Input Mask Name: Phone Number

Input Mask: !(999) 000-0000

What placeholder character do you want the field to display?

Placeholders are replaced as you enter data into the field.

Placeholder character: _

Default Placeholder Character

Try It:

Cancel   < Back   Next >   Finish

FIGURE AC 2.30

8. The next step in the wizard shows the code for the input mask. Click **Next** again to continue without making any customizations to the input mask as shown in Figure AC 2.30.

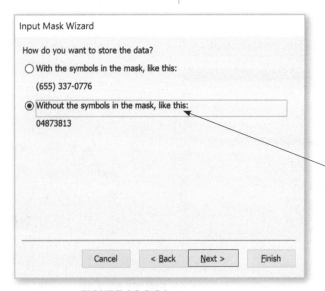

Input Mask Wizard

How do you want to store the data?

○ With the symbols in the mask, like this:

(655) 337-0776

◉ Without the symbols in the mask, like this:

04873813

Accept the option to store the data without the input mask symbols.

Cancel   < Back   Next >   Finish

FIGURE AC 2.31

9. In the next step, you specify how Access will store the data—with or without the input mask symbols. Unless you truly need the symbols stored in the database, select the second option as shown in Figure AC 2.31. This will help reduce the size of the database. Click **Finish**. You can also click **Next** and then click **Finish** on the final step of the wizard.

10. Save the table.

The input mask code is displayed in the *Input Mask* box in the Field Properties pane.

FIGURE AC 2.32

tips & tricks

> The *Input Mask* property is available for *Short Text* or *Date/Time* data type fields only. If you want to use the Social Security input mask, use the *Short Text* data type for the field that stores the Social Security numbers.

> If the field has a format specified through the *Format* property, the format takes precedence over the input mask format.

let me try

If the database is not already open, open the data file **AC02-14-Spa** and try this skill on your own:

1. If necessary, open the *Customers* table.

2. Switch to Design view.

3. Apply the **Phone Number** input mask format to the *Phone* field. Do not change default format or placeholder characters. Store the data without the symbols.

4. Save the table.

5. Switch to Datasheet view and enter a new record in the *Customers* table, using any customer information you want. The *CustomerID* field has an input mask applied that requires three letters followed by three numbers. Input in the *Phone* field is controlled by the input mask you applied in step 3.

6. Keep the *Customers* table open if you are moving on to the next skill. Close it if you are finished working with these skills.

Skill 2.15 Working with Attachment Fields

One of the most useful enhancements to recent versions of Access is the ability to create *Attachment* fields to store files as attachments to records. Attachments can be pictures, Word documents, or almost any other type of data file. For security reasons, Access will not allow program files (for example, .exe or .bat files) or any files greater than 256 MB as attachments.

To add an *Attachment* field from Datasheet view:

1. At the far right side of the table, there is a column with the header *Click to Add*. Click the arrow to expand the list of available field types, and click **Attachment**.

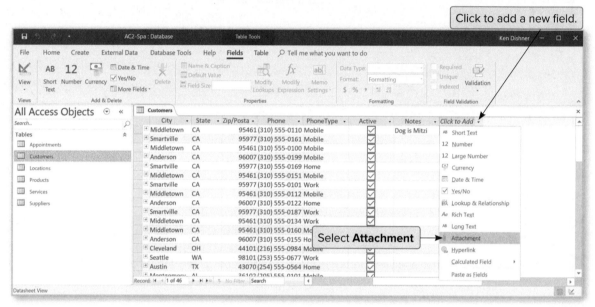

FIGURE AC 2.33

2. Notice that you cannot rename the *Attachment* field. It is designated by a paperclip icon. (You can, however, rename the field in Design view.)

FIGURE AC 2.34

Once you've added the *Attachment* field, use the *Attachments* dialog to add and manage attachments for each record.

To add an attachment:

1. Double-click the *Attachment* field in the record to which you want to add the attachment.

2. The *Attachments* dialog opens.

3. Click the **Add...** button and browse for the file you want to add.

4. Double-click the file to add it, or click the file once, and then click the **Open** button.

5. Click **OK** to save the attachment and close the *Attachments* dialog.

In Datasheet view, the number next to the attachment icon in each record tells you how many attachments there are. Records can have multiple attachments in a single *Attachment* field.

FIGURE AC 2.35

FIGURE AC 2.36

tips & tricks

Attachment fields cannot be changed to another data type.

tell me **more**

The attachment is not visible in the table. However, when you start working with forms and reports, the attachment is available for display in those database objects.

let me **try**

If the database is not already open, open the data file **AC02-15-Spa** and try this skill on your own:

1. If necessary, open the *Customers* table in Datasheet view.

2. Add an *Attachment* field at the far right of the table.

3. Add the JPEG image file **BerniceJames** to the customer record for Bernice James. The image file is located with your student data files for this chapter.

4. Save and close the table.

Skill 2.16 Adding a Lookup Field from Another Table

A **lookup field** allows the user to select data from a list of items. One type of lookup list presents values from a field in another table or a query.

Whether you begin with a new field or modify the data type for an existing field, the process using the *Lookup Wizard* is the same.

To create a new lookup field from Datasheet view:

1. On the *Table Tools Fields* tab, in the *Add & Delete* group, click the **More Fields** button.

2. From the *Basic Types* section of the *Field Types* gallery, click **Lookup & Relationship**.

3. The *Lookup Wizard* opens.

To create a new lookup field from Design view, type the name for the new field to expand the **Data Type** list, and select **Lookup Wizard...** to open the *Lookup Wizard*.

To modify an existing field to use a lookup list:

1. Open the table in Design view.

2. Select the field you want to change to use a lookup list.

3. Expand the **Data Type** list, and select **Lookup Wizard...** to open the *Lookup Wizard*.

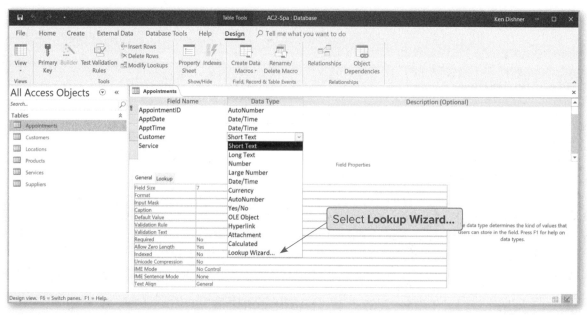

FIGURE AC 2.37

To add the lookup field using the *Lookup Wizard*:

1. The first step of the wizard asks you to determine where your lookup list data will come from. The **I want the lookup field to get the values from another table or query.** radio button is selected by default. Click **Next** to go to the next step.

Select the option to get the values from another table or query.

FIGURE AC 2.38

2. Click the name of the table or query that includes the field you want to use for your lookup field values. Click **Next**.

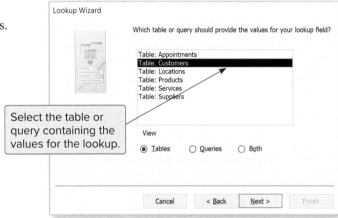

Select the table or query containing the values for the lookup.

FIGURE AC 2.39

3. Double-click each field name you want to include in the lookup. When you have selected all the fields you want, click **Next**. If you do not select the primary key field, Access will include it automatically.

Double-click a field in the *Available Fields* list to add it to the *Selected Fields* list.

FIGURE AC 2.40

FIGURE AC 2.41

4. If you want items in the lookup list sorted in a particular order, select the field to sort by. The sort order is ascending by default. Click the **Ascending** button if you want to switch the sort order to descending. Click **Next**.

FIGURE AC 2.42

5. By default, the **Hide key column (recommended)** check box is checked. This hides the primary key in the lookup list.

6. Adjust the column width as necessary to display the values in the lookup list. Click and drag the right border of the column header to make the column wider or narrower. You can double-click the right column border to autofit the column to the data. Click **Next** to continue.

FIGURE AC 2.43

7. If you are modifying an existing field, Access keeps the original field name. If this is a new field, Access gives the field a generic field name such as *Field1*. You should change the name of the new field to something more meaningful.

8. Click the **Enable Data Integrity** check box to require that only values from the lookup list are allowed in the field.

9. Verify that the *Restrict Delete* radio button is selected to prevent any deletions in the table containing the lookup values that would invalidate data in the table containing the lookup field.

10. Click the **Finish** button to add the new lookup field to the table.

11. Access will prompt you to save the table so table relationships can be created. Click **Yes**.

Switch to Datasheet view to test the new lookup field. You may need to adjust the column width to display the lookup data properly.

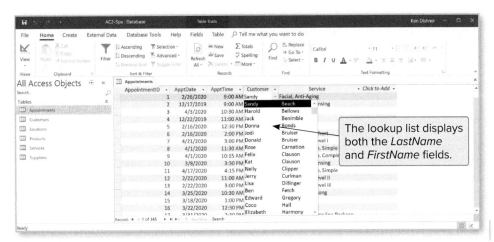

FIGURE AC 2.44

tell me **more**

When you create a lookup field that references data in another table, Access automatically creates a one-to-many relationship between the table that contains the list data (the "one") and the table that includes the lookup list (the "many"). This concept is discussed further in the skill *Creating Relationships*.

let me **try**

If the database is not already open, open the data file **AC02-16-Spa** and try this skill on your own:

1. If necessary, open the *Appointments* table in Design view.

2. Modify the *Customer* field to use a lookup list with the following parameters:
   - The lookup data will come from the **Customers** table.
   - Include the **CustomerID**, **FirstName**, and **LastName** fields in the lookup list in that order.
   - Sort the lookup list by the **LastName** field.
   - Hide the key column as suggested.
   - Enforce data integrity.
   - Do not allow deletions in the *Customers* table that would violate the integrity of records in the *Appointments* table.

3. Save the table.

4. Switch to Datasheet view and observe the new lookup list.

5. Close the table.

Skill 2.17 Adding a Lookup Field from a List

Lookup fields are useful for fields that reference a specific list of items. A lookup field does not need to reference data in another table or query. You can enter your own values to create a custom list.

To review the procedures for creating new lookup fields, refer to the skill *Adding a Lookup Field from another Table.*

To modify an existing field to use a lookup field with values you specify:

1. Open the table in Design view.
2. Click the field you want to modify to use a lookup list.
3. Click the **Data Type** drop-down arrow and select **Lookup Wizard...**
4. The first step of the wizard asks you to determine where your lookup list data will come from. Click the **I will type in the values that I want**. radio button. Click **Next** to go to the next step.

FIGURE AC 2.45

5. Observe that Access enters *1* as the default number of columns for the list. If you want more than one column, you can change this value.
6. Press (Tab ⭾) to go to the first cell in the first blank column.
7. Type the values in the table exactly as you want them to appear in the lookup field. Click and drag the right border of the column header to make the column wider or narrower. You can double-click the right column border to autofit the column to the data. Click **Next** to continue.

FIGURE AC 2.46

8. Access will keep the original field name. If you want to change it, type a new name.

9. If you want to restrict data entry to only items in the list, click the **Limit To List** check box.

10. Click the **Finish** button to complete the lookup list.

11. Save the table.

Switch to Datasheet view to test the new lookup field. You may need to adjust the column width to display the lookup data properly.

FIGURE AC 2.47

FIGURE AC 2.48

tell me **more**

If the field you want to change to a lookup field uses the *Date/Time* or *Currency* data type, you will need to change the data type to *Number* before you can modify it to be a lookup field.

let me **try**

If the database is not already open, open the data file **AC02-17-Spa** and try this skill on your own:

1. If necessary, open the *Customers* table in Design view.
2. Modify the *Phone Type* field to use a lookup list with the following values: **Home, Work, Mobile, Other**
3. Limit the lookup list to values in the list.
4. Save the table.
5. Switch to Datasheet view and observe the new lookup list.
6. Close the table.

Skill 2.18 Creating Relationships

When a lookup field in one table references values in a field in another table, Access will automatically create a one-to-many relationship between the tables for you. In other cases, you may need to manually create a relationship between two tables.

Enforcing **referential integrity** ensures that related database records remain accurate. If a relationship has *Enforce Referential Integrity* checked, then the tables will conform to the following rules:

❭ You cannot add a record to the secondary table without an associated record in the primary table.

❭ You cannot make changes to the primary table that would cause records in the secondary table to become unmatched.

❭ You cannot delete records from the primary table if there are related records in the secondary table.

To create a new table relationship and enforce referential integrity between the two tables:

1. Open the Relationships window. On the *Database Tools* tab, in the *Relationships* group, click the **Relationships** button.

2. To create a new relationship, click the primary key field name in the primary table and drag to the related field name in the secondary table.

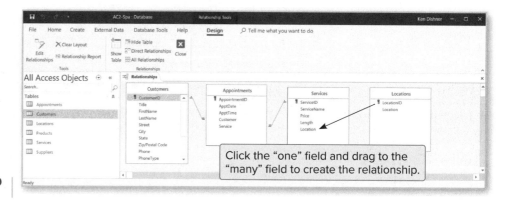

FIGURE AC 2.49

3. Review the relationship in the *Edit Relationships* dialog. Note the type of relationship.

4. Click the **Enforce Referential Integrity** check box.

5. Click the **Create** button.

FIGURE AC 2.50

Notice the change to the relationship line. The 1 indicates the "one" table in the one-to-many relationship. The infinity symbol indicates the "many" table. When these symbols appear, you know that the relationship has referential integrity enforced.

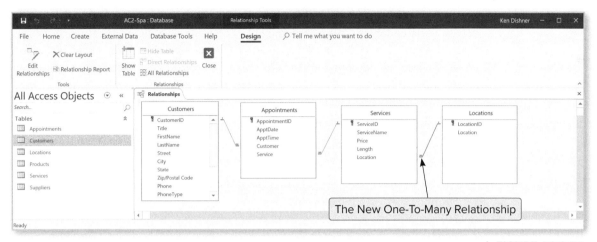

The New One-To-Many Relationship

FIGURE AC 2.51

tell me **more**

To delete the relationship between two tables, right-click the relationship line, and select **Delete**.

another **method**

To open the *Edit Relationships* dialog, you can also:

❯ Double-click any field name showing in the Relationships window.

❯ Double-click any empty area of the Relationships window.

When you open the *Edit Relationships* dialog with either of these methods, you will need to select the primary table from the *Table/Query* list at the left side of the dialog. When you make a selection, Access will populate the dialog with the existing relationships.

let me **try**

If the database is not already open, open the data file **AC02-18-Spa** and try this skill on your own:

1. If necessary, save and close all open database objects.
2. Open the Relationships window.
3. If necessary, show the *Locations* table and the *Services* table.
4. Create a new relationship between the *LocationID* field in the *Locations* table and the *Location* field in the *Services* table.
5. Enforce data integrity between the two fields.
6. Keep the Relationships window open if you are moving on to the next skill; save and close it if you are finished working with these skills.

Skill 2.19 Enforcing Deletions and Updates in Relationships

In the skill *Creating Relationships*, you learned how enforcing referential integrity between related tables ensures accuracy by preventing deleting or updating of records that would cause a violation of the relationship between the primary and secondary tables. Instead of preventing updates or deletions, you can set relationship options to delete or update the related records in the secondary table. These options are known as **cascading options** because when they are enforced, an action on one table cascades to affect records in the related table.

If you want related records to update automatically, enforce the **cascade update** option:

1. On the *Database Tools* tab, in the *Relationships* group, click the **Relationships** button to open the Relationships window.
2. Double-click the line connecting the two related tables to open the *Edit Relationships* dialog.
3. To update related records in the "many" table when the "one" record is updated, click the **Cascade Update Related Fields** check box.
4. Click **OK** to apply the changes and close the *Edit Relationships* dialog.

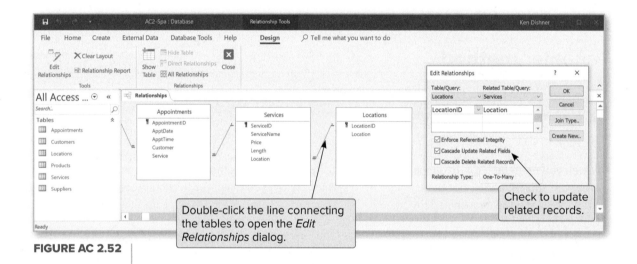

FIGURE AC 2.52

If you want related records to delete automatically, enforce the **cascade delete** option:

1. On the *Database Tools* tab, in the *Relationships* group, click the **Relationships** button to open the Relationships window.
2. Double-click the line connecting the two related tables to open the *Edit Relationships* dialog.
3. To delete records in the "many" table when the "one" record is deleted in the primary table, click the **Cascade Delete Related Records** check box.
4. Click **OK** to apply the changes and close the *Edit Relationships* dialog.

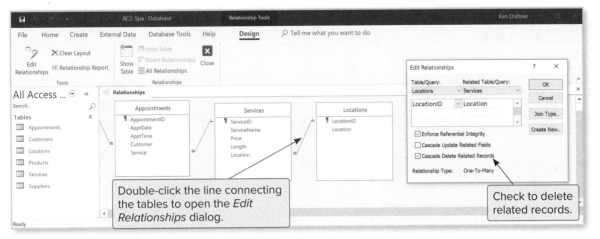

Double-click the line connecting the tables to open the *Edit Relationships* dialog.

Check to delete related records.

FIGURE AC 2.53

tips & tricks

Be careful when activating the *Cascade Delete* and *Cascade Update* options, as they may have unintended consequences. For example, deleting a customer from a table may also delete all related appointments linked to that customer name. Automatically removing future appointments may be desirable, but you may not want to delete past appointments.

another **method**

Right-click the line connecting the tables in the Relationships window and select **Edit Relationship...**

If you have trouble double-clicking the line connecting the tables in the Relationships window, open the *Edit Relationships* dialog by clicking the **Edit Relationships** button on the *Relationship Tools Design* tab, in the *Tools* group. When you open the *Edit Relationships* dialog, you may need to select the primary table from the *Table/Query* list at the left side of the dialog. When you make a selection, Access will populate the dialog with the existing relationships.

let me **try**

If the database is not already open, open the data file **AC02-19-Spa** and try this skill on your own:

1. If necessary, open the Relationships window.
2. Modify the relationship between the *Locations* and *Services* tables so when a record in the *Locations* table is updated, related records in the *Services* table will also be updated.
3. Modify the relationship between the *Services* and *Appointments* tables so when a record in the *Services* table is deleted, related records in the *Appointments* table will also be deleted.
4. Close the Relationships window.

key terms

AutoNumber data type
Short Text data type
Long Text data type
Number data type
Large Number data type
Date/Time data type
Currency data type
Yes/No data type
OLE Object data type
Hyperlink data type
Attachment data type
Calculated Field data type
Field name
Caption property
Quick Start fields

Field Properties pane
Primary key
Format field property
Currency format
Percent format
Comma Style format
Default Value property
Field Size property
Input mask
Lookup field
Referential integrity
Cascading options
Cascade update
Cascade delete

concept review

1. A well-designed database _____.

    a. repeats important data in multiple tables

    b. stores each unique piece of data in only one table

    c. uses the AutoNumber data type for primary key fields

    d. both b and c

2. Users can enter and edit data in an AutoNumber field.

    a. true

    b. false

3. To rename a field, _____.

    a. click the column header, and type the new field name

    b. double-click the column header, and type the new field name

    c. right-click the column header, select Rename Field, and type the new field name

    d. both b and c

4. Moving a field in Design view also changes the field order in Datasheet view.

    a. true

    b. false

5. A table's primary key must _____.

    a. be unique for every record in the table

    b. use the AutoNumber data type

    c. be linked to other tables

    d. be named ID

6. Which data type should be used to include an image file with each record in a table?

    a. Hyperlink

    b. Photo

    c. Attachment

    d. Memo

7. The Currency field format is the same as the Currency data type.

    a. true

    b. false

8. To control the number of characters a user can enter into a table field, use _____.

    a. the Field Width property

    b. the Field Size property

    c. the Long Text data type

    d. Rich Text Formatting

9. An input mask _____.

    a. creates a relationship between two tables

    b. modifies the field Format property

    c. changes the field data type to Short Text

    d. forces users to input data in a consistent format

10. If two tables have referential integrity enforced, _____.

    a. you cannot add a record to the secondary table without an associated record in the primary table

    b. you cannot make changes to the primary table that would cause records in the secondary table to become unmatched

    c. both a and b

    d. none of the above

skill review **2.1**

In this project, you will continue to work with the Computer Science department database from the *Chapter 1 Skill Review 1.1*. You will create new tables and modify fields in existing tables. You will also create lookup lists—one where you enter the values yourself and another where the values come from a field in another table. You will modify the relationship created by the lookup field to ensure that deletions in one table carry through to the related table.

Skills needed to complete this project:

- Designing a Table (Skill 2.1)
- Creating and Saving a Table in Datasheet View (Skill 2.2)
- Renaming Fields (Skill 2.3)
- Adding Fields in Datasheet View (Skill 2.4)
- Using Quick Start to Add Related Fields (Skill 2.5)
- Changing Data Type (Skill 2.10)
- Applying an Input Mask (Skill 2.14)
- Adding a Lookup Field from a List (Skill 2.17)
- Inserting, Deleting, and Moving Fields in Design View (Skill 2.9)
- Formatting Fields (Skill 2.11)
- Adding a Lookup Field from Another Table (Skill 2.16)
- Modifying the Field Size Property (Skill 2.13)
- Working with Attachment Fields (Skill 2.15)
- Deleting Fields in Datasheet View (Skill 2.6)
- Creating a Table in Design View and Setting the Primary Key (Skill 2.8)
- Creating Relationships (Skill 2.18)
- Enforcing Deletions and Updates in Relationships (Skill 2.19)

1. Open the start file **AC2019-SkillReview-2-1**.
2. If the database opens in Protected View, click the **Enable Content** button in the Message Bar at the top of the database so you can modify it.
3. Save a copy of the file to work on named: **[your initials] AC-SkillReview-2-1**
   If necessary, enable active content in the new database by clicking the **Enable Content** button in the Message Bar.
4. The file will be renamed automatically to include your name. Change the project file name if directed to do so by your instructor. If necessary, enable active content in the new database by clicking the **Enable Content** button in the Message Bar.
5. Create a table in Datasheet view to store vendor company data.
   a. On the *Create* tab, in the *Tables* group, click the **Table** button.
   b. You are now in the Datasheet view of a new table. Notice that Access has created a new field named *ID* with the *AutoNumber* data type.

6. Save the table.

    a. On the Quick Access Toolbar, click the **Save** button.

    b. In the *Save As* dialog, type **Vendors** in the *Table Name* box.

    c. Click **OK**.

7. Continue adding fields to the new table.

    a. Create the next field by typing **Amazon** in the cell directly underneath the *Click to Add* heading.

    b. Press (Tab ⭾) to go to the next field in this record.

    c. Create another new field by typing: **www.amazon.com**

    d. Press (Tab ⭾) again.

    e. Go to the next row in the table and enter another record with the following:

       Staples

       www.staples.com

8. Rename the fields.

    a. Click anywhere in the **ID** field.

    b. On the *Fields* tab, in the *Properties* group, click the **Name & Caption** button.

    c. Type **VendorID** in the *Name* box and press (Tab ⭾).

    d. Type **Vendor ID** in the *Caption* box and click **OK**.

    e. Repeat the process for **Field1**, renaming it **CompanyName** with the caption **Company Name**.

    f. Repeat the process for **Field2**, renaming it **WebSite** with the caption **Web Site**.

9. Add a group of related fields using *Quick Start*.

    a. Click the cell underneath the last *Click to Add* heading.

    b. On the *Table Tools Fields* tab, in the *Add & Delete* group, click the **More Fields** button.

    c. Scroll down and select **Address** from the *Quick Start* category.

10. Close the table.

11. In the *Employees* table, modify the data type for the *Email* field to *Hyperlink*.

    a. In the Navigation Pane, double-click **Employees : Table** to open it in Datasheet view.

    b. Click anywhere in the **Email** column to select the field. Observe that the data type for this field is *Short Text*.

    c. On the *Table Tools Fields* tab, in the *Formatting* group, expand the **Data Type** list, and select **Hyperlink**.

12. Add an input mask to the new *Phone* field to force users to enter data in the (206) 555-1212 format.

    a. On the *Home* tab, in the *Views* group, click the **View** button to switch to Design view.

    b. Select the **Phone** field by clicking anywhere in that row.

    c. In the Field Properties pane, click the **Input Mask** box, and then click the **Build...** button to start the *Input Mask Wizard*.

    d. The first input mask sample is the phone number format you want. Test it by typing any sample phone number in the *Try It* box. Click **Next** to continue.

    e. Click the **Next** button to continue without making any changes to the input mask or the placeholder character.

f. Verify that the radio button to store the data without the symbols is selected, and click **Next**.

g. Click **Finish**.

h. Observe that the *Input Mask* box now displays the input mask format:
!\(999″) ″000\- 0000;;_

i. Save the table.

j. Switch back to Datasheet view by clicking the **Datasheet View** button at the lower right part of the status bar. Observe the change to the *Phone* field. Enter a new record with any data you want. Observe the input mask as you enter data in the *Phone* field.

13. Close the *Employees* table.

14. In the *Items* table, move the *Category* field so it is between the *ItemName* and *Description* fields.

a. In the Navigation Pane, right-click **Items : Table** and select **Design View**.

b. Click the row selector at the left of the *Category* field.

c. Click and drag until the black line is between the *ItemName* and *Description* fields.

d. Release the mouse button.

15. Modify the *Category* field to use a lookup list.

a. Click in the **Data Type** column next to *Category* and select **Lookup Wizard...**

b. In the *Lookup Wizard*, click the **I will type in the values I want**. radio button. Click **Next**.

c. Use only 1 column and enter the following values:

Type **Equipment** and then press (Tab ⇆).

Type **Software** and then press (Tab ⇆).

Type **Textbook** and then press (Tab ⇆).

Type **Other** and then click **Next**.

d. Verify that *Category* is the label for the lookup field.

e. Limit data entry to the values in the list by clicking the **Limit to List** check box.

f. Click **Finish**.

g. Save the table.

16. Modify the *Cost* field to use the **Currency** format.

a. On the *Home* tab, in the *Views* group, click the **View** button to switch to Datasheet view.

b. Select the **Cost** field by clicking anywhere in that column.

c. On the *Table Tools Fields* tab, in the *Formatting* group, click the **Apply Currency Format** button.

d. Notice that the *Format* box now displays *Currency*.

17. Modify the size of the *ItemID* field.

a. Click anywhere in the **ItemID** field.

b. On the *Table Tools Fields* tab, in the *Properties* group, type **4** in the *Field Size* box. Press (← Enter).

c. Click **Yes** to continue.

18. Add an *Attachment* field.

    a. Click the arrow next to the *Click to Add* heading in the last available field to expand the list of field types.

    b. Select the **Attachment** option.

19. Add an attachment to a record.

    a. Find the record with an ID of **PRJ1**.

    b. Double-click the paperclip icon for this record, which is located in the new *Attachment* column you just created.

    c. Click **Add** in the *Attachments* dialog and then find the file named **projector.jpg** in your student data files folder.

    d. Double-click the file and then click **OK**. Note the (**1**) added to the paperclip icon to indicate that the record has one attachment.

20. Delete the *Location* field from the *Items* table.

    a. Click the **Location** field column heading to select the field.

    b. On the *Table Tools Fields* tab, in the *Add & Delete* group, click the **Delete** button.

    c. Click **Yes** to confirm the deletion.

21. Save and close the *Items* table.

22. Modify the *ItemID* field in the *Loans* table to use a lookup list of values from the *Items* table.

    a. In the Navigation Pane, right-click **Loans : Table** and select **Design View**.

    b. Click in the **Data Type** column next to *ItemID* and select **Lookup Wizard...**

    c. In the *Lookup Wizard*, verify that the **I want the lookup field to get the values from another table or query.** radio button is selected, and click **Next**.

    d. Select **Table: Items** as the table that will provide the values for your lookup field, and click **Next**.

    e. From the *Available Fields* list, select the **ItemID** field and click the single **>** button to add it to the *Selected Fields* list. Select the **ItemName** field and click the single **>** button to add it to the *Selected Fields* list. Click **Next**.

    f. Click the arrow to expand the **1** list and choose **ItemName** as the sort field. Click **Next**.

    g. Uncheck the **Hide key column (recommended)** check box. Verify that both *ItemID* and *ItemName* field data appear in the list.

    h. Double-click the right edge of the **ItemName** column to autofit the column width to the data. Click **Next**.

    i. Verify that the *ItemID* field is selected to store in the database. Click **Next**.

    j. Limit data entry to the values in the list by clicking the **Enable Data Integrity** check box.

    k. Click **Finish**.

    l. Click **Yes** to save the table. Click **Yes** again to continue.

23. Close the *Loans* table.

24. Create a table in Design view:

    a. On the *Create* tab, in the *Tables* group, click the **Table Design** button.

    b. Type **RoomNo** for the first field name. Press (Tab ⇄).

    c. Accept the default data type, *Short Text*.

d. With the cursor still in this row, on the *Design* tab, in the *Tools* group, click the **Primary Key** button.

e. Create the following fields in Design view:

FieldName	DataType	Description
Capacity	Number	Maximum number of seats
ComputerLab	Yes/No	Is this room a computer lab?

25. Save the table.

  a. On the Quick Access Toolbar, click the **Save** button.

  b. In the *Save As* dialog, type **Classrooms** in the *Table Name* box.

  c. Click **OK**.

26. Switch to Datasheet view to review the fields you entered and then close the table.

27. Create a new relationship between the *EmployeeID* field in the *Employees* table and the *EmployeeID* field in the *Loans* table.

  a. Open the Relationships window. On the *Database Tools* tab, in the *Relationships* group, click the **Relationships** button.

  b. Click the **EmployeeID** field in the *Employees* table and drag it to the *EmployeeID* field in the *Loans* table.

  c. The *Edit Relationships* dialog opens.

  d. Click the **Enforce Referential Integrity** check box.

  e. Click **Create**.

  f. Observe the new line connecting the *Employees* table and the *Loans* table.

28. Modify the relationship between the *Loans* table and the *Items* table so when an item is deleted any loans for that item are deleted as well.

  a. There is a relationship between the *ItemID* field in the *Items* table and the *ItemID* field in the *Loans* table. This relationship was created when you created the *ItemID* lookup field in the *Loans* table. Double-click the line connecting the two field names to open the *Edit Relationships* dialog.

  b. Look at the *Relationship Type* box near the bottom of the dialog and note that the relationship type is one-to-many.

  c. Click the **Cascade Delete Related Records** check box.

  d. Click **OK**.

29. Close the Relationships window. If Access prompts you to save changes to the layout, click **Yes**.

30. Close the database and exit Access.

skill review 2.2

In this project you will continue working with the health insurance database from *Chapter 1 Skill Review 1.2*. You will work with tables: creating tables, adding fields, and modify field properties. You will also create a new table relationship and modify an existing relationship to ensure that updates to the primary key in one table will update the foreign key field in the related table.

Skills needed to complete this project:

- Designing a Table (Skill 2.1)
- Creating and Saving a Table in Datasheet View (Skill 2.2)
- Adding Fields in Datasheet View (Skill 2.4)
- Renaming Fields (Skill 2.3)
- Using Quick Start to Add Related Fields (Skill 2.5)
- Modifying the Field Size Property (Skill 2.13)
- Setting the Default Value Property (Skill 2.12)
- Inserting, Deleting, and Moving Fields in Design View (Skill 2.9)
- Applying an Input Mask (Skill 2.14)
- Changing Data Type (Skill 2.10)
- Adding a Lookup Field from Another Table (Skill 2.16)
- Deleting Fields in Datasheet View (Skill 2.6)
- Working with Attachment Fields (Skill 2.15)
- Creating a Table in Design View and Setting the Primary Key (Skill 2.8)
- Formatting Fields (Skill 2.11)
- Adding a Lookup Field from a List (Skill 2.17)
- Creating Relationships (Skill 2.18)

1. Open the start file **AC2019-SkillReview-2-2**.

2. If the database opens in Protected View, click the **Enable Content** button in the Message Bar at the top of the database so you can modify it.

3. Save a copy of the file to work on named: **[your initials] AC-SkillReview-2-2**

   If necessary, enable active content in the new database by clicking the **Enable Content** button in the Message Bar.

4. Create a table in Datasheet view to store hospital data.

   a. On the *Create* tab, in the *Tables* group, click the **Table** button.

   b. You are now in the Datasheet view of a new table. Notice that Access has created a new field named *ID* with the *AutoNumber* data type.

   c. Create the next field by typing *Miami City Hospital* in the cell directly underneath the *Click to Add* heading.

   d. Press `Tab ⇥` to go to the next field in this record.

   e. Create another new field by typing: **88**

   f. Press `Tab ⇥` again.

   g. Enter two more records in the table with the following data:

Central Lauderdale Hospital	60
West Palm Hospital	62

5. Save the table.

   a. On the Quick Access Toolbar, click the **Save** button.

   b. In the *Save As* dialog, type **Hospitals** in the *Table Name* box.

   c. Click **OK**.

6. Rename the fields.

   a. Click anywhere in the **ID** field.

   b. On the *Fields* tab, in the *Properties* group, click the **Name & Caption** button.

c. Type **HospitalID** in the *Name* box and press (Tab ⇥).

d. Type **Hospital ID** in the *Caption* box and click **OK**.

e. Repeat the process for **Field1**, renaming it **HospitalName** with the caption **Hospital Name**.

f. Repeat the process for **Field2**, renaming it **MemberVisits** with the caption **Member Visits**.

7. Add a group of related fields using *Quick Start*.

a. Click the cell underneath the last *Click to Add* heading.

b. On the *Table Tools Fields* tab, in the *Add & Delete* group, click the **More Fields** button.

c. Scroll down and select **Address** from the *Quick Start* category.

d. Observe the five new fields. Type the following data into these new fields:

Address	City	StateProvince	ZipPostal	CountryRegion
4500 Miami Blvd	Miami	FL	33126	USA
320 Palmer Rd	Ft. Lauderdale	FL	33301	USA
800 Jefferson Street	West Palm Beach	FL	33403	USA

8. Modify the size of the *State Province* field.

a. Click the **State Province** field heading.

b. On the *Table Tools Fields* tab, in the *Properties* group, type **2** in the *Field Size* box. Press (← Enter).

c. Click **Yes** to continue.

d. If Access shows additional messages, click **OK** to dismiss each one. Changing the field size to 2 will not delete any data or delete the field.

9. Set the default value for the *State Province* field.

a. Verify that the *State Province* field is still selected.

b. On the *Table Tools Fields* tab, in the *Properties* group, click the **Default Value** button.

c. In the *Expression Builder*, type **FL** after the = sign.

d. Click **OK**.

10. Save and close the *Hospitals* table.

11. Change the order of fields in the *Physicians* table. Move the *Phone* field so it is between the *LastName* and *StreetAddress* fields.

a. In the Navigation Pane, under the *Tables* category, right-click **Physicians** and select **Design View**.

b. Click the row selector at the left of the *Phone* field.

c. Click and drag until the black line is between the *LastName* and *StreetAddress* fields.

d. Release the mouse button.

e. Save the table.

12. Add an input mask to the *Phone* field to force users to enter data in the (206) 555-1212 format.

a. If necessary, select the **Phone** field by clicking anywhere in that row.

b. In the Field Properties pane, click the **Input Mask** box, and then click the **Build...** button to start the *Input Mask Wizard*.

c. The first input mask sample is the phone number format you want. Test it by typing any sample phone number in the *Try It* box. Click **Next** to continue.

d. Click the **Next** button to continue without making any changes to the input mask or the placeholder character.

e. Verify that the radio button to store the data without the symbols is selected, and click **Next**.

f. Click **Finish**.

g. Observe that the *Input Mask* box now displays the input mask format:
!\(999") "000\-0000;;_

h. Save the table.

i. Switch back to Datasheet view by clicking the **Datasheet View** button at the lower right part of the status bar. Observe the change to the *Phone* field. Enter a new record with any data you want. Observe the input mask as you enter data in the *Phone* field.

13. Modify the *MemberCount* field to use the *Number* data type instead of the *Currency* data type.

a. Click the **MemberCount** column header to select the field.

b. On the *Table Tools Fields* tab, in the *Formatting* group, expand the **Data Type** list, and select **Number**.

c. Notice that the *Format* box no longer displays *Currency*. It is not necessary to specify a format for this field.

14. Create a *HospitalName* lookup field in the *Physicians* table using values from the *Hospitals* table.

a. Click the arrow next to the *Click to Add* heading in the last available field, and select **Lookup & Relationship**.

b. In the *Lookup Wizard*, verify that the **I want the lookup field to get the values from another table or query.** radio button is selected, and click **Next**.

c. Select **Table: Hospitals** as the table that will provide the values for your lookup field, and click **Next**.

d. From the *Available Fields* list, select the **HospitalName** field and click the single > button to add it to the right. Click **Next**.

e. Click the arrow to expand the **1** list and choose **HospitalName** as the sort field. Observe that even though you added only the *HospitalName* field to the lookup list, Access included the *HospitalID* field (the primary key) automatically. Click **Next**.

f. Verify that the *Hide key column (recommended)* check box is checked and that the three hospitals you entered in the table earlier appear in the lookup field preview. Click **Next**.

g. In the last screen, type **HospitalName** as the label for this new field.

h. Limit data entry to the values in the list by clicking the **Enable Data Integrity** check box.

i. Click **Finish**.

j. Use this new lookup field to add *HospitalName* values for the first three records. Choose **West Palm Hospital** for the first two and **Central Lauderdale Hospital** for the third.

k. Adjust the width of the *HospitalName* field to best fit the data by double-clicking the right edge of the field heading.

15. Delete the *YearsInPractice* field.

  a. Click the **YearsInPractice** field column heading to select the field.

  b. On the *Table Tools Fields* tab, in the *Add & Delete* group, click the **Delete** button.

  c. Click **Yes** to confirm the deletion.

16. Add an *Attachment* field and an attachment to the *Physicians* table.

  a. Click the arrow next to the *Click to Add* heading in the last available field. Select the **Attachment** option.

  b. Go to the record for **Antonio Gonzalez**, and double-click the paperclip icon, which is located in the new *Attachment* column you just created.

  c. Click **Add** in the *Attachments* dialog and then find the file named **Gonzalez.jpg** in your student data files folder.

  d. Double-click the file and then click **OK**. Note the (**1**) added to the paperclip icon to indicate that the record has one attachment.

17. Close any open tables. If Access prompts you to save changes, click **Yes**.

18. Create a table in Design view:

  a. On the *Create* tab, in the *Tables* group, click the **Table Design** button.

  b. Type *MemberID* for the first field name. Press [Tab ⇆].

  c. Accept the default data type, *Short Text*. Press [Tab ⇆].

  d. Enter the following in the Description: **First letter of last name followed by a randomly generated seven-digit number**

  e. With the cursor still in this row, on the *Design* tab, in the *Tools* group, click the **Primary Key** button.

  f. Create the following fields in Design view. None of these fields require a description.

FieldName	DataType
FirstName	ShortText
LastName	ShortText
Address	ShortText
City	ShortText
State	ShortText
Zip	Number
DOB	Date/Time

19. Save the table.

  a. On the Quick Access Toolbar, click the **Save** button.

  b. In the *Save As* dialog, type **Patients** in the *Table Name* box.

  c. Click **OK**.

20. Modify field properties and formatting in Design view.

  a. Expand the **Data Type** list for the **Zip** field and select **Short Text**.

  b. Click anywhere in the **DOB** row. In the Field Properties pane, click in the **Format** box. Click the arrow to expand the selection list, and select **Short Date**.

  c. Click anywhere in the **State** row. In the Field Properties pane, click in the **Default Value** box and type: **FL**

21. Add a new lookup field to the *Patients* table to use values you enter yourself.

    a. Click in the first empty cell in the **Field Name** column and type: `Gender`

    b. Press `Tab` or click in the **Data Type** cell. Expand the selection list, and select **Lookup Wizard. . .**

    c. In the *Lookup Wizard*, click the **I will type in the values I want**. radio button. Click **Next**.

    d. Click in the first cell under Col1 and type: `Female`

    e. Press `Tab` and then type: `Male`

    f. Click **Next**, and verify that *Gender* is the label for the lookup field.

    g. Click **Finish**.

    h. Save and close the table.

22. Create a new relationship between the *ProcedureID* field in the *Procedures* table and the *ProcedureID* field in the *Orders* table.

    a. Open the Relationships window. On the *Database Tools* tab, in the *Relationships* group, click the **Relationships** button.

    b. Click the **ProcedureID** field in the *Procedures* table and drag it to the *ProcedureID* field in the *Orders* table.

    c. The *Edit Relationships* dialog opens.

    d. Click the **Enforce Referential Integrity** check box.

    e. Click **Create**.

    f. Observe the new line connecting the *Procedures* table and the *Orders* table.

    g. Click the **Save** button on the Quick Access Toolbar.

23. Modify the relationship between the *Physicians* table and the *Hospitals* table so changes to the *Hospitals* table will be updated in the *Physicians* table.

    a. There is a relationship between the *HospitalID* field in the *Hospitals* table and the *HospitalName* field in the *Physicians* table. This relationship was created when you created the *HospitalName* lookup field in the *Physicians* table. *Hint*: If you cannot see this relationship, on the *Relationship Tools Design* tab, in the *Relationships* group, click the **All Relationships** button. You may want to click and drag the *Hospitals* box to reposition it below the *Position* box to make it easier to work with the relationship between the *Hospitals* table and the *Physicians* table.

    b. Double-click the line connecting the two field names to open the *Edit Relationships* dialog.

    c. Click the **Cascade Update Related Records** check box.

    d. Click **OK**.

24. Close the Relationships window. If Access prompts you to save changes to the layout, click **Yes**.

25. Close the database and exit Access.

challenge yourself 2.3

In this project you will continue working with the greenhouse database from *Chapter 1 Challenge Yourself 1.3*. You will add a new table to keep track of the fertilizers used in the greenhouse and the plants that use them. You will make changes to the *Plants*, *Employees*, and *MaintenanceLog* tables including adding fields, deleting fields, and modifying field properties. You will also create and modify table relationships.

Skills needed to complete this project:

- Creating a Table in Design View and Setting the Primary Key (Skill 2.8)
- Modifying the Field Size Property (Skill 2.13)
- Renaming Fields (Skill 2.3)
- Setting the Default Value Property (Skill 2.12)
- Adding Fields in Datasheet View (Skill 2.4)
- Adding a Lookup Field from Another Table (Skill 2.16)
- Deleting Fields in Datasheet View (Skill 2.6)
- Working with Attachment Fields (Skill 2.15)
- Adding a Lookup Field from a List (Skill 2.17)
- Inserting, Deleting, and Moving Fields in Design View (Skill 2.9)
- Using Quick Start to Add Related Fields (Skill 2.5)
- Moving Fields in Datasheet View (Skill 2.7)
- Changing Data Type (Skill 2.10)
- Formatting Fields (Skill 2.11)
- Creating Relationships (Skill 2.18)
- Enforcing Deletions and Updates in Relationships (Skill 2.19)

1. Open the start file **AC2019-ChallengeYourself-2-3**.

2. If the database opens in Protected View, click the **Enable Content** button in the Message Bar at the top of the database so you can modify it.

3. Save a copy of the file to work on named: **[your initials] AC-ChallengeYourself-2-3**

   If necessary, enable active content in the new database by clicking the **Enable Content** button in the Message Bar.

4. Create a new table in Design view using the following information.

Field Name	Data Type	Caption
FertID	Short Text	
FertilizerName	Short Text	Fertilizer Name
NutrientRatio	Short Text	Nutrient Ratio
Price	Currency	

   a. Set the **FertID** field as the primary key.

   b. Save the table with the name: **Fertilizers**

   c. Close the table.

5. Open the *Plants* table and make the following changes. You may work in Datasheet view or Design view as appropriate.

   a. Set the field size for the *PlantID* field to: **10**

   b. Rename the *FlowerColor* field to: **PrimaryColor**

   c. Set the *Default Value* property for the *PrimaryColor* field to **white**.

   d. Add a lookup field named **PreferredFertilizer** to the end of the *Plants* table to reference the *FertilizerName* field in the *Fertilizers* table. The lookup list should be sorted alphabetically by the *FertilizerName* data. The primary key field should be hidden. Enforce referential integrity.

e. Add an *Attachment* field after the *PreferredFertilizer* field. Add the image **azaleas.jpg** to the record for the **Wild azalea**.

f. Delete the *MaxHeightFeet* field.

g. Save and close the table.

6. Open the *Employees* table and make the following changes. You may work in Datasheet view or Design view as appropriate.

a. Move the *LastName* field so it appears before the *FirstName* field. *Hint*: Make the change in Design view so the change is applied to the underlying structure of the table.

b. Add the **Phone** *Quick Start* fields between the *FirstName* and *Position* fields.

c. Modify the *Position* field to use a lookup list **limited to** the following values: Supervisor, Greenhouse Tech 1, and Greenhouse Tech 2. *Hint*: Use the *Lookup Wizard* to create the lookup list and enter the values yourself. Double-click the right border of the *Col1* column in the wizard to AutoFit the column to the data. Don't forget to limit data entries to the value in the list.

d. Save and close the table.

7. Open the *MaintenanceLog* table and make the following changes:

a. Change the data type for the *Watered* field from *Short Text* to **Yes/No**.

b. Change the data type for the *Inspected* field from *Short Text* to **Yes/No**.

c. Change the data type for the *Pruned* field from *Short Text* to **Yes/No**.

d. Change the format for the *MaintenanceDate* field to **Medium Date**.

e. Save and close the table.

8. Review the table relationships and make the following changes.

a. Create a one-to-many relationship between the *PlantID* field in the *Plants* table and the *PlantID* field in the *MaintenanceLog* table. Enforce referential integrity.

b. Modify the relationship between the *EmployeeID* field in the *Employees* table and the *EmployeeID* field in the *MaintenanceLog* table so any deletions or changes to the *EmployeeID* in the *Employees* table will be carried through to the *EmployeeID* field in the *MaintenanceLog* table.

c. Close the Relationships window, saving the layout changes.

9. Close the database and exit Access.

challenge yourself 2.4

In this project you will continue working with the vaccines database from *Chapter 1 Challenge Yourself 1.4*. You will add a table to the database to track volunteer information.

Skills needed to complete this project:

- Designing a Table (Skill 2.1)
- Creating and Saving a Table in Datasheet View (Skill 2.2)
- Renaming Fields (Skill 2.3)
- Adding Fields in Datasheet View (Skill 2.4)
- Using Quick Start to Add Related Fields (Skill 2.5)
- Adding a Lookup Field from a List (Skill 2.17)
- Setting the Default Value Property (Skill 2.12)
- Working with Attachment Fields (Skill 2.15)

- Adding a Lookup Field from Another Table (Skill 2.16)
- Changing Data Type (Skill 2.10)
- Formatting Fields (Skill 2.11)
- Creating Relationships (Skill 2.18)
- Enforcing Deletions and Updates in Relationships (Skill 2.19)

1. Open the start file **AC2019-ChallengeYourself-2-4**.

2. If the database opens in Protected View, click the **Enable Content** button in the Message Bar at the top of the database so you can modify it.

3. Save a copy of the file to work on named: **[your initials] AC-ChallengeYourself-2-4**

If necessary, enable active content in the new database by clicking the **Enable Content** button in the Message Bar.

4. Create a new table to keep track of volunteer information. Use Datasheet view and Design view as appropriate.

a. Name the table: **Volunteers**

b. Enter the following data and fields as shown below. If you use the **Name** *Quick Start* option to add the first name and last name fields be sure to rename them to match the format shown below.

VolunteerID	LastName	FirstName	DOB
R56624	Dougherty	Tyra	5/9/82
G33391	Green	Susan	3/28/74
H58893	Hernandez	Maria	5/11/66

c. Add a caption for each field as follows:

VolunteerID	LastName	FirstName	DOB
Volunteer ID	Last Name	First Name	Date of Birth

d. Set the *VolunteerID* field as the primary key.

e. Add a lookup field to display the following values. Limit the list to these values. **Clerical, Manager, Nurse**

f. Name the new lookup field: **Position**

g. Set the default value of the *Position* field to **Nurse**.

h. Add a new *Attachment* field. Attach the photo **sgreen.jpg** to the **Susan Graham** record.

5. Save and close the *Volunteers* table.

6. Make the following changes to the *Shipments* table. Work in Datasheet view or Design view as appropriate.

a. Modify the **LocationID** field in the *Shipments* table to be a lookup field. Values should come from the *Locations* table. Include both the *LocationID* and the *City* fields. Sort the list alphabetically A to Z by values in the *City* field. Both fields should be visible in the list. *Hint*: Do not hide the key column. Store the *LocationID* value. Enforce referential integrity in the relationship between the *LocationID* field in the *Shipments* table and the *LocationID* field in the *Locations* table.

b. Change the data type of the *Cost* field from *Number* to **Currency**. If Access warns about potential data loss, just click **Yes** to proceed.

c. Apply the **ShortDate** format to the *DateShipped* field.

7. Save and close the *Shipments* table.

8. Create a one-to-many relationship between the *VaccineID* field in the *Vaccines* table and the *VaccineID* field in the *Shipments* table.

a. Enforce referential integrity.

b. Set the option so any changes to values in the *VaccineID* field in the *Vaccines* table will be updated in the *Shipments* table as well.

c. Set the option to delete records in the *Shipments* table when a related value in the *VaccineID* field in the *Vaccines* table is deleted.

d. Close the Relationships window, saving any layout changes.

9. Close the database and exit Access.

on your own 2.5

In this project, you will create a new database from scratch to track your textbook purchases. You will work with this database again in projects in later chapters.

Skills needed to complete this project:

- Designing a Table (Skill 2.1)
- Creating and Saving a Table in Datasheet View (Skill 2.2)
- Renaming Fields (Skill 2.3)
- Adding Fields in Datasheet View (Skill 2.4)
- Creating a Table in Design View and Setting the Primary Key (Skill 2.8)
- Inserting, Deleting, and Moving Fields in Design View (Skill 2.9)
- Adding a Lookup Field from a List (Skill 2.17)
- Modifying the Field Size Property (Skill 2.13)
- Setting the Default Value Property (Skill 2.12)
- Formatting Fields (Skill 2.11)
- Working with Attachment Fields (Skill 2.15)
- Adding a Lookup Field from Another Table (Skill 2.16)
- Creating Relationships (Skill 2.18)

1. Create a new Access database and name it: **[your initials] AC-OnYourOwn-2-5**

2. Create a **textbooks** table and add at least five fields that you believe are appropriate for this type of table. At a minimum, you must have:

a. A unique identifier for each textbook. This field will serve as the primary key.

b. A title

c. The purchase price

d. The purchase date

e. Additional fields of your choice

3. Demonstrate your knowledge of lookup fields by creating a value list in one of your fields. *Hint*: Create a **Condition** field to track the condition of the book

4. Enter data for at least two textbooks. They can be real or fictional.

5. Set the default value for at least one of the fields.

6. Modify the field size for at least one of the fields.

7. Change the field *Format* property for at least one of the fields.

8. Add an attachment field and an attachment file to at least one of the fields.

9. Create a second table to track information for places you purchase textbooks.

10. Add a field to the textbooks table to relate the two tables. Consider creating a lookup field to track a purchase location for each book. Review the relationship in the Relationships window.

11. Close the database and exit Access.

fix it 2.6

In this project, you will continue working with the pet store database from *Chapter 1 Fix It 1.6*. Once again, one of the employees has messed up the database, and it's up to you to fix it. This time, you'll implement a few changes to make it harder for employees to make data entry errors.

Skills needed to complete this project:

- Adding a Lookup Field from a List (Skill 2.17)
- Renaming Fields (Skill 2.3)
- Deleting Fields in Datasheet View (Skill 2.6)
- Inserting, Deleting, and Moving Fields in Design View (Skill 2.9)
- Adding Fields in Datasheet View (Skill 2.4)
- Working with Attachment Fields (Skill 2.15)
- Formatting Fields (Skill 2.11)
- Using Quick Start to Add Related Fields (Skill 2.5)
- Applying an Input Mask (Skill 2.14)
- Changing Data Type (Skill 2.10)
- Setting the Default Value Property (Skill 2.12)
- Creating Relationships (Skill 2.18)
- Enforcing Deletions and Updates in Relationships (Skill 2.19)

1. Open the start file **AC2019-FixIt-2-6**.

2. If the database opens in Protected View, click the **Enable Content** button in the Message Bar at the top of the database so you can modify it.

3. Save a copy of the file to work on named: **[your initials] AC-FixIt-2-6**

   If necessary, enable active content in the new database by clicking **Enable Content** button in the Message Bar.

4. The file will be renamed automatically to include your name. Change the project file name if directed to do so by your instructor. If necessary, enable active content in the new database by clicking the **Enable Content** button in the Message Bar.

5. Fix the *Pets* table as follows:

   a. In this store, there are only two types of pets: cats and dogs. Edit the **AnimalType** field so that **Cat** and **Dog** are the only two choices for this field. Do not allow any other type of animal to be entered.

   b. The pets aren't really sold; they are adopted. Please change the name of the *Price* field to: **AdoptionFee**

c. The store realizes it rarely types in the cage number for each animal it receives. Therefore, remove the **CageNum** field from the table. Click **Yes** to confirm that the index on this field will also be removed.

d. Modify the **AgeInMonths** field so the field caption is: `Age (Months)`

e. Add another new field that can store photographs and insert the **Newfoundland.jpg** image for the record with the **Newfoundland** breed.

f. Save and close the table.

6. Fix the *Adoptions* table as follows:

a. The dates in the *Adoptions* table should look like this: **30-Jun-19**

b. The pets aren't really sold; they are adopted. Please change the name of the *SaleDate* field to: `AdoptionDate`

c. Add a new field in Datasheet view using the **Payment Type** *Quick Start* option.

d. The *Payment Type* field should be the last field in the table in both Design view and Datasheet view. Move the field if necessary.

e. Save and close the table.

7. Fix the *Customers* table as follows:

a. The *Phone* field should use the **Phone Number** input mask to display all phone numbers in the format similar to (202) 555-1212. Store the data without the symbols.

b. The data type for the *Newsletter* field should be **Yes/No**, not *Short Text*. In Datasheet view, the field should display a check box.

c. The default value for the *Newsletter* field should be **Yes** so that it appears checked every time you create a new record.

d. Save and close the table.

8. Review the table relationships and fix them as follows:

a. Create a new one-to-many relationship between the *PetID* field in the *Pets* table and the *PetID* field in the *Adoptions* table. Be sure to enforce referential integrity.

b. Check the relationship between the *CustomerID* field in the *Customers* table and the *CustomerID* field in the *Adoptions* table. If a customer record is deleted, any related records in the *Adoptions* table should ***not*** be deleted. Make any necessary changes to the table relationship.

9. Close the database and exit Access.

chapter **3**

Using Queries and Organizing Information

In this chapter, you will learn the following skills:

❭ Create a simple query

❭ Add criteria to a query

❭ Organize the data in a query

❭ Create Unmatched and Find Duplicate queries

❭ Create a parameter query

❭ Filter data in a datasheet

❭ Export data to Excel and text file formats

❭ Import table data from Excel and text file formats

❭ Import data from an Access database

❭ Link to a table in an Access database

Skill **3.1**   Using the Simple Query Wizard

Skill **3.2**   Creating a Query in Design View

Skill **3.3**   Adding Text Criteria to a Query

Skill **3.4**   Adding Numeric and Date Criteria to a Query

Skill **3.5**   Using AND in a Query

Skill **3.6**   Using OR in a Query

Skill **3.7**   Combining AND and OR in a Query

Skill **3.8**   Adding a Calculated Field to a Query

Skill **3.9**   Specifying the Sort Order in a Query

Skill **3.10** Hiding and Showing Fields in a Query

Skill **3.11** Using a Parameter Query

Skill **3.12** Finding Unmatched Data Using a Query

Skill **3.13** Finding Duplicate Data Using a Query

Skill **3.14** Filtering Data Using AutoFilter

Skill **3.15** Filtering Data Using Filter by Selection

Skill **3.16** Exporting Data to Excel

Skill **3.17** Exporting Data to a Text File

Skill **3.18** Importing Data from Excel

Skill **3.19** Importing Data from a Text File

Skill **3.20** Adding Records to a Table by Importing

Skill **3.21** Importing Data from an Access Database

Skill **3.22** Linking to a Table in an Access Database

skills

introduction

This chapter shows you how to find information quickly by using queries and filtering in Access. You will learn to create a variety of select queries and add criteria. You will also use filtering techniques to organize data in Datasheet view. Finally, you will learn to export and import data to and from Excel, text files, and other Access databases.

Skill 3.1 Using the Simple Query Wizard

Queries allow you to display and manipulate a subset of data from a table. A table of customer information may include many fields that you don't need on a daily basis. You can use a query to generate a more manageable list displaying just the customer first names, last names, and phone numbers.

Queries can also be used to combine data from related tables into a single database object. If you want a list of appointments including the full customer name, use a query to show fields from both the *Appointments* and *Customers* tables. A query can combine data from both tables because there is a one-to-many relationship between the *Customer* field in the *Appointments* table (which stores the customer ID number) and the *CustomerID* field in the *Customers* table. To review the concept of a one-to-many relationship, refer to the skill *Understanding and Viewing Table Relationships.*

Use the *Simple Query Wizard* to create a simple **select query**. A select query displays data from one or more related tables or queries, based on the fields that you select.

To create a query using the *Simple Query Wizard*:

1. On the *Create* tab, in the *Queries* group, click the **Query Wizard** button.
2. In the *New Query* dialog, *Simple Query Wizard* is selected by default. Click **OK**.

FIGURE AC 3.1

FIGURE AC 3.2

3. Click the **Tables/Queries** drop-down arrow. Click the first table or query from which you want to add data.

4. To add a field to the query, double-click the field name in the *Available Fields* list to add it to the *Selected Fields* list, or click the field name and then click the ➤ button.

FIGURE AC 3.3

5. To add data from another table or query, click the **Tables/Queries** drop-down arrow again and make your selection.

6. Add the field or fields you want to include in the query.

7. When you have added all the fields you want, click **Next**.

FIGURE AC 3.4

8. The radio button to create a detail query is selected by default. The detail query shows every field you selected for every record. Click **Next**.

9. Give the query a meaningful title.

10. To see the results of the query immediately, verify that the *Open the query to view information.* radio button is selected.

11. Click **Finish**.

Notice that the query results datasheet looks like a table datasheet. It has the same navigation buttons at the bottom. However, the *Table Tools Fields* tab and the *Table Tools Table* tab are not available when you are viewing the query results datasheet. You cannot manipulate the structure of the underlying tables when you are viewing query results.

FIGURE AC 3.5

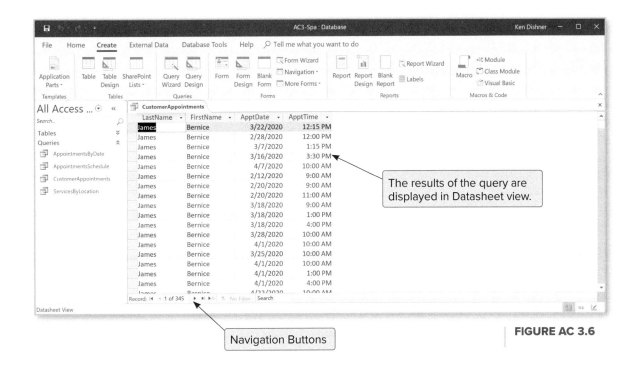

FIGURE AC 3.6

tips & tricks

You do not need to include the related primary key field and foreign key field(s) in the query.

let me try

Open the data file **AC03-01-Spa** and try this skill on your own:

1. Use the *Simple Query Wizard* to create a select query showing the details for every record in the results. Include these fields in this order: **LastName** and **FirstName** from the *Customers* table and **ApptDate** and **ApptTime** from the *Appointments* table. Select the option to open the query to view information. Use the query title: CustomerAppointments

2. Review the query results, and then close the query.

Skill 3.2 Creating a Query in Design View

You can create a new query from scratch using Design view. As shown in Figure AC 3.7, the query Design window has two parts. The upper pane shows the tables referenced in the query. The lower pane shows the **query grid** where you specify which fields to include in the query.

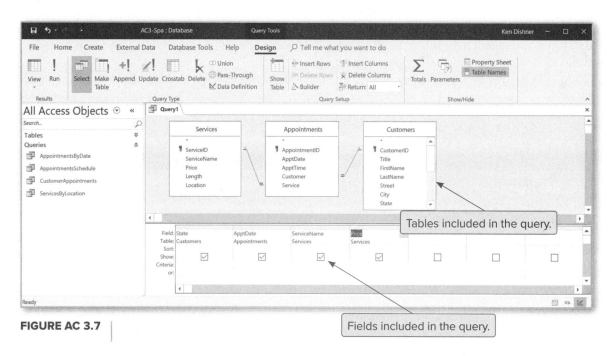

FIGURE AC 3.7

To create a select query in Design view:

1. On the *Create* tab, in the *Queries* group, click the **Query Design** button.

Query Design Button

FIGURE AC 3.8

2. Query Design view opens with the *Show Table* dialog active. Double-click the name of each table you want to include in the query (or click the table name once, and then click the **Add** button). Click the **Close** button when you have added the tables you want. You must close the *Show Table* dialog before continuing to build the query.

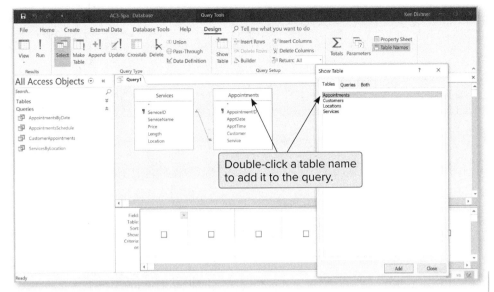

FIGURE AC 3.9

3. A complete field list for each table appears in the upper pane of the query Design window. When a relationship exists between two tables, a line connects the related fields.

4. You may find it necessary to adjust the layout of the query Design window.

   • Adjust the relative size of the two panes in the query Design window by clicking and dragging the horizontal border just above the query grid.

   • Adjust the size of a table box to see more fields by clicking and dragging the bottom boundary of the box downward.

   • Rearrange the table boxes in the upper pane of the query Design window by clicking the box header and dragging the box to a new location (similar to rearranging tables in the Relationships window).

   • Remove a table from the query Design window by right-clicking the table box header and selecting **Remove Table**.

FIGURE AC 3.10

5. Add fields to the query using one of these methods:

   • Double-click the field name in the table box.

   • Click the field name and drag it to the design grid.

   • Click in an empty cell in the *Field* row of the design grid, expand the list of available fields by clicking the arrow, and click the field name you want.

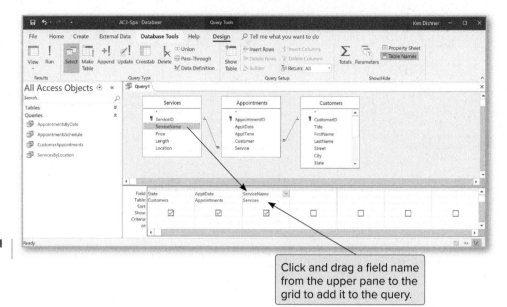

FIGURE AC 3.11

Click and drag a field name from the upper pane to the grid to add it to the query.

- To rearrange the order of fields in the query, move the mouse pointer to the top of the field column in the grid. When the mouse pointer changes to the ↓ shape, click to select the entire column, and then click and drag the column to the new position in the grid.

- To remove a field from the query grid, move the mouse pointer to the top of the field column in the grid. When the mouse pointer changes to the ↓ shape, click to select the entire column, and then press ⟨Delete⟩.

6. When you have added all the fields you want, run the query by clicking the **Run** button near the left side of the Ribbon (on the *Query Tools Design* tab, in the *Results* group).

Run Button

FIGURE AC 3.12

7. Press ⟨Ctrl⟩ + ⟨S⟩ to save the query. In the *Save As* dialog, enter a name for the query in the *Query Name* box. Click **OK**.

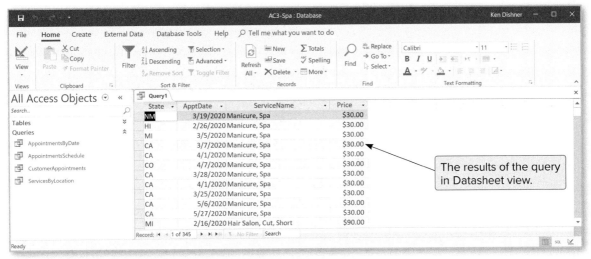

FIGURE AC 3.13

tips & tricks

If you want to include all the fields from a table in your query, click and drag the * symbol from the top of the table box to the field row. Notice that rather than listing each field from the table separately, there is only one field called **table.*** (where "table" is the name of the table). The * symbol represents a wildcard. Rather than look for specific field names, the query will look for all the fields in that table. So, if you later add fields to or delete fields from the table, you won't need to change the query design.

tell me **more**

To display the *Show Table* dialog again to add other tables to the query, on the *Query Tools Design* tab, in the *Query Setup* group, click the **Show Table** button.

another **method**

You can also view the results of a query by switching to Datasheet view using one of these methods:

❭ On the *Query Tools Design* tab, in the *Results* group, click the **View** button.

❭ Click the **View** button arrow, and select **Datasheet View**.

❭ Right-click the query tab, and select **Datasheet View**.

❭ Click the **Datasheet View** button in the status bar.

let me **try**

If the database is not already open, open the data file **AC03-02-Spa** and try this skill on your own:

1. Begin a new query in Design view.

2. Add these tables: **Services**, **Appointments**, and **Customers**.

3. If necessary, adjust the size of the **Customers** table box so you can see the *State* field.

4. Add these fields to the query grid, in this order: **State** from the *Customers* table, **ApptDate** from the *Appointments* table, and **ServiceName** and **Price** from the *Services* table.

5. Run the query.

6. Save the query with the name: ServicesByState

7. Keep the *ServicesByState* query open if you are moving on to the next skill; close it if you are finished working with these skills.

Skill 3.3 Adding Text Criteria to a Query

You can refine a select query in Design view so it shows only records that meet specific criteria. **Criteria** are conditions that the records must meet in order to be included in the query results. Each field data type takes a certain type of **criterion**. Text criteria are used for text and hyperlink fields.

To add text criteria to your query:

1. Open the query in Design view.

2. In the *Criteria* row, enter the text you want to match in the column for the appropriate field. For example, to include only records where the state is Colorado, enter the text criterion **"CO"** in the *Criteria* row under the *State* field. If you do not include the quotation marks when you enter text in the *Criteria* row, Access will place the text in quotation marks for you.

3. Run the query to see the results.

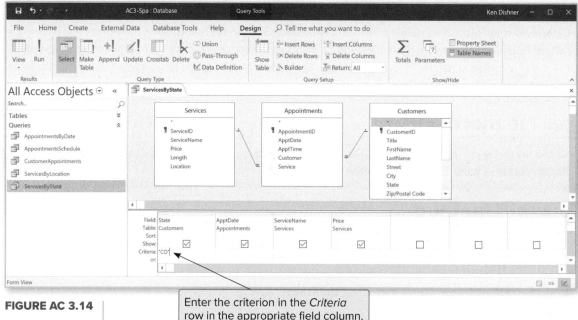

FIGURE AC 3.14

Enter the criterion in the *Criteria* row in the appropriate field column.

When the query is limited to records where the value in the *State* field is CO, there are 15 records in the results as shown in Figure AC 3.15.

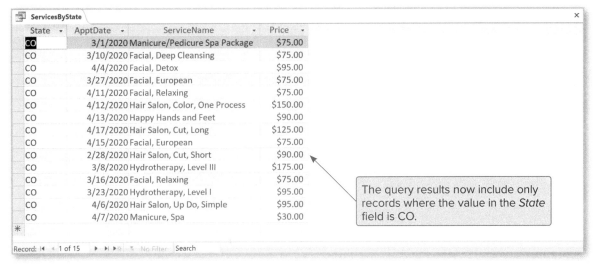

The query results now include only records where the value in the *State* field is CO.

FIGURE AC 3.15

You can use the **wildcard** characters asterisk (*) and question mark (?) and the "like" construction in the query criteria to find inexact text matches. The * wildcard replaces any string of characters. The ? wildcard replaces a single character.

To include all records where the data in the *State* field begins with the letter C followed by one unknown letter, enter the criterion **Like "C?"**. The query in Figure AC 3.16 will return records for CA and CO. (There are no customers from CT in this database.)

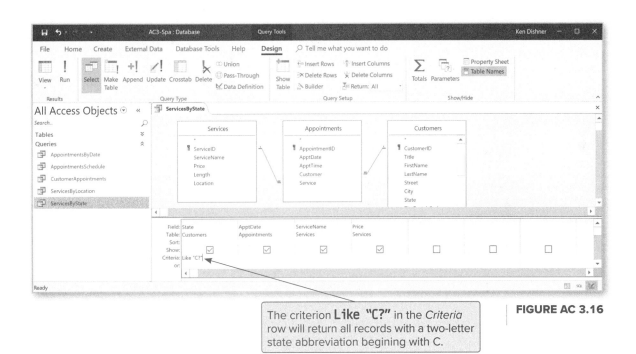

The criterion **Like "C?"** in the *Criteria* row will return all records with a two-letter state abbreviation begining with C.

FIGURE AC 3.16

When the query criterion is expanded to include any record where the value in the *State* field is any two-letter abbreviation beginning with C, there are 172 records in the results as shown in Figure AC 3.17.

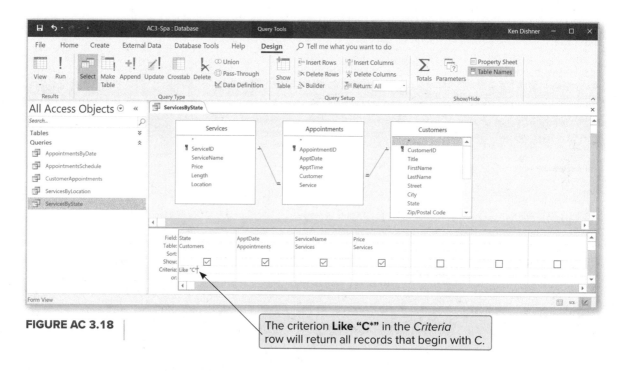

ServicesByState			
State	ApptDate	ServiceName	Price
CA	3/29/2020	Hydrotherapy, Level III	$175.00
CA	4/2/2020	Hydrotherapy, Level II	$125.00
CA	4/10/2020	Hydrotherapy, Level I	$95.00
CA	4/10/2020	Facial, Deep Cleansing	$75.00
CO	3/1/2020	Manicure/Pedicure Spa Package	$75.00
CO	3/10/2020	Facial, Deep Cleansing	$75.00
CO	4/4/2020	Facial, Detox	$95.00
CO	3/27/2020	Facial, European	$75.00
CO	4/11/2020	Facial, Relaxing	$75.00
CO	4/12/2020	Hair Salon, Color, One Process	$150.00
CO	4/13/2020	Happy Hands and Feet	$90.00
CO	4/17/2020	Hair Salon, Cut, Long	$125.00
CO	4/15/2020	Facial, European	$75.00
CA	3/2/2020	Facial, European	$75.00
CA	3/11/2020	Hair Salon, Color, Two Process	$150.00
CA	3/28/2020	Facial, European	$75.00
CA	4/3/2020	Facial, European	$75.00

Record: 1 of 172   No Filter   Search

The query results now include records with both CA and CO in the *State* field.

FIGURE AC 3.17

Use the * wildcard instead of the ? wildcard if you're not sure of the exact number of characters you're looking for. The query in Figure AC 3.18 will return records where the data in the *State* field begins with the letter C—including CA, California, CO, and Colorado.

The criterion **Like "C*"** in the *Criteria* row will return all records that begin with C.

FIGURE AC 3.18

When the query criterion is expanded further to include any record where the value in the *State* field is any value beginning with C, there are 184 records in the results as shown in Figure AC 3.19.

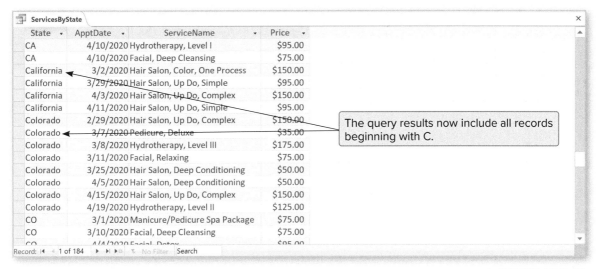

The query results now include all records beginning with C.

tips & tricks

When you begin typing in the criteria cell, Access may display a list of possible functions you could use if you were building an expression. This can be annoying if you're trying to enter text criteria instead. To prevent this, type the text criteria within quotation marks.

tell me **more**

Wildcard characters are not limited to the beginning of a text string. You can place them at the end or at both the beginning and end of the text.

1. The criteria construction **Like "*Spa"** will find all records with data that end with the letters *Spa*.
2. The criteria construction **Like "*Spa*"** will find all records with the letters *Spa* anywhere within the data.
3. The criteria construction **Not Like "*Spa*"** will find all records with data that do not include *Spa* anywhere within the text string.

let me **try**

If the database is not already open, open the data file **AC03-03-Spa** and try this skill on your own:

1. If necessary, open the *ServicesByStateQuery* query in Design view. If your database does not include this query, create it following the steps in *Creating a Query in Design View.*
2. Add a criterion to the query so the results will include only records where the value of the *State* field is equal to the text CO.
3. Run the query and review the results.
4. Return to Design view and modify the query so the results will include any record where the value of the *State* field begins with the letter C.
5. Run the query and review the results.
6. Save and close the query.

Skill 3.4 Adding Numeric and Date Criteria to a Query

Criteria are not limited to text fields. You can also add criteria to fields with Number, Currency, or Date/Time data types. When entering numeric or date criteria, you can enter values for exact matches, or you can enter an expression using comparison operators to broaden the criteria.

To add numeric or date criteria to your query:

1. Open the query in Design view.

2. In the *Criteria* row, enter the value or the expression in the column for the appropriate field. For example, to find all appointments that are longer than 75 minutes, enter **>75** in the *Criteria* row for the *Length* field.

3. Run the query to see the results.

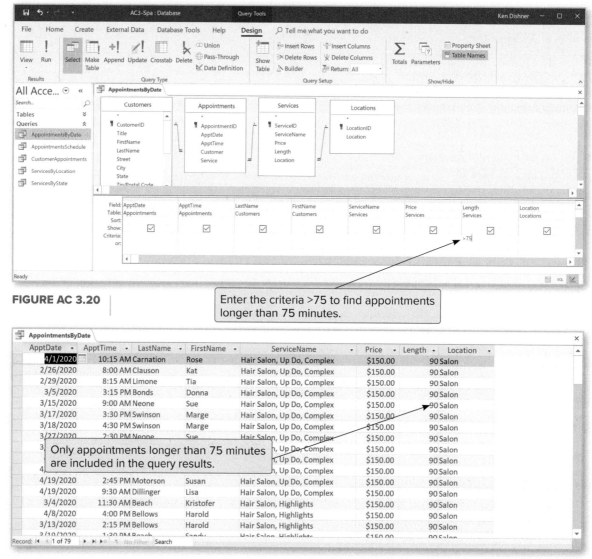

FIGURE AC 3.20

Enter the criteria >75 to find appointments longer than 75 minutes.

Only appointments longer than 75 minutes are included in the query results.

FIGURE AC 3.21

You can also use comparison operators with dates. To find all appointments that are scheduled for April 1, 2020 or later, enter the criterion **>=4/1/2020** in the *Criteria* row for the *ApptDate* field. When you enter dates in the *Criteria* row, Access places # symbols around the date. It is not necessary to type the # symbols yourself.

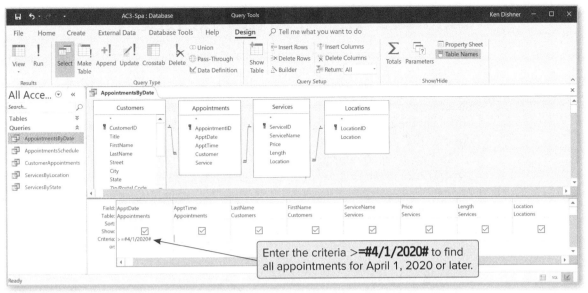

FIGURE AC 3.22

FIGURE AC 3.23

Note in Figure AC 3.23:

> Only appointments for April 1, 2020 or later are included in the query results.

tips & tricks

Common comparison operators are:

> greater than	= equal to	>= greater than or equal to
< less than	< > not equal to	<= less than or equal to

let me try

If the database is not already open, open the data file **AC03-04-Spa** and try this skill on your own:

1. Open the **AppointmentsByDate** query in Design view.

2. Add criteria to limit the query to appointments longer than **75** minutes.

3. Run the query and review the results.

4. Return to Design view and add criteria to show appointments for **April 1, 2020** and later. Be sure to remove the criteria from the *Length* field first.

5. Run the query and review the results.

6. Save the query.

7. Keep the *AppointmentsByDate* query open if you are moving on to the next; save and close it if you are finished working with these skills.

skill 3.4   Adding Numeric and Date Criteria to a Query

Skill 3.5 Using AND in a Query

Use *and* in your criteria construction to make a query more specific by limiting query results to records that meet multiple criteria.

To find records that meet two or more conditions in different fields, enter each of the criteria in the *Criteria* row under the appropriate field. When you enter multiple criteria in the *Criteria* row, the query will return only those records that meet the first criterion *and* the second criterion.

To find all appointments scheduled for April 1, 2020 or later in the Salon, enter **>=4/1/2020** in the *Criteria* row under *ApptDate* and **"Salon"** in the *Criteria* row under *Location.* The query in Figures AC 3.24 and AC 3.25 returns records where both of these conditions are met: appointments on April 1, 2020 or later *AND* the service location is Salon.

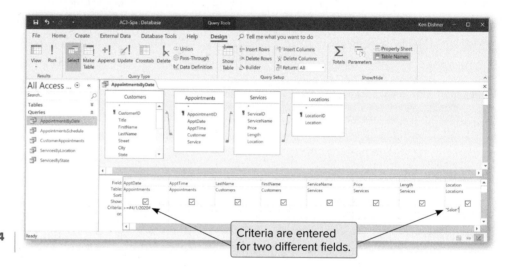

FIGURE AC 3.24

Criteria are entered for two different fields.

FIGURE AC 3.25

Only appointments on April 1, 2020 or later AND in the Salon are included in the query results.

To find records that meet more than one condition in the same field, enter both criteria separated by the word *And* in the *Criteria* row.

To find all appointments scheduled from April 1, 2020 to April 7, 2020, enter **>=4/1/2020 And <=4/7/2020** in the *Criteria* row under *ApptDate. Hint*: If you need more room to enter the criteria, you can click and drag the column header to make the column wider in the query Design grid.

The query in Figures AC 3.26 and AC 3.27 returns records where both of these conditions are met: appointments on April 1, 2020 or later *and* appointments on April 7, 2020 or earlier.

access 365   chapter 3 Using Queries and Organizing Information

FIGURE AC 3.26

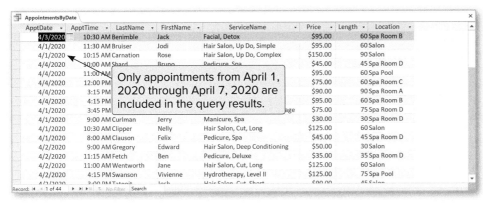

FIGURE AC 3.27

tips & tricks

If you need more room to enter criteria, press (↑ Shift) + (F2) to open the *Zoom* window. When you are finished working in the *Zoom* window, click **OK** to return to the query Design grid.

tell me **more**

When you create a query in Design view, you are generating programming code in a language called **Structured Query Language (SQL)**. To view the SQL behind the query, switch to SQL view. On the *Query Tools Design* tab, in the *Results* group, click the **View** button and select **SQL View**.

let me **try**

If the database is not already open, open the data file **AC03-05-Spa** and try this skill on your own:

1. If necessary, open the *AppointmentsByDate* query in Design view.
2. Remove any existing criteria.
3. Add criteria to find appointments scheduled for **April 1, 2020 or later** where the location is **Salon**.
4. Run the query and review the results.
5. Return to Design view and remove the criteria.
6. Add new criteria to find all appointments scheduled from **April 1, 2020** to **April 7, 2020**. Include both April 1, 2020 and April 7, 2020 in the criteria.
7. Run the query and review the results.
8. Keep the *AppointmentsByDate* query open if you are moving on to the next skill; save and close it if you are finished working with these skills.

Skill 3.6 Using OR in a Query

Use *or* in your criteria construction to make a query broader by expanding the query results to records that meet any one of multiple criteria.

To find records that meet any of the conditions, enter the criteria on separate rows in the query grid:

1. Enter the first criterion in the *Criteria* row.

2. Enter the second criterion in the *or* row (the row immediately below the *Criteria* row).

To find all appointments for customers with the last name Smith or Clauson, enter **Swanson** in the *Criteria* row for the *LastName* field, and then enter **Clauson** in the *or* row for the *LastName* field as shown in Figure AC 3.28.

FIGURE AC 3.28

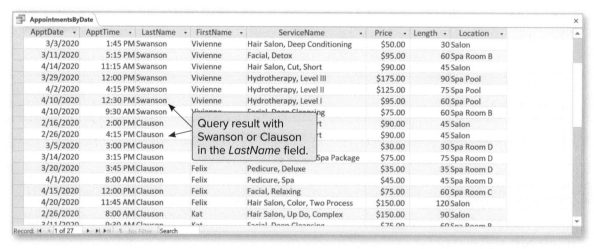

FIGURE AC 3.29

Criteria do not need to be in the same field. When using an *or* construction with multiple fields, make sure that each criterion is on its own row. The query shown in Figure AC 3.30 will return records where the value of the *LastName* field is Swanson or the value of the *Location* field is Salon.

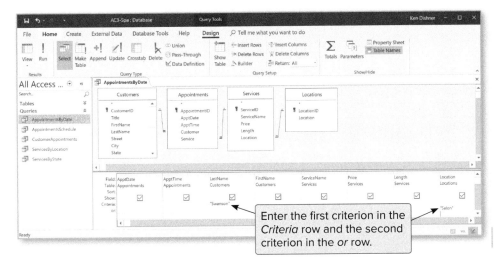

Enter the first criterion in the *Criteria* row and the second criterion in the *or* row.

FIGURE AC 3.30

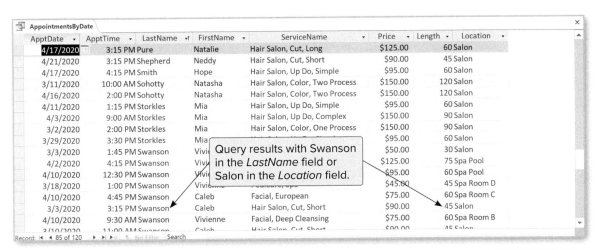

Query results with Swanson in the *LastName* field or Salon in the *Location* field.

FIGURE AC 3.31

tell me **more**

You can add more *or* criteria by continuing to add criteria to the rows under the first *or* row.

let me **try**

If the database is not already open, open the data file **AC03-06-Spa** and try this skill on your own:

1. If necessary, open the *AppointmentsByDate* query in Design view.
2. Remove any existing criteria.
3. Add criteria to find appointments for customers with the last name **Swanson** or **Clauson**.
4. Run the query and review the results.
5. Return to Design view and delete the *or* criterion for the *LastName* field (Clauson).
6. Modify the query criteria to show all appointments for customers with the last name **Swanson** or the location **Salon**.
7. Run the query and review the results.
8. Keep the *AppointmentsByDate* query open if you are moving on to the next skill; save and close it if you are finished working with these skills.

Skill 3.7 Combining AND and OR in a Query

You can combine the *and* and *or* query constructions to create a very precise query.

1. Enter the first set of criteria in the *Criteria* row.

2. Enter the second set of criteria in the *or* row (the row immediately below the *Criteria* row).

The query results will include records that meet **all** the criteria in the *Criteria* row **or** **all** the criteria in the *or* row.

The query in Figure AC 3.32 will return records with appointments between April 1, 2020 and April 7, 2020 for customers with the last name Swanson or the location Salon. Because the date range criterion is the same for both *or* criteria, it must be repeated in both rows.

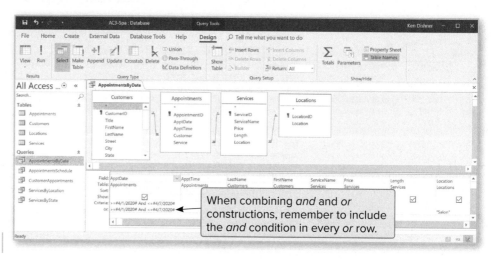

FIGURE AC 3.32

> When combining *and* and *or* constructions, remember to include the *and* condition in every *or* row.

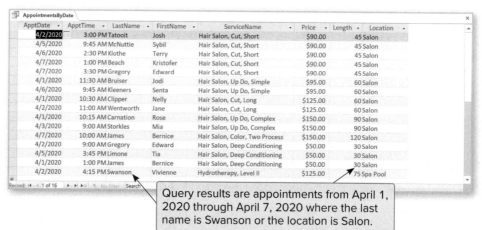

FIGURE AC 3.33

> Query results are appointments from April 1, 2020 through April 7, 2020 where the last name is Swanson or the location is Salon.

let me try

If the database is not already open, open the data file **AC03-07-Spa** and try this skill on your own:

1. If necessary, open the *AppointmentsByDate* query in Design view.

2. Remove any existing criteria.

3. Add criteria to find appointments from **April 1, 2020** through **April 7, 2020** (inclusive) for any customer with the last name **Swanson** or where the location is **Salon**.

4. Run the query and review the results.

5. Save and close the query.

Skill 3.8 Adding a Calculated Field to a Query

Database fields generally display the data that are entered into them. However, a **calculated field** displays a value returned by an **expression** (a formula). Expressions can reference fields, mathematical operators, functions, and constants. You use the *Expression Builder* to create calculated fields in tables and queries and calculated controls in forms and reports.

[Price]*.15	Calculates a value equal to the value in the *Price* field multiplied by .15.
[FirstName]+" "+[LastName]	Combines the value of the *FirstName* and *LastName* fields with a space in between them.
[Price]+[SuggestedTip]	Calculates the sum of the value in the *Price* field plus the value in the *SuggestedTip* field.

To create a calculated field in a query, you can type the expression directly in the query grid or you can use the *Expression Builder* to build it.

To use the *Expression Builder* to create a calculated field in a query:

1. Open the query in Design view.

2. Click in an empty cell in the *Field* row in the query grid. If a cell with a field name is selected when you build the expression, you will replace the field with the calculated field.

3. On the *Query Tools Design* tab, in the *Query Setup* group, click the **Builder** button to open the *Expression Builder*.

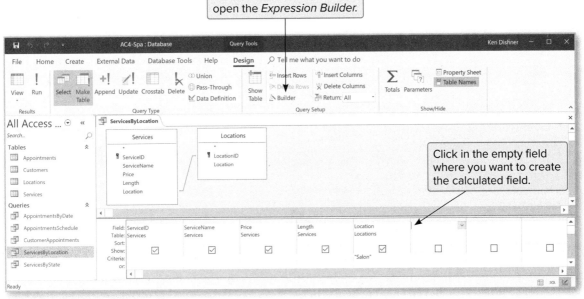

Click the **Builder** button to open the *Expression Builder*.

Click in the empty field where you want to create the calculated field.

FIGURE AC 3.34

4. The center box in the *Expression Builder* lists fields in the query. In the *Expression Categories* box, double-click a field name to add it to the expression box at the top of the dialog. When referencing a field name in an expression, the field name is always enclosed in brackets.

5. Finish entering the expression.

6. Click **OK** to add the expression to the query.

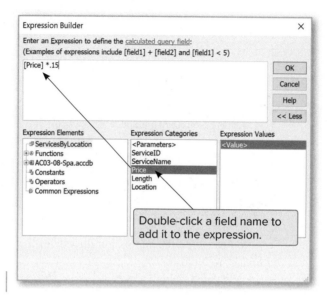

FIGURE AC 3.35

7. Notice that the new calculated field begins with *Expr1:*, this is the temporary name for the field. Click in the field and change **Expr1** to something more meaningful. Be careful not to delete the colon. Click and drag to make the column wider if you need more room to enter the field name.

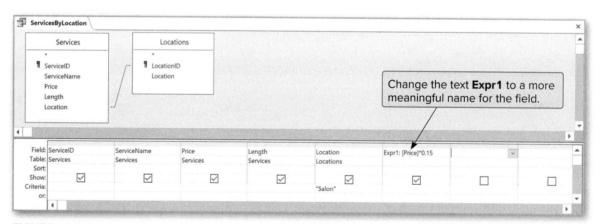

FIGURE AC 3.36

8. Run the query to see the results of the calculated field.

In Figure AC 3.37, the value in the *SuggestedTip* field is equal to the value of the *Price* field multiplied by .15. In the first record, the price is $90.00 and the suggested tip is 13.5 (90 * .15).

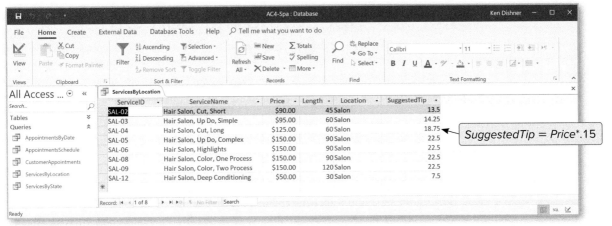

FIGURE AC 3.37

SuggestedTip = Price*.15

tips & tricks

When you add a calculated field to a query, the field can be used in forms and reports based on that query.

tell me **more**

The *Expression Builder* can be used to create complex expressions including functions similar to those in Excel.

another **method**

Press (Ctrl) + (F2) to open the *Expression Builder*.

let me **try**

If the database is not already open, open the data file **AC03-08-Spa** and try this skill on your own:

1. Open the **ServicesByLocation** query in Design view.
2. Add a new calculated field named **SuggestedTip** in the first empty column to the right of the *Length* field. The new field should calculate a value that is .15 times the value in the *Price* field.
3. Run the query and review the results. If necessary, click and drag to make the field column wider so the entire field name is visible.
4. Save the query.
5. Keep the *ServicesByLocation* query open if you are moving on to the next skill; close it if you are finished working with these skills.

skill 3.8   Adding a Calculated Field to a Query

Skill 3.9 Specifying the Sort Order in a Query

Query results may display records in an unexpected order. If you want to control how records are displayed, set the sort order as part of the query design. The sort order will be applied every time the query is run.

To add a sort order to a query:

1. Open the query in Design view.

2. Click in the *Sort* row for the field you want to sort. Click the arrow to expand the sort options list and select **Ascending** or **Descending**.

    • *Ascending* sorts text in alphabetical order from A to Z, numbers from smallest to largest, and dates from oldest to newest.

    • *Descending* sorts text in reverse alphabetical order from Z to A, numbers from largest to smallest, and dates from newest to oldest.

3. Run the query.

FIGURE AC 3.38

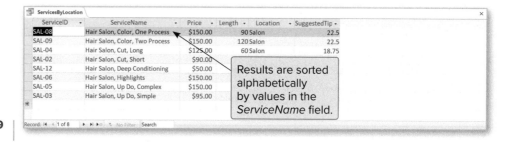

FIGURE AC 3.39

let me try

If the database is not already open, open the data file **AC03-09-Spa** and try this skill on your own:

1. If necessary, open the *ServicesByLocation* query in Design view.

2. Set the sort order so the results will display records sorted alphabetically by values in the *ServiceName* field.

3. Run the query and review the results.

4. Keep the *ServicesByLocation* query open if you are moving on to the next skill; save and close it if you are finished working with these skills.

Skill 3.10 Hiding and Showing Fields in a Query

If you want to include a field in your query but do not want that field to show in Datasheet view, click the **Show** box to remove the checkmark. By hiding the field, you can use it to define criteria for the query without making the field visible in the final query results.

FIGURE AC 3.40

FIGURE AC 3.41

tips & tricks

Run the query to verify that it returns results as you expect before hiding the field.

let me try

If the database is not already open, open the data file **AC03-10-Spa** and try this skill on your own:

1. If necessary, open the *ServicesByLocation* query in Design view.
2. Run the query and review the results.
3. Return to Design view and hide the **Location** field so it does not appear in the query results.
4. Run the query. Notice that the results are the same, but now the *Location* field is hidden. It was not necessary as every record in the result had the same value.
5. Save and close the query.

Skill 3.11 Using a Parameter Query

A **parameter query** is a type of select query that allows the user to provide the criteria. When you create a parameter query, you specify the field or fields the query will use to limit the records in the results just as you would if you were entering the criteria yourself. However, you don't specify the exact criteria. Instead, you enter a prompt the user will see when the query is run. The user then enters the exact value or values to use as the criteria.

To create a parameter query:

1. In Design view, create a select query or open the existing query that you want to change to a parameter query.

2. In the appropriate cell in the *Criteria* row, instead of entering specific criteria, type the prompt the user will see, enclosed in brackets. Ideally, the prompt will give the user direction as to what data to enter. Examples of parameter query prompts include **[Enter last name]** and **[Enter appointment date]**.

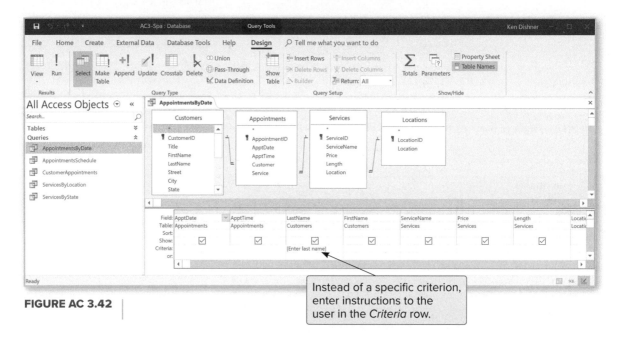

Instead of a specific criterion, enter instructions to the user in the *Criteria* row.

FIGURE AC 3.42

FIGURE AC 3.43

3. Run the query to test it. Notice that before results display, the *Enter Parameter Value* dialog appears with the prompt you created. Enter a value in the box and click **OK**.

4. The results of the query display only records that match the value you typed in the *Enter Parameter Value* dialog.

In Figure AC 3.44, the query results are limited to records where the value in the *LastName* field is *Swanson*. Typing **Swanson** in the *Enter Parameter Value* dialog has the same effect as typing **Swanson** in the *Criteria* row for the *LastName* field.

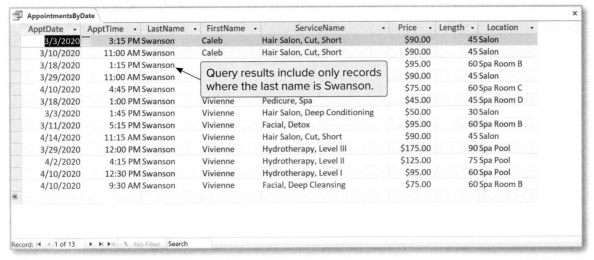

ApptDate	ApptTime	LastName	FirstName	ServiceName	Price	Length	Location
3/3/2020	3:15 PM	Swanson	Caleb	Hair Salon, Cut, Short	$90.00	45	Salon
3/10/2020	11:00 AM	Swanson	Caleb	Hair Salon, Cut, Short	$90.00	45	Salon
3/18/2020	1:15 PM	Swanson			$95.00	60	Spa Room B
3/29/2020	11:00 AM	Swanson			$90.00	45	Salon
4/10/2020	4:45 PM	Swanson			$75.00	60	Spa Room C
3/18/2020	1:00 PM	Swanson	Vivienne	Pedicure, Spa	$45.00	45	Spa Room D
3/3/2020	1:45 PM	Swanson	Vivienne	Hair Salon, Deep Conditioning	$50.00	30	Salon
3/11/2020	5:15 PM	Swanson	Vivienne	Facial, Detox	$95.00	60	Spa Room B
4/14/2020	11:15 AM	Swanson	Vivienne	Hair Salon, Cut, Short	$90.00	45	Salon
3/29/2020	12:00 PM	Swanson	Vivienne	Hydrotherapy, Level III	$175.00	90	Spa Pool
4/2/2020	4:15 PM	Swanson	Vivienne	Hydrotherapy, Level II	$125.00	75	Spa Pool
4/10/2020	12:30 PM	Swanson	Vivienne	Hydrotherapy, Level I	$95.00	60	Spa Pool
4/10/2020	9:30 AM	Swanson	Vivienne	Facial, Deep Cleansing	$75.00	60	Spa Room B

Query results include only records where the last name is Swanson.

Record: 1 of 13   No Filter   Search

FIGURE AC 3.44

tips & tricks

When you use a parameter query as the record source for a form or report, the user will see the *Enter Parameter Value* prompt whenever the form or report is opened.

tell me **more**

You can prevent users from entering a parameter input in the wrong data type.

1. On the *Query Tools Design* tab, in the *Show/Hide* group, click the **Parameters** button.
2. The *Query Parameters* dialog opens.
3. In the *Parameter* column, enter the parameter prompt exactly as you entered it in the query grid.
4. In the *Data Type* column, select the appropriate data type.
5. Click **OK**.

Now if a user attempts to use a parameter value with the wrong data type, he or she will see an error message rather than incorrect query results.

let me **try**

If the database is not already open, open the data file **AC03-11-Spa** and try this skill on your own:

1. Open the **AppointmentsByDate** query in Design view.
2. If necessary, clear all criteria.
3. Create a parameter query where the user will enter a value to use as the criterion for the **Last Name** field. Use the prompt Enter Last Name. Don't forget to enclose the prompt in brackets.
4. Test the parameter query using the last name **Swanson**.
5. Save and close the query.

Skill 3.12 Finding Unmatched Data Using a Query

Use the **Find Unmatched Query** Wizard to create a query that shows records from one table that have no corresponding records in another table. This type of query is useful for scenarios such as finding employees who have no sales records or customers who have no appointments.

To run the *Find Unmatched Query Wizard*:

1. On the *Create* tab, in the *Queries* group, click the **Query Wizard** button.

2. In the *New Query* dialog, click **Find Unmatched Query Wizard**, and click **OK**.

FIGURE AC 3.45

3. First, select the table or query that includes the records you want to match. Click **Next**.

FIGURE AC 3.46

4. Select the table or query that contains the related records. The query will return results from the first table that *do not* have corresponding records in this table. Click **Next**.

Select the table or query that may not have matching records.

5. Now, find the fields in the two tables that might contain matches. If there is an obvious field (fields with the same name in both tables or fields with an established relationship), Access will automatically suggest it. Keep in mind that the fields might be named differently in the two tables. In Figure AC 3.48, the *CustomerID* field in the *Customers* table contains the same values as the *Customer* field in the *Appointments* table. Click **Next**.

Select the matching fields.

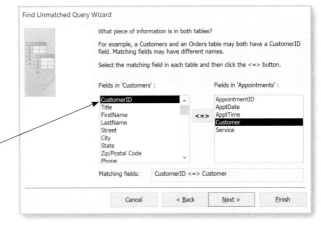

6. Add additional fields that you want to include in the query results. Double-click a field name in the *Available fields* list to add it to the *Selected fields* list. Add the fields that will help identify how the field values are related or fields that you need to identify the records accurately. Click **Next**.

Include additional fields to identify the records.

FIGURE AC 3.50

7. Access will suggest a name for the query based on the tables selected. You can enter a new name or accept the suggestion. Verify that the *View the results.* radio button is selected, and click **Finish** to view the results.

The results of the *Unmatched Query Wizard* display the specified fields from the first table for records that do not have corresponding records in the second table. The query results shown in Figure AC 3.51 include the *CustomerID*, *LastName*, and *FirstName* fields from the *Customers* table where the customer does not have any matching records in the *Appointments* table.

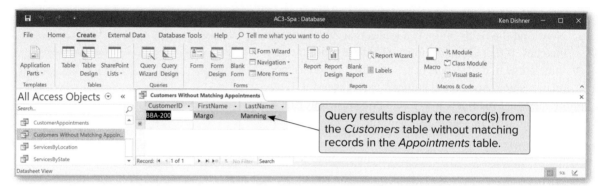

FIGURE AC 3.51

tell me **more**

You can create a select query yourself to find records that are missing data in a particular field. Type **Is Null** in the *Criteria* cell for the field you want to find. When you run the query, the results will show all records that are missing data in that field. To return only records that have data in the field, type **Is Not Null** in the *Criteria* cell instead.

let me **try**

If the database is not already open, open the data file **AC03-12-Spa** and try this skill on your own:

1. Create a new query using the *Unmatched Query Wizard* to find records in the **Customers** table without corresponding records in the **Appointments** table.

2. Include the **CustomerID**, **FirstName**, and **LastName** fields from the *Customers* table in that order.

3. Accept the suggested name for the query.

4. View the query results and then close the query.

Skill 3.13 Finding Duplicate Data Using a Query

You can create a query to find all the records that have duplicate values in one or more fields. A **Find Duplicates query** is useful for finding records that may have been entered more than once or for scenarios such as finding all employees who live in the same city (duplicates in the city field) or locating customers who may have duplicate appointments on the same day (duplicates in name and date fields).

To run the *Find Duplicates Query Wizard*:

1. On the *Create* tab, in the *Queries* group, click the **Query Wizard** button.
2. In the *New Query* dialog, click **Find Duplicates Query Wizard**. Click **OK**.

FIGURE AC 3.52

3. Select the table or query that you want to search for duplicate values. To view the list of queries in the database, click the **Queries** radio button. In Figure AC 3.53, we are selecting a query that includes fields from multiple tables. This allows us to include additional useful information in the query results, such as the length of the service selected for the appointment. Click **Next**.

Select the table or query that includes the records that may contain duplicates.

Click the **Queries** radio button to display the list of queries in the database.

FIGURE AC 3.53

FIGURE AC 3.54

The query will return records with the same data in the *ApptDate*, *FirstName*, and *LastName* fields.

4. Add the field(s) where there may be duplicate data. Double-click a field name in the *Available fields* list to add it to the *Duplicate-value fields* list. When you include more than one field, data in all fields must be duplicates in order for the record to be included in the query results. Click **Next**.

FIGURE AC 3.55

Add fields that provide useful information about the duplicate records.

5. Add additional fields that you want to include in the query results. Double-click a field in the *Available fields* list to add it to the *Additional query fields* list. Add the fields that will help identify how the duplicate values are related or provide more information about the results. Click **Next**.

FIGURE AC 3.56

Access suggests a name for the query.

6. Access will suggest a name for the query based on the table or query selected. You can enter a new name or accept the suggestion. Verify that the *View the results.* radio button is selected, and click **Finish** to view the results.

The results of the *Find Duplicates Query Wizard* display the specified fields from records with duplicate values in the specified fields. The query results shown in Figure AC 3.57 include appointments with duplicate values in the *ApptDate*, *LastName*, and *FirstName* fields. The *ApptTime*, *ServiceName*, and *Length* fields are included to provide more information about the possible duplicate appointments.

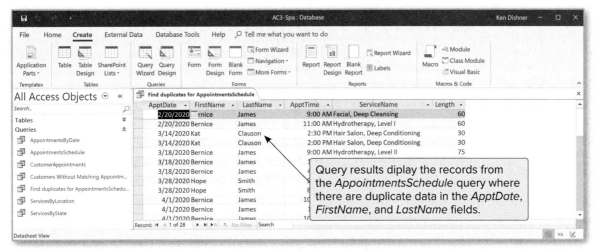

FIGURE AC 3.57

let me **try**

If the database is not already open, open the data file **AC03-13-Spa** and try this skill on your own:

1. Create a query using the *Find Duplicates Query Wizard* to find appointments on the same day for the same customer. Use the **AppointmentsSchedule** query.

2. Find duplicate values in the **ApptDate**, **FirstName**, and **LastName** fields.

3. Include the **ApptTime**, **ServiceName**, and **Length** fields to provide more information about the appointment.

4. Accept the suggested name for the query.

5. View the query results and then close the query.

from the perspective of. . .

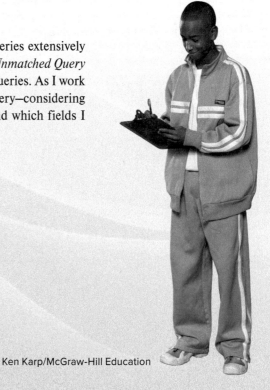

PERSONAL TRAINER

I use Access to keep track of client appointments and billing. I use queries extensively as the basis for invoices and to create reports for specific clients. The *Unmatched Query Wizard* and the *Find Duplicates Query Wizard* help me create complex queries. As I work through the steps of a wizard, I think about the logic behind the query—considering which table or query contains the fields I want to apply criteria to and which fields I need to include in the results so I can make sense of them.

Ken Karp/McGraw-Hill Education

skill 3.13   Finding Duplicate Data Using a Query

Skill 3.14 Filtering Data Using AutoFilter

By applying a **filter** to a database object, you display a subset of records that meet the filter criteria. AutoFilter displays a list of all the unique values in the field. This feature is available for table, queries, and forms. If you have used Microsoft Excel, AutoFilter will be familiar to you.

To filter a datasheet using AutoFilter:

1. Open the database object in Datasheet view.

2. Click the arrow at the top of the column in the column that contains the data you want to filter for.

3. At first, all of the filter options are checked. Click the **(Select All)** check box to remove all the checkmarks.

4. Click the check box or check boxes in front of the values you want to filter for.

5. Click **OK**.

FIGURE AC 3.58

As shown in Figure AC 3.59, Access displays only the records that include the value(s) you selected. The field that is filtered displays a filter icon next to the arrow in the field header.

On the *Home* tab, in the *Sort & Filter* group, click the **Toggle Filter** button to clear the filter. Click the **Toggle Filter** button again to reapply the filter.

Notice that when the database object has a filter applied, the *Filtered* button is highlighted next to the navigation buttons at the bottom of the object. You can also click this button to toggle back and forth between the filtered view and the unfiltered view.

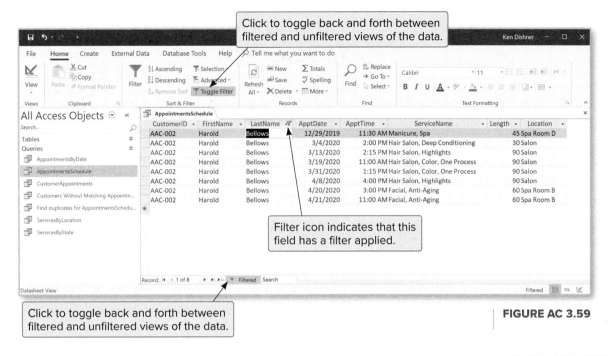

Click to toggle back and forth between filtered and unfiltered views of the data.

Filter icon indicates that this field has a filter applied.

Click to toggle back and forth between filtered and unfiltered views of the data.

FIGURE AC 3.59

To remove the filter, display the AutoFilter list again, and select the **Clear filter** option. Once you use the *Clear filter* command, you cannot use the *Toggle Filter* or *Filtered* button to show the filter again. You have to re-create it.

Click the **Clear filter** option to remove the filter from the field.

FIGURE AC 3.60

tips & tricks

Filtering with AutoFilter is temporary. When you close the database object, the filter is not saved. If you want a more permanent filter applied to a query, add criteria in Design view instead.

another **method**

To display the AutoFilter list, on the *Home* tab, in the *Sort & Filter* group, click the **Filter** button.

let me **try**

If the database is not already open, open the data file **AC03-14-Spa** and try this skill on your own:

1. If necessary, open the *AppointmentsSchedule* query in Datasheet view.
2. Use AutoFilter to filter the query results to show only records where the last name is **Bellows**.
3. Clear the filter from the field.
4. Keep the *AppointmentsSchedule* query open if you are moving on to the next skill; close it if you are finished working with these skills.

skill 3.14   Filtering Data Using AutoFilter

Skill 3.15 Filtering Data Using Filter by Selection

If a record that contains the data you want to filter for is visible, you can click the field and use the *Filter by Selection* feature. Besides filtering by matching exact values, you can filter for values that meet broader criteria.

To filter by selection:

1. Select the data you want to use as the filter criteria.

2. On the *Home* tab, in the *Sort & Filter* group, click the **Selection** button and select a filtering option.

    - The first option is to filter for only records that match the selected field value exactly.

    - The second option is to filter for all records that do not match the selected field value.

    - The other options will vary depending on the data type of the selected field.

        - A *Short Text* field will include options to filter for records that contain or do not contain the text in the selected field.

        - A *Number* or *Currency* field will include options to filter for records that are less than or greater than the selected field value.

        - A *Date/Time* field will include options to filter for records that include a date/time on or before or after the selected date as shown in Figure AC 3.61.

FIGURE AC 3.61

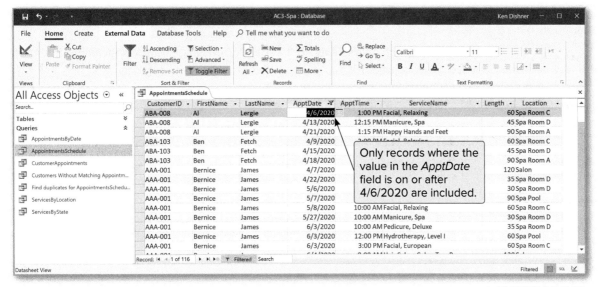

FIGURE AC 3.62

To remove all filters from a database object, on the *Home* tab, in the *Sort & Filter* group, click the **Advanced** button arrow and select **Clear All Filters**.

tips & tricks

You can apply filters to more than one field at a time.

another **method**

The filter options available by right-clicking a value are more extensive than those available from the *Selection* button menu.

1. Right-click anywhere in the field you want to filter.

2. Point to the **Filters** option and then click the filter option you want from the submenu. The *Filters* option will include the data type (for example, if the field is a *Short Text* field, the right-click menu will include *Text Filters*; if it is a *Date/Time* field, the right-click menu will include *Date Filters*).

3. When you make a selection from the submenu, a dialog may open, allowing you to enter specific filter criteria.

let me **try**

If the database is not already open, open the data file **AC03-15-Spa** and try this skill on your own:

1. If necessary, open the *AppointmentsSchedule* query in Datasheet view.

2. Clear any filters that may have been applied to the query results.

3. Filter the query results to show only appointment dates on or after **4/6/2020**. *Hint:* Find a record where the value in the *ApptDate* field is 4/6/2020 and then use *Filter by Selection*.

4. Clear the filter from the field.

5. Keep the *AppointmentsSchedule* query open if you are moving on to the next skill; close it if you are finished working with these skills.

Skill 3.16 Exporting Data to Excel

You can **export** Access data to a variety of other applications including Microsoft Excel. This is helpful if you want to share the data with someone who may not have Access or may not need to see the entire database.

FIGURE AC 3.63

To export data to Excel:

1. Open the database object or select it in the Navigation Pane.

2. On the *External Data* tab, in the *Export* group, click the **Excel** button.

3. In the *Export - Excel Spreadsheet* dialog, Access automatically suggests a file name based on the name of the object you selected. If you want to change the file name or the location of the saved file, click the **Browse...** button and make your changes in the *File Save* dialog.

4. When exporting to Excel, be sure to check the **Export data with formatting and layout** check box to maintain data formats such as dates and currency styles.

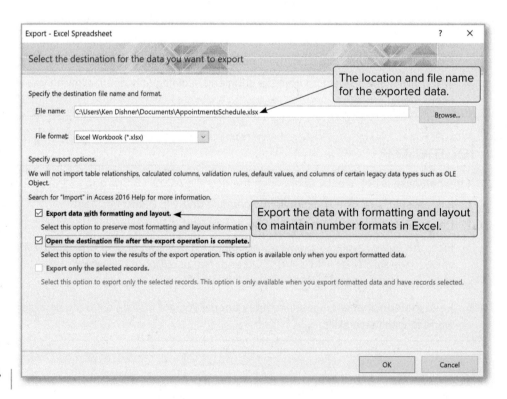

FIGURE AC 3.64

5. When the *Export data with formatting and layout.* option is checked, you also have the option to check the box to **Open the destination file after the export operation is complete**.

6. If you have a table, query, or form open with specific records selected, you can elect to export only those records. Click the **Export only the selected records.** check box.

7. Click **OK** to begin the export process.

8. After the export is complete, you have the option to save the export steps so you can easily run the same export again later. Check the **Save export steps** check box. If you save your export specifications, you can run the export again later by clicking the **Saved Exports** button on the *External Data* tab, *Export* group.

9. Click the **Close** button to close the *Export - Excel Spreadsheet* dialog.

FIGURE AC 3.65

tips & tricks

If you are exporting a report, the *Export data with formatting and layout.* check box is checked automatically. You do not have the option to uncheck it.

another **method**

In the Navigation Pane, right-click the database object you want to export, point to **Export**, and select the export format you want to use.

let me **try**

If the database is not already open, open the data file **AC03-16-Spa** and try this skill on your own:

1. Export the *AppointmentsSchedule* query to Excel, maintaining all data formatting and layouts.

2. Keep the *AppointmentsSchedule* query open if you are moving on to the next skill; close it if you are finished working with these skills.

Skill 3.17 Exporting Data to a Text File

If you need to use Access data in another database or a spreadsheet program other than Microsoft Excel, export the data as plain text. When you export as text, data fields may be separated by a specific character called a **delimiter**. The *Export Text Wizard* allows you to export the data separated by common delimiters such as commas, tabs, and spaces. It is the most flexible export option.

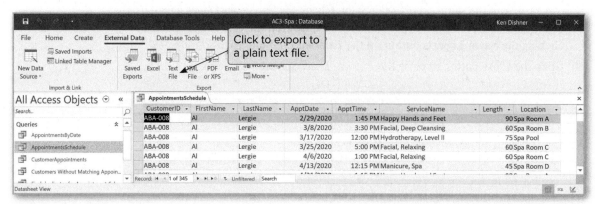

FIGURE AC 3.66

To export data to a text file:

1. Open the database object or select it in the Navigation Pane.

2. On the *External Data* tab, in the *Export* group, click the **Text File** button.

3. In the *Export - Text File* dialog, Access automatically suggests a file name based on the name of the object you selected. If you want to change the file name or the location of the saved file, click the **Browse...** button and make your changes in the *File Save* dialog.

4. Click **OK** to begin the export process.

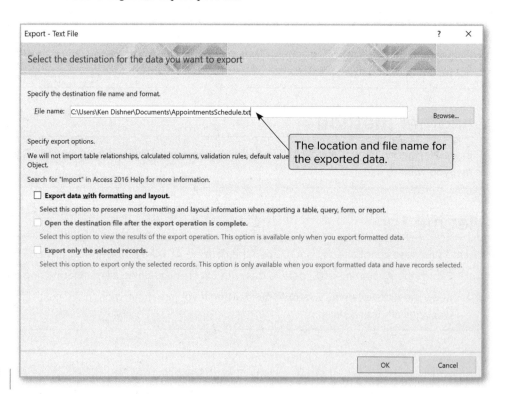

FIGURE AC 3.67

5. In the first step of the *Export Text Wizard*, select how you want the data exported—using a delimiter character or using a fixed width. The most common text file formats use a delimiter character such as a comma, tab, or space. The radio button for **Delimited** is selected by default. Click **Next**.

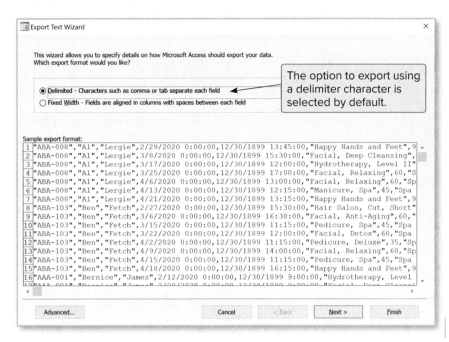

FIGURE AC 3.68

6. In the next step, select the options for the export.

    a. Select the radio button for the delimiter character you want to use.

    b. If you want to include field names in the export, click the **Include Field Names on First Row** check box.

    c. By default, all text fields in the export will be enclosed with quotation marks. If you require that text fields do not include the " character, expand the **Text Qualifier** list and select **{none}** or ' instead.

    d. Review the text file format in the preview box. Click **Next**.

FIGURE AC 3.69

7. Verify the file name and location and then click **Finish** to export the data.

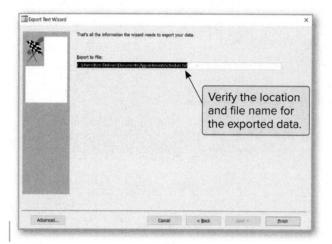

FIGURE AC 3.70

Verify the location
and file name for
the exported data.

8. After the export is complete, you have the option to save the export steps so you can easily run the same export again later. Check the **Save export steps** check box. If you save your export specifications, you can run the export again later by clicking the **Saved Exports** button on the *External Data* tab, *Export* group.

9. Click the **Close** button to close the *Export - Text File* dialog.

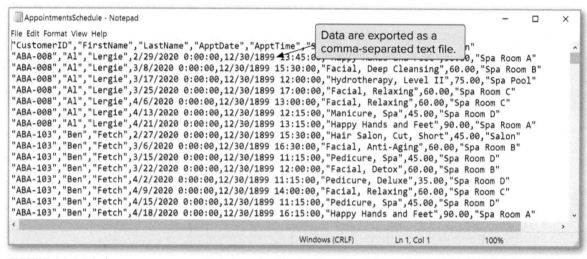

Data are exported as a
comma-separated text file.

FIGURE AC 3.71

tips & tricks

Most text file formats will not maintain formatting and layout options, so when exporting to a text file, you usually do not check the *Export data with formatting and layout.* check box in the *Export - Text File* dialog.

let me try

If the database is not already open, open the data file **AC03-17-Spa** and try this skill on your own:

1. Export the *AppointmentsSchedule* query to a comma-separated text file. Include field names in the export. You do not need to change the location of the saved file or save the export steps.

2. Save and close any open database objects and then close the *AC3-Spa* database.

Skill 3.18 Importing Data from Excel

Many small companies try to keep data in Excel spreadsheets. Eventually, however, the data and the needs of the organization may outgrow the functionality of Excel. Their data should be moved to a database. By **importing** data from individual worksheets into separate database tables, you can define relationships and create user-friendly forms for future data entry.

To import data from Excel into a new table:

1. On the *External Data* tab, in the *Import & Link* group, click the **New Data Source** button. Point to **From File** and click **Excel**.

FIGURE AC 3.72

2. The *Get External Data - Excel Spreadsheet* dialog opens. Click the **Browse...** button to open the *File Open* dialog. Navigate to find the spreadsheet that contains the data you want to import. Click the file name and then click **Open**, or double-click the file name.

3. The option to import the source data into a new table is selected by default. Click **OK**.

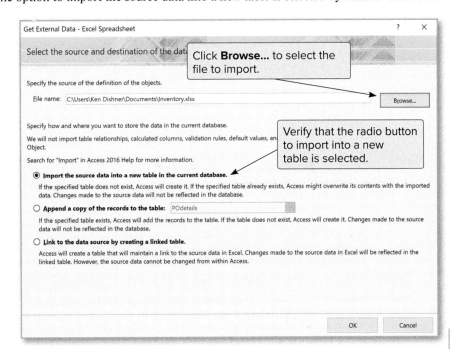

FIGURE AC 3.73

4. If your spreadsheet contains more than one worksheet, select the worksheet you want to import. If you want to import a specific named range instead of an entire worksheet, click the **Show Named Ranges** radio button and then select the named range you want to import. The preview box shows the columns in the worksheet you selected. Click **Next**.

FIGURE AC 3.74

5. If the first row of your spreadsheet corresponds to field names, click the **First Row Contains Column Headings** check box, and Access will automatically use the column headings as field names. If you forget to check this option, Access will name the fields *Field1*, *Field2*, etc., and the spreadsheet heading row will be imported as the first record in the table. Click **Next**.

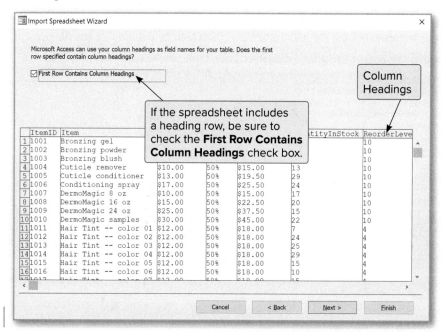

FIGURE AC 3.75

6. The next step allows you to specify properties for each of the fields. You can make changes here or modify field properties after the data import is complete. Click **Next** when you are finished modifying field properties.

- To rename a field, click to select the field in the preview image and then type the new name in the *Field Name* box.

- To specify a data type for a field, click to select the field in the preview image and then select the data type from the *Data Type* drop-down list.

- To exclude a field from the import, click to select the field in the preview image and then click the **Do not import field (Skip)** check box.

FIGURE AC 3.76

7. By default, Access will add a new AutoNumber field to the table to use as the primary key. If the worksheet already includes a column with a unique identifier for each record, click the **Choose my own primary key** radio button and select the column name from the drop-down list. Click **Next** to finish the import.

FIGURE AC 3.77

8. Access will suggest a name for the table using the Excel file name. You can modify the name or accept the suggestion. Click **Finish**.

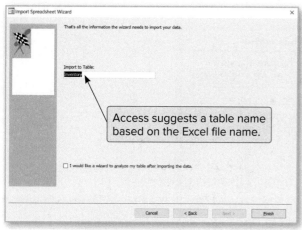

Access suggests a table name based on the Excel file name.

FIGURE AC 3.78

9. After the import is complete, you have the option to save the import steps so you can easily run the same import again later. Check the **Save import steps** check box. If you save your export specifications, you can run the export again later by clicking the **Saved Imports** button on the *External Data* tab, *Import* group.

10. Click the **Close** button to close the *Import - Excel Spreadsheet* dialog.

Each row in the Excel spreadsheet is imported as a record in the new table. If there are errors, and Access is unable to import some of the data, you will see a warning message.

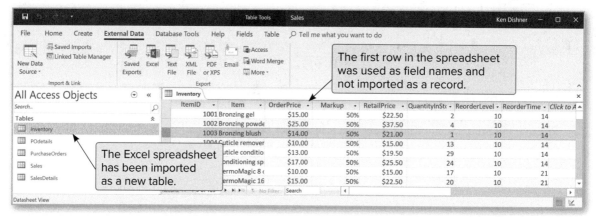

The first row in the spreadsheet was used as field names and not imported as a record.

The Excel spreadsheet has been imported as a new table.

FIGURE AC 3.79

tips & tricks

When you import data, a separate copy of the data is inserted into your database. Changes you make to the records in your database do not affect the original copy of the data.

tell me **more**

You can also import data from Excel and append the records to an existing table. Refer to the skill *Adding Records to a Table by Importing* for more information.

another **method**

To import data from an Excel spreadsheet, right-click any table in the Navigation Pane, point to **Import**, and click **Excel**.

let me **try**

If the database is not already open, open the data file **AC03-18-Sales** and try this skill on your own:

1. Import data from the **Inventory** Excel file to a new table in the current database. The file is located with the data files for this book.

2. Import all of the fields from the **Inventory** worksheet. Use the first row as column headings. Do not change any field information.

3. Use the **ItemID** field as the primary key. Accept the suggested table name **Inventory**. Do not save the import.

4. Open the table and review the imported data and then close the table.

Skill 3.19 Importing Data from a Text File

Text files are a common format used when passing data between organizations because they can be read by many different application programs. A text file that includes multiple data fields may separate the fields with a specific character called a **delimiter.** Common delimiters are commas, tabs, semicolons, and spaces. Text files that use tabs, spaces, or semicolons as the delimiter are stored as text files with the .txt file extension. Text files that use a comma as the delimiter may be saved as a **CSV (comma-separated value)** file with the .csv extension.

To import data from a delimited text file into a new table:

1. On the *External Data* tab, in the *Import & Link* group, click the **New Data Source** button. Point to **From File** and click **Text File**.

FIGURE AC 3.80

2. The *Get External Data - Text File* dialog opens. Click the **Browse...** button to open the *File Open* dialog. Navigate to find the text file that contains the data you want to import. Click the file name and then click **Open**, or double-click the file name.

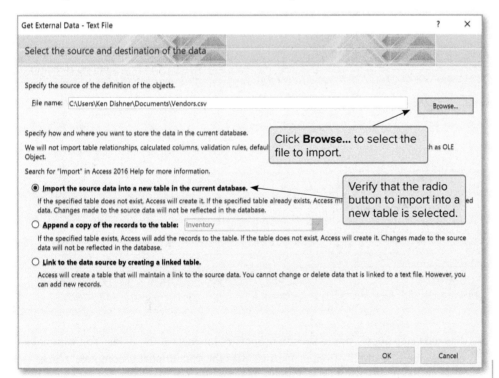

FIGURE AC 3.81

3. The option to import the source data into a new table is selected by default. Click **OK**.

4. Access will try to detect if the file includes an obvious delimiter character and select that import option for you. Click **Next** to continue.

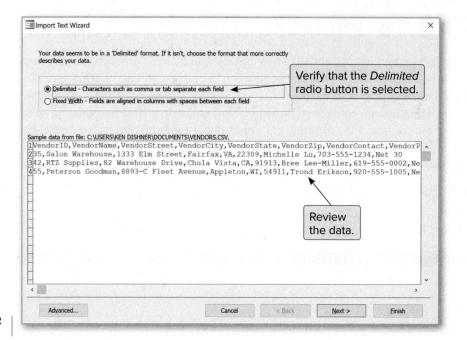

FIGURE AC 3.82

5. If necessary, click the radio button for the delimiter character used in the text file.

6. If the first row of the text file corresponds to field names, click the **First Row Contains Field Names** check box. Access will automatically use the column headings as field names. Review the import preview and then click **Next**.

FIGURE AC 3.83

7. The next step allows you to specify properties for each of the fields. You can make changes here or modify field properties after the data import is complete. Click **Next** when you are finished modifying field properties.

- To rename a field, click to select the field in the preview image and then type the new name in the *Field Name* box.

- To specify a data type for a field, click to select the field in the preview image and then select the data type from the *Data Type* drop-down list.
- To exclude a field from the import, click to select the field in the preview image and then click the **Skip Import** check box.

FIGURE AC 3.84

8. By default, Access will add a new AutoNumber field to the table to use as the primary key. If the file already includes a field with a unique identifier for each record, click the **Choose my own primary key** radio button, and select the field name from the drop-down list. Click **Next** to finish the import.

FIGURE AC 3.85

9. Access will suggest a name for the table using the text file name. You can modify the name or accept the suggestion. Click **Finish**.

FIGURE AC 3.86

10. Click the **Close** button to close the wizard. If you want to save these import steps to repeat again later, be sure to check the **Save Import Steps** check box first.

Each line in the text file is imported as a record in the new table. If there are errors, and Access is unable to import some of the data, you will see a warning message.

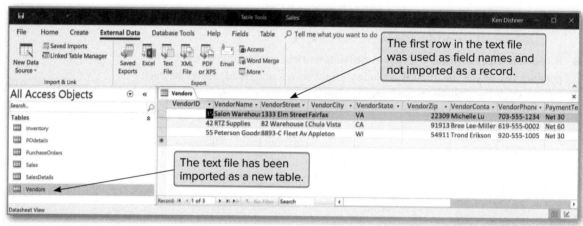

FIGURE AC 3.87

another **method**

To import data from a text file, right-click any table in the Navigation Pane, point to **Import**, and click **Text File**.

let me **try**

If the database is not already open, open the data file **AC03-19-Sales** and try this skill on your own:

1. Import data from the **Vendors** comma-delimited text file to a new table in the current database.

2. Import all of the fields from the **Vendors** file. Use the first row as column headings. Do not change any field information.

3. Use the **VendorID** field as the primary key. Accept the new table **Vendors**. Do not save the import.

4. Open the table and review the imported data and then close the table.

access 365   chapter 3 Using Queries and Organizing Information

Skill 3.20 Adding Records to a Table by Importing

The skills *Importing Data from Excel* and *Importing Data from a Text File* focus on importing data into a new table. If you receive data from an external source, you may need to import new data periodically. In that case, the first time you import the data, you will create a new table. For later imports, you will want to add (append) the data to the existing table.

To add records to a table by importing:

1. On the *External Data* tab, in the *Import & Link* group, click the **New Data Source** button. Point to **From File**, and select the type of file you are importing.

2. The *Get External Data* dialog opens (based on the type of file you are importing). Click the **Browse...** button to open the *File Open* dialog. Navigate to find the text file that contains the data you want to import. Click the file name and then click **Open**, or double-click the file name.

3. Click the **Append a copy of the records to the table:** radio button and then expand the list and select the table to which you want to add the records. Click **OK**.

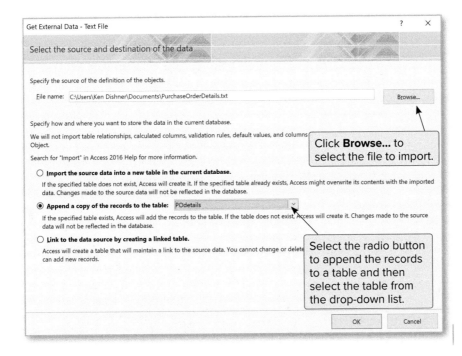

FIGURE AC 3.88

4. The next step is the same as if you were importing into a new table. If you are importing from Excel, select the worksheet or named range to import. If you are importing a text file, select whether the fields are separated by a delimiter character or by fixed width. Click **Next** to continue.

5. Again, the next step is the same as if you were importing into a new table. If the first row of the import corresponds to field names or column headings, click the check box. If you are importing from a text file, select the delimiter character or set the column width in the preview box. Click **Next**.

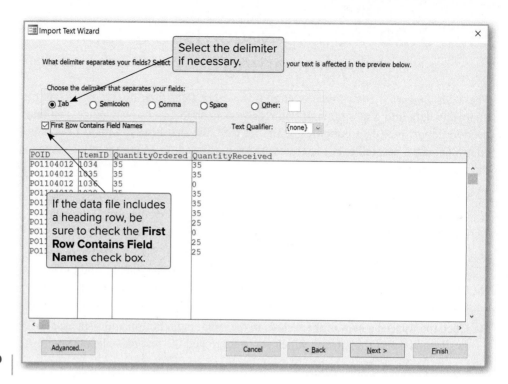

FIGURE AC 3.89

6. Because you are appending data to an existing table, you do not have the option to change the data type for any of the fields or to select a primary key. The final step is to click **Finish** to import the records and add them to the table.

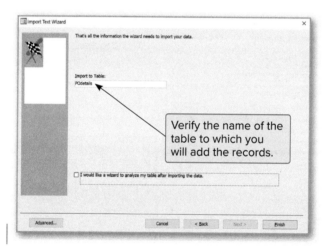

FIGURE AC 3.90

7. To save these import steps to repeat again later, check the **Save Import Steps** check box. If not, click the **Close** button to close the *Get External Data* dialog.

8. When you click the *Save Import Steps* check box, the dialog updates to include details for the saved import. Verify the name for the saved import in the *Save as* box. You can change the name if you want and add a description of the import in the *Description* box. Click the **Save Import** button to save the import or click **Cancel** to close the dialog without saving. At this point, the data have already been imported, so clicking the *Cancel* button cancels the process of saving the import steps only.

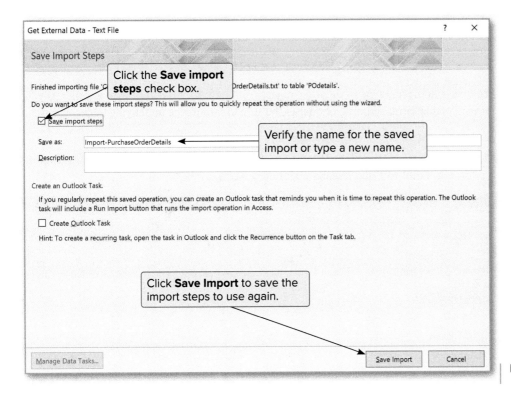

Get External Data - Text File

Save Import Steps

Finished importing file 'C ___ OrderDetails.txt' to table 'POdetails'.

Click the Save import steps check box.

Do you want to save these import steps? This will allow you to quickly repeat the operation without using the wizard.

☑ Save import steps

Save as: Import-PurchaseOrderDetails ◄ **Verify the name for the saved import or type a new name.**

Description:

Create an Outlook Task.

If you regularly repeat this saved operation, you can create an Outlook task that reminds you when it is time to repeat this operation. The Outlook task will include a Run Import button that runs the import operation in Access.

☐ Create Outlook Task

Hint: To create a recurring task, open the task in Outlook and click the Recurrence button on the Task tab.

Click Save Import to save the import steps to use again.

Manage Data Tasks... Save Import Cancel

FIGURE AC 3.91

tips & tricks

When importing data to append to an existing table, only the fields that match the original table will be imported. If a new field has been added to the data and you want to include it in the database, you will need to create the new field in the Access table before importing.

tell me **more**

To run the import again later, click the **Saved Imports** button on the *External Data* tab and select the import to run. The saved import includes the name of the external file containing the data, so if necessary, be sure to rename the data file each time you run the import.

let me **try**

If the database is not already open, open the data file **AC03-20-Sales** and try this skill on your own:

1. Open the **PODetails** table and note the number of records in the table. Close the table.
2. Import data from the **PurchaseOrderDetails** text file and append the records to the **PODetails** table.
3. The data fields in the text file are separated by tabs. The first row in the text file is the header row.
4. Save the import steps. Use the default name suggested by Access.
5. Open the **PODetails** table and note the number of records. Close the table.

Skill 3.21 Importing Data from an Access Database

You can import any type of database object from one Access database to another. If you are importing forms, reports, or queries, be sure to import the underlying table(s) as well.

To import data from an Access database:

1. On the *External Data* tab, in the *Import & Link* group, click the **New Data Source** button. Point to **From Database** and click **Access**.

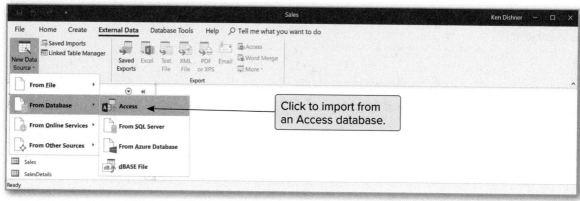

FIGURE AC 3.92

2. The *Get External Data - Access Database* dialog opens. Click the **Browse...** button to open the *File Open* dialog. Navigate to find the Access database that contains the object(s) you want to import. Click the database file name and then click **Open**, or double-click the file name.

3. Click **OK**.

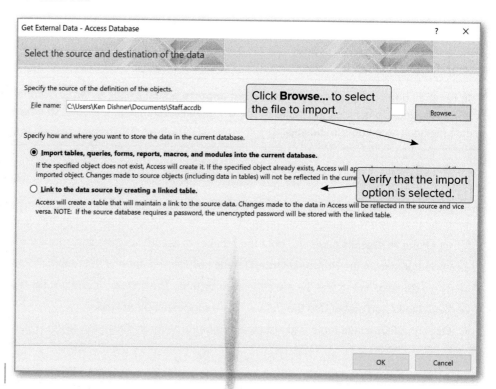

FIGURE AC 3.93

4. The *Import Objects* dialog appears with a tab for each database object type. Click the database object(s) you want to import and then click **OK**.

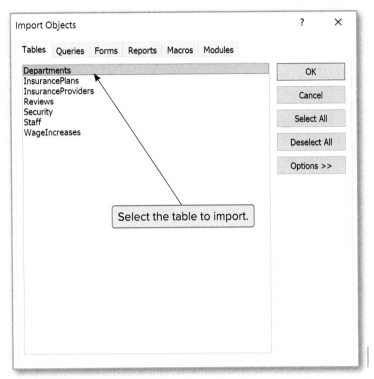

FIGURE AC 3.94

The database object now appears in your Access database. This object is completely independent of the object in the original database.

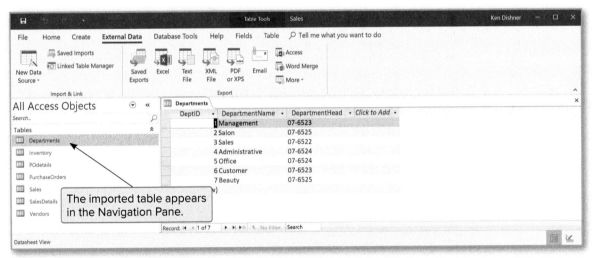

FIGURE AC 3.95

another **method**

To import data from an Access database, right-click any table in the Navigation Pane, point to **Import**, and click **Access Database**.

let me **try**

If the database is not already open, open the data file **AC03-21-Sales** and try this skill on your own:

1. Import the **Departments** table from the **Staff** database. The *Staff* database is located with the data files for this book.

2. Open the **Departments** table and observe the records.

3. Close the table.

skill 3.21   Importing Data from an Access Database

Skill 3.22 Linking to a Table in an Access Database

When you import data, a separate copy of the data is inserted into your database. Changes you make to the records in your database do not affect the original copy of the data. However, keeping two independent versions of the data may not always be the best choice. If multiple databases share a common list of customers or employees, it makes more sense to maintain the data in one database and then create **linked tables** in the other databases.

When you link to a table in another Access database, the data remain in the original source file. You cannot change any properties in the linked table, including adding or removing a primary key, because all table properties are defined in the source file. However, any changes made to the record data in the current database will appear in the source file. Conversely, any changes made to the source database will appear in the linked table automatically, including both table property changes and additions, updates, and deletions to table record data.

To link to a table in another Access database:

1. On the *External Data* tab, in the *Import & Link* group, click the **New Data Source** button. Point to **From Database** and click **Access**.

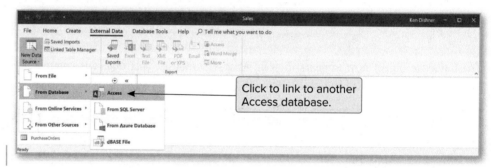

FIGURE AC 3.96

2. The *Get External Data - Access Database* dialog opens. Click the **Browse...** button to open the *File Open* dialog. Navigate to find the Access database that contains the table to which you want to link. Click the file name and then click **Open**, or double-click the file name.

3. Click the **Link to the data source by creating a linked table**. radio button.

4. Click **OK**.

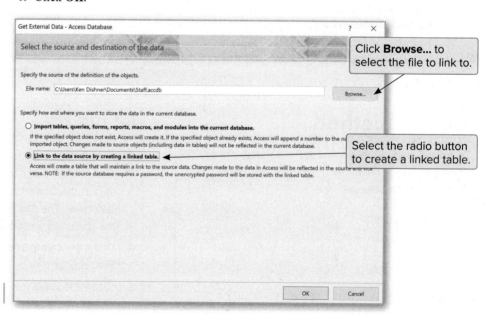

FIGURE AC 3.97

access 365   chapter 3 Using Queries and Organizing Information

5. The *Link Tables* dialog appears. Click the table(s) you want to link to and then click **OK**.

The linked table now appears in your Access database with an arrow to the left of the icon in the Navigation Pane. When you add, edit, and delete records in the linked table, those changes will appear in the table in the original data source as well. However, you are very limited in the types of changes you can make. You cannot add or remove fields or change data types or formatting properties. You can modify the structure of the table only in the original source file.

FIGURE AC 3.98

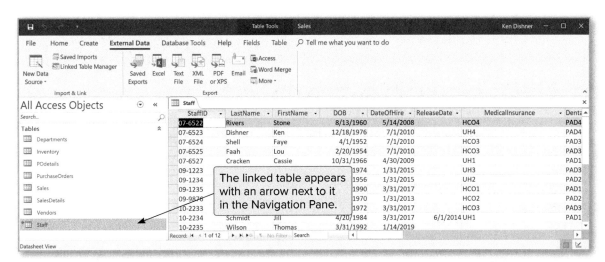

FIGURE AC 3.99

tips & tricks

> Although you will most commonly link to tables in other Access databases, you can also link to Excel worksheets, Microsoft Outlook contacts and address books, text files, XML files, or other types of databases. If the table is a link to a non-Access file, the icon will reflect the file type. You will not be able to make changes to the data in the linked table; you can make changes only in the original source file. However, when you make changes in the original source file, those changes will appear in the Access table automatically.

> When you delete a linked table, you are only deleting the link, not the table. The table will remain in the original source file.

tell me **more**

When you link to an external data source, Access stores the complete file path including the network name or drive letter. If you move the data source file, use the **Linked Table Manager** to update the file's location.

To update the location of a linked table:

1. On the *External Data* tab, in the *Import & Link* group, click the **Linked Table Manager** button.

2. Click the check boxes in front of the linked tables you want to update and then click **OK**.

3. If Access is unable to find and update the links, it will prompt you to select a new location. Navigate to the updated location, select the source file, and click **Open**.

4. Once Access is able to find and update the links successfully, it will display a message. Click **OK** to dismiss the message.

5. Click the **Close** button to close the Linked Table Manager.

let me try

from the perspective of. . .

SPORTING GOODS STORE PURCHASING MANAGER

Our store keeps inventory, purchasing, and sales in separate databases. We use a series of linked tables to keep tables up-to-date between database files. When I receive a shipment of goods from a purchase order, I import the information from the shipper (usually provided in a CSV file) into a linked table in my database. The original table in the inventory database is then updated automatically. A similar process happens with sales. When a sale is recorded in the sales database, the inventory database is updated automatically through the linked tables, which then updates the linked table in my database so I know when it's time to submit another purchase order. Without these links between databases, it would be a nightmare to keep track of inventory and to know when to order more.

Cultura/Image Source

Select Query
Query grid
Criteria
Criterion
Wildcard
Structured Query Language (SQL)
Calculated field
Expression
Parameter query

Find Unmatched query
Find Duplicates query
Filter
Export
Delimiter
Import
CSV (comma-separated value)
Linked tables
Linked Table Manager

concept review

1. A _____ displays data from one or more tables or queries, based on the fields that you select.

   a. select query

   b. crosstab query

   c. Find Unmatched query

   d. Find Duplicates query

2. The upper pane in query Design view shows the query grid where you specify which fields to include in the query.

   a. true

   b. false

3. _____ are conditions that the records must meet in order to be included in the query results.

   a. Data

   b. Fields

   c. Records

   d. Criteria

4. Entering < >100 as the criteria for a query will return results that are _____.

   a. greater than 100

   b. less than 100

   c. equal to 100

   d. not equal to 100

5. To limit query results to only records that meet all the criteria, enter criteria for multiple fields on the Criteria row, or enter multiple criteria for the same field separated by the word And.

   a. true

   b. false

6. A _____ displays a value returned by an expression.

   a. calculated field

   b. formula

   c. parameter query

   d. query

7. If you want to create a query that shows records from one table that have no corresponding records in another table, use a _____.

    a. select query

    b. parameter query

    c. Find Unmatched query

    d. Find Duplicate query

8. If you wanted to display records of all employees who live in the same city (from the City field in the table), you would use a _____.

    a. select query

    b. parameter query

    c. Find Unmatched query

    d. Find Duplicate query

9. When you create a _____, you specify the field or fields that the query will use, but you don't specify the exact criteria.

    a. select query

    b. parameter query

    c. Find Unmatched query

    d. Find Duplicate query

10. AutoFilter and Filter by Selection settings are saved with the database object.

    a. true

    b. false

Data files for projects can be found by logging into your SIMnet account and going to the *Library* section.

projects

skill review **3.1**

In this project, you will work with a Computer Science department database. You will add queries to the database to organize the *Employees* table and to manage equipment on loan. You will use filtering techniques to analyze the *Employees* and *Items* tables. You will also import a new table from an Excel spreadsheet and link to a table in another Access database.

Skills needed to complete this project:

- Using the Simple Query Wizard (Skill 3.1)
- Adding Text Criteria to a Query (Skill 3.3)
- Using OR in a Query (Skill 3.6)
- Specifying the Sort Order in a Query (Skill 3.9)
- Exporting Data to Excel (Skill 3.16)
- Creating a Query in Design View (Skill 3.2)
- Adding Numeric and Date Criteria to a Query (Skill 3.4)
- Hiding and Showing Fields in a Query (Skill 3.10)
- Using AND in a Query (Skill 3.5)
- Adding a Calculated Field to a Query (Skill 3.8)
- Finding Unmatched Data Using a Query (Skill 3.12)
- Finding Duplicate Data Using a Query (Skill 3.13)
- Filtering Data Using AutoFilter (Skill 3.14)
- Filtering Data Using Filter by Selection (Skill 3.15)
- Importing Data from Excel (Skill 3.18)
- Linking to a Table in an Access Database (Skill 3.22)

1. Open the start file **AC2019-SkillReview-3-1**.

2. If the database opens in Protected View, click the **Enable Content** button in the Message Bar at the top of the database so you can modify it.

3. Save a copy of the file to work on named: **[your initials] AC-SkillReview-3-1**. If necessary, enable active content again.

4. Use the Query Wizard to create a select query from the *Employees* table.

   a. On the *Create* tab, in the *Queries* group, click the **Query Wizard** button. In the *New Query* dialog, verify that *Simple Query Wizard* is selected. Click **OK**.

   b. Expand the *Tables/Queries* list and select **Table: Employees**. Click the **>>** button to add all the fields to the *Selected Fields* list. In the *Selected Fields* list, click the **EmployeeID** field and then click the **<** button to remove the *EmployeeID* field from the list. Click **Next**.

   c. In this step, verify that *Detail* is selected and click **Next**.

   d. In the last step, type **Tenure** for the title. Select the radio button to **Modify the query design**. and click **Finish**.

5. Add criteria to the query to return records where the value of the *Position* field is *Adjunct* or *Faculty*.

    a. Type **Adjunct** in the *Criteria* row under the *Position* field. Below that, in the *or* area, type: **Faculty**

    b. Click the drop-down arrow in the *Sort* row under the *LengthOfService* field. Select **Ascending**.

    c. Click the **Run** button and review the query results. There should be 22 records in the results.

    d. Save the query.

6. Export the *InstructorsByTenure* query to Excel. Include formatting and layout.

    a. On the *External Data* tab, in the *Export* group, click the **Excel** button.

    b. Click the **Browse…** button.

    c. If necessary, navigate to the location where you save your personal project files.

    d. In the *File name* box, type: **[your initials]Tenure**

    e. Click **Save**.

    f. In the *Export - Excel Spreadsheet* dialog, click the **Export data with formatting and layout**. check box.

    g. Click the **Open the destination file after the export operation is complete**. check box.

    h. Click **OK**.

    i. Review the Excel spreadsheet, and then close it.

    j. In the *Export - Excel Spreadsheet* dialog, click the **Close** button to finish without saving the export steps.

    k. Close the query.

7. Create a query in Design view to return records from the *Items* table where the value of the *Category* field is *Software* and the value of the *Cost* field is less than $200.

    a. On the *Create* tab, in the *Queries* group, click the **Query Design** button. In the *Show Table* dialog, double-click the **Items** table. Click the **Close** button.

    b. Notice the *Items* table in the upper pane of the query Design view window. Double-click these field names in order to add them to your query: **ItemName, ItemCost, Category,** and **Description**

    c. Type **Software** in the *Criteria* row under the *Category* field.

    d. Type <200 in the *Criteria* row under the *ItemCost* field.

    e. Uncheck the **Show** box under the *Category* field.

8. Create a calculated field to display a value that is 85% of the *Price* field value.

    a. Next to the *Description* field, create a new calculated field by typing the following in the *Field* row: **OurCost:[ItemCost]*0.85**

    b. Click the **Run** button to check your work, and then return to Design view.

    c. On the *Query Tools Design* tab, in the *Query Setup* group, click the **Show Table** button. Double-click the **Loans** table and then click the **Close** button.

    d. Click the **Run** button and observe the new query results. There should be two records in the results.

    e. Save the query with the name: **ExpensiveSoftwareOnLoan**

    f. Close the query.

9. Use the *Unmatched Query Wizard* to find items from the *Items* table that do not have corresponding records in the *Loans* table.

   a. On the *Create* tab, in the *Queries* group, click the **Query Wizard** button. In the *New Query* dialog, click **Find Unmatched Query Wizard** and click **OK**.

   b. Select **Table: Items**. Click **Next**.

   c. Select **Table: Loans**. Click **Next**.

   d. Confirm that Access has selected **ItemID** in the *Items* table and **Item** in the *Loans* table. Click **Next**.

   e. Add the following fields to the query by double-clicking each in this order: **ItemName**, **Description**, **Category**. Click **Next**.

   f. Change the name to `ItemsNotOnLoan` and Click **Finish**.

   g. Observe the query results. There should be 14 records in the results.

   h. Close the query.

10. Use the *Find Duplicates Query Wizard* to find employees who have more than one entry in the *Loans* table.

    a. On the *Create* tab, in the *Queries* group, click the **Query Wizard** button. In the *New Query* dialog, click **Find Duplicates Query Wizard** and click **OK**.

    b. Select **Table: Loans**. Click **Next**.

    c. Select **Employee** and add it to the right side by clicking the **>** button. Click **Next**.

    d. Add all fields by clicking the **>>** button. Click **Next**.

    e. Change the name to `EmployeeMultipleLoans` and click **Finish**.

    f. Observe the query results. There should be four records in the results.

    g. Close the query.

11. Use AutoFilter to filter the *Employees* table to show only records where the value of the *Position* field is *Technician*.

    a. Open the **Employees** table in Datasheet view.

    b. Click the arrow in the **Position** field header. Use the check boxes to make sure that only the **Technician** option is checked. Click **OK** and observe the results. There should be five records in the results.

12. Use *Filter by Selection* to filter the table further to include only employees where the length of service is 10 years or greater.

    a. Click in the *LengthOfService* field for any record where the value is **10**.

    b. On the *Home* tab, in the *Sort & Filter* group, click the **Selection** button.

    c. Click **Greater Than or Equal To 10**. Observe the results. There should be four records in the results.

    d. Save and close the table.

13. Import data from the *Class* Excel file into a new table. The first row in the *Class* worksheet should be used as the field names. Use the *Class Code* field as the primary key. You do not need to save the import steps.

    a. On the *External Data* tab, in the *Import & Link* group, click the **New Data Source** button. Point to **From File** and select **Excel**.

    b. In the *Get External Data - Excel Spreadsheet* dialog, click the **Browse...** button.

    c. Navigate to the folder where the resource files for this project are stored and double-click the **Class** Excel file.

d. Verify that the *Import the source data into a new table in the current database.* radio button is selected and click **OK**.

e. In the *Import Spreadsheet Wizard,* verify that the *Class* worksheet is selected and click **Next**.

f. Click the **First Row Contains Column Headings** checkbox. Click **Next**.

g. Include all the fields in the import. You do not need to change any of the data types. Click **Next**.

h. Click the **Choose my own primary key.** check box and verify that *ClassCode* is selected. Click **Next**.

i. Verify the table name *Class* and click **Finish** to complete the import.

j. Click **Close**.

14. Create a linked table to link to the *Departments* table in the *Departments* database.

a. On the *External Data* tab, in the *Import & Link* group, click the **New Data Source** button. Point to **From Database** and select **Access**.

b. In the *Get External Data - Access Database* dialog, click the **Browse** button.

c. Navigate to the folder where the resource files for this project are stored and double-click the **Departments** Access file.

d. Click the **Link to the data source by creating a linked table.** radio button. Click **OK**.

e. In the *Link Tables* dialog, click **Departments**. Click **OK**.

15. Close the database and exit Access.

skill review **3.2**

In this project you work with a health insurance database. You will improve the functionality of the database by creating a variety of queries. You will also import data from a text file and link to a table in another Access database.

Skills needed to complete this project:

- Using the Simple Query Wizard (Skill 3.1)
- Adding Numeric and Date Criteria to a Query (Skill 3.4)
- Using OR in a Query (Skill 3.6)
- Using AND in a Query (Skill 3.5)
- Creating a Query in Design View (Skill 3.2)
- Adding Text Criteria to a Query (Skill 3.3)
- Hiding and Showing Fields in a Query (Skill 3.10)
- Adding a Calculated Field to a Query (Skill 3.8)
- Finding Unmatched Data Using a Query (Skill 3.12)
- Finding Duplicate Data Using a Query (Skill 3.13)
- Using a Parameter Query (Skill 3.11)
- Importing Data from a Text File (Skill 3.19)
- Linking to a Table in an Access Database (Skill 3.22)
- Importing Data from an Access Database (Skill 3.21)

access 365   chapter 3 Using Queries and Organizing Information

1. Open the start file **AC2019-SkillReview-3-2**.

2. If the database opens in Protected View, click the **Enable Content** button in the Message Bar at the top of the database so you can modify it.

3. Save a copy of the file to work on named: **[your initials] AC-SkillReview-3-2**. If necessary, enable active content again.

4. Use the Query Wizard to create a select query from the *Physicians* table.

   a. On the *Create* tab, in the *Queries* group, click the **Query Wizard** button. In the *New Query* dialog, verify that *Simple Query Wizard* is selected. Click **OK**.

   b. Click the **Tables/Queries** drop-down arrow. Select **Table: Physicians**. Click the **>>** button to add all the fields to the *Selected Fields* list. In the *Selected Fields* list, click the **PhysicianID** field and then click the **<** button to remove the *PhysicianID* field from the list. Click **Next**.

   c. In this step, verify that *Detail* is selected and click **Next**.

   d. In the last step, type **DrsByZipCode** for the title. Select the radio button to **Modify the query design** and click **Finish**.

5. Add criteria to the query to limit the query to physicians with the zip code *33176* or *33186*.

   a. Type **33176** in the *Criteria* row under the *ZipCode* field.

   b. Below that, in the *or* row, type: **33186**

   c. Click the drop-down arrow in the **Sort** row under the *LastName* field. Select **Ascending**.

   d. Click the **Run** button and review the query results. There should be four records in the results.

   e. Save and close the query.

6. Create a query in Design view:

   a. On the *Create* tab, in the *Queries* group, click the **Query Design** button. In the *Show Table* dialog, double-click the **Procedures** table. Click the **Close** button.

   b. Notice the *Procedures* table in the upper pane of the query Design view window. Double-click each field name in the field list except *ProcedureID* in order to add them to your query.

   c. Type **Yes** in the *Criteria* row under the *Covered* field.

   d. Type **<=30** in the *Criteria* row under the *ReimbursementAmt* field.

   e. Uncheck the **Show** box under the *Covered* field.

   f. Click the **Run** button to check your work. There should be six records in the results.

   g. Return to Design view.

7. Add a calculated field to the query to display the result of a 7% increase in the reimbursement amount.

   a. Next to the *ReimbursementAmt* field, create a new calculated field by typing the following in the *Field* row: **7% Increase:[ReimbursementAmt]*1.07**

   Hint: If you need more room to type the expression, press ⬆ Shift + F2 to open the *Zoom* window.

   b. Click the **Run** button to check your work and then return to Design view.

8. Add the *OrderDate* field from the *Orders* table to the query.

   a. On the *Query Tools Design* tab, in the *Query Setup* group, click the **Show Table** button. Double-click the **Orders** table and then click the **Close** button.

b. Double-click the **OrderDate** field in the *Orders* table to add it to the query.

c. Click the **Run** button and observe the new query results.

d. Save the query with the name: `InexpensiveProcedures`

e. Close the query.

9. Use the *Unmatched Query Wizard* to find records in the *Procedures* table without corresponding records in the *Orders* table.

   a. On the *Create* tab, in the *Queries* group, click the **Query Wizard** button. In the *New Query* dialog, click **Find Unmatched Query Wizard** and click **OK**.

   b. Select **Table: Procedures**. Click **Next**.

   c. Select **Table: Orders**. Click **Next**.

   d. Confirm that Access has matched the **ProcedureID** field in the *Procedures* table and the **Procedure** field in the *Orders* table, and then click **Next**.

   e. Add all of the fields to the query by clicking the **>>** button. Click **Next**.

   f. Change the name to `ProceduresNotOrdered` and click **Finish**.

   g. Observe the query results. There should be 10 records in the results.

   h. Close the query.

10. Use the *Find Duplicates Query Wizard* to find records in the *Orders* table with the same values in the *Physician* and *OrderDate* fields.

    a. On the *Create* tab, in the *Queries* group, click the **Query Wizard** button. In the *New Query* dialog, click **Find Duplicates Query Wizard** and click **OK**.

    b. Select **Table: Orders**. Click **Next**.

    c. Select **OrderingPhysician** and add it to the right side by clicking the **>** button. Do the same for **OrderDate**. Click **Next**.

    d. Add all fields by clicking the **>>** button. Click **Next**.

    e. Change the name to `SameDateOrders` and click **Finish**.

    f. Observe the query results. There should be two records in the results.

    g. Close the query.

11. Create a parameter query to allow database users to find records in the *Physicians* table by entering a city name.

    a. On the *Create* tab, in the *Queries* group, click the **Query Design** button. In the *Show Table* dialog, double-click the **Physicians** table. Click the **Close** button.

    b. Notice the *Physicians* table in the upper pane of the query Design view window. Double-click the following field names in order to add them to your query: **FirstName**, **LastName**, **City**, **Phone**

    c. Click the **Criteria** row under the *City* field and type the following: `[Enter the city name]`

    d. Click the **Run** button. In the *Enter Parameter Value* dialog, type: `Miami` and then click **OK**. Observe the query results. There should be 12 records in the results.

    e. Save the query with the name: `DrsByCity`

    f. Close the query.

12. Import data from the *EmployeeTransfers* tab-delimited text file and append the records to the *Physicians* table.

    a. On the *External Data* tab, in the *Import & Link* group, click the **New Data Source** button. Point to **From File** and select **Text File**.

    b. In the *Get External Data - Text File* dialog, click the **Browse...** button.

c. Navigate to the folder where the resource files for this project are stored and double-click the **EmployeeTransfers** text file.

d. Click the **Append a copy of the records to the table:** radio button and verify that *Physicians* is selected. Click **OK**.

e. Verify that the *Delimited* radio button is selected. Click **Next**.

f. Verify that the *Tab* radio button is selected. Click the **First Row Contains Field Names** check box. Click **Next**.

g. Verify that *Physicians* is listed in the *Import to Table:* box. Click **Finish**.

h. Click **Close**.

i. Open the **Physicians** table. There should now be 38 records in the table. Close the table.

13. Import the *HealthPlan* and *DentalPlan* tables in the *InsurancePlans* database as linked tables.

a. On the *External Data* tab, in the *Import & Link* group, click the **New Data Source** button. Point to **From Database**, and select **Access**.

b. In the *Get External Data - Access Database* dialog, click the **Browse...** button.

c. Navigate to the folder where the resource files for this project are stored and double-click the **InsurancePlans** Access file.

d. Click the **Link to the data source by creating a linked table**. radio button. Click **OK**.

e. In the *Link Tables* dialog, click **HealthPlan** and **DentalPlan**.

f. Click **OK**.

14. Import the *PlanChange* table and the *PlanChangeDetail* form from the *InsurancePlans* database. Do not link the table.

a. On the *External Data* tab, in the *Import & Link* group, click the **New Data Source** button. Point to **From Database**, and select **Access**.

b. In the *Get External Data - Access Database* dialog, click the **Browse...** button.

c. Navigate to the folder where the resource files for this project are stored and double-click the **InsurancePlans** Access file.

d. Verify that the *Import tables, queries, forms, reports, macros, and modules into the current database.* radio button is selected. Click **OK**.

e. In the *Import Objects* dialog, *Tables* tab, click **PlanChange**. Click the **Forms** tab and click **PlanChangeDetail**.

f. Click **OK**.

g. Click **Close**.

15. Close the database and exit Access.

challenge yourself 3.3

In this project you work with a greenhouse database. Improve the functionality of this database by creating a variety of queries and exporting the query results to both an Excel spreadsheet and a tab-delimited text file.

Skills needed to complete this project:

- Using the Simple Query Wizard (Skill 3.1)
- Creating a Query in Design View (Skill 3.2)

- Adding Text Criteria to a Query (Skill 3.3)
- Adding Numeric and Date Criteria to a Query (Skill 3.4)
- Using AND in a Query (Skill 3.5)
- Specifying the Sort Order in a Query (Skill 3.9)
- Exporting Data to Excel (Skill 3.16)
- Using OR in a Query (Skill 3.6)
- Combining AND and OR in a Query (Skill 3.7)
- Exporting Data to a Text File (Skill 3.17)
- Hiding and Showing Fields in a Query (Skill 3.10)
- Adding a Calculated Field to a Query (Skill 3.8)
- Finding Unmatched Data Using a Query (Skill 3.12)
- Using a Parameter Query (Skill 3.11)
- Filtering Data Using AutoFilter (Skill 3.14)
- Filtering Data Using Filter by Selection (Skill 3.15)

1. Open the start file **AC2019-ChallengeYourself-3-3**.

2. If the database opens in Protected View, click the **Enable Content** button in the Message Bar at the top of the database so you can modify it.

3. Save a copy of the file to work on named: **[your initials] AC-ChallengeYourself-3-3**. If necessary, enable active content again.

4. Create a new query named: **GreenhouseTechsFT**

   a. Add all the fields from the *Employees* table.

   b. The query should list all employees whose *Position* begins with the word **greenhouse** and whose weekly hours are greater than or equal to 20. *Hint:* Include a wildcard character in the criterion for the *Position* field.

   c. Modify the query design so results are sorted alphabetically by last name.

   d. Add the **MaintenanceLog** table to this query and include the **MaintenanceDate** field after the *WeeklyHours* field.

   e. Run the query to review the results. There should be 16 records in the results.

   f. Save and close the query.

5. Export the **GreenhouseTechsFT** query to an Excel spreadsheet.

   a. Name the Excel file: **GreenhouseTechsFT**

   b. Include formatting and layout.

   c. Save the export steps with the name: **GreenhouseTechsFTExport**

6. Create a new query named: **NewPlants**

   a. Add all the fields from the *Plants* table except *ScientificName*.

   b. The query should list all **white** or **blue** colored plants whose *DatePlanted* is greater than or equal to **1/1/2019**.

   c. Modify the query design so results are sorted by values in the *DatePlanted* field with the newest plants listed first.

   d. Run the query to review the results. There should be three records in the results.

   e. Save and close the query.

7. Export the **NewPlants** query to a text file.

   a. Name the text file: **NewPlants**

   b. Use **Tab** as the delimiter.

c. Include the field names in the first row.

d. Save the export steps with the name: `NewPlantsExport`

8. Create a new query named: `RedPlantSale`

   a. Add the following fields from the *Plants* table to the query: **CommonName**, **PrimaryColor**, **PurchasePrice**

   b. Select only those plants with a **red** color, but don't show this field in the query results.

   c. Add a calculated field that displays a sale price that is **75 percent** of the purchase price. *Hint*: Use an expression that calculates the value of the *PurchasePrice* field multiplied by 0.75. Use the name `SalePrice` for the new field.

   d. Run the query to review the results. There should be five records in the results.

   e. Save and close the query.

9. Use the **Find Unmatched Query Wizard** to create a new query that identifies the plants that have no entry in the *MaintenanceLog*.

   a. Include all fields from the *Plants* table except the *PlantID*.

   b. Name this query: `PlantsMissingMaintenance`

   c. Review the query results. There should be 15 records in the results.

   d. Close the query.

10. Create a new parameter query named: `PlantsByColor`

    a. Add the following fields from the *Plants* table to the query: **CommonName**, **PrimaryColor**, **DatePlanted**, **PurchasePrice**

    b. Configure the **PrimaryColor** field so the user is prompted to enter the primary plant color with this message: `Enter plant color`

    c. Test the query using the color violet. There should be three records in the results.

    d. Save and close the query.

11. Open the **MaintenanceLog** table. Apply a filter that shows only those plants that have been watered and pruned. Close the table. There should be one record in the results.

12. Close the database and exit Access.

challenge yourself 3.4

In this project you will work with a vaccines database. Improve the functionality of this database by creating queries, linking to a table in another Access database, and importing new volunteers from an Excel spreadsheet.

Skills needed to complete this project:

- Using the Simple Query Wizard (Skill 3.1)
- Creating a Query in Design View (Skill 3.2)
- Adding Numeric and Date Criteria to a Query (Skill 3.4)
- Using AND in a Query (Skill 3.5)
- Using OR in a Query (Skill 3.6)
- Combining AND and OR in a Query (Skill 3.7)

- Adding Text Criteria to a Query (Skill 3.3)
- Adding a Calculated Field to a Query (Skill 3.8)
- Specifying the Sort Order in a Query (Skill 3.9)
- Hiding and Showing Fields in a Query (Skill 3.10)
- Finding Unmatched Data Using a Query (Skill 3.12)
- Finding Duplicate Data Using a Query (Skill 3.13)
- Using a Parameter Query (Skill 3.11)
- Linking to a Table in an Access Database (Skill 3.22)
- Importing Data from Excel (Skill 3.18)

1. Open the start file **AC2019-ChallengeYourself-3-4**.
2. If the database opens in Protected View, click the **Enable Content** button in the Message Bar at the top of the database so you can modify it.
3. Save a copy of the file to work on named: **[your initials] AC-ChallengeYourself-3-4**. If necessary, enable active content again.
4. Create a new query named: **LargeSummerShipments**
   a. Add all the fields from the *Shipments* table.
   b. Add criteria to the query so it returns only those orders from **6/1/19** to **8/31/19** (inclusive) that have a quantity greater than **75**.
   c. Run the query and review the results. There should be two records in the results.
   d. Save and close the query.
5. Create a new query named: **YouthShipments**
   a. Add all the fields from the *Vaccines* table.
   b. The query should list the vaccines where the value in the *PatientGroup* field is either **Children** or **Teenagers**.
   c. Add the *Shipments* table to this query and include the *DateShipped* field after the *PatientGroup* field.
   d. Limit the query to only records where the value in the *DateShipped* field is greater than or equal to **February 1, 2020**.
   e. Run the query and review the results. There should be three records in the results.
   f. Save and close the query.
6. Create a new query named: **PatientIncrease**
   a. Add all the fields from the *Locations* table.
   b. Add a calculated field named **PatientIncrease** to calculate a patient increase that is 15 percent higher than the current *PatientAvg*. *Hint*: Use an expression to calculate the value in the *PatientAvg* field multiplied by 1.15.
   c. Sort the query (descending) by this new calculated field.
   d. Hide the *PatientAvg* field from the query results.
   e. Run the query and review the results.
   f. Save and close the query.
7. Use the **Find Unmatched Query Wizard** to create a new query that identifies the vaccines in the *Vaccines* table that have no entry in the *Shipments* table.
   a. Include all fields from the *Vaccines* table except the *PatientGroup*.
   b. Name this query: **VaccinesNotShipped**
   c. Review the results. There should be 12 records in the results.
   d. Close the query.

8. Use the **Find Duplicates Query Wizard** to find out which Location IDs referenced in the *Shipments* table have received multiple shipments.

   a. Show all fields from the *Shipments* table.

   b. Name this query: `CountriesMultipleShipments`

   c. Review the results. There should be two records in the results.

   d. Close the query.

9. Create a new parameter query that displays the city and country from the *Locations* table and the vaccine, date shipped, and quantity from the *Shipments* table. Configure the *Country* field so that it requests the name of the country from the user when the query is run.

   a. Use the user prompt: `Enter country name`

   b. Test the query using the country Bolivia. There should be two records in the results.

   c. Save the query as: `CountrySearch`

   d. Close the query.

10. Add a linked table to display data from the *Diagnosis* table in the **Influenza** Access database. The file is located with the data files for this project.

11. Add new records to the *Volunteers* table by importing data from the **Volunteers** Excel file. The file is located with the data files for this project. The first row contains column headings. After the import, verify that the *Volunteers* table now has 11 records.

12. Close the database and exit Access.

on your own 3.5

In this project, you will work with a textbook database. Now that you have entered all of your textbooks, you will search for particular data using queries and filters.

Skills needed to complete this project:

- Finding Unmatched Data Using a Query (Skill 3.12)
- Finding Duplicate Data Using a Query (Skill 3.13)
- Using a Parameter Query (Skill 3.11)
- Using the Simple Query Wizard (Skill 3.1)
- Creating a Query in Design View (Skill 3.2)
- Adding Text Criteria to a Query (Skill 3.3)
- Adding Numeric and Date Criteria to a Query (Skill 3.4)
- Using AND in a Query (Skill 3.5)
- Using OR in a Query (Skill 3.6)
- Combining AND and OR in a Query (Skill 3.7)
- Specifying the Sort Order in a Query (Skill 3.9)
- Hiding and Showing Fields in a Query (Skill 3.10)
- Adding a Calculated Field to a Query (Skill 3.8)
- Filtering Data Using AutoFilter (Skill 3.14)
- Filtering Data Using Filter by Selection (Skill 3.15)

1. Open the start file **AC2019-OnYourOwn-3-5**.

2. If the database opens in Protected View, click the **Enable Content** button in the Message Bar at the top of the database so you can modify it.

3. Save a copy of the file to work on named: **[your initials] AC-OnYourOwn-3-5**. If necessary, enable active content again.

4. Create at least six queries. Of those six, you must have at least one parameter, one unmatched, and one duplicate query. For the other three select queries, you must demonstrate the use of the following features in a way that creates meaningful/useful queries:

    a. Apply text and numeric criteria, including using wildcards as well as *and* and *or* constructions.

    b. Creation of one calculated field.

    c. Hide a field in the query results.

    d. Sort the query results.

5. Apply a filter to one table.

6. Close the database and exit Access.

fix it 3.6

In this project, you will work with a pet store database. The store is currently having trouble with some queries. Find and fix their problems. Be sure to save the database objects after you make changes.

Skills needed to complete this project:

- Using a Parameter Query (Skill 3.11)
- Adding a Calculated Field to a Query (Skill 3.8)
- Hiding and Showing Fields in a Query (Skill 3.10)
- Adding Numeric and Date Criteria to a Query (Skill 3.4)
- Specifying the Sort Order in a Query (Skill 3.9)
- Adding Text Criteria to a Query (Skill 3.3)
- Using AND in a Query (Skill 3.5)
- Using OR in a Query (Skill 3.6)
- Combining AND and OR in a Query (Skill 3.7)
- Importing Data from Excel (Skill 3.18)

1. Open the start file **AC2019-FixIt-3-6**.

2. If the database opens in Protected View, click the **Enable Content** button in the Message Bar at the top of the database so you can modify it.

3. Save a copy of the file to work on named: **[your initials] AC-FixIt-3-6**. If necessary, enable active content again.

4. The *CustomersByPhone* query is not working properly. Fix it so when this query is run, it prompts the user to enter a phone number in order to find a particular customer. Use the prompt: **Enter customer phone**

5. Fix the *FeeIncrease* query to correctly display a calculated field that increases the pet adoption fees by 15 percent and hides the original adoption fee. (*Hint*: Multiply the original adoption fee times 1.15 to calculate the increase.) Change the name of the calculated field to: **NewFee**

6. The *OlderDogAdoptions* query has several problems. Fix it so it correctly displays only dogs that are at least four months of age. Sort the results by pet age from the youngest to the oldest.

7. Fix the *Customers-W&B* query so only customers whose last names begin with a **W** or a **B** appear in the query results.

8. A previous volunteer kept the employee list in an Excel spreadsheet. Import the data from the **Staff** Excel spreadsheet into a new table named: **Staff**

   The Excel file is located with the data files for this project.

   a. The first row of the Excel file contains column headings.

   b. The *HourlyRate* field should be imported using the *Currency* data type.

   c. The table should use the *StaffID* field as the primary key.

   d. The imported table should be named: **Staff**

9. Close the database and exit Access.

chapter 4

Working with Forms and Reports

In this chapter, you will learn the following skills:

❭ Create a variety of forms

❭ Create a variety of reports

❭ Add controls to forms and reports

❭ Add formatting to forms and reports

❭ Resize and arrange controls

❭ Add header and footer elements

❭ Group and total data in a report

❭ Modify the page settings and print a report

❭ Export a report to PDF and Word RTF formats

skills

introduction

In this chapter, you will learn to create a variety of forms and reports. You will work in Layout view to add and modify controls. Many skills, such as formatting, resizing, moving, and arranging controls, are applicable to both forms and reports. Other skills, such as adding grouping and totals and using Print Preview view, are available for reports only. Finally, you will export a report to both PDF and Word RTF formats.

Skill 4.1 Creating a Single Record Form Based on a Table or Query

While you can enter data directly in a table in Datasheet view, a form provides a more user-friendly data entry format. Remember, a form displays data from an underlying table or query and allows database users to enter, edit, and delete data, but it does not contain records or data itself. It is only an interface to the underlying table or query (the **record source**). The easiest form to create is a simple **Single Record form**. A Single Record form displays one record at a time.

To create a Single Record form based on a table or query:

1. In the Navigation Pane, select the table or query record source for your form.
2. On the *Create* tab, in the *Forms* group, click the **Form** button.
3. When you save the form, notice that the default name in the *Form Name* box is the same as the name of the table or query on which the form is based. Type a new name if you want to use something else.

FIGURE AC 4.1

tips & tricks

If Access finds a one-to-many relationship between the table on which the form is based and another table, Access automatically inserts a Datasheet subform at the bottom of the form. The Datasheet subform displays the records from the related table.

let me try

Open the data file **AC04-01-Spa** and try this skill on your own:

1. Create a Single Record form from the *Services* table.
2. Save the form as: **ServicesSingle**
3. Close the form.

Skill 4.2 Creating a Multiple Items Form

Some form types display all the records at once. A **Datasheet form** reproduces the exact look and layout of the table datasheet as a form. A **Multiple Items form** has a similar layout displaying multiple records at once. However, a Multiple Items form is more flexible than a Datasheet form because you can modify the layout and design of a Multiple Items form. Use a Multiple Items form when you need to see multiple records at the same time.

To create a Multiple Items form:

1. In the Navigation Pane, select the table or query record source for your form.

2. On the *Create* tab, in the *Forms* group, click the **More Forms** button, and select **Multiple Items**.

3. When you save the form, notice that the default name in the *Form Name* box is the same as the name of the table or query on which the form is based. Type a new name if you want to use something else.

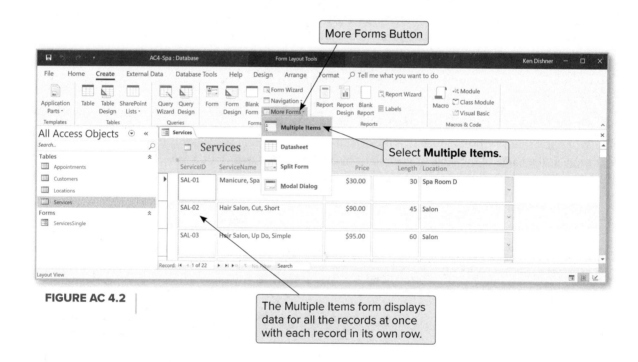

FIGURE AC 4.2

The Multiple Items form displays data for all the records at once with each record in its own row.

let me try

If the database is not already open, open the data file **AC04-02-Spa** and try this skill on your own:

1. Create a Multiple Items form from the *Services* table.

2. Save the form as: **ServicesMulti**

3. Close the form.

Skill 4.3 Creating a Split Form

A **Split form** combines the convenience of a continuous Datasheet form with the usability of a Single Record form displaying one record at a time. In a Split form, both formats are displayed and work together, so when you navigate records in one section, the other section synchronizes. Use a Split form when you need to see a large group of records at one time while having quick access to an individual record's details.

To create a Split form:

1. In the Navigation Pane, select the table or query record source for your form.

2. On the *Create* tab, in the *Forms* group, click the **More Forms** button, and select **Split Form**.

3. When you save the form, notice that the default name in the *Form Name* box is the same as the name of the table or query on which the form is based. Type a new name if you want to use something else.

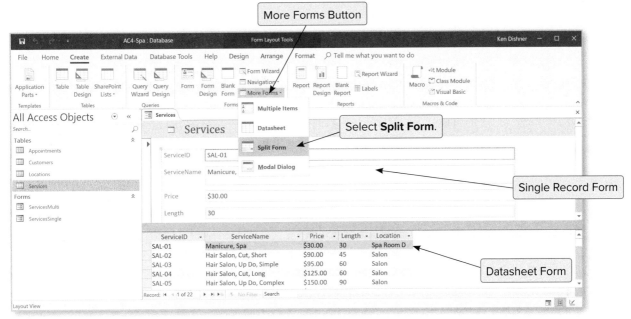

FIGURE AC 4.3

tips & tricks

The Datasheet form at the bottom of the Split form is not a subform; it is a special form view showing the same dataset.

let me try

If the database is not already open, open the data file **AC04-03-Spa** and try this skill on your own:

1. Create a Split form from the *Services* table.

2. Save the form as: **ServicesSplit**

3. Close the form.

Skill 4.4 Creating a Form Using the Form Wizard

Another easy way to begin a new form is to use the **Form Wizard**. Instead of automatically creating a form that includes every field in the underlying table, the *Form Wizard* walks you through the steps of creating the form, including selecting fields and a layout. You can use the *Form Wizard* to create a form combining fields from multiple related tables.

To create a new form using the *Form Wizard*:

1. On the *Create* tab, in the *Forms* group, click the **Form Wizard** button.

FIGURE AC 4.4

2. The *Form Wizard* opens. The first step is to expand the *Tables/Queries* list and select the underlying table or query for your form.

3. The *Available Fields* box displays all the fields from the table or query you selected. Double-click a field to move it to the *Selected Fields* box or click the field name once to select it and then click the ⟩ button. Click the ⟩⟩ button to add all the available fields with a single click.

4. If you want to include fields from more than one table or query, repeat steps 2 and 3 until you have selected all the fields you want in your form. Click the **Next** button to go to the next step.

FIGURE AC 4.5

5. If you selected fields from related tables, the next step in the wizard asks how you want to organize the data in the form. To create a form with a subform, in the *How do you want to view your data?* box, select the table that is the "one" part of the one-to-many relationship. The wizard will create a **subform**—a form within the form—to display the related records from the "many" table. Verify that the *Form with subform(s)* radio button is selected, and then click **Next**.

In Figure AC 4.6, the records in the *Locations* table are related to records in the *Services* table in a one-to-many relationship where the record in the *Locations* table is the "one" part of the relationship. The *Form with subform(s)* option will create a Single Record form for each *Locations* record with a subform displaying all the related records from the *Services* table.

If you selected fields from only one table or query, you will not see this step.

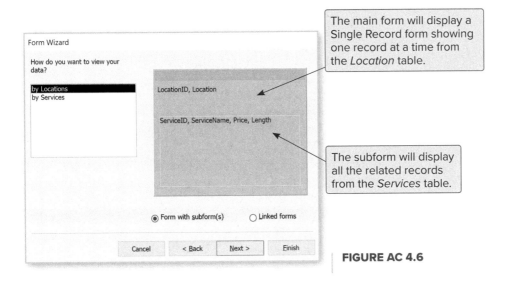

FIGURE AC 4.6

6. The next step asks you to select layout options. If your form includes a subform, select a layout for the subform: **Tabular** or **Datasheet**. If the form does not include a subform, you can select from a list of layout options for the main form: **Columnar**, **Tabular**, **Datasheet**, or **Justified**. Click the radio button for the layout option you want, and then click **Next**.

FIGURE AC 4.7

7. Enter a title for the form. If your form includes a subform, enter the title for the subform as well. The subform will be saved as a separate database object. Select whether you want to open the form to view and enter information (Form view) or modify the form's design (Design view).

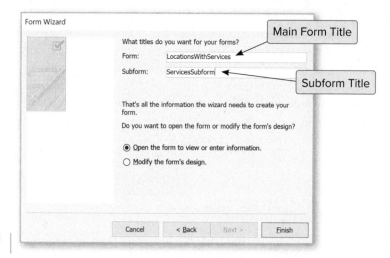

FIGURE AC 4.8

8. Click **Finish** to save the form.

FIGURE AC 4.9

tips & tricks

If you try to combine fields from tables that are not related, the *Form Wizard* will prompt you to open the Relationships window to create the appropriate relationships between the tables.

let me try

If the database is not already open, open the data file **AC04-04-Spa** and try this skill on your own:

1. Use the *Form Wizard* to create a new form. Include the **ServiceID**, **ServiceName**, **Price**, and **Length** fields from the *Services* table and the **LocationID** and **Location** fields from the *Locations* table.

2. View the data by the *Locations* table with related data from the *Services* table as a subform.

3. Use the **Datasheet** layout option for the subform.

4. Name the main form: **LocationsWithServices** and the subform: **ServicesSubform**

5. Close the form.

Skill 4.5 Creating a New Blank Form in Layout View

One way to start a new form is to begin with a blank form and add fields from tables and queries manually in Layout view.

To create a new blank form directly in Layout view, on the *Create* tab, in the *Forms* group, click the **Blank Form** button.

Create a new blank form in Layout view.

FIGURE AC 4.10

Notice that there are no records in the new form. The new blank form does not have a record source defined. The form is an empty layout until you add controls.

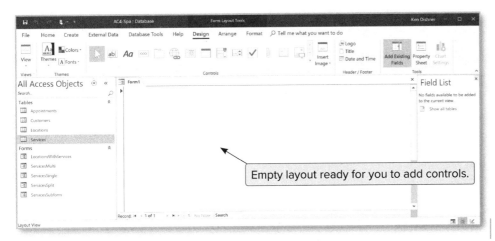

Empty layout ready for you to add controls.

FIGURE AC 4.11

tips & tricks

> Access will sometimes select a table or query to use as the record source for the form based on the object selected in the Navigation Pane or based on the first table listed in the Navigation Pane. If this is not the record source you want to use for the form, don't worry. The record source will be updated as you add fields.

> You can start a new blank form directly in either Layout view or Design view. Layout view may be easier to work with, but if you need to add advanced controls, you'll need to work in Design view instead.

let me try

If the database is not already open, open the data file **AC04-05-Spa** and try this skill on your own:

1. Create a new blank form so it opens directly in Layout view.
2. Save the form as: **AppointmentDetails**
3. Keep the *AppointmentDetails* form open if you are moving on to the next skill; close it if you are finished working with these skills.

Skill 4.6 Adding Fields to a Form in Layout View

If you are starting with a blank form, you will need to add **controls** to display field data. The most common type of control is the text box control. Text box controls can display text, numbers, dates, and similar data. A **text box control** that displays data from a table or query field is called a **bound control** because it is connected (bound) to the field. **Unbound controls** are not connected to field data directly.

Adding a field to a blank form places two controls in a **stacked layout**. A **label control** displays the name of the field on the left and a bound text box control displays the field data on the right.

To add a field to a form in Layout view:

1. If necessary, on the *Form Layout Tools Design* tab, in the *Tools* group, click the **Add Existing Fields** button to display the *Field List* pane.

2. In the *Field List* pane, click the + in front of the table or query that contains the field(s) you want to add. If the table you want is not visible, click the **Show all tables** link in the *Field List* pane.

3. Double-click a field name to add it to the form. A new bound control is automatically created at the top of the form, along with a label control.

FIGURE AC 4.12

4. To add a second column to the stacked layout, click a field name in the *Field List*, and drag it to the right of the field you just added. Access displays an I-bar shape to indicate where the controls will be placed.

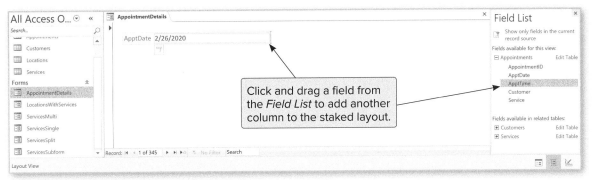

FIGURE AC 4.13

If you double-click the field name instead of dragging it, Access will maintain the single-column stacked layout and add the new controls below the currently selected control.

5. Continue adding fields and editing labels until your form is complete. You can add fields to any space in the layout grid using the click-and-drag method. If you look closely, you can see the dotted lines outlining the grid. Use these lines as a guide when you are dragging fields to the layout.

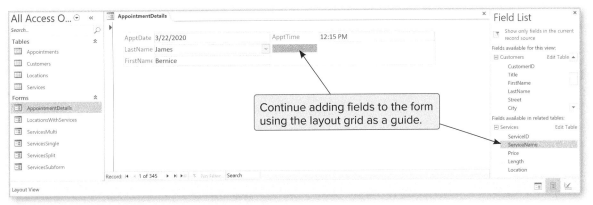

FIGURE AC 4.14

6. To edit the text in a label control, double-click the control to place the cursor within the text. Edit the text normally.

FIGURE AC 4.15

7. Save the form, and then switch to Form view to verify that it looks and behaves as you expect.

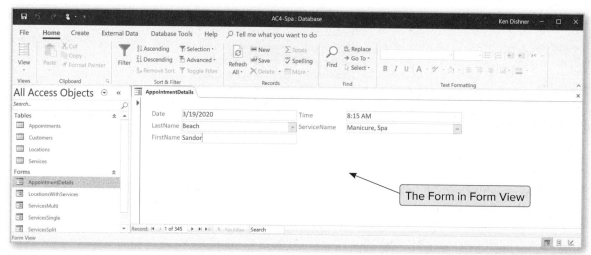

FIGURE AC 4.16

tips & tricks

You don't have to start with a blank form. Use these same techniques to add fields to any form.

tell me **more**

To delete a control, click the control once to select it and then press (Delete) or (← Backspace). If you delete a bound text box control, Access will delete the associated label control as well, if there is one.

another **method**

If you prefer working in Design view, you can add fields using the same procedures as described for working in Layout view.

let me **try**

If the database is not already open, open the data file **AC04-06-Spa** and try this skill on your own:

1. If necessary, open the **AppointmentDetails** form in Layout view.
2. If necessary, display the *Field List* pane.
3. Add the **ApptDate** field from the *Appointments* table to the form.
4. Add the **ApptTime** field from the *Appointments* table to the form, creating another layout column to the right of the *ApptDate* control.
5. Add the **LastName** and **FirstName** fields from the *Customers* table so they appear below the *ApptDate* controls. *Hint*: Click and drag the fields from the *Field List* to control the placement.
6. Add the **ServiceName** field from the *Services* table so it appears in the same column as the *ApptTime* controls in the same row as the *LastName* controls.
7. Change the text in the *ApptDate* label control to: **Date**
8. Change the text in the *ApptTime* label control to: **Time**
9. Save the form.
10. Switch to Form view and observe the new form.
11. Close the form.

Skill 4.7 Creating a Basic Report Based on a Table or Query

A report displays data from a table or query in a format suitable for printing. Like forms, reports depend on a record source for their data. Unlike forms, you cannot enter new data into a report. The easiest way to create a new report is to use the *Report* button.

To create a basic report based on a table or query:

1. In the Navigation Pane, select the table or query record source for your report.

2. On the *Create* tab, in the *Reports* group, click the **Report** button.

3. When you save the report, notice that the default name in the *Report Name* box is the same as the name of the table or query on which the report is based. Type a new name if you want to use something else.

In addition to the report title at the upper left side of the report header, the report includes the date and time in the upper right corner of the header and the page number centered in the page footer.

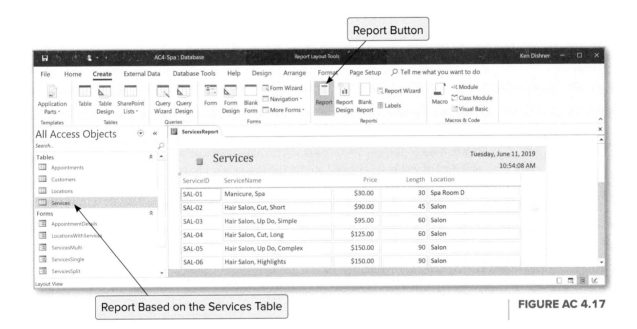

FIGURE AC 4.17

tips & tricks

The basic report layout is a simple tabular grid with each record displayed as a new row similar to the Multiple Items form. If your report has many columns, this format may not fit on a single page.

let me try

If the database is not already open, open the data file **AC04-07-Spa** and try this skill on your own:

1. Create a basic report from the *Services* table.

2. Save the report as: **ServicesReport**

3. Close the report.

Skill 4.8 Creating a Report Using the Report Wizard

The **Report Wizard** walks you step by step through the process of creating a report. The *Report Wizard* allows you to combine fields from more than one table or query and gives you more layout and design options than using the basic *Report* button from the *Create* tab.

To create a report using the *Report Wizard*:

1. On the *Create* tab, in the *Reports* group, click the **Report Wizard** button.

FIGURE AC 4.18

2. The *Report Wizard* opens. The first step is to expand the *Tables/Queries* list and select the underlying table or query for your report.

3. The *Available Fields* box displays all the fields from the table or query you selected. Double-click a field name to move it to the *Selected Fields* box or click the field name once to select it and then click the ⟩ button. Click the ⟩⟩ button to add all the available fields with a single click.

4. If you want to include fields from more than one table or query, repeat steps 2 and 3 until you have selected all the fields you want in your report. Click the **Next** button to go to the next step.

FIGURE AC 4.19

5. If you selected fields from related tables, the next step in the wizard asks how you want to organize the data in the report. Select the table that contains the field you want to use as the main grouping in the report, and then click **Next**. You will have the opportunity to add additional grouping levels in the next step. If you selected fields from only one table or query, you will not see this step.

The data in the report will be grouped by the *ServiceName* field from the *Services* table.

FIGURE AC 4.20

6. Use grouping levels to organize the data into subgroups by the value of a specific field. Select the field you want to group by and then click the ⟩ button. You can add multiple grouping levels and reorder them if necessary using the *Priority* up and down arrows. When you are finished selecting grouping levels, click **Next**.

For each service, appointment data will be grouped by month based on the *ApptDate* field.

FIGURE AC 4.21

7. Next, specify how you want the data in each subgroup sorted. Expand the sort level list and select the field you want. You can include up to four fields to sort by. Click **Next**.

FIGURE AC 4.22

8. Select the report layout and select whether you want to print in **Portrait** or **Landscape** orientation. Click **Next**.

FIGURE AC 4.23

9. Give your report a meaningful title and choose whether to preview how the report will look when printed (Print Preview view) or to modify its design (Design view).

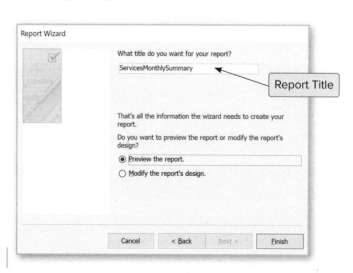

FIGURE AC 4.24

10. Click **Finish** to save the report.

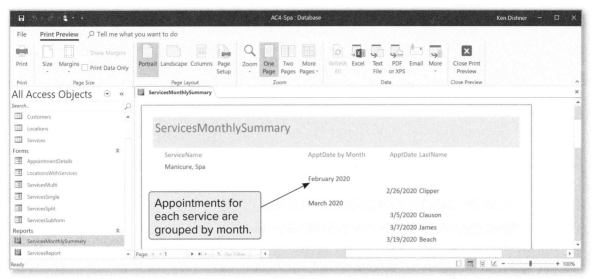

FIGURE AC 4.25

tips & tricks

❭ Use Portrait orientation for reports with few columns; use Landscape orientation for reports with many columns.

❭ If you selected to open the report in Print Preview, when you close Print Preview view, the report will display in Design view. If you want to modify the report design, switch to Layout view where you can see report data in the layout.

tell me **more**

❭ You can modify your grouping or sorting choices later by editing the report in Layout view. For more information, refer to the skill *Grouping Records in a Report*.

❭ If the report does not look exactly the way you want, you can resize and move controls. Refer to the skills *Resizing Controls* and *Moving and Arranging Controls*.

let me **try**

If the database is not already open, open the data file **AC04-08-Spa** and try this skill on your own:

1. Use the *Report Wizard* to create a new report. Include the **ServiceName** field from the *Services* table, the **ApptDate** field from the *Appointments* table, and the **LastName** field from the *Customers* table.

2. View the report data by the *Services* table.

3. Create subgroups by the **ApptDate** field.

4. Sort each subgroup by **ApptDate**.

5. Use the **Stepped** layout and **Portrait** orientation for the report.

6. Name the report **ServicesMonthlySummary** and preview it in Print Preview view.

7. Close Print Preview and then close the report.

Skill 4.9 Creating a New Blank Report in Layout View

One way to start a new report is to begin with a blank report and add fields from tables and queries manually in Layout view.

To create a new blank report directly in Layout view, on the *Create* tab, in the *Reports* group, click the **Blank Report** button.

Create a new blank report in Layout view.

FIGURE AC 4.26

Notice that there are no records in the new report. The new blank report does not have a record source defined. The report is an empty layout until you add controls.

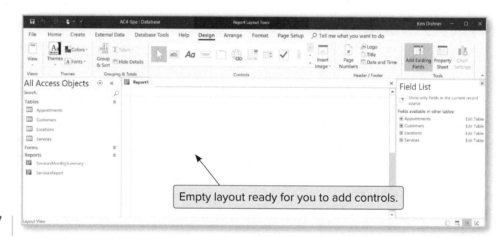

Empty layout ready for you to add controls.

FIGURE AC 4.27

tips & tricks

❯ Access will sometimes select a table or query to use as the record source for the report based on the object selected in the Navigation Pane or based on the first table listed in the Navigation Pane. If this is not the record source you want to use for the report, don't worry. The record source will be updated as you add fields.

❯ You can start a new blank report in either Layout view or Design view. Layout view may be easier to work with because you can see data in the report as you work.

let me try

If the database is not already open, open the data file **AC04-09-Spa** and try this skill on your own:

1. Create a new blank report so it opens directly in Layout view.

2. Save the report as: `AppointmentsSchedule`

3. Keep the *AppointmentsSchedule* report open if you are moving on to the next skill; close it if you are finished working with these skills.

Skill 4.10 Adding Fields to a Report in Layout View

If you are starting with a blank report, you will need to add controls to display field data. By default, blank reports use a **tabular layout** in which the data are arranged similar to a table with the label controls at the top of each column.

To add fields to a report in Layout view:

1. If necessary, on the *Report Layout Tools Design* tab, in the *Tools* group, click the **Add Existing Fields** button to display the *Field List* pane.

2. In the *Field List* pane, click the + in front of the table or query that contains the field(s) you want to add.

3. Double-click a field name to add it. A new label control is automatically created at the top of the report with a bound text box control below it. In Layout view, Access displays values for multiple records in the column.

4. Continue double-clicking fields in the *Field List* to add them to the report.

5. When you are finished adding fields, save the report.

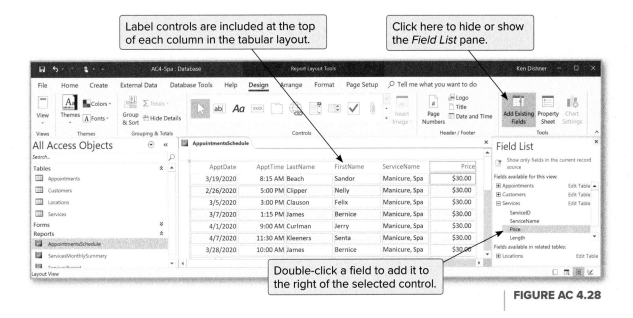

> Label controls are included at the top of each column in the tabular layout.

> Click here to hide or show the *Field List* pane.

> Double-click a field to add it to the right of the selected control.

FIGURE AC 4.28

let me try

If the database is not already open, open the data file **AC04-10-Spa** and try this skill on your own:

1. If necessary, open the *AppointmentsSchedule* report in Layout view.
2. If necessary, display the *Field List* pane.
3. From the *Appointments* table, add the **ApptDate** field and then the **ApptTime** field.
4. From the *Customers* table, add the **LastName** field and then the **FirstName** field.
5. From the *Services* table, add the **ServiceName** field and then the **Price** field.
6. Save the report.
7. Keep the *AppointmentsSchedule* report open if you are moving on to the next skill; close it if you are finished working with these skills.

Skill 4.11 Formatting Controls

Once you have created your form or report, it is easy to change formatting in Layout view. Click the control you want to change, and then make your formatting selections from the Ribbon. While these formatting techniques also work in Design view, in Layout view you can immediately see the formatting change. The formatting options discussed in this skill are available for both forms and reports.

❭ For forms, these commands are found on the *Form Layout Tools Format* tab.

❭ For reports, these commands are found on the *Report Layout Tools Format* tab.

To apply the same formatting to multiple controls at the same time, press [Ctrl] as you click each control.

From the *Font* group, click the buttons to apply standard text formatting such as **bold**, *italic*, and underline, change the font, font size, or font color, and align text to the left, center, or right side of the control box.

FIGURE AC 4.29

For bound text box controls with the *Date/Time* data type, you can apply a specific date/time format from the *Number Format* list in the *Number* group.

FIGURE AC 4.30

For bound text box controls with the *Number* or *Currency* data type, you can apply specific number formatting from the *Number* group by clicking the **Apply Currency Format $**, **Apply Percent Format %**, or **Apply Comma Number Format** ⁹ button. More number formats are available from the *Number Format* list.

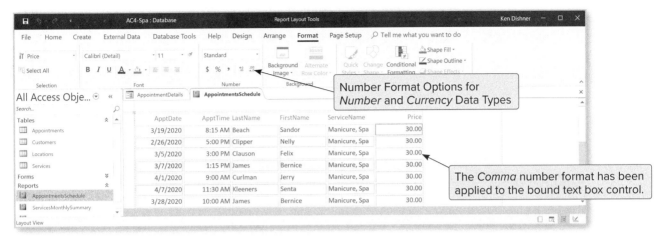

FIGURE AC 4.31

tips & tricks

You can use *Format Painter* to copy the formatting from one control and apply it to another. The *Format Painter* button 🖌 is located in the *Font* group to the right of the *Font Size* list.

another **method**

Common keyboard shortcuts that you may be familiar with in other applications (such as Ctrl + B to apply bold formatting) also work in Access.

let me **try**

If the database is not already open, open the data file **AC04-11-Spa** and try this skill on your own:

1. If necessary, open the *AppointmentDetails* form in Layout view.
2. Select all the label controls in the form and apply **bold** formatting.
3. With the label controls still selected, apply the **Dark Blue** font color. Use the fourth color from the left in the first row of standard colors.
4. Select only the **ApptDate** bound text box control and apply the **Long Date** format.
5. Save and close the form.
6. If necessary, open the *AppointmentsSchedule* report in Layout view. If your database does not include this report, create it following the steps in *Creating a New Blank Report in Layout View* and *Adding Fields to a Report in Layout View*.
7. Apply the **Comma Number** format to the **Price** bound text box control.
8. Save the report.
9. Keep the *AppointmentsSchedule* report open if you are moving on to the next skill; close it if you are finished working with these skills.

Skill 4.12 Applying a Theme

A **theme** is a unified color and font scheme. Working with themes in Layout view allows you to see the effects of the new theme immediately.

To apply a theme to a form or report in Layout view:

1. On the *Form Layout Tools Design* tab or the *Report Layout Tools Design* tab, in the *Themes* group, click the **Themes** button to expand the gallery.
2. Roll your mouse over each theme to preview the formatting changes.
3. Click one of the themes to apply it to the entire database at once. *Hint*: If you want to apply the new theme to the active database object only, right-click the theme and select **Apply Theme to This Object Only**.

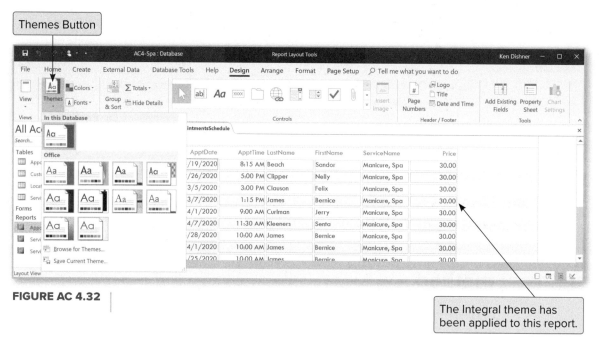

FIGURE AC 4.32

The Integral theme has been applied to this report.

tips & tricks

If you change the theme, you may need to resize some controls to display the data completely.

tell me **more**

From the *Themes* group, you can apply specific aspects of a theme by making a selection from the *Theme Colors* or *Theme Fonts* gallery.

Theme Colors—limits the colors available from the color palette for fonts, borders, and shading. Notice that when you change themes, the color palette changes for background colors, fills, outlines, and fonts.

Theme Fonts—affects the fonts used for titles, label controls, bound controls, and other text in the form. Changing the theme fonts does not limit the fonts available to you from the *Font* list.

let me **try**

If the database is not already open, open the data file **AC04-12-Spa** and try this skill on your own:

1. If necessary, open the *AppointmentsSchedule* report in Layout view.
2. Apply the **Integral** theme.
3. Save the report.
4. Keep the *AppointmentsSchedule* report open if you are moving on to the next skill; close it if you are finished working with these skills.

Skill 4.13 Resizing Controls

When designing forms and reports, you should ensure that the controls are sized to fit the data properly. You can change the width and height of controls as necessary. When the control is part of a layout, changing the height of a single control affects all the controls in the layout. For example, in a tabular layout, changing the width of any control in a column will change the width of the entire column including the label control at the top of the column.

To change the width of a control in Layout view, move the cursor to the right or left edge of the control, and when the mouse pointer changes to the double-arrow ↔, click and drag to make the control wider or narrower. Use the same technique to make rows taller or shorter.

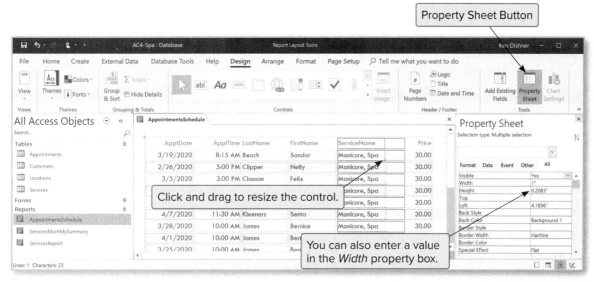

FIGURE AC 4.33

Clicking and dragging to resize controls can be imprecise. Use the *Property Sheet* if you need to specify an exact width or height:

1. If the *Property Sheet* is not visible, in the *Form Layout Tools Design* tab or the *Report Layout Tools Design* tab, in the *Tools* group, click the **Property Sheet** button. If necessary, click the *Property Sheet* **Format** tab.

2. Click anywhere in the control you want to resize.

3. Type the value you want (in inches) in the *Width* or *Height* box. Press ⟵ Enter to apply the change.

let me try

If the database is not already open, open the data file **AC04-13-Spa** and try this skill on your own:

1. If necessary, open the *AppointmentsSchedule* report in Layout view.

2. Use the *Property Sheet* to resize the **ServiceName** column to exactly 1.5 inches wide.

3. Save the report.

4. Keep the *AppointmentsSchedule* report open if you are moving on to the next skill; close it if you are finished working with these skills.

Skill 4.14 Moving and Arranging Controls

By default, all controls in a form or a report are included in the control layout. The **control layout** restricts movement of controls to the layout rows and columns ensuring that controls align with one another.

To rearrange columns in a tabular layout:

1. Click anywhere in the column you want to move.

2. On the *Report Layout Tools Arrange* tab or the *Form Layout Tools Arrange* tab, in the *Rows & Columns* group, click the **Select Column** button. This ensures that you will move the label control along with the bound text box control.

3. Move the mouse pointer over the column. When the cursor changes to ⬚, click and drag the column to the new location. Access displays an I-bar shape to indicate where the controls will be placed.

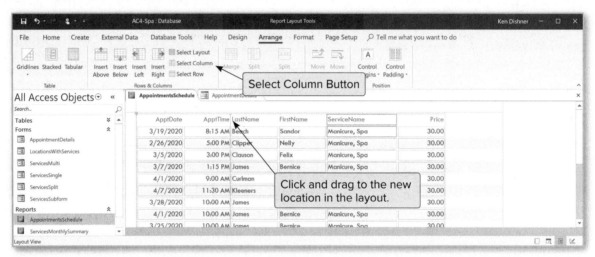

FIGURE AC 4.34

In a stacked layout, it is more common to move individual controls rather than an entire column.

1. Select the control or controls you want to move. To move both a bound control and its label control, select both controls by clicking one and pressing Ctrl as you click the other.

2. Move the mouse pointer over the selected controls. When the cursor changes to ⬚, click and drag to the new location. Access highlights the cell in the layout where the control will be placed. When you move multiple controls, Access maintains the relative layout of the controls.

FIGURE AC 4.35

tips & tricks

Use the layout grid as a guide when moving controls. If the gridlines are not visible, on the *Form Layout Tools Arrange* tab or the *Report Layout Tools Arrange* tab, in the *Table* group, click the **Gridlines** button.

tell me **more**

There may be times you want to move a single control outside the control layout. You must remove the control from the layout before you can manipulate it individually.

❯ In form or report Design view, click the control you want to remove from the control layout. On the *Form Design Tools Arrange* tab or the *Report Design Tools Arrange* tab, in the *Table* group, click the **Remove Layout** button to remove the control from the layout.

❯ The *Remove Layout* command is available in Layout view, but only from the right-click menu. Right-click the control you want to remove from the layout, point to **Layout**, and click **Remove Layout**.

let me **try**

If the database is not already open, open the data file **AC04-14-Spa** and try this skill on your own:

1. If necessary, open the *AppointmentsSchedule* report in Layout view.
2. Move the **ServiceName** column to place it between the *ApptTime* and *LastName* columns.
3. Save the report. Keep the *AppointmentsSchedule* report open if you are moving on to the next skill; close it if you are finished working with these skills.
4. If necessary, open the *AppointmentDetails* form in Layout view.
5. Move the **ServiceName** control and its label control down one row in the layout to the area to the right of the *FirstName* control.
6. Save the form. Keep the *AppointmentDetails* form open if you are moving on to the next skill; close it if you are finished working with these skills.

Skill 4.15 Modifying the Layout of a Form or Report

The default layouts created by Access may not provide the layout you want for your form or report. Use the features available from the *Form Layout Tools Arrange* tab and the *Report Layout Tools Arrange* tab to modify the layout to suit your needs.

To add a new empty row or column to the control layout:

1. Select a control in the layout.

2. On the *Form Layout Tools Arrange* tab or the *Report Layout Tools Arrange* tab, in the *Rows & Columns* group, click the appropriate button to control where the new row or column will be inserted: **Insert Above**, **Insert Below**, **Insert Left**, or **Insert Right**.

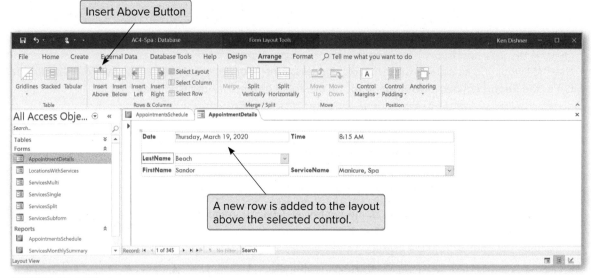

FIGURE AC 4.36

To remove a row or column from the control layout, right-click anywhere in the row or column, and select **Delete Row** or **Delete Column** from the right-click menu.

Padding refers to the space between the layout rows and columns. By default, Access uses the *Narrow* padding setting which includes a little space between layout rows and columns, but not much.

To modify the padding for the entire form or report:

1. On the *Form Layout Tools Arrange* tab or the *Report Layout Tools Arrange* tab, in the *Rows & Columns* group, click the **Select Layout** button to select the entire layout.

2. On the *Form Layout Tools Arrange* tab or the *Report Layout Tools Arrange* tab, in the *Position* group, click the **Control Padding** button and select the padding option you want: **None**, **Narrow**, **Medium**, or **Wide**.

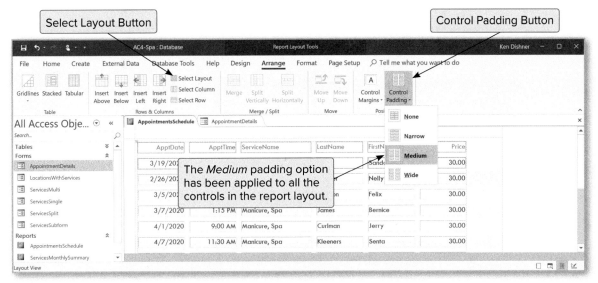

FIGURE AC 4.37

tell me **more**

❯ To split a layout column into two columns, on the *Form Layout Tools Arrange* tab or the *Report Layout Tools Arrange* tab, in the *Merge/Split* group, click the **Split Horizontally** button.

❯ To split a layout row into two rows, on the *Form Layout Tools Arrange* tab or the *Report Layout Tools Arrange* tab, in the *Merge/Split* group, click the **Split Vertically** button.

❯ To merge two layout areas into a single row or column, select the layout areas you want to merge, and then on the *Form Layout Tools Arrange* tab or the *Report Layout Tools Arrange* tab, in the *Merge/Split* group, click the **Merge** button. Access will merge layout areas only if at least one of them is empty.

another **method**

You can modify the form or report layout by right-clicking a control or layout area. Point to **Insert** and select an option to insert a layout row or column.

let me **try**

If the database is not already open, open the data file **AC04-15-Spa** and try this skill on your own:

1. If necessary, open the *AppointmentDetails* form in Layout view.
2. Insert a new row into the form layout above the *LastName* controls.
3. Save the form. Keep the *AppointmentDetails* form open if you are moving on to the next skill; close it if you are finished working with these skills.
4. If necessary, open the *AppointmentsSchedule* report in Layout view.
5. Apply the **Medium** padding option to the entire report layout.
6. Save the report. Keep the *AppointmentsSchedule* report open if you are moving on to the next skill; close it if you are finished working with these skills.

Skill 4.16 Adding Design Elements to Form and Report Headers

The **form header** or **report header** is the section directly above the detail section where the data are displayed. Access allows you to add three common design elements to the header quickly and easily: a logo or other small image, a title, and the current date and/or time.

To add a logo or other small image to the header:

1. On the *Form Layout Tools Design* tab or the *Report Layout Tools Design* tab, in the *Header/Footer* group, click the **Logo** button.

2. In the *Insert Picture* dialog, browse to find the image you want to use as the logo, select the file, and then click the **Open** button.

3. The image is added to the upper left corner of the header.

FIGURE AC 4.38

To add a title to the header:

1. On the *Form Layout Tools Design* tab or the *Report Layout Tools Design* tab, in the *Header/Footer* group, click the **Title** button.

2. An unbound text control with the name of the database object is added to the header, just to the right of the logo (if there is one).

3. To change the title, click in the box and modify the text.

FIGURE AC 4.39

To add the date and/or time to the header:

1. On the *Form Layout Tools Design* tab or the *Report Layout Tools Design* tab, in the *Header/Footer* group, click the **Date and Time** button.

2. The *Date and Time* dialog opens. Check the boxes for the date and/or time formats you want.

3. Click **OK** to add the date and time options you selected to the upper right corner of the header.

FIGURE AC 4.40

FIGURE AC 4.41

tell me **more**

While these features are available from both Layout view and Design view, it is much easier to work in Layout view because you will see a live preview of the formatted header. In Design view, you will not see the actual date and time in the date and time controls. Instead, Design view displays the formulas used in the unbound text controls to calculate the current date and time: =Date( ) and =Time( ).

let me **try**

If the database is not already open, open the data file **AC04-16-Spa** and try this skill on your own:

1. If necessary, open the *AppointmentDetails* form in Layout view.

2. Add the image **SpaLogo25** to the form header as a logo. The image file is located with the data files for this book.

3. Add a title to the form header and change the text to: **Appointments**

4. Save and close the form.

5. If necessary, open the *AppointmentsSchedule* report in Layout view.

6. Add the date and time to the report header using the date format similar to **Monday, June 10, 2019**, and the time format similar to **1:58 PM**.

7. Save the report. Keep the *AppointmentsSchedule* report open if you are moving on to the next skill; close it if you are finished working with these skills.

Skill 4.17 Adding Page Numbers to Reports

Because reports are intended for printing, they include additional header and footer sections unavailable in forms. Data in the **page header section** and **page footer section** appear at the top and bottom of every printed page in the report; data in the **report header section** and **report footer section** appear only at the very beginning and the very end of the report.

To add page numbers to the page\footer section:

1. On the *Report Layout Tools Design* tab, in the *Header/Footer* group, click the **Page Numbers** button.

2. In the *Page Numbers* dialog, select the page number options you want. Be sure to select the **Bottom of Page (Footer)** radio button to place the page number at the bottom of the page.

3. Click **OK** to insert the page numbers.

4. If necessary, scroll down to see the page number at the bottom of the report.

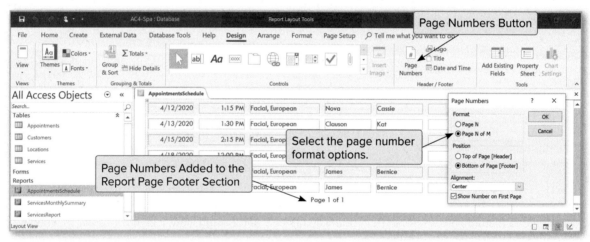

FIGURE AC 4.42

tips & tricks

If you use the page number format **Page N of M**, where **N** is the current page number and **M** is the total number of pages, you will always see Page 1 of 1 in Layout view. To test the page number format with the actual number of printed pages, switch to Print Preview view.

let me try

If the database is not already open, open the data file **AC04-17-Spa** and try this skill on your own:

1. If necessary, open the *AppointmentsSchedule* report in Layout view.

2. Add automatic page numbers centered at the bottom of the page footer on every page. Use the format Page **N of M**.

3. Save the report. Keep the *AppointmentsSchedule* report open if you are moving on to the next skill; close it if you are finished working with these skills.

Skill 4.18 Grouping Records in a Report

If you have used the *Report Wizard* to create a report, you should already be somewhat familiar with the concept of **grouping**. Adding grouping organizes the report into sections (groups) by the value of a specific field. Grouping can make a long report much easier to follow. Grouping also allows you to add group-specific headers and footers where you can calculate totals for each group.

To add grouping to a report:

1. On the *Report Layout Tools Design* tab, in the *Grouping & Totals* group, click the **Group & Sort** button to display the *Group, Sort, and Total* pane at the bottom of the report window.

2. Click the **Add a group** button in the *Group, Sort, and Total* pane to display a list of available fields to group by. Click the field you want.

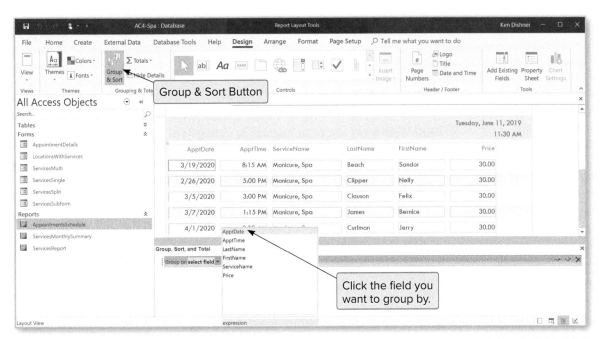

FIGURE AC 4.43

Access adds grouping to the report, including a group header for each group with a title. How the data are grouped depends on the type of field you selected. If you selected a text field, Access may group the data by specific text values. If you selected a date/time field, Access may group the data by year, quarter, month, week, or day.

To change the grouping level Access selected:

1. Click the arrow next to the grouping level description, and select a new option from the menu.

2. Click outside the menu to accept the change.

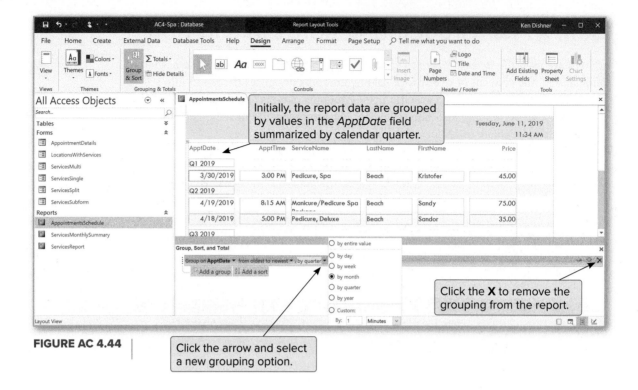

FIGURE AC 4.44

Initially, the report data are grouped by values in the *ApptDate* field summarized by calendar quarter.

Click the arrow and select a new grouping option.

Click the **X** to remove the grouping from the report.

To delete a grouping, click the **X** at the far right side of the group in the *Group, Sort, and Total* pane.

When you are finished adding grouping to the report, hide the *Group, Sort, and Total* pane by clicking the **Group & Sort** button again.

tips & tricks

You can also add groupings from Design view. However, it's always easier to work with grouping in Layout view so you can preview how the data will look.

let me try

If the database is not already open, open the data file **AC04-18-Spa** and try this skill on your own:

1. If necessary, open the *AppointmentsSchedule* report in Layout view.

2. Add grouping by the **ApptDate** field.

3. Change the grouping level for the *ApptDate* field to **by month**.

4. Save the report. Keep the *AppointmentsSchedule* report open if you are moving on to the next skill; close it if you are finished working with these skills.

Skill 4.19 Adding Totals to a Report

Totals in a report display a calculation such as the sum or average of the values in a field or group. The formula to calculate the total is added to the report in a type of control called a **calculated control**—an unbound text box control that contains an expression (a formula). You do not need to know how to add a calculated control, however, in order to add totals to a report. Report Layout view provides a tool that adds totals for you.

To add totals to a report in Layout view:

1. Click any value in the control to which you want to add a total.
2. On the *Report Layout Tools Design* tab, in the *Grouping & Totals* group, click the **Totals** button.
3. Select the function you want to use for the total.

   Access automatically inserts the new calculated control into the report footer. The calculated control in the report footer calculates a grand total for all the values in the report. If the report includes grouping, Access also adds a calculated control in each group footer to calculate the total for records in that group.

FIGURE AC 4.45

tips & tricks

In Design view, the *Totals* button is also available on the *Report Design Tools Design* tab, in the *Grouping & Totals* group. However, in Design view, you will not see the total values. Instead, Design view displays the formulas used in the unbound text controls.

let me try

If the database is not already open, open the data file **AC04-19-Spa** and try this skill on your own:

1. If necessary, open the *AppointmentsSchedule* report in Layout view.
2. Add totals to the *Price* column to calculate the sum of prices.
3. Save the report. Keep the *AppointmentsSchedule* report open if you are moving on to the next skill; close it if you are finished working with these skills.

Skill 4.20 Previewing and Printing a Report

Print Preview view shows you exactly how the report will look when it is printed. It is always a good idea to preview the report before printing. There are three main methods for switching to Print Preview view:

❱ Right-click the report tab, and select **Print Preview**.

❱ Click the **Print Preview** view button on the status bar.

❱ On the *Home* tab, in the *Views* group, click the **View** button, and select **Print Preview**.

Use the navigation buttons at the lower left corner of the Print Preview window to navigate through the pages of the report.

If your report will print on more than one page, it is a good practice to preview the report in a multiple page layout.

To preview more than one page at a time, in the *Zoom* group, click the **Two Pages** button or click the **More Pages** button and select an option to see **Four**, **Eight**, or **Twelve** pages at once.

FIGURE AC 4.46

To print the report:

❱ From Print Preview view, click the **Print** button at the far left side of the Ribbon to open the *Print* dialog. In the *Print* dialog you can specify which pages to print and how many copies to print. Click **OK** to send the report to the printer.

❱ To close Print Preview view, click the **Close Print Preview** button at the far right side of the Ribbon.

tips & tricks

If the printed report will result in blank pages, Access will display a warning message when you switch to Print Preview view. Click **OK** to dismiss the warning and continue to Print Preview view. You can use Print Preview view to adjust print settings as necessary.

another **method**

Print options are also available from Backstage.

1. With the report open in any view, click the **File** tab to open Backstage view.
2. Click **Print**.
3. Select the print option you want.

   Quick Print sends the report to the printer without opening the *Print* dialog first.

   Print opens the *Print* dialog so you can check the printer settings before printing.

   Print Preview opens the report in Print Preview view.

let me **try**

If the database is not already open, open the data file **AC04-20-Spa** and try this skill on your own:

1. If necessary, open the *AppointmentsSchedule* report in Layout view.
2. Switch to Print Preview view.
3. Change the view to show two pages at once.
4. Keep the *AppointmentsSchedule* report open if you are moving on to the next skill; close it if you are finished working with these skills.

from the perspective of. . .

LAWYER

I use Access to track time and billing for my law practice. I use forms to enter client information and to track time spent on each case, and I use reports to generate client invoices. I always check the invoice report in Print Preview view before printing. You never know when an adjustment to a column width will cause the report to spill over to a second page. When that happens, I can usually adjust the margins or switch the page orientation to keep the invoice to no more than one page wide.

Shutterstock/Andrey_Popov

Skill 4.21 Controlling the Page Setup of a Report for Printing

When you create a new report from scratch, the default page orientation is **portrait**. This means the height of the page is greater than the width. You may want to change the page orientation to **landscape** to print sideways on the page if your report contains multiple columns of data.

Use Print Preview view to adjust page orientation for your reports before printing:

1. Switch to Print Preview view.

2. To change the page orientation, in the *Page Layout* group, click the **Portrait** or **Landscape** button.

FIGURE AC 4.47

Margins are the blank spaces at the top, bottom, left, and right of the printed page. If your report is just a little bit too wide to fit on one page, try adjusting the margins to a narrower setting. This will give you more room on the page for printed data.

Use Print Preview view to adjust the margins for your reports before printing:

1. Switch to Print Preview view.

2. To use a preset margin option, in the *Page Size* group, click the **Margins** button, and select an option: **Normal**, **Wide**, or **Narrow**.

FIGURE AC 4.48

tell me **more**

When you switch page orientation or margins, all the visible data in your report may fit on one page, but the report width may still be wider than the page. When that happens, Access will show a warning message that the report may print with blank pages.

To fix this problem:

1. Switch to Design view.

2. In Design view, you can clearly see that the report is wider than it needs to be.

3. Move the mouse pointer to the right side of the report detail section. When the cursor changes to the ↔ shape, click and drag the section boundary to the left to make it smaller. Access will not let you make the section so small that any controls are outside its border.

Another way to fix this problem is to allow Access to remove the excess space for you.

1. The green triangle in the report selector box at the upper left corner of the report indicates that there may be a problem. Click it to display the Smart Tag.

2. Hover the mouse pointer over the Smart Tag at the upper right corner of the report to see a description of the problem.

3. Click the **Smart Tag** to see the list of possible solutions.

4. Select **Remove Extra Report Space**.

another **method**

The *Page Setup* tab is also available from Layout view and Design view, but it is best to adjust print settings from Print Preview view where you can see the effect of changes.

let me **try**

If the database is not already open, open the data file **AC04-21-Spa** and try this skill on your own:

1. If necessary, open the *AppointmentsSchedule* report in Layout view.

2. Change the orientation so the report page is wider than it is tall.

3. Change the margins setting to the **Wide** option.

4. Keep the *AppointmentsSchedule* report open in Print Preview view if you are moving on to the next skill; close it if you are finished working with these skills.

Skill 4.22 Exporting a Report to Other Formats

You are probably familiar with **PDF (Portable Document Format)** files. This type of file can be read by anyone who has the Adobe Reader software installed (which is almost everyone with a computer nowadays). If you need a version of one of your database objects, particularly reports, to look exactly like it would when printed from Access, consider exporting the object to a PDF file.

To export a report to a PDF file:

1. Open the report in Print Preview view and review the layout.
2. On the *Print Preview* tab, in the *Data* group, click the **PDF or XPS** button.

FIGURE AC 4.49

3. In the *Publish as PDF or XPS* dialog, Access automatically suggests a file name based on the name of the object you selected. If necessary, make the location and file name changes in the dialog.
4. Click **Publish**.

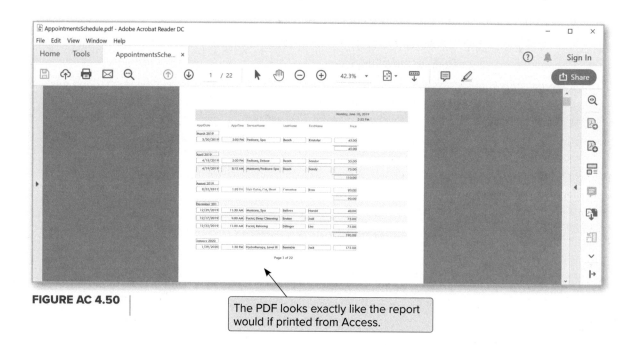

FIGURE AC 4.50

The PDF looks exactly like the report would if printed from Access.

5. When you return to Access, the *Export-PDF* window will be open. If you want to save the export steps to repeat again later, check the **Save export steps** check box.

6. Click the **Close** button to close the window.

Another option for exporting a report is to export to Microsoft Word. This is helpful if you want to share the data with someone who may need to modify or manipulate the data but does not have Microsoft Access. When you export Access data to Word, you are actually exporting to a text format called **Rich Text Format (RTF)**. This format can be used with any word processing program, not just Microsoft Word.

To export data to Word:

1. Open the report in Print Preview view and review the layout.

2. On the *Print Preview* tab, in the *Data* group, click the **More** button, and select **Word**.

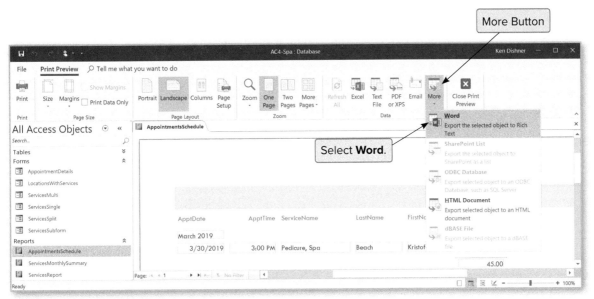

FIGURE AC 4.51

3. Access automatically suggests a file name based on the name of the object you selected. If you want to change the file name or the location of the saved file, click the **Browse...** button and make your changes in the *File Save* dialog.

4. If you are exporting a report, the *Export data with formatting and layout.* check box is checked automatically. You do not have the option to uncheck it.

5. When the *Export data with formatting and layout.* option is checked, you also have the option to check the box **Open the destination file after the export operation is complete**.

6. Click **OK** to begin the export process.

7. After the export is complete, you have the option to save the export steps so you can easily run the same export again later. Check the **Save export steps** check box.

8. Click the **Close** button.

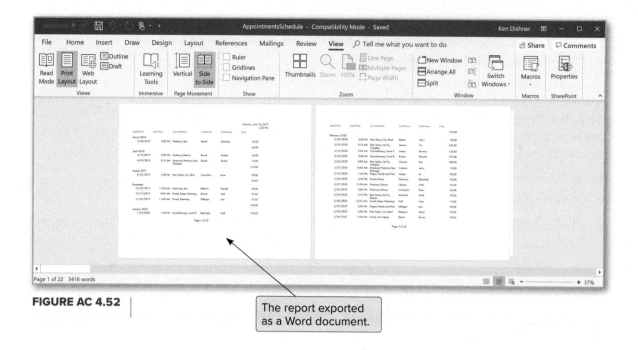

FIGURE AC 4.52

The report exported
as a Word document.

another **method**

> **To export to PDF:**

> In the Navigation Pane, click the object you want to export. On the *External Data* tab, in the *Export* group, click the **PDF or XPS** button.

> In the Navigation Pane, right-click the database object you want to export, point to **Export**, and select **PDF or XPS**.

> **To export to Word:**

> In the Navigation Pane, click the object you want to export. On the *External Data* tab, in the *Export* group, click the **More** button and select **Word**.

> In the Navigation Pane, right-click the database object you want to export, point to **Export**, and select **Word RTF File**.

let me **try**

If the database is not already open, open the data file **AC04-22-Spa** and try this skill on your own:

1. If necessary, open the *AppointmentsSchedule* report in Print Preview view.
2. Export the report as a PDF file.
3. Export the report to Word.
4. Save and close the report.
5. Close the database.

Record source
Single Record form
Datasheet form
Multiple Items form
Split form
Form Wizard
Subform
Control
Text box control
Bound control
Unbound control
Stacked layout
Label control
Report Wizard
Tabular layout
Theme
Theme colors

Theme fonts
Control layout
Padding
Form header
Report header
Page header section
Page footer section
Report header section
Report footer section
Grouping
Calculated control
Portrait
Landscape
Margins
PDF (Portable Document Format)
Rich Text Format (RTF)

concept review

1. A _____ combines the convenience of a continuous Datasheet form with the usability of a Single Record form displaying one record at a time.

   a. Datasheet form

   b. Split form

   c. Multiple Items form

   d. subform

2. A _____ is a form within a form that displays records related to the record in the main form.

   a. Datasheet form

   b. Split form

   c. Multiple Items form

   d. subform

3. A(n) _____ text control displays data from a field.

   a. label

   b. unbound

   c. bound

   d. calculated

4. A stacked layout places labels across the top, with columns of data (similar to a datasheet or a spreadsheet).

   a. true

   b. false

5. Click and drag fields from the _____ to add controls to a blank report.

   a. *Property Sheet*

   b. *Report Wizard*

   c. *Field List* pane

   d. none of the above

6. Each form and report in a database can have its own theme.

    a. true

    b. false

7. Page numbers can be added only to a footer section.

    a. true

    b. false

8. An unbound text box control that contains an expression (formula) is called a(n) _____ control.

    a. bound

    b. unbound

    c. label

    d. calculated

9. Grand totals in a report are added to the _____.

    a. group footer section

    b. group header section

    c. page footer section

    d. report footer section

10. To change the direction a report prints on the page, change the page _____.

    a. margins

    b. orientation

    c. zoom

    d. layout

Data files for projects can be found by logging into your SIMnet account and going to the *Library* section.

projects

skill review 4.1

In this project, you will work with a Computer Science department database. It uses Access to manage employees and various items that are loaned to students and faculty. You will create a variety of forms for entering employee, loan, and item information.

Skills needed to complete this project:

- Creating a Single Record Form Based on a Table or Query (Skill 4.1)
- Creating a Multiple Items Form (Skill 4.2)
- Creating a Split Form (Skill 4.3)
- Creating a Form Using the Form Wizard (Skill 4.4)
- Applying a Theme (Skill 4.12)
- Creating a New Blank Form in Layout View (Skill 4.5)
- Adding Fields to a Form in Layout View (Skill 4.6)
- Resizing Controls (Skill 4.13)
- Modifying the Layout of a Form or Report (Skill 4.15)
- Formatting Controls (Skill 4.11)
- Adding Design Elements to Form and Report Headers (Skill 4.16)

1. Open the start file **AC2019-SkillReview-4-1**.

2. If the database opens in Protected View, click the **Enable Content** button in the Message Bar at the top of the database so you can modify it.

3. Save a copy of the file to work on named: **[your initials] AC-SkillReview-4-1**. If necessary, enable active content again.

4. Create a Single Record form using the *Staff* table as the record source.

   a. In the Navigation Pane, select the **Staff** table.

   b. On the *Create* tab, in the *Forms* group, click the **Form** button.

   c. Save the form with the name: **StaffSingleRecord**

   d. Close the form.

5. Create a Multiple Items form using the *Staff* table as the record source.

   a. In the Navigation Pane, select the **Staff** table.

   b. On the *Create* tab, in the *Forms* group, click the **More Forms** button and select **Multiple Items** from the list.

   c. Save the form with the name: **StaffMultipleItems**

   d. Close the form.

6. Create a Split form using the *Staff* table as the record source.

   a. In the Navigation Pane, select the **Staff** table.

   b. On the *Create* tab, in the *Forms* group, click the **More Forms** button and select **Split Form** from the list.

   c. Save the form with the name: **StaffSplit**

   d. Close the form.

7. Create a form using the *Form Wizard* to show items on loan to each employee.

   a. On the *Create* tab, in the *Forms* group, click the **Form Wizard** button.

   b. In the first step of the wizard, verify that *Table: Staff* is selected from the *Tables/Queries* list.

   c. Double-click the following fields to add them to the *Selected Fields* box in this order: **EmployeeID**, **LastName**, **FirstName**

   d. Expand the *Tables/Queries* list and select **Table: Loans**.

   e. Double-click the following fields to add them to the *Selected Fields* box below the fields from the *Staff* table: **LoanID**, **Item**, **LoanDate**

   f. Click the **Next** button.

   g. Verify that the form will be organized by data in the *Staff* table as a form with a subform. Click **Next**.

   h. Verify that the *Datasheet* radio button is selected to use the Datasheet layout for the subform. Click **Next**.

   i. Enter the following title in the *Form* box: StaffLoans

   j. Enter the following title in the *Subform* box: StaffLoansSubform

   k. Verify that the *Open the form to view or enter information* radio button is selected.

   l. Click the **Finish** button. Do not close this form.

8. Apply a theme to the database.

   a. Switch to Layout view.

   b. Click the **Form Layout Tools Design** tab if it is not already selected.

   c. In the *Themes* group, click the **Themes** button. Select the **Facet** theme.

   d. Save and close the form.

9. Create a new blank form in Layout view.

   a. On the *Create* tab, in the *Forms* group, click the **Blank Form** button.

   b. Save the form with the name: ItemDetails

10. Add controls to the new *ItemDetails* form.

    a. If necessary, display the *Field List* pane. On the *Form Layout Tools Design* tab, in the *Tools* group, click the **Add Existing Fields** button.

    b. If necessary, click the **Show All Tables** link in the *Field List* pane.

    c. Click the + in front of **Items**.

    d. Add the *ItemID* field to the form by double-clicking **ItemID** in the *Field List* pane.

    e. Click the **ItemName** field and drag it to the form to the right of the *ItemID* control. Pay close attention to the placement guide so you drop the new controls to the right of the *ItemID* control, not below it.

    f. Click and drag the **ItemCost** field to the form so it is placed directly below the *ItemName* field. Make sure the label controls line up in the same column. *Hint*: If you make a mistake, press (Ctrl) + (z) to undo, and then try again.

    g. Click and drag the **Description** field to the form so it is placed directly below the *ItemCost* field. Make sure the label controls line up in the same column.

11. Modify the width of the *ItemID* bound text control.

    a. Click the **ItemID** bound text control to select it.

    b. Click and drag the right border to the left to make the control smaller. The control should be just large enough so the entire ACC1 is visible.

12. Increase the padding between all the controls in the form detail section.
   a. On the *Form Layout Tools Arrange* tab, in the *Rows & Columns* group, click the **Select Layout** button to select all the controls in the detail section at once.
   b. On the *Form Layout Tools Arrange* tab, in the *Position* group, click the **Control Padding** button and select **Medium**.

13. Apply a font color to all the labels in the form.
   a. Click the **ItemID** label control to select it. Press Ctrl and click each of the other label controls. All the label controls should be selected.
   b. On the *Form Layout Tools Format* tab, in the *Font* group, click the **Font Color** button arrow to view the color palette, and click the standard color **Purple** (the third color from the right in the first row of standard colors).

14. Add a title to the form header.
   a. On the *Form Layout Tools Design* tab, in the *Header/Footer* group, click the **Title** button.
   b. Change the title to: **Inventory**
   c. Save and close the form.

15. Close the database and exit Access.

16. Upload and save the project file.

17. Submit project for grading.

skill review **4.2**

In this project you will work with a health insurance database. You will create and modify a variety of reports.

Skills needed to complete this project:

- Creating a Basic Report Based on a Table or Query (Skill 4.7)
- Resizing Controls (Skill 4.13)
- Moving and Arranging Controls (Skill 4.14)
- Grouping Records in a Report (Skill 4.18)
- Adding Totals to a Report (Skill 4.19)
- Formatting Controls (Skill 4.11)
- Applying a Theme (Skill 4.12)
- Previewing and Printing a Report (Skill 4.20)
- Creating a Report Using the Report Wizard (Skill 4.8)
- Creating a New Blank Report in Layout View (Skill 4.9)
- Adding Fields to a Report in Layout View (Skill 4.10)
- Adding Design Elements to Form and Report Headers (Skill 4.16)
- Adding Page Numbers to Reports (Skill 4.17)

1. Open the start file **AC2019-SkillReview-4-2**.

2. If the database opens in Protected View, click the **Enable Content** button in the Message Bar at the top of the database so you can modify it.

3. Save a copy of the file to work on named: **[your initials] AC-SkillReview-4-2**. If necessary, enable active content again.

4. Create a basic report using the *Procedures* table as the data source.
   a. In the Navigation Pane, select the **Procedures** table.
   b. On the *Create* tab, in the *Reports* group, click the **Report** button.
   c. Save the report with the name: **ProceduresOverview**

5. Adjust the *ProcedureID* column width to 1 inch.

   a. If it is not already selected, click anywhere in the **ProcedureID** column.

   b. On the *Report Layout Tools Design* tab, in the *Tools* group, click the **Property Sheet** button.

   c. Verify that *ProcedureID* is selected in the drop-down list at the top of the *Property Sheet*.

   d. If necessary, click the **Format** tab.

   e. In the *Width* box, delete the current value and type: **1**

   f. Press (← Enter).

   g. Save and close the report.

6. Modify the *HospitalSummary* report so the *Hospital Name* column appears first in the report.

   a. Open the **HospitalSummary** report in Layout view.

   b. Click the **Hospital Name** label at the top of the column. On the *Report Layout Tools Arrange* tab, in the *Rows & Columns* group, click the **Select Column** button.

   c. Move the mouse pointer over the column. When the mouse pointer changes to the move shape ⁺⬍, click and drag the entire column to the left. Release the mouse button when the I-bar move indicator appears at the very left side of the report.

7. Add grouping to the report by values in the *HospitalName* field.

   a. If the *Group, Sort, and Total* pane is not visible, on the *Report Layout Tools Design* tab, in the *Grouping & Totals* group, click the **Group & Sort** button.

   b. In the *Group, Sort, and Total* pane at the bottom of the report, click **Add a Group**, and then click **HospitalName**.

8. Add totals to the report to calculate the total number of members. Calculate totals for each group as well as a grand total for the entire report.

   a. Click any **MemberCount** value.

   b. On the *Report Layout Tools Design* tab, in the *Grouping & Totals* group, click the **Totals** button, and click **Sum**.

9. Adjust the height of the controls displaying the totals.

   a. Click any of the controls displaying the total in one of the group footers.

   b. Drag the bottom boundary down so the entire number is visible.

   c. Scroll to the very bottom of the report.

   d. Click the grand total control at the very bottom of the report.

   e. Drag the bottom boundary down so the entire number is visible.

10. Apply bold formatting to all the total controls.

    a. Verify that the grand total control is still selected.

    b. Press (Ctrl) and click any of the group total controls.

    c. On the *Report Layout Tools Format* tab, in the *Font* group, click the **Bold** button.

11. Add page numbers to the center of the page footer section of the report. Use the format similar to Page 1 of 2.

    a. If necessary, scroll to the bottom of the report so you can see the page footer section.

    b. On the *Report Layout Tools Design* tab, in the *Header/Footer* group, click the **Page Numbers** button.

c. In the *Page Numbers* dialog, click the **Page N of M** radio button.

d. Click the **Bottom of Page [Footer]** radio button.

e. Verify that *Center* is selected from the *Alignment* list.

f. Verify that the *Show Number on First Page* check box is checked.

g. Click **OK**.

12. Apply the Gallery theme to the database.

    a. On the *Report Layout Tools Design* tab, in the *Themes* group, click the **Themes** button, and select **Gallery**.

    b. Save and close the report.

13. Use the Report Wizard to create a report combining information from the *Orders*, *Physicians*, and *Procedures* tables.

    a. On the *Create* tab, in the *Reports* group, click the **Report Wizard**.

    b. Expand the **Tables/Queries** list and select **Table: Orders**.

    c. Double-click the following fields to add them to the *Selected Fields* list in this order: **OrderID** and **OrderDate**.

    d. Expand the **Tables/Queries** list again and select **Table: Physicians**.

    e. Double-click the following fields to add them to the *Selected Fields* list in this order: **LastName** and **FirstName**

    f. Expand the **Tables/Queries** list and select **Table: Procedures**.

    g. Double-click the **ProcedureName** field to add it to the *Selected Fields* list.

    h. Click the **Next** button to continue to the next step of the Report Wizard.

    i. Verify that *by Orders* is selected in the *How do you want to view your data?* box. Click **Next**.

    j. Add grouping by order date. Double-click **OrderDate** in the *Do you want any grouping levels?* box. Observe that Access will group the orders by month. Click **Next**.

    k. Sort the records in the report by the procedure name. Next to the number **1**, click the arrow and select **ProcedureName** from the list of choices. Click **Next**.

    l. Verify that the report will use the *Stepped layout* with *Portrait orientation*. Click **Next**.

    m. Enter the following name in the *What title do you want for your report?* box: **ProcedureOrderDetails**

    n. If necessary, click the **Preview the report**. radio button so the report will open in Print Preview view.

    o. Click **Finish**.

14. Edit the text in the *OrderDatebyMonth* label in the report header section.

    a. Switch to Layout view so you can make changes to the report.

    b. Click the **OrderDatebyMonth** label control and change the text to: **Month**

15. Adjust the control widths in the report so all values are visible. *Hint*: If you want to know how wide a column is as you click and drag to adjust the width, open the *Property Sheet* to the *Format* tab and watch the value in the *Width* box.

    a. Click the **ProcedureName** label control. Press (Ctrl) and click any value in the column. Click and drag the **right** column border to the **left** until the column is just wide enough to display the entire text *Cardiac Stress Test*. The control should be approximately 1.6 inches wide.

    b. Click the **OrderID** label control. Press (Ctrl) and click any value in the column. Click and drag the **left** column border to the **left** to make the column just wide enough that the text in the label control is visible. The control should be approximately .8 inch wide.

 c. Click the **LastName** label control. Press Ctrl and click any value in the column. Click and drag the **left** column border to the **right** to make the column approximately 1 inch wide.

 d. Click the **Order Date** label control. Press Ctrl and click any value in the column. Click and drag the **right** column border to the **right** to make the column wide enough that the dates are visible. The control should be approximately .9 inch wide.

16. Modify the format used for the *OrderDate* control.

 a. Click any value in the *OrderDate* column.

 b. On the *Report Layout Tools Format* tab, in the *Number* group, expand the **Format** list, and select **Medium Date**.

 c. Save and close the report.

17. Create a new blank report and add controls to it.

 a. On the *Create* tab, in the *Reports* group, click the **Blank Report** button.

 b. If necessary, on the *Report Layout Tools Design* tab, in the *Tools* group, click the **Add Existing Fields** button to display the *Field List* pane.

 c. In the *Field List* pane, if necessary, click the **Show all tables** link and then click the **+** button to expand the **Physicians** table.

 d. Double-click the following fields from the *Physicians* table in order to add them to the report in this order: **LastName**, **FirstName**, **Phone**

 e. Save the report with the name: **PhoneDirectory**

18. Add a logo to the report header.

 a. On the *Report Layout Tools Design* tab, in the *Header/Footer* group, click the **Logo** button.

 b. In the *Insert Picture* dialog, navigate to the data files location for this project.

 c. Double-click the **InsuranceLogo** image file.

 d. Add a title to the report header.

 e. On the *Report Layout Tools Design* tab, in the *Header/Footer* group, click the **Title** button.

 f. Modify the title text so there is a space between *Phone* and *Directory*.

19. Add page numbers centered in the report page footer.

 a. On the *Report Layout Tools Design* tab, in the *Header/Footer* group, click the **Page Numbers** button.

 b. In the *Page Numbers* dialog, click the **Page N** radio button.

 c. Verify that the *Bottom of Page [Footer]* radio button is selected.

 d. Verify that *Center* is selected from the *Alignment* list.

 e. Verify that the *Show Number on First Page* check box is checked.

 f. Click **OK**.

20. Save and close the report.

21. Close the database and exit Access.

In this project you will work with a greenhouse database. You will create a variety of forms for entering plant and maintenance information.

Skills needed to complete this project:

- Creating a Single Record Form Based on a Table or Query (Skill 4.1)
- Moving and Arranging Controls (Skill 4.14)
- Creating a Multiple Items Form (Skill 4.2)
- Creating a Split Form (Skill 4.3)
- Adding Fields to a Form in Layout View (Skill 4.6)
- Creating a Form Using the Form Wizard (Skill 4.4)
- Creating a New Blank Form in Layout View (Skill 4.5)
- Resizing Controls (Skill 4.13)
- Applying a Theme (Skill 4.12)
- Modifying the Layout of a Form or Report (Skill 4.15)
- Formatting Controls (Skill 4.11)
- Adding Design Elements to Form and Report Headers (Skill 4.16)

1. Open the start file **AC2019-ChallengeYourself-4-3**.

2. If the database opens in Protected View, click the **Enable Content** button in the Message Bar at the top of the database so you can modify it.

3. Save a copy of the file to work on named:
   `[your initials] AC-ChallengeYourself-4-3`. If necessary, enable active content again.

4. Create a **Single Record form** using the *Plants* table as the record source. Save the form with the name `PlantsSingleForm` and close it.

5. Create a **Multiple Items form** using the *Plants* table as the record source. Save the form with the name `PlantsMultipleForm` and close it.

6. Create a **Split form** using the *MaintenanceLog* table as the record source. Save it with the name `MaintenanceLogSplit` and close it.

7. Use the **Form Wizard** button to create a form showing employee information in the main form with a subform showing related maintenance records.
   a. Add the following fields to the form in this order:
      From the *Employees* table: **EmployeeID**, **LastName**, **FirstName**, **WeeklyHours**
      From the *MaintenanceLog* table: **MaintenanceDate**, **Plant**, **Watered**, **Inspected**, **Pruned**
   b. Organize the form by the *Employees* table with data from the *MaintenanceLog* table as a subform.
   c. Format the subform as a **Datasheet** form.
   d. Name the main form: `EmployeeLog`
   e. Name the subform: `EmployeeLogSubform`
   f. Review the form in Form view, and then close it.

8. Create a form from scratch in Layout view.
   a. Start with a new blank form in Layout view. Save the form with the name:
      `EmployeeDetails`
   b. Add the following fields from the *Employees* table to the form in this order:
      EmployeeID, **LastName**, **FirstName**

c. Apply the **Slice** theme to the database.

d. Save and close the form.

9. Add controls to the *MaintenanceLog* form.

    a. Open the **MaintenanceLog** form in Layout view.

    b. Move the **Plant** label and bound text control above the *Employee* controls.

    c. Add the **Inspected** field immediately below the *Watered* control.

    d. Add the **Pruned** field immediately below the *Inspected* control.

    e. There is an extra row in the form layout. Delete it.

10. Format controls in the *MaintenanceLog* form.

    a. Change the **MaintenanceDate** label to: `Date`

    b. Change the font color for all the label controls to the standard color **Maroon** (the fifth color from the right in the first row of standard colors).

    c. Modify the **MaintenanceDate bound text box control** to use the **Long Date** format.

    d. Add the title `Maintenance Log` to the form header. Be sure to include a space between the words in the title.

    e. Save the form and close it.

11. Close the database and exit Access.

12. Upload and save the project file.

13. Submit project for grading.

challenge yourself 4.4

In this project you will work with a vaccines database. You will create an inventory report and reports to summarize shipments by country and by target audience. Complete the steps below to create and modify these objects.

Skills needed to complete this project:

- Creating a Basic Report Based on a Table or Query (Skill 4.7)
- Resizing Controls (Skill 4.13)
- Adding Totals to a Report (Skill 4.19)
- Formatting Controls (Skill 4.11)
- Creating a Report Using the Report Wizard (Skill 4.8)
- Creating a New Blank Report in Layout View (Skill 4.9)
- Adding Fields to a Report in Layout View (Skill 4.10)
- Moving and Arranging Controls (Skill 4.14)
- Grouping Records in a Report (Skill 4.18)
- Adding Totals to a Report (Skill 4.19)
- Adding Design Elements to Form and Report Headers (Skill 4.16)
- Adding Page Numbers to Reports (Skill 4.17)
- Applying a Theme (Skill 4.12)

1. Open the start file **AC2019-ChallengeYourself-4-4**.

2. If the database opens in Protected View, click the **Enable Content** button in the Message Bar at the top of the database so you can modify it.

3. Save a copy of the file to work on named:
`[your initials] AC-ChallengeYourself-4-4`. If necessary, enable active content again.

4. Create a basic report using the *Vaccines* table as the data source.

   a. Save the report with the name: `VaccineInventory`

   b. Adjust the width of the **VaccineID** column so it is just wide enough to display the column label (make the column narrower).

   c. Delete the page number control in the page footer section.

   d. Modify the total for the **CostPerUnit** field to calculate the average of the cost per unit for all vaccines instead of the Sum.

   e. Modify the height of the total control to .25 inches.

   f. Apply **bold** formatting to the total control.

   g. Save and close the report.

5. Use the Report Wizard to create a report summarizing the vaccine shipments to each country.

   a. Include these fields in this order:

   From the *Shipments* table: **DateShipped**, **ShipmentID**, **Quantity**

   From the *Locations* table: **Country**

   From the *Vaccines* table: **VaccineName**

   b. Organize the report data by location.

   c. Do not add any grouping.

   d. Sort the detail records by **DateShipped**.

   e. Use the **Stepped** layout and **Portrait** orientation.

   f. Name the report: `ShipmentsByLocation`

   g. Open the report in Print Preview view when the wizard is finished.

   h. Switch to Layout view.

   i. Modify the column widths so all the data are visible. Use any method you want. Ensure that the labels are completely visible.

   j. Save and close the report.

6. Create a new blank report in Layout view.

   a. Save the report with the name: `VolunteerAssignmentsByLocation`

   b. Add the following controls in this order:

   From the *Volunteers* table: **LastName**, **FirstName**, **Position**

   From the *Locations* table: **Country**

   c. Move the **Country** column so it is first in the table.

   d. Add grouping by the **Country** field.

   e. Add totals to the **Position** column to count the records in each group. Include a grand total at the end of the report in the report footer.

   f. Add **bold** formatting to the total controls. Don't forget to include the grand total in the report footer.

   g. Add a logo to the report header. Use the image file **GlobeLogo** included with the data files for this project.

   h. Add the title `Volunteer Assignments` to the report header.

   i. Add the date to the report header. Use the format similar to **11-Jun-19**. Do not include the time.

   j. Add page numbers centered in the page footer. Use the format **Page N of M**. Ensure that the page number will be included on the first page of the report.

k. Apply the **Retrospect** theme to the database.

l. Save and close the report.

7. Close the database and exit Access.

on your own 4.5

In this project, you will work with a textbook database. You will create forms to enter new purchases. You will also create reports to keep a printed record of your current textbook inventory. Save your changes often as you work through the project.

Skills needed to complete this project:

- Creating a Single Record Form Based on a Table or Query (Skill 4.1)
- Creating a Multiple Items Form (Skill 4.2)
- Creating a Split Form (Skill 4.3)
- Creating a Form Using the Form Wizard (Skill 4.4)
- Creating a New Blank Form in Layout View (Skill 4.5)
- Adding Fields to a Form in Layout View (Skill 4.6)
- Resizing Controls (Skill 4.13)
- Moving and Arranging Controls (Skill 4.14)
- Applying a Theme (Skill 4.12)
- Formatting Controls (Skill 4.11)
- Adding Design Elements to Form and Report Headers (Skill 4.16)
- Creating a Basic Report Based on a Table or Query (Skill 4.7)
- Creating a Report Using the Report Wizard (Skill 4.8)
- Creating a New Blank Report in Layout View (Skill 4.9)
- Adding Fields to a Report in Layout View (Skill 4.10)
- Grouping Records in a Report (Skill 4.18)
- Adding Totals to a Report (Skill 4.19)
- Previewing and Printing a Report (Skill 4.20)
- Controlling the Page Setup of a Report for Printing (Skill 4.21)

1. Open the textbook database you created in *Chapter 3, On Your Own 3.5* or use the start file **AC2019-OnYourOwn-4-5**.

2. If the database opens in Protected View, click the **Enable Content** button in the Message Bar at the top of the database so you can modify it.

3. Save a copy of the file to work on named: `[your initials] AC-OnYourOwn-4-5`. If necessary, enable active content again.

4. Create three forms: a Single Record form, a Multiple Items form, and a Split form. Use any table you want as the record source for each form.

5. Use the *Form Wizard* to create a form with all the fields from the *Stores* table and a subform displaying all the fields from the *Textbooks* table.

6. Create a new form in Layout view to use to enter new textbook purchases. Include any fields you want to create a form that will be easy to use. Resize controls as necessary. Apply a theme to the database. Apply formatting to the label controls so they stand out from the rest of the form. Be sure to add a form title.

7. Create a basic report using the *Textbooks* table as the record source.

8. Use the *Report Wizard* to create a report to summarize books in your textbook inventory. At a minimum, include the textbook ID, title, price, and condition. Organize the report by condition or another field of your choice. Resize and move controls as necessary. Preview how the report will look when printed and adjust the margins or orientation as you feel necessary.

9. Create another report starting from scratch in Layout view. Use this report to summarize your textbooks by topic or another field of your choice. Calculate the total value of the books in each group as well as the total value of all the books in your inventory. Resize controls as necessary. Add formatting to emphasize the labels for each group. Preview how the report will look when printed and adjust the margins or orientation as you feel necessary.

10. Close the database and exit Access.

fix it 4.6

In this project, you will work with a pet store database. The pet store employees tried to work with the database on their own, but their forms and reports need some help.

Skills needed to complete this project:

- Modifying the Layout of a Form or Report (Skill 4.15)
- Moving and Arranging Controls (Skill 4.14)
- Adding Fields to a Form in Layout View (Skill 4.6)
- Resizing Controls (Skill 4.13)
- Adding Design Elements to Form and Report Headers (Skill 4.16)
- Creating a Split Form (Skill 4.3)
- Adding Fields to a Report in Layout View (Skill 4.10)
- Grouping Records in a Report (Skill 4.18)
- Adding Totals to a Report (Skill 4.19)
- Formatting Controls (Skill 4.11)
- Adding Page Numbers to Reports (Skill 4.17)
- Previewing and Printing a Report (Skill 4.20)
- Controlling the Page Setup of a Report for Printing (Skill 4.21)
- Applying a Theme (Skill 4.12)

1. Open the start file **AC2019-FixIt-4-6**.

2. If the database opens in Protected View, click the **Enable Content** button in the Message Bar at the top of the database so you can modify it.

3. Save a copy of the file to work on named: **[your initials] AC-FixIt-4-6**. If necessary, enable active content again.

4. Fix the *Customers* form as follows:

    a. Add two columns to the form layout.

    b. Move the **LastName** controls to the right of the *FirstName* controls.

    c. Move the **ZipCode** controls to the right of the *City* controls.

    d. Move the **Phone** controls up so they are placed below the *City* controls.

e. Add the **Newsletter** field to the form, right below the *Phone* control.

f. Delete any empty rows or columns from the form layout.

g. The form is missing the store logo. Use the image file **PetsLogo** located with the data files for this project.

h. Save and close the form.

5. The store owner would like a new form for the *Pets* table—one that shows both a datasheet and a single record in one screen. Create this form for her. Name the form: NewPets

6. Fix the *PetsReport* as follows:

a. The *PetID* field is missing from this report. Add it to the report between the *Animal Type* and *Breed* columns.

b. The report should be grouped by animal type with an average age for each group.

c. Adjust the height of the total controls as necessary. Don't forget the grand total at the bottom of the report.

d. Apply the **Comma** format to the total controls. Don't forget the grand total at the bottom of the report.

e. All adoption fees should be formatted using the **Currency** format.

f. The report is missing the store logo. Use the image file **PetsLogo** located with the data files for this project.

g. The report is also missing the title: Pet Inventory

h. Preview the report to make sure it will fit on no more than one page wide. If necessary, make the **MainColor** column narrow enough that the report will fit on one page wide without cutting off the information in the report. If necessary, switch to Design view and adjust the report width to remove the extra space.

i. The report is missing the page numbers. The page number should be centered in the page footer, and it should use the format **Page N**.

j. Save your changes.

7. The store owner would like all forms and reports to use the **Wisp** theme. Apply the theme to the database. Save the changes as necessary.

8. Close any open database objects, close the database, and exit Access.

powerpoint 365

chapter 1

Getting Started with PowerPoint

In this chapter, you will learn the following skills:

❱ Use the different view options

❱ Navigate between slides

❱ Create a new presentation from a template

❱ Add slides to the presentation

❱ Change the layout of slides

❱ Add content to slides

❱ Format text

❱ Change the layout of text

❱ Find and replace text

Skill **1.1** Introduction to PowerPoint

Skill **1.2** Designing Presentations

Skill **1.3** Understanding Views

Skill **1.4** Working with Thumbnails

Skill **1.5** Creating a New Presentation Using a Template

Skill **1.6** Adding Slides to Presentations

Skill **1.7** Changing Slide Layouts

Skill **1.8** Adding Text to Slides

Skill **1.9** Changing the Size of a Placeholder

Skill **1.10** Applying Character Effects

Skill **1.11** Changing Fonts and Font Sizes

Skill **1.12** Changing the Color of Text

Skill **1.13** Using Format Painter

Skill **1.14** Clearing Formatting

Skill **1.15** Changing Line Spacing

Skill **1.16** Aligning Text

Skill **1.17** Adding Columns to Placeholders

Skill **1.18** Using Find

Skill **1.19** Using Replace

Skill **1.20** Using Undo and Redo

skills

introduction

This chapter provides you with the basic skills necessary to navigate through and edit a basic PowerPoint presentation. The first step is to become familiar with the different views and how to navigate between and work with slides in the Normal view. After you become familiar with PowerPoint's user interface, you will learn how to create a new presentation using one of Microsoft's templates. Once you have the template framework of your presentation, you will add slides and modify the slides in the presentation. Next, you'll learn basic formatting techniques for changing the look of text in a presentation. You will also learn how to find and replace text in a presentation and undo and redo actions.

Skill 1.1 Introduction to PowerPoint

Whether used for a marketing campaign or as a teaching tool, a presentation incorporating graphics, animation, sound, and video is much more compelling than paper handouts or a "talking head" lecture. Microsoft Office PowerPoint enables you to create robust multimedia presentations. A **presentation** is made up of a series of **slides**. Each slide contains content, including text, graphics, audio, and video. You can then manipulate that content by adding transitions, animations, and graphic effects. Before diving in and creating a presentation, you should familiarize yourself with some of PowerPoint's basic features.

When you first start PowerPoint, the presentation is shown in the **working space**, or *Normal* view. You will notice the working space is divided into three areas:

❭ **Thumbnails pane**—Displays thumbnails of the slides in the presentation and provides a quick way to navigate between slides.

❭ **Slide pane**—Area where you can modify slides, including adding and formatting text, images, SmartArt, tables, charts, and media.

❭ **Notes pane**—Area where you can type notes about the current slide displayed in the *Slide* pane. The text you type in the *Notes* pane will not appear to your audience when you play your presentation.

FIGURE PP 1.1

A **placeholder** is a container on a slide that holds text or other content, such as a table, chart, or image. When you click in a placeholder, it becomes active and is outlined with a dotted line. You can then work with the individual elements of the placeholder. When you click the edge of the placeholder, the entire placeholder is selected, and it appears with a solid line around it. When the entire placeholder is selected, any formatting changes you make will affect all the elements in the placeholder. Each slide contains placeholders for you to add content to, including:

> **Title**—Use to display the title of the presentation or the title for the slide.

> **Subtitle**—Use to display the subtitle of the presentation.

FIGURE PP 1.2

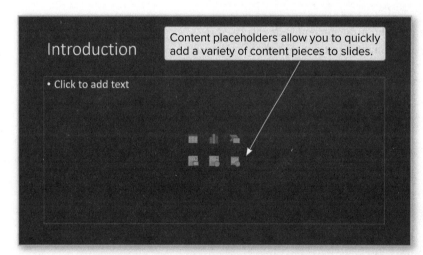

FIGURE PP 1.3

> **Text**—Use to add text to a slide. Be sure to keep your points brief and use bulleted lists to emphasize text.

> **Tables**—Organize information in a table to give your audience a clear picture of your data.

> **Charts**—Use charts to create a visual display of your information.

> **SmartArt**—Use to display lists in a more graphic format, including processes, cycles, hierarchical diagrams, and matrices.

> **Pictures**—Add your own photographs or other images to slides.

> **Online Pictures**—Add illustrations or photographs from online resources, such as *Bing* search or your *OneDrive*.

> **Video**—Add video files from a file or from an online resource.

Presentations can be simple or complex, but they all follow some basic steps:

Plan Your Presentation	Decide what you want to include and in what order you want to present the information.
Create Your Slides	You can create slides from sophisticated templates, or start with a blank slide and create your own design.
Add Your Content	Be sure to keep your message focused and your content brief.
Format Your Content	Use formatting effects, transitions, and animation effects to add sizzle to your presentation.
Review and Rehearse	Always check your slides for errors.
Practice	Practicing your presentation will give you confidence when it comes time to give it in front of an audience.

tips & tricks

You do not need to be a graphic artist to create beautiful presentations that will impress your audience. PowerPoint comes with a number of pre-built templates, effects, and animations that you can quickly apply to content to make it more engaging for your viewers.

tell me more

〉 In past versions of PowerPoint, the default aspect ratio for slides was 4:3. In PowerPoint 2013, Microsoft changed the default aspect ratio to widescreen 16:9. A 4:3 slide has a squarer appearance, while a 16:9 slide is more rectangular in shape with the width being much longer than the height.

〉 In PowerPoint 2010 and earlier versions, the *Notes* pane was displayed by default. In PowerPoint 2013, this changed so the *Notes* pane is hidden by default. To display the *Notes* pane, click the *Notes* button at the bottom of the PowerPoint window.

let me try

Open the student data file **pp1-01-SpaServices** and try this skill on your own:

1. Click the part of the PowerPoint interface where you would add content to slides.

2. Click the part of the PowerPoint interface that shows a thumbnail of each slide in the presentation.

3. If you will be moving on to the next skill in this chapter, leave the presentation open to continue working. If not, close the file.

Skill 1.2 Designing Presentations

In this book, you will learn the skills needed to create PowerPoint presentations. You will learn to create slides, add text and images, animate objects, and add transitions to slides. You also will learn how to run a presentation using PowerPoint's built-in navigation and presentation tools.

Before you learn the mechanics of creating and giving a presentation, some basic design principles will help you create more effective PowerPoint presentations:

Balance. Distribute the elements on your slides in a balanced layout. Don't crowd the elements to one side or the other.	
Flow. Elements on your slides should guide your audience's eyes from one point to another in a natural progression. Think of reading a line of text on the page. Your eye is naturally led from one word to the next.	
Distinction. If all elements on your slides are the same size, nothing will stand out to your audience. Stress important elements by making them slightly larger than other elements.	
Recurrence. Repeat design elements (such as backgrounds, slide title styles, and bullet styles) throughout a presentation to give your presentation a unified and professional look.	

In addition to these design principles, there are some basic dos and don'ts to follow when designing presentations:

	DO	DON'T
Color choice	Use PowerPoint's built-in color themes.	Use too many colors or colors that do not work well together.
Text amount	Use short bullet points.	Use long paragraphs of text.
Text size	Use large fonts.	Use 10 pt. or 11 pt. fonts.
Animation	Animate important elements for emphasis.	Animate every element on a slide.
Slides	Keep the number of slides to a minimum (10 to 20 slides at the most).	Create a slide for every minor point in the presentation.
Presentation	Make unrehearsed comments	Read your slides word for word.

tips & tricks

Use the presentation templates available from *Office.com* as a starting point for your presentations. Many of these templates come with built-in styles and slides that incorporate the design principles discussed here. To learn more about PowerPoint templates, see the skill *Creating a New Presentation Using a Template* later in this chapter.

Skill 1.3 Understanding Views

PowerPoint has four main ways to view your presentation: Normal view, Slide Sorter view, Reading view, and Slide Show view. **Normal view** is the view in which you will typically create and edit your content. **Slide Sorter view** displays thumbnail pictures of the slides in your presentation and is useful in rearranging the order of the slides. **Reading view** allows you to run your presentation within the PowerPoint application window. **Slide Show view** displays your slides full screen and allows you to see your presentation the way your audience will see it.

The easiest way to switch between views is to click one of the view buttons located at the right side of the status bar, near the zoom slider.

- Click the **Normal** view button to add or edit content.
- Click the **Slide Sorter** view button to view thumbnails of your presentation.
- Click the **Reading** view button to view your presentation within the current PowerPoint window.
- Click the **Slide Show** view button to view your presentation at full screen as your audience will. To exit Slide Show view, press the (Esc) key on the keyboard.

Normal View

FIGURE PP 1.4

Slide Sorter View

FIGURE PP 1.5

Reading View

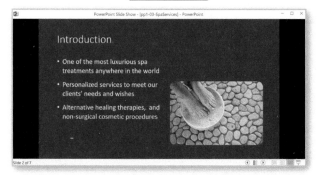

FIGURE PP 1.6

Slide Show View

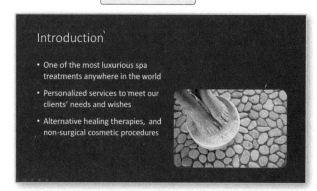

FIGURE PP 1.7

tips & tricks

When you first open a presentation, PowerPoint will display your slides so they fit in the *Slide* pane. The **zoom slider** (located at the bottom of the PowerPoint window) allows you to change how your slides are displayed in the *Slide* pane. Use the zoom slider to magnify your slides to check alignment of text and graphics or to see how your slides will appear when you play your presentation.

tell me **more**

In addition to the four main views, PowerPoint also includes the following:

❭ **Notes Page view**—Allows you to add notes for each slide in your presentation. Each slide appears on its own screen with a large text area for your notes about the slide. The text you type in Notes Page view will not appear when you are playing your presentation. However, you can choose to print your notes along with your slides to hand out to your audience.

❭ **Master views**—Include Slide Master view, Handout Master view, and Notes Master view. The master views contain universal settings for the presentation. If you want to make changes that will affect the entire presentation, you should use a master view.

another **method**

❭ To switch views, you can also click the **View** tab and click a view button in the *Presentation Views* group.

❭ To switch to Slide Show view, you can also click the **Slide Show** tab and click a button in the *Start Slide Show* group.

let me **try**

If you do not have the data file from the first skill open, open the student data file **pp1-03-SpaServices** and try this skill on your own:

1. Switch to **Slide Sorter** view.
2. Switch to **Reading** view.
3. Switch to **Slide Show** view.
4. Switch to **Normal** view.
5. If you will be moving on to the next skill in this chapter, leave the presentation open to continue working. If not, close the file.

Skill 1.4 Working with Thumbnails

The *Thumbnails* pane displays thumbnails of all the slides in a presentation. Use the pane to quickly navigate between slides, rearrange the slide order, and review and edit content. To make changes to a specific slide, it must first be displayed in the *Slide* pane.

To navigate to a slide using the *Thumbnails* pane:

1. Click the thumbnail of the slide you want to display.

2. The slide appears in the *Slide* pane ready for editing.

FIGURE PP 1.8

tell me **more**

Each thumbnail in the pane has a number next to it. This number is the slide's place in the presentation. When you rearrange slides, PowerPoint automatically renumbers the slides for you. If the slide number appears faded with a slash through it, this indicates that the slide is in a hidden state and will not display in the presentation when played normally. In addition, if a star appears next to the slide number, this indicates that either a transition or an animation has been applied to the slide.

another **method**

To navigate between slides one slide at a time, you can also:

❭ Click the **Next Slide** and **Previous Slide** buttons on the vertical scroll bar in the *Slide* pane.

❭ Click a slide in the *Thumbnails* pane and press the up and down arrow keys on the keyboard.

let me **try**

If you do not have the data file from the previous skill open, open the student data file **pp1-04-SpaServices** and try this skill on your own:

1. Using the *Thumbnails* pane, navigate to **Slide 4**.

2. Using the *Thumbnails* pane, navigate back to **Slide 1**.

3. Save the file as directed by your instructor and close it.

Skill 1.5 Creating a New Presentation Using a Template

A **template** is a file with predefined settings that you can use as a pattern to create a new presentation of your own. Using a template makes creating a fully formatted and designed new presentation easy, saving you time and effort. There are templates available for sales presentations, product presentations, academic presentations, personal presentations, and almost any other type of presentation you can imagine.

To create a new file from a template:

1. Click the **File** tab to open Backstage view.

2. Click **New**. PowerPoint includes a variety of templates that are copied to your computer when you install the application. These templates are always available from the *New* page. Additional templates that you download are also displayed on the *New* page, so your screen may look different than the one in Figure PP 1.9.

3. Click each template preview picture for a brief description of the template.

4. When you find the template you want to use, click a color option (if available) and click the **Create** button.

5. A new presentation opens, prepopulated with all of the template elements.

FIGURE PP 1.9

FIGURE PP 1.10

powerpoint 365   chapter 1 Getting Started with PowerPoint

You can search for more presentation templates online. (You must have an active Internet connection.)

1. Near the top of the *New* page, in the *Search for online templates and themes* box, type a keyword or phrase that describes the template you want.

2. Click the **Start searching** button (the magnifying glass image at the end of the *Search for online templates and themes* box).

3. The search results display previews of the templates that match the keyword or phrase you entered. To further narrow the results, click one of the categories listed in the *Categories* pane at the right side of the window. Notice that each category lists the number of templates available.

4. When you find the template you want, click it to display the larger preview with detailed information about the template, and then click **Create**.

FIGURE PP 1.11

tell me **more**

Some PowerPoint templates are design templates and contain a single slide with all the design elements included. Use one of these templates if you have planned out the content of your presentation. If you know the topic of your presentation but have not outlined the content, there are other presentations that include both the design elements and multiple slides for you to add your content.

let me **try**

Try this skill on your own:

1. Create a new presentation based on the **Berlin** template.

2. Create the presentation using the **blue theme**.

3. Search for online templates using the keywords `project plan`

4. Create the presentation from the **Business project planning overview presentation** template (the one highlighted in Figure PP 1.11). If you do not see this template, select a different option from your results.

5. Save both files as directed by your instructor and close them.

Skill 1.6 Adding Slides to Presentations

A presentation consists of several slides filled with text and graphics. If you start with a template, your presentation may include some slides ready to add content. But what if you need to add more information to your presentation? How do you add more slides? PowerPoint makes it easy.

To add a slide to a presentation:

1. On the *Home* tab, in the *Slides* group, click the **New Slide** button arrow.
2. Select a slide layout from the *New Slide* gallery.
3. Add your content to the slide.
4. Continue adding and modifying slides until your presentation is complete.

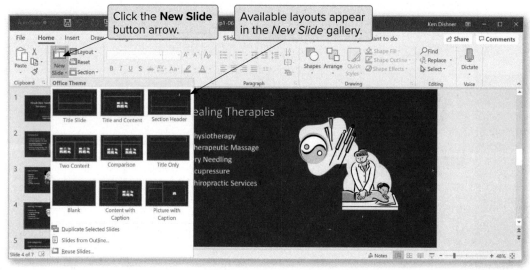

FIGURE PP 1.12

tips & tricks

When you add slides through the *New Slide* gallery, each slide layout includes design elements from the presentation's theme. This helps create a consistent look and feel for the entire presentation. If you switch themes, the look of the new slide layouts will change to match that theme.

another method

To add a slide to a presentation, you can also:

❯ Click the top half of the **New Slide** button.

❯ Press Ctrl + M on the keyboard.

NOTE: When you use either of these methods, the new slide added to the presentation will use the same layout as the last slide you added.

tell me more

There are a number of slide layouts for you to choose from, including title only slides, blank slides, title and content slides, comparison slides, picture with caption slides, and content with caption slides.

let me try

Open the student data file **pp1-06-SpaServices** and try this skill on your own:

1. Navigate to **Slide 4**.
2. Add a slide to the presentation that uses the **Comparison** layout.
3. If you will be moving on to the next skill in this chapter, leave the presentation open to continue working. If not, save the file as directed by your instructor and close it.

Skill 1.7 Changing Slide Layouts

After you have created your presentation, you can modify the information displayed on an individual slide. If you add or delete elements, you may want to change the **slide layout** to accommodate the new content. PowerPoint comes with a number of slide layouts for you to use. Choose the one that best suits the content for each slide.

To change the slide layout:

1. Select the slide you want to change.
2. On the *Home* tab, in the *Slides* group, click the **Slide Layout** button.
3. Select a slide layout from the *Slide Layout* gallery.

FIGURE PP 1.13

tips & tricks

Once you have selected a new slide layout, you can move and resize placeholders to fit your content. If you have made a number of changes and decide you want to undo your changes, you can revert the slide to its original design. Click the **Reset** button on the *Home* tab in the *Slides* group to return the slide layout to its default layout.

another method

To change the layout of a slide, you can also right-click any area of the *Slide* pane without a placeholder, point to *Layout*, and select a slide layout.

let me try

If you do not have the data file from the previous skill open, open the student data file **pp1-07-SpaServices** and try this skill on your own:

1. Change the layout of **Slide 5** to use the **Title and Content** layout.
2. If you will be moving on to the next skill in this chapter, leave the presentation open to continue working. If not, save the file as directed by your instructor and close it.

Skill 1.8 Adding Text to Slides

A good presentation consists of a balance of text and graphics. It is important to keep text brief. Short, clear points convey your message to your audience better than rambling paragraphs of text. You can add text to slides by using **text placeholders** and **text boxes**. Text placeholders are predefined areas in slide layouts where you enter text. Text boxes are boxes you add to the slide layout to enter text where you want it.

To add text to a text placeholder, click inside the text placeholder and type the text you want to add. Click outside the placeholder to deselect it.

FIGURE PP 1.14

To edit text in a text placeholder:

1. Click the placeholder with the text you want to change.
2. Click and drag across the text to select it.
3. Type the new text for the placeholder.
4. Click outside the placeholder to deselect it.

To add a text box:

1. Click the **Insert** tab.
2. In the *Text* group, click the **Text Box** button.
3. Click on the slide where you want the text to appear.
4. Type your text.
5. Click outside the text box to deselect it.

FIGURE PP 1.15

tell me **more**

Text placeholders are a part of the slide layout and cannot be added directly to a slide. You can add text placeholders to slide layouts only in Slide Master view. To add a text placeholder, first switch to Slide Master view. On the *Slide Master* tab, click the **Insert Placeholder** button and select **Text**. As you can see from the *Insert Placeholder* menu, you can add placeholders for pictures, charts, tables, SmartArt, media, and online images, as well as text.

let me **try**

If you do not have the data file from the previous skill open, open the student data file **pp1-08-SpaServices** and try this skill on your own:

1. If necessary, navigate to **Slide 5,** and add the text **Cosmetic Procedures** to the slide title placeholder at the top of the slide.
2. Add the following bulleted list to the content placeholder:
   - **Laser Spot Removal**
   - **Wrinkle Reduction Therapies**
   - **Laser Hair Removal**
   - **Facial Plumping Therapies**
3. Navigate to **Slide 2** and add a **text box** to the right of the word **world**.
4. Type the text **Try one of our personalized services** in the text box. You may notice that the text is hard to read. You will adjust the look of this text later in the chapter.
5. If you will be moving on to the next skill in this chapter, leave the presentation open to continue working. If not, save the file as directed by your instructor and close it.

Skill 1.9 Changing the Size of a Placeholder

Placeholders can hold text, pictures, charts, tables, or other content. You may find that you want to resize the placeholder to improve the layout of the slide. When you resize a placeholder, you resize the content it contains. You can change the size of placeholders by entering values or by dragging one of the resize handles.

To resize a placeholder by manually entering values:

1. Click in the placeholder you want to resize.
2. Click the **Drawing Tools Format** tab.
3. In the *Size* group, type a value in the **Width** and/or **Height** box to resize the placeholder.

To change the size of a placeholder by dragging:

1. Point to one of the resize handles on the placeholder.
2. When the mouse changes to the resize cursor, click and drag the mouse:
    ❭ Drag the mouse toward the center of the placeholder to make it smaller.
    ❭ Drag the mouse away from the center of the placeholder to make it larger.
3. When the placeholder is the size you want, release the mouse button.

FIGURE PP 1.16

tips & tricks

When using one of the corner resize handles, press ⬆ Shift on the keyboard as you drag the mouse to constrain the aspect ratio of the image and prevent the image from becoming distorted.

another method

To manually resize a placeholder, you can also click the up and down arrows on the right side of the *Width* and *Height* boxes.

let me try

If you do not have the data file from the previous skill open, open the student data file **pp1-09-SpaServices** and try this skill on your own:

1. On **Slide 2**, resize the placeholder with the bulleted list so it is **4.6"** tall and **5.8"** wide.
2. If you will be moving on to the next skill in this chapter, leave the presentation open to continue working. If not, save the file as directed by your instructor and close it.

Skill 1.10 Applying Character Effects

When you add text to a slide, it is formatted according to the slide design. But what if you want the text to look different from the preset design? You can call attention to text in your presentation by using the bold, italic, underline, strikethrough, or shadow **character effects**. Remember, these effects are used to emphasize important text and should be used sparingly.

To add character effects to your text, on the *Home* tab, in the *Font* group:

COMMAND	KEYBOARD SHORTCUT	DESCRIPTION
Bold	Ctrl + B	**Gives the text a heavy appearance**
Italic	Ctrl + I	*Slants the text to the right*
Underline	Ctrl + U	<u>Draws a line under the text</u>
Text Shadow	NA	Applies a simple shadow to the text
Strikethrough	NA	~~Draws a line through the center of the text~~

When text has the bold, italic, underline, shadow, or strikethrough effect applied to it, the button highlights on the Ribbon. To remove the effect, click the highlighted button.

FIGURE PP 1.17

tips & tricks

Character spacing refers to the amount of horizontal space that appears between characters when you type. In some cases, you will want to make the characters closer together to fit better on-screen. In other cases, you will want to make the characters farther apart for a visual effect. To change the spacing of the characters in text, in the *Font* group, click the **Character Spacing** button and select an option.

another **method**

❯ You can also apply character effects through the *Font* dialog. To open the *Font* dialog, on the *Home* tab, in the *Font* group, click the dialog launcher.

❯ To apply the bold, italic, or underline effect, you can also:

1. Right-click the text you want to change.

2. Click the **Bold**, **Italic**, or **Underline** button on the Mini toolbar.

let me **try**

If you do not have the data file from the previous skill open, open the student data file **pp1-10-SpaServices** and try this skill on your own:

1. On **Slide 2**, select the text **Try one of our personalized services**.

2. Apply the **Bold** formatting to the text.

3. Apply the **Italic** formatting to the text.

4. Apply the **Underline** formatting to the text.

5. Apply the **Shadow** formatting to the text.

6. If you will be moving on to the next skill in this chapter, leave the presentation open to continue working. If not, save the file as directed by your instructor and close it.

from the perspective of . . .

TEACHER

Presentations enable me to provide handouts for my students, quickly cover lecture material, and give a professional, visual experience to keep their attention. I always start with one of PowerPoint's templates and then fill in my own content. I follow the basic steps for creating a presentation and am always aware of the four basic design principles. I use notes in my slides to help me remember those important points that aren't part of my slide content.

Comstock/SuperStock

Skill 1.11 Changing Fonts and Font Sizes

A **font**, or typeface, refers to a set of characters of a certain design. The font is the shape of the character or number as it appears on-screen. PowerPoint offers many fonts. **Serif fonts**, such as Cambria and Times New Roman, have an embellishment at the end of each stroke. **Sans serif fonts**, such as Calibri and Arial, do not have an embellishment at the end of each stroke.

To change the font:

1. Select the text to be changed.
2. On the *Home* tab, in the *Font* group, click the arrow next to the **Font** box.
3. Scroll the list to find the new font.
4. Click the font name.

FIGURE PP 1.18

Fonts are measured in **points**, abbreviated "pt." On the printed page, 72 points equal one inch. Different text sizes are used for different slide elements, such as titles, subtitles, and text placeholders.

To change the size of the text:

1. Select the text to be changed.
2. On the *Home* tab, in the *Font* group, click the arrow next to the **Font Size** box.
3. Scroll the list to find the new font size.
4. Click the size you want.

FIGURE PP 1.19

tips & tricks

> When you add text to placeholders, PowerPoint will automatically resize the text to fit within the placeholder. It is a good idea to review the size of similar elements (such as slide titles) to ensure they are the same size.

> If you want to change all the text in a placeholder, click the edge of the placeholder to select it (it will appear with a solid line around it). When you select a new font or font size, all the text in the placeholder will change.

tell me more

When designing a presentation, it is good practice to limit the number of fonts. Using one font for slide titles and a second font for slide text is a good rule to follow. Using multiple fonts in one presentation can be distracting to your audience.

another method

> To change the font, right-click the text, click the arrow next to the **Font** box on the Mini toolbar, and select an option.

> To change the font size, right-click the text, click the arrow next to the **Font Size** box on the Mini toolbar, and select an option.

let me try

If you do not have the data file from the previous skill open, open the student data file **pp1-11-SpaServices** and try this skill on your own:

1. On **Slide 2**, verify the text **Try one of our personalized services** is selected.
2. Change the font to **Candara**.
3. Change the font size to **24**.
4. If you will be moving on to the next skill in this chapter, leave the presentation open to continue working. If not, save the file as directed by your instructor and close it.

skill 1.11   Changing Fonts and Font Sizes

Skill 1.12 Changing the Color of Text

The presentation's theme controls the color of the various slide elements. But what if you want a particular word to stand out on a slide? Adding color to text in your presentation adds emphasis to certain words and helps design elements stand out for your audience. It is important to be selective when adding color to text in your presentation. Using too many colors can often be distracting to your audience, and your message can be lost.

To change the color of the text:

1. Select the text to be changed.
2. On the *Home* tab, in the *Font* group, click the arrow next to the **Font Color** button.
3. Click the color you want.

FIGURE PP 1.20

tips & tricks

) When you change the color of text, the *Font Color* button changes to the color you selected. Click the **Font Color** button to quickly apply the same color to other text in the presentation.

) If you want to change text to a color that appears on your slide, click the **Eyedropper** at the bottom of the palette. The cursor changes to the shape of an eyedropper. Click a color on the slide to change the font color to that color.

tell me **more**

Theme colors are a group of predefined colors that work well together in a document. When you apply a theme in PowerPoint, you can then choose from a number of color variants for applying to slide elements. When you change the color variants in a presentation, the color palette changes and displays only colors that are part of the theme colors.

another **method**

To change the color of text, you can also right-click the text, click the arrow next to the **Font Color** button on the Mini toolbar, and select an option.

let me **try**

If you do not have the data file from the previous skill open, open the student data file **pp1-12-SpaServices** and try this skill on your own:

1. On **Slide 2**, verify the text **Try one of our personalized services** is selected.
2. Change the font color to **Light Gray, Background 2**. It is the third option in the first row under *Theme Colors*.
3. If you will be moving on to the next skill in this chapter, leave the presentation open to continue working. If not, save the file as directed by your instructor and close it.

Skill 1.13 Using Format Painter

PowerPoint gives you the ability to apply complex formatting to objects. If you want to use the same formatting for more than one object, you could select the second object and reapply all the effects to create the final result, or you could use **Format Painter** to copy the formatting from one object to another.

To use *Format Painter*:

1. Select the object that has the formatting you want to copy.
2. On the *Home* tab, in the *Clipboard* group, click the **Format Painter** button.
3. Click the object that you want to apply the formatting to.
4. The formats are automatically applied to the second object.

If you want to apply the formats more than once, double-click the **Format Painter** button when you select it. It will stay on until you click the **Format Painter** button again or press (Esc) to deselect it.

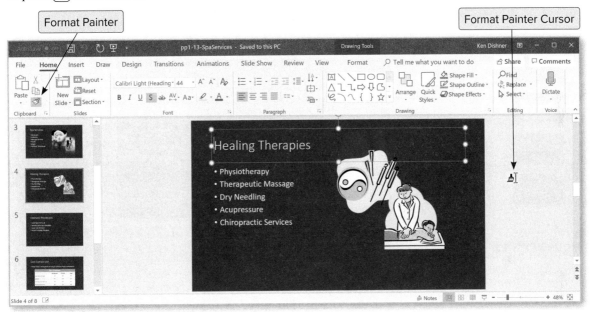

FIGURE PP 1.21

tips & tricks

If you are copying formatting from a text box, click in the text (so the text box appears with a dashed line around it) to copy and paste the formatting of just the text. Click the edge of the text box (so it appears with a solid line around it) to copy and paste the formatting of the entire text box.

another **method**

To activate *Format Painter*, you can also right-click the text with formatting you want to copy and click the **Format Painter** button on the Mini toolbar. If you are copying the formatting on a picture, you will not see the Mini toolbar.

let me **try**

If you do not have the data file from the previous skill open, open the student data file **pp1-13-SpaServices** and try this skill on your own:

1. Navigate to **Slide 4** and select the text **Healing Therapies**.
2. Use the **Format Painter** to copy the formatting of the text.
3. Navigate to **Slide 5** and paste the copied formatting to the text **Cosmetic Procedures**.
4. If you will be moving on to the next skill in this chapter, leave the presentation open to continue working. If not, save the file as directed by your instructor and close it.

Skill 1.14 Clearing Formatting

After you have applied a number of character formats and effects to text, you may find that you want to return your text to its original formatting. You could perform multiple Undo commands on the text, or you could use the **Clear All Formatting** command. The *Clear All Formatting* command removes any formatting that has been applied to text, including character formatting, text effects, and styles, and leaves only plain text.

To remove formatting from text:

1. Select the text you want to remove the formatting from.

2. On the *Home* tab, in the *Font* group, click the **Clear All Formatting** button.

FIGURE PP 1.22

tips & tricks

If you clear the formatting from text and then decide that you want to keep the formatting that was removed, you can use the *Undo* command to apply the previous formatting to the text.

let me try

If you do not have the data file from the previous skill open, open the student data file **pp1-14-SpaServices** and try this skill on your own:

1. On **Slide 8** select the text **http://www.hhspa.com**.

2. Clear all the formatting from the text.

3. If you will be moving on to the next skill in this chapter, leave the presentation open to continue working. If not, save the file as directed by your instructor and close it.

Skill 1.15 Changing Line Spacing

Line spacing is the white space between lines of text. The default line spacing in Microsoft PowerPoint is 0.9 line. This line spacing is a good choice to use for the items on a slide. It is a little tighter vertically than single spacing, giving you more room for text in a placeholder without crowding the text. Other commonly used spacing options include single spacing, double spacing, and 1.5 spacing. When you increase the line spacing, you are adding more white space between the items on the slide.

To change line spacing:

1. Select the text you want to change.
2. On the *Home* tab, in the *Paragraph* group, click the arrow next to the **Line Spacing** button.
3. Select the number of the spacing you want.

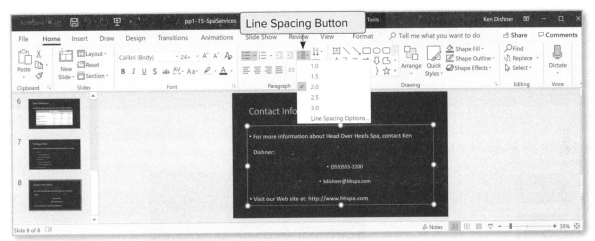

FIGURE PP 1.23

tips & tricks

You can control how much spacing appears before and after text through the *Paragraph* dialog:

1. Click the **Line Spacing** button and select **Line Spacing Options...**
2. In the *Paragraph* dialog, in the *Spacing* section, click the **Before** and **After** arrows to adjust the spacing between text.

another method

You can also change line spacing from the *Paragraph* dialog:

1. Click the **Line Spacing** button and select **Line Spacing Options...**
2. In the *Paragraph* dialog, in the *Spacing* section, click the **Line Spacing** arrow and select an option.

let me try

If you do not have the data file from the previous skill open, open the student data file **pp1-15-SpaServices** and try this skill on your own:

1. Navigate to **Slide 8** and select the text in the content placeholder.
2. Change the line spacing to **1.5**.
3. If you will be moving on to the next skill in this chapter, leave the presentation open to continue working. If not, save the file as directed by your instructor and close it.

Skill 1.16 Aligning Text

Text alignment refers to how text is lined up with regard to the left and right edges of a slide.

> **Left alignment** aligns the text on the left side, leaving the right side ragged.
>
> **Center alignment** centers each line of text relative to the margins.
>
> **Right alignment** aligns the text on the right side, leaving the left side ragged.
>
> **Justified alignment** evenly spaces the words, aligning the text on the right and left sides of the printed page.

To change the alignment of text:

1. Click in the text you want to change.
2. On the *Home* tab, in the *Paragraph* group, click an **alignment** button.

FIGURE PP 1.24

Vertical alignment refers to how text is aligned with regard to the top and bottom of the placeholder. **Top alignment** places the text at the top of the placeholder. **Middle alignment** centers the text vertically in the placeholder. **Bottom alignment** places the text at the bottom of the placeholder.

To change the vertical alignment of text:

1. Click in the text you want to change.
2. On the *Home* tab, in the *Paragraph* group, click the **Align Text** button and select an option: **Top**, **Middle**, or **Bottom**.

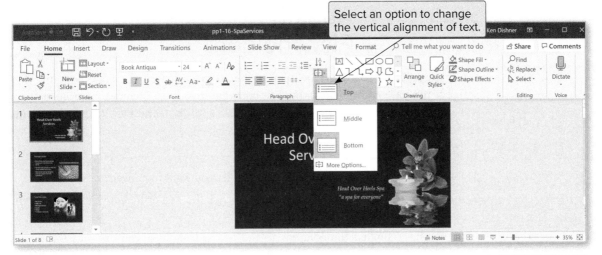

FIGURE PP 1.25

tips & tricks

When creating presentations, it is important to use consistent text alignment on every slide. For example, if a slide's title area is center-aligned, then every title throughout the presentation should also be center-aligned.

tell me **more**

Bulleted and numbered lists are typically left-aligned. When you apply left alignment to a list, the bullets and numbers align vertically, giving your slide a precise, organized appearance.

another **method**

To align text, you can also use the following keyboard shortcuts:

❯ Align Left: Ctrl + L

❯ Center: Ctrl + E

❯ Align Right: Ctrl + R

❯ Justify: Ctrl + J

To left-align, center-align, or right-align text, you can right-click the text and click an alignment button on the Mini toolbar.

let me **try**

If you do not have the data file from the previous skill open, open the student data file **pp1-16-SpaServices** and try this skill on your own:

1. On **Slide 8**, verify the text in the content placeholder is selected.

2. Change the vertical alignment of the text to be **middle-aligned**.

3. On **Slide 8**, select the phone number and the email address.

4. Change the horizontal alignment of the text so it aligned along the **left side** of the placeholder.

5. Navigate to **Slide 1** and select the text **Head Over Heels Spa "a spa for everyone"**.

6. Change the alignment on the text so it is **center-aligned** and aligned along the **top** of the placeholder.

7. If you will be moving on to the next skill in this chapter, leave the presentation open to continue working. If not, save the file as directed by your instructor and close it.

Skill 1.17 Adding Columns to Placeholders

When you add a list to a slide, the items in the list are displayed in a single column. This is fine if you have a few items in the list, but what if your list includes more items than will easily fit in a single vertical column? You can apply **columns** to text, giving you the flexibility of displaying lists across a slide.

To apply columns to text:

1. Select the text placeholder containing the list you want to convert.
2. On the *Home* tab, in the *Paragraph* group, click the **Add or Remove Columns** button and select an option.

After you have applied the columns to the text placeholder, you can resize the text placeholder, making it wider or shorter to even out the number of items in each column.

FIGURE PP 1.26

tips & tricks

In the *Columns* dialog, you can increase the number of columns to more than three. You can also control the spacing between the columns of text on the slide. To open the *Columns* dialog, click the **Add or Remove Columns** button and select **More Columns...**

let me try

If you do not have the data file from the previous skill open, open the student data file **pp1-17-SpaServices** and try this skill on your own:

1. Navigate to **Slide 7**.
2. Click in the placeholder with the bulleted list.
3. Change the text to display in **three columns**.
4. If you will be moving on to the next skill in this chapter, leave the presentation open to continue working. If not, save the file as directed by your instructor and close it.

Skill 1.18 Using Find

The **Find** command in PowerPoint allows you to locate specific instances of text in your presentation. With the *Find* command, you can find instances of a word or phrase throughout a presentation.

To find a word or phrase in a presentation:

1. On the *Home* tab, in the *Editing* group, click the **Find** button.

2. Type the word or phrase you want to find in the *Find what* box.

3. Click **Find Next** to find the first instance of the word or phrase.

4. Click **Find Next** again to find the next instance.

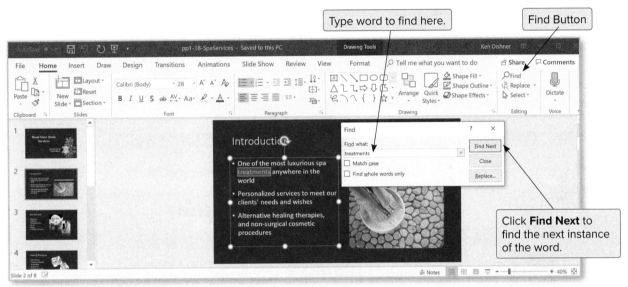

FIGURE PP 1.27

tips & tricks

To find an exact match for how a word is capitalized, select the **Match case** check box.

another **method**

To open the *Find* dialog, you can also press (Ctrl) + (F) on the keyboard.

let me **try**

If you do not have the data file from the previous skill open, open the student data file **pp1-18-SpaServices** and try this skill on your own:

1. Navigate to **Slide 1**.

2. Use the **Find** command to find the first instance of the word **treatments** in the presentation.

3. Find the next instance of the word **treatments** in the presentation.

4. Close the dialog.

5. If you will be moving on to the next skill in this chapter, leave the presentation open to continue working. If not, close the file.

Skill 1.19 Using Replace

The **Replace** command allows you to locate specific instances of text in your presentation and replace them with different text. With the *Replace* command, you can replace words or phrases one instance at a time. With the **Replace All** command, you can replace words or phrases all at once throughout the presentation.

To replace instances of a word in a presentation:

1. On the *Home* tab, in the *Editing* group, click the **Replace** button.
2. Type the word or phrase you want to change in the *Find what* box.
3. Type the new text you want in the *Replace with* box.
4. Click the **Find Next** button to find the first instance of the text.
5. Click **Replace** to replace just that one instance of the text.
6. Click **Replace All** to replace all instances of the text.
7. PowerPoint displays a message telling you how many replacements it made. Click **OK** to dismiss the message.
8. Click the **Close** button to close the *Replace* dialog.

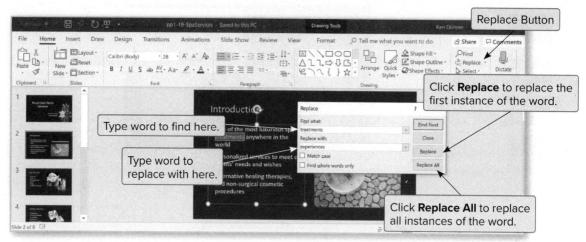

FIGURE PP 1.28

tips & tricks

The *Replace Fonts* command on the *Replace* menu allows you to quickly change the font for all text in a presentation with another font.

another method

To open the *Replace* dialog, you can also press (Ctrl) + (H) on the keyboard.

let me try

If you do not have the data file from the previous skill open, open the student data file **pp1-19-SpaServices** and try this skill on your own:

1. Navigate to **Slide 1**.
2. Open the **Replace** dialog.
3. Replace the first instance of the word **treatments** with **experiences**.
4. Do not change the second instance of the word **treatments**.
5. Close the dialog.
6. If you will be moving on to the next skill in this chapter, leave the presentation open to continue working. If not, save the file as directed by your instructor and close it.

Skill 1.20 Using Undo and Redo

If you make a mistake when working, the **Undo** command allows you to reverse the last action you performed. The **Redo** command allows you to reverse the undo command and restore the file to its previous state. The Quick Access Toolbar gives you immediate access to both of these commands.

To undo the last action taken, click the **Undo** button on the Quick Access Toolbar.

To redo the last action taken, click the **Redo** button on the Quick Access Toolbar.

To undo multiple actions at the same time:

1. Click the arrow next to the *Undo* button to expand the list of your most recent actions. These actions are listed in the reverse order of how they were done with the most recent action appearing at the top of the list.

2. Click an action in the list.

3. The action you click will be undone, along with all the actions completed after that. In other words, your presentation will revert to the state it was in before that action.

Click the **Undo** button to undo the last action taken.

Click the **Redo** button to redo the last action taken.

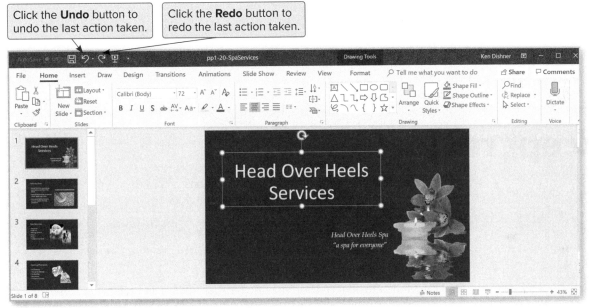

FIGURE PP 1.29

another **method**

❯ To undo an action, you can also press (Ctrl) + (Z) on the keyboard.

❯ To redo an action, you can also press (Ctrl) + (Y) on the keyboard.

let me **try**

If you do not have the data file from the previous skill open, open the student data file **pp1-20-SpaServices** and try this skill on your own:

1. On **Slide 1**, change the text size of the title **Head Over Heels Services** to **72 pt**.

2. Use the **Undo** command to reverse the text size change.

3. Use the **Redo** command to reapply the text size change.

4. Save the file as directed by your instructor and close it.

key terms

Presentation
Slides
Working space
Thumbnails pane
Slide pane
Notes pane
Placeholder
Normal view
Slide Sorter view
Reading view
Slide Show view
Zoom slider
Notes Page view
Master views
Template
Slide layout
Text placeholders
Text boxes
Character effects
Font
Serif fonts

Sans serif fonts
Points
Format Painter
Clear All Formatting
Line spacing
Text alignment
Left alignment
Center alignment
Right alignment
Justified alignment
Vertical alignment
Top alignment
Middle alignment
Bottom alignment
Columns
Find
Replace
Replace All
Undo
Redo

concept review

1. What is the final step in creating a presentation?

a. create your slides

b. plan your presentation

c. review your presentation

d. practice your presentation

2. Using the same font style on the title for each slide is an example of which design principle?

a. balance

b. flow

c. distinction

d. recurrence

3. Which view would you use to view the presentation as your audience will see it?

a. Normal view

b. Slide Sorter view

c. Slide Show view

d. Reading view

4. Which are predefined areas in slide layouts where you enter text?

a. text placeholders

b. text boxes

c. sections

d. slides

5. Which type of font has an embellishment at the end of each stroke?

    a. sans serif

    b. serif

    c. title

    d. body

6. Which command would you use to copy and paste formatting from one object to another?

    a. *Copy* and *Paste* commands

    b. *Cut* and *Paste* commands

    c. *Format Painter* command

    d. *Quick Styles* command

7. Which command aligns text along the upper edge of a text placeholder?

    a. Top

    b. Center

    c. Middle

    d. Justify

8. If a list includes more items than will easily fit vertically on a slide, you should use the _____ command to display the items side by side.

    a. Line spacing

    b. Columns

    c. Slide Layout

    d. Arrange

9. Which command would you use to locate specific instances of text in your presentation?

    a. Spelling

    b. Thesaurus

    c. Find

    d. Replace

10. What is the keyboard shortcut for reversing the last action you performed?

    a. Ctrl + W

    b. Ctrl + X

    c. Ctrl + Y

    d. Ctrl + Z

projects

Data files for projects can be found by logging into your SIMnet account and going to the *Library* section.

skill review **1.1**

In this project, you will be creating a new presentation from a template for Suarez Marketing. You will add and modify slides, add text, and format text. You will copy formatting using the *Format Painter* and paste the formatting to content on multiple slides. You will also review the presentation in Slide Sorter view.

Skills needed to complete this project:

- Creating a New Presentation from a Template (Skill 1.5)
- Adding Text to Slides (Skill 1.8)
- Changing the Size of a Placeholder (Skill 1.9)
- Working with Thumbnails (Skill 1.4)
- Changing Fonts and Font Sizes (Skill 1.11)
- Applying Character Effects (Skill 1.10)
- Changing the Color of Text (Skill 1.12)
- Using Format Painter (Skill 1.13)
- Changing Slide Layouts (Skill 1.7)
- Aligning Text (Skill 1.16)
- Changing Line Spacing (Skill 1.15)
- Using Undo and Redo (Skill 1.20)
- Understanding Views (Skill 1.3)

1. Open the start file **PP2019-SkillReview-1-1** presentation.
2. If the presentation opens in Protected View, click the **Enable Editing** button in the Message Bar at the top of the presentation so you can modify it.
3. Create a new presentation from a template.
   a. Click the **File** tab.
   b. Click **New**.
   c. Click in the **Search for online templates and themes** box at the top of the screen, type business plan, and press **Enter**.
   d. Select the **Business plan presentation (Ion green design, widescreen)** template.
   e. Click the **Create** button in the *Preview* window.
4. Save the presentation as [your initials]PP-SkillReview-1-1
5. Add text to slides.
   a. On **Slide 1**, click in the title placeholder.
   b. Click and drag across the text **Company Name** to select the text.
   c. Type: The Suarez Agency
6. Resize the company name placeholder so the top of the placeholder is closer to the top of the text you typed.

7. Using the *Thumbnails* pane, click **Slide 2** to display the second slide in the *Slide* pane.

8. Change the font and font size on text.

    a. Select the text **Business Concept**.

    b. On the *Home* tab, in the *Font* group, click the arrow next to the **Font** box and select **Verdana**.

    c. On the *Home* tab, in the *Font* group, click the arrow next to the **Font Size** box and select **54**.

9. Apply character effects to text.

    a. Verify that the text *Business Concept* is still selected.

    b. In the *Font* group, click the **Shadow** button.

10. Change the color of text.

    a. Verify that the text *Business Concept* is still selected.

    b. In the *Font* group, click the **Font Color** arrow and select **Green, Accent 4, Lighter 80%**. It is the third option from the right in the second row under *Theme Colors.*

11. Use *Format Painter* to copy and paste formatting.

    a. Verify that the text *Business Concept* is still selected.

    b. On the *Home* tab, in the *Clipboard* group, double-click the **Format Painter**.

    c. Apply the formatting to the titles of **Slide 4 through Slide 14**.

    d. Click the **Format Painter** once to turn it off.

12. Change the layout of a slide.

    a. On the *Thumbnails* pane, click **Slide 2**.

    b. On the *Home* tab, in the *Font* group, click the **Slide Layout** button and select **Content with Caption**.

13. Align text.

    a. On the *Thumbnails* pane, click **Slide 3**.

    b. Select the quote text (**Clearly state your company's long term mission.**).

    c. Type: **To provide our clients with a one of a kind campaign with outstanding results**

    d. On the *Home* tab, in the *Paragraph* group, click the **Center** alignment button.

    e. Delete the text box at the bottom of the slide (*Try to use words that will help. . .*).

14. Change the line spacing.

    a. On **Slide 3**, place the cursor in the quote.

    b. On the *Home* tab, in the *Paragraph* group, click the **Line Spacing** button and select **1.5**.

15. On the Quick Access Toolbar, click the **Undo** button.

16. On the Quick Access Toolbar, click the **Redo** button.

17. Switch between views.

    a. On the status bar, click the **Slide Sorter** button.

    b. Switch back to Normal view by clicking the **Normal** button on the status bar.

18. Save and close the business plan presentation. Close the blank presentation, but do not save the file

In this project you will be working on a personal fitness presentation. First, you will clear formatting from unattractive text. You will then format text, change the layout of slides, and use the *Find* and *Replace* commands. You will add a slide to the end of the presentation, add text to that slide, and format the text. Finally, you will start the presentation in Slide Show view and then return to Normal view.

Skills needed to complete this project:

- Clearing Formatting (Skill 1.14)
- Applying Character Effects (Skill 1.10)
- Changing Fonts and Font Sizes (Skill 1.11)
- Changing the Color of Text (Skill 1.12)
- Working with Thumbnails (Skill 1.4)
- Changing Slide Layouts (Skill 1.7)
- Using Format Painter (Skill 1.13)
- Adding Columns to Placeholders (Skill 1.17)
- Using Find (Skill 1.18)
- Using Replace (Skill 1.19)
- Adding Slides to Presentations (Skill 1.6)
- Adding Text to Slides (Skill 1.8)
- Aligning Text (Skill 1.16)
- Understanding Views (Skill 1.3)

1. Open the start file **PP2019-SkillReview-1-2** presentation and resave the file as: `[your initials]PP-SkillReview-1-2`

2. If the presentation opens in Protected View, click the **Enable Editing** button in the Message Bar at the top of the presentation so you can modify it.

3. Clear the formatting from text.

   a. On **Slide 1**, select the text **My Fitness Roadmap**.

   b. On the *Home* tab, in the *Font* group, click **Clear All Formatting**.

4. Apply character effects to text.

   a. On **Slide 1**, verify the text **My Fitness Roadmap** is still selected.

   b. On the *Shape Format* tab, in the *WordArt styles* group select any shadow text effect from the *Text Effects* menu.

5. Change the font size.

   a. Verify the text **My Fitness Roadmap** is still selected.

   b. On the *Home* tab, in the *Font* group, click the **Font Size** arrow and select **54**.

6. Change the font color.

   a. Verify the text **My Fitness Roadmap** is still selected.

   b. On the *Home* tab, in the *Font* group, click the **Font Color** arrow and select **Gold, Accent 2, Lighter 80%**. It is the sixth option in the second row under *Theme Colors*.

7. Navigate to a slide and change the slide layout.

   a. Using the *Thumbnails* pane, click **Slide 3** to navigate to that slide.

   b. On the *Home* tab, in the *Font* group, click the **Slide Layout** button and select **Title and Content**.

8. Change the font and change the size of text.

 a. Click **Slide 4**.

 b. Select the items in the bulleted list.

 c. On the *Home* tab, in the *Font* group, click the **Font** arrow and select **Calibri**.

 d. In the *Font* group, click the **Font Size** arrow and select **32**.

9. Use *Format Painter* to copy and paste formatting.

 a. Click **Slide 3**.

 b. Place the cursor in the slide title placeholder.

 c. On the *Home* tab, in the *Clipboard* group, click the **Format Painter** button.

 d. Navigate to **Slide 4** and click and drag across the word **Rest**.

10. Add columns to placeholders.

 a. Click **Slide 5** and click in the bulleted list.

 b. On the *Home* tab, in the *Paragraph* group, click the **Add or Remove Columns** button and select **Two Columns**.

11. Use the *Find* command.

 a. In the top right corner above the ribbon, click in the **Find In Presentation** box.

 b. Type **Routine** in the box and press ⏎ Enter .

 c. With the word *Routine* still selected, type **Roadmap**

 d. Press ⏎ Enter to advance to the next occurrence of the word.

12. Use the *Replace* command.

 a. On the *Home* tab, in the *Editing* group, click the **Replace** button.

 b. The word *Routine* should still be in the *Find what* box.

 c. Type **Roadmap** in the *Replace with* box.

 d. Click the **Replace All** button.

 e. A message box appears telling you two replacements have been made. Click **OK** in the message box.

 f. Close the *Replace* dialog.

13. Add slides to a presentation.

 a. Using the *Thumbnails* pane, click **Slide 7** to navigate to that slide.

 b. On the *Home* tab, in the *Slides* group, click the **New Slide** button arrow and select **Closing Slide**.

14. Add text to a placeholder.

 a. Click in the title placeholder.

 b. Type: **Only 8 weeks to go!**

15. Change the font size.

 a. Select the text you just typed.

 b. On the *Home* tab, in the *Font* group, click the **Font Size** arrow and select **60**.

16. Change the font color.

 a. Verify the text **Only 8 weeks to go!** is still selected.

 b. On the *Home* tab, in the *Font* group, click the **Font Color** arrow and select **Orange, Accent 5, Lighter 80%**. It is the second to last option in the second row under *Theme Colors*.

17. Align text.

 a. With the text still selected, on the *Home* tab, in the *Paragraph* group, click the **Center** button.

 b. In the *Paragraph* group, click the **Align Text** button and select **Middle**.

18. Switch to *Slide Show* view and then return back to *Normal* view.

    a. In the *Thumbnails* pane, click **Slide 1**.

    b. On the status bar, click the **Slide Show** button.

    c. Press the **Esc** key on the keyboard to return to *Normal view*.

19. Save and close the presentation.

challenge yourself 1.3

In this project you will be creating a new presentation from a template for presenting a healthy cookbook at a book festival. You will add and format text. Using the *Format Painter*, you will copy and paste formatting from one slide to another. Finally, you will use the *Undo* and *Redo* commands, and view the presentation in different PowerPoint views.

Skills needed to complete this project:

- Creating a New Presentation Using a Template (Skill 1.5)
- Adding Text to Slides (Skill 1.8)
- Changing Fonts and Font Sizes (Skill 1.11)
- Changing the Color of Text (Skill 1.12)
- Aligning Text (Skill 1.16)
- Working with Thumbnails (Skill 1.4)
- Using Format Painter (Skill 1.13)
- Applying Character Effects (Skill 1.10)
- Changing Line Spacing (Skill 1.15)
- Using Undo and Redo (Skill 1.20)
- Understanding Views (Skill 1.3)

1. Open the **PP2019-ChallengeYourself-1-3** presentation.

2. If the presentation opens in Protected View, click the **Enable Editing** button in the Message Bar at the top of the presentation so you can modify it.

3. Create a new presentation from a template.

    a. Search for template using the keyword **food**.

    b. Create a new presentation based on the **Fresh food presentation (widescreen)** template.

4. Save this presentation as: **[your initials]PP-ChallengeYourself-1-3**

5. Add text to slides.

    a. Change the title of the presentation to: **Healthy Cooking for a Healthy Life**

    b. Change the subtitle to: **Cooking Right For You**

6. Change the font, font size, and font color on text.

    a. Select the text **Healthy Cooking for a Healthy Life**.

    b. Change the font to **Calibri**.

    c. Change the font size to **48**.

    d. Change the font color to **Plum, Accent 5**. It is the second option from the right in the first row under *Theme Colors*.

7. Change the alignment of the **subtitle** on **Slide 1** to be center-aligned.

8. Navigate to a slide and add text.

   a. Using the *Thumbnails* pane, navigate to **Slide 2**.

   b. Change the title of the slide to: **Why this cookbook?**

   c. Replace the bullet items with the following:

   - **Unique recipes**
   - **Clean substitutions**
   - **Food metrics**
   - **Meal planning**

9. Use the Format Painter to copy and paste formatting and then change the size of text.

   a. Copy the formatting from the **presentation title** on **Slide 1** and apply the formatting to the title on **Slide 2**.

   b. Change the font size to **40**.

10. Apply character effects to text.

    a. On **Slide 2**, apply the **italic** character effect to the second word for each item in the bulleted list (**recipes**, **substitutions**, **metrics**, and **planning**).

    b. Apply the **underline** character effect to the second word for each item in the bulleted list.

11. Change the line spacing on the bulleted list to **1.5** line spacing.

12. **Undo** the line spacing action and then **Redo** the action so the line spacing returns to **1.5**.

13. Switch to **Reading** view, and then switch to **Slide Sorter** view. Switch back to **Normal** view.

14. Save and close the cookbook presentation. Close the blank presentation, but do not save the file.

challenge yourself **1.4**

In this project you will be working on a presentation about personal finance. You will add and modify slides, add and format text, and switch between different PowerPoint views.

Skills needed to complete this project:

- Clearing Formatting (Skill 1.14)
- Changing Fonts and Font Sizes (Skill 1.11)
- Aligning Text (Skill 1.16)
- Working with Thumbnails (Skill 1.4)
- Changing Slide Layouts (Skill 1.7)
- Changing the Size of a Placeholder (Skill 1.9)
- Using Format Painter (Skill 1.13)
- Adding Columns to Placeholders (Skill 1.17)
- Using Find (Skill 1.18)
- Using Replace (Skill 1.19)
- Adding Slides to Presentations (Skill 1.6)
- Adding Text to Slides (Skill 1.8)

- Changing the Color of Text (Skill 1.12)
- Understanding Views (Skill 1.3)

1. Open the **PP2019-ChallengeYourself-1-4** presentation and resave the file as: `[your initials]PP-ChallengeYourself-1-4`

2. If the presentation opens in Protected View, click the **Enable Editing** button in the Message Bar at the top of the presentation so you can modify it.

3. Clear the formatting from text.

   a. On **Slide 1**, select the text **The Smart & Easy Way to Save Money**.

   b. Clear the formatting from the text.

4. Change the size of text.

   a. Verify the text is still selected.

   b. Change the size of the text to **28 pt**.

   c. Change the size of the text **Ready? Set! Save!** to **72 pt**.

5. Change the alignment of the text in both placeholders to be right-aligned.

6. Navigate to a slide and change the slide layout.

   a. Navigate to **Slide 2**.

   b. Change the layout of the slide to **Title and Content**.

7. Change the size of a placeholder.

   a. Navigate to **Slide 3**.

   b. Change the size of the placeholder to be **5"** in height and **9"** in width.

8. Change the font and change the size of text.

   a. Verify the placeholder on **Slide 3** is still active.

   b. Change the bulleted list items to **Century Gothic**.

   c. Change the size of the text to **18 pt**.

9. Use the **Format Painter** to copy and paste formatting.

   a. Copy the formatting from the bulleted list on **Slide 3**.

   b. Apply the formatting to the bulleted lists on **Slide 2**, **Slide 4**, and **Slide 5**.

10. Add columns to placeholders and resize the placeholder.

    a. Change the bulleted list on **Slide 4** to display in two columns.

    b. Change the size of the placeholder to be **4.5"** in height and **10"** in width.

11. Use the **Find** command to find the word **money** in the presentation.

12. Use the **Replace** command to replace the word `Barter` with `Trade`.

13. Add a new blank slide to the end of the presentation.

14. Add a text box to the middle of the newly inserted slide and enter the text: `Take control and start now!`

15. Change the font size and color.

    a. Change the font size to **54 pt**.

    b. Change the color of the text to **Light Green, Accent 1, Lighter 40%**.

16. Navigate to **Slide 1**. Switch to Slide Show view and then return back to Normal view.

17. Save and close the presentation.

on your own **1.5**

In this project you will be creating a presentation from a template on the four steps in creating a PowerPoint presentation. You will add and modify slides, format text, use the *Find* command, and switch between different PowerPoint views.

Skills needed to complete this project:

- Creating a New Presentation Using a Template (Skill 1.5)
- Adding Text to Slides (Skill 1.8)
- Aligning Text (Skill 1.16)
- Adding Slides to Presentations (Skill 1.6)
- Changing Slide Layouts (Skill 1.7)
- Working with Thumbnails (Skill 1.4)
- Changing Fonts and Font Sizes (Skill 1.11)
- Changing the Color of Text (Skill 1.12)
- Using Format Painter (Skill 1.13)
- Applying Character Effects (Skill 1.10)
- Clearing Formatting (Skill 1.14)
- Using Find (Skill 1.18)
- Understanding Views (Skill 1.3)

1. Open the start file **PP2019-OnYourOwn-1-5** presentation.

2. If the presentation opens in Protected View, click the **Enable Editing** button in the Message Bar at the top of the presentation so you can modify it.

3. Create a new presentation from a single slide template based on a design of your choice. Be sure the template includes only one slide.

4. Save this presentation as: `[your initials]PP-OnYourOwn-1-5`

5. On **Slide 1**, add the title `Creating an Effective Presentation`. Add the subtitle `6 steps for creating a presentation`

6. If necessary, change the font size of the title so the entire title appears on a single line on the slide.

7. On **Slide 1**, change the alignment of the text in the **Title** and **Subtitle** placeholders.

8. Add a new slide with a layout of your choice.

9. Add the title `The 6 Steps` to the slide.

10. Add the following text to the content placeholder on the left:
    - `Plan Your Presentation`
    - `Create Your Slides`
    - `Add Your Content`
    - `Format Your Content`
    - `Review and Rehearse`
    - `Practice`

11. If you didn't choose the *Title and Content* layout in step 8, change the layout of the slide to the **Title and Content** layout.

12. Add a **Title and Content** slide for each item in the list you added on **Slide 2**. Add each item in the list as the title for each slide. For example, the title on **Slide 3** should be **Plan Your Presentation**, the title on **Slide 4** should be **Create Your Slides**, and so on.

13. On **Slide 2**, change the font, font size, and color of the text **The 6 Steps**.

14. Use the *Format Painter* to copy and paste the formatting to the titles of the other slides in the presentation.

15. Change the title on **Slide 1** to use the same font you used on the other slide titles.

16. Apply character formatting to the subtitle and then clear the formatting on the text.

17. Use the *Find* command to find where the word **practice** appears in the presentation.

18. Display your presentation in the different PowerPoint views.

19. Save and close the PowerPoint presentation. Close the blank presentation, but do not save the file.

fix it **1.6**

In this project, you will be editing a presentation on team orientation and team building. You will modify slides, add and format text, and switch between different PowerPoint views.

Skills needed to complete this project:

- Clearing Formatting (Skill 1.14)
- Changing the Color of Text (Skill 1.12)
- Applying Character Effects (Skill 1.10)
- Working with Thumbnails (Skill 1.4)
- Changing the Size of a Placeholder (Skill 1.9)
- Aligning Text (Skill 1.16)
- Changing Fonts and Font Sizes (Skill 1.11)
- Using Format Painter (Skill 1.13)
- Change Slide Layouts (Skill 1.7)
- Adding Text to Slides (Skill 1.8)
- Using Replace (Skill 1.19)
- Understanding Views (Skill 1.3)

1. Open the start file **PP2019-FixIt-1-6** presentation and resave the file as: **[your initials]PP-FixIt-1-6**

2. If the presentation opens in Protected View, click the **Enable Editing** button in the Message Bar at the top of the presentation so you can modify it.

3. On **Slide 1**, clear the formatting from the text **Team Orientation**.

4. Change the color of the text to **Blue, Accent 6, Darker 50%**. It is the last option in the last row under *Theme Colors*.

5. Apply the **Bold** character effect.

6. On **Slide 1**, change the size of the text **The Basics** to **48 pt**.

7. Change the list placeholder on **Slide 3** to be the same size as the list placeholder on **Slide 2**.

8. Change the list on **Slide 3** to be left-aligned.

9. Navigate to **Slide 2**. Change the list to **32 pt. Candara**.

10. Change vertical alignment on the list on **Slide 2** to be middle-aligned.

11. Use **Format Painter** to copy the formatting from the list placeholder on **Slide 2** and copy it to the lists on **Slides 3**, **4**, and **8**. **NOTE**: Be sure the placeholder is selected and appears with a solid outline and not a dashed outline before copying the formatting.

12. Change the layout of **Slide 7** to **Title and Content**.

13. Add SMART REVIEW as the title of **Slide 7**.

14. Add Scavenger hunts and Volunteer days as the fourth and fifth items in the list on **Slide 8**.

15. Use the **Replace** command to replace **attitude** with the word **approach**.

16. Display your presentation in the different PowerPoint views.

17. Save and close the presentation.

chapter 2

Adding Content to Slides

In this chapter, you will learn the following skills:

❱ Add slides and text from a Word Outline

❱ Use the Cut, Copy, and Paste commands

❱ Use the Clipboard

❱ Create bulleted and numbered lists

❱ Add WordArt to Slides

❱ Understand the content placeholder

❱ Add objects to slides including tables, charts, and SmartArt diagrams

❱ Add objects to slides including icons, shapes, pictures, and 3D models

❱ Add alt text to images for accessibility

❱ Change image alignment, size, and placement

❱ Display the ruler and gridlines

❱ Add audio and video to slides

skills

introduction

This chapter provides you with the skills to add content to presentations. You will learn to quickly fill out a presentation by adding slide content using a Word document. You will then move text around in the presentation using the *Copy and Paste* and *Cut and Paste* commands. You will apply bulleted and numbered lists to slide content and will add WordArt to slides. You will explore the content placeholder and then add objects to slides through the content placeholders. You will add tables, SmartArt diagrams, icons, pictures, 3D models, and shapes. You will work with images on the slide, changing alignment and using smart guides to move and place images. You will learn to display the ruler and gridlines to help with image placement and sizing. Finally, you will add audio and videos to a presentation.

Skill 2.1 Importing Slides from a Word Outline

When organizing the content for a presentation, you may find it helpful to write your text in a Word document and then import it into PowerPoint. Use heading styles in the Word document to ensure that the content will convert to a presentation in a uniform manner. Each Heading 1 style becomes the title on the slide, and each Heading 2 style becomes the main text on the slide. After you have saved the Word document, you can then import the content, creating the base slides for your presentation.

To insert slides from a Word outline:

1. Click in the presentation where you want to insert the slides.
2. On the *Home* tab, in the *Slides* group, click the arrow below the **New Slide** button and select **Slides from Outline…**
3. In the *Insert Outline* dialog, select the file you want to insert.
4. Click the **Insert** button.
5. The slides are added to the presentation based on the heading styles in the Word document.

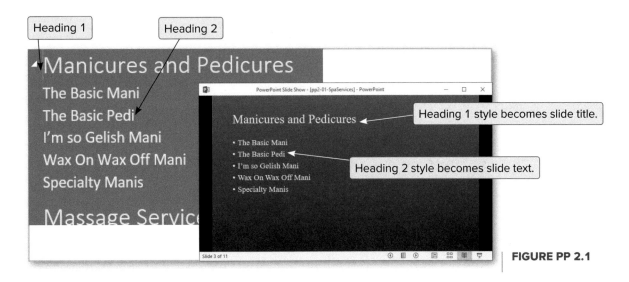

FIGURE PP 2.1

New Slide Button

FIGURE PP 2.2 | Select **Slides from Outline...**

tips & tricks

When you insert an outline, all the slides will use the default slide design. Click the **Layout** button on the *Home* tab to change the layout of a slide. Click the **Design** tab to make any changes to a slide's design.

tell me **more**

You can import many file formats from Word, including Word documents (both .docx and .doc), plain text (.txt), rich text format (.rtf), and HTML (.htm).

let me **try**

Open the student data file **pp2-01-SpaServices** and try this skill on your own:

1. Navigate to **Slide 2**.
2. Open the **Insert Outline** dialog.
3. Navigate to the location where you saved the data files for this book.
4. Insert the **SpaProductOutline** into the presentation.
5. If you will be moving on to the next skill in this chapter, leave the presentation open to continue working. If not, save the file as directed by your instructor and close it.

Skill 2.2 Using the Outline View

When working on a presentation, it's easy to focus on the graphic elements of your slides. Adding graphics, transitions, and animations may seem important, but the foundation of an effective presentation is a focused message. When working with text on slides, it is a good idea to keep the amount of text on each slide balanced and to concentrate on one clear message per slide. The **Outline view** displays the text from your slides in an outline, allowing you to concentrate on the text aspect of your slides without being distracted by the graphic elements. Use the *Outline* view to enter and edit your text directly in the outline.

To use the *Outline* view:

1. Click the **View** tab.
2. In the *Presentation Views* group, click the **Outline View** button.
3. Click in the text you want to change.
4. Type the new text for the slide. The *Slide* pane to the right updates with the new text.
5. In the *Presentation Views* group, click the **Normal View** button to return to Normal view.

FIGURE PP 2.3

tips & tricks

If your slides include a large amount of text, you can make the *Outline* pane wider to make it easier to write and edit your content. To change the width of the *Outline* pane, place your cursor over the right edge of the pane. When the cursor changes to the resize cursor, click and drag the mouse to the right to make the pane wider or to the left to make the pane narrower.

let me try

If you do not have the data file from the previous skill open, open the student data file **pp2-02-SpaServices** and try this skill on your own:

1. Display the slides in **Outline view**.
2. On **Slide 2**, add the text `cosmetic` before the word **procedures** in the last bullet point on the slide.
3. Switch back to **Normal** view.
4. If you will be moving on to the next skill in this chapter, leave the presentation open to continue working. If not, save the file as directed by your instructor and close it.

Skill 2.3 Using Copy and Paste

The **Copy** command places a duplicate of the selected text or object on the **Clipboard** but does not remove it from your presentation. You can then use the **Paste** command to insert the text or object into the same presentation, another presentation, or another Microsoft Office file, such as an Excel workbook or a Word document.

To copy text and paste it into the same presentation:

1. Select the text to be copied.
2. On the *Home* tab, in the *Clipboard* group, click the **Copy** button.
3. Place the cursor where you want to insert the text from the *Clipboard*.
4. On the *Home* tab, in the *Clipboard* group, click the **Paste** button.
5. These same steps apply whether you are copying and pasting text, pictures, shapes, video files, or any type of object in a presentation.

FIGURE PP 2.4

tell me **more**

The *Paste* button has two parts—the top part of the button pastes the most recently copied item into the current file. If you click the bottom part of the button (the *Paste* button arrow), you can control how the item is pasted.

Each type of object has different **paste options**. For example, if you are pasting text, you may have options to keep the source formatting, merge the formatting of the source and the current presentation, or paste only the text without any formatting.

another **method**

To apply the *Copy* or *Paste* command, you can also use the following shortcuts:

Copy = Press (Ctrl) + (C) on the keyboard, or right-click and select **Copy**.

Paste = Press (Ctrl) + (V) on the keyboard, or right-click and select **Paste**.

let me **try**

If you do not have the data file from the previous skill open, open the student data file **pp2-03-SpaServices** and try this skill on your own:

1. On **Slide 3**, copy the fourth bullet point on the slide (*Wax On Wax Off Mani*).
2. Press (←Enter) at the end of the fourth bullet.
3. Paste the text you copied. If necessary, delete the extra blank line.
4. Change the word **Mani** to **Pedi** in the text you pasted.
5. If you will be moving on to the next skill in this chapter, leave the presentation open to continue working. If not, save the file as directed by your instructor and close it.

Skill 2.4 Using Cut and Paste

The *Copy* command is great if you want to duplicate content in your presentation, but what if you want to move content from one place to another? The **Cut** command is used to move text and other objects within a file and from one file to another. Text or an object that is cut is removed from the file and placed on the *Clipboard* for later use. You can then use the *Paste* command to insert the text or object into the same presentation, another presentation, or another Microsoft Office file.

To cut text and paste it into the same presentation:

1. Select the text to be cut.

2. On the *Home* tab, in the *Clipboard* group, click the **Cut** button.

3. Place the cursor where you want to insert the text from the *Clipboard*.

4. On the *Home* tab, in the *Clipboard* group, click the **Paste** button.

FIGURE PP 2.5

another **method**

To apply the *Cut* or *Paste* command, you can also use the following shortcuts:

Cut = Press Ctrl + x on the keyboard, or right-click and select **Cut**.

Paste = Press Ctrl + v on the keyboard, or right-click and select **Paste**.

let me **try**

If you do not have the data file from the previous skill open, open the student data file **pp2-04-SpaServices** and try this skill on your own:

1. On **Slide 6**, cut the fourth bullet point from the slide (*The Mummy Wrap*).

2. On the same slide, paste the text as the second bullet point on the slide (below *The C-Weed Wrap*). If necessary, delete the extra blank line.

3. If you will be moving on to the next skill in this chapter, leave the presentation open to continue working. If not, save the file as directed by your instructor and close it.

Skill 2.5 Adding Bulleted Lists

When you create a PowerPoint presentation, limit each point you want to discuss to a few words. When you give your presentation, you can expand on the information displayed on your slide. This will keep your audience engaged and focused on what you are saying rather than reading your slides.

When you create slides, you will notice that text is organized in bulleted lists. **Bulleted lists** are used to organize information that does not have to be displayed in a particular order.

To add a bulleted list to a slide:

1. Select the text you want to display in a list.
2. On the *Home* tab, in the *Paragraph* group, click the arrow next to the **Bullets** button.
3. Select a **bullet style** from the gallery.

FIGURE PP 2.6

tips & tricks

Sometimes you will want to include subpoints in your bulleted and numbered lists. When a list includes point and subpoints, it is called a **multilevel list**. In PowerPoint, you can create a multilevel list by demoting and promoting points in lists. To move a point down a level in a list, click the **Increase Indent** button. To move a point up a level in a list, click the **Decrease Indent** button.

another **method**

To add a bulleted list, you can also right-click the selected text, point to **Bullets**, and select a style from the submenu.

let me **try**

If you do not have the data file from the previous skill open, open the student data file **pp2-05-SpaServices** and try this skill on your own:

1. Select the three list items on **Slide 2**.
2. Apply the **Checkmark Bullets** bulleted list style to the items.
3. If you will be moving on to the next skill in this chapter, leave the presentation open to continue working. If not, save the file as directed by your instructor and close it.

Skill 2.6 Adding Numbered Lists

Numbered lists are used to organize information that must be presented in a certain order, such as step-by-step instructions. When you apply numbering formatting to a list, PowerPoint displays a number or letter next to each list item using the format you chose. You can choose to number lists using Arabic numbers (1, 2, 3), Roman numerals (I, II, III), or letters (A, B, C).

To add a numbered list to a slide:

1. Select the text you want to display in a list.
2. On the *Home* tab, in the *Paragraph* group, click the arrow next to the **Numbering** button.
3. Select a **numbering style** from the gallery.

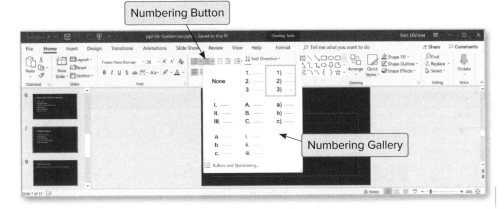

FIGURE PP 2.7

tips & tricks

Sometimes you will want to add more items to an existing list. To add another item to the list, place your cursor at the end of an item and press ← Enter to start a new line. The list will renumber itself to accommodate the new item.

tell me **more**

To change the numbering list type, click the **Numbering** button arrow and select an option from the *Numbering Library*.

another **method**

To add a numbered list, you can also right-click the selected text, point to **Numbering**, and select a style from the submenu.

let me **try**

If you do not have the data file from the previous skill open, open the student data file **pp2-06-SpaServices** and try this skill on your own:

1. Select the five list items on **Slide 7**.
2. Apply the **1) 2) 3)** numbered list style to the items.
3. If you will be moving on to the next skill in this chapter, leave the presentation open to continue working. If not, save the file as directed by your instructor and close it.

Skill 2.7 Adding WordArt

Sometimes you'll want to call attention to text that you add to a slide. You can format the text by using character effects, or if you want the text to really stand out, you can use **WordArt**. WordArt Quick Styles are predefined graphic styles you apply to text. These styles include a combination of color, fills, outlines, and effects. Be sure to limit the use of WordArt to a small amount of text. Overuse of WordArt can be distracting to your audience.

To add WordArt to slides:

1. Click the **Insert** tab.
2. In the *Text* group, click the **WordArt** button and select a Quick Style from the gallery.
3. Begin typing to replace the text **"Your Text Here"** with the text for your slide.

   After you have added WordArt to your presentation, you can modify it just as you would any other text. Use the *Font* box and *Font Size* box on the *Home* tab to change the font or font size of WordArt.

FIGURE PP 2.8

tips & tricks

When you add WordArt to a slide, it will appear centered in the middle of the slide. To move the WordArt you added, point to the WordArt and when the cursor changes to the move cursor ..⊹.., click and drag the WordArt to the new location.

let me try

If you do not have the data file from the previous skill open, open the student data file **pp2-07-SpaServices** and try this skill on your own:

1. On **Slide 11**, add WordArt to the document using the **Fill: White; Outline: Blue, Accent Color 5; Shadow** (the fourth option in the first row of the gallery).
2. Add the text **Call us today!** in the WordArt style.
3. If you will be moving on to the next skill in this chapter, leave the presentation open to continue working. If not, save the file as directed by your instructor and close it.

Skill 2.8 Understanding the Content Placeholder

A good presentation contains a balance of text, graphics, charts, and other subject matter. The **content placeholder** is a special type of placeholder that gives you a quick way to add a variety of material to your presentations. In PowerPoint, you can add several types of content to your slides through the content placeholder:

To add content to a slide through the content placeholder:

1. Click the icon of the type of content you want to add.

2. The associated dialog appears.

3. Add the content in the same manner as if you accessed the command from the Ribbon.

	Insert Table
	Insert Chart
	Insert a SmartArt Graphic
	Pictures
	Online Pictures
	Insert Video

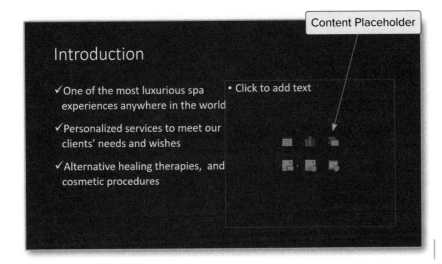

FIGURE PP 2.9

tips & tricks

When you add slides to a presentation, you can choose slides that are preformatted with content placeholders. Some slide layouts contain one content placeholder, but other layouts include multiple content placeholders, allowing you to add more than one content type to a slide.

let me try

If you do not have the data file from the previous skill open, open the student data file **pp2-08-SpaServices** and try this skill on your own:

1. Navigate to **Slide 2**.

2. Click the **Insert Chart** icon in the content placeholder. Click **Cancel** to close the dialog.

3. Click the **Online Pictures** icon in the content placeholder. Click the **Close** button in the upper right corner to close the dialog.

4. If you will be moving on to the next skill in this chapter, leave the presentation open to continue working. If not, save the file as directed by your instructor and close it.

Skill 2.9 Creating Tables in Presentations

When you have a large amount of information on one slide, you will want to organize the data so they are easier for your audience to understand. A **table** helps you organize information for effective display. Tables are organized by **rows**, which display horizontally, and **columns**, which display vertically. The intersection of a row and a column is referred to as a **cell**. Tables can be used to display everything from dates in a calendar to sales numbers to product inventory.

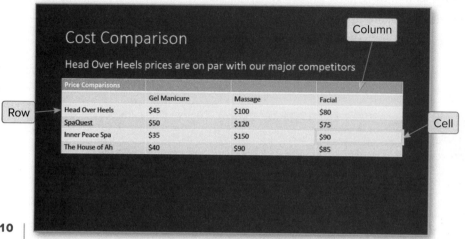

FIGURE PP 2.10

To add a table to a slide:

1. Click the **Insert** tab.
2. Click the **Table** button.
3. Select the number of cells you want by moving the cursor across and down the squares.
4. When the description at the top of the menu displays the number of rows and columns you want, click the mouse.
5. The table is inserted into your presentation.

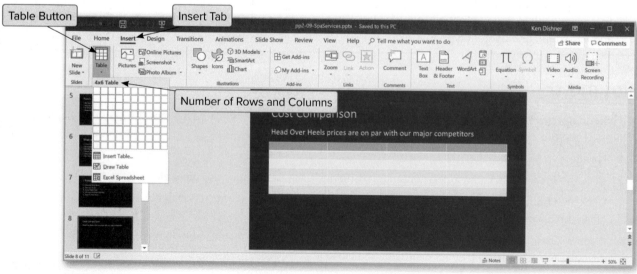

FIGURE PP 2.11

6. Place the cursor in the cell where you want to enter the data.

7. Type the data just as you would in normal text.

8. Press (Tab) to move to the next cell and enter more data.

9. Continue pressing (Tab) until all data are entered.

tell me **more**

When you add a table to a slide, the *Table Tools* contextual tabs display. These tabs contain commands for working with tables. From the *Design* tab, you can modify the rows and columns, apply table styles and effects, and change the table's borders. From the *Layout* tab, you can delete and add rows and columns, change the alignment of text in cells, change the size of cells, and change the size of the table.

another **method**

To add a table from the *Insert Table* dialog:

> Click the **Table** button and select **Insert Table...**

> Click the **Insert Table** icon in the content placeholder.

In the *Insert Table* dialog, enter the number of rows and columns for your table. Click **OK** to add the table to the slide.

let me **try**

If you do not have the data file from the previous skill open, open the student data file **pp2-09-SpaServices** and try this skill on your own:

1. On **Slide 8**, insert a table that has **four columns** and **six rows**.

2. Enter the following information for the table:

Price Comparisons			
	Gel Manicure	**Massage**	**Facial**
Head Over Heels Spa	$45	$100	$80
SpaQuest	$50	$120	$75
Inner Peace Spa	$35	$150	$90
The House of Ah	$40	$90	$85

3. If you will be moving on to the next skill in this chapter, leave the presentation open to continue working. If not, save the file as directed by your instructor and close it.

Skill 2.10 Adding Charts

When creating a PowerPoint presentation, you will want to display your data in the most visual way possible. One way to display data graphically is by using charts. A **chart** takes the information you have entered in a spreadsheet and converts it to a visual representation. In PowerPoint, you can create a wide variety of charts, including bar charts (both stack and 3D), pie charts, column charts, scatter charts, and line charts.

To add a chart to a presentation:

1. Click the **Insert** tab.
2. In the *Illustrations* group, click the **Chart** button.

FIGURE PP 2.12

3. In the *Insert Chart* dialog, click a chart type category to display that category in the right pane.
4. Click a chart type in the right pane to select it.
5. Click **OK** to add the chart to the slide.

FIGURE PP 2.13

PowerPoint automatically opens the *Chart in Microsoft PowerPoint* dialog. Think of this dialog as a simplified spreadsheet where you can enter the data for your chart. The dialog opens with sample data entered for you.

1. Replace the sample data with your own data.
2. Click the **Close** button to return to PowerPoint to see your finished chart.

FIGURE PP 2.14

tell me **more**

As you enter data in the *Chart in Microsoft PowerPoint* dialog, PowerPoint will update the chart as you enter data and move from cell to cell in the spreadsheet.

another **method**

To open the *Insert Chart* dialog, you can also click the **Insert Chart** icon in the content placeholder on the slide.

let me **try**

If you do not have the data file from the previous skill open, open the student data file **pp2-10-SpaServices** and try this skill on your own:

1. On **Slide 9**, insert a **pie chart**.
2. Enter the following information for the chart:

	Sales
Manicures and Pedicures	48
Massage Services	30
Facials	22
Wraps	10
Other	8

3. Close the **Chart in Microsoft PowerPoint** dialog.
4. If you will be moving on to the next skill in this chapter, leave the presentation open to continue working. If not, save the file as directed by your instructor and close it.

skill 2.10 Adding Charts

Skill 2.11 Adding SmartArt

SmartArt is a way to take your ideas and make them visual. Where presentations used to have plain bulleted and ordered lists, now they can have SmartArt. SmartArt images are visual diagrams containing graphic elements with text boxes in which you enter information. Using SmartArt not only makes your presentation look better but also helps convey the information in a more meaningful way.

To insert a SmartArt diagram:

1. Click the **Insert** tab.
2. In the *Illustrations* group, click the **SmartArt** button.

FIGURE PP 2.15

3. In the *Choose a SmartArt Graphic* dialog, click a SmartArt graphic type.
4. Click **OK**.
5. The SmartArt diagram is added to the slide.
6. Each shape in the diagram includes a text placeholder.
7. Click **[Text]** in a shape and enter the text for the item.
8. Enter the text for all the shapes in the diagram.

FIGURE PP 2.16

There are eight categories of SmartArt for you to choose from:

❭ **List**—Use to list items that *do not* need to be in a particular order.

❭ **Process**—Use to list items that *do* need to be in a particular order.

❭ **Cycle**—Use for a process that repeats over and over again.

❭ **Hierarchy**—Use to show branching, in either a decision tree or an organization chart.

❭ **Relationship**—Use to show relationships between items.

❭ **Matrix**—Use to show how an item fits into the whole.

❭ **Pyramid**—Use to illustrate how things relate to each other with the largest item being on the bottom and the smallest item being on the top.

❭ **Picture**—Use to show a series of pictures along with text in the diagram.

FIGURE PP 2.17

tips & tricks

When choosing a SmartArt diagram, it is important that the diagram type suits your content. In the *Choose a SmartArt Graphic* dialog, click a SmartArt type to display a preview of the SmartArt. The preview not only displays what the diagram will look like but also includes a description of the best uses for the diagram type.

another **method**

To insert a SmartArt diagram, you can also click the **SmartArt** icon in a content placeholder.

let me **try**

If you do not have the data file from the previous skill open, open the student data file **pp2-11-SpaServices** and try this skill on your own:

1. Navigate to **Slide 10** and open the **Choose a SmartArt Graphic** dialog.
2. Insert a **Grouped List** diagram. It is the second option in the fifth row of the dialog.
3. Enter the following information in the diagram:

Hand and Foot	Facials	Wraps
Single: $30–$60	Single: $75–$125	Single: $95–$150
Block of 3: $25–$50	Block of 3: $70–$110	Block of 3: $85–$130

4. If you will be moving on to the next skill in this chapter, leave the presentation open to continue working. If not, save the file as directed by your instructor and close it.

Skill 2.12 Adding Shapes

A **shape** is a drawing object that you can quickly add to your presentation. The PowerPoint *Shapes* gallery gives you access to a number of prebuilt shapes to add to your presentation. There are a number of types of shapes that you can add to slides, including lines, rectangles, block arrows, equation shapes, stars, banners, and callouts.

To add a shape to a slide:

1. On the *Home* tab, in the *Drawing* group, click the **Shapes** button and select an option from the *Shapes* gallery.

2. The cursor changes to a crosshair.

3. Click anywhere on the presentation to add the shape.

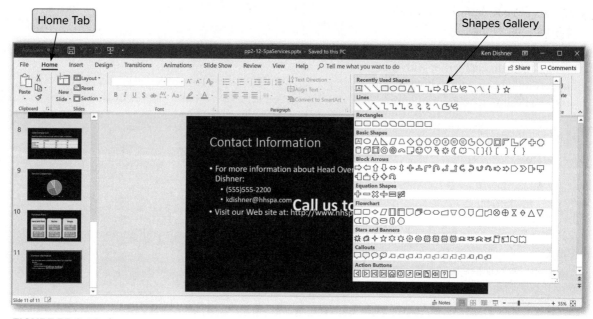

FIGURE PP 2.18

Once you have added a shape to a presentation, there are a number of ways you can work with it:

> To resize a shape: click a resize handle and drag toward the center of the image to make it smaller or away from the center of the image to make it larger.

> To rotate a shape: click the rotate handle and drag your mouse to the right to rotate the image clockwise or to the left to rotate the image counterclockwise.

> To move a shape: point to the graphic and when the cursor changes to the move cursor (⸱⸱⊹⸱⸱), click and drag the image to the new location.

FIGURE PP 2.19

tell me **more**

When you insert a shape into a presentation, the *Format* tab under *Drawing Tools* displays. This tab is called a contextual tab because it displays only when a drawing object is the active element. The *Format* tab contains tools to change the look of the shape, such as shape styles, effects, and placement on the slide.

another **method**

❯ To add a shape, you can also click the **Insert** tab. In the *Illustrations* group, click the **Shapes** button.

❯ The most recently used shapes category displays in a shortened version of the *Shapes* gallery on the Ribbon. If the shape you want to use is displayed, you can click the shape to select it and add it to the slide without opening the full *Shapes* gallery.

let me **try**

If you do not have the data file from the previous skill open, open the student data file **pp2-12-SpaServices** and try this skill on your own:

1. Navigate to **Slide 11**.
2. Add the **Arrow: Curved Right** shape to the slide so it appears below the text *www.hhspa.com*. It is in the *Block Arrows* section of the gallery.
3. If you will be moving on to the next skill in this chapter, leave the presentation open to continue working. If not, save the file as directed by your instructor and close it.

Skill 2.13 Inserting an Icon

Icons are SVG (Scalable Vector Graphics) images you can add to your presentations. They are simple drawings and because they use the SVG format, they can be enlarged, colored, and rotated without losing image quality.

To insert an icon:

1. Navigate to the slide where you want to add the icon.

2. Click the **Insert** tab.

3. In the *Illustrations* group, click the **Icons** button.

FIGURE PP 2.20

4. The *Insert Icons* dialog appears. Click a category on the left to navigate to that section.

5. Click an icon to select it.

6. Click the **Insert** button.

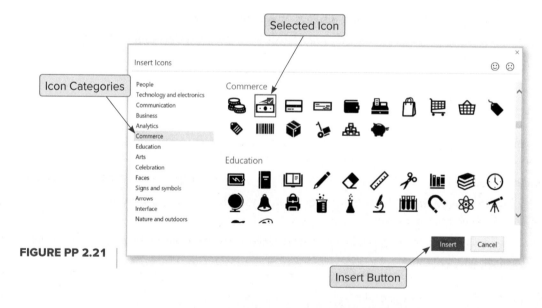

FIGURE PP 2.21

All icons are inserted with a black fill color, but you can modify icons from the *Graphics Tools Format* tab. This tab contains commands for changing the look of the icon, including applying a preset graphics style. Preset graphic styles are a combination of fill and outline settings that can be applied to a graphic at the same time.

To apply a preset graphics style to an icon:

1. With the icon selected, on the *Graphics Tools Format* tab, click the **Graphics Styles More** button.

2. The *Graphics Styles* gallery displays. Click a style in the gallery to apply it to the icon.

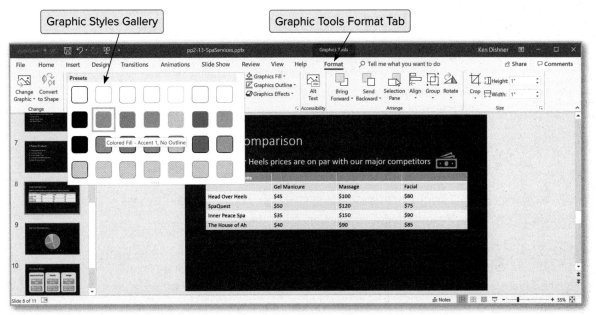

Graphic Styles Gallery

Graphic Tools Format Tab

FIGURE PP 2.22

tell me **more**

You can select more than one icon to insert. Selected icons appear with a box around the icon and a checkmark in the upper right corner.

another **method**

❭ You can also scroll the icons in the *Insert Icons* dialog rather than using the category list to jump to a section.

❭ To apply a preset graphics style, you can also click an option in the gallery on the Ribbon.

let me **try**

If you do not have the data file from the previous skill open, open the student data file **pp2-13-SpaServices** and try this skill on your own:

1. Navigate to **Slide 8**.
2. Add the icon of the **paper money**. It is the second icon in the *Commerce* category.
3. Move the icon so it appears at the right of the text *Head Over Heels prices are on par with our major competitors*.
4. Apply the **Colored Fill – Accent 1, No Outline** graphics style to the icon. It is the second icon in the second row of the gallery.
5. If you will be moving on to the next skill in this chapter, leave the presentation open to continue working. If not, save the file as directed by your instructor and close it.

Skill 2.14 Adding Pictures

Sometimes adding a photograph or an illustration to a slide will convey a message better than text alone. Use the *Insert Picture* dialog to insert pictures you created in another program or downloaded from your smartphone or digital camera into your presentation.

To insert a picture from a file:

1. Click the **Insert** tab.

2. In the *Images* group, click the **Pictures** button.

3. The *Insert Picture* dialog opens.

4. Navigate to the file location, select the file, and click **Insert**.

FIGURE PP 2.23

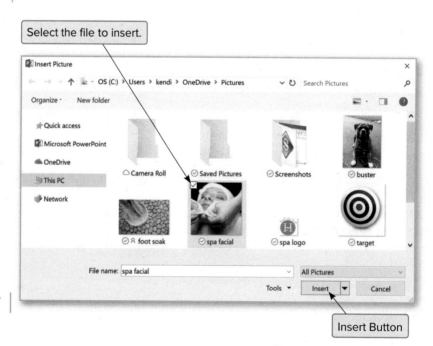

FIGURE PP 2.24

powerpoint 365   chapter 2 Adding Content to Slides

tell me **more**

You can create a slide show of photographs including captions using PowerPoint's **Photo Album** feature. On the *Insert* tab, in the *Images* group, click the **Photo Album** button. Use the *Photo Album* dialog to add photos, create captions, and modify the layout. Click the **Create** button to create the photo album as a new presentation.

another **method**

To open the *Insert Picture* dialog, you can also click the **Pictures** icon in the content placeholder.

let me **try**

If you do not have the data file from the previous skill open, open the student data file **pp2-14-SpaServices** and try this skill on your own:

1. Navigate to **Slide 2** and open the **Insert Picture** dialog.
2. Navigate to the location where you saved the data files for this book.
3. Insert the **spa facial** picture.
4. If you will be moving on to the next skill in this chapter, leave the presentation open to continue working. If not, save the file as directed by your instructor and close it.

from the perspective of . . .

DENTAL HYGIENIST

In my profession as a dental hygienist, I created a fun presentation showing good oral hygiene habits. First, I created all my content in Word and then imported the outline to save time creating all the slides in the presentation. I added information in bulleted lists and tables, and I added a chart to visually display how good hygiene decreases the chance of cavities. I was able to add pictures, music, and videos. My young patients love it!

Mike Kemp/Getty Images

Skill 2.15 Adding Alt Text to Pictures

Adding alt text to pictures in your presentations makes your presentations accessible to a wider audience, including those that are blind. **Alt text** is a description of a picture, chart, or other object that can be read by screen readers. When creating alt text, write a description that is thorough and to the point. Do not include any unnecessary words. A good rule of thumb is to think of how you would describe the picture to someone who cannot see it.

To add alt text to a picture:

1. Right-click the picture and select **Edit Alt Text...**

FIGURE PP 2.25

Right-click the picture and select **Edit Alt Text...**

2. In the *Alt Text* task pane, type a detailed description of the picture in the text box.

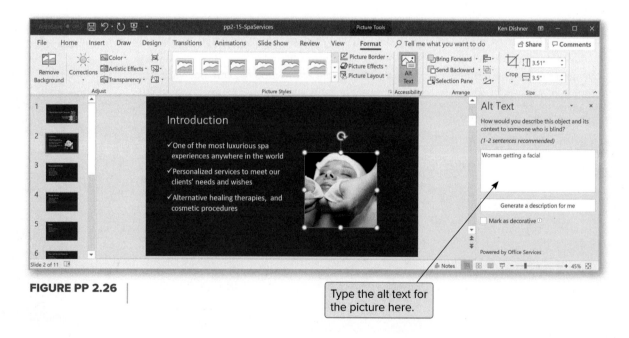

FIGURE PP 2.26

Type the alt text for the picture here.

tips & tricks

PowerPoint's *Accessibility Checker* feature reviews your document looking for anything that does not meet accessibility standards. To run the *Accessibility Checker*, click the **Review** tab. In the *Accessibility* group, click the **Check Accessibility** button. Issues that might interfere with a screen reader's ability to read the document appear in the *Warnings* section, including any figures that do not include an alt text description.

tell me **more**

If you have an Office 365 subscription, PowerPoint's intelligent services automatically analyzes any picture that is added to the presentation and creates an alt text description for the picture. However, the description that PowerPoint's intelligent services creates is not always accurate. It is important to check the alt text for the pictures in your presentations and edit them as necessary.

another **method**

To add alt text to images, you can also:

1. Select the picture to which you want to add the description.
2. Click the **Picture Tools Format** tab.
3. In the *Accessibility* group, click the **Alt Text** button.

let me **try**

If you do not have the data file from the previous skill open, open the student data file **pp2-15-SpaServices** and try this skill on your own:

1. Select the picture on **Slide 2**.
2. Open the **Alt Text** task pane.
3. Add the following description as alt text and then close the task pane when you are done: `Woman getting a facial`
4. If you will be moving on to the next skill in this chapter, leave the presentation open to continue working. If not, save the file as directed by your instructor and close it.

Skill 2.16 Adding Online Pictures

In addition to adding pictures from your computer, you can also search online to find more pictures to add to presentations. Using PowerPoint's **Online Pictures** feature, you can search for pictures through *Bing Image Search*, or from your OneDrive. When you search using *Bing Image Search*, you will be searching for images from across the Internet and will return images that have the Creative Commons licensing tag. Searching for images on your OneDrive will return images that you have added to your OneDrive for use in presentations.

To add an online picture:

1. Click the **Insert** tab.
2. In the *Illustrations* group, click the **Online Pictures** button.

FIGURE PP 2.27

3. The *Online Pictures* dialog opens.
4. Type a word describing the image you want to search for in the *Search* box and press ⏎Enter.
5. PowerPoint displays thumbnail results that match the search criteria.
6. Click a thumbnail to select it and click the **Insert** button to add the image to your presentation.

FIGURE PP 2.28

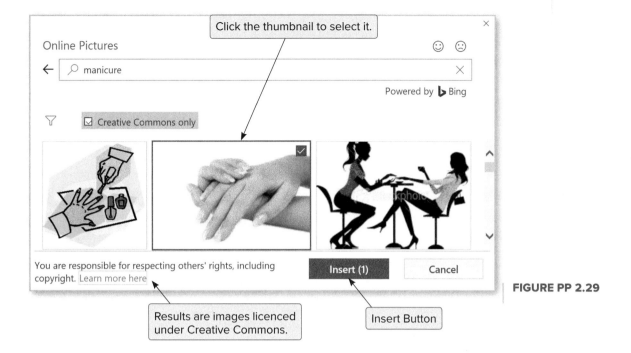

Click the thumbnail to select it.

Results are images licenced under Creative Commons.

Insert Button

FIGURE PP 2.29

tips & tricks

❯ If you use *Bing Image Search*, you will be searching the Internet for images that have been filtered based on the Creative Commons licensing system. However, the results you see may not include images that are royalty free. Always check the source of the image to be sure you use only images in your presentations that you know you have the proper rights to use.

❯ Rather than entering search terms, you can browse online pictures by subject matter. On the first screen of the *Online Pictures* dialog, under the *Search* box, you will see a grid of categories. Click a category to view the online pictures related to that subject.

tell me **more**

In previous versions of PowerPoint, you were able to search Microsoft's free Clip Art collection. In 2014, Microsoft stopped offering access to this collection of images.

another **method**

To open the *Online Pictures* dialog, you can also click the **Online Pictures** icon in the content placeholder.

let me **try**

If you do not have the data file from the previous skill open, open the student data file **pp2-16-SpaServices** and try this skill on your own:

1. Navigate to **Slide 3** and open the **Online Pictures** dialog.
2. Search for images using the keyword **manicure**.
3. Insert the image of your choice.
4. If you will be moving on to the next skill in this chapter, leave the presentation open to continue working. If not, save the file as directed by your instructor and close it.

Skill 2.17 Adding 3D Models

A **3D model** is a mathematical representation of an object created by special 3D modeling software. The resulting graphic object can be very realistic and detailed. In addition, the object can be rotated along three axes, allowing for it to be viewed from a number of different angles.

FIGURE PP 2.30

To add a 3D model to a slide:

1. Click the **Insert** tab.
2. In the *Illustrations* group, click the top half of the **3D Models** button.

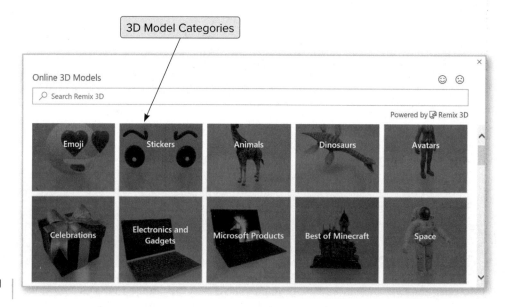

FIGURE PP 2.31

3. The *Online 3D Models* dialog opens.
4. Click a category of 3D models.
5. Click a thumbnail to select it and click the **Insert** button to add the 3D model to your presentation.

Click a thumbnail to select it.

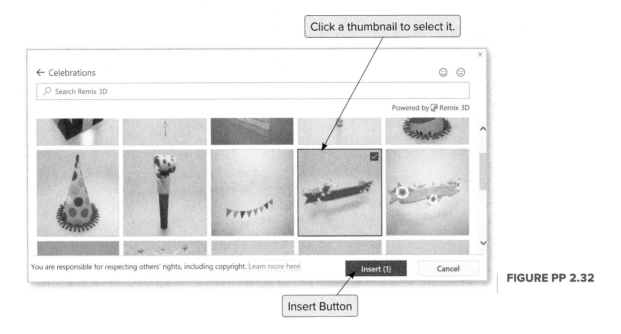

FIGURE PP 2.32

Insert Button

tips & tricks

❯ You can also search for 3D models using keywords. Type a word describing the image you want to search for in the *Search* box and press ⏎ Enter . PowerPoint displays thumbnail results that match the search criteria.

❯ 3D models are complex images that can be rotated along three different axes, but this also means that the images contain a large amount of data and can increase the size of your presentation. The more complex the model, the larger your presentation will be, so be careful when choosing which models to add to a presentation.

tell me **more**

The online 3D models in PowerPoint come from Microsoft's Remix 3D website. Remix 3D is a site created by Microsoft to allow users to share and download 3D models.

another **method**

To open the *Online 3D Models* dialog, you can also click the bottom part of the **3D Models** button and select **From Online Sources...**

let me **try**

If you do not have the data file from the previous skill open, open the student data file **pp2-17-SpaServices** and try this skill on your own:

1. Navigate to **Slide 2** and open the **Online 3D Models** dialog.
2. Navigate to the **Celebrations** category and insert the purple banner with the purple flowers. It is the fourth option in the second row of the dialog.
3. If you will be moving on to the next skill in this chapter, leave the presentation open to continue working. If not, save the file as directed by your instructor and close it.

Skill 2.18 Changing the Size of Images

When you first add an image to a slide, more than likely it is not the size you want. It will either be too small or too large. You can resize images in a presentation by either manually entering the values for the size of the picture or by dragging a **resize handle** on the image to resize it.

To resize an image using the drag method:

1. Select the picture you want to resize.

2. Point to one of the resize handles on the image.

3. When the mouse changes to the resize cursor, click and drag the mouse:
   - Drag the mouse toward the center of the image to make it smaller.
   - Drag the mouse away from the center of the image to make it larger.

4. When the image is the size you want, release the mouse button.

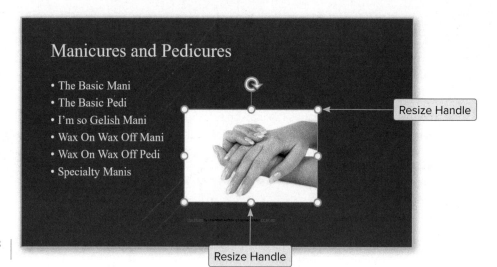

FIGURE PP 2.33

To resize a picture by manually entering values:

1. Select the picture you want to resize.

2. Click the **Picture Tools Format** tab.

3. In the *Size* group, type a value in the *Width* or *Height* box to resize the picture.

4. Press (←Enter) to resize the picture.

FIGURE PP 2.34

tips & tricks

❯ When resizing by dragging, be sure to use one of the resize handles on the four corners of the picture to maintain the aspect ratio of the picture. If you use a resize handle along one of the sides of the picture, you will be resizing the width of the picture only. If you use a resize handle along the top or bottom of the picture, you will be resizing the height of the picture only.

❯ When you enter a value in the *Width* or *Height* box on the Ribbon, the value in the other box will change to maintain the aspect ratio for the picture.

tell me **more**

You can use these same steps to resize drawing objects. On the *Drawing Tools Format* tab, in the *Size* group, enter the size values in the *Shape Height* and *Shape Width* boxes.

let me **try**

If you do not have the data file from the previous skill open, open the student data file **pp2-18-SpaServices** and try this skill on your own:

1. Select the picture of the manicure on **Slide 3**.
2. Click and drag the upper left corner resize handle and drag toward the middle of the picture to make the picture smaller until it is approximately 3 inches in height.
3. If necessary, manually change the size of the picture to be exactly **3"** in height and allow PowerPoint to automatically resize the width.
4. If you will be moving on to the next skill in this chapter, leave the presentation open to continue working. If not, save the file as directed by your instructor and close it.

Skill 2.19 Aligning Objects

When designing a presentation, it is important to place your slide objects so they will have the most impact on your audience. Any objects that appear in a straight line should be aligned to ensure they are precisely placed. You can also distribute objects on a slide ensuring they are evenly spaced.

To align objects on a slide:

1. Select the objects you want to align. To select more than one object, click the first object, press the ⇧ Shift key, click the second object, and release the ⇧ Shift key.
2. On the *Picture Tools Format* tab, in the *Arrange* group, click the **Align** button.
3. Verify the **Align Selected Objects** option is selected and select an option:
   - The *Align Left*, *Align Center*, and *Align Right* commands align objects along an invisible vertical line.
   - The *Align Top*, *Align Middle*, and *Align Bottom* commands align objects along an invisible horizontal line.

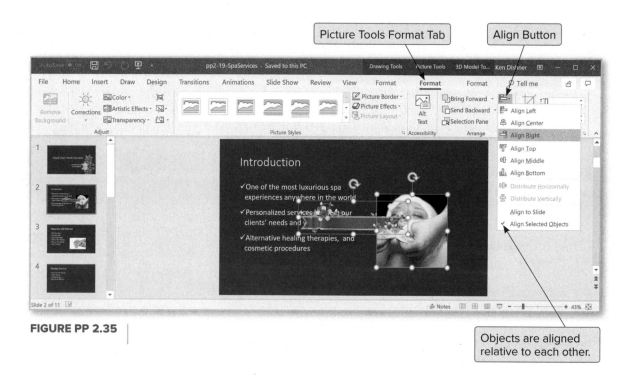

Picture Tools Format Tab

Align Button

FIGURE PP 2.35

Objects are aligned relative to each other.

To distribute objects on a slide:

1. Select the objects you want to align.
2. On the *Picture Tools Format* tab, in the *Arrange* group, click the **Align** button.
3. Select **Align to Slide**.
4. The *Distribute Horizontally* and *Distribute Vertically* options become active.
5. Click the **Align** button again and select an option.

FIGURE PP 2.36

tips & tricks

From the *View* tab you can display gridlines in the *Slide* pane, which is helpful when you have many objects you want to align.

tell me **more**

You can use these same steps to align drawing objects. On the *Drawing Tools Format* tab, in the *Arrange* group, click the **Align** button and select an option.

another **method**

To align objects on a slide, you can also:

1. Click the **Drawing Tools Format** tab for drawing objects, click the **Picture Tools Format** tab for pictures, or click the **3D Model Tools** tab for 3D models.

2. In the *Arrange* group, click the **Align** button and select an option.

let me **try**

If you do not have the data file from the previous skill open, open the student data file **pp2-19-SpaServices** and try this skill on your own:

1. Select the picture and the 3D model on **Slide 2**.

2. Change the alignment on the images to be **right-aligned**. Be sure to align the pictures relative to each other and not the slide.

3. Change the distribution of the pictures so they are evenly spaced **vertically**.

4. If you will be moving on to the next skill in this chapter, leave the presentation open to continue working. If not, save the file as directed by your instructor and close it.

Skill 2.20 Moving Objects Using Smart Guides

When you first add an image to a slide, you may find it is not positioned where you want it. You can change the position of images by dragging and dropping the image where you want it on the slide. When you drag an image, you will see horizontal and vertical dotted lines. These lines are the **smart guides**. They appear when the image's edge is aligned with another object or area on the slide.

To move images on a slide:

1. Select the image you want to move.

2. Rest your mouse over the image.

3. When the cursor changes to the **move cursor**, click and drag the image to the new location.

4. When a smart guide appears aligning it with the desired element on the slide, release the mouse button to snap the image in place and align it on the slide.

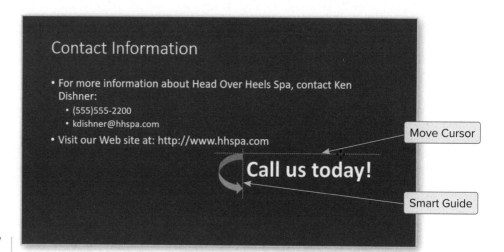

FIGURE PP 2.37

tips & tricks

To turn off smart guides, click the **View** tab. In the *Show* group, click the **dialog launcher**. In the *Grid and Guides* dialog, click the **Display smart guides when shapes are aligned** check box to deselect it.

tell me more

PowerPoint also includes **drawing guides** that are different from smart guides. Drawing guides divide the slide into four quadrants to help you place images on a slide. To turn on drawing guides, click the **View** tab. In the *Show* group, click the **Guides** check box.

let me try

If you do not have the data file from the previous skill open, open the student data file **pp2-20-SpaServices** and try this skill on your own:

1. On **Slide 10**, click and drag the WordArt (**Call Us Today!**) so the top of the text box is aligned with the top of the arrow shape. Use smart guides to help place the image (see Figure PP 2.37).

2. If you will be moving on to the next skill in this chapter, leave the presentation open to continue working. If not, save the file as directed by your instructor and close it.

Skill 2.21 Using Gridlines and the Ruler

When you are designing slides in your presentation, aligning placeholders and images can be the difference between a polished presentation and one that looks thrown together. Use PowerPoint's rulers and gridlines as visual tools to check the placement of text and images on your slides. The **ruler** allows you to control the placement of text in placeholders, including tabs and indents. **Gridlines** are a series of dotted vertical and horizontal lines that divide the slide into small boxes, giving you visual markers for aligning placeholders and images.

To display gridlines:

1. Click the **View** tab.
2. In the *Show* group, click the **Gridlines** check box to select it.
3. Click the **Gridlines** check box again to hide the gridlines.

To display the ruler:

1. Click the **View** tab.
2. In the *Show* group, click the **Ruler** check box to select it.
3. Click the **Ruler** check box again to hide the ruler.

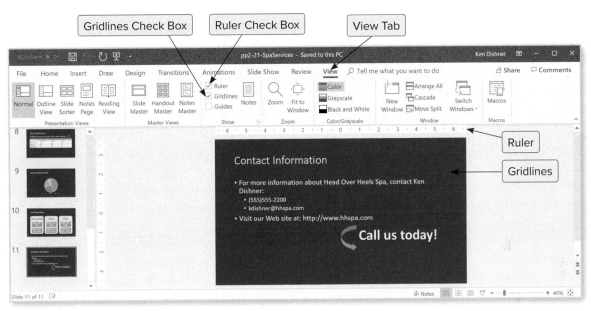

FIGURE PP 2.38

tell me **more**

The gridlines and ruler are visible only when you are working on the presentation. They do not appear when you show the presentation in Slide Show view or when you print handouts.

let me **try**

If you do not have the data file from the previous skill open, open the student data file **pp2-21-SpaServices** and try this skill on your own:

1. Display the **ruler**.
2. Display the **gridlines**.
3. Hide the **ruler** and **gridlines**.
4. If you will be moving on to the next skill in this chapter, leave the presentation open to continue working. If not, save the file as directed by your instructor and close it.

Skill 2.22 Adding Audio

An **audio file**, such as music or sound effects, can enhance your slides, making them more engaging to your audience. You can add audio to a presentation by inserting sound files from your computer.

To insert sound files from your computer:

1. Click the **Insert** tab.
2. In the *Media* group, click the **Insert Audio** button and select **Audio on My PC...**

FIGURE PP 2.39

3. The *Insert Audio* dialog opens.
4. Navigate to the file location, select the file, and click **Insert**.
5. The sound icon along with a playbar appears on the slide.

FIGURE PP 2.40

When you add a sound to a slide, the *Audio Tools* contextual tabs display. These tabs contain commands for working with sound objects in PowerPoint:

〉 The *Format* tab allows you to change the look of the sound icon in the presentation, including applying artistic effects and Quick Styles to the icon.

〉 The *Playback* tab provides tools for editing the audio file within PowerPoint. From the *Playback* tab, you can change the slide show volume, fade the audio in and out, loop the sound, and preview the sound.

When you add a sound to a slide, a sound icon is added to the slide. When you run your presentation, this icon will display as part of the slide, and a play bar will display when you rest your pointer over it.

To hide the icon:

1. Click the **Playback** tab under *Audio Tools*.

2. In the *Audio Options* group, click the **Hide During Show** check box.

3. Click the **Play in Background** button to hide the icon and play bar, play the sound file automatically, and play it across all slides in a continuous loop.

FIGURE PP 2.41

tips & tricks

Rest your mouse over an icon in the *Insert Audio* dialog to hear a sample of the sound file.

tell me **more**

There are a number of audio file types you can choose to add to your presentations. Some of the more common types include MP3 audio file (mp3), MP4 Audio, Windows audio file (wav), and Windows Media Audio file (wma).

let me **try**

If you do not have the data file from the previous skill open, open the student data file **pp2-22-SpaServices** and try this skill on your own:

1. On **Slide 1**, open the **Insert Audio** dialog to add an audio file from your computer.

2. Navigate to the location where you saved the data files for this book.

3. Insert the **spa opener** audio file.

4. Change the playback settings to have the clip **play in the background**.

5. If you will be moving on to the next skill in this chapter, leave the presentation open to continue working. If not, save the file as directed by your instructor and close it.

Skill 2.23 Adding Video

Today, almost everyone with a smartphone has the ability to take digital videos. Now more than ever you can take your own video, save it to your computer, and then add it to your presentations. If you have a **video file** you want to use in your presentation, you can add the file to your presentation from your computer. When you add a video file, PowerPoint adds the image of the first frame of the video with the playback controls under it.

To add video from your computer:

1. Click the **Insert** tab.
2. In the *Media* group, click the **Insert Video** button and select **Video on My PC...**

FIGURE PP 2.42

3. The *Insert Video* dialog opens.
4. Navigate to the file location, select the file, and click **Insert**.

FIGURE PP 2.43

When you add a video to a slide, the *Video Tools* contextual tabs display. These tabs contain commands for working with video objects in PowerPoint:

》 The *Format* tab allows you to change the look of the video frame in the presentation, including applying artistic effects and Quick Styles.

》 The *Playback* tab provides tools for editing the video file within PowerPoint. From the Playback tab, you can change the video volume, fade the video in and out, loop the video, and preview the video.

Video Tools Playback Tab

FIGURE PP 2.44

tips & tricks

When you add a video to a presentation, it is treated as if it is a picture. You can move and position the video using alignment guides, as well as apply picture Quick Styles from the *Picture Tools Format* tab.

tell me **more**

There are a number of video file types you can choose to add to your presentations. Some of the more common types include QuickTime (mov) and MPEG (mp4).

another **method**

You can also add a video from your computer using the content placeholder. Click the **Insert Video** button in the content placeholder. In the dialog that opens, click the **Browse...** button next to *From a file*.

let me **try**

If you do not have the data file from the previous skill open, open the student data file **pp2-23-SpaServices** and try this skill on your own:

1. On **Slide 3**, open the **Insert Video** dialog.
2. Navigate to the location where you saved the data files for this book.
3. Insert the **spa pedicure** video file.
4. Save the file as directed by your instructor and close it.

key terms

Outline view
Copy
Clipboard
Paste
Paste Options
Cut
Bulleted lists
Multilevel list
Numbered lists
WordArt
Content placeholder
Table
Rows
Columns
Cell

Chart
SmartArt
Shape
Icons
Alt text
Online Pictures
3D model
Resize handle
Smart guides
Drawing guides
Ruler
Gridlines
Audio file
Video file

concept review

1. When creating slides from a Word outline, text with which style applied to it will become the title text for each slide?

   a. Heading 1

   b. Heading 2

   c. Heading 3

   d. Title

2. Which command would you use to copy text to the Clipboard and not remove it from the presentation?

   a. Copy

   b. Cut

   c. Undo

   d. Redo

3. Which would you use to display items in a list in a particular order?

   a. bulleted list

   b. numbered list

   c. SmartArt diagram

   d. table

4. Text that includes predefined graphic styles, such as shadows, reflections, and glows, is known as _____.

   a. SmartArt

   b. shapes

   c. WordArt

   d. fonts

5. Which of the following is a special type of placeholder that gives you a quick way to add a variety of material to your presentations?

    a. text

    b. slide

    c. content

    d. title

6. What is the intersection of a row and column in a table called?

    a. placeholder

    b. data point

    c. cell

    d. axis

7. Which of the following are visual diagrams containing graphic elements with text boxes in which you enter information?

    a. SmartArt

    b. tables

    c. charts

    d. 3D models

8. Which of the following are added to a document as an SVG image?

    a. charts

    b. SmartArt

    c. icons

    d. shapes

9. Which of the following graphic objects can be rotated along three different axes?

    a. icons

    b. charts

    c. SmartArt

    d. 3D models

10. Which command hides the sound icon and plays an audio file across the entire presentation?

    a. *Hide During Show* check box

    b. *Play in Background* button

    c. *Volume* button

    d. No Style

projects

Data files for projects can be found by logging into your SIMnet account and going to the *Library* section.

skill review 2.1

In this project you will be adding content to a presentation for Suarez Marketing. First you will create slides by importing an outline from Word. You will then edit the content using Outline view and move content using the Cut and Paste commands. You will add visual elements including shapes, pictures, icons, and SmartArt as well as add a table of information to the presentation. Finally, you will add an audio file to the presentation and have it play in background.

Skills needed to complete this project:

- Importing Slides from a Word Outline (Skill 2.1)
- Using the Outline View (Skill 2.2)
- Using Cut and Paste (Skill 2.4)
- Adding Numbered Lists (Skill 2.6)
- Adding Shapes (Skill 2.12)
- Changing the Size of Images (Skill 2.18)
- Understanding the Content Placeholder (Skill 2.8)
- Adding SmartArt (Skill 2.11)
- Inserting an Icon (Skill 2.13)
- Creating Tables in Presentations (Skill 2.9)
- Adding Pictures (Skill 2.14)
- Adding Alt Text to Pictures (Skill 2.15)
- Moving Objects Using Smart Guides (Skill 2.20)
- Adding WordArt (Skill 2.7)
- Adding Audio (Skill 2.22)

1. Open the start file **PP2019-SkillReview-2-1** presentation and resave the file as: [your initials]PP-SkillReview-2-1

2. If the presentation opens in Protected View, click the **Enable Editing** button in the Message Bar at the top of the presentation so you can modify it.

3. Insert slide content from a Word outline.

   a. On the *Home* tab, in the *Slides* group, click the **New Slide** button.

   b. Select **Slides from Outline...**

   c. In the *Insert Outline* dialog, navigate to the location where you saved the data files for this book.

   d. Select the **SuarezMarketingOutline** document and click the **Insert** button.

4. Add text to a slide from Outline view.

   a. Click the **View** tab.

   b. In the *Presentation Views* group, click the **Outline View** button.

c. Place the cursor before **PHONE** on **Slide 1**. Press (←Enter) and move the cursor to the empty line that was added.

d. Type: PUTTING YOUR NEEDS FIRST

e. In the *Presentation Views* group, click the **Normal** button to return to Normal view.

5. Cut and paste text from one slide to another.

   a. Navigate to **Slide 3**.

   b. Select the first bullet point: **We are dedicated to listening to your needs and working with you to develop a strategic plan to grow your business.**

   c. Click the **Home** tab.

   d. In the *Clipboard* group, click the **Cut** button. If there is an empty line where the text was, delete the empty line so there are two bulleted items on the slide.

   e. Navigate to **Slide 2**, click in the text placeholder. In the *Clipboard* group, click the **Paste** button.

6. Create a numbered list.

   a. Navigate to **Slide 4** and select the bullet points on the slide.

   b. On the *Home* tab, in the *Paragraph* group, click the **Numbering** button arrow and select the **1), 2), 3)** format.

7. Add a shape to a slide.

   a. Navigate to **Slide 5**.

   b. On the *Home* tab, in the *Drawing* group, click the **More** button on the *Shapes* gallery and select the **Speech Bubble: Oval** shape (it is the third option under *Callouts*).

   c. Add the shape to the right of the slide title.

8. Resize the shape.

   a. Verify the callout you added is still selected.

   b. Click the **Drawing Tools Format** tab.

   c. In the *Size* group, enter **1"** in the *Shape Height* box and **2"** in the *Shape Width* box.

9. Change the layout of a slide to include a content placeholder.

   a. Navigate to **Slide 8**.

   b. On the *Home* tab, in the *Slides* group, click the **Slide Layout** button and select **Title and Content**.

10. Add a SmartArt diagram.

    a. On **Slide 8**, click the **SmartArt** icon in the content placeholder.

    b. In the *Choose a SmartArt Graphic* dialog, click the **Process** category.

    c. Click the **Basic Chevron Process** diagram. It is the second option in the fourth row of the dialog.

    d. Click **OK** to add the SmartArt diagram to the slide.

    e. In the first rectangle, type: Analyze

    f. In the second rectangle, type: Design

    g. In the third rectangle, type: Implement

11. Add an icon to a slide.

    a. Verify you are still on **Slide 8**.

    b. Click the **Insert** tab.

c. In the *Illustrations* group, click the **Icons** button.

d. In the *Insert Icons* dialog, click the **Analytics** category.

e. Click the icon of the **two gears**. It is the ninth icon in the category.

f. Click the **Insert** button.

12. Apply a style to the icon and move it on the slide.

a. On the *Graphics Tools Format* tab, click the **Light 1 Fill, Colored Outline - Accent 1** graphics style. It is the second option in gallery.

b. Move the icon to the right of the slide's title (after *The Suarez Process*).

13. Change the layout of a slide to include a content placeholder.

a. Navigate to **Slide 9**.

b. On the *Home* tab, in the *Slides* group, click the **Slide Layout** button and select **Title and Content**.

14. Add a table.

a. On **Slide 9**, click the **Insert Table** icon.

b. In the *Insert Table* dialog, in the *Number of columns* box, type **2**. In the *Number of rows* box, type **4**.

c. Click **OK**.

d. Enter the following information in the table:

Belief	What it means at Suarez
Commitment	Doing everything possible for the client
Teamwork	Working together for success
Trust	Openness and honesty above all

15. Add a picture from your computer.

a. Click the **Insert** tab.

b. In the *Images* group, click the **Pictures** button.

c. In the *Insert Picture* dialog, navigate to the location where you saved your data files.

d. Select the **teamwork** image and click **Insert**.

16. Add alt text to a picture.

a. Right-click the picture and select **Edit Alt Text...**

b. In the *Alt Text* task pane, type `silhouette of two business people high fiving each other`

17. Change the size of the image.

a. Verify the picture you added is still selected.

b. Click the **Picture Tools Format** tab.

c. In the Size group, enter **2.5"** in the *Shape Height* box and **1.77"** in the *Shape Width* box.

18. Move the picture to the lower right corner of the slide so it appears below the table. Use the smart guides to align the right edge of the picture with the right edge of the table.

19. Add WordArt to a slide.

a. Navigate to **Slide 1.**

b. Select the **title placeholder** and press (Delete). The text is deleted.

c. Select the **title placeholder** again and press (Delete) to remove the placeholder.

d. Click the **Insert** tab.

e. In the *Text* group, click the **WordArt** button and select the **Fill: White; Outline: Plum, Accent color 1; Glow: Plum, Accent color 1** option (the fourth option in the second row of the gallery).

f. Type: Suarez Marketing

20. Insert an audio file.

a. Verify you are still on **Slide 1**.

b. Click the **Insert** tab.

c. In the *Media* group, click the **Audio** button and select **Audio on my PC...**

d. In the *Insert Audio* dialog, navigate to the location where you saved the data files for this book.

e. Select the **intro music** audio file and click **Insert**.

21. Adjust the settings of the audio file.

a. Verify the **audio icon** on **Slide 1** is selected.

b. On the *Audio Tools Playback* tab, in the *Audio Styles* group, click the **Play in Background** button.

22. Save and close the presentation.

skill review 2.2

In this project you will be modifying the *My Fitness Plan* presentation by adding content. You will change text using Outline view and the Copy and Paste commands. You will add pictures both from your computer and from online. You will then resize and move the pictures you add. You will change a numbered list into a bulleted list. You will display data in a chart and add WordArt and a shape to a slide. Finally, you will add an audio file from your computer and have the audio play in the background.

Skills needed to complete this project:

- Using the Outline View (Skill 2.2)
- Using Copy and Paste (Skill 2.3)
- Adding Bulleted Lists (Skill 2.5)
- Adding Pictures (Skill 2.14)
- Adding Alt Text to Pictures (Skill 2.15)
- Changing the Size of Images (Skill 2.18)
- Aligning Objects (Skill 2.19)
- Inserting an Icon (Skill 2.13)
- Moving Objects Using Smart Guides (Skill 2.20)
- Understanding the Content Placeholder (Skill 2.8)
- Adding Charts (Skill 2.10)
- Adding WordArt (Skill 2.7)
- Adding Shapes (Skill 2.12)
- Adding Audio (Skill 2.22)

1. Open the start file **PP2019-SkillReview-2-2** presentation and resave the file as: `[your initials]PP-SkillReview-2-2`

2. If the presentation opens in Protected View, click the **Enable Editing** button in the Message Bar at the top of the presentation so you can modify it.

3. Add text to a slide through Outline view.

   a. Click the **View** tab.

   b. In the *Presentation Views* group, click the **Outline View** button.

   c. Click next to the square for **Slide 2** on the *Outline* pane.

   d. Type: `Eating Habits`

   e. In the *Presentation Views* group, click the **Normal View** button.

4. Copy and paste text from one slide to another.

   a. Navigate to **Slide 4**.

   b. Select the third bullet point: **Take a nap when possible.**

   c. Click the **Home** tab.

   d. In the *Clipboard* group, click the **Copy** button.

   e. Navigate to **Slide 6**.

   f. Place the cursor after the last bullet point (**Quiet time**) and press `← Enter`.

   g. In the *Clipboard* group, click the **Paste** button.

5. Convert a numbered list into a bulleted list.

   a. Navigate to **Slide 7**.

   b. Select the numbered list.

   c. On the *Home* tab, in the *Paragraph* group, click the **Bullets** button arrow.

   d. Select the **Hollow Square Bullets** option.

6. Add a picture from your computer.

   a. Navigate to **Slide 2**.

   b. Click the **Insert** tab.

   c. In the *Images* group, click the **Pictures** button.

   d. In the *Insert Picture* dialog, navigate to the location where you saved your data files.

   e. Select the **fruits and veggies** image and click **Insert**.

7. Add alt text to the picture.

   a. Right-click the picture and select **Edit Alt Text...**

   b. In the *Alt Text* task pane, if necessary, delete any text that appear in the text box. Type `fruits and veggies on a table`

8. Resize the image.

   a. Verify the image is still selected.

   b. On the *Picture Tools Format* tab, in the *Size* group, type **5.5"** in the *Width* box.

   c. Press `← Enter`.

9. Align an image.

   a. Verify the image is still selected.

   b. On the *Picture Tools Format* tab, in the *Arrange* group, click the **Align** button and select **Align Left**.

   c. Click the **Align** button again and select **Align Bottom**.

10. Add an icon.

    a. Navigate to **Slide 7**.

    b. Click the **Insert** tab.

    c. In the *Illustrations* group, click the **Icons** button.

    d. Click the **Analytics** category.

    e. Click the icon of the **target with an arrow**. It is the fifth option in the *Analytics* category.

    f. Click the **Insert** button.

    g. Resize the icon so it is **4"** wide and **4"** tall.

11. Apply a style to the icon.

    a. On the *Graphics Tools Format* tab, in the *Graphics Styles* group, click the **More** button to expand the gallery.

    b. Click the **Colored Fill - Accent 1, Dark 1 Outline** graphics style. It is the second option in the third row of the gallery.

12. Move an object using smart guides.

    a. Verify the icon you inserted is still selected.

    b. Move the icon so it appears to the right of the bulleted list. Use the smart guides to align the top of the icon object with the top of the bulleted list.

13. Add a chart to a slide.

    a. Navigate to **Slide 8**.

    b. Click in the title placeholder and type `Calories in and Calories Out`

    c. Click the **Insert Chart** icon in the content placeholder.

    d. In the *Insert Chart* dialog, select a **Clustered Column** chart (the first option in the Column category), and click **OK**.

    e. In the *Chart in Microsoft PowerPoint* dialog, delete the **Series 3** column.

    f. Insert the following data for the chart. **NOTE:** When you add Thursday through Saturday, you may see a message box indicating a problem with the data. Click **OK** in the message box to continue adding the information:

	Calories Consumed	Calories Burned
Sunday	1525	475
Monday	1675	320
Tuesday	1400	365
Wednesday	1250	200
Thursday	1740	426
Friday	1760	230
Saturday	2200	705

    g. Close the **Chart in Microsoft PowerPoint** dialog.

14. Add WordArt to a slide.

    a. Navigate to **Slide 9**.

    b. Click the **Insert** tab.

    c. In the *Text* group, click the **WordArt** button and select the **Fill: Turquoise, Accent color 1; Shadow** option (the second option in the first row of the gallery).

d. Type: **I know I can do it!**

e. Click outside the text box to deselect it.

15. Add a shape to a slide.

    a. Click the **Insert** tab.

    b. In the *Illustrations* group, click the **Shapes** button and select the **Smiley Face** (it is located in the third row under *Basic Shapes*).

    c. Add the shape on the lower right side of the WordArt you added.

16. Insert an audio file.

    a. Click the **Insert** tab.

    b. In the *Media* group, click the **Audio** button and select **Audio on My PC...**

    c. In the *Insert Audio* dialog, navigate to the location where you saved the data files for this book.

    d. Select the **closing song** audio file.

    e. Click the **Insert** button.

17. Adjust the settings of the audio file.

    a. Verify the audio file is selected on the slide.

    b. On the *Audio Tools Playback* tab, in the *Audio Styles* group, click the **Play in Background** button.

18. Save and close the presentation.

challenge yourself 2.3

In this project you will be adding content to a presentation for the Greenscapes landscaping company. First, you will import slide content from an outline created in Word. You will add a 3D model and adjust the placement of the model. You will work in Outline view and use the Cut and Paste commands to move text. You will convert text to a numbered list and add a SmartArt diagram and a table. You will insert a picture and add alt text to the picture. You will add WordArt and position the WordArt on the slide using smart guides. Finally, you will add an audio file and have the audio play in the background.

Skills needed to complete this project:

- Importing Slides from a Word Outline (Skill 2.1)
- Using Gridlines and the Ruler (Skill 2.21)
- Adding 3D Models (Skill 2.17)
- Moving Objects Using Smart Guides (Skill 2.20)
- Using the Outline View (Skill 2.2)
- Using Cut and Paste (Skill 2.4)
- Adding Numbered Lists (Skill 2.6)
- Understanding the Content Placeholder (Skill 2.8)
- Adding SmartArt (Skill 2.11)
- Creating Tables in Presentations (Skill 2.9)
- Adding Pictures (Skill 2.14)
- Adding Alt Text to Pictures (Skill 2.15)
- Changing the Size of Images (Skill 2.18)

- Aligning Objects (Skill 2.19)
- Adding WordArt (Skill 2.7)
- Adding Audio (Skill 2.22)

1. Open the start file **PP2019-ChallengeYourself-2-3** presentation and resave the file as:
   [your initials]PP-ChallengeYourself-2-3

2. If the presentation opens in Protected View, click the **Enable Editing** button in the Message Bar at the top of the presentation so you can modify it.

3. Open the *Insert Outline* dialog. Navigate to the location where you saved your data files and insert the **greenscapesOutline** document.

4. In the **Title placeholder** on **Slide 1**, type **Greenscapes**

5. In the **Subtitle placeholder** on **Slide 1**, type **natural, organic, beautiful**

6. If necessary, display the **ruler**.

7. Add the 3D model of the **purple flowers** to **Slide 1**. It is the first option in the *Spring* category of the *Online 3D Models* dialog.

8. Move the model to the lower left corner of the slide aligning the top of the model at **0** on the ruler. You will know the object is aligned when you see the horizontal smart guide appear.

9. Switch to Outline view. Add the text **Recycle and Reuse** as the last bullet point on **Slide 2**. Switch back to Normal view.

10. On **Slide 5**, select the first bullet point: **Water Landscapes**. Cut the text and paste it after the last bullet point (**Leaf Removal**) on **Slide 3**.

11. Select the bulleted list on **Slide 3**. Convert the list to a numbered list using the **1. 2. 3.** format.

12. Change the layout of **Slide 4** to the **Title and Content** layout.

13. Insert a **Chevron Accent Process** SmartArt diagram. In the box on the left, type **Blow and Rake**. In the middle box, type **Gather and Haul Away** In the box on the right, type **Compost**

14. Change the layout of **Slide 6** to the **Title and Content** layout.

15. Insert a table with **two columns** and **five rows**.

16. Enter the following information in the table:

Service	Price
Lawn Care	$25.00 per service
Lawn Maintenance	$99.00 per treatment
Leaf Removal	$25.00 per hour
Arborist	$125.00 per hour

17. Change the layout of **Slide 7** to the **Blank** layout.

18. Insert the **garden** image from the location where you saved the data files for this book.

19. Add the following as alt text for the picture: **garden landscape with red and yellow flowers**

20. Change the size of the image so it is **3" tall** and **4.48" wide**.

21. Align the picture so it appears along the left edge of the slide.

22. Align the picture so it is vertically aligned in the middle of the slide.

23. Add WordArt to the slide using the **Fill: Green, Accent color 1; Shadow** option (the second option in the first row of the gallery) that reads **Thank you!**

24. Drag the WordArt object up so the middle of the object is aligned with the middle of the picture you inserted. You will know the objects are aligned when you see the horizontal smart guide displayed across the WordArt and the picture.

25. Insert the **garden music** audio file from the locations where you saved the data files for this book.

26. Change the playback settings for the audio file so it will play in background during the presentation.

27. Save and close the presentation.

challenge yourself 2.4

In this project you will be adding content to a presentation about personal finance. You will add slide content by importing an outline from Word. You will then change the text using Outline view and the Cut and Paste commands. You will add an icon and adjust the position and look of the icon. You will add pictures both from your computer and from an online source. You will then add alt text, resize, and position the pictures on the slide. You will convert a bulleted list into a numbered list. Finally, you will add a table of information and display the data in a chart.

Skills needed to complete this project:

- Importing Slides from a Word Outline (Skill 2.1)
- Using the Outline View (Skill 2.2)
- Inserting an Icon (Skill 2.13)
- Aligning Objects (Skill 2.19)
- Using Cut and Paste (Skill 2.4)
- Adding Pictures (Skill 2.14)
- Adding Alt Text to Pictures (Skill 2.15)
- Changing the Size of Images (Skill 2.18)
- Adding Online Pictures (Skill 2.16)
- Using Gridlines and the Ruler (Skill 2.21)
- Moving Objects Using Smart Guides (Skill 2.20)
- Adding Numbered Lists (Skill 2.6)
- Understanding the Content Placeholder (Skill 2.8)
- Creating Tables in Presentations (Skill 2.9)
- Adding Charts (Skill 2.10)

1. Open the start file **PP2019-ChallengeYourself-2-4** presentation and resave the file as:
   [your initials]PP-ChallengeYourself-2-4

2. If the presentation opens in Protected View, click the **Enable Editing** button in the Message Bar at the top of the presentation so you can modify it.

3. Open the *Insert Outline* dialog. Navigate to the location where you saved your data files and insert the **PersonalFinanceOutline** document.

4. Switch to Outline view and replace the text **MY BUDGET** with the text The Smart and Easy Way to Save as the subtitle on **Slide 1**. Switch back to Normal view.

5. On **Slide 1**, insert the **piggy bank** icon. It is the last icon in the *Commerce* section of the dialog.

6. Use the alignment options to align the icon along the right side and the bottom of the slide.

7. Apply the **Colored Fill – Accent 1, Dark 1 Outline** graphics style to the icon. It is the second option in the third row of the gallery.

8. On **Slide 9**, cut the last bullet point (**Turn a hobby into a business**).

9. On **Slide 6**, paste the text you cut so it appears last in the list.

10. On **Slide 2**, insert the **save** image downloaded from the **Resources** link.

11. Add the following as alt text for the picture: SAVE tile letters on top of one dollar bills

12. Resize the image to be **2.3" tall** and **3.45" wide**.

13. On the same slide, search for a picture of a **piggy bank** through *Bing Image Search*. Insert a picture of your choice. If necessary, resize the image you inserted to be **3.36" wide** and allow PowerPoint to set the height, so it resizes proportionally.

14. Display the ruler and drag both images to the **3 mark** to the right of **0** on the ruler.

15. Select both pictures and align them along the **left** relative to each other.

16. Using the smart guides, drag the picture of the **piggy bank** below the **save image**. The side of the images should be aligned, and the top of the **piggy bank** image should be touching the bottom of the **save image**.

17. Navigate to **Slide 10** and convert the five items in the list to a numbered list using the **1., 2., 3.** format.

18. Navigate to **Slide 4** and change the layout of the slide to use the **Two Content** layout.

19. In the content placeholder on the left, add a table with **2 columns** and **6 rows**.

20. Enter the following information in the table:

Expense	Budget
Rent	$750
Utilities	$225
Credit Cards	$90
Groceries	$315
Entertainment	$125

21. In the placeholder on the right, add a **3-D pie chart** using the same information as the table.

22. Save and close the presentation.

In this project you will be modifying a presentation for a cookbook. First, you will add text using Outline view. You will then move text using cut and paste. You will convert text to a bulleted list. You will add a chart, table, and SmartArt diagram to the presentation. You will add an online picture, shape, icon, and WordArt. You will then resize, align, and move the objects you added.

Skills needed to complete this project:

- Using the Outline View (Skill 2.2)
- Using Cut and Paste (Skill 2.4)
- Adding Bulleted Lists (Skill 2.5)
- Understanding the Content Placeholder (Skill 2.8)
- Adding Charts (Skill 2.10)
- Creating Tables in Presentations (Skill 2.9)
- Adding SmartArt (Skill 2.11)
- Adding WordArt (Skill 2.7)
- Adding Online Pictures (Skill 2.16)
- Adding Alt Text to Pictures (Skill 2.15)
- Adding Shapes (Skill 2.12)
- Inserting an Icon (Skill 2.13)
- Changing the Size of Images (Skill 2.18)
- Aligning Objects (Skill 2.19)
- Moving Objects Using Smart Guides (Skill 2.20)

1. Open the start file **PP2019-OnYourOwn-2-5** presentation and resave the file as: `[your initials]PP-OnYourOwn-2-5`

2. If the presentation opens in Protected View, click the **Enable Editing** button in the Message Bar at the top of the presentation so you can modify it.

3. Using Outline view, add a subtitle to **Slide 1** of the presentation.

4. Navigate to **Slide 2** and reorder the points to an order of your choice.

5. On **Slide 2**, change the list to a **bulleted list** using a style of your choice.

6. Navigate to **Slide 3** and add a **chart** in the placeholder on the right. Base the data for the chart on the table on the left side of the slide.

7. Navigate to **Slide 4** and replace the text on the slide with a **table** using the same information.

8. Navigate to **Slide 5** and add a **SmartArt diagram** to the placeholder using a cycle diagram of your choice. Use the information on the *Clipboard* to fill in the diagram. Be sure to remove any extra SmartArt shapes in the diagram.

9. Navigate to **Slide 6** and add the text `Enjoy!` using a WordArt style of your choice.

10. On **Slide 6**, search **online** for pictures of **healthy food** and add an image of your choice.

11. Add appropriate alt text to the picture.

12. On **Slide 6**, add a shape of your choice to the slide.

13. On **Slide 6**, add an icon of your choice to the slide and apply a graphic style of your choice.

14. Resize the picture, shape, and icon you added to **Slide 6** so they are approximately the same size.

15. Use the **alignment** and **distribution** commands and **smart guides** to rearrange the objects on the slide.

16. Save and close the presentation.

fix it **2.6**

In this project you will be fixing a presentation about team building. First, you will fix mistakes in text using Outline view. You will then add an icon and modify the icon. You will move text around using cut and paste and fix missing text using copy and paste. You will convert a numbered list into a bulleted list. You will change the way information is presented. You will display information in a table, next you will create a chart to visually display data, and then you will create a SmartArt graphic to convey information. Finally, you will add a shape to fill out the look of the presentation and resize and align the shape on the slide.

Skills needed to complete this project:

- Using the Outline View (Skill 2.2)
- Using Cut and Paste (Skill 2.4)
- Using Copy and Paste (Skill 2.3)
- Adding Bulleted Lists (Skill 2.5)
- Creating Tables in Presentations (Skill 2.9)
- Understanding the Content Placeholder (Skill 2.8)
- Adding Charts (Skill 2.10)
- Adding SmartArt (Skill 2.11)
- Adding Shapes (Skill 2.12)
- Changing the Size of Images (Skill 2.18)
- Moving Objects Using Smart Guides (Skill 2.20)
- Aligning Objects (Skill 2.19)

1. Open the start file **PP2019-FixIt-2-6** presentation and resave the file as: `[your initials]PP-FixIt-2-6`

2. If the presentation opens in Protected View, click the **Enable Editing** button in the Message Bar at the top of the presentation so you can modify it.

3. Use Outline view to change the subtitle on **Slide 1** from **A PRIMER** to **AN OVERVIEW**

4. On **Slide 1**, add the icon of the **three people from the shoulders up**. It is the fifth option in the *People* category of the dialog.

5. Resize the icon to be **3"** wide and **3"** tall.

6. Apply the **Colored Fill - Accent 1, No Outline** graphics style to the icon. It is the second option in the second row of the gallery.

7. Display the ruler and move the icon so it is positioned at the **.5"** mark above 0 on the vertical ruler and the **2"** mark on the horizontal ruler. The icon should appear just above and to the right of the last letter in the title (*Team Orientation*).

8. On **Slide 3**, cut the first point (**Member introduction**) and paste it as the last bullet point on **Slide 2**.

9. Copy the slide title from **Slide 5** and paste the text in the title placeholder on **Slide 7**.

10. Convert the **numbered list** on **Slide 3** to a bulleted list using the **Arrow Bullets** style.

11. On **Slide 5**, move the text from the tabbed list into a new table. *Hint*: You can cut the text and then paste it into the table you add. You can then cut and paste each piece of text into the proper cell in the table. If you use this method, be sure to remove any extra line breaks and spaces.

12. On **Slide 6**, create a **Pie chart** from the data on the slide. Have the title of the chart read `Time`

13. On **Slide 7**, delete the bulleted list on the slide and add a **Nondirectional Cycle** SmartArt diagram. Include the following points (starting at the top and moving clockwise in the diagram):
    - `Specific`
    - `Measurable`
    - `Attainable`
    - `Relevant`
    - `Time Bound`

14. On **Slide 8**, add a **sun** shape to the right side of the slide title.

15. Resize the shape to be **2" tall** and **2" wide**.

16. Using smart guides, move the shape so the top of the shape is aligned with the top of the bulleted list.

17. Change the shape to be **center-aligned** on the slide.

18. Save and close the presentation.

chapter 3

Formatting Presentations

In this chapter, you will learn the following skills:

- Change themes
- Customize a theme
- Change the size of slides in a presentation
- Change the slide background
- Use Designer
- Apply slide transitions
- Modify the look of drawing objects
- Apply Quick Styles to drawing objects, tables, and pictures
- Modify SmartArt diagrams
- Format charts
- Add and modify animations

skills

introduction

This chapter provides you with the skills to modify the look of content in presentations. First, you will change the theme of a presentation and then modify the look of the theme. You will change the slide size and background in a presentation. You will use PowerPoint's Designer feature to change the look of a slide. You will apply transitions to all the slides in the presentation. You will learn how to change the look of objects by applying Quick Styles, changing the fill color, and modifying the outline. Finally, you will learn how to apply and modify animations including animations applied to 3D models.

Skill 3.1 Changing the Presentation Theme

A **theme** is a group of formatting options that you apply to a presentation. Themes include font, color, and effect styles that are applied to specific elements of a presentation. In PowerPoint, themes also include background styles. When you apply a theme, all the slides in the presentation are affected.

To apply a theme to the presentation:

1. Click the **Design** tab.
2. In the *Themes* group, click the **More** button ⌄.
3. Select an option in the *Themes* gallery.
4. All the slides in your presentation now use the new theme.

FIGURE PP 3.1

tell me **more**

Although themes are designed to make it easy for you to create a cohesive look for presentations, you may find that the themes available in the Microsoft Office applications are close to what you want, but not quite right for your presentation. To create your own version of a theme, all you need to do is change the theme's color, font, effect styles, or background style.

another **method**

To apply a theme, you can also click a theme on the Ribbon without opening the gallery.

let me **try**

Open the student data file **pp3-01-SpaServices** and try this skill on your own:

1. Change the presentation theme to the **Office Theme**.

2. If you will be moving on to the next skill in this chapter, leave the presentation open to continue working. If not, save the file as directed by your instructor and close it.

Skill 3.2 Customizing the Theme

When you apply a theme, it comes with a set of colors applied to text, the background, and objects in the presentation. But what if you like the layout of a theme, but you don't like the colors? PowerPoint allows you to choose from a number of theme variants to apply to a presentation. A **theme variant** is a set of color variations and backgrounds you can change for a theme.

To change the theme variant:

1. Click the **Design** tab.
2. In the *Variants* group, select a theme variant option.

FIGURE PP 3.2

You can further customize the theme by changing the other aspects of the theme:

Color themes—A **color theme** is a set of colors that are designed to work well together in a presentation. A color theme will change the color of text, tables, and drawing objects in a presentation.

Font themes—A **font theme** includes default fonts for titles and slide text.

Effects themes—An **effects theme** consists of line and fill effects that you apply to objects on your slides.

Background Styles—Each theme comes with a number of preset **background styles** you can apply to the presentation. Backgrounds range from light to dark colors and can be a solid color or a gradient.

To customize parts of the theme:

1. Click the **Design** tab.
2. In the *Variants* group, click the **More** button.
3. Point to an option on the menu to display a gallery of options.
4. Click an option to apply it to the theme.

Point to a menu item and select an option to further modify the theme.

FIGURE PP 3.3

tips & tricks

When you create a presentation from a template, you can choose the theme variant before you create the new presentation.

tell me **more**

After you have modified a theme, you can save it as your own custom theme by clicking the **More** button in the *Themes* group and selecting **Save Current Theme...** The file will be saved with the *thmx* file extension. The theme will be saved in the *Document Themes* folder and will be available from Excel, Word, and Outlook as well as PowerPoint.

let me **try**

If you do not have the data file from the previous skill open, open the student data file **pp3-02-SpaServices** and try this skill on your own:

1. Change the variant for the theme to use the third theme variant. It is the first one with a black background.

2. Change the background style for the presentation to use the **Style 7** style.

3. If you will be moving on to the next skill in this chapter, leave the presentation open to continue working. If not, save the file as directed by your instructor and close it.

Skill 3.3 Changing the Size of Slides

In past versions of PowerPoint, the default aspect ratio for slides was 4:3. This aspect ratio is square in appearance and does not translate well to widescreen displays. The default slide size in PowerPoint is now **widescreen 16:9**.

To change the size of slides in a presentation:

1. Click the **Design** tab.
2. In the *Customize* group, click the **Slide Size** button and select an option.

FIGURE PP 3.4

tips & tricks

Click **Custom Slide Size...** to open the *Slide Size* dialog where you can manually adjust the size of the slides in a presentation or select from a number of other preset options.

tell me more

If you change your slide size from widescreen (16:9) to standard (4:3), PowerPoint will give you the option of maximizing the content on the new slide size or to reduce the content size to ensure it will fit in the new slide size.

let me try

If you do not have the data file from the previous skill open, open the student data file **pp3-03-SpaServices** and try this skill on your own:

1. Change the slide size for the presentation to **Standard (4:3)**.
2. Ensure the content will fit the slides.
3. This is not the size you want. Click the **Undo** button on the Quick Access Toolbar to undo the change.
4. If you will be moving on to the next skill in this chapter, leave the presentation open to continue working. If not, save the file as directed by your instructor and close it.

Skill 3.4 Changing the Color of Slide Backgrounds

A **background** is the graphic element that fills a slide. Backgrounds can be solid colors, textures, or even images. From the *Format Background* task pane, you can adjust the look of the slide backgrounds.

To change the slide background to a solid color:

1. Click the **Design** tab.
2. In the *Customize* group, click the **Format Background** button.
3. The *Format Background* task pane displays.
4. In the *Fill* section, click the **Solid fill** radio button.
5. Click the **Color** button and select an option from the color palette.
6. Click the **Apply to All** button to change the background for all the slides in the presentation.

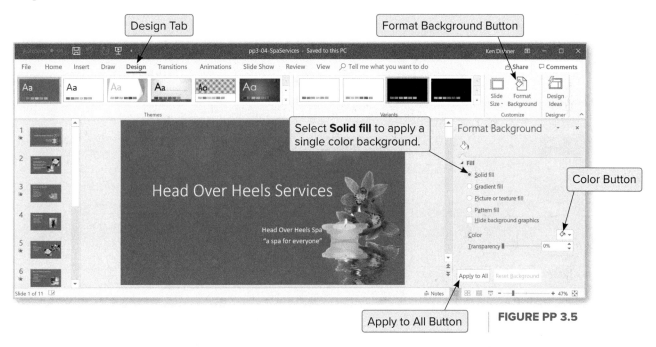

FIGURE PP 3.5

another **method**

To open the *Format Background* task pane, you can also right-click the background of a slide and select **Format Background...**

let me **try**

If you do not have the data file from the previous skill open, open the student data file **pp3-04-SpaServices** and try this skill on your own:

1. Display the **Format Background** task pane.
2. Apply a **solid fill** background using the **Blue-Gray, Background 2, Darker 25%** option (it is the third option in the second to last row under *Theme Colors*).
3. Apply the background to all the slides in the presentation.
4. If you will be moving on to the next skill in this chapter, leave the presentation open to continue working. If not, save the file as directed by your instructor and close it.

Skill 3.5 Applying a Pattern to Slide Backgrounds

In addition to solid color backgrounds, there are a number of other graphic treatments you can add to slide backgrounds in presentations. PowerPoint comes with a number of pattern fills you can apply. A **pattern fill** is a geometric pattern that repeats across the background of the slide. You can change the look of the pattern by adjusting the foreground and background colors.

To apply a pattern to a background:

1. Click the **Design** tab.
2. In the *Customize* group, click the **Format Background** button.
3. The *Format Background* task pane displays.
4. In the *Fill* section, click **Pattern fill**.
5. Click a pattern to apply to the slide background.
6. Click the **Foreground Color** button arrow and select a color.
7. Click the **Background Color** button arrow and select a color.

FIGURE PP 3.6

tips & tricks

❭ Click the **Reset Background** button to remove the changes you made and return the background to its original state.

❭ Click the **Apply to All** button to apply the custom background to all the slides in the presentation.

another **method**

To open the *Format Background* task pane, you can also right-click the background of a slide and select **Format Background...**

let me **try**

If you do not have the data file from the previous skill open, open the student data file **pp3-05-SpaServices** and try this skill on your own:

1. Verify you are on the first slide of the presentation.
2. Display the **Format Background** task pane.
3. Apply the **Horizontal Bricks** pattern to the background. It is the fourth option in the sixth row.
4. Change the foreground color to **Blue, Accent 1** (the fifth option in the first row under *Theme Colors*).
5. Change the background color to **Black, Background 1, Lighter 35%** (the first option in the third row under *Theme Colors*).
6. If you will be moving on to the next skill in this chapter, leave the presentation open to continue working. If not, save the file as directed by your instructor and close it.

from the perspective of . . .

MARKETING MANAGER

Working in the marketing field, I need to advertise to clients and present at business meetings. My boss used to tell me that my presentations were too plain and were putting the clients to sleep. Now I've added transitions and animations to my slides along with customized backgrounds. I use Designer to create highly stylized slides, and I use Quick Styles to apply formatting to pictures and shapes, making my presentations look great without a lot of work. Now when I give a presentation, I can see how engaged the clients are and my boss notices too!

Mike Kemp/Rubberball/Getty Images

Skill 3.6 Applying a Gradient to Slide Backgrounds

Applying a gradient to a slide background can give your slides more visual depth than just using a solid color. A **gradient** is the gradual transition of one color to another. In PowerPoint, a gradient background uses one color and then transitions from one shade of that color to other shades of the same color. The point where the gradient changes from one shade of the color to another is called a **gradient stop**.

To apply a gradient to a background:

1. Click the **Design** tab.
2. In the *Customize* group, click the **Format Background** button.
3. The *Format Background* task pane displays.
4. In the *Fill* section, click **Gradient fill**.
5. Click the **Preset gradients** button arrow to select from a set of gradients based on the presentation's theme.
6. Click the **Type** button arrow to choose a type of gradient. There are five basic types of gradients to choose from—*Linear*, *Radial*, *Rectangular*, *Path*, and *Shade from title*.
7. Click the **Direction** button arrow to change the position where the first gradient stop will appear and the direction the gradient will draw.
8. Click the **Apply to All** button to apply the gradient background to all the slides in the presentation.

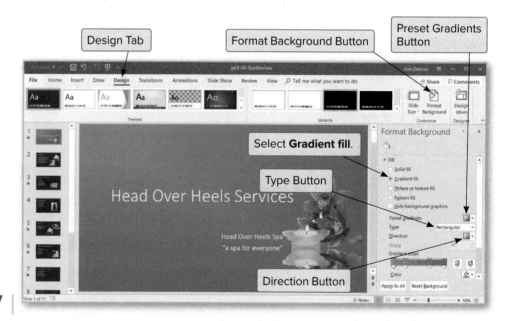

FIGURE PP 3.7

When choosing the gradient's colors and style, keep in mind the content that will appear on top of the background. If the text color in your presentation is white or another light color, choose darker colors to allow the text to stand out. If the text color in your presentation is a dark color, choose lighter colors for the gradient.

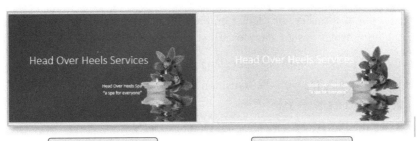

FIGURE PP 3.8

Good Color Choice

Bad Color Choice

tips & tricks

You can further adjust the gradient by adjusting the gradient stops. Click a slider tab and drag it to the left or right to adjust how quickly the gradient blends from one shade to another. You can also adjust the brightness and transparency of the gradient color in the *Format Background* task pane.

tell me **more**

Background gradients are composed of shades of the same color. This ensures that the gradient will smoothly transition from one shade to another, making for a subtle background that won't distract from the content of the presentation.

another **method**

To open the *Format Background* task pane, you can also right-click the background of a slide and select **Format Background...**

let me **try**

If you do not have the data file from the previous skill open, open the student data file **pp3-06-SpaServices** and try this skill on your own:

1. Verify you are on the first slide of the presentation.
2. Display the **Format Background** task pane.
3. Apply a **gradient fill** to the slide background.
4. Choose the **Radial Gradient - Accent 5** preset option. It is the fifth option in the last row under *Preset gradients*.
5. Change the gradient type to **rectangular**.
6. Change the direction of the gradient so the gradient starts from the top left corner of the slide.
7. If you will be moving on to the next skill in this chapter, leave the presentation open to continue working. If not, save the file as directed by your instructor and close it.

Skill 3.7 Using Designer

The **Designer** feature in PowerPoint analyzes the current slide and presents several slide layout options from which you can choose. When you add a picture to a slide, the *Design Ideas* task pane will display automatically and present you with a number of layout options for using the picture on the slide. Click a layout to apply it to the slide. You can also display design ideas for any slide in the presentation.

To use a design suggestion from *Designer*:

1. Select the slide with the transition you want to modify.
2. Click the **Design** tab.
3. In the *Designer* group, click the **Design Ideas** button.
4. The *Design Ideas* task pane displays. Several slide layouts appear in the task pane.
5. Click a layout to apply it to the slide.

FIGURE PP 3.9

tips & tricks

Not all slides will have suggested design ideas. With the *Designer* task pane open, select different thumbnails to see the different design ideas for each slide. If *Designer* cannot create any design ideas, you will see the message *Sorry, no design ideas for this slide.*

tell me **more**

The *Designer* feature is available only for users who have an Office 365 subscription. If you purchased the on-premises version of Office, then you will not see the *Design Ideas* button on the *Design* tab.

let me **try**

If you do not have the data file from the previous skill open, open the student data file **pp3-07-SpaServices** and try this skill on your own:

1. Verify you are on Slide 1 of the presentation.

2. Display the **Design Ideas** task pane. **NOTE:** If you are using the Office 2019 on-premises version of PowerPoint, skip steps 2 and 3.

3. Apply the third design to the slide (the one shown in *Figure PP 3.9*). If you do not see the same design idea as the one shown in the figure, use a design idea of your choice.

4. If you will be moving on to the next skill in this chapter, leave the document open to continue working. If not, save the file as directed by your instructor and close it.

Skill 3.8 Applying Slide Transitions

A **transition** is an effect that occurs when one slide leaves the screen and another one appears. Transitions add movement to your presentation and can keep audiences interested, but remember that overusing transitions can be distracting. Add transitions only where they will improve your presentation.

FIGURE PP 3.10

Transitions Gallery

To apply transitions to a slide:

1. Select the slide to which you want to add the transition.
2. Click the **Transitions** tab.
3. In the *Transition to This Slide* group, click the **More** button and select a transition to apply to the slide. PowerPoint automatically previews the transition for you.
4. Click the **Preview** button to play the transition again.
5. To add a sound effect to a slide, click the arrow next to the *Sound* box and select a sound effect.
6. To add the transition to all the slides of a presentation, select the slide with the transition you want to apply, and click the **Apply to All** button.

FIGURE PP 3.11

Preview Button

Transitions Tab

Sound Box

More Button

Apply to All Button

tips & tricks

When you select a transition, PowerPoint applies the default settings for that transition to the slide. You can customize the settings for a transition to create the exact effect you want:

❭ Click the **Effect Options** button to view the different options for the transition. When you select an option, PowerPoint will automatically play a preview of the new transition.

❭ Enter a time in seconds in the *Duration* box or click the up or down arrows to adjust how quickly or slowly the transition happens. Click the **Preview** button to view the new transition speed.

tell me **more**

PowerPoint offers a number of transitions for you to choose from. There are simple fades and dissolves, any number of directional wipes (including shapes and rotations), pushes and covers, stripes and bars, and random transitions. In PowerPoint 2016, Microsoft introduced a new transition, Morph. The **Morph transition** allows you to move and transform objects on a slide when transitioning from one slide to another.

When choosing transitions for your presentation, it is important to keep in mind who your audience will be. If you are presenting in a formal business environment, you will probably want to use more understated transitions, such as fades and dissolves. If your audience expects more "sizzle" in the presentation, then you may want to choose a complex wipe, such as the Vortex transition.

another **method**

To apply a transition, you can also click a transition in the *Transition to This Slide* group without opening the *Transitions* gallery.

let me **try**

If you do not have the data file from the previous skill open, open the student data file **pp3-08-SpaServices** and try this skill on your own:

1. Apply the **Split** transition to **Slide 1**. It is located in the *Subtle* category.
2. Add the **Chime** sound to the transition.
3. Preview the slide.
4. Remove the sound effect on the transition.
5. Apply the transition to all the slides in the presentation.
6. If you will be moving on to the next skill in this chapter, leave the presentation open to continue working. If not, save the file as directed by your instructor and close it.

Skill 3.9 Applying Quick Styles to Drawing Objects

Quick Styles are a combination of formatting that give elements of your presentation a more polished, graphical look without a lot of work. Quick Styles can be applied to **drawing objects**, such as text boxes, shapes, and WordArt, and include a combination of fill colors, borders, and transparency settings. Instead of applying each of these formatting elements one at a time, you can apply a combination of elements at one time using a preset Quick Style.

To apply a Quick Style to a drawing object:

1. Select the drawing object to which you want to apply the Quick Style.
2. Click the **Drawing Tools Format** tab.
3. In the *Shape Styles* group, click the **More** button.
4. In the *Shape Styles* gallery, click a Quick Style to apply it to the drawing object.

FIGURE PP 3.12

tell me **more**

Drawing objects in PowerPoint include shapes, text boxes, placeholders, and WordArt. When you insert or select a drawing object in a presentation, the *Drawing Tools Format* tab displays. This tab is called a contextual tab because it displays only when a drawing object is the active element. The *Format* tab contains tools to change the look of the selected drawing object, such as shape styles, WordArt styles, sizing, and arrangement options.

another **method**

To apply a Quick Style to a drawing object, you can also:

❯ On the *Home* tab, in the *Drawing* group, click the **Shape Quick Styles** button and select an option.

❯ Right-click the drawing object, click the **Shape Quick Styles** button, and select an option.

let me **try**

If you do not have the data file from the previous skill open, open the student data file **pp3-09-SpaServices** and try this skill on your own:

1. Select the rounded rectangle shape on **Slide 11**.
2. Apply the **Colored Outline - Gold, Accent 4** Quick Style to the shape. It is the fifth option in the first row under *Theme Styles*.
3. If you will be moving on to the next skill in this chapter, leave the presentation open to continue working. If not, save the file as directed by your instructor and close it.

Skill 3.10 Applying Fill Colors to Drawing Objects

When you add a drawing object to a slide, PowerPoint uses the default object **fill color** from the presentation's theme. But what if you want your object to be a different color? You can customize the fill color for objects from the *Drawing Tools Format* tab.

To change the fill color for a drawing object:

1. Select the drawing object you want to change.
2. Click the **Drawing Tools Format** tab.
3. In the *Shape Styles* group, click the **Shape Fill** button.
4. Select an option from the color palette.

FIGURE PP 3.13

tell me **more**

You can use these same steps to change the fill color on icons. On the *Graphics Tools Format* tab, in the *Graphics Styles* group, click the **Graphics Fill** button to access the same options.

another **method**

To change the fill color of a drawing object, you can also:

❭ On the *Home* tab, in the *Drawing* group, click the **Shape Fill** button and select an option.

❭ Right-click the drawing object, click the **Fill** button, and select an option.

let me **try**

If you do not have the data file from the previous skill open, open the student data file **pp3-10-SpaServices** and try this skill on your own:

1. Select the rounded rectangle shape on **Slide 11**.
2. Apply the **Gold, Accent 4, Lighter 80%** fill color to the shape. It is the eighth option in the second row under *Theme Colors*.
3. If you will be moving on to the next skill in this chapter, leave the presentation open to continue working. If not, save the file as directed by your instructor and close it.

Skill 3.11 Applying Outlines to Drawing Objects

When you add a drawing object to a slide, PowerPoint uses the default object outline style from the presentation's theme. This may not be the look you want for your drawing object. You can customize the weight and style of **outlines** for drawing objects from the *Drawing Tools Format* tab.

To change the shape outline of a drawing object:

1. Select the drawing object you want to change.
2. Click the **Drawing Tools Format** tab.
3. In the *Shape Styles* group, click the **Shape Outline** button.
4. Select an option from the color palette to change the color of the outline.
5. Point to **Weight** and select a thickness option for the outline.
6. Point to **Dashes** and select a dash style for the outline.

FIGURE PP 3.14

tell me **more**

You can use these same steps to change the outline style on icons. On the *Graphics Tools Format* tab, in the *Graphics Styles* group, click the **Graphics Outline** button to access the same options.

another **method**

To change the outline of a drawing object, you can also:

❯ On the *Home* tab, in the *Drawing* group, click the **Shape Outline** button, and select an option.

❯ Right-click the drawing object, click the **Outline** button, and select an option.

let me **try**

If you do not have the data file from the previous skill open, open the student data file **pp3-11-SpaServices** and try this skill on your own:

1. Select the rounded rectangle shape on **Slide 11**.
2. Change the outline color for the shapes to **Orange, Accent 2**. It is the sixth option in the first row under *Theme Colors*.
3. Change the weight of the outline to **6 pt**.
4. If you will be moving on to the next skill in this chapter, leave the presentation open to continue working. If not, save the file as directed by your instructor and close it.

Skill 3.12 Using the Eyedropper Tool

A presentation's theme comes with a set of colors that work well together. In addition, you can create your own custom colors in PowerPoint. But what if the color you want is already in use in your presentation or on another part of your screen? The **Eyedropper** allows you to select any color from your screen and apply it to an object. The Eyedropper can be used for changing the color of text, slide backgrounds, WordArt fill and outlines, as well as shape fill and outlines.

To select the fill color for a drawing object using the Eyedropper:

1. Select the drawing object or text you want to change.
2. Click the **Drawing Tools Format** tab.
3. In the *Shape Styles* group, click the **Shape Fill** button. Click **Eyedropper**.
4. The cursor turns to an eyedropper with a magnification box showing the active area:

    ❭ Click the area of the slide that contains the color you want to use.

    ❭ Click and drag the mouse to select an area outside the main slide area, such as the Slides tab or the Ribbon.

FIGURE PP 3.15

FIGURE PP 3.16

tips & tricks

When you pause over an area, a tool tip displays with the color value of the area you are over.

another **method**

To use the Eyedropper to change the fill color of a drawing object, you can also:

❭ On the *Home* tab, in the *Drawing* group, click the **Shape Fill** button, and select **Eyedropper**.

❭ Right-click the drawing object, click the **Fill** button, and select **Eyedropper**.

let me **try**

If you do not have the data file from the previous skill open, open the student data file **pp3-12-SpaServices** and try this skill on your own:

1. Select the rounded rectangle shape on **Slide 11**.

2. Using the Eyedropper, change the fill color of the shape to the color of the title text on the slide (*Contact Information*).

3. If you will be moving on to the next skill in this chapter, leave the presentation open to continue working. If not, save the file as directed by your instructor and close it.

Skill 3.13 Applying Quick Styles to Tables

Just as you can apply complex formatting to drawing objects using Quick Styles, you can also apply complex formatting to tables using Quick Styles for tables. With Quick Styles for tables, you can apply the borders and shading for a table with one command, giving your table a professional, sophisticated look without a lot of work.

To apply a Quick Style to a table:

1. Select the table to which you want to apply the Quick Style.
2. Click the **Table Tools Design**.
3. In the *Table Styles* group, click the **More** button.
4. In the *Table Styles* gallery, click a Quick Style to apply it to the table.

FIGURE PP 3.17

tips & tricks

To remove all formatting from the table, click the **Clear Table** button at the bottom of the *Table Quick Styles* gallery.

tell me more

When you insert a table into a presentation, the *Table Tools Design* and *Layout* tabs display. These tabs are called contextual tabs because they display only when a table is the active element. The *Design* tab contains tools to change the look of the table, such as Quick Styles, WordArt, and borders. The *Layout* tab contains tools for changing the structure of a table, including adding and removing rows and columns, resizing the table, and changing the alignment of text.

let me try

If you do not have the data file from the previous skill open, open the student data file **pp3-13-SpaServices** and try this skill on your own:

1. Select the table on **Slide 8**.
2. Apply the **Medium Style 1 - Accent 5** Quick Style to the table (it is the sixth option in the *Medium* section of the *Quick Styles* gallery).
3. If you will be moving on to the next skill in this chapter, leave the presentation open to continue working. If not, save the file as directed by your instructor and close it.

Skill 3.14 Using the Picture Styles Gallery

When creating a presentation, you want to grab the audience's attention. What makes one presentation stand out from another isn't necessarily the content of the slides, but the images used to convey that content. PowerPoint comes with a number of picture Quick Styles you can apply to pictures, instantly giving them a more sophisticated look. **Picture Quick Styles** include a combination of graphic effects, such as borders, shadows, 3-D rotation, and reflections.

To apply a picture Quick Style to a picture:

1. Select the picture to which you want to apply the Quick Style.
2. Click the **Picture Tools Format** tab.
3. In the *Picture Styles* group, click the **More** button ⥥.
4. In the *Picture Styles* gallery, click a Quick Style to apply it to the picture.

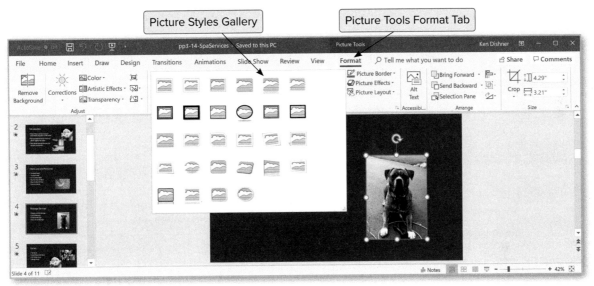

FIGURE PP 3.18

tell me **more**

When you insert a picture into a presentation, the *Picture Tools Format* tab displays. This tab is called a contextual tab because it displays only when a picture is the active element. The *Format* tab contains tools to change the look of a picture, such as applying artistic effects, changing the color, and cropping the image.

another **method**

To apply a Quick Style to a picture, you can also right-click the picture, click the **Picture Styles** button, and select an option.

let me **try**

If you do not have the data file from the previous skill open, open the student data file **pp3-14-SpaServices** and try this skill on your own:

1. Select the picture on **Slide 4**.
2. Apply the **Simple Frame, White** Quick Style to the picture (it is the first option in the gallery).
3. If you will be moving on to the next skill in this chapter, leave the presentation open to continue working. If not, save the file as directed by your instructor and close it.

Skill 3.15 Applying Preset Picture Effects

PowerPoint allows you to add a number of **picture effects** to images. These effects include shadows, reflections, glows, soft edges, bevels, and 3-D rotation. You can add these effects individually, or you can apply one of PowerPoint's preset effects that include a combination of multiple effects in one style.

To apply preset effects to a picture:

1. Select the picture to which you want to apply the effect.
2. Click the **Picture Tools Format** tab.
3. In the *Picture Styles* group, click the **Picture Effects** button.
4. Point to **Preset** and select a predetermined combination of shape effects.

FIGURE PP 3.19

tips & tricks

To apply individual picture effects, point to any other options on the *Picture Effects* menu and select an option.

another **method**

To change picture effects, you can also click the **Shape Effects** button in the *Drawing* group on the *Home* tab.

let me **try**

If you do not have the data file from the previous skill open, open the student data file **pp3-15-SpaServices** and try this skill on your own:

1. Select the picture on **Slide 6**.
2. Apply the **Preset 4** picture effects to the picture.
3. If you will be moving on to the next skill in this chapter, leave the presentation open to continue working. If not, save the file as directed by your instructor and close it.

Skill 3.16 Customizing Charts

All charts include common chart elements that you can adjust to change the display of your charts. These common elements include:

❯ The **plot area** is the area where the data series are plotted.

❯ The **chart area** is the area that encompasses the entire chart including the plot area and optional layout elements, such as the title and legend.

❯ The **chart title** is a text box above or overlaying the chart.

❯ The **legend** tells you which data point or data series is represented by each color in the chart.

❯ The **data labels** display data values for each visual element of the chart (such as the column, bar, pie slice, or line depending on the type of chart in the presentation).

PowerPoint includes a number of Quick Layout options for charts. These Quick Layouts include a combination of chart elements that you can apply to charts with one command.

To apply a Quick Layout to a chart:

1. Click an empty area of the chart area to select the chart.
2. Click the **Chart Tools Design** tab.
3. In the *Chart Layouts* group, click the **Quick Layout** button and select an option.

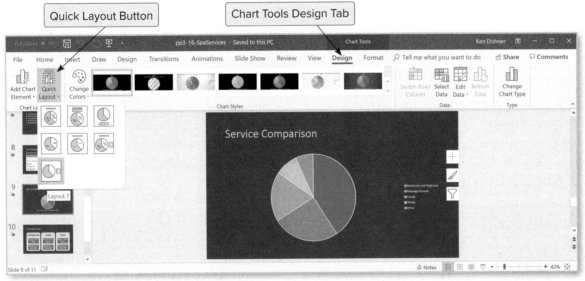

FIGURE PP 3.20

After you have applied a Quick Layout, you may find that your chart appears too cluttered. You can show and hide chart elements, making the chart easier to read.

To show or hide chart elements:

1. Click an empty area of the chart area to select the chart.
2. Click the **Chart Elements** button that appears near the upper right corner of the chart.
3. Click the check boxes to show or hide chart elements.

tips & tricks

To change the chart title, click the box to select it and edit the text directly in the text box.

tell me more

When a chart is selected, two tabs are available: the *Chart Tools Design* tab and the *Chart Tools Format* tab. The *Chart Tools Design* tab gives you access to commands for working with the design elements for the chart including the color, style, and data. The *Chart Tools Formatting* tab allows you to apply formatting to parts of the chart. On the *Chart Tools Formatting* tab, in the *Current Selection* group, the *Chart Elements* box displays the name of the chart element that is currently selected. This can be helpful if you need to ensure that you have selected the chart area, plot area, or another chart element to be formatted.

another method

You can hide or show chart elements and control their appearance and position from the *Chart Tools Design* tab. In the *Chart Layouts* group, click the **Add Chart Element** button, point to the chart element you want, and click an option.

let me try

If you do not have the data file from the previous skill open, open the student data file **pp3-16-SpaServices** and try this skill on your own:

1. On **Slide 9**, select the chart by clicking an empty part of the chart area.
2. Apply the **Layout 7** Quick Layout to the chart.
3. Hide the **title** for the chart.
4. If you will be moving on to the next skill in this chapter, leave the presentation open to continue working. If not, save the file as directed by your instructor and close it.

Skill 3.17 Modifying SmartArt

When you add SmartArt to a presentation, the diagram uses a default style and the default colors pulled from the presentation's theme. You can modify the look of SmartArt diagrams by changing the style of the diagram as well as selecting from a number of color sets.

To change the style of a SmartArt diagram:

1. Select the SmartArt you want to change.
2. Click the **SmartArt Tools Design** tab.
3. In the *SmartArt Styles* gallery, click the **More** button to display the gallery.
4. Click a style to apply to the diagram.

FIGURE PP 3.22

To change the colors of a SmartArt diagram:

1. Click the **SmartArt Tools Design** tab.
2. In the *SmartArt Styles* group, click the **Change Colors** button and select a color set to apply to the diagram.

FIGURE PP 3.23

tips & tricks

❯ Selections made from the *Colors* and *Styles* galleries affect the entire SmartArt diagram. If you want to format a specific shape in the diagram, first select the part of the diagram you want to change. Next, click the *SmartArt Tools Format* tab. In the *Shapes Styles* group, you can change the shape style, shape color, and shape outline just as you would for any other drawing object.

❯ Click the **Reset Graphic** button on the *SmartArt Tools Design* tab to restore the SmartArt diagram to the original state.

tell me **more**

There are a variety of SmartArt styles to choose from. These styles include a combination of outlines and effects (such as gradients and bevels) that you can apply with a single command.

another **method**

❯ To change the style of SmartArt, you can also right-click an empty area of the diagram, click the **SmartArt Quick Style** button on the Mini toolbar, and select an option.

❯ To change the color of SmartArt, you can also right-click an empty area of the diagram, click the **Color** button on the Mini toolbar, and select an option.

let me **try**

If you do not have the data file from the previous skill open, open the student data file **pp3-17-SpaServices** and try this skill on your own:

1. Select the SmartArt diagram on **Slide 10**.
2. Apply the **Polished** SmartArt style to the diagram. It is the first option in the *3D* section of the gallery.
3. Apply the **Colored Fill - Accent 2** color set to the diagram.
4. If you will be moving on to the next skill in this chapter, leave the presentation open to continue working. If not, save the file as directed by your instructor and close it.

Skill 3.18 Applying Animation Effects

Adding **animations** to slides can help emphasize important points and grab your audience's attention. In PowerPoint you can animate individual objects on a slide, including text, images, charts, tables, and SmartArt.

There are four basic types of animation schemes:

》 **Entrance**—Animates the object coming onto the slide; starts with the object not visible and ends with the object visible. Examples of **Entrance animations** include *Fade In*, *Split*, *Fly In*, and *Appear*.

》 **Emphasis**—Animates the object on the screen. Examples of **Emphasis animations** include *Pulse*, *Spin*, *Grow/Shrink*, and *Teeter*.

》 **Exit**—Animates the object leaving the slide; starts with the object visible and ends with the object not visible. Examples of **Exit animations** include *Fade*, *Disappear*, *Float Out*, and *Wipe*.

》 **Motion Paths**—Animates the object along an invisible line. Examples of **Motion Path animations** include *Lines*, *Arcs*, and *Loops*.

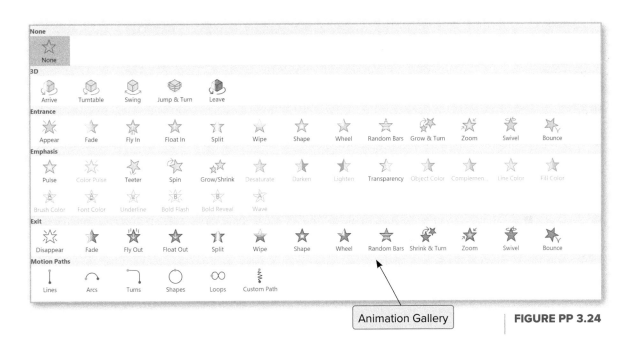

Animation Gallery

FIGURE PP 3.24

To add an animation to an object:

1. Select the object you want to animate.
2. Click the **Animations** tab.
3. In the *Animation* group, click the More button ⊟.
4. In the *Animation* gallery, click an option to apply it to the object.

FIGURE PP 3.25

tips & tricks

〉 When you first apply an animation effect, a preview of the animation plays in the *Slide* pane. To view the animation again, click the **Preview** button on the *Animations* tab.

〉 To remove an animation, select **None** in the gallery.

tell me more

A star appears next to the thumbnails in the *Slides* pane that contain animations or transitions.

let me try

If you do not have the data file from the previous skill open, open the student data file **pp3-18-SpaServices** and try this skill on your own:

1. Select the SmartArt diagram on **Slide 10**.
2. Apply the **Zoom** entrance animation to the SmartArt diagram.
3. If you will be moving on to the next skill in this chapter, leave the presentation open to continue working. If not, save the file as directed by your instructor and close it.

Skill 3.19 Modifying Animations

Although PowerPoint comes with a number of easy-to-use, prebuilt animations, you may find that you want to further customize those animations to better suit your needs. You can adjust the behavior of an animation by adjusting the effect options.

To modify the effect options of an animation:

1. Select the object with the animation you want to modify.
2. Click the **Animations** tab.
3. Click the **Effect Options** button and select an option to change the default behavior of the animation.

FIGURE PP 3.26

tips & tricks

Click the arrow next to the *Start* box and select when the animation will play—*On Click*, *With Previous*, or *After Previous*.

let me try

If you do not have the data file from the previous skill open, open the student data file **pp3-19-SpaServices** and try this skill on your own:

1. Select the SmartArt diagram on **Slide 10**.
2. Change the animation effects to have the diagram animate **one by one**.
3. If you will be moving on to the next skill in this chapter, leave the presentation open to continue working. If not, save the file as directed by your instructor and close it.

Skill 3.20 Animating 3D Models

Just as you can animate other objects on a slide, you can also animate 3D models. When a 3D model is selected, a specific set of animation options displays.

To animate a 3D model:

1. Select the model you want to animation.
2. Click the **Animations** tab.
3. The first several animation options in the gallery on the Ribbon are animations that can be applied to 3D models.
4. Click an option to apply the animation to the model.

FIGURE PP 3.27

You can further modify a 3D model by changing the direction the object is animated along its axis.

To change the direction of the animation of a 3D model:

1. On the *Animations* tab, in the *Animation* group, click the **Effect Options** button.
2. Select an option from the *Direction* section of the gallery.

tips & tricks

From the *Effect Options* gallery, you can also choose the amount the object will animate—subtle (little movement), moderate (the default), or strong (a lot of movement). You can also choose to rotate the object around the view's center or the object's center.

let me try

If you do not have the data file from the previous skill open, open the student data file **pp3-20-SpaServices** and try this skill on your own:

1. Select the 3D model of the fireworks on **Slide 7**.
2. Apply the **Arrive** 3D animation to the model.
3. Change the animation direction to rotate **Down**.
4. If you will be moving on to the next skill in this chapter, leave the presentation open to continue working. If not, save the file as directed by your instructor and close it.

Skill 3.21 Using Animation Painter

Animations can become complex very quickly. You can invest a lot of time working on an animation to get it just right. What if you want to use those same animation effects on another slide? The **Animation Painter** works similarly to the *Format Painter*, but instead of copying and pasting formatting, the *Animation Painter* copies and pastes the animations that have been applied to an object.

To use the *Animation Painter* to copy and paste animations:

1. Select the object that has the animation you want to copy.

2. Click the **Animations** tab.

3. In the *Advanced Animation* group, click the **Animation Painter** button.

4. Click the object to which you want to apply the animation.

5. The animation is automatically applied to the second object.

If you want to apply the animation more than once, double-click the **Animation Painter** button when you select it. It will stay on until you click the **Animation Painter** button again or press (Esc) to deselect it.

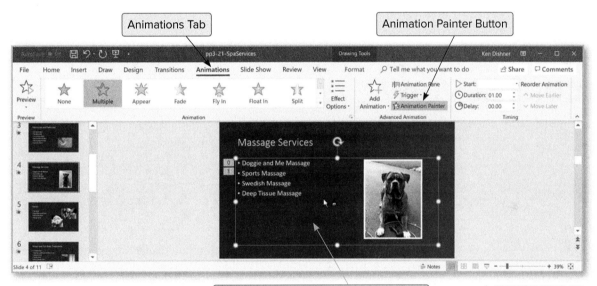

Animations Tab

Animation Painter Button

When the *Animation Painter* is active, the cursor changes to paintbrush cursor.

FIGURE PP 3.28

tips & tricks

To remove an animation, on the *Animations* tab, in the *Animation* group, click the **None** option in the gallery.

let me try

If you do not have the data file from the previous skill open, open the student data file **pp3-21-SpaServices** and try this skill on your own:

1. Select the text placeholder on **Slide 5**.

2. Use the **Animation Painter** to copy the animation.

3. Apply the animation to the text placeholder on **Slide 4**.

4. Save the file as directed by your instructor and close it.

key terms

Theme
Theme variant
Color theme
Font theme
Effects theme
Background styles
Widescreen 16:9
Background
Pattern fill
Gradient
Gradient stop
Designer
Transition
Morph transition
Quick Styles
Drawing objects

Fill color
Outlines
Eyedropper
Picture Quick Styles
Picture effects
Plot area
Chart area
Chart title
Legend
Data labels
Animations
Entrance animations
Emphasis animations
Exit animations
Motion Path animations
Animation Painter

concept review

1. Which of the following is a group of formatting options, including font, color, backgrounds, and effect styles, that you apply to a presentation?

a. style

b. theme

c. Quick Style

d. variant

2. Which of the following is a set of color variations and backgrounds you can change for a theme?

a. effects theme

b. theme variant

c. color theme

d. background

3. Which of the following is the default size for slides?

a. 3:4

b. 3:6

c. 12:4

d. 16:9

4. A _____ is the graphic element that fills a slide.

a. fill color

b. drawing object

c. background

d. transition

5. The gradual transition from one color to another is known as a _____.

    a. fill color

    b. gradient

    c. variant

    d. background

6. Which of the following is a combination of formatting settings you apply to objects?

    a. theme colors

    b. Quick Styles

    c. theme effects

    d. theme variants

7. An animation is an effect that occurs when one slide leaves the screen and another one appears.

    a. true

    b. false

8. The Eyedropper tool allows you to capture colors from any part of your computer screen.

    a. true

    b. false

9. The Quick Layout button allows you to quickly apply a combination of chart elements with one command.

    a. true

    b. false

10. Which would you use to copy and paste animation settings from one object to another?

    a. *Format Painter*

    b. *Animation Painter*

    c. *Animation task* pane

    d. none of the above

projects

skill review **3.1**

In this project you will be modifying the look of the marketing presentation from Suarez Marketing. First, you will change the look of the presentation by changing the theme, adjusting the colors, and applying a pattern to the slide background. You will then apply transitions to all the slides in the presentation. You will adjust the look of a drawing object, SmartArt diagram, picture, and a table. Finally, you will animate a SmartArt diagram and change the effects of the animation.

Skills needed to complete this project:

- Changing the Presentation Theme (Skill 3.1)
- Customizing the Theme (Skill 3.2)
- Applying a Pattern to Slide Backgrounds (Skill 3.5)
- Applying Slide Transitions (Skill 3.8)
- Applying Quick Styles to Drawing Objects (Skill 3.9)
- Applying Fill Colors to Drawing Objects (Skill 3.10)
- Applying Outlines to Drawing Objects (Skill 3.11)
- Modifying SmartArt (Skill 3.17)
- Applying Animation Effects (Skill 3.18)
- Modifying Animations (Skill 3.19)
- Applying Quick Styles to Tables (Skill 3.13)
- Using the Picture Styles Gallery (Skill 3.14)

1. Open the start file **PP2019-SkillReview-3-1** and resave the file as: `[your initials]PP-SkillReview-3-1`
2. If the presentation opens in Protected View, click the **Enable Editing** button in the Message Bar at the top of the presentation so you can modify it.
3. Change the presentation theme and variant.
   a. Click the **Design** tab.
   b. In the *Themes* group, click the **More** button and select the **Berlin** theme.
   c. In the *Variants* group, select the **blue** option (the second option in the *Variants* gallery).
4. Apply a pattern background to a slide.
   a. If necessary, navigate to **Slide 1**.
   b. In the *Customize* group, click the **Format Background** button.
   c. In the *Format Background* task pane, select the **Pattern fill** radio button under *Fill*.
   d. In the *Pattern* section, click the **Dotted: 50%** option (the first option in the second row of the gallery).
   e. Click the **Foreground** button and select **Turquoise, Background 2**. It is the third option in the first row under *Theme Colors*.

f. Click the **Background** button and select **Black, Background 1, Lighter 50%**. It is the first option in the second row under *Theme Colors*.

g. Click the **Apply To All** button.

h. Click the **Close** button at the top of the task pane.

5. Apply a slide transition to all the slides in the presentation.

a. Click the **Transitions** tab.

b. In the *Transition to This Slide* group, click the **Wipe** transition. If the *Wipe* transition does not appear on the Ribbon, click the **More** button to see all the available transitions.

c. In the *Timing* group, click the **Apply to All** button.

6. Apply a Quick Style to a drawing object.

a. Navigate to **Slide 5**.

b. Select the callout shape at the top of the slide.

c. On the *Drawing Tools Format* tab, in the *Shape Styles* group, click the **More** button and select **Light 1 Outline, Colored Fill - Turquoise, Accent 1** (the second option in the third row).

7. Change the shape fill color of a drawing object.

a. Verify the callout shape is still selected.

b. In the *Shape Styles* group, click the **Shape Fill** button and select **Turquoise, Accent 1, Lighter 60%** (it is the fifth option in the third row of the color palette).

8. Change the outline of a drawing object.

a. Verify the callout shape is still selected.

b. In the *Shape Styles* group, click the **Shape Outline** button, point to **Weight**, and select the **6 pt**. option.

9. Modify the look of a SmartArt diagram.

a. Select the **SmartArt** diagram on **Slide 8**.

b. Click the **SmartArt Tools Design** tab.

c. In the *SmartArt Styles* group, click the **Intense Effect** style. It is the fifth option in the gallery.

10. Apply an animation effect.

a. Verify the SmartArt diagram is still selected.

b. Click the **Animations** tab.

c. In the *Animation* group, click the **Float In** animation effect.

11. Change the effects of an animation.

a. Verify the SmartArt diagram is still selected.

b. On the *Animations* tab, in the *Animation* group, click the **Effect Options** button and select **Float Down**.

c. Click the **Effect Options** button again and select **One By One**.

12. Apply a Quick Style to a table.

a. Select the table on **Slide 9**.

b. Click the **Table Tools Design** tab.

c. In the *Table Styles* group, click the **More** button. In the *Dark* section, click the **Dark Style 1 - Accent 1** style (it is the second option in the *Dark* section).

13. Apply a picture style to an image.

    a. Select the picture on **Slide 9**.

    b. Click the **Picture Tools Format** tab.

    c. In the *Picture Styles* group, click the **Drop Shadow Rectangle** option. It is the fourth option in the gallery. If this option does not appear on the Ribbon, click the **More** button to see all the available Quick Styles.

14. Save and close the presentation.

skill review **3.2**

In this project you will be modifying the look of the My Fitness Plan presentation. You will change the size of the slides in the presentation. You will change the look of the presentation by changing the theme and variant and background color. You will use PowerPoint's *Designer* feature to change the layout of the title slide and then you will add a transition to the slide. You will apply an animation, adjust the animation, and then copy the animation to other objects in the presentation using the *Animation Painter.* You will adjust the look of objects in the presentation including a chart, picture, and drawing object.

Skills needed to complete this project:

- Changing the Size of Slides (Skill 3.3)
- Changing the Presentation Theme (Skill 3.1)
- Customizing the Theme (Skill 3.2)
- Changing the Color of Slide Backgrounds (Skill 3.4)
- Using Designer (Skill 3.7)
- Applying Slide Transitions (Skill 3.8)
- Customizing Charts (Skill 3.16)
- Applying Animation Effects (Skill 3.18)
- Modifying Animations (Skill 3.19)
- Using Animation Painter (Skill 3.21)
- Using the Picture Styles Gallery (Skill 3.14)
- Applying Preset Picture Effects (Skill 3.15)
- Applying Quick Styles to Drawing Objects (Skill 3.9)
- Applying Fill Colors to Drawing Objects (Skill 3.10)
- Applying Outlines to Drawing Objects (Skill 3.11)

1. Open the start file **PP2019-SkillReview-3-2** and resave the file as:
   `[your initials]PP-SkillReview-3-2`

2. If the presentation opens in Protected View, click the **Enable Editing** button in the Message Bar at the top of the presentation so you can modify it.

3. Change the size of slides in the presentation.

    a. Click the **Design** tab.

    b. In the *Customize* group, click the **Slide Size** button and select **Widescreen (16:9)**.

4. Change the presentation theme and variant.

    a. On the *Design* tab, in the *Themes* group, click the **More** button and select the **Retrospect** theme.

    b. In the *Variants* group, select the **green variant option** (the second option in the *Variants* gallery).

5. Change the background color of slides.

   a. On the *Design* tab, in the *Customize* group, click the **Format Background** button.

   b. In the *Format Background* task pane, verify the **Solid Fill** radio button is selected.

   c. Click the **Color** button and select **Dark Green, Text 2, Lighter 80%**. It is the fourth color in the second row under *Theme Colors*.

   d. Click the **Apply to All** button.

   e. Click the **Close** button at the top of the task pane.

6. Use Designer to change the layout of a slide. **NOTE**: If you are using the Office 2019 on-premises version of PowerPoint, skip this step.

   a. Verify you are on **Slide 1**.

   b. On the *Design* tab, in the *Designer* group, click the **Design Ideas** button.

   c. Click the slide design with the barbell. If you do not see one with a barbell, select a slide design of your choice.

7. Apply a slide transition to the first slide in the presentation.

   a. Verify you are on **Slide 1**.

   b. Click the **Transitions** tab.

   c. In the *Transition to This Slide* group, click the **More** button. In the *Exciting* group, click the **Cube** option.

8. Apply a Quick Layout to a chart.

   a. Select the chart on **Slide 8**.

   b. Click the **Chart Tools Design** tab.

   c. In the *Chart Layouts* group, click the **Quick Layout** button and select **Layout 5**.

9. Change the elements that display on a chart.

   a. Click the **Chart Elements** button to the right of the chart on **Slide 8**.

   b. Click the **Axis Titles** check box so it is not selected.

   c. Click the **Chart Title** check box so it is not selected.

10. Apply an animation effect.

    a. Navigate to **Slide 2** and select the **text placeholder** with the list.

    b. Click the **Animations** tab.

    c. In the *Animation* group, click the **Split** animation effect.

11. Modify the animation effect.

    a. Verify the text placeholder on **Slide 2** is selected.

    b. In the *Animation* group, click the **Effect Options** button and select **Vertical Out**.

12. Apply the animation to other slides using the *Animation Painter*.

    a. Select the **text placeholder** on Slide 2 that you applied the animation to.

    b. In the *Advanced Animation* group, double-click the **Animation Painter** button so it will remain active until you turn it off.

    c. Navigate to **Slide 3** and click the **text placeholder** with the list.

    d. Use the *Animation Painter* to apply the animation to the lists on **Slides 4, 5, 6,** and **7**.

    e. Press (Esc) to turn off the *Animation Painter*.

13. Change the look of an image.

    a. Select the image of the nail polish on **Slide 6**.

    b. Click the **Picture Tools Format** tab.

    c. In the *Picture Styles* group, apply the **Soft Edge Rectangle** Quick Style to the picture (it is the sixth option displayed on the Ribbon). If this option does not appear on the Ribbon, click the **More** button to see all the available Quick Styles.

14. Apply a Quick Style to a drawing object.

    a. Select the WordArt **I know I can do it!** on **Slide 9**.

    b. Click the **Drawing Tools Format** tab.

    c. In the *Shape Styles* group, click the **Colored Outline - Green, Accent 2** Quick Style.

15. Change the fill color of a drawing object.

    a. Verify the WordArt is still selected.

    b. In the *Shape Styles* group, click the **Shape Fill** button and select **Green, Accent 2, Darker 50%** (it is the sixth option in the last row of the color palette).

16. Change the outline of a drawing object.

    a. Verify the WordArt is still selected.

    b. In the *Shape Styles* group, click the **Shape Outline** button, point to **Weight**, and select the **6 pt**. option.

17. Save and close the presentation.

challenge yourself 3.3

In this project you will be modifying the look of a presentation for Greenscapes landscaping company. First, you will change the theme and theme variant for the presentation. You will apply a gradient background and a transition to all the slides in the presentation. You will modify the look of a SmartArt diagram and then animate the diagram. You will animate a 3D model as well as change the look of a table, drawing object, and picture. Finally, you will use PowerPoint's *Designer* to change the layout of a slide.

Skills needed to complete this project:

- Changing the Presentation Theme (Skill 3.1)
- Customizing the Theme (Skill 3.2)
- Applying a Gradient to Slide Backgrounds (Skill 3.6)
- Applying Slide Transitions (Skill 3.8)
- Modifying SmartArt (Skill 3.17)
- Applying Animation Effects (Skill 3.18)
- Modifying Animations (Skill 3.19)
- Animating 3D Models (Skill 3.20)
- Applying Quick Styles to Tables (Skill 3.13)
- Applying Quick Styles to Drawing Objects (Skill 3.9)
- Applying Fill Colors to Drawing Objects (Skill 3.10)
- Applying Outlines to Drawing Objects (Skill 3.11)
- Using the Picture Styles Gallery (Skill 3.14)
- Using Designer (Skill 3.7)

1. Open the start file **PP2019-ChallengeYourself-3-3** presentation and resave the file as: `[your initials]PP-ChallengeYourself-3-3`

2. If the presentation opens in Protected View, click the **Enable Editing** button in the Message Bar at the top of the presentation so you can modify it.

3. Change the presentation theme to **Retrospect**.

4. Change the variant to use the **green option** (the second option in the *Variants* gallery).

5. Change the background of all the slides in the presentation to use a **gradient fill**. Apply the **Light Gradient - Accent 5** preset gradient to all the slides in the presentation. It is the fifth option in the first row of the *Preset gradients* gallery. Close the *Format Background* task pane when you are done.

6. Apply a **Push** slide transition to all the slides in the presentation.

7. Change the style of the SmartArt diagram on **Slide 4** to use the **Inset** style.

8. Apply the **Fly In** animation to the SmartArt diagram on **Slide 4**.

9. Change the animation on the SmartArt diagram to use the **One by One** option.

10. Select the table on **Slide 6**. Change the table to use the **Medium Style 1 - Accent 2** Quick Style (it is the third option under *Medium*).

11. Select the star shape on **Slide 3**. Apply the **Colored Outline - Green, Accent 3** Quick Style to the object (the fourth option in the first row).

12. Apply the **Lime, Accent 1, Lighter 80%** fill color to the star shape. It is the fifth option in the second row of the color palette.

13. Change the star shape outline color to **Lime, Accent 1, Darker 50%**. It is the fifth option in the last row of under *Theme Colors*.

14. Change the star shape outline weight to **3 pt**.

15. Select the picture on **Slide 5**. Apply the **Reflected, Rounded Rectangle** Quick Style to the picture (it is the fifth option in the *Picture Styles* gallery).

16. Navigate to **Slide 7** and display the **Design Ideas** task pane. Apply a design of your choice to the slide. *NOTE*: If you are using the Office 2019 on-premises version of PowerPoint, skip this step.

17. Save and close the presentation.

challenge yourself 3.4

In this project you will be modifying the look of a presentation about emotional intelligence. First, you will change the theme and theme variant for the presentation. You will change the size of the slides in the presentation. You will apply a transition to the opening slide and adjust the transition. You will apply a color to all the slides in the presentation. You will animate a placeholder and use the *Animation Painter* to apply the animation to other placeholders in the presentation. Finally, you will modify the look of a SmartArt diagram, picture, and shape.

Skills needed to complete this project:

- Changing the Presentation Theme (Skill 3.1)
- Customizing the Theme (Skill 3.2)
- Changing the Size of Slides (Skill 3.3)
- Applying Slide Transitions (Skill 3.8)
- Changing the Color of Slide Backgrounds (Skill 3.4)

- Applying Animation Effects (Skill 3.18)
- Modifying Animations (Skill 3.19)
- Using Animation Painter (Skill 3.21)
- Using the Picture Styles Gallery (Skill 3.14)
- Modifying SmartArt (Skill 3.17)
- Applying Fill Colors to Drawing Objects (Skill 3.10)
- Applying Outlines to Drawing Objects (Skill 3.11)

1. Open the start file **PP2019-ChallengeYourself-3-4** presentation and resave the file as:
   `[your initials]PP-ChallengeYourself-3-4`

2. If the presentation opens in Protected View, click the **Enable Editing** button in the Message Bar at the top of the presentation so you can modify it.

3. Change the presentation theme to **Facet**.

4. Change the variant to use the one with the **blue background** (the second option in the *Variants* gallery).

5. Change the size of slides in the presentation to be **Widescreen (16:9)**.

6. Apply the **Vortex** slide transition to the first slide in the presentation.

7. Change the transition effect to **From Bottom**.

8. Change the background of all the slides in the presentation to use a **solid fill**. Apply the **Blue, Accent 2, Lighter 80%** color to all the slides in the presentation. It is the sixth color in the second row under *Theme Colors.* Close the *Format Background* task pane when you are done.

9. Apply and modify an animation effect.
   a. Select the **text placeholder** with the bulleted list on **Slide 3**.
   b. Apply the **Wipe** entrance animation effect to the placeholder.
   c. Change the direction of the animation to **From Left**.

10. Use the *Animation Painter* to copy the animation from the text placeholder on **Slide 3** to the text placeholders on **Slide 4**, **Slide 5**, **Slide 6**, **Slide 7**, **Slide 10**, and **Slide 11**.

11. Select the picture on **Slide 2**. Apply the **Beveled Oval, Black** Picture Style to the picture.

12. Change the style of the SmartArt diagram on **Slide 8** to use the **Polished** style.

13. Change the colors of the SmartArt diagram on **Slide 8** to use the **Gradient Range - Accent 2** color set.

14. Change the style of the SmartArt diagram on **Slide 9** to use the **Polished** style.

15. Change the colors of the SmartArt diagram on **Slide 9** to use the **Gradient Range - Accent 2** color set.

16. Select the **thought bubble shape** on **Slide 3**. Change the fill color to **Turquoise, Accent 1**. It is the fifth color in the first row under *Theme Colors.*

17. Verify the shape is still selected. Change the outline color to **White, Background 1**. It is the first color in the first row under *Theme Colors.*

18. Change the weight of the outline of the shape to **3 pt**.

19. Save and close the presentation.

In this project you will be modifying the look of a presentation about a healthy cookbook. First, you will change the size of the slides in the presentation. You will then change the theme and theme variant for the presentation. You will apply a transition to all the slides in the presentation. You will use PowerPoint's *Designer* to change the layout of the title slide. You will adjust the look of a picture, chart, table, SmartArt diagram, and shape. Finally, you will animate a diagram and adjust the animation you applied.

Skills needed to complete this project:

- Changing the Size of Slides (Skill 3.3)
- Changing the Presentation Theme (Skill 3.1)
- Customizing the Theme (Skill 3.2)
- Applying Slide Transitions (Skill 3.8)
- Using Designer (Skill 3.7)
- Using the Picture Styles Gallery (Skill 3.14)
- Customizing Charts (Skill 3.16)
- Applying Quick Styles to Tables (Skill 3.13)
- Modifying SmartArt (Skill 3.17)
- Applying Animation Effects (Skill 3.18)
- Modifying Animations (Skill 3.19)
- Applying Quick Styles to Drawing Objects (Skill 3.9)
- Applying Fill Colors to Drawing Objects (Skill 3.10)
- Applying Outlines to Drawing Objects (Skill 3.11)

1. Open the start file **PP2019-OnYourOwn-3-5** presentation and resave the file as: `[your initials]PP-OnYourOwn-3-5`

2. If the presentation opens in Protected View, click the **Enable Editing** button in the Message Bar at the top of the presentation so you can modify it.

3. Change the presentation to use the **Widescreen (16:9)** slide size.

4. Apply a theme and variant of your choice to the presentation.

5. Apply a slide transition of your choice to all the slides in the presentation.

6. Navigate to **Slide 1** and use the *Designer* feature to change the layout of the slide.

7. Select the chart on **Slide 3**. Apply a Quick Layout of your choice. Hide chart elements that display generic labels (for example, *Axis Title*).

8. Select the table on **Slide 3** and apply a table Quick Style of your choice.

9. Apply the same Quick Style to the table on **Slide 4**.

10. Change the look of the SmartArt diagram on **Slide 5** by applying a style of your choice.

11. Change the colors of the SmartArt dialog on **Slide 5**.

12. Animate the SmartArt diagram on **Slide 5** using an animation of your choice.

13. Change the effects of the animation so each piece of the diagram appears **one by one**.

14. Adjust the look of the **sun shape** on **Slide 6** by applying a Quick Style of your choice.

15. Further adjust the look of the shape by adjusting the fill color and outline.

16. Select the heart-shaped picture on **Slide 6**. Apply a Quick Style of your choice to the picture.

17. Save and close the presentation.

fix it 3.6

In this project you will be modifying the look of a project about team orientation. First, you will change the theme and theme variant for the presentation. You will fix the size of the slides in the presentation. You will add transition and animation effects. You will change the look of objects, including a table, chart, SmartArt diagram, picture, and shape.

Skills needed to complete this project:

- Changing the Presentation Theme (Skill 3.1)
- Customizing the Theme (Skill 3.2)
- Changing the Size of Slides (Skill 3.3)
- Applying Slide Transitions (Skill 3.8)
- Applying Quick Styles to Tables (Skill 3.13)
- Applying Animation Effects (Skill 3.18)
- Modifying Animations (Skill 3.19)
- Using Animation Painter (Skill 3.21)
- Applying Quick Styles to Drawing Objects (Skill 3.9)
- Applying Outlines to Drawing Objects (Skill 3.11)
- Modifying SmartArt (Skill 3.17)
- Using the Picture Styles Gallery (Skill 3.14)

1. Open the start file **PP2019-FixIt-3-6** presentation and resave the file as: `[your initials]PP-FixIt-3-6`

2. If the presentation opens in Protected View, click the **Enable Editing** button in the Message Bar at the top of the presentation so you can modify it.

3. Change the presentation theme to **Ion Boardroom**.

4. Change the variant to use the blue option (the third option in the *Variants* gallery).

5. Change the presentation to use the **Widescreen (16:9)** slide size.

6. Navigate to **Slide 1**. Apply the **Cover** transition. Adjust effect options on the transition to be **From Top-Left**. Apply the transition to all the slides in the presentation.

7. Apply the **Medium Style 1 - Accent 1** table Quick Style to the table on **Slide 5** (it is the second option under *Medium*).

8. Apply the **Wipe** entrance animation effect to the text placeholder on **Slide 2**.

9. Change the animation effects so the text animates from the **top** and as **one object**.

10. Use the *Animation Painter* to copy the animation from the text placeholder on **Slide 2** to the text placeholders on **Slide 3**, **Slide 4**, and **Slide 8**.

11. Select the chart on **Slide 6**. Change the layout for the chart to use the **Layout 7** Quick Layout.

12. Show the **chart title** on the chart.

13. Select the sun shape on **Slide 7**. Apply the **Light 1 Outline, Colored Fill - Gold, Accent 2** Quick Style to the shape (it is the third option in the third row of the gallery).

14. Change the color of the outline of the sun shape to be **Orange, Accent 3** (it is the seventh option in the first row under *Theme Colors*).

15. Change the weight of the outline of the sun shape to **3 pt**.

16. Select the SmartArt diagram on **Slide 7**. Apply the **Moderate Effect** style to the diagram.

17. Select the picture on **Slide 8**. Apply the **Reflected Rounded Rectangle** Quick Style to the picture (it is the fifth option in the *Picture Styles* gallery).

18. Save and close the presentation.

chapter 4

Managing and Delivering Presentations

In this chapter, you will learn the following skills:

❯ Delete and reorder slides

❯ Hide and unhide slides

❯ Copy and paste slides

❯ Add hyperlinks to slides

❯ Check for spelling errors

❯ Add footer information, including slide numbers and the current date

❯ Rehearse timings, use slide show tools, and use Presenter view

❯ Add notes, modify the handout master, and print handouts

❯ Package a presentation to run on another computer

skills

introduction

This chapter provides you with the skills to give a professional presentation. First, you will learn to change the structure of a presentation by reordering slides, deleting slides, copying and pasting slides, and hiding slides. You will add footer content to slides, including slide numbers and the current date. You will rehearse the slide show using PowerPoint's Rehearse Timings feature. You will then start the presentation, navigate through the slides, and use presentation tools. You will add notes to slides and then use those notes when giving the presentation in Presenter view. You will learn to modify and print handouts as well as print the presentation's slides. Finally, you will learn how to package a presentation to run the presentation on another computer.

Skill 4.1 Deleting Slides from Presentations

After you have created all the content for your presentation, it is a good idea to carefully review the slides. As you make a final review, you may find that a slide you created is not necessary, and you want to permanently remove it. You can remove an entire slide of content by deleting it from the *Slides* tab.

To delete a slide:

1. On the *Thumbnails* pane, right-click the slide you want to delete.
2. Click **Delete Slide** on the menu that appears.

You can delete multiple slides at once:

1. Click a slide you want to delete and press (↑ Shift) on the keyboard.
2. With the (↑ Shift) key still pressed, click another slide.
3. Notice, all the slides between the two slides you clicked have been selected.
4. Right-click any of the selected slides and select **Delete Slide**.
5. If you want to select slides that are not next to each other, press (Ctrl) on the keyboard instead of (↑ Shift) and click each slide you want to delete. Only the slides you clicked are selected.

FIGURE PP 4.1

another **method**

To delete a slide, you can also select the slide and press (Delete) on the keyboard.

let me **try**

Open the student data file **pp4-01-SpaServices** and try this skill on your own:

1. Delete **Slide 7**.
2. If you will be moving on to the next skill in this chapter, leave the presentation open to continue working. If not, save the file as directed by your instructor and close it.

Skill 4.2 Changing the Order of Slides

One of the most important aspects of a presentation is the flow of the information. It is important that your slides appear in a logical, grouped order for your audience to fully grasp the message you are presenting. After you have reviewed your presentation, you may find you want to switch the order of some of your slides. You can change the slide order from Slide Sorter view.

To change the slide order in Slide Sorter view:

1. Click the **Slide Sorter** button on the status bar.
2. Click and drag the slide until it appears where you want it in the slide order. Release the mouse button.

Each slide thumbnail appears with a number next to it indicating its location in the presentation. When you change the order of slides, PowerPoint automatically renumbers the slides for you.

Click and drag the slide to the new location.

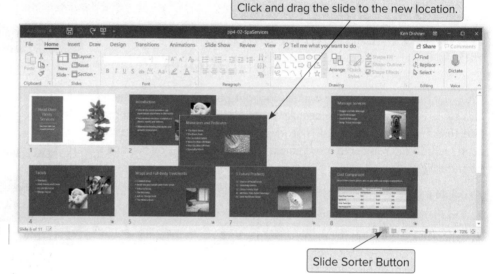

Slide Sorter Button

FIGURE PP 4.2

tips & tricks

To move or copy a slide by dragging, right-click the slide you want to move and drag it to the new location. When you release the mouse button, a menu of options will appear, allowing you to move the slide, copy the slide, or cancel the action.

another **method**

❯ To switch to Slide Sorter view, you can also click the **View** tab, in the *Presentation Views* group, click the **Slide Sorter** button.

❯ You can also reorder slides by clicking and dragging the slide thumbnails on the *Slides* tab in Normal view.

let me **try**

If you do not have the data file from the previous skill open, open the student data file **pp4-02-SpaServices** and try this skill on your own:

1. Switch to **Slide Sorter** view.
2. Move **Slide 6** so it appears between **Slide 2** and **Slide 3**.
3. Return to **Normal** view.
4. If you will be moving on to the next skill in this chapter, leave the presentation open to continue working. If not, save the file as directed by your instructor and close it.

Skill 4.3 Hiding and Unhiding Slides

When you practice your presentation, you may find that you want to omit certain slides, but that you do not want to delete them from your presentation in case you need them later. The **Hide Slide** command allows you to prevent slides from being seen without permanently removing them.

To hide slides:

1. Select the slide you want to hide.
2. Click the **Slide Show** tab.
3. In the *Set Up* group, click the **Hide Slide** button. The button toggles to the "on" state.
4. When a slide is hidden, the thumbnail appears washed out with a slash over the slide number in the *Slides* tab.
5. To unhide the slide, click the **Hide Slide** button again.

FIGURE PP 4.3

tips & tricks

To unhide a slide during a presentation, right-click any slide, and select **See All Slides**. Hidden slides will appear in the list with parentheses around the number. For example, if the third slide in a presentation is hidden, the menu will display the number as (3). Click the slide you want to display.

another method

To hide a slide, you can also right-click the slide on the *Slides* tab and select **Hide Slide**. To unhide a slide, right-click the slide and select **Hide Slide** again.

let me try

If you do not have the data file from the previous skill open, open the student data file **pp4-03-SpaServices** and try this skill on your own:

1. Hide **Slide 8**.
2. Unhide **Slide 8**.
3. If you will be moving on to the next skill in this chapter, leave the presentation open to continue working. If not, save the file as directed by your instructor and close it.

Skill 4.4 Copying and Pasting Slides

You may find when you are creating your presentation that one slide's content and layout are similar to another slide's content and layout that you need to add. Instead of having to recreate all the content for the second slide, you can copy the first slide, paste it into the presentation where you want it to appear, and then change the content you need to change.

To copy and paste slides:

1. On the *Slides* tab, select the slide thumbnail you want to copy.

2. On the *Home* tab, in the *Clipboard* group, click the **Copy** button.

3. Click the slide thumbnail that you want to appear before the new slide.

4. Click the **Paste** button.

5. The new slide has been added to the presentation.

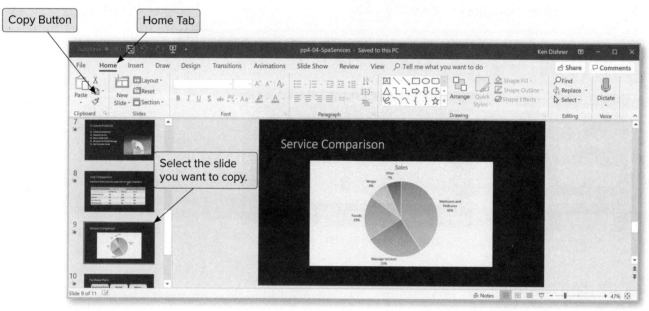

FIGURE PP 4.4

The *Paste* button includes a menu of options for pasting slides. You can choose to use the current presentation's theme, keep the formatting for the copied slide, or paste the slide as a picture. If you paste the slide as a picture, it will be inserted as a single image and you will not be able to edit the content.

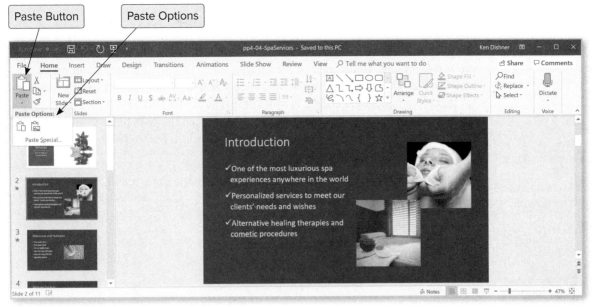

FIGURE PP 4.5

tips & tricks

❯ If you want the copy of the slide to appear directly after the slide you are copying, click the arrow next to the *Copy* button and select **Duplicate**.

❯ Click **Cut** in the *Clipboard* group to copy the slide to the Office *Clipboard* and remove it from its current location in the presentation.

another **method**

To copy a slide:

❯ Click the arrow next to the **Copy** button and select **Copy**.

❯ Press (Ctrl) + (C) on the keyboard.

❯ Right-click the slide and select **Copy**.

To paste a slide:

❯ Click the arrow below the **Paste** button and select a paste option.

❯ Press (Ctrl) + (V) on the keyboard.

❯ Right-click the slide and select a paste option.

let me **try**

If you do not have the data file from the previous skill open, open the student data file **pp4-04-SpaServices** and try this skill on your own:

1. Copy **Slide 9**.

2. Paste the copied slide so it appears after **Slide 2**.

3. Click the **Undo** button on the Quick Access Toolbar to undo the change.

4. If you will be moving on to the next skill in this chapter, leave the presentation open to continue working.
   If not, save the file as directed by your instructor and close it.

Skill 4.5 Adding Hyperlinks to Slides

A **hyperlink** is text or a graphic that, when clicked, takes you to a new location. You can use hyperlinks to navigate to Web pages, other PowerPoint presentations, custom shows, or any slide in the presentation. When you point to a hyperlink, your mouse cursor turns to a hand, indicating it is something that can be clicked.

Some hyperlinks include **ScreenTips**. A ScreenTip is a bubble with text that appears when the mouse is placed over the link. Add a ScreenTip to include a more meaningful description of the hyperlink.

To add a hyperlink from one slide to another slide in the same presentation:

1. Place the cursor where you want the hyperlink to appear.
2. Click the **Insert** tab.
3. In the *Links* group, click the **Link** button.

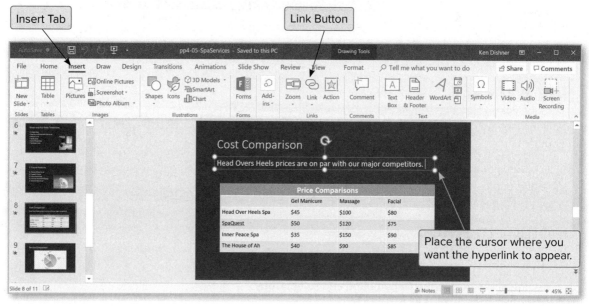

FIGURE PP 4.6

4. The *Insert Hyperlink* dialog opens.
5. Under *Link to* select **Place in This Document**.
6. Select the slide to link to.
7. Type the text for the hyperlink in the *Text to display* box.
8. Click **OK** to insert the hyperlink into your presentation.

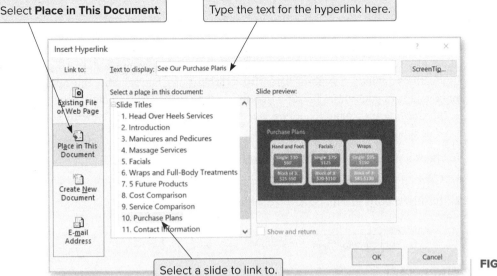

FIGURE PP 4.7

tips & tricks

To remove a hyperlink, first select the hyperlink you want to remove. In the *Links* group, click the **Link** button. In the *Edit Hyperlink* dialog, click the **Remove Hyperlink** button.

tell me **more**

Hyperlinks do not work in Normal view. In order to test your hyperlink, you must be in Slide Show view.

another **method**

To open the *Insert Hyperlink* dialog, you can also:

〉 Right-click the text or object and select **Hyperlink...** from the menu.

〉 Press (Ctrl) + (K) on the keyboard.

〉 Click the **Link** button arrow and select **Insert link...**

let me **try**

If you do not have the data file from the previous skill open, open the student data file **pp4-05-SpaServices** and try this skill on your own:

1. Navigate to **Slide 8** and place the cursor after the text *our major competitors*. Be sure there is a space after the period.

2. Open the **Insert Hyperlink** dialog.

3. Add a hyperlink that will navigate to **Slide 10** when clicked. Have the text read **See Our Purchase Plans**.

4. If you will be moving on to the next skill in this chapter, leave the presentation open to continue working. If not, save the file as directed by your instructor and close it.

Skill 4.6 Checking Spelling

Regardless of the amount of work you put into a presentation, a spelling error or typo can make the entire presentation appear sloppy and unprofessional. All the Office applications include a built-in **spelling checker**. In PowerPoint, the *Spelling* command analyzes your entire presentation for spelling errors. It presents any errors it finds in the *Spelling* task pane, enabling you to make decisions about how to handle each error or type of error in turn.

To check a presentation for spelling errors:

1. Click the **Review** tab.
2. In the *Proofing* group, click the **Spelling** button.

FIGURE PP 4.8

3. The first spelling error appears in the *Spelling* task pane.
4. Review the spelling suggestions and then select an action:
   - Click **Ignore** to make no changes to this instance of the word.
   - Click **Ignore All** to make no changes to all instances of the word.
   - Click **Add** to make no changes to this instance of the word and add it to the main dictionary, so future uses of this word will not show up as misspellings. When you add a word to the main dictionary, it is available for all of the Office applications.
   - Click the correct spelling in the list of suggestions, and click **Change** to correct just this instance of the misspelling in your document.
   - Click the correct spelling in the list of suggestions, and click **Change All** to correct all instances of the misspelling in your document.
5. After you select an action, the spelling checker automatically advances to the next suspected spelling error.
6. When the spelling checker finds no more errors, it displays a message telling you the check is complete. Click **OK** to close the dialog and return to your file.

FIGURE PP 4.9

tips & tricks

❭ Whether or not you use the *Spelling* tool, you should always proofread your files. Spelling checkers are not infallible, especially if you misuse a word yet spell it correctly—for instance, writing "bored" instead of "board."

❭ If you have repeated the same word in a sentence, PowerPoint will flag the second instance of the word as a possible error. In the *Spelling* task pane, the *Change* button will switch to a *Delete* button. Click the **Delete** button to remove the duplicate word.

tell me **more**

When you select an option in the list of suggestions, PowerPoint displays a list of words that have the same meaning as the selected word along with an audio file of the pronunciation of the word.

another **method**

To display the *Spelling* task pane, you can also press ⏺F7⏺.

let me **try**

If you do not have the data file from the previous skill open, open the student data file **pp4-06-SpaServices** and try this skill on your own:

1. Navigate to **Slide 1**.
2. Start the spelling checker.
3. Correct any misspellings found in the presentation. Ignore any suggestions on company names in the presentation.
4. If you will be moving on to the next skill in this chapter, leave the presentation open to continue working. If not, save the file as directed by your instructor and close it.

Skill 4.7 Adding Notes

Speaker notes are hidden notes you can add to slides. They do not appear as part of the presentation. Speaker notes can be used to help remind you to go to a certain slide in the presentation or to mention a specific detail that may not be included on the slide.

To add speaker notes to slides:

1. Click the **Notes** button on the status bar to display the *Notes* pane.

2. Click in the **Notes** pane.

3. Type your note for the slide.

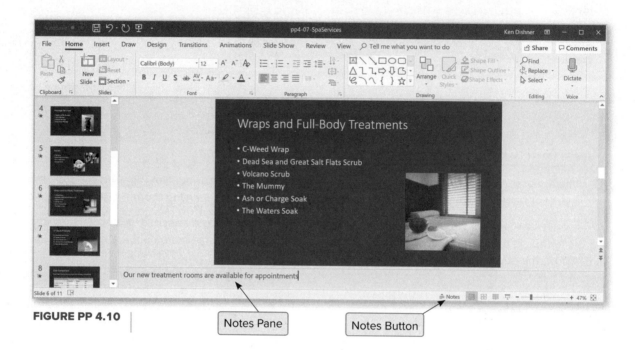

FIGURE PP 4.10

Notes Pane

Notes Button

Speaker notes can also be used to create handouts for your audience. You can then print your speaker notes and distribute them to your audience. The **Notes Page view** allows you to view how your speaker notes will look when printed. In Notes Page view, the image of the slide appears at the top of the screen and the speaker notes appear directly below the slide. You can add and format note text in Notes Page view, but you cannot edit the content of the slides.

To switch to Notes Page view:

1. Click the **View** tab.

2. In the *Presentation Views* group, click the **Notes Page** button.

3. The current slide is displayed with the note below it.

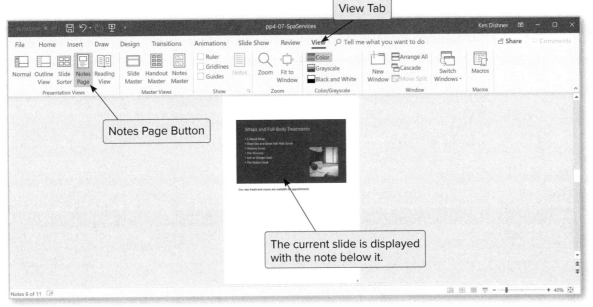

FIGURE PP 4.11

tips & tricks

To hide the *Notes* pane, click the **Notes** button on the status bar again.

tell me **more**

Presenter view allows you to use two monitors to display your presentation. One monitor shows the presentation as your audience sees it, while the other includes presentation tools, navigation tools, and any notes that have been added to slides.

another **method**

To display the *Notes* pane, you can also click the **View** tab. In the *Show* group, click the **Notes** button.

let me **try**

If you do not have the data file from the previous skill open, open the student data file **pp4-07-SpaServices** and try this skill on your own:

1. Display the **Notes** pane.
2. Add a note to **Slide 6** that reads `Our new treatment rooms are available for appointments.`
3. Switch to **Notes Page** view.
4. Return to **Normal** view and hide the **Notes** pane.
5. If you will be moving on to the next skill in this chapter, leave the presentation open to continue working. If not, save the file as directed by your instructor and close it.

Skill 4.8 Adding Footers

A **footer** is text that appears on every slide. Typically, footers appear at the bottom of the slide, but they can also appear along the side of a slide. Use footers when you want to display the same text on every slide, such as the name of your company.

To add text to the footer of all the slides in a presentation:

1. Click the **Insert** tab.
2. In the *Text* group, click the **Header & Footer** button.

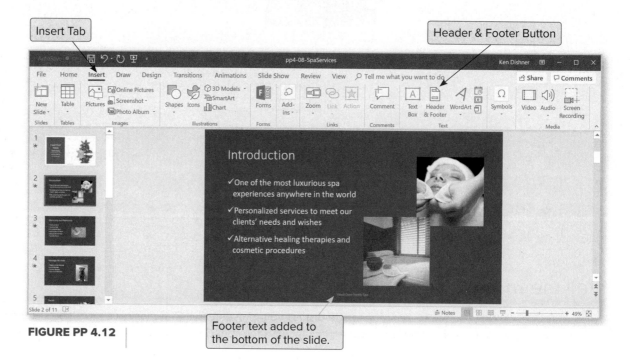

FIGURE PP 4.12

3. On the *Slide* tab of the *Header and Footer* dialog, select the **Footer** check box.
4. Type the text for the footer in the *Footer* text box.
5. If you do not want your footer to display on the title slide of the presentation, select the **Don't show on title slide** check box.
6. Click the **Apply to All** button to add the footer to every slide in the presentation.

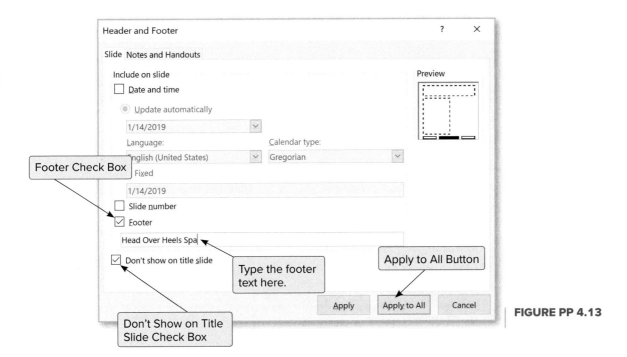

Footer Check Box

Type the footer text here.

Apply to All Button

Don't Show on Title Slide Check Box

FIGURE PP 4.13

tips & tricks

If you want the footer to appear only on the current slide and not every slide in the presentation, click the **Apply** button.

tell me **more**

A **header** is used to display information in a handout printed from a presentation. Headers appear on the top of every handout. They do not display in the slide show. The footer text you add to slides will appear at the bottom of the handouts as well as the bottom of the slides in the presentation.

let me **try**

If you do not have the data file from the previous skill open, open the student data file **pp4-08-SpaServices** and try this skill on your own:

1. Navigate to **Slide 2**.
2. Open the **Header and Footer** dialog.
3. Add a footer to every slide in the presentation except the title slide that reads **Head Over Heels Spa**.
4. If you will be moving on to the next skill in this chapter, leave the presentation open to continue working. If not, save the file as directed by your instructor and close it.

Skill 4.9 Adding the Date to the Footer

It is common practice to include the current date in the footer of slides. You could manually type the date in the footer of each slide and then update the date every time you work on the presentation, or you could add the date to the footer.

To add the date to the footer of a presentation:

1. Click the **Insert** tab.

2. In the *Text* group, click the **Date & Time** button.

3. In the *Header and Footer* dialog, click the **Date and time** check box to select it.

4. Verify the **Update automatically** radio button is selected.

5. Click the drop-down list under the *Update automatically* radio button and select a format for the date.

6. Click **Apply to All** to add the date to all the slides in the presentation.

Date & Time Button

FIGURE PP 4.14

Date and Time Check Box

Update Automatically Radio Button

Select a format here.

Apply to All Button

FIGURE PP 4.15

tell me **more**

When you select the **Update automatically** option in the *Header and Footer* dialog, PowerPoint pulls the current date from the computer's system clock and displays the date on the slide. The date is then automatically updated when the computer's date changes.

let me **try**

If you do not have the data file from the previous skill open, open the student data file **pp4-09-SpaServices** and try this skill on your own:

1. Open the **Header and Footer** dialog.

2. Add the current date to all the slides in the presentation except the title slide. Use the **Month Day, Year** format (for example January 1, 2020) and have the date update automatically.

3. If you will be moving on to the next skill in this chapter, leave the presentation open to continue working. If not, save the file as directed by your instructor and close it.

Skill 4.10 Inserting Slide Numbers

When giving a presentation, it is easy to lose track of where you are in it. You can add **slide numbers** to the footer area of each slide to display how far along you are in your presentation. You could manually type the number for each slide in the footer area, but what if you add or delete slides from your presentation? You would have to manually renumber each slide. Instead, you can add slide numbers from the *Header and Footer* dialog; when you add or remove slides, the slide numbers will be updated automatically.

To add slide numbers to the footer of a presentation:

1. Click the **Insert** tab.
2. In the *Text* group, click the **Slide Number** button.
3. In the *Header and Footer* dialog, click the **Slide number** check box.
4. Click **Apply to All** to add slide numbers to all the slides in the presentation.

FIGURE PP 4.16

FIGURE PP 4.17

tell me **more**

Depending on which theme you have applied to the presentation, the slide number may appear at the bottom of the slide, but it may also appear at the top, at the right side, at the left side, or next to a slide element, such as the slide's title.

let me **try**

If you do not have the data file from the previous skill open, open the student data file **pp4-10-SpaServices** and try this skill on your own:

1. Open the **Header and Footer** dialog.
2. Add a slide number to every slide in the presentation except the title slide.
3. If you will be moving on to the next skill in this chapter, leave the presentation open to continue working. If not, save the file as directed by your instructor and close it.

Skill 4.11 Rehearsing Timings

Timing is an important part of your presentation. For example, you wouldn't want to be part way through explaining the content of a slide and have your presentation advance before you are ready. Before you give your presentation, it is a good idea to rehearse what you will say and set up the timing for the slide show. Use PowerPoint's **Rehearse Timings** feature to synchronize your verbal presentation with your slides.

To use PowerPoint's Rehearse Timings feature:

1. Click the **Slide Show** tab.

2. In the *Set Up* group, click the **Rehearse Timings** button.

FIGURE PP 4.18

FIGURE PP 4.19

3. When the first slide appears, begin rehearsing your presentation.

4. Click the **Pause** button if you want to stop the timer.

5. Click the **Next** button to advance to the next slide.

6. Continue rehearsing each slide, clicking the **Next** button to advance the slides, until you reach the end of the presentation.

7. At the end of the presentation, you will be asked if you want to keep the timings as part of your slide show. Click **Yes** to include the timings as part of the presentation. If you do not want to keep the timings, click **No**.

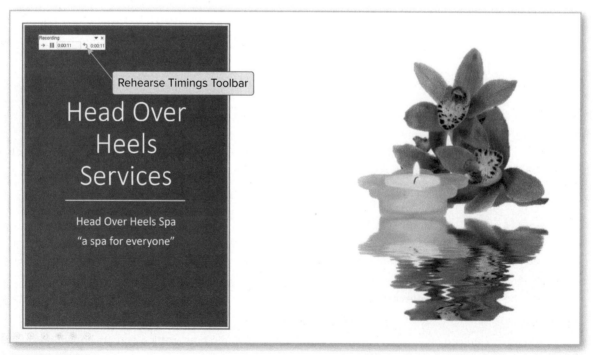

FIGURE PP 4.20

powerpoint 365   chapter 4 Managing and Delivering Presentations

tips & tricks

When you are timing your presentation, be sure to speak slowly and carefully, and to pause slightly before you advance to the next slide.

another **method**

You can also enter the timing for a slide directly into the **Slide Time** box on the *Rehearse Timings* toolbar.

let me try

If you do not have the data file from the previous skill open, open the student data file **pp4-11-SpaServices** and try this skill on your own:

1. Start the **Rehearse Timings** feature.
2. Click the **Next** button to navigate to the next slide.
3. Pause the presentation.
4. Start the timings again.
5. Finish navigating through the presentation using the toolbar.
6. Do not save the timings.
7. If you will be moving on to the next skill in this chapter, leave the presentation open to continue working. If not, save the file as directed by your instructor and close it.

from the perspective of . . .

A HEALTH CLUB MANAGER

The first time I gave a presentation to a potential customer, it was a disaster! All my slides were out of order, and I had one slide in the presentation three times. Since then, I've learned to carefully practice my PowerPoint slide shows before presenting them before customers. I can then reorder and delete slides and even hide slides that I don't want to show but want to keep as part of the presentation. I always add notes and then use two screens to show the presentation in Presenter view—this helps me stay on track when presenting.

Ryan McVay/Photodisc/Getty Images

Skill 4.12 Starting the Slide Show

You can choose to start your presentation from the beginning, playing it all the way through. But what if you find you don't have as much time as you originally planned to present? You can also choose to start the presentation from any slide in the presentation.

To start a presentation from the beginning:

1. Click the **Slide Show** tab.
2. In the *Start Slide Show* group, click the **From Beginning** button.

To start a presentation from the current slide:

1. Click the **Slide Show** tab.
2. In the *Start Slide Show* group, click the **From Current Slide** button.

FIGURE PP 4.21

tips & tricks

Another way to start a presentation from the beginning is to select the first slide in the presentation and use any of the methods for playing the presentation from the current slide.

another method

❭ To start a slide show from the current slide, you can also click the **Slide Show** view button on the status bar.

❭ To start the slide show from the beginning, you can also press (F5) on the keyboard.

let me try

If you do not have the data file from the previous skill open, open the student data file **pp4-12-SpaServices** and try this skill on your own:

1. Start the slide show from the beginning.
2. Press (Esc) to exit the slide show.
3. Navigate to **Slide 3**.
4. Start the slide show from the current slide.
5. Press (Esc) to exit the slide show.
6. If you will be moving on to the next skill in this chapter, leave the presentation open to continue working. If not, save the file as directed by your instructor and close it.

Skill 4.13 Navigating the Slide Show

Once you have started the slide show, you will need a way to advance through the slides as you talk. You can use the *Rehearse Timings* feature to automatically advance the slide show for you. However, if you want the freedom to depart from your script, you will want to navigate the slide show yourself. This table lists commands for navigating a presentation in Slide Show view using the mouse and the keyboard:

SLIDE SHOW NAVIGATION		
Command	**Mouse Command**	**Keyboard Command**
Next Slide	Left-click on the slide. Right-click and select **Next**.	Press **Enter**. Press the **Spacebar**.
Previous Slide	Right-click and select **Previous**.	Press **Backspace**.
Specific Slide	Right-click and select **See All Slides**. Select the slide.	Press the number of the slide and press **Enter**.
Exit the Presentation	Right-click and select **End Show**.	Press **Escape**.

When running a slide show, you can also use the Slide Show toolbar, located in the lower-left corner of the slide, to navigate through a presentation.

❭ Click the **Next** button to navigate to the next slide in the presentation.

❭ Click the **Previous** button to navigate to the previous slide in the presentation.

❭ Click the **Zoom** button to magnify a part of a slide.

❭ Click the **See All Slides** button to display thumbnails of all the slides in the presentation. Click a thumbnail to navigate to that slide.

FIGURE PP 4.22

FIGURE PP 4.23

tips & tricks

If you want to see the last slide you viewed, but it is not part of the slide order, right-click the presentation and select **Last Viewed** on the menu.

let me try

If you do not have the data file from the previous skill open, open the student data file **pp4-13-SpaServices** and try this skill on your own:

1. Start the slide show.
2. Navigate to the next slide.
3. Navigate to the previous slide.
4. Navigate to **Slide 6**.
5. Continue navigating through the presentation.
6. When you get to the end, exit the presentation.
7. If you will be moving on to the next skill in this chapter, leave the presentation open to continue working. If not, save the file as directed by your instructor and close it.

Skill 4.14 Using Presentation Tools

When you are presenting, you may find you want to take a break to discuss a point or answer a question, but you do not want your audience to be distracted by the current slide's information. While presenting at this point, you can cover the current slide's content by turning the screen black or white.

To change the screen to black or white:

1. Click the **Slide Show Options** button.

2. Click **Screen** and **Black Screen** to fill the screen with black or **White Screen** to fill the screen with white.

3. To return to your slide, display *Slide Show Options* menu, and click **Screen**. Select either **Unblack Screen** or **Unwhite Screen**.

FIGURE PP 4.24

The presentation tools in PowerPoint allow you to write on your slides while you are giving your presentation. You can use the **Pen** tool to underline or circle important points as you discuss them. Use the **Highlighter** tool to add color behind text on slides and emphasize parts of your slides. PowerPoint also includes a **laser pointer** tool. This tool turns the mouse pointer into a red dot that you can use to call attention to important parts of your slides.

To make notations on slides using the presentation tools:

1. In Slide Show view, click the **Pointer Options** button.

2. Select a pointer option: **Laser Pointer**, **Pen**, or **Highlighter**.

FIGURE PP 4.25

3. Click and drag the mouse to write on the slide or highlight part of the slide.

4. To return to the arrow pointer, press the **Esc** key on the keyboard.

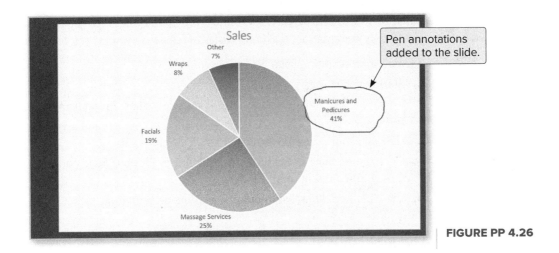

FIGURE PP 4.26

tips & tricks

When you end your presentation, PowerPoint will ask if you want to keep the annotations you added. Click the **Keep** button to include the annotations as part of the presentation. Click the **Discard** button to delete the annotations.

another **method**

To use presentation tools, you can also right-click the slide, point to **Pointer Options**, and select an option.

let me **try**

If you do not have the data file from the previous skill open, open the student data file **pp4-14-SpaServices** and try this skill on your own:

1. Start the slide show.
2. Navigate to **Slide 9**.
3. Change the screen to be all black.
4. Unblack the screen.
5. Use the **Pen** tool to circle the *Manicures and Pedicures* information on the chart.
6. Exit the presentation. Do not save the annotations.
7. If you will be moving on to the next skill in this chapter, leave the presentation open to continue working. If not, save the file as directed by your instructor and close it.

Select **Show Presenter View.**

Slide Show Options Button

FIGURE PP 4.27

Skill 4.15 Using Presenter View

You can use two monitors to display your presentation. When you use two monitors your audience will see your presentation in Slide Show view, while you will see the presentation in **Presenter view**. Presenter view allows you to see your notes while you are giving your presentation, making it easier to refer to any notes you have added to slides.

To show a presentation using Presenter view:

1. Start the slide show.
2. Click the **Slide Show Options** button and select **Show Presenter View**.
3. Presenter view displays with the presentation on the left and a preview of the next slide and your notes for the current slide on the right.
4. Click the **Advance to Next Slide** and **Return to Previous Slide** button to navigate through the presentation.
5. Click the **End Slide Show** button to exit the presentation.

Presenter View

Next Slide in Presentation

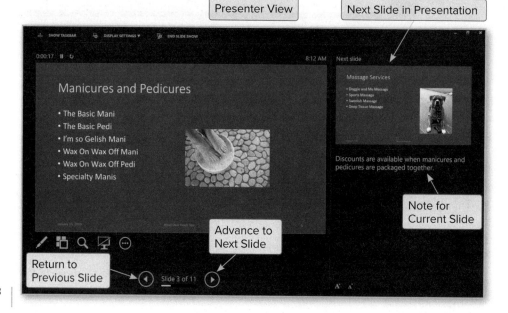

Note for Current Slide

Advance to Next Slide

Return to Previous Slide

FIGURE PP 4.28

tips & tricks

If you need to change which display shows the presentation and which display shows Presenter view, click the **Display Settings** button and select **Swap Presenter View and Slide Show**.

another **method**

To open Presenter view, you can also right-click a slide in Slide Show view and select **Show Presenter View**.

let me **try**

If you do not have the data file from the previous skill open, open the student data file **pp4-15-SpaServices** and try this skill on your own:

Start the slide show from the beginning.

1. Open **Presenter view**.
2. Navigate through the presentation using Presenter view.
3. Exit the slide show.
4. If you will be moving on to the next skill in this chapter, leave the presentation open to continue working. If not, save the file as directed by your instructor and close it.

Skill 4.16 Recording a Slide Show

Rather than presenting a slide show live, you can choose to record your slide show, including the timings, narrations, and an inset video of you giving the presentation. When you play the recorded slide show, PowerPoint will automatically play any recorded narration or video and navigate through the slides using the timings you created when you recorded the slide show.

NOTE: To record narration, you will need to have a microphone or headset with a microphone attached to your computer. To include a video of yourself giving the presentation, you will need a camera attached to your computer. Please be sure these are working before doing the following steps.

To record a slide show:

1. Click the **Slide Show** tab.

2. In the *Set Up* group, click the **Record Slide Show** button.

3. The *Recording* window opens.

4. Click the **Turn Camera On/Off** button to choose whether to record video of yourself as you give the presentation.

5. Click the **Turn Microphone On/Off** button to choose whether to record narration with the presentation.

6. When you are ready to begin recording the presentation, click the **Record** button.

FIGURE PP 4.29

7. After the countdown, work through your presentation as if you were presenting to an audience.

8. Click the **Advance to the next slide** button to advance to the next slide.

9. Continue narrating each slide, clicking the **Advance to the next slide** button to advance the slides, until you reach the end of the presentation.

FIGURE PP 4.30

tips & tricks

> To remove timings from a presentation, click the **Record Slide Show** button arrow, point to **Clear**, and select **Clear Timings on All Slides**.

> To remove narration and video from a presentation, click the **Record Slide Show** button arrow, point to **Clear**, and select **Clear Narrations on All Slides**.

tell me **more**

When you record a presentation, PowerPoint will use the timings, narration, and video you recorded as the default playback options for the presentation. To change these options, on the *Slide Show* tab, in the *Set Up* group, click the **Play Narrations** check box to deselect it and not use the recorded narration and video. Click the **Use Timings** check box to deselect it and not use the recorded timings.

let me **try**

If you do not have the data file from the previous skill open, open the student data file **pp4-16-SpaServices** and try this skill on your own:

1. Verify **Slide 1** is selected.
2. Open the **Recording window**.
3. Turn off the **camera** while recording.
4. Begin recording the presentation.
5. Navigate through the presentation recording each slide until you reach the end.
6. If you will be moving on to the next skill in this chapter, leave the presentation open to continue working. If not, save the file as directed by your instructor and close it.

from the perspective of . . .

STUDENT

I was terrified when I found out I had to present in front of my entire class. I always do well when I practice, but when I get in front of a live audience, I freeze up. I talked to my instructor and she said I could record my presentation and play it for the class instead. That was such a relief! I spent so many hours on my presentation, adding both entry and exit animations and getting the timings just right. I even animated a chart! When it came time to record the presentation, I wasn't nervous at all. I spoke slowly and clearly with no "ums" or "uhs." When I played the presentation for the class, I got a really great response, but the best response of all was the A I got from my instructor.

Imagerymajestic/Alamy Stock Photo

Skill 4.17 Printing Presentations

In PowerPoint, all the print settings are combined in a single page along with a preview of how the printed presentation will look. From the *Print* page in Backstage view, you can preview and print all the slides in your presentation.

To preview and print a presentation:

1. Click the **File** tab to open Backstage view.
2. Click **Print**.
3. Verify that the correct printer name is displayed in the *Printer* section.
4. In the *Settings* section, the last button displays the color options for printing the presentation. By default, *Color* is selected. To change the print selection, click the button, and then click an option: **Color**, **Grayscale**, or **Pure Black and White**.
5. Click the **Print** button to print.

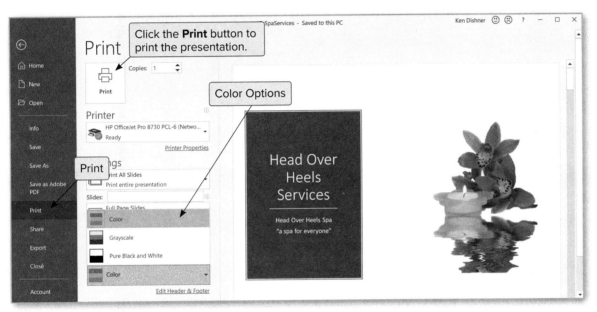

FIGURE PP 4.31

tips & tricks

Click the **Next Page** and **Previous Page** buttons at the bottom of the preview to navigate through your presentation to see how all the slides will appear when printed.

another **method**

To open the *Print* page in Backstage view, you can use the keyboard shortcut (Ctrl) + (P).

let me **try**

If you do not have the data file from the previous skill open, open the student data file **pp4-17-SpaServices** and try this skill on your own:

1. Open Backstage view and display the **Print** page.
2. Change the color of the printed presentation to **Grayscale**.
3. Print the presentation. **NOTE**: If you are using this in class or in your school's computer lab, check with your instructor about printing permissions before completing this step.
4. If you will be moving on to the next skill in this chapter, leave the presentation open to continue working. If not, save the file as directed by your instructor and close it.

Skill 4.18 Customizing Handout Masters

The **Handout Master** view allows you to modify how the printed version of your presentation will look. When you open the presentation in Handout Master view, you will see a preview of the printed page with dotted placeholders for the slides, header, footer, page number, and date.

To work in Handout Master view:

1. Click the **View** tab.
2. In the *Master Views* group, click the **Handout Master** button.

FIGURE PP 4.32

3. The Handout Master view displays.
4. On the *Handout Master* tab, in the *Placeholders* group, click a placeholder check box to remove the checkmark and hide the placeholder. Click the placeholder check box again to display the placeholder.
5. In the *Page Setup* group, click the **Slides Per Page** button and select an option to change the number of slides that will appear on each printed page.
6. Click the **Close Master View** button to return to *Normal* view.

Placeholders you can hide and show include:

> **Header**–appears in the upper-left corner of the page. To add header text for a handout, click in the **Header** box and type the text you want to appear in the upper left corner of each handout.

> **Date**–appears in the upper-right corner of the page and displays the date.

> **Footer**–appears in the lower-left corner of the page and displays the text you entered for the footer.

> **Page Number**–appears in the lower-right corner of the page and displays the current number of the printed page (not the slide number).

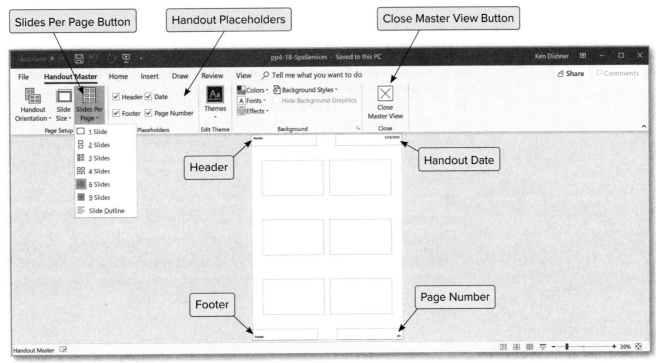

Slides Per Page Button · Handout Placeholders · Close Master View Button

Header · Handout Date · Footer · Page Number

FIGURE PP 4.33

tips & tricks

By default, handouts appear in portrait orientation, meaning the page is taller than it is wide. If you want your handouts to appear in landscape orientation (with the page being more wide than tall), in the *Page Setup* group, click the **Handout Orientation** button and select **Landscape**.

another **method**

To return to Normal view, you can also click the **Normal** button on the status bar.

let me **try**

If you do not have the data file from the previous skill open, open the student data file **pp4-18-SpaServices** and try this skill on your own:

1. Switch to the **Handout Master** view.
2. Hide the **page number** on the handout.
3. Change the handout master so **four slides** appear on each printed page.
4. Add the text **Head Over Heels Spa** to the header of the handout. If necessary, increase the zoom percentage in the view to see the header area more clearly.
5. Close **Handout Master** view.
6. If you will be moving on to the next skill in this chapter, leave the presentation open to continue working. If not, save the file as directed by your instructor and close it.

Skill 4.19 Printing Handouts

In addition to printing slides, PowerPoint also gives you the ability to print handouts, notes, and an outline of the presentation. A **handout** is a printout of your presentation with anywhere from one to nine slides per page and with areas for taking notes. The **Notes Pages** option will print a copy of the slide with its associated note, if there is one. Select *Outline* when you want to print a text outline of your presentation. As with printing presentations, printing of handouts, notes pages, and outlines are all done from the *Print* page in Backstage view.

To preview and print handouts:

1. Click the **File** tab to open Backstage view.
2. Click **Print**.
3. Verify that the correct printer name is displayed in the *Printer* section.
4. In the *Settings* section, the second button displays the page options for printing the presentation. By default, *Full Page Slides* is selected. To change the print selection, click the button and then select an option.
5. Click the **Print** button to print.

FIGURE PP 4.34

tips & tricks

The Handouts (3 Slides) layout includes lines next to the slide image. This layout is useful if you want to print your presentation for your audience and include an area where they can easily write notes to correspond with each slide.

another **method**

To open the *Print* page in Backstage view, you can use the keyboard shortcut Ctrl + P.

let me **try**

If you do not have the data file from the previous skill open, open the student data file **pp4-19-SpaServices** and try this skill on your own:

1. Open Backstage view.
2. Display the **Print** page.
3. Change the print settings to print **3 Slides per page**.
4. Print the presentation. **NOTE**: If you are using this in class or in your school's computer lab, check with your instructor about printing permissions before completing this step.
5. If you will be moving on to the next skill in this chapter, leave the presentation open to continue working. If not, save the file as directed by your instructor and close it.

Skill 4.20 Packaging a Presentation

PowerPoint's **Package for CD** feature allows you to copy and package all the elements of your presentation to a folder. When you package a presentation, the PowerPoint viewer is included by default, allowing you to run your presentation from any computer. You can then save the presentation to a removable USB drive, a shared network location, or a cloud storage location, such as your OneDrive account.

To use the Package for CD feature to package a presentation to a folder:

1. Click the **File** tab to open Backstage view.
2. Click **Export**.
3. Under *Export*, click **Package Presentation for CD**.
4. Under *Package Presentation for CD*, click **Package for CD**.

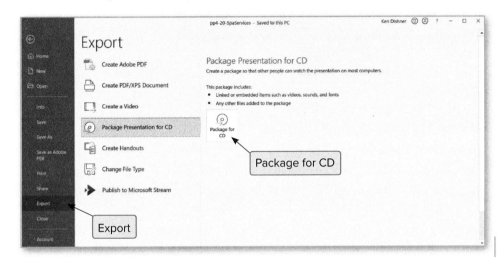

FIGURE PP 4.35

5. The *Package for CD* dialog opens.
6. Type the name for the folder in the *Name the CD* box.
7. Click the **Copy to Folder...** button.

FIGURE PP 4.36

8. In the *Copy to Folder* dialog, click the **Browse...** button.

9. In the *Choose Location* folder, navigate to the location where you want to save the presentation. Choose a location that will be accessible from another computer, such as a folder in your OneDrive location.

10. Click **Select** in the *Choose Location* dialog.

FIGURE PP 4.37

11. Click **OK** in the *Copy to Folder* dialog.

12. Click the **Close** button to close the *Package for CD* dialog.

13. You can also package your presentation to a CD. However, many computers no longer include built-in CD drives. Before choosing this option, be sure the computer you will be presenting on has a CD drive.

tips & tricks

❭ Click the **Add...** button in the *Package for CD* dialog to copy more than one presentation to the folder.

❭ Click the **Options...** button in the *Package for CD* dialog to change the options for including linked files and embedding True Type fonts. In the *Options* dialog, you can also add passwords for opening the presentation and modifying the presentation.

let me try

If you do not have the data file from the previous skill open, open the student data file **pp4-20-SpaServices** and try this skill on your own:

1. Open **Backstage** view and navigate to the **Export** page.

2. Open the **Package for CD** dialog.

3. Name the presentation: **SpaServices**

4. Package the presentation to a folder in your OneDrive account.

5. If you see a message asking if you want to include linked files, click **Yes**.

6. Close the **Package for CD** dialog.

7. Save the file as directed by your instructor and close it.

Hide Slide
Hyperlink
ScreenTips
Spelling checker
Speaker notes
Notes Page view
Footer
Header
Slide numbers

Rehearse Timings
Pen
Highlighter
Laser pointer
Presenter view
Handout Master
Handout
Notes Pages
Package for CD

concept review

1. Which command do you use to keep a slide in a presentation but not show it by default when you are in Slide Show view?

a. *Delete*

b. *Reorder*

c. *Hide*

d. *Cut*

2. Which of the following is a text or a graphic that, when clicked, takes you to a new location?

a. comment

b. hyperlink

c. ScreenTip

d. note

3. Which area of the slide would you add an automatic date or slide number to in order to have it appear on every slide?

a. header

b. footer

c. slide placeholder

d. title

4. Which key do you press to exit a slide show?

a. Escape

b. Backspace

c. Enter

d. spacebar

5. Press the spacebar to navigate to the next slide in Slide Show view.

a. true

b. false

6. When giving a presentation, you can write on slides and save annotations by using PowerPoint's pen options, which include the _____ tool.

   a. laser pointer

   b. pen

   c. highlighter

   d. all of the above

7. Which view allows you to give a presentation on two screens, with one screen showing the slide show along with speaker notes and other tools?

   a. Slide Show view

   b. Slide Sorter view

   c. Presenter view

   d. Presentation view

8. Which feature would you use to practice your presentation and record how long you spend on each slide?

   a. Rehearse Timings

   b. Record narration

   c. Slide Show

   d. Presenter view

9. Which of the following print layouts displays lines next to the slides for taking notes?

   a. Outline

   b. Notes Pages

   c. 3 Slides

   d. 4 Slides Horizontal

10. To package a presentation to a shared folder to play on another computer, you would use the Package to CD feature.

   a. true

   b. false

projects

skill review **4.1**

In this project you will be working on the structure for the marketing presentation from Suarez Marketing. You will add footer information. You will rehearse the presentation and practice navigating through the slide show using the keyboard and mouse. You will change the handout master and print handouts for your audience.

Skills needed to complete this project:

- Changing the Order of Slides (Skill 4.2)
- Hiding and Unhiding Slides (Skill 4.3)
- Adding Hyperlinks to Slides (Skill 4.5)
- Deleting Slides from Presentations (Skill 4.1)
- Checking Spelling (Skill 4.6)
- Adding Footers (Skill 4.8)
- Adding Notes (Skill 4.7)
- Rehearsing Timings (Skill 4.11)
- Starting the Slide Show (Skill 4.12)
- Navigating the Slide Show (Skill 4.13)
- Customizing Handout Masters (Skill 4.18)
- Printing Handouts (Skill 4.19)

1. Open the start file **PP2019-SkillReview-4-1** and resave the file as: [your initials]PP-SkillReview-4-1

2. If the presentation opens in Protected View, click the **Enable Editing** button in the Message Bar at the top of the presentation so you can modify it.

3. Change the order of slides in a presentation.

    a. Select **Slide 9** in the *Slides* pane.

    b. Click and drag the slide thumbnail up in the list until it appears above the **The Suarez Marketing Belief** slide. The slide should now appear with an *8* next to it.

4. Unhide a slide in a presentation.

    a. Navigate to **Slide 10**.

    b. Click the **Slide Show** tab.

    c. In the *Set Up* group, click the **Hide Slide** button.

5. Add a hyperlink to slides.

    a. Navigate to **Slide 4**.

    b. Click at the end of the second bullet point and press the Spacebar one time.

    c. Click the **Insert** tab.

    d. In the *Links* group, click the **Link** button.

    e. Under *Link to*, click **Place in This Document**.

    f. In the *Select a place in this document* box, click **Slide 8. Client Quotes**.

g. In the *Text to display* box, delete the text *Client Quotes.* Type **(See Client Quotes)**

h. Click **OK**.

6. Delete a slide from the presentation.

a. Navigate to **Slide 12**.

b. Right-click the slide thumbnail and select **Delete Slide**.

7. Check the presentation for spelling errors.

a. Navigate to **Slide 1**.

b. Click the **Review** tab.

c. In the *Proofing* group, click the **Spelling** button.

d. Click the **Change** button to change the first misspelling from **busines** to **business**.

e. Click the **Change** button to change the second misspelling from **organisation** to **organization**.

f. Click the **Change** button to change the third misspelling from **Asociation** to **Association**.

g. The next possible error is not a misspelling. Click the **Ignore Once** button to keep the spelling.

h. A message box appears when the spell check is complete. Click **OK** in the message box.

8. Add a footer to the presentation.

a. Click the **Insert** tab.

b. In the *Text* group, click the **Header & Footer** button.

c. Click the check box next to **Footer** and type **Suarez Marketing** in the text box.

d. Click **Apply to All**.

9. Add notes to a slide.

a. Navigate to **Slide 2**.

b. Click the **Notes** button on the status bar.

c. Click in the *Notes* pane and type **Give specific client examples**

10. Use PowerPoint's Rehearse Timing feature.

a. Click the **Slide Show** tab.

b. In the *Set Up* group, click the **Rehearse Timings** button.

c. When the first slide appears, begin rehearsing your presentation.

d. Click the **Pause** button if you want to stop the timer.

e. Click the **Next** button to advance to the next slide.

f. Continue rehearsing each slide, clicking the **Next** button to advance the slides, until you reach the end of the presentation.

g. At the end of the presentation, you will be asked if you want to keep the timing as part of your slide show. Click **No**.

11. Start the slide show from the beginning and navigate through the presentation using the mouse.

a. On the *Slide Show* tab, in the *Start Slide Show* group, click the **From Beginning** button.

b. To advance to the next slide, click the mouse or click the **Next** button.

c. To go to the previous slide, click the **Previous** button.

d. To jump to a specific slide, click the **See All Slides** button and select a slide.

e. To exit the presentation, click the **Slide Show Options** button and select **End Show**.

12. Hide a slide.

   a. Navigate to **Slide 11**.

   b. On the *Slide Show* tab, in the *Set Up* group, click the **Hide Slide** button to hide the slide.

13. Start the slide show from the current slide and navigate through the presentation using the keyboard.

   a. Navigate to **Slide 9**.

   b. On the *Slide Show* tab, in the *Start Slide Show* group, click the **From Current Slide** button.

   c. To advance to the next slide: press ⏎ Enter or the **Spacebar**.

   d. To go to the previous slide: press ← Backspace.

   e. To jump to a specific slide: type the number of the slide and press Enter.

   f. To exit the presentation: press Esc.

14. Customize the handout master.

   a. Click the **View** tab.

   b. In the *Master Views* group, click the **Handout Master** button.

   c. Click in the handout header box and type `Suarez Marketing Presentation`

   d. Click the **Close Master View** button.

15. Print handouts.

   a. Click the **File** tab. Click the **Print** button.

   b. Click the second button under *Settings* and select the **4 Slides Horizontal** option in the *Handouts* section.

   c. Click the **Print** button. **NOTE:** If you are using this in class or in your school's computer lab, check with your instructor about printing permissions before completing this step.

16. Save and close the presentation.

skill review **4.2**

In this project you will be working on the structure for a personal fitness plan presentation. You will add footer information. You will rehearse the presentation and practice navigating through the slide show in Presenter view. You will change the handout master and print handouts for your audience.

Skills needed to complete this project:

- Changing the Order of Slides (Skill 4.2)
- Copying and Pasting Slides (Skill 4.4)
- Deleting Slides from Presentations (Skill 4.1)
- Hiding and Unhiding Slides (Skill 4.3)
- Adding Footers (Skill 4.8)

- Adding the Date to the Footer (Skill 4.9)
- Checking Spelling (Skill 4.6)
- Adding Notes (Skill 4.7)
- Rehearsing Timings (Skill 4.11)
- Starting the Slide Show (Skill 4.12)
- Navigating the Slide Show (Skill 4.13)
- Using Presentation Tools (Skill 4.14)
- Using Presenter View (Skill 4.15)
- Customizing Handout Masters (Skill 4.18)
- Printing Handouts (Skill 4.19)

1. Open the start file **PP2019-SkillReview-4-2** and resave the file as: `[your initials]PP-SkillReview-4-2`

2. If the presentation opens in Protected View, click the **Enable Editing** button in the Message Bar at the top of the presentation so you can modify it.

3. Change the order of slides in a presentation.

   a. Select **Slide 4** in the *Slides* pane.

   b. Click and drag the slide thumbnail up in the list until it is the first slide in the presentation.

4. Copy and paste a slide.

   a. Select **Slide 8**.

   b. On the *Home* tab, in the *Clipboard* group, click the **Copy** button.

   c. Select **Slide 2**.

   d. In the *Clipboard* group, click the **Paste** button.

5. Delete a slide from the presentation.

   a. Navigate to **Slide 10**.

   b. Right-click the slide thumbnail and select **Delete Slide**.

6. Hide a slide in a presentation.

   a. Navigate to **Slide 7**.

   b. Click the **Slide Show** tab.

   c. In the *Set Up* group, click the **Hide Slide** button.

7. Add a footer.

   a. Click the **Insert** tab.

   b. In the *Text* group, click the **Header & Footer** button.

   c. Click the check box next to *Footer* and type `My Six Week Fitness Plan` in the text box.

   d. If necessary, select the **Don't show on title slide** check box.

   e. Click **Apply to All**.

8. Add an automatic date to the footer.

   a. On the *Insert* tab, in the *Text* group, click the **Header & Footer** button.

   b. Click the **Date and Time** check box.

   c. Verify the *Update automatically* radio button is selected.

   d. Click the drop-down arrow and select the **MM/DD/YYYY** format. For example, *1/1/2020*.

   e. Click **Apply to All**.

9. Check the presentation for spelling errors.

   a. Navigate to **Slide 1**.

   b. Click the **Review** tab.

   c. In the *Proofing* group, click the **Spelling** button.

   d. Click the **Change** button to change the first misspelling from **bedtim** to **bedtime**.

   e. Click the **Change** button to change the second misspelling from **frend** to **friend**.

   f. Click the **Change** button to change the third misspelling from **massege** to **massage**.

   g. Click the **Change** button to change the fourth misspelling from **triathalon** to **triathlon**.

   h. A message box appears when the spell check is complete. Click **OK** in the message box.

10. Add notes to a slide.

    a. Navigate to **Slide 5**.

    b. Click the **Notes** button on the status bar.

    c. Click in the *Notes* pane and type `Use app to log nutritional info and exercise`

11. Use PowerPoint's Rehearse Timing feature.

    a. Click the **Slide Show** tab.

    b. In the *Set Up* group, click the **Rehearse Timings** button.

    c. When the first slide appears, begin rehearsing your presentation.

    d. Click the **Pause** button if you want to stop the timer.

    e. Click the **Next** button to advance to the next slide.

    f. Continue rehearsing each slide, clicking the **Next** button to advance the slides until you reach the end of the presentation.

    g. At the end of the presentation, you will be asked if you want to keep the timing as part of your slide show. Click **No**.

12. Start the slide show from the beginning and navigate through the presentation using the mouse.

    a. On the *Slide Show* tab, in the *Start Slide Show* group, click the **From Beginning** button.

    b. To advance to the next slide, click the mouse or click the **Next** button.

    c. To go to the previous slide, click the **Previous** button.

    d. Click the **See All Slides** button and select a **Slide 3**.

    e. Click the **Pointer Options** button and select **Pen**.

    f. Click and drag the mouse around the bars for **Saturday**, circling the day on the chart.

13. Switch to **Presenter view**.

    a. Click the **Slide Show Options** button and select **Show Presenter View**.

    b. Click the **Advance to Next Slide** button to move forward in the presentation. Click the **Return to Previous Slide** button to move backward in the presentation.

    c. To exit the presentation, click the **Slide Show Options** button and select **End Show**. In the message box that appears, click the **Discard** button to remove the pen annotation you made.

14. Customize the handout master.
    a. Click the **View** tab.
    b. In the *Master Views* group, click the **Handout Master** button.
    c. Click in the upper left box of the handout header and type: `My Six Week Fitness Plan`
    d. In the *Placeholders* group, click the **Date** check box to remove the date from the printed handout.
    e. Click the **Close Master View** button.
15. Print handouts.
    a. Click the **File** tab.
    b. Click the **Print** button.
    c. Click the second button under *Settings* and select the **6 Slides** option in the *Handouts* section.
    d. Click the **Print** button. **NOTE:** If you are using this in class or in your school's computer lab, check with your instructor about printing permissions before completing this step.
16. Save and close the presentation.

challenge yourself **4.3**

In this project you will be working on the structure for a presentation for Greenscapes landscaping company. You will add footer information. You will rehearse the presentation and practice navigating through the slide show. You will change the handout master and print handouts for your audience.

Skills needed to complete this project:
- Changing the Order of Slides (Skill 4.2)
- Deleting Slides from Presentations (Skill 4.1)
- Adding Hyperlinks to Slides (Skill 4.5)
- Adding Footers (Skill 4.8)
- Adding the Date to the Footer (Skill 4.9)
- Checking Spelling (Skill 4.6)
- Adding Notes (Skill 4.7)
- Rehearsing Timings (Skill 4.11)
- Starting the Slide Show (Skill 4.12)
- Navigating the Slide Show (Skill 4.13)
- Using Presentation Tools (Skill 4.14)
- Hiding and Unhiding Slides (Skill 4.3)
- Customizing Handout Masters (Skill 4.18)
- Printing Handouts (Skill 4.19)

1. Open the start file **PP2019-ChallengeYourself-4-3** and resave the file as: `[your initials]PP-ChallengeYourself-4-3`
2. If the presentation opens in Protected View, click the **Enable Editing** button in the Message Bar at the top of the presentation so you can modify it.
3. Move **Slide 4** so it comes after **Slide 1**.
4. Delete **Slide 4**.

5. Add a hyperlink to slides.

   a. Select **Slide 3**.

   b. Place the cursor in the blank line under the numbered list.

   c. Insert a hyperlink to **Slide 7** that reads `See our pricing`

6. Add a footer to every slide except the title slide that reads `Greenscapes Landscaping`

7. Add a date to the footer using the *Day Month Year* format (for example, 1 January 2020). Have the date update automatically.

8. Check the presentation for spelling errors.

   a. Do not change the suggested misspelling on **Greenscapes**.

   b. Correct the misspelling on the word **organic**.

   c. Correct the misspelling on the word **carbon**.

   d. Correct the misspelling on the word **Maintenance**.

   e. Correct the misspelling on the word **Specialty**.

   f. Correct the misspelling on the word **maintenance**.

9. Add notes to a slide.

   a. Navigate to **Slide 2**.

   b. Display the *Notes* pane and add a note that reads: `We use biodynamic principles`

10. Start the **Rehearse Timings** feature. Navigate through the presentation using the toolbar. Do not save the timings.

11. Start the presentation and use presentation tools.

    a. Start the slide show from the beginning.

    b. Navigate through the presentation using the mouse.

    c. When you come to the **Specialty Services** slide, use the **Highlighter** tool to highlight **Water landscapes** and **Compost Silos** on the slide.

    d. When the slide show ends, do not save the annotations.

12. Hide **Slide 6**.

13. Customize the handout master.

    a. Hide the date on the handout master.

    b. Hide the footer on the handout master

    c. Add the text `Greenscapes Landscaping` to the header.

14. Print handouts.

    a. Change the printing options so three slides appear on each page with lines next to the image of each slide.

    b. Print the handouts. **NOTE:** If you are using this in class or in your school's computer lab, check with your instructor about printing permissions before completing this step.

15. Save and close the presentation.

challenge yourself 4.4

In this project you will be working on the structure for a presentation about emotional intelligence. You will add footer information. You will rehearse the presentation and practice navigating through the slide show in Presenter view. You will change the handout master and print handouts for your audience.

Skills needed to complete this project:

- Changing the Order of Slides (Skill 4.2)
- Deleting Slides from Presentations (Skill 4.1)
- Hiding and Unhiding Slides (Skill 4.3)
- Checking Spelling (Skill 4.6)
- Adding Footers (Skill 4.8)
- Inserting Slide Numbers (Skill 4.10)
- Adding the Date to the Footer (Skill 4.9)
- Adding Notes (Skill 4.7)
- Rehearsing Timings (Skill 4.11)
- Starting the Slide Show (Skill 4.12)
- Navigating the Slide Show (Skill 4.13)
- Using Presentation Tools (Skill 4.14)
- Using Presenter View (Skill 4.15)
- Customizing Handout Masters (Skill 4.18)
- Printing Handouts (Skill 4.19)

1. Open the start file **PP2019-ChallengeYourself-4-4** and resave the file as: `[your initials]PP-ChallengeYourself-4-4`

2. If the presentation opens in Protected View, click the **Enable Editing** button in the Message Bar at the top of the presentation so you can modify it.

3. Move **Slide 11** so it appears below **Slide 12**.

4. Delete **Slide 13**.

5. Hide **Slide 7**.

6. Check the presentation for spelling errors and make corrections to the misspellings found.

   a. Correct the misspelling on the word **Stressors**.

   b. Correct the misspelling on the word **purpose**.

   c. Correct the misspelling on the word **Neocortex**.

   d. Correct the misspelling on the word **decision**.

7. Add a footer to every slide that reads `Emotional Intelligence`

8. Add slide numbers to every slide in the presentation.

9. Add a date to the footer of every slide in the presentation using the **Month Day, Year** format (for example, January 1, 2020). Have the date update automatically.

10. Add notes to a slide.

   a. Navigate to **Slide 2**.

   b. Display the **Notes** pane and add a note that reads `Give three examples of over the top situations.`

11. Start the **Rehearse Timings** feature. Navigate through the presentation using the toolbar. Do not save the timings.

12. Start the presentation and use presentation tools.

   a. Start the slide show from the beginning.

   b. Navigate through the presentation using the keyboard.

   c. Use the **Show All Slides** command to navigate to **Slide 4**.

d. Use the **Highlighter** tool to highlight **'right' emotion**, **'right' time**, **'right' intensity**, **'right' purpose**, and **'right' way** on the slide.

e. Switch to Presenter view and navigate through the presentation.

f. End the slide show and do not save the annotations.

13. Customize the handout master by adding the text `Emotional Intelligence` to the header box.

14. Show the footer on the handout master and the text `Presentation Handout` to the footer box.

15. Print handouts.

a. Change the printing options so four slides appear on each page.

b. Print the handouts. **NOTE:** If you are using this in class or in your school's computer lab, check with your instructor about printing permissions before completing this step.

16. Save and close the presentation.

on your own 4.5

In this project you will be modifying a presentation about creating PowerPoint presentations. You will add footer information. You will rehearse the presentation and practice navigating through the slide show in Presenter view. You will change the handout master and print handouts for your audience.

Skills needed to complete this project:

- Deleting Slides from Presentations (Skill 4.1)
- Changing the Order of Slides (Skill 4.2)
- Checking Spelling (Skill 4.6)
- Adding Hyperlinks to Slides (Skill 4.5)
- Adding Notes (Skill 4.7)
- Adding Footers (Skill 4.8)
- Adding the Date to the Footer (Skill 4.9)
- Inserting Slide Numbers (Skill 4.10)
- Rehearsing Timings (Skill 4.11)
- Starting the Slide Show (Skill 4.12)
- Navigating the Slide Show (Skill 4.13)
- Using Presenter View (Skill 4.15)
- Customizing Handout Masters (Skill 4.18)
- Printing Handouts (Skill 4.19)

1. Open the start file **PP2019-OnYourOwn-4-5** and resave the file as: `[your initials]PP-OnYourOwn-4-5`

2. If the presentation opens in Protected View, click the **Enable Editing** button in the Message Bar at the top of the presentation so you can modify it.

3. Delete the empty slide in the presentation.

4. Reorder the slides in the presentation so they follow the four steps outlined on **Slide 2**.

5. Check the presentation for spelling errors and correct any misspellings found.

6. Convert each step on **Slide 2** to a hyperlink and link the text to its appropriate slide.

7. Add notes for each slide with further talking points about steps in creating a presentation.

8. Add the title of the presentation as a footer that will appear on every slide except the title slide.

9. Add a date to the footer of every slide except the title slide using a format of your choice. Have the date update automatically.

10. Add slide numbers to the footer of every slide except the title slide of the presentation.

11. Use the Rehearse Timings feature to practice the presentation. Do not save the timings.

12. Start the slide show from the beginning and navigate through the presentation using the keyboard.

13. Navigate to any slide and start the presentation from the current slide.

14. Switch to **Presenter view** and use the navigation tools to move through the presentation.

15. Customize the handout master to include a header. Change any other options in the handout you want.

16. Print copies of the handouts using a setting of your choice. **NOTE**: If you are using this in class or in your school's computer lab, check with your instructor about printing permissions before selecting **Print**.

17. Save and close the presentation.

fix it 4.6

In this project you will be working on the structure for a presentation about team building. You will practice navigating through the slide show and using annotation tools. You will change the handout master and print handouts for your audience.

Skills needed to complete this project:
- Changing the Order of Slides (Skill 4.2)
- Deleting Slides from Presentations (Skill 4.1)
- Hiding and Unhiding Slides (Skill 4.3)
- Checking Spelling (Skill 4.6)
- Adding Notes (Skill 4.7)
- Adding Footers (Skill 4.8)
- Adding the Date to the Footer (Skill 4.9)
- Inserting Slide Numbers (Skill 4.10)
- Starting the Slide Show (Skill 4.12)
- Navigating the Slide Show (Skill 4.13)
- Using Presentation Tools (Skill 4.14)
- Printing Presentations (Skill 4.17)
- Customizing Handout Masters (Skill 4.18)
- Printing Handouts (Skill 4.19)

1. Open the start file **PP2019-FixIt-4-6** and resave the file as: `[your initials]PP-FixIt-4-6`

2. If the presentation opens in Protected View, click the **Enable Editing** button in the Message Bar at the top of the presentation so you can modify it.

3. Move **Slide 7** so it appears below **Slide 8**.

4. There is a duplicate slide in the presentation. Delete **Slide 9**.

5. Unhide **Slide 5**.

6. Check the presentation for spelling errors and correct any misspellings found.

7. The slide number and presentation title have been added manually to the bottom of every slide except the title slide. This is not the correct way to add footer information to a presentation. Delete the text boxes on *Slide 2* through *Slide 8*.

8. Add a footer to every slide in the presentation except the title slide. Include the information that was in the text boxes you deleted.

9. Start the slide show from the beginning and navigate through the presentation using the mouse. When you get to the **Project Objectives** slide, use the **Pen** tool to circle each objective as it is discussed. End the slide show but do not save the annotations.

10. Print one grayscale copy of all the slides in the presentation (each slide should appear on its own page). **NOTE**: If you are using this in class or in your school's computer lab, check with your instructor about printing permissions before selecting **Print**.

11. Change the handout master so the **date** and **page number** appear on the printed handouts.

12. Change the handout master so the presentation title appears in the header area.

13. Print handouts so three slides appear on each page with lines next to the image of each slide. **NOTE**: If you are using this in class or in your school's computer lab, check with your instructor about printing permissions before completing this step.

14. Save and close the presentation.

Office 365 Shortcuts

Office Keyboard Shortcuts

ACTION	KEYBOARD SHORTCUT
Display Open page in Backstage view	Ctrl + O
Create a new blank file (bypassing Backstage view)	Ctrl + N
Copy	Ctrl + C
Cut	Ctrl + X
Paste	Ctrl + V
Undo	Ctrl + Z
Redo	Ctrl + Y
Save	Ctrl + S
Select All	Ctrl + A
Help	F1
Bold	Ctrl + B
Italic	Ctrl + I
Underline	Ctrl + U
Close Start page or Backstage view	Esc
Close a file	Ctrl + W
Minimize the Ribbon	Ctrl + F1
Switch windows	Alt + Tab

Word Keyboard Shortcuts

ACTION	KEYBOARD SHORTCUT
Open a new blank Word document	`Ctrl` + `N`
Display Open page in Backstage view	`Ctrl` + `O`
Open the *Open* dialog	`Ctrl` + `F12`
Select All	`Ctrl` + `A`
Open *Spelling and Grammar* task pane	`F7`
Undo	`Ctrl` + `Z`
Redo	`Ctrl` + `Y`
Open *Navigation* task pane with the search results section displayed	`Ctrl` + `F`
Open *Find and Replace* dialog with the *Replace* tab displayed	`Ctrl` + `H`
Open *Find and Replace* dialog with the *Go To* tab selected	`Ctrl` + `G` or `F5`
Copy	`Ctrl` + `C`
Cut	`Ctrl` + `X`
Paste	`Ctrl` + `V`
Bold	`Ctrl` + `B`
Italic	`Ctrl` + `I`
Underline	`Ctrl` + `U`
Save	`Ctrl` + `S`
Open *Save As* dialog	`F12`
Open *Font* dialog	`Ctrl` + `D`
Increase font size	`Ctrl` + `↑ Shift` + `>`
Decrease font size	`Ctrl` + `↑ Shift` + `<`
Left align text	`Ctrl` + `L`
Center text	`Ctrl` + `E`
Right align text	`Ctrl` + `R`
Justify text	`Ctrl` + `J`
Single line spacing	`Ctrl` + `1`
Double line spacing	`Ctrl` + `2`

ACTION	KEYBOARD SHORTCUT
Show formatting marks	Ctrl + ↑ Shift + 8
Open *Insert Hyperlink* dialog	Ctrl + K
Open *Thesaurus* pane	↑ Shift + F7
Open Word Help	F1
Insert line break	↑ Shift + ←┘ Enter
Insert page break	Ctrl + ←┘ Enter
Insert non-breaking space	Ctrl + ↑ Shift + Space
Copy formatting	Ctrl + ↑ Shift + C
Paste formatting	Ctrl + ↑ Shift + V
Insert an endnote	Alt + Ctrl + D
Insert a footnote	Alt + Ctrl + F
Move the insertion point to the beginning of the document	Ctrl + Home
Move the insertion point to the end of the document	Ctrl + End
Display print page	Ctrl + P
Close a document	Ctrl + W

Excel Keyboard Shortcuts

ACTION	KEYBOARD SHORTCUT
Open a new blank workbook	Ctrl + N
Display Open page in Backstage view	Ctrl + O
Open the *Open* dialog	Ctrl + F12
Move to cell A1	Ctrl + Home
Save	Ctrl + S
Cut	Ctrl + X
Copy	Ctrl + C
Paste	Ctrl + V
Undo	Ctrl + Z
Redo	Ctrl + Y
Bold	Ctrl + B
Italic	Ctrl + I
Underline	Ctrl + U
Open the Quick Analysis tool	Ctrl + Q
Open the *Find and Replace* dialog with the *Find* tab displayed	Ctrl + F
Open the *Find and Replace* dialog with the *Replace* tab displayed	Ctrl + H
Edit mode (insertion point appears within the cell)	F2
Add a line break within a cell	Alt + ← Enter
Hide row	Ctrl + 9
Hide column	Ctrl + 0
Unhide row	Ctrl + ↑ Shift + 9
Insert dialog (cell, row, or column)	Ctrl + ↑ Shift + =
Insert worksheet	↑ Shift + F11
Insert chart	Alt + F1
Fill selected cell(s) with the value from the cell above it	Ctrl + D
Fill selected cell(s) with the value from the cell to the left of it	Ctrl + R
Open *Insert Function* dialog	↑ Shift + F3

ACTION	KEYBOARD SHORTCUT
Toggle between displaying formulas in cells and showing the formula results	[Ctrl] + [`]
Apply percent style	[Ctrl] + [↑ Shift] + [5]
Insert the SUM function	[Alt] + [=]
Toggle between cell reference states in a formula (absolute, mixed with relative column and absolute row, mixed with absolute column and relative row, relative)	[F4]
Open *Paste Name* dialog	[F3]
Open the *Spelling* dialog	[F7]
Open the Print page in Backstage view	[Ctrl] + [P]
Close	[↑ Shift] + [F11]

Access Keyboard Shortcuts

ACTION	KEYBOARD SHORTCUT
Open a new blank database	Ctrl + N
Open an existing database	Ctrl + O
Go to the next field in the record	→
Go to the previous field in the record	←
Go to the next record	↓
Go to the previous record	↑
Go to the first record	Ctrl + ↑
Go to the last record	Ctrl + ↓
Navigate from field to field within a record	Tab
Navigate from the last field in the record to the first field in the next record	Tab
Create a new blank record from the last record in the dataset	Tab
Add a new blank record to a table or form	Ctrl + ↑ Shift + =
Cut	Ctrl + X
Copy	Ctrl + C
Paste	Ctrl + V
Undo	Ctrl + Z
Redo	Ctrl + Y
Delete a record	Delete or Ctrl + -
Open the *Spelling* dialog	F7
Open or close *Navigation* pane	F11
Open selected object in Design view	Ctrl + ← Enter
Save a database object. If first time saving the object, opens the *Save As* dialog.	Ctrl + S
Open the *Save As* dialog	F12
Open shortcut menu for the selected object	↑ Shift + F10
Move to preceding cell in a table, query, or form	↑ Shift + Tab
Insert line break when entering data in a *Short Text* or *Long Text* field	Ctrl + ← Enter

ACTION	KEYBOARD SHORTCUT
Undo changes to current field and all changes if more than one field on current record has been changed.	`Esc`
Switch between Edit mode (insertion point displayed) and Navigation mode	`F2`
Increase selection to add adjacent column to the right	`↑ Shift` + `→`
Increase selection to add adjacent column to the left	`↑ Shift` + `←`
Open *Find and Replace* dialog	`Ctrl` + `F`
Open *Find and Replace* dialog with the *Replace* tab selected	`Ctrl` + `H`
Find next	`↑ Shift` + `F4`
Open Expression Builder	`Ctrl` + `F2`
Open Zoom window	`↑ Shift` + `F2`
Open or close the Properties window for the selected control	`F4`
Show or hide Field list	`Alt` + `F8`
Open *Page Setup* dialog from Print Preview view	`S`
Open *Print* dialog from Print Preview view	`Ctrl` + `P`
Switch to Form view from Design view	`F5`

PowerPoint Keyboard Shortcuts

ACTION	KEYBOARD SHORTCUT
Open a new blank presentation	Ctrl + N
Display Open page in Backstage view	Ctrl + O
Open the *Open* dialog	Ctrl + F12
Exit Slide Show view	Esc
Bold	Ctrl + B
Italic	Ctrl + I
Underline	Ctrl + U
Align text left	Ctrl + L
Center text	Ctrl + E
Align text right	Ctrl + R
Justify text	Ctrl + J
Open *Find* dialog	Ctrl + F
Open *Replace* dialog	Ctrl + H
Save	Ctrl + S
Undo	Ctrl + Z
Redo	Ctrl + Y
Cut	Ctrl + X
Copy	Ctrl + C
Paste	Ctrl + V
Open *Insert Hyperlink* dialog	Ctrl + K
Display the *Spelling* task pane	F7
Duplicate slides	Ctrl + D
Soft return, causes text to wordwrap to the next line	↑ Shift + ← Enter
Open the Print page in Backstage view	Ctrl + P
Open *Save As* dialog	F12
Move to first slide	Home
Move to last slide	End
Move to next slide	Page down or ↓

ACTION	KEYBOARD SHORTCUT
Move to previous slide	[Page up] or [↑]
Move from the slide title to the body placeholder	[Ctrl] + [← Enter]
Start a presentation slide show from the beginning	[F5]
Open Presenter view and start a slide show	[Alt] + [F5]
In Slide Show view, advance to the next slide	[N], [Space], [→], [↓], [← Enter] or [Page down]
In Slide Show view, go to the previous slide	[P], [← Backspace], [←], [↑], or [Page up]
In Slide Show view, go to a particular slide	Slide number, [← Enter]
In Slide Show view, open the *All Slides* dialog	[Ctrl] + [S]
In Slide Show view, blanks the screen to black	[B] or [·]
In Slide Show view, blanks the screen to white	[W] or [·]
In Slide Show view, stop or restart an automatic show	[S] or [+]
In Slide Show view, change pointer to pen	[Ctrl] + [P]
In Slide Show view, change pointer to arrow	[Ctrl] + [A]
In Slide Show view, change pointer to laser pointer	[Ctrl] + [L]
In Slide Show view, change pointer to highlighter	[Ctrl] + [I]
In Slide Show view, change pointer to eraser	[Ctrl] + [E]
In Slide Show view, show or hide ink markup	[Ctrl] + [M]
In Slide Show view, erase markings on the screen	[E]
In Slide Show view, zoom in on a slide	[Ctrl] + [=]
In Slide Show view, zoom out on a slide	[Ctrl] + [−]

Mouse Commands and Touch Gestures

When working on a device with touch capability, Office includes the ability to switch the user interface between one optimized for using a mouse or one optimized for using touch gestures. In Touch Mode, the buttons on the Ribbon appear more spread out making it easier to select using your finger rather than the mouse pointer.

To switch between touch and mouse mode:

1. Click the **Touch/Mouse Mode** button on the Quick Access Toolbar.
2. Select the mode you want to use.

FIGURE AB-1

The following table lists some of the more common mouse commands and their corresponding gestures:

DESCRIPTION	MOUSE COMMAND	GESTURE	EXAMPLE
Make a selection or place the insertion point	Left-click	Tap	
Select a word	Double-click	Double tap	x2
Select a paragraph	Triple-click	Triple tap	x3

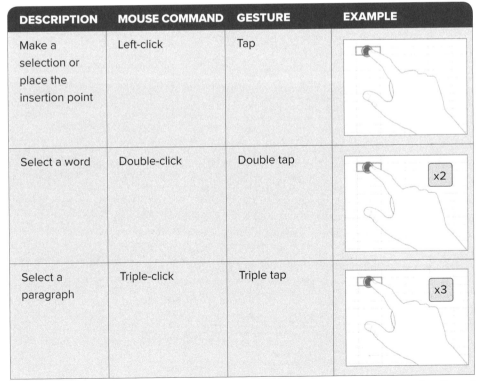

(continued)

DESCRIPTION	MOUSE COMMAND	GESTURE	EXAMPLE
Display a shortcut menu	Right-click	Press and hold then release	hold and release
Drag an object	Left-click > drag to new location while holding the button down > release the mouse button	Tap object > Slide finger to new location > lift	
Zoom Out	Drag Zoom Slider to the right	Stretch	
Zoom In	Drag Zoom Slider to the left	Pinch	

Source of screenshots: Microsoft Office 365: Word, Excel, Access, and PowerPoint.

Overview 365 Glossary

a

Account page: Page in Backstage view that lists information for the user currently logged in to Office. This account information comes from the Microsoft account you used when installing Office.

AutoSave: Feature in Office where version files are automatically saved. In order for AutoSave to be active, the file must be saved to a OneDrive account.

b

Backstage view: Tab that contains the commands for managing and protecting files, including Save, Open, Close, New, Share, Export, and Print.

c

Cloud storage: File storage that is online rather than on your computer's hard drive. You can access the files from any computer or device as long as you have an Internet connection.

Contextual tabs: Contain commands specific to the type of object selected and are visible only when the commands might be useful.

d

Desktop apps: Full-featured version of the Office apps that you download and install on your computer.

Dialog launcher: Button in the lower right corner of a Ribbon group that, when clicked, opens the associated dialog for that group.

e

Enhanced ScreenTip: A ScreenTip that displays the name of the command, the keyboard shortcut (if there is one), and a short description of what the button does and when it is used.

f

File Properties: Information about a file such as the location of the file, the size of file, when the file was created and when it was last modified, the title, and the author. File properties can be found on the Info page in Backstage view.

File tab: Tab located at the far left side of the Ribbon. Opens the Microsoft Office Backstage view.

g

Groups: Subsections of a tab on the Ribbon; organizes commands with similar functions together.

h

Help task pane: Office task pane where you can look up topics to learn about features and how to perform certain tasks.

Home page: Page in Backstage view that displays a list of recently opened files along with common templates. The Home page displays be default on the Start page (the page that displays when you first open an app).

Home tab: Contains the most commonly used commands for each Office application.

i

Intelligent services: Services in Office that rely on the cloud to continually update the information they provide.

k

Keyboard shortcuts: Keys or combinations of keys that, when pressed, execute a command.

l

Live Preview: Displays formatting changes in a file before actually committing to the change.

m

Metadata: All the information about a file that is listed under the Properties section of the Info page in Backstage view.

Microsoft Access: A database program. Database applications allow you to organize and manipulate large amounts of data.

Microsoft Excel: A spreadsheet program. Originally, spreadsheet applications were viewed as electronic versions of an accountant's ledger. Today's spreadsheet applications can do much more than just calculate numbers—they include powerful charting and data analysis features. Spreadsheet programs can be used for everything from managing personal budgets to calculating loan payments.

Microsoft PowerPoint: A presentation program. Such applications enable you to create robust, multimedia presentations.

Microsoft Word: A word processing program. Word processing software allows you to create text-based documents. Word processing software also offers more powerful formatting and design tools, allowing you to create complex documents, including reports, résumés, brochures, and newsletters.

Mini toolbar: Provides access to common tools for working with text. When text is selected and then the mouse is rested over the text, the Mini toolbar fades in.

Mobile apps: Free apps available for your tablet device. Similar in features and functionality to the online app, these apps are designed to run on the iOS and android operating systems.

n

New command: Creates a new file in an Office application without exiting and reopening the program.

o

Office 2019 (on-premises): Version of Microsoft Office that is paid for one time. It includes full versions of the apps, but only receives security and bug fixes in updates. No new feature updates are included with the on-premises version of Office.

Office 365: Version of Microsoft Office that is paid on a subscription basis (either monthly or annually). It includes the full versions of the Office apps and is updated twice a year with new features.

Office background: Image that displays in the upper right corner of the application Window near the username.

Office theme: The color scheme for Office that affects the look of the Ribbon, task panes, and main working areas.

OneDrive: Microsoft's free cloud storage where you can save files and access those files from any computer or device or share the files with others.

Online apps: Apps that are accessed through a web browser (no install required) and allow you to create and save files online using your OneDrive account. Available at https://office.com.

Online collaboration: Ability for multiple people to work on a shared file at the same time. All changes made are combined into a single file.

Options dialog: Place where you can control settings for the Office application. When you make a change in the Options dialog, the setting applies to the application, not the current active file.

p

Protected View: Provides a read-only format that protects your computer from becoming infected by a virus or other malware.

q

Quick Access Toolbar: Toolbar located at the top of the application window above the File tab. The Quick Access Toolbar gives quick one-click access to common commands.

r

Ribbon: Located across the top of the application window and organizes common features and commands into tabs.

s

ScreenTip: A small information box that displays the name of the command when the mouse is rested over a button on the Ribbon.

Sharing link: Link to a shared file on OneDrive that can be sent to others to collaborate on a file.

Shortcut menus: Menus of commands that display when an area of the application window is right-clicked.

Smart Lookup: Tool that allows you to quickly search the Internet about any word or phrase in a document, spreadsheet, or presentation.

Start page: Screen that displays when you launch an Office application. From the Start page you can open a recently opened file or create a new file from a template.

t

Tab: Subsection of the Ribbon; organizes commands further into related groups.

Tags: Keywords used for grouping common files together or for searching.

Tell Me: Feature that offers a quick way to access command and help topics in Office.

v

Versions: Backups of files that are autosaved in Office and can be accessed to either copy and paste content or save as a new file.

glossary of key terms

Word 365 Glossary

a

Alignment guides: Horizontal and vertical green lines that appear when an object is dragged and the object's edge is aligned with another element on the page.

Alt text: A description of a picture, chart, or other object that can be read by screen readers.

AutoCorrect: Feature that analyzes each word as it is entered in a document. Each word is compared to a list of common misspellings, symbols, and abbreviations. If a match is found, AutoCorrect automatically replaces the text in the document with the matching replacement entry.

AutoFit: Command used for resizing a table's column width to either the cell's content or the size of the window.

Automatic date stamp: Pulls the current date from the computer's system clock and displays the date in the document.

b

Bar Tab: Displays a vertical line through the text at the tab stop.

Bibliography: A compiled list of sources referenced in a document.

Bold: Character formatting that gives the text a heavier, thicker appearance.

Border Painter: Feature that allows you to quickly apply the currently selected border styles to tables by clicking a border along the edge of a cell. When the Border Painter is active, the cursor changes to a paintbrush.

Border styles: Predefined styles you can add to a table. Border styles come in a number of colors and weights.

Borders: Lines that appear along the top, bottom, left side, and right side of the paragraph.

Building block: A piece of content that is reusable in any document. Building blocks can be text, such as AutoText, or can include graphics, such as a cover page.

Building Blocks Organizer: Lists the building blocks in alphabetical order by the gallery in which they appear; includes Bibliographies, Cover Pages, Equations, Footers, Headers, Page Numbers, Table of Contents, Tables, Text Boxes, and Watermarks.

Bullet: A symbol that is displayed before each item in a list.

Bulleted list: List where the items do not need to be displayed in a specific order. In a bulleted list, a symbol appears before each list item.

c

Caption: A brief description of an illustration, chart, equation, or table.

Cell: The intersection of a row and column in a table.

Center alignment: Paragraph alignment that centers each line of text relative to the margins.

Center Tab: Displays text centered over the tab stop.

Change Case: Command in Word that manipulates the typed characters, changing how the letters are displayed.

Character effects: Effects applied to individual characters or words rather than paragraphs. Common character effects include bold, italic, and underline effects.

Chart data labels: Display the values that go with the data series in the chart.

Chart legend: A key for a chart defining which data series is represented by each color.

Chart styles: A combination of layout styles and formatting options you apply to charts.

Chart title: A text box that overlays the chart and is typically located above the chart.

Chart: A graphic that transforms numerical data into a more visual representation.

Citations: A reference to source material in a document. Citations include information such as the author, title, publisher, and the publish date.

Clear All Formatting: Command that removes any formatting that has been applied to text, including character formatting, text effects, and styles, and leaves only plain text.

Clipboard: Task pane that displays up to 24 copied or cut items for use in any Office application.

Color theme: A set of colors that complement each other and are designed to work well together.

Column break: Break that marks where one column ends and moves the following text to the top of the next column.

Columns: A vertical arrangement of text on-screen. Text at the bottom of one column continues on to the top of the next column.

Columns: Groups of cells that display vertically in a table.

Comment: A note you add to a document that is not meant to be a part of the document.

Copy: Command that places a duplicate of the selected text or object on the Clipboard without changing the file.

Cover page: First page in a document that contains brief information about the document, including the title and the date.

Creative Commons: Licensing system through which Bing Image Search filter results when searching for pictures online.

Cut: Command that removes the selected text or object from the file and places it on the Office Clipboard for later use.

d

Decimal Tab: Aligns the text along the decimal point.

Decrease Indent: Moves text to the left by one level (0.5 inch).

Distribute Columns: Command that resizes all the columns in a table so they have the same width.

Distribute Rows: Command that resizes all the rows in a table so they have the same height.

Draft view: Simplified view in Word that is designed for typing and formatting text. Draft view does not display headers and footers, page edges, backgrounds, or drawing objects.

e

Editor: A tool in Word that analyzes your entire document for spelling, grammar, clarity, and conciseness errors and displays any potential errors for you to decide how to handle them.

Endnotes: References in a document that provide the reader with further information. Endnotes are composed of two parts: a reference mark and the associated text. Endnotes appear at the end of the document.

f

Find: Command that locates specific text or formatting in a document.

First Line Indent: Indents only the first line of a paragraph and leaves the remainder of the paragraph left aligned.

Font theme: A set of fonts that complement each other and are designed to work well together.

Font: Refers to a set of characters of a certain design. The font is the shape of the character or number as it appears on-screen.

Footer: Text that appears at the bottom of every page.

Footnotes: References in a document that provide the reader with further information. Footnotes are composed of two parts: a reference mark and the associated text. Footnotes appear at the bottom of a page.

Format Painter: Tool that copies and pastes formatting styles.

Formatting marks: Hidden marks in a document that indicate spaces, paragraphs, tabs, and page breaks.

g

Grammar error: Error in punctuation or capitalization that is displayed in the Editor pane after the Spelling & Grammar checker analyzes a document looking for errors.

Graphics: Photographs, SmartArt, or line drawings that can be added to documents, spreadsheets, presentations, and database forms and reports.

Gridlines: A series of vertical and horizontal lines that divide the page into small boxes, giving you visual markers for aligning graphics, tables, and other elements on the page.

h

Hanging Indent: Leaves the first line of a paragraph left-aligned while indenting the remaining lines of text in the paragraph.

Hard page break: Command that forces the text to a new page no matter how much content is on the present page.

Header: Text that appears at the top of every page.

Highlighting: Tool in Word that changes the background color of the selected area to make it stand out on the page.

Hyperlink: Text or a graphic that, when clicked, opens another file or jumps to another place in the document.

i

Icons: Simple drawings (Scalable Vector Graphics) that you can add to your documents. They can be enlarged, colored, and rotated without losing image quality.

Increase Indent: Moves text to the right by one level (0.5 inch).

Index: A list of topics and associated page numbers that typically appears at the end of a document.

Insert controls: Used to quickly add rows and columns to tables. Insert Controls appear when you roll your mouse over the left edge of a row or the top edge of a column.

Intelligent Services: Cloud-enhanced features in Office that can offer recommendations to help you work more efficiently. In Word, the Editor and Smart Lookup features rely on intelligent services.

Italic: Character formatting that makes text slant to the right.

j

Justified alignment: Paragraph alignment where the words are evenly spaced between the page margins, aligning the text on the right and left sides of the printed page.

l

Layout Options: Options for changing how objects appear with text, either in line or with text wrapping.

Left alignment: Text alignment where the text is aligned on the left side, leaving the right side ragged.

Left Tab: Displays text to the right of the tab stop.

Line spacing: The white space between lines of text.

Lock Tracking: Feature that adds a password to a document that will be required to be entered in order to disable Track Changes.

m

Margin: The blank spaces at the top, bottom, left, and right of a page.

Merge cells: Combines multiple cells in a table into a single cell.

Move cursor: Cursor that appears when the mouse is resting over an object that can be moved. When the move cursor displays, clicking the left mouse button and dragging the mouse will move the object to a new location in the document.

Multifunction printer: A device that combines either inkjet or laser printing capabilities with scanning, photocopying, and faxing capabilities.

n

Numbered lists: List type used to organize information that must be presented in a certain order.

o

Online pictures: Pictures that are added from a source on the Internet, such as Bing Image Search or a OneDrive account.

Outline view: View in Word that is designed to check the structure of a document. In Outline view, the document's structure can be collapsed to view just the top-level headings or expanded to see the document's framework.

p

Page borders: The decorative graphic element along the top, right, bottom, and left edges of the page. Borders can be simple lines or include 3-D effects and shadows.

Page Break: Marker in a document that identifies where one page ends and another page begins.

Paragraph alignment: How text is aligned with regard to the left and right margins of a document.

Paragraph: Any text separated by a hard return. A hard return refers to pressing the Enter key to create a new paragraph.

Paste options: Options for pasting text and objects in Word. Paste options allow you to choose to keep the source formatting, merge the formatting of the source and the current document, paste the text as a single picture object, or paste only the text without any formatting.

Paste: Command that is used to insert text or an object from the Clipboard into a file.

Points: Measurement for the height of a font. Abbreviated pt.

Print Layout view: Displays how document elements will appear on a printed page.

Print page: Page in Backstage view where you can preview and print all the pages in your document.

Property control: An element that is added to a document to save time entering the same information over and over again.

Property controls can be used as shortcuts for entering long strings of text that are difficult to type, such as email addresses, phone numbers, and street addresses.

q

Quick Styles: Groups of formatting, including character and paragraph formatting, that can be easily applied to text, tables, drawings, or other objects.

Quick Tables: Preformatted, complex table objects ready for you to enter your own data.

r

Read Mode: View in Word that is designed for reading documents in electronic format. In Read Mode, documents are displayed as screens rather than pages.

Redo: Reverses the Undo command and restores the file to its previous state.

Reference mark: The superscript character placed next to the text for a footnote or endnote.

Reference style: A set of rules used to display references in a bibliography. These rules include the order of information, when and how punctuation is used, and the use of character formatting.

Replace All: Command used to replace words or phrases all at once throughout the document.

Replace: Used with the Find command to replace specified text in a file with new text.

Researcher: Feature that uses Microsoft's Bing search to find information on the Internet and allows you to automatically add citations to documents.

Resize handle: One of the six squares that appear when an object is selected. Clicking and dragging a resize handle toward the center of the object will make the object smaller. Clicking and dragging the resize handle away from the center of the object will make the object larger.

Reviewing pane: Task pane that displays all the changes in a document and shows a summary of the revisions in a document, including the number of insertions, deletions, moves, formatting changes, and comments.

Right alignment: Paragraph alignment where the text is aligned on the right side, leaving the left side ragged.

Right Tab: Displays the text to the left of the tab stop.

Rows: Groups of cells that display horizontally in a table.

Ruler: Displays horizontally across the top of the window just below the Ribbon and vertically along the left side of the window. The ruler gives you a quick view of the margins and position of elements in your document.

S

Sans serif fonts: Fonts that do not have an embellishment at the end of each stroke. Includes Calibri and Arial.

ScreenTip: A bubble with text that appears when the mouse hovers over a hyperlink. Typically, a ScreenTip provides a description of the hyperlink.

Section page break: Inserts a hard page break and starts a new section in the document.

Section: A designated part of a document that can be formatted separately from the rest of the document.

Serif fonts: Fonts that have an embellishment at the end of each stroke. Includes Cambria and Times New Roman.

Shading: Color that appears behind the text of the paragraph.

Shape: A drawing object that can be quickly added to a document.

Side to side layout: A setting in Word that displays pages in a horizontal layout to allow for scrolling right and left to navigate between pages in a document.

SmartArt: Visual diagrams containing graphic elements with text boxes to enter information in.

Sorting: Arranges the rows in a table in either ascending (A–Z) or descending (Z–A) alphabetical or numeric order.

Source Manager: Dialog for saving source information to a master list of sources. When you open or create new documents, you can add the sources in the master list to the document, so there is no need to reenter the same source information.

Spelling error: Misspelled word that is displayed in the Editor pane after the Spelling & Grammar checker analyzes a document looking for errors.

Split cells: Divides a cell in a table in Word into multiple cells.

Style set: Formatting options for changing the font and paragraph formatting for an entire document based on styles.

Style: Complex formatting, including font, color, size, and spacing, that can be applied to Office files.

Styles: Complex formatting, including font, color, size, and spacing, that can be applied to Office files.

t

Tab leaders: Element that fills in the space between tab stops with solid, dotted, or dashed lines.

Tab stop: The location along the horizontal ruler that indicates how far to indent text when the Tab key is pressed.

Tab: Content element that helps to organize information by rows, which display horizontally, and columns, which display vertically.

Table move handle: appears at the upper left corner of the table when it is active.

Table of contents: Lists the topics in a document and the associated page numbers, so readers can easily locate information.

Table: Content element that helps to organize information by rows, which display horizontally, and columns, which display vertically.

T

Template: A file with predefined settings that can be used as a pattern to create a new file.

Theme: A group of formatting options that is applied to an entire Office file. Themes include font, color, and effect styles that are applied to specific elements in a file.

Thesaurus: Reference tool that provides a list of synonyms (words with the same meaning) and antonyms (words with the opposite meaning) for a selected word or phrase.

Track Changes: Word feature that marks text and formatting changes in a document.

U

Underline: Character formatting that draws a single line under the text.

Undo: Reverses the last action performed.

V

Vertical layout: A setting in Word that displays pages one above another to allow for scrolling up and down to navigate between pages in a document.

W

Watermark: A graphic or text that appears as part of the page background. Watermarks appear faded so the text that appears on top of the watermark is legible when the document is viewed or printed.

Web Layout view: Displays all backgrounds, drawing objects, and graphics as they will appear on-screen if the document is saved as a Web page.

Word Count: Feature that provides the current statistics of the document you are working on, including the number of pages, number of words, number of characters, (with and without spaces), number of paragraphs, and number of lines.

Word wrap: Automatically places text on the next line when the right margin of the document has been reached.

WordArt: Predefined graphic styles that are applied to text. These styles include a combination of colors, fills, outlines, and effects.

Z

Zoom slider: Slider bar that controls how large or small the file appears in the application window.

Zooming: The act of changing the size of text and images on-screen. Zooming a document affects only how the document appears on-screen. It does not affect how the document will print.

Excel 365 Glossary

#

3-D reference: A formula that references the same cell(s) on multiple sheets.

a

Absolute reference: A cell reference whose location remains constant when the formula is copied. The $ character before a letter or number in the cell address means that part of the cell's address is absolute (nonchanging).

Accounting Number Format: Aligns the $ at the left side of the cell, displays two places after the decimal, and aligns all numbers at the decimal point. Zero amounts are displayed as dashes (-).

Alignment: Refers to how text and numbers are positioned within the cell both horizontally and vertically.

Argument: The part of the formula (input) that the function uses to calculate a value.

AutoFill: Feature used to fill a group of cells with the same data or to extend a data series.

AutoSum: Allows you to insert common functions (SUM, AVERAGE, COUNT, MIN, and MAX) with a single mouse click.

AVERAGE: A statistical function that is used to calculate the average value of a group of values. A formula using the AVERAGE function looks like this: =AVERAGE(A3:A6)

b

Banding: Applies a fill color to alternating rows or columns, making a table easier to read.

Bar charts: Chart type that works best with data that are organized into rows and columns like a table. The categories are displayed on the vertical (y) axis, and the data points are plotted along the horizontal (x) axis.

Bottom Rules: Excel conditional formatting style that automatically finds and highlights the highest or lowest values or values that are above or below the average in the specified range of cells.

c

Cascade: Places the windows in a staggered, overlapping, diagonal arrangement.

Cell address: The column and row position that defines a cell. For example, the cell at the intersection of column B and row 4 has a cell address of B4.

Cell range: A contiguous group of cells. A cell range is identified by the address of the cell in the upper left corner of the range, followed by a colon, and then the address of the cell in the lower right corner of the range. The cell range B3:D5 includes cells B3, B4, B5, C3, C4, C5, D3, D4, and D5.

Cell reference: A cell's address when it is used in a formula.

Cell style: A combination of effects that can be applied at one time. Styles can include formatting such as borders, fill color, font size, and number formatting.

Cell: The intersection of a row and column in a spreadsheet.

Chart area: Encompasses the entire chart including the plot area and optional layout elements, such as title and legend.

Chart sheet: A special type of worksheet that contains only the chart object.

Chart title: A text box above or overlaying the chart.

Chart: A graphic that represents numeric data visually.

Clustered column chart: Chart type where each column represents a single data point. The data points are grouped (clustered) together by category. Each data series is represented by a single color.

Color Scales: A conditional formatting style in Excel that colors cells according to one of the color scales (e.g., red to green [bad/low to good/high] or blue to red [cold/low to hot/high]).

Column charts: Chart type that works best with data that are organized into rows and columns like a table. Data point values are transformed into columns, with the values plotted along the vertical (y) axis. Each row in the table is grouped as a data series. Excel uses the column labels as the categories along the horizontal (x) axis.

Column input cell: The cell that contains the original value for which you want to substitute the data table values when the substitute values are listed in a column.

Column selector: The box with the column letter at the top of the worksheet grid. Clicking this box will select the entire column.

Column: A vertical group of cells. Columns are identified by letters. For example, the fourth column is labeled with the letter D.

Comma Style format: Number format similar to the Accounting Number Format, but without the currency symbol.

CONCAT: A Text function used to combine the text values of cells. For example, if you have two columns for the first name and last name, but you need a third column displaying the full name, you can use CONCAT to combine the values of the first two columns. In Excel 2016, CONCAT replaced CONCATENATE.

Concatenate: To link items together.

Conditional formatting: Provides a visual analysis of data by applying formatting to cells that meet specific criteria (conditions).

Copy: Command that places a duplicate of the selected text or object on the Clipboard without changing the file.

COUNT: A Statistical function that counts the number of cells that contain numbers within a specified range of cells. A formula using the COUNT function looks like this: =COUNT(A2:A106)

COUNTA: A Statistical function that counts the number of cells that are not blank within a specified range of cells. Use

COUNTA if your cell range includes both numbers and text data. A formula using the COUNTA function looks like this: =COUNTA(B2:B106)

COUNTBLANK: A Statistical function that counts the number of blank cells within a specified range of cells. A formula using the COUNTBLANK function looks like this: =COUNTBLANK(D2:D106)

Currency format: Number format that places the $ immediately to the left of the number, so columns of numbers do not align at the $ and at the decimal as they do with Accounting Number Format.

Cut: Command that removes the selected text or object from the file and places it on the Office Clipboard for later use.

d

Data Bars: A conditional formatting style in Excel that displays a color bar (gradient or solid) representing the cell value in comparison to other values (cells with higher values have longer data bars).

Data labels: Display data values for each data marker in a chart.

Data markers: Columns, bars, pie pieces, or other visual elements in a chart that represent data point values.

Data points: Values from a cell range plotted on a chart.

Data series: A group of related data points plotted on a chart.

Data series: A sequence of cells with a recognizable pattern (used with the AutoFill feature).

Data table: Displays a table of the data point values below the chart.

Data table: Provides a quick what-if analysis of the effects of changing one or two variables within a formula. The data table is organized with a series of values for the variable(s) in a column or a row or both.

Defined name: The names you created and names that Excel creates automatically when you define a print area or print titles.

Delimiter: A specific character that separates text values. Delimiters are used in text files to separate fields and when combining text values using the TEXTJOIN function. Common delimiters are commas, tabs, semicolons, and spaces.

Dependent: The cell containing a formula that references the value or formula in the selected cell.

Doughnut charts: Chart type similar to a pie chart with the capability to display more than one series. Each series is represented by a ring around the doughnut. Each data point in the series is represented by a piece of the ring proportional to the total.

e

Edit mode: The data entry method used in Excel to change only part of the cell data by double-clicking the cell, and then moving the cursor within the cell to insert or delete data.

f

Fill color: Solid color that shades a cell.

Fill Handle: Appears at the lower-right corner of a selected cell or group of cells and can be used to implement the AutoFill feature.

Filter: Limits the spreadsheet rows displayed to only those that meet specific criteria.

Find: Command that locates specific text, data, or formatting in a spreadsheet.

Font: Refers to a set of characters of a certain design. The font is the shape of the character or number as it appears on-screen.

Footer: Text that appears at the bottom of every page.

Format Painter: Tool that copies and pastes formatting styles.

Formula AutoComplete: Displays a list of potential matches (functions and other valid reference names) after an = has been typed in a cell in Excel.

Formula bar: Data entry area directly below the Ribbon and above the worksheet grid.

Formula: An equation used to calculate a value.

Freeze: Excel command that keeps column headings and row labels visible as you scroll through your data.

Functions: Preprogrammed shortcuts for calculating complex equations (like the average of a group of numbers).

g

General horizontal alignment: Default alignment of cells. When cells are formatted using the General horizontal alignment, Excel detects the type of content in the cell. Cells that contain text are aligned to the left, and cells that contain numbers are aligned to the right.

General number format: Number format that right-aligns numbers in the cells but does not maintain a consistent number of decimal places (43.00 will appear as 43, while 42.25 appears as 42.25) and does not display commas (so 1,123,456 appears as 1123456).

Goal Seek: Feature that lets you enter a desired value (outcome) for a formula and specify an input cell that can be modified in order to reach that goal.

Gridlines: The lines that appear on the worksheet defining the rows and columns.

Group: Multiple worksheets with the same structure that you can make changes to at the same time.

h

Header: Area that appears at the top of every page.

Headings: The numbers at the left of rows and the letters at the top of columns.

Highlight Cells Rules: A conditional formatting style in Excel that allows you to define formatting for cells that meet specific numerical or text criteria (e.g., greater than a specific value or containing a specific text string).

HLOOKUP: Function that finds a value or cell reference in a cell range and returns another value from the same column.

Horizontal scroll bar: The scrollbar located at the bottom of the window. Click the arrows at the ends of the scroll bars to move left and right to see more cells in an individual worksheet.

Horizontal: Places the windows in a row next to each other.

i

Icon Sets: Conditional formatting style in Excel that displays a graphic in each cell representing the cell value in relation to other values.

IF: A Logical function that returns one value if a condition is true and another value if the condition is false. A formula using the IF function looks like this: =IF(TOTAL_SALES > 50000,10%,5%)

l

Landscape orientation: Page orientation where the width of the page is greater than the height.

Legend: A key for a chart defining which data series is represented by each color.

Line charts: Chart type that features a line connecting each data point showing the movement of values over time.

Line with markers: Line chart type that includes dots along the line for each data point.

Long Date format: Excel date format that displays the day of the week, and then the name of the month, the two-digit date, and the four-digit year (Sunday, June 30, 2019).

LOWER: A Text function that converts the text string to all lowercase letters. A formula using the LOWER function looks like this: =LOWER(E2)

m

Margins: The blank spaces at the top, bottom, left, and right of a page.

MAX: A Statistical function that gives the highest value in a range of values. A formula using the MAX function looks like this: =MAX(A3:A6)

Mean: The sum of a group of values divided by the number of values in the group.

Median: The middle value of a set of values.

Message Bar: Displays a warning at the top of the window, below the Ribbon, when a file is opened in Protected View.

MIN: A Statistical function that gives the lowest value in a range of values. A formula using the MIN function looks like this: =MIN(A3:A6)

Mixed reference: A combination cell reference with a row position that stays constant with a changing column position (or vice versa).

Mode: The value that appears most often in a group of values.

n

Name box: Appears at the left side of the formula bar and displays the address of the selected cell or the name of a named range.

Name Manager: Lists all the named ranges used in your workbook, the current value for each, the cells to which the name refers (including the sheet name), the scope of the name (whether it is limited to a specific worksheet or applies to the entire workbook), and comments (if there are any).

Name: A word or group of words that is assigned to cells or ranges of cells to give your cell references names that are more user-friendly. Also called a named range or a range name.

Named range: A word or group of words that is assigned to cells or ranges of cells to give your cell references names that are more user-friendly. Also called a name or a range name.

Normal view: The typical working view in Excel. In Normal view, Excel shows the aspects of the worksheet that are visible only on-screen. Elements that are visible only when printed (like headers and footers) are hidden.

NOW: Function that inserts the current date and time. A formula using the NOW function looks like this: =NOW()

Number format: An Excel cell format that stores data as numbers and shows two decimal places by default (so 43 displays as 43.00) but does not include commas.

o

Order of operations: A mathematical rule stating that mathematical operations in a formula are calculated in this order (1) exponents and roots, (2) multiplication and division, and (3) addition and subtraction.

Orientation: Refers to the direction the worksheet prints.

p

Page Break Preview view: Allows you to manipulate where page breaks occur when the worksheet is printed.

Page Layout view: Shows all the worksheet elements as they will print. Page Layout view includes headers and footers.

Paste: Command that is used to insert text or an object from the Clipboard into a file.

Percent Style format: Displays numbers as % with zero places to the right of the decimal point.

Pie charts: Chart type that represents data as parts of a whole. Pie charts do not have x and y axes like column charts. Instead, each value is a visual slice of the pie.

PivotChart: A graphic representation of a PivotTable.

PivotTable: A special report view that summarizes data and calculates the intersecting totals. In Excel, PivotTables do not contain any data themselves—they summarize data from a range or a table in another part of your workbook.

Plot area: The area of the chart where the data series are plotted.

PMT: Function that can be used to calculate loan payments. The PMT function is based upon constant payments and a constant interest rate. A formula using the PMT function looks like this =PMT(7%/12,120,250000)

Portrait orientation: Page orientation where the height of the page is greater than the width.

Precedent: The cell containing the formula or value the selected cell refers to.

Print area: A range of cells that you designate as the default print selection.

PROPER: A Text function that converts the text string to proper case (the first letter in each word is capitalized). A formula using the PROPER function looks like this: PROPER(C2)

Protected View: Provides a read-only format that protects your computer from becoming infected by a virus or other malware.

q

Quick Analysis tool: Feature that helps you easily apply formatting, create charts, and insert formulas based on the selected data.

Quick Layouts: Predefined chart layouts that apply combinations of data labels, titles, and data tables.

Quick Style: A group of formatting, including character and paragraph formatting, that can easily apply to text, tables, drawings, or other objects.

r

Range name: A word or group of words assigned to cells or ranges of cells to give your cell references names that are more user-friendly. Also called a name or a named range.

Ready mode: The data entry method used in Excel to change the contents of the entire cell by clicking the cell once and then typing the data.

Redo: Reverses the Undo command and restores the file to its previous state.

Relative reference: A cell reference that adjusts to the new location in the worksheet when the formula is copied.

Replace: Used with the Find command to replace specified data or formatting in a file with new data or formatting.

Row input cell: The cell that contains the original value for which you want to substitute the data table values when the substitute values are listed in a row.

Row selector: The box with the row number at the left side of the worksheet grid. Clicking this box will select the entire row.

Row: A horizontal group of cells. Rows are identified by numbers. For example, the third row is labeled with the number 3.

s

Scale: Specifies that the worksheet will print at a percentage of the original size or at a maximum number of pages wide and/or tall.

Short Date format: Excel number format that displays the one- or two-digit number representing the month, followed by the one- or two-digit number representing the day, followed by the four-digit year (6/30/2019).

Slicer: A visual representation of filtering options. You can display multiple slicers and filter by multiple values from each. Slicers are only available when the data have been formatted as a table or PivotTable.

Smart Tag: Icon that appears next to a formula with a potential error and displays a menu for resolving the issue.

Sort: Arranges the rows in a table, worksheet, or datasheet in either ascending (A–Z) or descending (Z–A) alphabetical or numeric order.

Sparklines: Represent a series of data values as an individual graphic within a single cell.

Stacked bar chart: Similar to a Stacked Column chart, a stacked bar chart combines the data points of each data series into a single horizontal bar.

Stacked column chart: Chart type that shows each data point as part of a whole where the column represents the sum of the values in the series. Use a stacked column chart instead of a pie chart when you want the chart to show multiple series.

Status bar: Appears at the bottom of the worksheet grid and can display information about the selected data, including the number of cells selected that contain data (count) and the average and sum (total) of the selected values (when appropriate).

String: Text in a function.

t

Table: A range of cells may be explicitly defined as a table in Excel with additional functionality such as a Total row.

Template: A file with predefined settings that can be used as a pattern to create a new file.

Text string: Text in a function.

TEXTJOIN: A Text function used to combine the text values of cells including defining the delimiter character to use between cell values.

Theme Colors: Aspect of the theme that limits the colors available from the color palette for fonts, borders, and shading.

Theme Effects: Aspect of the theme that controls how graphic elements appear.

Theme Fonts: Aspect of the theme that controls which fonts are used for built-in text styles. Changing the theme fonts does not limit the fonts available from the Font group on the Ribbon.

Theme: A group of formatting options that is applied to an entire Office file. Themes include font, color, and effect styles that are applied to specific elements in a file.

Tiled: Places the windows in a grid pattern.

TODAY: A Date & Time function that inserts the current date. A formula using the TODAY function looks like this: =TODAY( )

Total row: A row that calculates an aggregate function, such as the sum or average, of all the values in the column. Total rows can be added to defined tables in Excel.

Trusted Document: A document originally displayed in Protected View that has been marked as safe for editing.

Two-variable data table: Provides a quick what-if analysis of the effects of changing two variables within a formula. The data table is organized with a series of values for the variables in both a column and a row.

u

Undo: Reverses the last action performed.

UPPER: A Text function that converts the text string to all uppercase letters. A formula using the UPPER function looks like this: =UPPER(D2)

v

Vertical scroll bar: The scrollbar located along the right side of the window. Click the arrows at the ends of the scroll bars to move up and down to see more cells in an individual worksheet.

Vertical: Places the windows in a row next to each other.

VLOOKUP: Function that finds a value or cell reference in a cell range and returns another value from the same row. A formula using the VLOOKUP function looks like this: =VLOOKUP(D13,LoanRange,7)

Volatile: Functions that recalculate whenever the worksheet recalculates. Volatile functions include DATE and TIME which update each time the workbook is opened.

w

Workbook: An Excel file made up of a collection of worksheets.

Worksheet: An electronic ledger where you enter data in Excel (also called a sheet). The worksheet appears as a grid made up of rows and columns where you can enter and then manipulate data using functions, formulas, and formatting.

x

X axis: The horizontal axis in a chart. It goes from left to right.

y

Y axis: The vertical axis in a chart. It goes from bottom to top.

z

Zoom slider: Slider bar that controls how large or small the file appears in the application window.

Access 365 Glossary

a

Attachment data type: Stores files as attachments to records. Attachments can be images, Word documents, or almost any other type of data file.

AutoNumber data type: Fields with this data type are automatically assigned their values by Access incrementally. Database users cannot edit or enter data in an AutoNumber field. AutoNumber fields are often used as a primary key if no other unique field exists in the table.

b

Bound control: Control that displays a value from a specific field.

c

Calculated control: An unbound text control in a form or report that contains an expression (formula).

Calculated Field (in a query): Displays a value returned by an expression (a formula). The field values are calculated each time the query is run.

Calculated Field data type: Displays a value returned by an expression (a formula).

Caption property: The field name as it will appear in labels and column headings.

Cascade delete: Table relationships option to delete records in the "many" table when the "one" record is deleted in the primary table.

Cascade update: Table relationships option to update related records in the "many" table when the "one" record is updated in the primary table.

Cascading options: Delete and update options that may be applied to relationships between tables. When they are enforced, actions on one table affect records in the related table.

Comma Style format: Displays the comma symbol (,) within the number and two digits to the right of the decimal.

Compact and Repair: Database utility that removes unused space from a database to help improve performance; can be used to repair a database in which some objects have become corrupted.

Control: Displays data or allows user to enter and edit data in a form or report. Controls can be bound, unbound, or calculated.

Control layout: Combines multiple controls in your database form or report into a single layout object in one of two formats: tabular or stacked.

Criteria: Conditions that the records must meet in order to be included in the query results. Criteria is a plural word that refers to more than one criterion.

Criterion: Singular form of the word criteria.

CSV (comma-separated value): File format for saving text files that uses a comma as the delimiter. These files have a .csv file extension.

Currency data type: Fields with this data type store a numerical value with a high degree of accuracy (up to four decimal places to the right of the decimal). Access will not round the values stored in Currency fields, regardless of the format in which the value displays.

Currency format: Displays a $ symbol before the number and two digits to the right of the decimal place.

d

Database: A collection of data. An effective database allows you to enter, store, organize, and retrieve large amounts of related data.

Datasheet form: Form that reproduces the exact look and layout of the table datasheet.

Datasheet view: View to use when entering data in a table or to sort and filter data. By default, tables open in Datasheet view.

Datasheets: Table data and query results displayed in Datasheet view.

Date/Time data type: Fields with this data type store a numerical value that is displayed as a date and time. The format in which the date and/or time displays is controlled by the Format property.

Default Value property: Adds a preset value to the field.

Delimiter: A specific character that separates the fields in a text file with multiple data fields. Common delimiters are commas, tabs, semicolons, and spaces.

Design view: View option that allows you to build or modify the basic structure or functionality of a database object.

e

Export: To save data in a file format accessible to other applications.

Expression: A formula used in a calculated field in a table or query or a calculated control in a form or report.

f

Field: Each column in a table in a database.

Field name: The name by which other database objects reference the field. This is the name you use when you build a query or add fields to a form or report.

Field Properties pane: Allows you to set field properties in table Design view.

Field Size property: Limits the number of characters that can be entered in a text field.

Filter: Limits the database records displayed to only those that meet specific criteria. Filters are temporary and are not saved with the database object unless they are defined in the object's properties.

Find Duplicates query: Finds duplicate records in a table.

Foreign key: In a one-to-many relationship, the field in the secondary table that relates to the primary key in the primary table.

Form: Allows database users to input data through a friendly interface.

Form header: The section directly above the detail section where the data are displayed in a form.

Form view: Provides a user-friendly interface for entering data in a database. From Form view, you cannot change the form layout or formatting.

Form Wizard: Wizard that walks you through the steps of creating the form, including selecting fields and a layout. You can use the Form Wizard to create a form combining fields from multiple related tables.

Format field property: Controls the way the data are displayed to the end user. It does not affect the data stored in the table.

g

Grouping: Feature that organizes records into distinct sections within an Access report.

h

Hyperlink data type: Fields with this data type store a Web address or email address.

i

Import: To bring data into the database from another file format. The process of importing converts the data from the original file format into the format required by Access.

Innermost sort: In a multilevel sort, the last field the data are sorted on.

Input mask: Ensures that users enter data in a database field in a particular format.

Insert controls: Used to quickly add rows and columns to tables. Insert Controls appear when you roll your mouse over the left edge of a row or the top edge of a column.

l

Label control: Unbound control that displays the field name or other text.

Landscape: Page orientation where the width of the page is greater than the height.

Large Number data type: Fields with this data type hold a very large numerical value. Use the Large Number data type for compatibility with the SQL_BIGINT data type in ODBC.

Layout view: View where you can modify some (but not all) structural elements in a form or report.

Linked Table Manager: Tool that allows you to update the connection to linked data.

Linked tables: A link to a table in another Access database. All of the data remain in the original source file. You cannot change any properties in the linked table, because all table properties are defined in the source file. However, any changes made to the record data in the current database will appear in the source file. Any changes made to the source database will appear in the linked table automatically, including both table property changes and changes to table data.

Long Text data type: Holds text and numbers like a Short Text field, except you can enter up to 65,535 characters in a Long Text field. Text in Long Text fields can be formatted using Rich Text Formatting. In Access 2010 and earlier, the Long Text data type was called the Memo data type.

Lookup field: Allows the user to select data from a list of items.

m

Macro: Programming instruction that can be run from within a file. Macros are used to automate data entry and formatting processes and to execute commands from buttons in database forms and reports.

Margins: The blank spaces at the top, bottom, left, and right of a page.

Message Bar: Security warning that displays at the top of the window, below the Ribbon.

Multiple Items form: Displays multiple records at once. The layout and design of a Multiple Items form can be modified.

n

Navigation Pane: Pane that organizes all the objects for a database. The Navigation Pane is docked at the left side of the screen.

Number data type: Fields with this data type hold a numerical value. The default number is described as a long integer, a number between $-2,147,483,648$ and $2,147,483,647$.

o

OLE Object data type: Fields with this data type store OLE files such as Word documents or Excel spreadsheets. Unless you need backward compatibility with a legacy database, use the newer and more flexible Attachment data type instead.

Outermost sort: In a multilevel sort, the first field the data are sorted on.

p

Padding: Space between the layout rows and columns in a form or report.

Page footer section: Section that appears at the bottom of every printed page in a report.

Page header section: Section that appears at the top of every printed page in a report.

Parameter query: A query with user-controlled criteria input. When the query is run, the user is prompted to enter a value for a specific field (the parameter input) that will be used as the criterion when generating results.

PDF (Portable Document Format): Type of file that can be read by anyone who has the Adobe Reader software installed.

Percent format: Displays the number as a percentage, so .05 displays as 5, and 5 displays as 500. This format displays the % symbol.

Portrait: Page orientation where the height of the page is greater than the width.

Primary key: The field that contains data unique to each record in a table. In a one-to-many relationship, the field in the main table that is also included in the secondary table.

Print Preview: A specific report view that shows how the database report will appear when printed.

q

Queries: Extracts data from a table or multiple related tables.

Query grid: The lower pane in query Design view where the fields and criteria for the query are defined.

Quick Start application parts: A table template that you can use to start building a database. There are five Quick Start application parts to choose from: Comments, Contacts, Issues, Tasks, and Users. Most also include forms for data entry.

Quick Start field types: Provide an easy way to add address fields and other common field groups to your table.

r

Record: Each row in a table in a database.

Record source: The associated table or query for a database form or report.

Redo: Reverses the Undo command and restores the file to its previous state.

Referential integrity: The policy that ensures that related database records remain accurate. If a relationship has referential integrity enforced, then no modification can be made to either table that would violate the relationship structure.

Relational database: A database that allows you to relate tables and databases to one another through common fields.

Relationship: A relationship between two database tables where the primary table contains a primary key field that is included as a field (the foreign key) in the secondary table. Thus, one record in the first table can relate to many records in the second table.

Relationships window: Window that provides a visual representation of the relationships in your database.

Report: Displays database information for printing or viewing on-screen.

Report footer section: The section directly below the detail section where the data are displayed in a report.

Report header section: The section directly above the detail section where the data are displayed in a report.

Report view: Shows a static view of the database report. You cannot change the layout or formatting of the report from Report view.

Report Wizard: Wizard that walks you step by step through the process of creating a report. The Report Wizard allows you to combine fields from more than one table or query and gives you more layout and design options than using the basic Report button from the Create tab.

s

Select query: Displays data from one or more tables or queries, based on the fields that you select.

Short Text data type: Can hold up to 255 characters. Short Text fields are used for short text data or numbers that should be treated as text.

Single Record form: Form that displays one record at a time.

Split form: Combines the convenience of a continuous datasheet form with the usability of a single form displaying one record at a time.

SQL view: Shows the code used to build the query.

Stacked layout: Places the form or report labels at the left side with data to the right (similar to many paper forms or reports).

Structured Query Language (SQL): Programming language used in Access and other relational database management systems to define queries.

Subform: A form within the form, to display the related records from the "many" table in a one-to-many relationship.

t

Table: Stores all the database data. Tables are the basic building blocks of the database.

Tabular layout: Places the form or report labels across the top, with columns of data (similar to a datasheet or a spreadsheet).

Template: A file with predefined settings that you can use as a base to create a new database of your own.

Text box control: Control that displays text, numbers, dates, and similar data. Text box controls can be bound or unbound.

Theme: A unified font and color scheme applied to the entire database.

u

Unbound control: A control that is not linked to a field.

Undo: Reverses the last action performed.

w

Wildcard: Special characters used in criteria to substitute for any character. The * wildcard replaces any string of characters. The ? wildcard replaces a single character.

y

Yes/No data type: Fields with this data type store a true/false value as a −1 for yes and 0 for no.

PowerPoint 365 Glossary

#

3D model: A mathematical representation of an object created by special 3D modeling software.

a

Alt text: A description of a picture, chart, or other object that can be read by screen readers.

Animation Painter: Tool that copies and pastes animations from one object to another.

Animations: Movement of an object or text in a presentation. There are four basic types of animation schemes: Entrance, Emphasis, Exit, and Motion Paths.

Audio file: Music, sound effect, or narration file that can be added to a slide or presentation. Common audio file formats include MP3 audio file (mp3), MP4 Audio, Windows audio file (wav), and Windows Media Audio file (wma).

b

Background styles: Preset backgrounds that come as part of a theme. They range from light to dark colors and can be a solid color or gradient.

Background: The graphic element that fills a slide. Backgrounds can be solid colors, textures, or images.

Bottom alignment: Text alignment that places the text at the bottom of the placeholder.

Bulleted lists: List type used to organize information that does not have to be displayed in a particular order.

c

Cell: The intersection of a row and column in a table.

Center alignment: Text alignment that centers each line of text relative to the margins.

Character effects: Effects applied to individual characters or words rather than paragraphs. Common character effects include bold, italic, and underline effects.

Chart area: Encompasses the entire chart including the plot area and optional layout elements, such as title and legend.

Chart title: A text box above or overlaying the chart.

Chart: A graphic that transforms numerical data into a more visual representation.

Clear All Formatting: Command that removes any formatting that has been applied to text, including character formatting, text effects, and styles, and leaves only plain text.

Clipboard: Task pane that displays up to 24 copied or cut items for use in any Office application.

Color theme: A set of colors that complement each other and are designed to work well together.

Columns: A vertical arrangement of text on-screen. Text at the bottom of one column continues on to the top of the next column.

Columns (Table): Groups of cells that display vertically in a table.

Content placeholder: A special type of placeholder that provides a quick way to add a variety of material to presentations, including tables, charts, SmartArt diagrams, pictures, and videos.

Copy: Command that places a duplicate of the selected text or object on the Clipboard without changing the file.

Creative Commons: Licensing system through which Bing Image Search filter results when searching for pictures online.

Cut: Command that removes the selected text or object from the file and places it on the Office Clipboard for later use.

d

Data labels: Display data values for each data marker in a chart.

Designer: Feature in PowerPoint that analyzes the current slide and presents several slide layout options from which you can choose.

Drawing guides: Lines that can be turned on and off that divide the slide into four quadrants to help you place images on a slide.

Drawing objects: Objects that when selected display the Drawing Tools contextual tab. Drawing objects include text boxes, shapes, and WordArt.

e

Effects theme: A set of line and fill effects that you apply to objects on your slides.

Emphasis animation: Animates the object on the screen. Examples include Pulse, Spin, Grow/Shrink, and Teeter.

Entrance animations: Animates the object coming on to the slide; starts with the object not visible and ends with the object visible. Examples include Fade In, Split, Fly In, and Appear.

Exit animation: Animates the object leaving the slide; starts with the object visible and ends with the object not visible. Examples include Fade, Disappear, Float Out, and Wipe.

Eyedropper: Tool that allows you to select any color from your screen and apply it to an object.

f

Fill color: Solid color that fills a drawing object.

Find: Command that locates specific text in a presentation.

Font theme: A set of fonts that complement each other and are designed to work well together.

Font: Refers to a set of characters of a certain design. The font is the shape of the character or number as it appears on-screen.

Footer: Text that appears on every slide or handout. Typically, a footer appears at the bottom of a slide or handout.

Format Painter: Tool that copies and pastes formatting styles.

g

Gradient stop: The point where the gradient changes from one shade of the color to another.

Gradient: The gradual transition of one color to another.

Gridlines: A series of dotted vertical and horizontal lines that divide the slide into small boxes. Used as visual markers for aligning placeholders and graphics.

h

Handout Master: Master that controls how the slides in a presentation look when printed.

Handout: A printout of a presentation with one to nine slides per page and with areas for taking notes.

Header: Used to display information in a handout printed from a presentation. Headers appear on the top of every handout. They do not display in the slide show.

Hide Slide: Command that hides the slide when in Slide Show view, but does not delete the slide in Normal view.

Highlighter: Slide show tool used to add color behind text on slides in Slide Show view and emphasize parts of a slide.

Hyperlink: Text or a graphic that, when clicked, opens another file or jumps to another place in the presentation.

i

Icons: Simple drawings (Scalable Vector Graphics) that you can add to your presentations. They can be enlarged, colored, and rotated without losing image quality.

j

Justified alignment: Text alignment where the words are evenly spaced between the right and left side of the placeholder.

l

Laser pointer: Slide show tool that turns the mouse pointer into red dot you can use to call attention to important parts of your slides

Left alignment: Text alignment where the text is aligned on the left side, leaving the right side ragged.

Legend: A key for a chart defining which data series is represented by each color.

Line spacing: The white space between lines of text.

m

Master views: Special views that contain universal settings for the presentation. These views include Slide Master view, Handout Master view, and Notes Master view.

Middle alignment: Text alignment that centers the text vertically in the placeholder.

Morph transition: Transition that allows you to move and transform objects on a slide when transitioning from one slide to another.

Motion Path animation: Animates the object along an invisible line. Examples include Lines, Arcs, and Loops.

Multilevel list: List type that includes points and subpoints.

n

Normal view: The view where content is created and edited. Normal view consists of the Thumbnails pane, Slide pane, and Notes pane.

Notes Page view: View that allows you to add notes for each slide in your presentation. Each slide appears on its own screen with a large text area for your notes about the slide.

Notes Pages: The printed copy of the slide with its associated note.

Notes pane: Area where you can type notes about the current slide displayed in the Slide pane. The text you type in the Notes pane will not appear when you play your presentation.

Numbered lists: List type used to organize information that must be presented in a certain order.

o

Online Pictures: Images located on the Internet that can be accessed by searching through a Bing Image Search or from your OneDrive.

Outline view

Outline view: Displays only the text from the slides in a presentation in an outline format. Use the Outline view to enter and edit text directly in the outline.

Outlines: Line that surrounds the shape of a drawing object. You can adjust the weight and style of outlines.

p

Package for CD: Feature that allows you to copy and package all the elements of your presentation to a folder. When you package a presentation, the PowerPoint viewer is included by default, allowing you to run your presentation from any computer.

Paste options: Options for pasting text and objects in PowerPoint. Paste options allow you to choose to keep the source formatting, merge the formatting of the source and the current document, or paste only the text without any formatting.

Paste: Command that is used to insert text or an object from the Clipboard into a file.

Pattern fill: A geometric pattern that repeats across the background of the slide.

Pen: Slide show tool used to underline or circle important points in Slide Show view as they are discussed.

Picture effects: Effects including shadows, reflections, glows, soft edges, bevels, and 3-D rotation that you apply to pictures.

Picture Quick Styles: A combination of graphic effects, such as borders, shadows, 3-D rotation, and reflections that you apply to pictures.

Placeholder: A container on a slide that holds text or other content, such as a table, chart, or image.

Plot area: Area of the chart where the data series are plotted.

Points: Measurement for the height of a font. Abbreviated pt.

Presentation: A multimedia slide show that combines text, images, charts, audio, video, animations, and transition effects to convey information.

Presenter view: View that allows you to see your notes while you are giving your presentation, making it easier to refer to any notes you have added to slides.

q

Quick Styles: A group of formatting, including character and paragraph formatting, that can easily apply to text, tables, drawings, or other objects.

r

Reading view: The view that runs the presentation within the PowerPoint application window.

Redo: Reverses the Undo command and restores the file to its previous state.

Rehearse Timings: Feature that runs the presentation while recording the time spent on each slide.

Replace All: Command used to replace words or phrases all at once throughout the presentation.

Replace: Used with the Find command to replace specified text in a file with new text.

Resize handle: One of the six squares that appear when an object is selected. Clicking and dragging a resize handle toward the center of the object will make the object smaller. Clicking and dragging the resize handle away from the center of the object will make the object larger.

Right alignment: Text alignment where the text is aligned on the right side, leaving the left side ragged.

Rows: Groups of cells that display horizontally in a table.

Ruler: Displays horizontally across the top of the window just below the Ribbon and vertically along the left side of the window. The ruler gives you a quick view of the position of elements on a slide.

S

Sans serif fonts: Fonts that do not have an embellishment at the end of each stroke. Includes Calibri and Arial.

ScreenTip: A bubble with text that appears when the mouse hovers over a hyperlink. Typically, a ScreenTip provides a description of the hyperlink.

Serif fonts: Fonts that have an embellishment at the end of each stroke. Includes Cambria and Times New Roman.

Shape: A drawing object that can be quickly added to a presentation.

Slide layout: Slide templates with predefined placeholders for content such as titles, subtitles, pictures, tables, charts, SmartArt, and video.

Slide numbers: Information added to the footer area of each slide to display how far along you are in your presentation. Slide numbers are added through the Header and Footer dialog and are automatically updated when slides are added, deleted, or moved.

Slide pane: Area where you can modify slides, including adding and formatting text, images, SmartArt, tables, charts, and media.

Slide Show view: The view that displays the slides full-screen and displays the presentation as the audience will see it.

Slide Sorter view: The view that displays a grid of thumbnail pictures of the slides in a presentation, and is useful in rearranging the order of slides in a presentation.

Slides: Units within a presentation. Each slide contains content, including text, graphics, audio, and video.

Smart guides: Horizontal and vertical dotted lines that appear when an object is dragged and the object's edge is aligned with another element on the slide.

SmartArt: Visual diagrams containing graphic elements with text boxes to enter information in.

Speaker notes: Hidden notes that do not appear as part of the presentation.

Spelling checker: Command that analyzes your entire presentation for spelling errors. It presents any errors it finds in the Spelling task pane, enabling you to make decisions about how to handle each error or type of error in turn.

t

Table: Content element that helps to organize information by rows, which display horizontally, and columns, which display vertically.

Template: A file with predefined settings that can be used as a pattern to create a new file.

Text alignment: Refers to how text is lined up with regard to the left and right edges of a slide.

Text boxes: Boxes that are added to the slide layout to enter text anywhere on the slide.

Text placeholders: Predefined areas in slide layouts where text is entered.

Theme variant: A set of color variations you can change for a theme.

Theme: A group of formatting options that is applied to an entire presentation. Themes include font, color, and effect styles that are applied to specific elements in a presentation.

Thumbnails pane: Displays thumbnails of all the slides in a presentation. Use the Thumbnails pane to quickly navigate between slides and rearrange the slide order of slides in a presentation.

Top alignment: Text alignment that places the text at the top of the placeholder.

Transition: An effect that occurs when one slide leaves the screen and another one appears.

u

Undo: Reverses the last action performed.

V

Vertical alignment: Refers to how text is aligned with regard to the top and bottom of the placeholder.

Video file: Movies that can be added to a slide. Common types include QuickTime (mov) and MPEG (mp4).

W

Widescreen: Display where the width of the slide is larger than the height of the slide designed for widescreen monitors and projectors. Widescreen 16:9 is the default size for slides.

WordArt: Predefined graphic styles that are applied to text. These styles include a combination of colors, fills, outlines, and effects.

Working space: Another name for Normal view.

z

Zoom slider: Slider bar that controls how large or small the file appears in the application window.

office index

word index

excel index

, EX-170
#DIV/0!, EX-135
( ), EX-19
$, EX-13, EX-26
*, EX-18
+, EX-18
-, EX-18
/, EX-18
, EX-28
!, EX-121
% Total, EX-30
3-D reference, EX-122

a

Absolute reference, EX-26
Access
   export to, AC-149 to AC-152
   import from, AC-144 to AC-145
Accounting Number Format, EX-12,
   EX-13
Accounting underline format, EX-72 to
   EX-73, EX-77
Add Chart Elements button, EX-215
Add to Dictionary, EX-40
Addition (+), EX-18
Align Left, EX-68
Align Right, EX-68
Alignment, EX-68 to EX-69
Alignment group, EX-66, EX-68,
   EX-70
Alignment Settings dialog launcher,
   EX-66, EX-69, EX-70
All Borders, EX-76
Annual percentage rate (APR), EX-132
Argument, EX-28
Arrange All button, EX-38, EX-39
Arrange Windows dialog, EX-38
Arranging workbooks, EX-38 to EX-39
Ascending sort, EX-227
AutoFill, EX-16 to EX-17
AutoFill Options button, EX-17
Automatic Color, EX-74
AutoSum, EX-29, EX-109, EX-113,
   EX-114
Average, EX-30, EX-113
AVERAGE function, EX-113

b

Backspace key, EX-11, EX-89
Backstage view
   adjust margins, EX-184

new workbook, EX-35
   print, EX-41, EX-187
Bar chart, EX-205 to EX-207
Bold, EX-72 to EX-73
Border, EX-73, EX-76 to EX-77
Borders button, EX-76, EX-77
Bottom Align, EX-68
Bottom Border, EX-76
Breaks button, EX-180, EX-181

c

Calculation style, EX-80
Cancel button, EX-11
Cascade window arrangement, EX-38
Cell
   angling text, EX-68, EX-69
   background color, EX-78 to EX-79
   clear content, EX-89
   definition of, EX-3
   delete, EX-64 to EX-65
   entering text and numbers, EX-10
     to EX-11
   horizontal alignment, EX-68
   insert, EX-63 to EX-64
   merge/unmerge, EX-70 to EX-71
   number formats, EX-12 to EX-13
   select, EX-5
   split, EX-71
   text wrapping, EX-66
   vertical alignment, EX-68
Cell address, EX-3, EX-7
Cell range, EX-3, EX-6
Cell reference, EX-26 to EX-27
Cell styles, EX-13, EX-80
Cell Styles button, EX-13, EX-80
Cell Styles gallery, EX-80
Cell underline formats, EX-72 to
   EX-73
Cells group, EX-164, EX-166 to
   EX-167, EX-173, EX-174
Center, EX-68
Center Across Selection, EX-70
Change Chart Type button, EX-217
Change Chart Type dialog, EX-217
Change Colors button, EX-216
Chart, EX-18 to EX-23, EX-205 to
   EX-221
   bar, EX-205 to EX-207
   change type, EX-217
   color scheme, EX-216
   column, EX-205 to EX-207
   common elements, EX-19
   definition of, EX-18

delete, EX-23
doughnut, EX-209
filtering data, EX-218 to EX-219
hide/unhide elements, EX-215
highlighting, EX-20
line, EX-210
move, EX-211 to EX-213
perception/presentation, EX-20
pie, EX-18, EX-209
PivotChart, EX-236 to EX-237
Quick Analysis tool, EX-21, EX-23
Quick Layouts, EX-214
Quick Styles, EX-216
recommended charts features,
   EX-21 to EX-23
resize, EX-211
Sparklines, EX-220 to EX-221
stacked, EX-207
switch data series and categories,
   EX-206 to EX-207, EX-210
x axis/y axis, EX-19
Chart area, EX-19
Chart Elements box, EX-19
Chart Elements button, EX-215
Chart Filters button, EX-218 to
   EX-219
Chart Layouts group, EX-214, EX-215
Chart Options dialog, EX-21
Chart sheet, EX-212, EX-213
Chart Styles button, EX-216
Chart title, EX-19, EX-22
Chart Title box, EX-22
Chart Tools Design tab
   color, EX-216
   contextual tab, EX-19
   move, EX-211
   Quick Layout, EX-214
   Quick Styles, EX-216
   show/hide chart elements, EX-215
   switch row/column, EX-206
Chart Tools Format tab, EX-19
Charts group, EX-205, EX-206,
   EX-209, EX-210
Choose Format from Cell..., EX-93
Clear All, EX-89
Clear button, EX-89, EX-228
Clear cell content, EX-89
Clear Comments, EX-89
Clear conditional formatting, EX-88
Clear Contents, EX-89
Clear Filter button, EX-231
Clear Filter From "Name of Column,"
   EX-228
Clear Format button, EX-88
Clear Formats, EX-89

Name box, EX-3, EX-4, EX-5
Name Manager, EX-126, EX-126 to
    EX-128
Name Manager button, EX-126,
    EX-128
Name worksheet, EX-160
Named range
    create, EX-123 to EX-124
    delete name, EX-128
    duplicate name, EX-127
    edit name, EX-127
    filter list of names, EX-128
    formula, EX-125
    Name Manager, EX-126 to EX-128
    uniqueness of name, EX-127
    update, EX-126
Narrow margins, EX-184
Navigating a workbook, EX-5 to EX-7
Navigation group, EX-178
New Name dialog, EX-124
New sheet, EX-159
New sheet radio button, EX-211
No Border, EX-76
No Borders paste option, EX-61
No Fill, EX-78
Normal margins, EX-184
Normal view, EX-177, EX-180
NOW, EX-115
Nper argument, EX-132
Number format, EX-13
Number Format menu, EX-12 to
    EX-13
Number formats, EX-12 to EX-13
Number group, EX-14

o

Object in radio button, EX-211
Office theme, EX-168
One-variable data table, EX-238
Online templates, EX-36
Orange gradient data bars, EX-84
Order of operations (precedence),
    EX-19
Orientation
    angling text, EX-68, EX-69
    portrait/landscape, EX-183
Orientation button, EX-68, EX-183
Orientation dial, EX-69
Outside Borders, EX-76

p

Page break, EX-180 to EX-181
Page Break Preview view, EX-177,
    EX-180
Page Layout button, EX-178

Page Layout tab
    margins, EX-184
    orientation, EX-183
    page break, EX-180, EX-181
    print titles, EX-186
    scaling, EX-185
    show/hide worksheet elements,
        EX-182
    theme, EX-169
Page Layout view, EX-177, EX-178
Page Setup dialog, EX-179, EX-183,
    EX-184, EX-186
Page Setup group, EX-180, EX-181,
    EX-183, EX-184, EX-186
Parentheses ( ), EX-19
Paste
    copy (copy and paste), EX-59 to
        EX-60
    default command, EX-61
    move (cut and paste), EX-59 to
        EX-60
    options, EX-61
Paste button, EX-60, EX-62
Paste Names dialog, EX-125
Paste Options, EX-61 to EX-62
Paste Options button, EX-62
Paste Special dialog, EX-62
Paste Values command, EX-118
Pattern styles, EX-79
Percent Style format, EX-12, EX-13
Percent (%) Total, EX-30
Percentage format, EX-13
Picture paste option, EX-61
Pie chart, EX-18, EX-209
PivotChart, EX-236 to EX-237
PivotChart button, EX-236
PivotTable, EX-233 to EX-235
PivotTable Fields pane, EX-233,
    EX-234, EX-235, EX-237
PivotTable Tools Analyze tab, EX-235,
    EX-236
Plot area, EX-19
PMT financial function, EX-131 to
    EX-132
Portrait orientation, EX-183
Precedence, EX-19
Precedent, EX-137 to EX-138
Precedent tracer arrows, EX-137,
    EX-138
Present value, EX-132
Preview
    Cell Styles gallery, EX-80
    chart layout, EX-214
    conditional formatting, EX-82,
        EX-85
    filtering chart data, EX-218
    PivotChart, EX-236 to EX-237
    print, EX-41, EX-94, EX-95
Print

basic print function, EX-41
    gridlines, EX-182
    headings, EX-182
    margins, EX-184
    orientation, EX-183
    portion of worksheet, EX-94 to
        EX-95
    portrait/landscape, EX-183
    preview, EX-41, EX-94, EX-95
    print area, EX-94 to EX-95
    Quick Print, EX-41
    repeat rows/columns on every page,
        EX-186
    scaling, EX-185
    selection, EX-187
    titles, EX-186
    workbook, EX-187
    worksheet, EX-187
Print Active Sheets, EX-187
Print area, EX-94 to EX-95
Print Area button, EX-94 to EX-95
Print Entire Workbook, EX-187
Print Selected Table, EX-187
Print Selection, EX-187
Print Titles button, EX-186
Proofing group, EX-40
Proofreading, importance of,
    EX-40
PROPER function, EX-118
Protected View, EX-8 to EX-9
Pv argument, EX-132

q

Quick Access toolbar
    print, EX-41
    redo, EX-67
    undo, EX-67
Quick Analysis tool
    conditional formatting, EX-82 to
        EX-83, EX-88
    overview, EX-30 to EX-31,
        EX-109
    recommended charts, EX-21,
        EX-23
    Sparklines, EX-220
    types of calculations, EX-30
Quick Analysis Tool button
    calculate totals, EX-30
    conditional formatting, EX-82,
        EX-88
    recommended charts, EX-21,
        EX-23
    show, EX-31
    Sparklines, EX-220
Quick Layout button, EX-214
Quick Layouts, EX-214
Quick Print command, EX-41

access index

powerpoint index